1956	1958	1960	1962	1964	1966	1968	1970	1972	1974	1976	1978	1979	1980
437.5	467.2	526.4	585.6	663.6	787.8	910.0	1,038.5	1,238.3	1,500.0	1,825.3	2,294.7	2,563.3	2,789.5
271.7	296.2	331.7	363.3	411.4	480.9	558.0	648.5	770.6	933.4	1,151.9	1,428.5	1,592.2	1,757.1
72.0	64.5	78.9	88.1	102.1	131.3	141.2	152.4	207.6	249.4	292.0	438.0	492.9	479.3
91.4	106.0	111.6	130.1	143.2	171.8	209.4	233.8	263.5	317.9	383.0	453.6	500.8	566.2
2.4	0.5	4.2	4.1	6.9	3.9	1.4	4.0	−3.4	−0.8	−1.6	−25.4	−22.5	−13.1
391.1	415.2	470.8	526.4	598.6	712.2	821.6	931.8	1,111.8	1,137.5	1,620.1	2,032.4	2,263.2	2,446.6
395.6	416.8	474.9	530.1	602.7	711.0	823.2	930.9	1,111.2	1,342.1	1,611.8	2,027.4	2,249.1	2,439.3
244.5	259.5	296.4	327.1	370.7	442.7	524.3	617.2	725.1	890.2	1,059.3	1,336.1	1,500.8	1,651.8
14.2	15.4	17.1	18.8	19.6	20.8	20.9	21.4	23.4	24.3	22.3	22.1	23.8	30.0
6.9	9.5	10.6	14.2	17.4	22.4	27.1	39.1	47.9	70.8	85.5	115.0	138.9	181.8
48.5	43.5	53.8	63.3	76.5	93.2	98.8	83.6	112.1	115.8	163.3	216.6	232.2	201.1
45.8	50.1	50.7	51.2	59.0	63.9	74.3	78.4	95.9	113.1	132.2	166.6	180.1	174.1
35.6	38.6	46.3	55.8	64.4	71.7	77.8	91.2	106.9	127.8	149.2	171.0	182.3	200.5
339.6	369.0	411.5	456.7	514.6	603.9	712.0	838.8	992.7	1,222.6	1,474.8	1,837.7	2,062.2	2,307.9
303.0	350.5	365.4	405.1	462.5	537.5	625	735.7	869.1	1,071.6	1,302.5	1,608.3	1,793.5	2,009.0
1,801.0	1,898.0	2,022.0	2,171.0	2,410.0	2,734.0	3,114.0	3,587.0	4,140.0	5,010.0	5,972.0	7,224.0	7,967.0	8,822.0
8.5	8.6	7.3	8.3	8.8	8.3	8.4	9.4	8.9	10.6	9.4	8.9	8.9	10.0

1956	1958	1960	1962	1964	1966	1968	1970	1972	1974	1976	1978	1979	1980
2,255.8	2,279.7	2501.8	2,715.2	2,998.6	3,399.1	3,652.7	3,771.9	4,105.0	4,319.6	4,540.9	5,015.0	5,173.4	5,161.7
1.9	−1.0	2.5	6.1	5.8	6.5	4.8	0.2	5.3	−0.5	5.3	5.6	3.2	−0.2
27.2	28.9	29.6	30.2	31.0	32.4	34.8	38.8	41.8	49.3	56.9	65.2	72.6	82.4
1.5	2.8	1.7	1.0	1.3	2.9	4.2	5.7	3.2	11.0	5.8	7.6	11.3	13.5
136.0	138.4	140.7	145.2	160.3	172.0	197.4	214.4	249.2	274.2	306.2	357.3	381.8	408.5
2.73	1.57	3.21	2.71	3.5	5.11	5.66	7.17	4.44	10.51	5.05	7.94	11.3	13.35
3.77	3.83	4.82	4.5	4.5	5.63	5.63	7.91	5.72	8.03	6.84	9.06	12.67	15.27
168.9	174.9	180.7	186.5	191.9	196.6	200.7	205.1	209.9	213.9	218.0	222.6	225.1	227.7
66.6	67.6	69.6	70.6	73.1	75.8	78.7	82.8	87.0	91.9	96.2	102.3	105.0	106.9
63.8	63.0	65.8	66.7	69.3	72.9	75.9	78.7	82.2	86.8	88.8	96.0	98.8	99.3
2.8	4.6	3.9	3.9	3.8	2.9	2.8	4.1	4.9	5.2	7.4	6.2	6.1	7.6
4.1	6.8	5.5	5.5	5.2	3.8	3.6	4.9	5.6	5.6	7.7	6.1	5.8	7.1
0.1	2.8	1.7	4.6	3.4	4.1	3.4	2.0	3.2	−1.6	3.1	1.1	0.0	−0.2
5.3	4.2	4.4	4.5	5.2	5.6	5.1	4.0	4.3	5.5	5.4	5.4	5.7	4.8
2.94	3.0	2.91	2.85	3.0	3.1	3.18	3.39	2.85	9.25	13.1	14.95	25.1	37.42
3.9	−2.8	0.3	−7.1	−5.9	−3.7	−25.2	−2.8	−23.4	−6.1	−73.7	−59.2	−40.7	−73.8
272.7	279.7	290.5	302.9	316.1	328.5	368.7	380.9	435.9	483.9	629.0	776.6	829.5	909.1
2.7	0.8	2.8	3.4	6.8	3.0	0.6	2.3	−5.8	2.0	4.3	−15.1	−0.3	2.3

(Continued in back of book)

Seventeenth Edition

Macroeconomics

Principles, Problems, and Policies

Campbell R. McConnell

University of Nebraska

Stanley L. Brue

Pacific Lutheran University

Boston   Burr Ridge, IL   Dubuque, IA   Madison, WI   New York   San Francisco   St. Louis
Bangkok   Bogotá   Caracas   Kuala Lumpur   Lisbon   London   Madrid   Mexico City
Milan   Montreal   New Delhi   Santiago   Seoul   Singapore   Sydney   Taipei   Toronto

To **Mem** and to **Terri** and **Craig**

McGraw-Hill
Irwin

MACROECONOMICS: PRINCIPLES, PROBLEMS, AND POLICIES

Published by McGraw-Hill/Irwin, a business unit of The McGraw-Hill Companies, Inc., 1221
Avenue of the Americas, New York, NY, 10020. Copyright © 2008 by The McGraw-Hill
Companies, Inc. All rights reserved. No part of this publication may be reproduced or distributed
in any form or by any means, or stored in a database or retrieval system, without the prior written
consent of The McGraw-Hill Companies, Inc., including, but not limited to, in any network or
other electronic storage or transmission, or broadcast for distance learning.
Some ancillaries, including electronic and print components, may not be available to customers
outside the United States.

This book is printed on acid-free paper.

1 2 3 4 5 6 7 8 9 0 DOW/DOW 0 9 8 7 6

ISBN   978-0-07-327308-2
MHID   0-07-327308-2

Editorial director: *Brent Gordon*
Executive editor: *Douglas Reiner*
Developmental editor II: *Rebecca Hicks*
Media producer: *Jennifer Wilson*
Lead project manager: *Lori Koetters*
Lead production supervisor: *Michael R. McCormick*
Director of design BR: *Keith J. McPherson*
Photo research coordinator: *Lori Kramer*
Photo researcher: *Keri Johnson*
Lead media project manager: *Becky Szura*
Cover design: *Sayles Graphics*
Interior design: *Maureen McCutcheon/Kay Fulton*
Cover image: *Gettyimages Paul Harris Photographer*
Typeface: *10/12 Jansen*
Compositor: *GTS – New Delhi, India Campus*
Printer: *R. R. Donnelley*

Library of Congress Cataloging-in-Publication Data

McConnell, Campbell R.
    Macroeconomics : principles, problems, and policies / Campbell R. McConnell, Stanley L.
Brue.– 17th ed.
        p. cm.
    Includes index.
    ISBN-13: 978-0-07-327308-2 (alk. paper)
    ISBN-10: 0-07-327308-2 (alk. paper)
    1. Macroeconomics. I. Brue, Stanley L., 1945- II. Title.
HB171.5.M473 2008
338.5–dc22

                                    2006024944

www.mhhe.com

About the Authors

Campbell R. McConnell earned his Ph.D. from the University of Iowa after receiving degrees from Cornell College and the University of Illinois. He taught at the University of Nebraska–Lincoln from 1953 until his retirement in 1990. He is also coauthor of *Contemporary Labor Economics*, seventh edition, and *Essentials of Economics*, first edition (both The McGraw-Hill Companies), and has edited readers for the principles and labor economics courses. He is a recipient of both the University of Nebraska Distinguished Teaching Award and the James A. Lake Academic Freedom Award and is past president of the Midwest Economics Association. Professor McConnell was awarded an honorary Doctor of Laws degree from Cornell College in 1973 and received its Distinguished Achievement Award in 1994. His primary areas of interest are labor economics and economic education. He has an extensive collection of jazz recordings and enjoys reading jazz history.

Stanley L. Brue did his undergraduate work at Augustana College (South Dakota) and received its Distinguished Achievement Award in 1991. He received his Ph.D. from the University of Nebraska–Lincoln. He is a professor at Pacific Lutheran University, where he has been honored as a recipient of the Burlington Northern Faculty Achievement Award. Professor Brue has also received the national Leavey Award for excellence in economic education. He has served as national president and chair of the Board of Trustees of Omicron Delta Epsilon International Economics Honorary. He is coauthor of *Economic Scenes*, fifth edition (Prentice-Hall), *Contemporary Labor Economics*, seventh edition, *Essentials of Economics*, first edition (both The McGraw-Hill Companies), and *The Evolution of Economic Thought*, seventh edition (South-Western). For relaxation, he enjoys international travel, attending sporting events, and skiing with family and friends.

List of Key Graphs

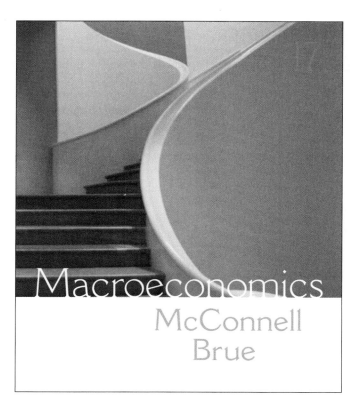

Fundamental Objectives

We have three main goals for *Economics*:

- Help the beginning student master the principles essential for understanding the economizing problem, specific economic issues, and the policy alternatives.
- Help the student understand and apply the economic perspective and reason accurately and objectively about economic matters.
- Promote a lasting student interest in economics and the economy.

What's New and Improved?

One of the benefits of writing a successful text is the opportunity to revise—to delete the outdated and install the new, to rewrite misleading or ambiguous statements, to introduce more relevant illustrations, to improve the organizational structure, and to enhance the learning aids. A chapter-by-chapter list of changes is available at our Web site, **www.mcconnell17.com.** The more significant changes include the following.

New Analysis of Monetary Policy

We have revised the discussion of monetary policy to help the student understand the Federal Reserve Board's focus on the Federal funds rate and how changes in that rate affect other interest rates and the overall economy. In "Interest Rates and Monetary Policy" (Chapter 14), we demonstrate how the Fed targets a specific Federal funds rate and then uses open-market operations to drive the rate to that level and hold it there (see Figure 14.3). This new analysis will help students interpret the news as it relates to Fed announcements about the Federal funds rates.

Chapter-Level Learning Objectives

Several learning objectives have been included on the first page of each chapter. After reading a chapter, students should have mastered these core concepts. Questions in Test Banks I and II are organized according to these learning objectives, as are the narrated PowerPoint presentations.

Worked Problems

We continue to integrate the book and our Web site with in-text Web buttons that direct readers to Web site content. Specifically, we have added a third Web button consisting of a set of 50 worked problems. Written by Norris Peterson of Pacific Lutheran University, these pieces

Welcome to the seventeenth edition of *Macroeconomics*, the macro portion of *Economics*, the nation's best-selling economics textbook. An estimated 13 million students worldwide have now used this book. *Economics* has been adapted into Australian and Canadian editions and translated into Italian, Russian, Chinese, French, Spanish, Portuguese, and other languages. We are pleased that *Economics* continues to meet the market test: nearly one out of four U.S. students in principles courses used the sixteenth edition.

A Note about the Cover

The seventeenth edition cover includes a photograph of a staircase in the Musée des Beaux-Arts in Nancy, France. The photo is a metaphor for the step-by-step approach that we use to present basic economic principles. It also represents the simplicity, beauty, and power of basic economic models. Our goal is to entice the student to walk up the staircase. The floors above contain hundreds of years of accumulated economic knowledge, a portion of which we have captured for you here.

consist of side-by-side computational questions and the computational procedures used to derive the answers. In essence, they extend the textbook's explanations involving computations—for example, of real GDP, real GDP per capita, the unemployment rate, the inflation rate, per-unit production costs, economic profit, and more. From a student perspective, they provide "cookbook" help for problem solving.

This new content joins two carryover Web buttons from the prior edition. "Interactive Graphs" (developed under the supervision of Norris Peterson) depict more than 30 major graphs and instruct students to shift the curves, observe the outcomes, and derive relevant generalizations. "Origins of the Idea" are brief histories (written by Randy Grant of Linfield College) of

70 major ideas identified in the book. Students are interested in learning about the economists who first developed ideas such as opportunity costs, equilibrium price, the multiplier, comparative advantage, and elasticity.

New Internet Chapter

A new Internet chapter, along with an existing Web chapter, is available for free use at our Web site, **www.mcconnell17. com.** "Financial Economics" (Chapter 14Web), examines ideas such as compound interest, present value, arbitrage, risk, diversification, and the risk-return relationship.

This new Internet chapter was written by Sean Masaki Flynn. Sean is an important new member of the McConnell and Brue author team. He did his undergraduate work at USC, obtained his Ph.D. from the University of California–Berkeley (2002), and teaches at Vassar College. He is the author of the best-selling *Economics for Dummies*. We are very excited to have Sean on the authorship team, since he shares our desire to present economics in a way that is understandable to all.

The second Internet chapter, "The Economics of Developing Countries" (16Web), is updated and available for instructors and students who have a special interest in that topic. Developing economies are often in the news, and many college students have a keen interest in them. (For the chapter outlines for these three chapters, see pages 283, and 319 of this book.)

The two Web chapters have the same design, color, and features as regular book chapters, are readable in Adobe Acrobat format, and can be printed if desired. All are supported by the *Study Guide*, *Test Banks*, and other supplements to the book.

Consolidated Chapters

With overwhelming support of reviewers, we have consolidated the first two chapters of the prior edition into a single chapter, "Limits, Alternatives, and Choices" (Chapter 1). This new chapter quickly and directly moves the student into the subject matter of economics, demonstrating its methodology. This consolidation has the side benefit of reducing Part 1 (the common chapters in *Economics*, *Macroeconomics*, and *Microeconomics*) from six chapters to five.

We also combined the prior edition's separate chapters on fiscal policy and the public debt into a single chapter, "Fiscal Policy, Deficits, and Debt" (Chapter 11). The topics are closely related, and consolidation integrates them logically and smoothly.

New and Relocated "Consider This" and "Last Word" Boxes

Our "Consider This" boxes are used to provide analogies, examples, or stories that help drive home central economic ideas in a student-oriented, real-world manner. For instance, the idea of inflation is described with the story of feudal princes who clipped coins, while McDonald's "McHits" and "McMisses" demonstrate the idea of consumer sovereignty. These brief vignettes, each accompanied by a photo, illustrate key points in a lively, colorful, and easy-to-remember way.

CONSIDER THIS . . .

Unprincipled Agents

In the 1990s many corporations addressed the principal-agent problem by providing a substantial part of executive pay either as shares of the firm's stock or as stock options. Stock options are contracts that allow executives or other key employees to buy shares of their employers' stock at fixed, lower prices when the stock prices rise. The intent was to align the interest of the executives and other key employees more closely with those of the broader corporate owners. By pursuing high profits and share prices, the executives would enhance their own wealth as well as that of all the stockholders.

This isolution to the principal-agent problem had an unexpected negative side effect. It prompted a few unscrupulous executives to inflate their firms' share prices by hiding costs, overstating revenues, engaging in deceptive transactions, and, in general, exaggerating profits. These executives then sold large quantities of those inflated stock, making quick personal fortunes. In some cases, independent outside auditing firms turned out to be not so independent, because they held valuable consulting contracts with the firms being audited.

When the stock-market bubble of the late 1990s burst, many instances of business manipulations and fraudulent accounting were exposed. Several executives of large U.S. firms were indicted and a few large firms collapsed, among them Enron (energy trading), WorldCom (communications), and Arthur Andersen (accounting and business consulting). General stockholders of those firms were left holding severely depressed or even worthless stock.

In 2002 Congress strengthened the laws and penalties against executive misconduct. Also, corporations have improved their accounting and auditing procedures. But seemingly endless revelations of executive wrongdoings make clear that the principal-agent problem is not an easy problem to solve.

New "Consider This" boxes include such disparate topics as fast-food lines (Chapter 1), the economics of war (Chapter 1), "buying American" (Chapter 2), ticket scalping (Chapter 3), salsa and coffee beans (Chapter 3), unprincipled agents (Chapter 4), a CPA and a house painter (Chapter 5), high European unemployment rates (Chapter 7), the Fed as a sponge (Chapter 14), returns on ethical investing (Chapter 14Web), and women and economic growth (Chapter 16).

Our "Last Word" pieces are lengthier applications and case studies located toward the end of each chapter.

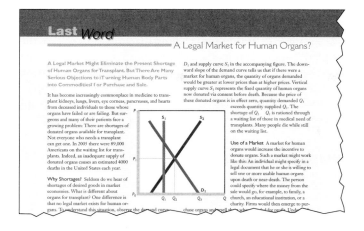

Last Word — A Legal Market for Human Organs?

A Legal Market Might Eliminate the Present Shortage of Human Organs for Transplant. But There Are Many Serious Objections to iTurning Human Body Parts into Commodities I for Purchase and Sale.

It has become increasingly commonplace in medicine to transplant kidneys, lungs, livers, eye corneas, pancreases, and hearts from deceased individuals to those whose organs have failed or are failing. But surgeons and many of their patients face a growing problem: There are shortages of donated organs available for transplant. Not everyone who needs a transplant can get one. In 2005 there were 89,000 Americans on the waiting list for transplants. Indeed, an inadequate supply of donated organs causes an estimated 4000 deaths in the United States each year.

Why Shortages? Seldom do we hear of shortages of desired goods in market economies. What is different about organs for transplant? One difference is that no legal market exists for human organs. To understand this situation, observe the demand curve...

D_1 and supply curve S_1 in the accompanying figure. The downward slope of the demand curve tells us that if there were a market for human organs, the quantity of organs demanded would be greater at lower prices than at higher prices. Vertical supply curve S_1 represents the fixed quantity of human organs now donated via consent before death. Because the price of these donated organs is in effect zero, quantity demanded Q_3 exceeds quantity supplied Q_1. The shortage of Q_3 ... Q_1 is rationed through a waiting list of those in medical need of transplants. Many people die while still on the waiting list.

Use of a Market A market for human organs would increase the incentive to donate organs. Such a market might work like this: An individual might specify in a legal document that he or she is willing to sell one or more usable human organs upon death or near-death. The person could specify where the money from the sale would go, for example, to family, a church, an educational institution, or a charity. Firms would then emerge to purchase organs and resell them where needed for profit. Under...

In this edition, we included photos to pique student interest. New and relocated Last Words include those on pitfalls to sound economic reasoning (Chapter 1), a market for human organs (Chapter 3), the long-run problem of financing Social Security (Chapter 4), the diminishing impact of oil prices on the overall economy (Chapter 10), the relative performance of index funds versus actively managed funds (Chapter 14Web), a supply-side anecdote on who gets tax cuts (Chapter 15), and economic growth in China (Chapter 16).

Contemporary Discussions and Examples

The seventeenth edition refers to and discusses many current topics. Examples include the economics of the war in Iraq, China's rapid growth rate, large Federal budget deficits, the Doha Round, recent Fed monetary policy, the debate over inflation targeting, the productivity acceleration, the recent profit paths of Wal-Mart and General Motors, rapidly expanding and disappearing U.S. jobs, rising oil prices, immigration impacts, large U.S. trade deficits, offshoring of American jobs, and many more.

Distinguishing Features

Comprehensive Explanations at an Appropriate Level *Macroeconomics* is comprehensive, analytical, and challenging yet fully accessible to a wide range of students. The thoroughness and accessibility enable instructors to select topics for special classroom emphasis with confidence that students can read and comprehend other independently assigned material in the book. Where needed, an extra sentence of explanation is provided. Brevity at the expense of clarity is false economy.

Fundamentals of the Market System Many economies throughout the world are making difficult transitions from planning to markets. Our detailed description of the institutions and operation of the market system in Chapter 2 is even more relevant than before. We pay particular attention to property rights, entrepreneurship, freedom of enterprise and choice, competition, and the role of profits because these concepts are often misunderstood by beginning students.

Early and Full Integration of International Economics We give the principles and institutions of the global economy early treatment. Chapter 5 examines the growth of world trade and its major participants, specialization and comparative advantage, the foreign exchange market, tariffs and subsidies, and various trade agreements. This strong introduction to international economics permits "globalization" of later discussions. Then, we delve into the more difficult, graphical analysis of international trade and finance in Chapters 18 and 19.

Early and Extensive Treatment of Government Government is an integral component of modern capitalism. This book introduces the economic functions of government early and accords them systematic treatment in Chapter 4. Government's role (including the role of the "Fed") in promoting full employment, price-level stability, and economic growth is central to the macroeconomic policy chapters.

Step-by-Step, Two-Path Macro We systematically present macroeconomics by:

- Examining the national income and product accounts and previewing economic growth, unemployment, and inflation.
- Discussing three key macro relationships.
- Presenting the aggregate expenditures model (AE model) in a single chapter.
- Developing the aggregate demand–aggregate supply model (AD-AS model).
- Using the AD-AS model to discuss fiscal policy.
- Introducing monetary considerations into the AD-AS model.
- Using the AD-AS model to discuss monetary policy.
- Extending the AD-AS model to include both short-run and long-run aggregate supply.
- Applying the "extended AD-AS model" to macroeconomic instability, economic growth, and disagreements on macro theory and policy.

We organized Chapters 8, 9, and 10 to provide two alternative paths through macro. We know that nearly all instructors like to cover somewhere in their macro course the basic relationships between income and consumption, the real interest rate and investment, and changes in spending and changes in output (the multiplier, conceptually presented). All of these topics are found in Chapter 8, "Basic Macroeconomic Relationships." The instructor can proceed from Chapter 8 directly to either Chapter 9, "The Aggregate Expenditures Model," or Chapter 10, "Aggregate Demand and Aggregate Supply." This organization allows those instructors who prefer not to teach the equilibrium AE model to skip it without loss of continuity. As before, the remainder of the macro is AD-AS based.

Emphasis on Technological Change and Economic Growth

This edition continues to emphasize economic growth. Chapter 1 uses the production possibilities curve to show the basic ingredients of growth. Chapter 7 explains how growth is measured and presents the facts of growth. Chapter 16 discusses the causes of growth, looks at productivity growth, and addresses some controversies surrounding economic growth. Chapter 7's Last Word examines the rapid economic growth in China. Chapter 16Web focuses on developing countries and the growth obstacles they confront.

Integrated Text and Web Site

Macroeconomics and its Web site are highly integrated through in-text Web buttons, Web-based end-of-chapter questions, bonus Web chapters, multiple-choice self-tests at the Web site, online newspaper articles, math notes, and other features. Our Web site is part and parcel of our student learning package, customized to the book.

Organizational Alternatives

Although instructors generally agree on the content of principles of economics courses, they sometimes differ on how to arrange the material. *Macroeconomics* includes 6 parts, and thus provides considerable organizational flexibility. For example, the two-path macro enables covering the full aggregate expenditures model or advancing directly from the basic macro relationships chapter to the AD-AS model. Also, the section of Chapter 15 that discusses the intricacies of the relationship between short-run and long-run aggregate supply can easily be appended to Chapter 10 on AD and AS.

Pedagogical Aids

Macroeconomics is highly student-oriented. The "To the Student" statement at the beginning of Part 1 details the book's many pedagogical aids. The seventeenth edition is also accompanied by a variety of high-quality supplements that help students master the subject and help instructors implement customized courses.

Supplements for Students and Instructors

Study Guide

One of the world's leading experts on economic education, William Walstad of the University of Nebraska–Lincoln, prepared the seventeenth edition of the *Study Guide*. Many students find the *Study Guide* indispensable. Each chapter contains an introductory statement, a checklist of behavioral objectives, an outline, a list of important terms, fill-in questions, problems and projects, objective questions, and discussion questions.

The *Guide* comprises a superb "portable tutor" for the principles student. Separate *Study Guides* are available for the macro and micro paperback editions of the text.

McGraw-Hill's Homework Manager Plus™

Homework Manager is a Web-based supplement that duplicates problem sets directly from the end-of-chapter material in your textbook. Using algorithms to provide a limitless supply of online self-graded assignments and graphing exercises, McGraw-Hill's Homework Manager™ can be used for practice, homework, and testing.

All assignments can be delivered over the Web and are graded automatically. Instructors can see all of the results stored in a private grade book. Detailed results let you see  at a glance how each student does on an assignment or an individual problem. Homework Manager Plus is an extension of McGraw-Hill's popular Homework Manager System. With McGraw-Hill's Homework Manager Plus™ you get all of the power of Homework Manager with an integrated online version of the text. Students receive one single access code which provides access to all of the resources available through Homework Manager Plus.

McGraw-Hill's Homework Manager Plus™ is a complete online homework solution, offering online graphing exercises, practice tests correlated with the key Learning Objectives, and full integration for Blackboard and WebCT courses.

Aplia McGraw-Hill/Irwin and Aplia (**www.aplia.com/mhhe**) are working together to bring you high-quality content and graphing tools in economics. Aplia provides:

- High-quality problem sets.
- Detailed news analyses with exercises.
- Math tutorials with testing.
- Online synchronous experiments.

Aplia will help increase student effort and enhance greater understanding and success in the course. This new partnership enables the bundling of Aplia with McGraw-Hill economics textbooks, including the comprehensive principles texts, one-semester splits, and the essentials books. An integrated eBook version of the text is included when access to Aplia is purchased as part of a McGraw-Hill package. New *value editions*, available directly from Aplia, include a one-color version of the complete text accompanied by full access to the Aplia application. The interactive tools and engaging materials are highly correlated to match the language and style of each McGraw-Hill book. Easy to use and set up, these new package options provide professors with even more flexibility and purchasing solutions for their students. To learn more about the McGraw-Hill/Aplia partnership, please visit **www.aplia.com.**

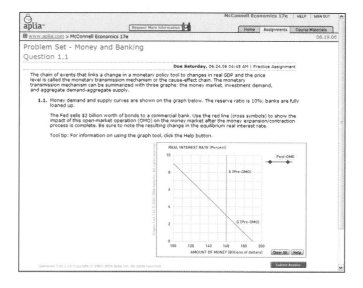

Online Learning Center (www.mcconnell17.com) The Web site accompanying this book contains a host of features. For example, the three kinds of highly visible "Web buttons" in the text alert the students to points in the book where they can springboard to the

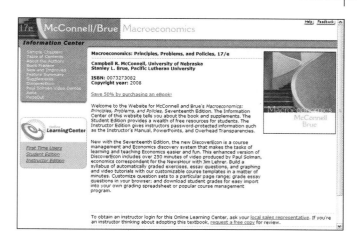

 **Online Learning Center with POWERWEB** Web site to get more information. Students can test their knowledge of a chapter's concepts with three self-graded multiple-choice quizzes per chapter. The "See the Math" section, written by Professor Norris Peterson, enables students to explore the mathematical details of the concepts in the text. Students can also access the Solman Videos, a set of more than 250 minutes of video covering key concepts from this text. Created by Paul Solman of *The News Hour with Jim Lehrer*, the videos cover core economic concepts such as elasticity, deregulation, and perfect competition.

New to the seventeenth edition site:

- Narrated PowerPoint presentations, which students can view on the site or download to their video iPod. The PowerPoints are correlated to the key Learning Objectives for every chapter. (Premium Content)
- The Solman Videos can also be downloaded to a video iPod or mp3 player. (Premium Content)
- Standard PowerPoint Presentations, answers to Web-based questions, and self-grading tests—all specific to *Economics*.
- Two optional Web chapters: "Financial Economics" and "The Economics of Developing Countries."

Zinio eBook Experience the speed, convenience, affordability, and intelligence of Zinio eBooks (**www.textbooks.zinio.com**). Digital textbooks are exact replicas of the print version, and better. They are easy to navigate,  allowing you to flip back and forth between pages, offer continual access to the Table of Contents with a toolbar button to jump directly to a chapter, topic, or page of interest. The Smart Zoom button allows you to easily zoom in and out, taking full advantage of crisp text and

high-resolution diagrams and images. Rich media offer an experience beyond simply reading, with flash, video, and audio. Embedded Web links also allow you to learn more about topics of interest and, when you are finished, return to exactly where you were in the book. Find relevant information quickly and easily with the search function, which allows you to get information on specific topics, phrases, and key words. You can write electronic notes with the Zinio annotation tool as well as highlight important topics. You can also print sections in high resolution and full color. Digital textbooks will become part of your lifestyle! The Zinio reader automatically saves your textbook in your own personal library on your computer. Textbooks can be easily referenced at any time, anywhere. To learn more or to download a free sample, visit **www.textbooks.zinio.com.**

iPod Content Harness the power of one of the most popular technology tools students use today–the Apple iPod. Our innovative approach enables students to download audio and video presentations right into their iPod and take learning materials with them wherever they go. This makes review and study time as easy as putting on headphones. Visit **www.mcconnell17.com** to learn more details on available iPod content—and enhance your learning experience today. (Premium Content)

McGraw-Hill PrepCenter™ The innovative McGraw-Hill PrepCenter™ offers a dynamic Web-based solution for managing all of the digital assets that accompany this textbook. The PrepCenter serves as a digital locker for your course materials, enabling you to consolidate the resources you need into readily accessible folders that are hosted in a secure and easy-to-use online environment. To learn more about McGraw-Hill's PrepCenter™, please visit **http://prepcenter.mhhe.com/.**

Enhanced Cartridges Enhanced WebCT and Blackboard course cartridges allow instructors to manage their course and administer online examinations. Some of the new features include:

- Pretest and posttest question banks: Administer comprehensive and chapter-specific pretests and posttests to evaluate student understanding. Pre- and posttest questions are tied to the chapter learning objectives and Association to Advance Collegiate Schools of Business (AACSB) guidelines.
- Question feedback: Answer feedback directs students back to the text for concept review. Feedback comments are linked to the Narrated PowerPoint presentations by learning objective.
- Administer tests and quizzes online: You decide how students are tested. Select the questions, time limit, and feedback options.
- Narrated PowerPoint presentations: Students can view these slides on the site or download the material to their video iPod. The PowerPoints are correlated to the key learning objectives for every chapter.

- The Solman Videos can also be downloaded to a video iPod or mp3 player.
- Flashcards enhance practice and preparation.

Instructor's Manual

Randy Grant of Linfield College revised and updated the *Instructor's Resource Manual*. The revised IM includes:

- Chapter summaries.
- Listings of "what's new" in each chapter.
- Teaching tips and suggestions.
- Learning objectives.
- Chapter outlines.
- Data and visual aid sources with suggestions for classroom use.
- Extra questions and problems.
- End-of-chapter correlation guides mapping content to the learning objectives and important AACSB standards.

The *Instructor's Manual* is available in hard copy or in electronic format on the Instructor's Resource CD-ROM as well as the Instructor's Side of the Online Learning Center.

Instructor's Resource CD-ROM

This CD contains everything the instructor needs, including PowerPoint slides, all the charts and figures from the text, Test Banks I and III, and the *Instructor's Manual*.

Three Test Banks

Test Bank I contains about 6650 multiple-choice and true-false questions, most of which were written by the text authors. *Instructor's Manual* author Randy Grant revised Test Bank I for the seventeenth edition. Test Bank II contains around 6300 multiple-choice and true-false questions, written by William Walstad. All Test Bank I and II questions are organized by learning objective, type, level of difficulty, relevant text page number, and general AACSB classifications. Test Bank III contains more than 600 pages of short-answer questions and problems created in the style of the book's end-of-chapter questions. Test Bank III can be used to construct student assignments or design essay and problem exams. Suggested answers to the essay and problem questions are included. In all, more than 14,000 questions give instructors maximum testing flexibility while ensuring the fullest possible text correlation.

Test Banks I and II are available in computerized EZ Test versions, as well as in MS Word. EZ Test allows professors to create multiple versions of the same test by scrambling questions and answer choices. The EZ Test software will meet the various needs of the widest spectrum of computer users. Test Bank III is available in printed and MS Word formats.

Classroom Performance Systems by eInstruction

This is a revolutionary system that brings ultimate interactivity to the classroom. CPS is a wireless response system that gives you immediate feedback from every student in the class. CPS units include easy-to-use

software for creating and delivering questions and assessments to your class. With CPS you can ask subjective and objective questions. Then every student responds with an individual, wireless response pad, providing instant results. CPS is the perfect tool for engaging students while gathering important assessment data.

Instructor's can access eInstruction questions in two formats—CPS and PowerPoint. Motivate student preparation, interactivity, and active learning with these lecture-formatted questions.

Color Transparencies

More than 200 new full-color transparencies were prepared for the seventeenth edition. They encompass all the figures appearing in *Economics*. Additionally, the figures and tables from the text are found on the Instructor's Resource CD-ROM.

Acknowledgments

We give special thanks to Sean Masaki Flynn of Vassar for the two new Internet chapters and Norris Peterson of Pacific Lutheran University and Randy Grant of Linfield College, who created the "button" content on our Web site. We again thank James Reese of the University of South Carolina at Spartanburg, who wrote the original Internet exercises. Although many of those questions were replaced or modified in the typical course of revision, several remain virtually unchanged. We also thank C. Norman Hollingsworth at Georgia Perimeter College for his ever-popular and creative PowerPoint slides and Terry Christesson at Clovis Community College for his Narrated PowerPoint slides. Finally, we thank William Walstad and Tom Barbiero (the coauthor of our Canadian edition) for their helpful ideas and insights.

We are greatly indebted to an all-star group of professionals at McGraw-Hill—in particular Gary Burke, Lucille Sutton, Rebecca Hicks, Lori Koetters, Keith McPherson, Douglas Reiner, and Brent Gordon—for their publishing and marketing expertise. To Lucille and Gary, we express our deepest gratitude for helping us keep *Economics* "number one" over the past 12 years.

We thank Keri Johnson for her selection of the Consider This and Last Word photos. Keith McPherson provided the vibrant cover.

The seventeenth edition has benefited from a number of perceptive formal reviews. The contributors, listed at the end of the Preface, were a rich source of suggestions for this revision. To each of you, and others we may have inadvertently overlooked, thank you for your considerable help in improving *Economics*.

Stanley L. Brue
Campbell R. McConnell

Contributors

Reviewers

Basil Al-Hashimi, *Mesa Community College*

Ayman Amer, *Mount Mercy College*

Len Anyanwu, *Union College*

Greg Arburn, *University of Findlay*

William Ashley, *Mississippi Delta Community College*

John Atkins, *Pensacola Junior College*

Hamid Azari-Rad, *State University of New York–New Paltz*

Asatar Bair, *City College of San Francisco*

Paul Ballantyne, *University of Colorado at Colorado Springs*

Carl Bauer, *Oakton Community College*

Charles A. Bennett, *Gannon University*

Jay Bhattacharya, *Okaloosa-Walton College*

Antonio Bos, *Tusculum College*

David Bourne, *Northwest Mississippi Community College*

Douglas M. Brown, *Georgetown University*

Lara Bryant, *Florida Atlantic University*

Rebecca Cline, *Middle Georgia College Dublin Campus*

Rosa Lea Danielson, *College of DuPage*

Mahmoud R. Davoudi, *North Harris College*

Mark DeHainaut, *California University of Pennsylvania*

Kruti Dholakia, *University of Texas at Dallas*

Richard W. Dixon, *Thomas Nelson Community College*

Amrik Singh Dua, *Mt. San Antonio College*

James Dulgeroff, *San Bernardino Valley College*

Kevin C. Duncan, *Colorado State University–Pueblo*

Eugene Elander, *Plymouth State University*

Christopher A. Erickson, *New Mexico State University*

James Fallon, *Gwynedd-Mercy College*

Nikki M. Finlay, *Clayton State University*

John Francis, *Auburn University Montgomery*

S.N. Gajanan, *University of Pittsburgh*

Maria V. Gamba, *University of Findlay*

Michael G. Goode, *Central Piedmont Community College*

William D. Goodman, *Bluefield State College*

Gary Greene, *Manatee Community College–Venice*

Lisa Grobar, *California State University–Long Beach*

Phillip J. Grossman, *St. Cloud State University*

Shiv K. Gupta, *University of Findlay*

David W. Hedrick, *Central Washington University*

Elizabeth Hill, *Pennsylvania State University–Mont Alto*

Steven R. Hoagland, *Mount Union College*

Tracy Hofer, *University of Wisconsin–Stevens Point*

Jack W. Hou, *California State University–Long Beach*

Andy Howard, *Rio Hondo College*

Greg Hunter, *Cal Poly Pomona*

Tim Justice, *Columbus Technical College*

Veronica Kalich, *Baldwin-Wallace College*

Carol King, *Dana College*

Jack Kinworthy, *Concordia University*

Tori H. Knight, *Carson-Newman College*

Jacob Kurien, *Rockhurst University*

Felix B. Kwan, *Maryville University*

James Lacey, *Hesser College*
Chris Lawrey, *Williams Baptist College*
Bozena Leven, *College of New Jersey*
Patricia Lindsey, *Butte College*
Kenneth E. Long, *New River Community College*
KT Magnusson, *Salt Lake Community College*
Monica Malanoski, *Winston Churchill High School*
Gretchen Mester, *Anne Arundel Community College*
Meghan Millea, *Mississippi State University*
Amlan Mitra, *Purdue University Calumet*
Carl B. Montano, *Lamar University*
Antoni Moskwa, *Allegheny College*
Thaddeaus Mounkurai, *Daytona Beach Community College*
Panos Mourdoukoutas, *Long Island University*
Annette Najjar, *Lindenwood University*
Louis V. Palacios-Salguero, *Rutgers University*
James E. Payne, *Illinois State University*
Wesley A. Payne, *Delgado Community College*
Joseph S. Pomykala, *Towson University*
Joe Prinzinger, *Lynchburg College*
Jeffrey Reed, *Columbia College of Missouri*
Charles A. Reichheld, *Cuyahoga Community College*
Timothy Jay Reynolds, *Alvin Community College*
Kathryn Roberts, *Chipola College*
Mike Romzy, *Waynesburg College*
Barbara Ross, *Kapi'olani Community College*
Henry Ryder, *Gloucester County College*
William C. Schaniel, *University of West Georgia*
Jerry Schwartz, *Broward Community College*
Edward M. Shaffer, *Gwynedd Mercy College*
Calvin Shipley, *Henderson State University*
Carl Simkonis, *Northern Kentucky University*
Garvin Smith, *Daytona Beach Community College*
Thomas P. Soos, *Pennsylvania State University–McKeesport*
Joanne Spitz, *University of Massachusetts–Boston*
Robert E. Tansky, *St. Clair County Community College*
Donna Thompson, *Brookdale Community College*
Lee J. Van Scyoc, *University of Wisconsin–Oshkosh*
Debra Way, *University of Cincinnati Clermont College*
Janice E. Weaver, *Drake University*
W. Parker Wheatley, *Saint John's University*
Thomas G. Wier, *Northeastern State University*
Krissa Wrigley, *University of Phoenix*

User Survey Respondents

Basil Al-Hashimi, *Mesa Community College*
Len Anyanwu, *Union College*
John Baffoe-Bonnie, *Pennsylvania State University–Delaware County*
Paul Ballantyne, *University of Colorado at Colorado Springs*
Emil Berendt, *Friends University*
John E. Bowen, *Park University*

Joyce Bremer, *Oakton Community College*
Stacey Brook, *University of Sioux Falls*
W. Todd Brotherson, *Southern Virginia University*
Douglas D. Brown, *Scottsdale Community College*
Mark Buenafe, *Mesa Community College*
Francine Butler, *Grand View College*
Chris Cusatis, *Gwynedd Mercy College*
Mahmoud R. Davoudi, *North Harris College*
Mark DeHainaut, *California University of Pennsylvania*
Richard Dempsey, *Ohio State University at Lima*
Manfred Dix, *Tulane University*
Amrik Singh Dua, *Mt. San Antonio College*
James Dulgeroff, *San Bernardino Valley College*
Erick M. Elder, *University of Arkansas at Little Rock*
Loretta Fairchild, *Nebraska Wesleyan University*
Abdollah Ferdowsi, *Ferris State University*
Lawrence Frateschi, *College of DuPage*
Arthur Friedberg, *Mohawk Valley Community College*
Yoshi Fukasawa, *Midwestern State University*
S.N. Gajanan, *University of Pittsburgh*
Maria V. Gamba, *University of Findlay*
Leticia Garcia, *Elgin Community College*
David G. Garraty, *Virginia Wesleyan College*
Philip J Grossman, *St. Cloud State University*
Lydia Harris, *Goucher College*
Charles F. Hawkins, *Lamar University*
Mark L. Healy, *William Rainey Harper College*
Michael G. Heslop, *Northern Virginia Community College*
Thomas Hiestand, *Concordia College*
Elizabeth Hill, *Pennsylvania State University–Mont Alto*
Tracy Hofer, *University of Wisconsin–Stevens Point*
Naphtali Hoffman, *Elmira College*
Andy Howard, *Rio Hondo College*
Mahshid Jalilvand, *University of Wisconsin–Stout*
R. Bruce Johnson, *Southwest Missouri State University*
Frederick M. Jungman, *Northwestern Oklahoma State University*
Veronica Kalich, *Baldwin-Wallace College*
Theodore C. Kariotis, *Towson University*
Alan Kessler, *Providence College*
Jack Kinworthy, *Concordia University*
Barry Kotlove, *Edmonds Community College*
Felix B. Kwan, *Maryville University*
Fritz Laux, *Northeastern State University*
Chris Lawrey, *Williams Baptist College*
Bozena Leven, *College of New Jersey*
KT Magnusson, *Salt Lake Community College*
Monica Malanoski, *Winston Churchill High School*
John E. Martinez, *Midwestern State University*
Jerome McElroy, *St. Mary's College*
Meghan Mille, *Mississippi State University*
Masoud Moallem, *Rockford College*
Carl B. Montano, *Lamar University*
Panos Mourdoukoutas, *Long Island University*

Joseph S. Pomykala, *Towson University*
Mitchell Redlo, *Rochester Institute of Technology*
Charles A. Reichheld, *Cuyahoga Community College*
Kathryn Roberts, *Chipola College*
Mike Romzy, *Waynesburg College*
Barbara Ross, *Kapi'olani Community College*
Henry Ryder, *Gloucester County College*
Calvin Shipley, *Henderson State University*
Carl Simkonis, *Northern Kentucky University*
Thomas P. Soos, *Pennsylvania State University–McKeesport*

Joanne Spitz, *University of Massachusetts–Boston*
Donna Thompson, *Brookdale Community College*
Michael Twomey, *University of Michigan–Dearborn*
Lee J. Van Scyoc, *University of Wisconsin–Oshkosh*
Debra Way, *University of Cincinnati Clermont College*
Janice E. Weaver, *Drake University*
Thomas G. Wier, *Northeastern State University*
Wendy Wood, *Bevill State Community College*
Krissa Wrigley, *University of Phoenix*

Brief Contents

PART ONE

Introduction to Economics and the Economy

Chapter 1

Contents

WEB Chapter 16   www.mcconnell17.com

Chapter 17

PART SIX
International Economics

Chapter 18

This book and its ancillaries contain several features designed to help you learn economics:

- *Web buttons* A glance through the book reveals many pages with symbols in the margins. These "buttons" alert you to helpful learning aids available with the book. The graph button denotes "Interactive Graphs" found at the text's Web site, **www.mcconnell17.com.** Brief exercises have you interact with the graphs, for example, by clicking on a specific curve and dragging it to a new location. These exercises will enhance your understanding of the underlying concepts. The light-bulb button symbolizes "Worked Problems." Numeric problems are presented and then solved, side-by-side, step-by-step. Seeing how the problems are worked will help you solve similar problems on quizzes and exams. The egg button stands for "Origin of the Idea." Each of these pieces traces a particular idea to the person or persons who first developed it.

| Interactive Graphs | Worked Problems | Origin of the Idea |

After reading a chapter, thumb back through it to note the Web buttons and the number that follows them. On the home page of our Internet site select Student Edition and use the pull-down list under "Choose one" to find the Web button content for each chapter.

- *Other Internet aids* Our Internet site contains many other aids. In the Student Edition you will find self-testing multiple-choice quizzes, links to relevant news articles, and much more. For those of you with very strong mathematics background, be sure to note the "See the Math" section on the Web site. There you will find nearly 50 notes that develop the algebra and, in a few cases, the calculus that underlie the economic concepts.
- *Appendix on graphs* Be assured, however, that you will need only basic math skills to do well in the principles course. In particular, you will need to be comfortable with basic graphical analysis and a few quantitative concepts. The appendix at the end of

Chapter 1 reviews graphs and slopes of curves. You may want to read it before starting Chapter 1.

- *Reviews* Each chapter contains two or three Quick Reviews and an end-of-chapter summary. These reviews will help you focus on essential ideas and study for exams.
- *Key terms and Key Graphs* Key terms are set in boldface type within the chapters, listed at the end of each chapter, and again defined in the glossary at the end of the book. Graphs with special relevance are labeled Key Graphs, and each includes a multiple-choice Quick Quiz. Your instructor may or may not emphasize all of these figures, but you should pay special attention to those that are discussed in class; you can be certain there will be exam questions on them.
- *Consider This and Last Word boxes* Many chapters include a Consider This box. These brief pieces provide commonplace analogies, examples, and stories that help you understand and remember central economic ideas. Each chapter concludes with a Last Word box. Some of them are revealing applications of economic ideas; others are short case studies. While it is tempting to ignore in-text boxes, don't. Most are fun to read, and all will improve your grasp of economics.
- *Questions* A comprehensive list of study questions is located at the end of each chapter. Several of the questions are designated Key Questions and are answered in the *Study Guide* and also at our Internet site. Also at the Internet site are three multiple-choice quizzes for each chapter.
- *Study Guide* We enthusiastically recommend the *Study Guide* accompanying this text. This "portable tutor" contains not only a broad sampling of various kinds of questions but a host of useful learning aids. Software-driven tutorials (Aplia, for example) are also available with the text.

Our two main goals are to help you understand and apply economics and help you improve your analytical skills. An understanding of economics will enable you to comprehend a whole range of economic, social, and political problems that otherwise would seem puzzling and perplexing. Also, your study will enhance reasoning skills that are highly prized in the workplace.

Good luck with your study. We think it will be well worth your effort.

IN THIS CHAPTER YOU WILL LEARN:

- **The definition of economics and the features of the economic perspective.**

- **The role of economic theory in economics.**

- **The distinction between microeconomics and macroeconomics.**

- **The categories of scarce resources and the nature of the economizing problem.**

- **About production possibilities analysis, increasing opportunity costs, and economic growth.**

Limits, Alternatives, and Choices

(An appendix on understanding graphs follows this chapter. If you need a quick review of this mathematical tool, you might benefit by reading the appendix first.) People's wants are numerous and varied. Biologically, people need only air, water, food, clothing, and shelter. But in modern society people also desire goods and services that provide a more comfortable or affluent standard of living. We want bottled water, soft drinks, and fruit juices, not just water from the creek. We want salads, burgers, and pizzas, not just berries and nuts. We want jeans, suits, and coats, not just woven reeds. We want apartments, condominiums, or houses, not just mud huts. And, as the saying goes, "that is not the half of it." We also want DVD players, Internet service, education, homeland security, cell phones, health care, and much more.

Fortunately, society possesses productive resources, such as labor and managerial talent, tools and machinery, and land and mineral deposits. These resources, employed in the economic system (or simply the economy), help us produce goods and services that satisfy many of our economic wants. But the blunt reality is that our economic wants far exceed the productive capacity of our scarce (limited) resources. We are forced to make choices. This unyielding truth underlies the definition of **economics,** which is the social science concerned with how individuals, institutions, and society make optimal (best) choices under conditions of scarcity.

O 1.1
Origin of the term
"Economics"

The Economic Perspective

Economists view things from a unique perspective. This **economic perspective,** or economic way of thinking, has several critical and closely interrelated features.

Scarcity and Choice

From our definition of economics, we can easily see why economists view the world through the lens of scarcity. Scarce economic resources mean limited goods and services. Scarcity restricts options and demands choices. Because we "can't have it all," we must decide what we will have and what we must forgo.

At the core of economics is the idea that "there is no free lunch." You may be treated to lunch, making it "free" from your perspective, but someone bears a cost—ultimately, society. Scarce inputs of land, equipment, farm labor, the labor of cooks and waiters, and managerial talent are required. Because society could have used these resources to produce something else, it sacrifices those other goods and services in making the lunch available. Economists call such sacrifices **opportunity costs:** To obtain more of one thing, society forgoes the opportunity of getting the next best thing. That sacrifice is the opportunity cost of the choice.

Purposeful Behavior

Economics assumes that human behavior reflects "rational self-interest." Individuals look for and pursue opportunities to increase their **utility**—the pleasure, happiness, or satisfaction obtained from consuming a good or service. They allocate their time, energy, and money to maximize their satisfaction. Because they weigh costs and benefits, their economic decisions are "purposeful" or "rational," not "random" or "chaotic."

O 1.2
Utility

Consumers are purposeful in deciding what goods and services to buy. Business firms are purposeful in deciding what products to produce and how to produce them. Government entities are purposeful in deciding what public services to provide and how to finance them.

"Purposeful behavior" does not assume that people and institutions are immune from faulty logic and therefore are perfect decision makers. They sometimes make mistakes. Nor does it mean that people's decisions are unaffected by emotion or the decisions of those around them. "Purposeful behavior" simply means that people make decisions with some desired outcome in mind.

Rational self-interest is not the same as selfishness. In the economy, increasing one's own wage, rent, interest, or

---

Free for All?

Free products are seemingly everywhere. Sellers offer free software, free cell phones, and free checking accounts. Dentists give out free toothbrushes. At state visitor centers, there are free brochures and maps.

Does the presence of so many free products contradict the economist's assertion "There is no free lunch"? No! Resources are used to produce each of these products, and because those resources have alternative uses, society gives up something else to get the "free" good. Where resources are used to produce goods or services, there is no free lunch.

So why are these goods offered for free? In a word: marketing! Firms sometimes offer free products to entice people to try them, hoping they will then purchase those goods later. The free software may eventually entice you to buy the producer's upgraded software. In other instances, the free brochures contain advertising for shops and restaurants, and that free e-mail program is filled with ads. In still other cases, the product is free only in conjunction with a larger purchase. To get the free bottle of soda, you must buy the large pizza. To get the free cell phone, you need to sign up for a year's worth of cell phone service.

So "free" products may or may not be truly free to individuals. They are never free to society.

---

profit normally requires identifying and satisfying *somebody else's* wants! Also, people make personal sacrifices to others. They contribute time and money to charities because they derive pleasure from doing so. Parents help pay for their

Fast-Food Lines

The economic perspective is useful in analyzing all sorts of behaviors. Consider an everyday example: the behavior of fast-food customers. When customers enter the restaurant, they go to the shortest line, believing that line will minimize their time cost of obtaining food. They are acting purposefully; time is limited, and people prefer using it in some way other than standing in line.

If one fast-food line is temporarily shorter than other lines, some people will move to that line. These movers apparently view the time saving from the shorter line (marginal benefit) as exceeding the cost of moving from their present line (marginal cost). The line switching tends to equalize line lengths. No further movement of customers between lines occurs once all lines are about equal.

Fast-food customers face another cost-benefit decision when a clerk opens a new station at the counter. Should they move to the new station or stay put? Those who shift to the new line decide that the time saving from the move exceeds the extra cost of physically moving. In so deciding, customers must also consider just how quickly they can get to the new station compared with others who may be contemplating the same move. (Those who hesitate in this situation are lost!)

Customers at the fast-food establishment do not have perfect information when they select lines. Thus, not all decisions turn out as expected. For example, you might enter a short line and find someone in front of you is ordering hamburgers and fries for 40 people in the Greyhound bus parked out back (and the employee is a trainee)! Nevertheless, at the time you made your decision, you thought it was optimal.

Finally, customers must decide what food to order when they arrive at the counter. In making their choices, they again compare marginal costs and marginal benefits in attempting to obtain the greatest personal satisfaction for their expenditure.

Economists believe that what is true for the behavior of customers at fast-food restaurants is true for economic behavior in general. Faced with an array of choices, consumers, workers, and businesses rationally compare marginal costs and marginal benefits in making decisions.

children's education for the same reason. These self-interested, but unselfish, acts help maximize the givers' satisfaction as much as any personal purchase of goods or services. Self-interested behavior is simply behavior designed to increase personal satisfaction, however it may be derived.

Marginal Analysis: Benefits and Costs

The economic perspective focuses largely on **marginal analysis**—comparisons of marginal benefits and marginal costs, usually for decision making. To economists, "marginal" means "extra," "additional," or "a change in." Most choices or decisions involve changes in the status quo, meaning the existing state of affairs.

Should you attend school for another year? Should you study an extra hour for an exam? Should you supersize your fries? Similarly, should a business expand or reduce its output? Should government increase or decrease its funding for a missile defense system?

Each option involves marginal benefits and, because of scarce resources, marginal costs. In making choices rationally, the decision maker must compare those two amounts. Example: You and your fiancée are shopping for an engagement ring. Should you buy a $\frac{1}{2}$-carat diamond, a $\frac{5}{8}$-carat diamond, a $\frac{3}{4}$-carat diamond, a 1-carat diamond, or something even

O 1.3
Marginal analysis

larger? The marginal cost of a larger-size diamond is the added expense beyond the cost of the smaller-size diamond. The marginal benefit is the perceived lifetime pleasure (utility) from the larger-size stone. If the marginal benefit of the larger diamond exceeds its marginal cost (and you can afford it), buy the larger stone. But if the marginal cost is more than the marginal benefit, buy the smaller diamond instead, even if you can afford the larger stone!

In a world of scarcity, the decision to obtain the marginal benefit associated with some specific option always includes the marginal cost of forgoing something else. The money spent on the larger-size diamond means forgoing some other product. Opportunity costs are present whenever a decision is made. **(Key Question 3)**

Theories, Principles, and Models

Like the physical and life sciences, as well as other social sciences, economics relies on the **scientific method.** That procedure consists of several elements:

- The observation of real-world behavior and outcomes.
- Based on those observations, the formulation of a possible explanation of cause and effect (hypothesis).

- The testing of this explanation by comparing the outcomes of specific events to the outcome predicted by the hypothesis.
- The acceptance, rejection, or modification of the hypothesis, based on these comparisons.
- The continued testing of the hypothesis against the facts. As favorable results accumulate, the hypothesis evolves into a theory. A very well-tested and widely accepted theory is referred to as an economic law or an **economic principle**—a statement about economic behavior or the economy that enables prediction of the probable effects of certain actions. Combinations of such laws or principles are incorporated into models, which are simplified representations of how something works, such as a market or segment of the economy.

Economists develop theories of the behavior of individuals (consumers, workers) and institutions (businesses, governments) engaged in the production, exchange, and consumption of goods and services. Theories, principles, and models are "purposeful simplifications." The full scope of economic reality itself is too complex and bewildering to be understood as a whole. In developing theories, principles, and models economists remove the clutter and simplify.

Economic principles and models are highly useful in analyzing economic behavior and understanding how the economy operates. They are the tools for ascertaining cause and effect (or action and outcome) within the economic system. Good theories do a good job of explaining and predicting. They are supported by facts concerning how individuals and institutions actually behave in producing, exchanging, and consuming goods and services.

There are some other things you should know about economic principles.

- *Generalizations* Economic principles are generalizations relating to economic behavior or to the economy itself. Economic principles are expressed as the tendencies of typical or average consumers, workers, or business firms. For example, economists say that consumers buy more of a particular product when its price falls. Economists recognize that some consumers may increase their purchases by a large amount, others by a small amount, and a few not at all. This "price-quantity" principle, however, holds for the typical consumer and for consumers as a group.
- *Other-Things-Equal Assumption* In constructing their theories, economists use the *ceteris paribus* or **other-things-equal assumption**—the assumption that factors other than those being considered do not change. They assume that all variables except those under immediate consideration are held constant for a particular analysis. For example, consider the relationship between the price of Pepsi and the amount of it purchased. Assume that of all the factors that might influence the amount of Pepsi purchased (for example, the price of Pepsi, the price of Coca-Cola, and consumer incomes and preferences), only the price of Pepsi varies. This is helpful because the economist can then focus on the "price of Pepsi–purchases of Pepsi" relationship without being confused by changes in other variables.

O 1.4
Ceteris paribus

- *Graphical Expression* Many economic models are expressed graphically. Be sure to read the special appendix at the end of this chapter as a review of graphs.

Macroeconomics and Microeconomics

Economists develop economic principles and models at two levels.

Macroeconomics

Macroeconomics examines either the economy as a whole or its basic subdivisions or aggregates, such as the government, household, and business sectors. An **aggregate** is a collection of specific economic units treated as if they were one unit. Therefore, we might lump together the millions of consumers in the U.S. economy and treat them as if they were one huge unit called "consumers."

In using aggregates, macroeconomics seeks to obtain an overview, or general outline, of the structure of the economy and the relationships of its major aggregates. Macroeconomics speaks of such economic measures as total output, total employment, total income, aggregate expenditures, and the general level of prices in analyzing various economic problems. No or very little attention is given to specific units making up the various aggregates.

Figuratively, macroeconomics looks at the beach, not the pieces of sand, the rocks, and the shells.

Microeconomics

Microeconomics is the part of economics concerned with individual units such as a person, a household, a firm, or an industry. At this level of analysis, the economist observes the details of an economic unit, or very small segment of the economy, under a figurative microscope. In microeconomics we look at decision making by individual customers, workers, households, and business firms. We measure the price of a specific product, the number of workers employed by a single firm, the revenue or income of a particular firm or household, or the expenditures of a specific firm, government entity, or family. In microeconomics, we examine the sand, rock, and shells, not the beach.

The macro–micro distinction does not mean that economics is so highly compartmentalized that every topic can be readily labeled as either macro or micro; many topics and subdivisions of economics are rooted in both. Example: While the problem of unemployment is usually treated as a macroeconomic topic (because unemployment relates to aggregate production), economists recognize that the decisions made by *individual* workers on how long to search for jobs and the way *specific* labor markets encourage or impede hiring are also critical in determining the unemployment rate. (**Key Question 5**)

Positive and Normative Economics

Both macroeconomics and microeconomics contain elements of positive economics and normative economics. **Positive economics** focuses on facts and cause-and-effect relationships. It includes description, theory development, and theory testing (theoretical economics). Positive economics avoids value judgments, tries to establish scientific statements about economic behavior, and deals with what the economy is actually like. Such scientific-based analysis is critical to good policy analysis.

Economic policy, on the other hand, involves **normative economics,** which incorporates value judgments about what the economy should be like or what particular policy actions should be recommended to achieve a desirable goal (policy economics). Normative economics looks at the desirability of certain aspects of the economy. It underlies expressions of support for particular economic policies.

Positive economics concerns *what is*, whereas normative economics embodies subjective feelings about *what ought to be*. Examples: Positive statement: "The unemployment rate in France is higher than that in the United States." Normative statement: "France ought to undertake policies to make its labor market more flexible to reduce unemployment rates." Whenever words such as "ought" or "should" appear in a sentence, you are very likely encountering a normative statement.

Most of the disagreement among economists involves normative, value-based policy questions. Of course, economists sometime disagree about which theories or models best represent the economy and its parts; but they agree on a full range of economic principles. Most economic controversy thus reflects differing opinions or value judgments about what society should be like.

Individuals' Economizing Problem

A close examination of the **economizing problem**—the need to make choices because economic wants exceed economic means—will enhance your understanding of economic models and the difference between microeconomic and macroeconomic analysis. Let's first build a microeconomic model of the economizing problem faced by an individual.

Limited Income

We all have a finite amount of income, even the wealthiest among us. Even Donald Trump must decide how to spend his money! And the majority of us have much more limited means. Our income comes to us in the form of wages, interest, rent, and profit, although we may also receive money from government programs or family members. As Global Perspective 1.1 shows, the average income of Americans in 2004 was $41,400. In the poorest nations, it was less than $500.

Unlimited Wants

For better or worse, most people have virtually unlimited wants. We desire various goods and services that provide utility. Our wants extend over a wide range of products, from *necessities* (for example, food, shelter, and clothing) to *luxuries* (for example, perfumes, yachts, and sports cars).

Average Income, Selected Nations

Average income (total income/population) and therefore typical individual budget constraints vary greatly among nations.

Country	Per Capita Income, 2004 (U.S. dollars, based on exchange rates)
Switzerland	$48,230
United States	41,400
Japan	37,180
France	30,090
South Korea	13,980
Mexico	6,770
Brazil	3,090
China	1,290
Pakistan	600
Nigeria	390
Rwanda	220
Liberia	110

Source: World Bank, **www.worldbank.org.**

Some wants such as basic food, clothing, and shelter have biological roots. Other wants, for example, specific kinds of food, clothing, and shelter, arise from the conventions and customs of society.

Over time, as new products are introduced, economic wants tend to change and multiply. Only recently have people wanted MP3 players, Internet service, digital cameras, or camera phones because those products did not exist a few decades ago. Also, the satisfaction of certain wants may trigger others: the acquisition of a Ford Focus or a Honda Civic has been known to whet the appetite for a Lexus or a Mercedes.

Services, as well as goods, satisfy our wants. Car repair work, the removal of an inflamed appendix, legal and accounting advice, and haircuts all satisfy human wants. Actually, we buy many goods, such as automobiles and washing machines, for the services they render. The differences between goods and services are often smaller than they appear to be.

For most people, the desires for goods and services cannot be fully satisfied. Bill Gates may have all that he wants for himself, but his massive charitable giving suggests that he keenly wants better health care for the world's poor. Our desires for a particular good or service can be satisfied; over a short period of time we can surely get enough toothpaste or pasta. And one appendectomy is plenty. But our desire for goods and services in general seem to be another story.

Because we have only limited income (usually through our work) but seemingly insatiable wants, it is in our self-interest to economize: to pick and choose goods and services that create maximum utility.

A Budget Line

We can clarify the economizing problem facing consumers by visualizing a **budget line** (or, more technically, a *budget constraint*). It is a schedule or curve that shows various combinations of two products a consumer can purchase with a specific money income. Although we assume two products, the analysis generalizes to the full range of products available to an individual consumer.

To understand the idea of a budget line, suppose that you received a Barnes & Noble (or Borders) gift card as a birthday present. The $120 card is soon to expire. You take the card to the store and confine your purchase decisions to two alternatives: DVDs and paperback books. DVDs are $20 each and paperback books are $10 each. Your purchase options are shown in the table in Figure 1.1.

At one extreme, you might spend all of your $120 "income" on 6 DVDs at $20 each and have nothing left to spend on books. Or, by giving up 2 DVDs and thereby gaining $40, you can have 4 DVDs at $20 each and 4 books at $10 each. And so on to the other extreme, at which you could buy 12 books at $10 each, spending your entire gift card on books with nothing left to spend on DVDs.

The graph in Figure 1.1 shows the budget line. Note that the graph is not restricted to whole units of DVDs and books as is the table. Every point on the graph represents a possible combination of DVDs and books, including fractional quantities. The slope of the graphed budget line measures the ratio of the price of books (P_b) to the price of DVDs (P_{dvd}); more precisely, the slope is $P_b/P_{dvd} = \$ - 10/\$ + 20 = -\frac{1}{2}$, or $-.5$. So you must forgo 1 DVD (measured on the vertical axis) to buy 2 books (measured on the horizontal axis). This yields a slope of $-\frac{1}{2}$ or $-.5$.

The budget line illustrates several ideas.

Attainable and Unattainable Combinations

All the combinations of DVDs and books on or inside the budget line are *attainable* from the $120 of money income. You can afford to buy, for example, 3 DVDs at $20 each

FIGURE 1.1 A consumer's budget line. The budget line (or budget constraint) shows all the combinations of any two products that can be purchased, given the prices of the products and the consumer's money income.

The Budget Line: Whole-Unit Combinations of DVDs and Paperback Books Attainable with an Income of $120		
Units of DVDs (Price = $20)	Units of Books (Price = $10)	Total Expenditure
6	0	($120 = $120 + $0)
5	2	($120 = $100 + $20)
4	4	($120 = $80 + $40)
3	6	($120 = $60 + $60)
2	8	($120 = $40 + $80)
1	10	($120 = $20 + $100)
0	12	($120 = $0 + $120)

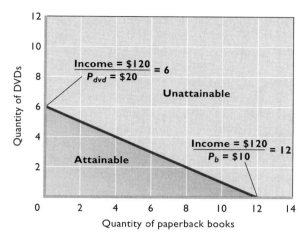

and 6 books at $10 each. You also can obviously afford to buy 2 DVDs and 5 books, if so desired, and not use up the value on the gift card. But to achieve maximum utility you will want to spend the full $120.

In contrast, all combinations beyond the budget line are *unattainable*. The $120 limit simply does not allow you to purchase, for example, 5 DVDs at $20 each and 5 books at $10 each. That $150 expenditure would clearly exceed the $120 limit. In Figure 1.1 the attainable combinations are on and within the budget line; the unattainable combinations are beyond the budget line.

Tradeoffs and Opportunity Costs The budget line in Figure 1.1 illustrates the idea of tradeoffs arising from limited income. To obtain more DVDs, you have

O 1.5
Opportunity costs

to give up some books. For example, to obtain the first DVD, you trade off 2 books. So the opportunity cost of the first DVD is 2 books. To obtain the second DVD the opportunity cost is also 2 books. The straight-line budget constraint, with its constant slope, indicates constant opportunity cost. That is, the opportunity cost of 1 extra DVD remains the same (= 2 books) as more DVDs are purchased. And, in reverse, the opportunity cost of 1 extra book does not change (= $\frac{1}{2}$ DVD) as more books are bought.

Choice Limited income forces people to choose what to buy and what to forgo to fulfill wants. You will select the combination of DVDs and paperback books that you think is "best." That is, you will evaluate your marginal benefits and marginal costs (here, product price) to make choices that maximize your satisfaction. Other people, with the same $120 gift card, would undoubtedly make different choices.

CONSIDER THIS ...

Did Gates, Winfrey, and Rodriguez Make Bad Choices?

Opportunity costs come into play in decisions well beyond simple buying decisions. Consider the different choices people make with respect to college. College graduates usually earn about 50 percent more during their lifetimes than persons with just high school diplomas. For most capable students, "Go to college, stay in college, and earn a degree" is very sound advice.

Yet Microsoft cofounder Bill Gates and talk show host Oprah Winfrey* both dropped out of college, and baseball star Alex Rodriguez ("A-Rod") never even bothered to start classes. What were they thinking? Unlike most students, Gates faced enormous opportunity costs for staying in college. He had a vision for his company, and his starting work young helped ensure Microsoft's success. Similarly, Winfrey landed a spot in local television news when she was a teenager, eventually producing and starring in the *Oprah Winfrey Show* when she was 32 years old. Getting a degree in her twenties might have interrupted the string of successes that made her famous talk show possible. And Rodriguez knew that professional athletes have short careers. Therefore, going to college directly after high school would have taken away 4 years of his peak earning potential.

So Gates, Winfrey, and Rodriguez understood opportunity costs and made their choices accordingly. The size of opportunity costs greatly matters in making individual decisions.

*Winfrey eventually went back to school and earned a degree from Tennessee State University when she was in her thirties.

Income Changes The location of the budget line varies with money income. An increase in money income shifts the budget line to the right; a decrease in money income shifts it to the left. To verify this, recalculate the table in Figure 1.1, assuming the card value (income) is (a) $240 and (b) $60, and plot the new budget lines in the graph. No wonder people like to have more income: That shifts their budget lines outward and enables them to buy more goods and services. But even with more income, people will still face spending tradeoffs, choices, and opportunity costs. (Key Question 7)

W 1.1
Budget lines

QUICK REVIEW 1.2

- Because wants exceed incomes, individuals face an economizing problem; they must decide what to buy and what to forgo.
- A budget line (budget constraint) shows the various combinations of two goods that a consumer can purchase with a specific money income.
- Straight-line budget constraints imply constant opportunity costs associated with obtaining more of either of the two goods.

Society's Economizing Problem

Society must also make choices under conditions of scarcity. It, too, faces an economizing problem. Should it devote more of its limited resources to the criminal justice system (police, courts, and prisons) or to education (teachers, books, and schools)? If it decides to devote more resources to both, what other goods and services does it forgo? Health care? Energy development?

Scarce Resources

Society has limited or scarce **economic resources,** meaning all natural, human, and manufactured resources that go into the production of goods and services. This includes the entire set of factory and farm buildings and all the equipment, tools, and machinery used to produce manufactured goods and agricultural products; all transportation and communication facilities; all types of labor; and land and mineral resources.

Resource Categories

Economists classify economic resources into four general categories.

Land Land means much more to the economist than it does to most people. To the economist **land** includes all natural resources ("gifts of nature") used in the production process, such as arable land, forests, mineral and oil deposits, and water resources.

Labor The resource **labor** consists of the physical and mental talents of individuals used in producing goods and services. The services of a logger, retail clerk, machinist, teacher, professional football player, and nuclear physicist all fall under the general heading "labor."

Capital For economists, **capital** (or capital goods) includes all manufactured aids used in producing consumer goods and services. Included are all factory, storage, transportation, and distribution facilities, as well as tools and machinery. Economists refer to the purchase of capital goods as **investment.**

Capital goods differ from consumer goods because consumer goods satisfy wants directly, whereas capital goods do so indirectly by aiding the production of consumer goods. Note that the term "capital" as used by economists refers not to money but to tools, machinery, and other productive equipment. Because money produces nothing, economists do not include it as an economic resource. Money (or money capital or financial capital) is simply a means for purchasing capital goods.

Entrepreneurial Ability Finally, there is the special human resource, distinct from labor, called **entrepreneurial ability.** The entrepreneur performs several functions:

- The entrepreneur takes the initiative in combining the resources of land, labor, and capital to produce a good or a service. Both a sparkplug and a catalyst, the entrepreneur is the driving force behind production and the agent who combines the other resources in what is hoped will be a successful business venture.
- The entrepreneur makes the strategic business decisions that set the course of an enterprise.
- The entrepreneur is an innovator. He or she commercializes new products, new production techniques, or even new forms of business organization.
- The entrepreneur is a risk bearer. The entrepreneur has no guarantee of profit. The reward for the entrepreneur's time, efforts, and abilities may be profits or losses. The entrepreneur risks not only his or her invested funds but those of associates and stockholders as well.

Because land, labor, capital, and entrepreneurial ability are combined to produce goods and services, they are called the **factors of production,** or simply "inputs."

Production Possibilities Model

Society uses its scarce resources to produce goods and services. The alternatives and choices it faces can best be understood through a macroeconomic model of production possibilities. To keep things simple, let's initially assume:

- *Full employment* The economy is employing all its available resources.
- *Fixed resources* The quantity and quality of the factors of production are fixed.
- *Fixed technology* The state of technology (the methods used to produce output) is constant.
- *Two goods* The economy is producing only two goods: pizzas and industrial robots. Pizzas symbolize **consumer goods,** products that satisfy our wants directly; industrial robots (for example, the kind used to weld automobile frames) symbolize **capital goods,** products that satisfy our wants indirectly by making possible more efficient production of consumer goods.

Production Possibilities Table

A production possibilities table lists the different combinations of two products that can be produced with a specific set of resources, assuming full employment. Table 1.1 presents a simple, hypothetical economy that is producing pizzas and industrial robots; the data are, of course, hypothetical. At alternative A, this economy would be devoting all its available resources to the production of industrial robots (capital goods); at alternative E, all resources would go to pizza production (consumer goods). Those alternatives are unrealistic extremes; an economy typically produces both capital goods and consumer goods, as in B, C, and D. As we move from alternative A to E, we increase the production of pizzas at the expense of the production of industrial robots.

TABLE 1.1 **Production Possibilities of Pizzas and Industrial Robots**

	Production Alternatives				
Type of Product	**A**	**B**	**C**	**D**	**E**
Pizzas (in hundred thousands)	0	1	2	3	4
Robots (in thousands)	10	9	7	4	0

Because consumer goods satisfy our wants directly, any movement toward E looks tempting. In producing more pizzas, society increases the current satisfaction of its wants. But there is a cost: More pizzas means fewer industrial robots. This shift of resources to consumer goods catches up with society over time because the stock of capital goods does not expand at the current rate, with the result that some potential for greater future production is lost. By moving toward alternative E, society chooses "more now" at the expense of "much more later."

By moving toward A, society chooses to forgo current consumption, thereby freeing up resources that can be used to increase the production of capital goods. By building up its stock of capital this way, society will have greater future production and, therefore, greater future consumption. By moving toward A, society is choosing "more later" at the cost of "less now."

Generalization: At any point in time, a fully employed economy must sacrifice some of one good to obtain more of another good. Scarce resources prohibit such an economy from having more of both goods. Society must choose among alternatives. There is no such thing as a free pizza, or a free industrial robot.

Production Possibilities Curve

The data presented in a production possibilities table are shown graphically as a **production possibilities curve.** Such a curve displays the different combinations of goods and services that society can produce in a fully employed economy, assuming a fixed availability of supplies of resources and constant technology. We arbitrarily represent the economy's output of capital goods (here, industrial robots) on the vertical axis and the output of consumer goods (here, pizzas) on the horizontal axis, as shown in **Figure 1.2 (Key Graph).**

G 1.1

Production possibilities curve

Each point on the production possibilities curve represents some maximum output of the two products. The curve is a "constraint" because it shows the limit of attainable outputs. Points on the curve are attainable as long as the economy uses all its available resources. Points lying inside the curve are also attainable, but they reflect less total output and therefore are not as desirable as points on the curve. Points inside the curve imply that the economy could have more of both industrial robots and pizzas if it achieved full employment of its resources. Points lying beyond the production possibilities curve, like *W*, would represent a greater output than the output

keygraph

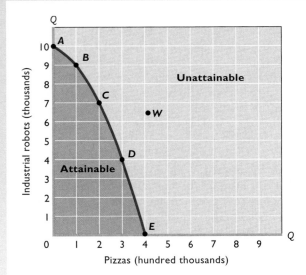

FIGURE 1.2 **The production possibilities curve.** Each point on the production possibilities curve represents some maximum combination of two products that can be produced if resources are fully employed. When an economy is operating on the curve, more industrial robots means less pizzas, and vice versa. Limited resources and a fixed technology make any combination of industrial robots and pizzas lying outside the curve (such as at W) unattainable. Points inside the curve are attainable, but they indicate that full employment is not being realized.

at any point on the curve. Such points, however, are unattainable with the current availability of resources and technology.

Law of Increasing Opportunity Cost

Figure 1.2 clearly shows that more pizzas means fewer industrial robots. The number of units of industrial robots that must be given up to obtain another unit of pizzas, of course, is the opportunity cost of that unit of pizzas.

In moving from alternative A to alternative B in Table 1.1, the cost of 1 additional unit of pizzas is 1 fewer unit of industrial robots. But when additional units are considered—B to C, C to D, and D to E—an important economic principle is revealed: For society, the opportunity cost of each additional unit of pizzas is greater than the opportunity cost of the preceding one. When we move from A to B, just 1 unit of industrial robots is sacrificed for 1 more unit of pizzas; but in going from B to C we sacrifice 2 additional units of industrial robots for 1 more unit of pizzas; then 3 more of industrial robots for 1 more of pizzas; and finally 4 for 1. Conversely, confirm that as we move from E to A, the cost of an additional unit of industrial robots (on average) is $\frac{1}{4}$, $\frac{1}{3}$, $\frac{1}{2}$, and 1 unit of pizzas, respectively, for the four successive moves.

Our example illustrates the **law of increasing opportunity costs.** As the production of a particular good increases, the opportunity cost of producing an additional unit rises.

Shape of the Curve   The law of increasing opportunity costs is reflected in the shape of the production possibilities curve: The curve is bowed out from the origin of the graph. Figure 1.2 shows that when the economy moves from *A* to *E*, it must give up successively larger amounts of industrial robots (1, 2, 3, and 4) to acquire equal increments of pizzas (1, 1, 1, and 1). This is shown in the slope of the production possibilities curve, which becomes steeper as we move from *A* to *E*.

Economic Rationale   The economic rationale for the law of increasing opportunity costs is that economic resources are not completely adaptable to alternative uses. Many resources are better at producing one type of good than at producing others. Some land is highly suited to growing the ingredients necessary for pizza production, but as pizza production expands society has to start using land that is less bountiful for farming. Other land is rich in mineral deposits and therefore well-suited to producing the materials needed to make industrial robots. As society steps up the production of robots, it must use land that is less and less adaptable to making their components.

If we start at *A* and move to *B* in Figure 1.2, we can shift resources whose productivity is relatively high in pizza production and low in industrial robots. But as we move from *B* to *C*, *C* to *D*, and so on, resources highly productive of pizzas become increasingly scarce. To get more pizzas, resources whose productivity in industrial robots is relatively great will be needed. Increasingly more of such resources, and hence greater sacrifices of industrial robots, will be needed to achieve each 1-unit increase in pizzas. This lack of perfect flexibility, or interchangeability, on the part of resources is the cause of increasing opportunity costs for society. **(Key Question 10)**

W 1.2

Production possibilities

Optimal Allocation

Of all the attainable combinations of pizzas and industrial robots on the curve in Figure 1.2, which is optimal (best)? That is, what specific quantities of resources should be allocated to pizzas and what specific quantities should be allocated to industrial robots in order to maximize satisfaction?

Recall that economic decisions center on comparisons of marginal benefit (MB) and marginal cost (MC). Any economic activity should be expanded as long as marginal benefit exceeds marginal cost and should be reduced if marginal cost exceeds marginal benefit. The optimal

amount of the activity occurs where MB = MC. Society needs to make a similar assessment about its production decision.

Consider pizzas. We already know from the law of increasing opportunity costs that the marginal costs of additional units of pizzas will rise as more units are produced. We also know that we obtain extra or marginal benefits from additional units of pizzas. However, although economic wants in the aggregate are insatiable, the assumption that successive units of a particular product yield fewer additional benefits to society than prior units is reasonable.

The optimal quantity of pizza production is indicated by point *e* at the intersection of the MB and MC curves: 200,000 units in Figure 1.3. Why is this amount the optimal quantity? If only 100,000 units of pizzas were produced, the marginal benefit of an extra unit of them (point *a*) would exceed its marginal cost (point *b*). In money terms, MB is $15, while MC is only $5. When society gains something worth $15 at a marginal cost of only $5, it is better off. In Figure 1.3, net gains can continue to be realized until pizza-product production has been increased to 200,000.

In contrast, the production of 300,000 units of pizzas is excessive. There the MC of an added unit is $15 (point *c*) and its MB is only $5 (point *d*). This means that 1 unit of pizzas is worth only $5 to society but costs it $15 to obtain. This is a losing proposition for society!

FIGURE 1.3   Optimal output: MB = MC. Achieving the optimal output requires the expansion of a good's output until its marginal benefit (MB) and marginal cost (MC) are equal. No resources beyond that point should be allocated to the product. Here, optimal output occurs at point e, where 200,000 units of pizzas are produced.

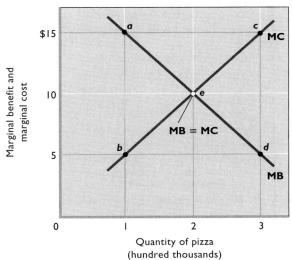

So resources are being efficiently allocated to any product when the marginal benefit and marginal cost of its output are equal (MB = MC). Suppose that by applying the same analysis to industrial robots, we find that the optimal (MB = MC) output of robots is 7000. This would

CONSIDER THIS …

The Economics of War

Production possibilities analysis is helpful in assessing the costs and benefits of waging the broad war on terrorism, including the wars in Afghanistan and Iraq. An October 2005 estimate places the total cost of these efforts, including rebuilding expenses, at $350 billion.

If we categorize all U.S. production as either "defense goods" or "civilian goods," we can measure them on the axes of a production possibilities diagram such as that shown in Figure 1.2. The opportunity cost of using more resources for defense goods is the civilian goods sacrificed. In a fully employed economy, more defense goods are achieved at the opportunity cost of fewer civilian goods—health care, education, pollution control, personal computers, houses, and so on. The cost of war and defense is the other goods forgone. The benefits are numerous and diverse but clearly include the gains from protecting against future loss of American lives, assets, income, and well-being.

Society must assess the marginal benefit (MB) and marginal cost (MC) of additional defense goods to determine their optimal amounts—where to locate on the defense goods–civilian goods production possibilities curve. Although estimating marginal benefits and marginal costs is an imprecise art, the MB-MC framework is a useful way of approaching choices. An optimal allocation of resources requires that society expand production of defense goods until MB = MC.

The events of September 11, 2001, and the future threats they foreshadowed increased the marginal benefits of defense goods, as perceived by Americans. If we label the horizontal axis in Figure 1.3 "defense goods" and draw in a rightward shift of the MB curve, you will see that the optimal quantity of defense goods rises. In view of the concerns relating to September 11, the United States allocated more of its resources to defense. But the MB-MC analysis also reminds us we can spend too much on defense, as well as too little. The United States should not expand defense goods beyond the point where MB = MC. If it does, it will be sacrificing civilian goods of greater value than the defense goods obtained.

mean that alternative C (200,000 units of pizzas and 7000 units of industrial robots) on the production possibilities curve in Figure 1.2 would be optimal for this economy. **(Key Question 11)**

QUICK REVIEW 1.3

- Economists categorize economic resources as land, labor, capital, and entrepreneurial ability.
- The production possibilities curve illustrates several ideas: (a) scarcity of resources is implied by the area of unattainable combinations of output lying outside the production possibilities curve; (b) choice among outputs is reflected in the variety of attainable combinations of goods lying along the curve; (c) opportunity cost is illustrated by the downward slope of the curve; (d) the law of increasing opportunity costs is implied by the bowed-outward shape of the curve.
- A comparison of marginal benefits and marginal costs is needed to determine the best or optimal output mix on a production possibilities curve.

Unemployment, Growth, and the Future

In the depths of the Great Depression of the 1930s, one-quarter of U.S. workers were unemployed and one-third of U.S. production capacity was idle. The United States has suffered a number of considerably milder downturns since then, the latest occurring in 2001. In that year total production fell one-half a percentage point and unemployment increased by about 2 million workers.

Almost all nations have experienced widespread unemployment and unused production capacity from business downturns at one time or another. Since 1995, for example, several nations—including Argentina, Japan, Mexico, Germany, and South Korea—have had economic downturns and unemployment.

How do these realities relate to the production possibilities model? Our analysis and conclusions change if we relax the assumption that all available resources are fully employed. The five alternatives in Table 1.1 represent maximum outputs; they illustrate the combinations of pizzas and industrial robots that can be produced when the economy is operating at full employment. With unemployment, this economy would produce less than each alternative shown in the table.

Graphically, we represent situations of unemployment by points inside the original production possibilities curve (reproduced here in Figure 1.4). Point U is one such point. Here the economy is falling short of the various maximum combinations of pizzas and industrial robots represented

FIGURE 1.4 **Unemployment and the production possibilities curve.** Any point inside the production possibilities curve, such as *U*, represents unemployment or a failure to achieve full employment. The arrows indicate that by realizing full employment, the economy could operate on the curve. This means it could produce more of one or both products than it is producing at point *U*.

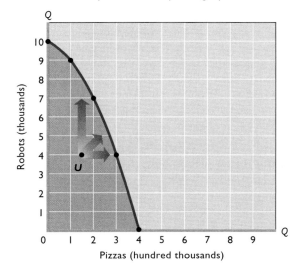

by the points on the production possibilities curve. The arrows in Figure 1.4 indicate three possible paths back to full employment. A move toward full employment would yield a greater output of one or both products.

A Growing Economy

When we drop the assumptions that the quantity and quality of resources and technology are fixed, the production possibilities curve shifts positions and the potential maximum output of the economy changes.

Increases in Resource Supplies
Although resource supplies are fixed at any specific moment, they change over time. For example, a nation's growing population brings about increases in the supplies of labor and entrepreneurial ability. Also, labor quality usually improves over time. Historically, the economy's stock of capital has increased at a significant, though unsteady, rate. And although some of our energy and mineral resources are being depleted, new sources are also being discovered. The development of irrigation programs, for example, adds to the supply of arable land.

The net result of these increased supplies of the factors of production is the ability to produce more of both consumer goods and capital goods. Thus 20 years from now, the production possibilities may supersede those shown in Table 1.1. The new production possibilities might look like those in the table in Figure 1.5. The

greater abundance of resources will result in a greater potential output of one or both products at each alternative. The economy will have achieved economic growth in the form of expanded potential output. Thus, when an increase in the quantity or quality of resources occurs, the production possibilities curve shifts outward and to the right, as illustrated by the move from the inner curve to curve *A'B'C'D'E'* in Figure 1.5. This sort of shift represents growth of economic capacity, which, when used, means **economic growth:** a larger total output.

Advances in Technology
An advancing technology brings both new and better goods and improved ways of producing them. For now, let's think of technological advance as being only improvements in the methods of production, for example, the introduction of computerized systems to manage inventories and schedule production. These advances alter our previous discussion of the economizing problem by allowing society to produce more goods with available resources. As with increases in

FIGURE 1.5 **Economic growth and the production possibilities curve.** The increase in supplies of resources, improvements in resource quality, and technological advances that occur in a dynamic economy move the production possibilities curve outward and to the right, allowing the economy to have larger quantities of both types of goods.

Type of Product	Production Alternatives				
	A'	**B'**	**C'**	**D'**	**E'**
Pizzas (in hundred thousands)	0	2	4	6	8
Robots (in thousands)	14	12	9	5	0

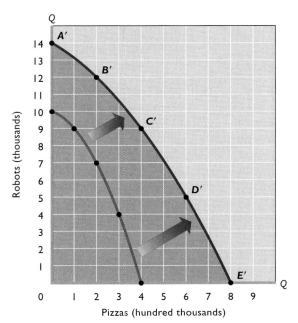

Last *Word*

Pitfalls to Sound Economic Reasoning

Because they affect us so personally, we often have difficulty thinking accurately and objectively about economic issues.

Here are some common pitfalls to avoid in successfully applying the economic perspective.

Biases Most people bring a bundle of biases and preconceptions to the field of economics. For example, some might think that corporate profits are excessive or that lending money is always superior to borrowing money. Others might believe that government is necessarily less efficient than businesses or that more government regulation is always better than less. Biases cloud thinking and interfere with objective analysis. All of us must be willing to shed biases and preconceptions that are not supported by facts.

Loaded Terminology The economic terminology used in

newspapers and broadcast media is sometimes emotionally biased, or loaded. The writer or spokesperson may have a cause to promote or an ax to grind and may slant comments accordingly. High profits may be labeled "obscene," low wages may be called "exploitive," or self-interested behavior may be "greed." Government workers may be referred to as "mindless bureaucrats" and those favoring stronger government regulations may be called "socialists." To objectively analyze economic issues, you must be prepared to reject or discount such terminology.

Fallacy of Composition Another pitfall in economic thinking is the assumption that what is true for one individual or part of a whole is necessarily true for a group of individuals or the whole. This is a logical fallacy called the *fallacy of composition*; the assumption is not correct. A statement that is valid for an individual or part is not necessarily valid for the larger group or whole. You may see the action better if you leap to your feet to see an

resource supplies, technological advances make possible the production of more industrial robots and more pizzas.

A real-world example of improved technology is the recent surge of new technologies relating to computers, communications, and biotechnology. Technological advances have dropped the prices of computers and greatly increased their speed. Improved software has greatly increased the everyday usefulness of computers. Cellular phones and the Internet have increased communications capacity, enhancing production and improving the efficiency of markets. Advances in biotechnology have resulted in important agricultural and medical discoveries. The sum of these new technologies is so significant that they may be contributing to greater-than-normal U.S. economic growth (larger rightward shifts of the nation's production possibilities curve).

Conclusion: Economic growth is the result of (1) increases in supplies of resources, (2) improvements in resource quality, and (3) technological advances. The consequence of growth is that a full-employment economy can enjoy a greater output of both consumption goods and

capital goods. Whereas static, no-growth economies must sacrifice some of one good to obtain more of another, dynamic, growing economies can have larger quantities of both goods. **(Key Question 13)**

Present Choices and Future Possibilities

An economy's current choice of positions on its production possibilities curve helps determine the future location of that curve. Let's designate the two axes of the production possibilities curve as "goods for the future" and "goods for the present," as in Figure 1.6. Goods for the future are such things as capital goods, research and education, and preventive medicine. They increase the quantity and quality of property resources, enlarge the stock of technological information, and improve the quality of human resources. As we have already seen, goods for the future, such as capital goods, are the ingredients of economic growth. Goods for the present are consumer goods, such as food, clothing, and entertainment.

outstanding play at a football game. But if all the spectators leap to their feet at the same time, nobody—including you—will have a better view than when all remained seated.

Here is an economic example: An individual farmer who reaps a particularly large crop is likely to realize a sharp gain in income. But this statement cannot be generalized to farmers as a group. The individual farmer's large "bumper" crop will not noticeably reduce crop prices because each farmer produces a negligible fraction of the total farm output. But for all farmers as a group, prices decline when total output increases. Thus, if all farmers reap bumper crops, the total output of farm products will increase, depressing crop prices. If the price declines are relatively large, total farm income might actually fall.

Post Hoc Fallacy You must think very carefully before concluding that because event A precedes event B, A is the cause of B. This kind of faulty reasoning is known as the *post hoc, ergo propter hoc,* or "after this, therefore because of this," fallacy. Noneconomic example: A professional football team hires a new coach and the team's record improves. Is the new coach the cause? Maybe. Perhaps the presence of more experienced and talented players or an easier schedule is the true cause. The rooster crows before dawn, but does not cause the sunrise.

Economic example: Many people blamed the Great Depression of the 1930s on the stock market crash of 1929. But the crash did not cause the Great Depression. The same severe weaknesses in the economy that caused the crash caused the Great Depression. The depression would have occurred even without the preceding stock market crash.

Correlation but not Causation Do not confuse correlation, or connection, with causation. Correlation between two events or two sets of data indicates only that they are associated in some systematic and dependable way. For example, we may find that when variable X increases, Y also increases. But this correlation does not necessarily mean that there is causation—that an increase in X is the cause of an increase in Y. The relationship could be purely coincidental or dependent on some other factor, Z, not included in the analysis.

Here is an example: Economists have found a positive correlation between education and income. In general, people with more education earn higher incomes than those with less education. Common sense suggests education is the cause and higher incomes are the effect; more education implies a more knowledgeable and productive worker, and such workers receive larger salaries.

But might the relationship be explainable in other ways? Are education and income correlated because the characteristics required for succeeding in education—ability and motivation— are the same ones required to be a productive and highly paid worker? If so, then people with those traits will probably both obtain more education and earn higher incomes. But greater education will not be the sole cause of the higher income.

FIGURE 1.6 Present choices and future locations of production possibilities curves. A nation's current choice favoring "present goods," as made by Presentville in (a), will cause a modest outward shift of the production possibilities curve in the future. A nation's current choice favoring "future goods," as made by Futureville in (b), will result in a greater outward shift of the curve in the future.

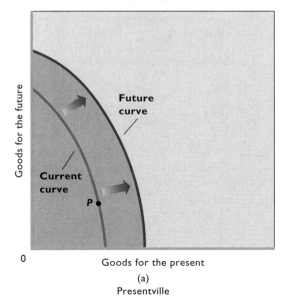

(a)
Presentville

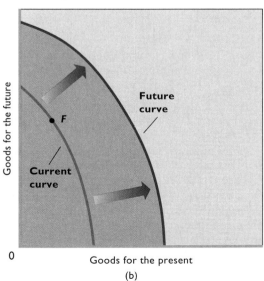

(b)
Futureville

Now suppose there are two hypothetical economies, Presentville and Futureville, which are initially identical in every respect except one: Presentville's current choice of positions on its production possibilities curve strongly

favors present goods over future goods. Point *P* in Figure 1.6a indicates that choice. It is located quite far down the curve to the right, indicating a high priority for goods for the present, at the expense of fewer goods for the future. Futureville, in contrast, makes a current choice that stresses larger amounts of future goods and smaller amounts of present goods, as shown by point *F* in Figure 1.6b.

G 1.2

Present choices and future possibilities

Now, other things equal, we can expect the future production possibilities curve of Futureville to be farther to the right than Presentville's curve. By currently choosing an output more favorable to technological advances and to increases in the quantity and quality of resources, Futureville will achieve greater economic growth than Presentville. In terms of capital goods, Futureville is choosing to make larger current additions to its "national factory" by devoting more of its current output to capital than Presentville. The payoff from this choice for Futureville is greater future production capacity and economic growth. The opportunity cost is fewer consumer goods in the present for Futureville to enjoy.

Is Futureville's choice thus necessarily "better" than Presentville's? That, we cannot say. The different outcomes simply reflect different preferences and priorities in the two countries. But each country will have to live with the economic consequences of its choice. **(Key Question 14)**

A Qualification: International Trade

Production possibilities analysis implies that an individual nation is limited to the combinations of output indicated by its production possibilities curve. But we must modify this principle when international specialization and trade exist.

You will see in later chapters that an economy can circumvent, through international specialization and trade, the output limits imposed by its domestic production possibilities curve. International specialization means directing domestic resources to output that a nation is highly efficient at producing. International trade involves the exchange of these goods for goods produced abroad. Specialization and trade enable a nation to get more of a desired good at less sacrifice of some other good. Rather than sacrifice 3 units of robots to get a third unit of pizza, as in Table 1.1, a nation might be able to obtain the third unit of pizza by trading only 2 units of robots for it. Specialization and trade have the same effect as having more and better resources or discovering improved production techniques; both increase the quantities of capital and consumer goods available to society. Expansion of domestic production possibilities and international trade are two separate routes for obtaining greater output.

QUICK REVIEW 1.4

- Unemployment causes an economy to operate at a point inside its production possibilities curve.
- Increases in resource supplies, improvements in resource quality, and technological advance cause economic growth, which is depicted as an outward shift of the production possibilities curve.
- An economy's present choice of capital and consumer goods helps determine the future location of its production possibilities curve.
- International specialization and trade enable a nation to obtain more goods than its production possibilities curve indicates.

Summary

1. Economics is the social science that examines how individuals, institutions, and society make optimal choices under conditions of scarcity.

2. The economic perspective includes three elements: scarcity and choice, purposeful behavior, and marginal analysis. It sees individuals and institutions making rational decisions based on comparisons of marginal costs and marginal benefits.

3. Economists employ the scientific method, in which they form and test hypotheses of cause-and-effect relationships to generate theories, laws, and principles. Economists often combine theories into representations called models.

4. Macroeconomics looks at the economy as a whole or its major aggregates. Microeconomics examines specific economic units or institutions.

5. Positive economic analysis deals with facts; normative economics reflects value judgments.

6. Individuals face an economizing problem. Because their wants exceed their income, they must decide what to purchase and what to forgo. Society also faces an economizing problem. Societal wants exceed the available resources necessary to fulfill them. Society therefore must decide what to produce and what to forgo.

7. Graphically, a budget line (or budget constraint) illustrates the economizing problem for individuals. The line shows the various combinations of two products that a consumer can purchase with a specific money income, given the prices of the two products.

8. Economic resources are inputs into the production process and can be classified as land, labor, capital, and entrepreneurial ability. Economics resources are also known as factors of production or inputs.

9. Economists illustrate society's economizing problem through production possibilities analysis. Production possibilities tables and curves show the different combinations of goods and services that can be produced in a fully employed economy, assuming that resource quantity, resource quality, and technology are fixed.

10. An economy that is fully employed and thus operating on its production possibilities curve must sacrifice the output of some types of goods and services to increase the production of others. The gain of one type of good or service is always accompanied by an opportunity cost in the form of the loss of some of the other type.

11. Because resources are not equally productive in all possible uses, shifting resources from one use to another creates increasing opportunity costs. The production of additional units of one product requires the sacrifice of increasing amounts of the other product.

12. The optimal (best) point on the production possibilities curve represents the most desirable mix of goods and is determined by expanding the production of each good until its marginal benefit (MB) equals its marginal cost (MC).

13. Over time, technological advances and increases in the quantity and quality of resources enable the economy to produce more of all goods and services, that is, to experience economic growth. Society's choice as to the mix of consumer goods and capital goods in current output is a major determinant of the future location of the production possibilities curve and thus of the extent of economic growth.

Terms and Concepts

economics	aggregate	capital
economic perspective	microeconomics	investment
opportunity cost	positive economics	entrepreneurial ability
utility	normative economics	factors of production
marginal analysis	economizing problem	consumer goods
scientific method	budget line	capital goods
economic principle	economic resources	production possibilities curve
other-things-equal assumption	land	law of increasing opportunity costs
macroeconomics	labor	economic growth

Study Questions

1. What is an opportunity cost? How does the idea relate to the definition of economics? Which of the following decisions would entail the greatest opportunity cost: Allocating a square block in the heart of New York City for a surface parking lot or allocating a square block at the edge of a typical suburb for such a lot? Explain.

2. What is meant by the term "utility" and how does the idea relate to purposeful behavior?

3. **KEY QUESTION** Cite three examples of recent decisions that you made in which you, at least implicitly, weighed marginal cost and marginal benefit.

4. What are the key elements of the scientific method and how does this method relate to economic principles and laws?

5. **KEY QUESTION** Indicate whether each of the following statements applies to microeconomics or macroeconomics:
   a. The unemployment rate in the United States was 5.2 percent in January 2005.
   b. A U.S. software firm discharged 15 workers last month and transferred the work to India.
   c. An unexpected freeze in central Florida reduced the citrus crop and caused the price of oranges to rise.
   d. U.S. output, adjusted for inflation, grew by 3.5 percent in 2005.
   e. Last week Wells Fargo Bank lowered its interest rate on business loans by one-half of 1 percentage point.
   f. The consumer price index rose by 3.4 percent in 2005.

6. State (a) a positive economic statement of your choice, and then (b) a normative economic statement relating to your first statement.

7. **KEY QUESTION** Suppose you won $15 on a lotto ticket at the local 7-Eleven and decided to spend all the winnings on candy bars and bags of peanuts. The price of candy bars is $.75 and the price of peanuts is $1.50.
   a. Construct a table showing the alternative combinations of the two products that are available.
   b. Plot the data in your table as a budget line in a graph. What is the slope of the budget line? What is the opportunity cost of one more candy bar? Of one more bag

of peanuts? Do these opportunity costs rise, fall, or remain constant as each additional unit of the product is purchased?

c. How, in general, would you decide which of the available combinations of candy bars and bags of peanuts to buy?

d. Suppose that you had won $30 on your ticket, not $15. Show the $30 budget line in your diagram. Why would this budget line be preferable to the old one?

8. What are economic resources? What categories do economists use to classify them? Why are resources also called factors of production? Why are they called inputs?

9. Why is money not considered to be a capital resource in economics? Why is entrepreneurial ability considered a category of economic resource, distinct from labor? What are the major functions of the entrepreneur?

10. **KEY QUESTION** Below is a production possibilities table for consumer goods (automobiles) and capital goods (forklifts):

Type of Production	Production Alternatives				
	A	B	C	D	E
Automobiles	0	2	4	6	8
Forklifts	30	27	21	12	0

a. Show these data graphically. Upon what specific assumptions is this production possibilities curve based?

b. If the economy is at point C, what is the cost of one more automobile? Of one more forklift? Explain how the production possibilities curve reflects the law of increasing opportunity costs.

c. If the economy characterized by this production possibilities table and curve were producing 3 automobiles and 20 fork lifts, what could you conclude about its use of its available resources?

d. What would production at a point outside the production possibilities curve indicate? What must occur before the economy can attain such a level of production?

11. **KEY QUESTION** Specify and explain the typical shapes of marginal-benefit and marginal-cost curves. How are these curves used to determine the optimal allocation of resources

to a particular product? If current output is such that marginal cost exceeds marginal benefit, should more or fewer resources be allocated to this product? Explain.

12. Explain how (if at all) each of the following events affects the location of a country's production possibilities curve:
a. The quality of education increases.
b. The number of unemployed workers increases.
c. A new technique improves the efficiency of extracting copper from ore.
d. A devastating earthquake destroys numerous production facilities.

13. **KEY QUESTION** Referring to the table in question 10, suppose improvement occurs in the technology of producing forklifts but not in the technology of producing automobiles. Draw the new production possibilities curve. Now assume that a technological advance occurs in producing automobiles but not in producing forklifts. Draw the new production possibilities curve. Now draw a production possibilities curve that reflects technological improvement in the production of both goods.

14. **KEY QUESTION** On average, households in China save 40 percent of their annual income each year, whereas households in the United States save less than 5 percent. Production possibilities are growing at roughly 9 percent annually in China and 3.5 percent in the United States. Use graphical analysis of "present goods" versus "future goods" to explain the differences in growth rates.

15. Suppose that, on the basis of a nation's production possibilities curve, an economy must sacrifice 10,000 pizzas domestically to get the 1 additional industrial robot it desires but that it can get the robot from another country in exchange for 9000 pizzas. Relate this information to the following statement: "Through international specialization and trade, a nation can reduce its opportunity cost of obtaining goods and thus 'move outside its production possibilities curve.'"

16. **LAST WORD** Studies indicate that married men on average earn more income than unmarried men of the same age and education level. Why must we be cautious in concluding that marriage is the cause and higher income is the effect?

Web-Based Questions

1. **NORMATIVE ECONOMICS—REPUBLICANS VERSUS DEMOCRATS** Visit both the Republicans' **www.rnc.org/** and the Democrats' **www.democrats.org/** Web sites. Identify an economic issue that both parties address, and compare and contrast their views on that issue. Generally speaking, how much of the disagreement is based on normative economics compared to positive economics? Give an example of loaded terminology from each site.

2. **MORE LABOR RESOURCES—WHAT IS THE EVIDENCE FOR THE UNITED STATES AND JAPAN?** Go to the Bureau of Labor Statistics' Web site at **www.bls.gov/** and select Get

Detailed Statistics. Look for Labor Force Statistics from the CPS and click the Most Requested Statistics icon. Find U.S. civilian employment data for the last 10 years. How many more workers were there at the end of the 10-year period than at the beginning? Next, return to the Detailed Statistics page. Use the Most Requested Statistics icon next to Foreign Labor Statistics (it's under Productivity and Technology) to find total employment growth in Japan over the last 10 years. In which of the two countries did "more labor resources" have the greatest impact in shifting the nation's production possibilities curve outward over the 10-year period?

Graphs and Their Meaning

If you glance quickly through this text, you will find many graphs. Some seem simple, while others seem more formidable. All are included to help you visualize and understand economic relationships. Physicists and chemists sometimes illustrate their theories by building arrangements of multicolored wooden balls, representing protons, neutrons, and electrons, which are held in proper relation to one another by wires or sticks. Economists most often use graphs to illustrate their models. By understanding these "pictures," you can more readily comprehend economic relationships. Most of our principles or models explain relationships between just two sets of economic facts, which can be conveniently represented with two-dimensional graphs.

Construction of a Graph

A *graph* is a visual representation of the relationship between two variables. The table in Figure 1 is a hypothetical illustration showing the relationship between income and consumption for the economy as a whole. Without even studying economics, we would expect intuitively that people would buy more goods and services when their incomes go up. Thus we are not surprised to find in the table that total consumption in the economy increases as total income increases.

The information in the table is expressed graphically in Figure 1. Here is how it is done: We want to show visually or graphically how consumption changes as income changes. Since income is the determining factor, we represent it on the **horizontal axis** of the graph, as is customary. And because consumption depends on income, we represent it on the **vertical axis** of the graph, as is also customary. Actually, what we are doing is representing the *independent variable* on the horizontal axis and the *dependent variable* on the vertical axis.

Now we arrange the vertical and horizontal scales of the graph to reflect the ranges of values of consumption and income, and we mark the scales in convenient increments. As you can see, the values marked on the scales cover all the values in the table. The increments on both scales are $100.

Because the graph has two dimensions, each point within it represents an income value and its associated consumption value. To find a point that represents one of the five income-consumption combinations in the table in Figure 1, we draw perpendiculars from the appropriate values on the vertical and horizontal axes. For example, to plot point *c* (the $200 income–$150 consumption point), we draw perpendiculars up from the horizontal (income) axis at $200 and across from the vertical (consumption) axis at $150. These perpendiculars intersect at point *c*, which represents this particular income-consumption combination. You should verify that the other income-consumption combinations shown in the table are properly located in the graph in Figure 1. Finally, by assuming that the same general relationship between income and

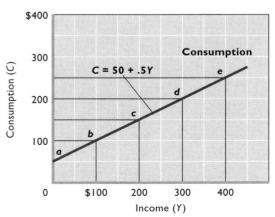

FIGURE 1 Graphing the direct relationship between consumption and income. Two sets of data that are positively or directly related, such as consumption and income, graph as an upsloping line.

Income per Week	Consumption per Week	Point
$ 0	$ 50	a
100	100	b
200	150	c
300	200	d
400	250	e

$$C = 50 + .5Y$$

consumption prevails for all other incomes, we draw a line or smooth curve to connect these points. That line or curve represents the income-consumption relationship.

If the graph is a straight line, as in Figure 1, we say the relationship is *linear*.

Direct and Inverse Relationships

The line in Figure 1 slopes upward to the right, so it depicts a direct relationship between income and consumption. By a **direct relationship** (or positive relationship) we mean that two variables—in this case, consumption and income—change in the *same* direction. An increase in consumption is associated with an increase in income; a decrease in consumption accompanies a decrease in income. When two sets of data are positively or directly related, they always graph as an *upsloping* line, as in Figure 1.

In contrast, two sets of data may be inversely related. Consider the table in Figure 2, which shows the relationship between the price of basketball tickets and game attendance at Gigantic State University (GSU). Here we have an **inverse relationship** (or negative relationship) because the two variables change in *opposite* directions. When ticket prices decrease, attendance increases. When ticket prices increase, attendance decreases. The six data points in the table in Figure 2 are plotted in the graph. Observe that an inverse relationship always graphs as a *downsloping* line.

Dependent and Independent Variables

Although it is not always easy, economists seek to determine which variable is the "cause" and which is the "effect." Or, more formally, they seek the independent variable and the dependent variable. The **independent variable** is the cause or source; it is the variable that changes first. The **dependent variable** is the effect or outcome; it is the variable that changes because of the change in the independent variable. As noted in our income-consumption example, income generally is the independent variable and consumption the dependent variable. Income causes consumption to be what it is rather than the other way around. Similarly, ticket prices (set in advance of the season) determine attendance at GSU basketball games; attendance at games does not determine the ticket prices for those games. Ticket price is the independent variable, and the quantity of tickets purchased is the dependent variable.

You may recall from your high school courses that mathematicians always put the independent variable (cause) on the horizontal axis and the dependent variable (effect) on the vertical axis. Economists are less tidy; their graphing of independent and dependent variables is more arbitrary. Their conventional graphing of the income-consumption relationship is consistent with mathematical presentation, but economists put price and cost data on

FIGURE 2 Graphing the inverse relationship between ticket prices and game attendance. Two sets of data that are negatively or inversely related, such as ticket price and the attendance at basketball games, graph as a downsloping line.

Ticket Price	Attendance, Thousands	Point
$50	0	a
40	4	b
30	8	c
20	12	d
10	16	e
0	20	f

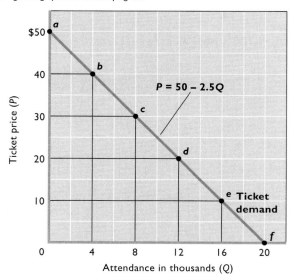

the vertical axis. Hence, economists' graphing of GSU's ticket price–attendance data conflicts with normal mathematical procedure.

Other Things Equal

Our simple two-variable graphs purposely ignore many other factors that might affect the amount of consumption occurring at each income level or the number of people who attend GSU basketball games at each possible ticket price. When economists plot the relationship between any two variables, they employ the *ceteris paribus* (other-things-equal) assumption. Thus, in Figure 1 all factors other than income that might affect the amount of consumption are presumed to be constant or unchanged. Similarly, in Figure 2 all factors other than ticket price that might influence attendance at GSU basketball games are assumed constant. In reality, "other things" are not equal; they often change, and when they do, the relationship represented in our two tables and graphs will change. Specifically, the lines we have plotted would shift to new locations.

Consider a stock market "crash." The dramatic drop in the value of stocks might cause people to feel less wealthy and therefore less willing to consume at each level of income. The result might be a downward shift of the consumption line. To see this, you should plot a new consumption line in Figure 1, assuming that consumption is, say, $20 less at each income level. Note that the relationship remains direct; the line merely shifts downward to reflect less consumption spending at each income level.

Similarly, factors other than ticket prices might affect GSU game attendance. If GSU loses most of its games, attendance at GSU games might be less at each ticket price. To see this, redraw Figure 2, assuming that 2000 fewer fans attend GSU games at each ticket price. (**Key Appendix Question 2**)

Slope of a Line

Lines can be described in terms of their slopes. The **slope of a straight line** is the ratio of the vertical change (the rise or drop) to the horizontal change (the run) between any two points of the line.

Positive Slope

Between point *b* and point *c* in Figure 1 the rise or vertical change (the change in consumption) is +$50 and the run or horizontal change (the change in income) is +$100. Therefore:

$$\text{Slope} = \frac{\text{vertical change}}{\text{horizontal change}} = \frac{+50}{+100} = \frac{1}{2} = .5$$

Note that our slope of $\frac{1}{2}$ or .5 is positive because consumption and income change in the same direction; that is, consumption and income are directly or positively related.

The slope of .5 tells us there will be a $1 increase in consumption for every $2 increase in income. Similarly, it indicates that for every $2 decrease in income there will be a $1 decrease in consumption.

Negative Slope

Between any two of the identified points in Figure 2, say, point *c* and point *d*, the vertical change is −10 (the drop) and the horizontal change is +4 (the run). Therefore:

$$\text{Slope} = \frac{\text{vertical change}}{\text{horizontal change}} = \frac{-10}{+4}$$
$$= -2\frac{1}{2} = -2.5$$

This slope is negative because ticket price and attendance have an inverse relationship.

Note that on the horizontal axis attendance is stated in thousands of people. So the slope of −10/+4 or −2.5 means that lowering the price by $10 will increase attendance by 4000 people. This is the same as saying that a $2.50 price reduction will increase attendance by 1000 persons.

Slopes and Measurement Units

The slope of a line will be affected by the choice of units for either variable. If, in our ticket price illustration, we had chosen to measure attendance in individual people, our horizontal change would have been 4000 and the slope would have been

$$\text{Slope} = \frac{-10}{+4000} = \frac{-1}{+400} = -.0025$$

The slope depends on the way the relevant variables are measured.

Slopes and Marginal Analysis

Recall that economics is largely concerned with changes from the status quo. The concept of slope is important in economics because it reflects marginal changes—those involving 1 more (or 1 less) unit. For example, in Figure 1 the .5 slope shows that $.50 of extra or marginal consumption is associated with each $1 change in income. In this example, people collectively will consume $.50 of any $1 increase in their incomes and reduce their consumption by $.50 for each $1 decline in income.

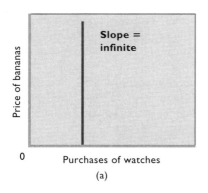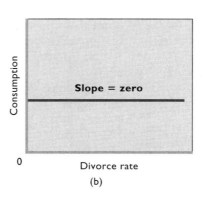

FIGURE 3 **Infinite and zero slopes.** (a) A line parallel to the vertical axis has an infinite slope. Here, purchases of watches remain the same no matter what happens to the price of bananas. (b) A line parallel to the horizontal axis has a slope of zero. Here, consumption remains the same no matter what happens to the divorce rate. In both (a) and (b), the two variables are totally unrelated to one another.

Infinite and Zero Slopes

Many variables are unrelated or independent of one another. For example, the quantity of wristwatches purchased is not related to the price of bananas. In Figure 3a we represent the price of bananas on the vertical axis and the quantity of watches demanded on the horizontal axis. The graph of their relationship is the line parallel to the vertical axis, indicating that the same quantity of watches is purchased no matter what the price of bananas. The slope of such a line is *infinite*.

Similarly, aggregate consumption is completely unrelated to the nation's divorce rate. In Figure 3b we put consumption on the vertical axis and the divorce rate on the horizontal axis. The line parallel to the horizontal axis represents this lack of relatedness. This line has a slope of *zero*.

Vertical Intercept

A line can be located on a graph (without plotting points) if we know its slope and its vertical intercept. The **vertical intercept** of a line is the point where the line meets the vertical axis. In Figure 1 the intercept is $50. This intercept means that if current income were zero, consumers would still spend $50. They might do this through borrowing or by selling some of their assets. Similarly, the $50 vertical intercept in Figure 2 shows that at a $50 ticket price, GSU's basketball team would be playing in an empty arena.

Equation of a Linear Relationship

If we know the vertical intercept and slope, we can describe a line succinctly in equation form. In its general form, the equation of a straight line is

$$y = a + bx$$

where y = dependent variable
a = vertical intercept
b = slope of line
x = independent variable

For our income-consumption example, if C represents consumption (the dependent variable) and Y represents income (the independent variable), we can write $C = a + bY$. By substituting the known values of the intercept and the slope, we get

$$C = 50 + .5Y$$

This equation also allows us to determine the amount of consumption C at any specific level of income. You should use it to confirm that at the $250 income level, consumption is $175.

When economists reverse mathematical convention by putting the independent variable on the vertical axis and the dependent variable on the horizontal axis, then y stands for the independent variable, rather than the dependent variable in the general form. We noted previously that this case is relevant for our GSU ticket price–attendance data. If P represents the ticket price (independent variable) and Q represents attendance (dependent variable), their relationship is given by

$$P = 50 - 2.5Q$$

where the vertical intercept is 50 and the negative slope is $-2\frac{1}{2}$, or -2.5. Knowing the value of P lets us solve for Q, our dependent variable. You should use this equation to predict GSU ticket sales when the ticket price is $15. (**Key Appendix Question 3**)

Slope of a Nonlinear Curve

We now move from the simple world of linear relationships (straight lines) to the more complex world of nonlinear relationships. The slope of a straight line is the same at all its points. The slope of a line representing a nonlinear relationship changes from one point to another. Such lines are referred to as *curves*. (It is also permissible to refer to a straight line as a "curve.")

Consider the downsloping curve in Figure 4. Its slope is negative throughout, but the curve flattens as we move down along it. Thus, its slope constantly changes; the curve has a different slope at each point.

To measure the slope at a specific point, we draw a straight line tangent to the curve at that point. A line is *tangent* at a point if it touches, but does not intersect, the curve at that point. Thus line *aa* is tangent to the curve in Figure 4 at point *A*. The slope of the curve at that point is equal to the slope of the tangent line. Specifically, the total vertical change (drop) in the tangent line *aa* is −20 and the total horizontal change (run) is +5. Because the slope of the tangent line *aa* is −20/+5, or −4, the slope of the curve at point *A* is also −4.

G 1.3

Curves and slopes

Line *bb* in Figure 4 is tangent to the curve at point *B*. Following the same procedure, we find the slope at *B* to be −5/+15, or −⅓. Thus, in this flatter part of the curve, the slope is less negative. **(Key Appendix Question 7)**

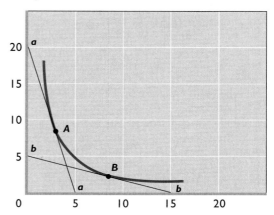

FIGURE 4 **Determining the slopes of curves.**
The slope of a nonlinear curve changes from point to point on the curve. The slope at any point (say, *B*) can be determined by drawing a straight line that is tangent to that point (line *bb*) and calculating the slope of that line.

Appendix Summary

1. Graphs are a convenient and revealing way to represent economic relationships.

2. Two variables are positively or directly related when their values change in the same direction. The line (curve) representing two directly related variables slopes upward.

3. Two variables are negatively or inversely related when their values change in opposite directions. The curve representing two inversely related variables slopes downward.

4. The value of the dependent variable (the "effect") is determined by the value of the independent variable (the "cause").

5. When the "other factors" that might affect a two-variable relationship are allowed to change, the graph of the relationship will likely shift to a new location.

6. The slope of a straight line is the ratio of the vertical change to the horizontal change between any two points. The slope of an upsloping line is positive; the slope of a downsloping line is negative.

7. The slope of a line or curve depends on the units used in measuring the variables. It is especially relevant for economics because it measures marginal changes.

8. The slope of a horizontal line is zero; the slope of a vertical line is infinite.

9. The vertical intercept and slope of a line determine its location; they are used in expressing the line—and the relationship between the two variables—as an equation.

10. The slope of a curve at any point is determined by calculating the slope of a straight line tangent to the curve at that point.

Appendix Terms and Concepts

horizontal axis

vertical axis

direct relationship

inverse relationship

independent variable

dependent variable

slope of a straight line

vertical intercept

Appendix Study Questions

1. Briefly explain the use of graphs as a way to represent economic relationships. What is an inverse relationship? How does it graph? What is a direct relationship? How does it graph? Graph and explain the relationships you would ex- pect to find between (*a*) the number of inches of rainfall per month and the sale of umbrellas, (*b*) the amount of tuition and the level of enrollment at a university, and (*c*) the popularity of an entertainer and the price of her concert tickets.

In each case cite and explain how variables other than those specifically mentioned might upset the expected relationship. Is your graph in previous part *b* consistent with the fact that, historically, enrollments and tuition have both increased? If not, explain any difference.

2. **KEY APPENDIX QUESTION** Indicate how each of the following might affect the data shown in the table and graph in Figure 2 of this appendix:
   a. GSU's athletic director schedules higher-quality opponents.
   b. An NBA team locates in the city where GSU plays.
   c. GSU contracts to have all its home games televised.

3. **KEY APPENDIX QUESTION** The following table contains data on the relationship between saving and income. Rearrange these data into a meaningful order and graph them on the accompanying grid. What is the slope of the line? The vertical intercept? Interpret the meaning of both the slope and the intercept. Write the equation that represents this line. What would you predict saving to be at the $12,500 level of income?

Income per Year	Saving per Year
$15,000	$1,000
0	−500
10,000	500
5,000	0
20,000	1,500

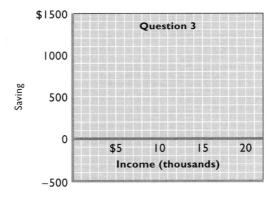

4. Construct a table from the data shown on the graph below. Which is the dependent variable and which the independent variable? Summarize the data in equation form.

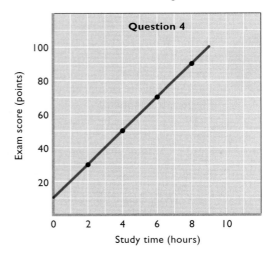

5. Suppose that when the interest rate on loans is 16 percent, businesses find it unprofitable to invest in machinery and equipment. However, when the interest rate is 14 percent, $5 billion worth of investment is profitable. At 12 percent interest, a total of $10 billion of investment is profitable. Similarly, total investment increases by $5 billion for each successive 2-percentage-point decline in the interest rate. Describe the relevant relationship between the interest rate and investment in words, in a table, on a graph, and as an equation. Put the interest rate on the vertical axis and investment on the horizontal axis. In your equation use the form $i = a + bI$, where i is the interest rate, a is the vertical intercept, b is the slope of the line (which is negative), and I is the level of investment. Comment on the advantages and disadvantages of the verbal, tabular, graphical, and equation forms of description.

6. Suppose that $C = a + bY$, where $C =$ consumption, $a =$ consumption at zero income, $b =$ slope, and $Y =$ income.
   a. Are C and Y positively related or are they negatively related?
   b. If graphed, would the curve for this equation slope upward or slope downward?
   c. Are the variables C and Y inversely related or directly related?
   d. What is the value of C if $a = 10$, $b = .50$, and $Y = 200$?
   e. What is the value of Y if $C = 100$, $a = 10$, and $b = .25$?

7. KEY APPENDIX QUESTION The accompanying graph shows curve XX' and tangents at points A, B, and C. Calculate the slope of the curve at these three points.

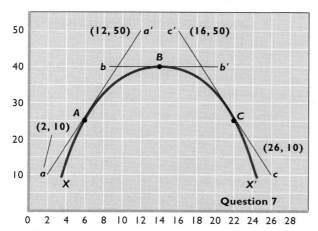

Question 7

8. In the accompanying graph, is the slope of curve AA' positive or negative? Does the slope increase or decrease as we move along the curve from A to A'? Answer the same two questions for curve BB'.

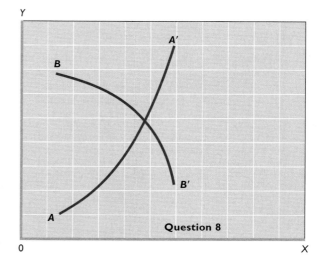

Question 8

2

IN THIS CHAPTER YOU WILL LEARN:

* The difference between a command system and a market system.
* The main characteristics of the market system.
* How the market system decides what to produce, how to produce it, and who obtains it.
* How the market system adjusts to change and promotes progress.
* The mechanics of the circular flow model.

The Market System and the Circular Flow

You are at the mall. Suppose you were assigned to compile a list of all the individual goods and services there, including the different brands and variations of each type of product. That task would be daunting and the list would be long! And even though a single shopping mall contains a remarkable quantity and variety of goods, it is only a tiny part of the national economy.

Who decided that the particular goods and services available at the mall and in the broader economy should be produced? How did the producers determine which technology and types of resources to use in producing these particular goods? Who will obtain these products? What accounts for the new and improved products among these goods? This chapter will answer these and related questions.

Economic Systems

Every society needs to develop an **economic system**—a particular set of institutional arrangements and a coordinating mechanism—to respond to the economizing problem. The economic system has to determine what goods are produced, how they are produced, who gets them, how to accommodate change, and how to promote technological progress.

Economic systems differ as to (1) who owns the factors of production and (2) the method used to motivate, coordinate, and direct economic activity. Economic systems have two polar extremes: the command system and the market system.

The Command System

The **command system** is also known as *socialism* or *communism*. In that system, government owns most property resources and economic decision making occurs through a central economic plan. A central planning board appointed by the government makes nearly all the major decisions concerning the use of resources, the composition and distribution of output, and the organization of production. The government owns most of the business firms, which produce according to government directives. The central planning board determines production goals for each enterprise and specifies the amount of resources to be allocated to each enterprise so that it can reach its production goals. The division of output between capital and consumer goods is centrally decided, and capital goods are allocated among industries on the basis of the central planning board's long-term priorities.

A pure command economy would rely exclusively on a central plan to allocate the government-owned property resources. But, in reality, even the preeminent command economy—the Soviet Union—tolerated some private ownership and incorporated some markets before its collapse in 1992. Recent reforms in Russia and most of the eastern European nations have to one degree or another transformed their command economies to capitalistic, market-oriented systems. China's reforms have not gone as far, but they have greatly reduced the reliance on central planning. Although government ownership of resources and capital in China is still extensive, the nation has increasingly relied on free markets to organize and coordinate its economy. North Korea and Cuba are the last prominent remaining examples of largely centrally planned economies. Other countries using mainly the command system include Turkmenistan, Laos, Belarus, Libya, Myanmar, and Iran. Later in this chapter, we will explore the main reasons for the general demise of the command systems.

The Market System

The polar alternative to the command system is the **market system,** or *capitalism*. The system is characterized by the private ownership of resources and the use of markets and prices to coordinate and direct economic activity. Participants act in their own self-interest. Individuals and businesses seek to achieve their economic goals through their own decisions regarding work, consumption, or production. The system allows for the private ownership of capital, communicates through prices, and coordinates economic activity through *markets*—places where buyers and sellers come together. Goods and services are produced and resources are supplied by whoever is willing and able to do so. The result is competition among independently acting buyers and sellers of each product and resource. Thus, economic decision making is widely dispersed. Also, the high potential monetary rewards create powerful incentives for existing firms to innovate and entrepreneurs to pioneer new products and processes.

In *pure* capitalism—or *laissez-faire* capitalism—government's role would be limited to protecting private property and establishing an environment appropriate to the operation of the market system. The term "laissez-faire" means "let it be," that is, keep government from interfering with the economy. The idea is that such interference will disturb the efficient working of the market system.

O 2.1

Laissez-faire

But in the capitalism practiced in the United States and most other countries, government plays a substantial role in the economy. It not only provides the rules for economic activity but also promotes economic stability and growth, provides certain goods and services that would otherwise be underproduced or not produced at all, and modifies the distribution of income. The government, however, is not the dominant economic force in deciding what to produce, how to produce it, and who will get it. That force is the market.

Characteristics of the Market System

An examination of some of the key features of the market system in detail will be very instructive.

Private Property

In a market system, private individuals and firms, not the government, own most of the property resources (land and capital). It is this extensive private ownership of capital that gives capitalism its name. This right of **private property,** coupled with the freedom to negotiate binding legal contracts, enables individuals and businesses to obtain, use, and dispose of property resources as they see fit. The right of property owners to designate who will receive their property when they die helps sustain the institution of private property.

Property rights encourage investment, innovation, exchange, maintenance of property, and economic growth. Nobody would stock a store, build a factory, or clear land for farming if someone else, or the government itself, could take that property for his or her own benefit.

Property rights also extend to intellectual property through patents, copyrights, and trademarks. Such long-term protection encourages people to write books, music, and computer programs and to invent new products and production processes without fear that others will steal them and the rewards they may bring.

Moreover, property rights facilitate exchange. The title to an automobile or the deed to a cattle ranch assures the buyer that the seller is the legitimate owner. Also, property rights encourage owners to maintain or improve their property so as to preserve or increase its value. Finally, property rights enable people to use their time and resources to produce more goods and services, rather than using them to protect and retain the property they have already produced or acquired.

Freedom of Enterprise and Choice

Closely related to private ownership of property is freedom of enterprise and choice. The market system requires that various economic units make certain choices, which are expressed and implemented in the economy's markets:

- **Freedom of enterprise** ensures that entrepreneurs and private businesses are free to obtain and use economic resources to produce their choice of goods and services and to sell them in their chosen markets.
- **Freedom of choice** enables owners to employ or dispose of their property and money as they see fit. It also allows workers to try to enter any line of work for which they are qualified. Finally, it ensures that consumers are free to buy the goods and services that best satisfy their wants and that their budgets allow.

These choices are free only within broad legal limitations, of course. Illegal choices such as selling human organs or buying illicit drugs are punished through fines and imprisonment. (Global Perspective 2.1 reveals that the degree of economic freedom varies greatly from economy to economy.)

Self-Interest

O 2.2
Self-interest

In the market system, **self-interest** is the motivating force of the various economic units as they express their free choices. Self-interest simply means that each economic unit tries to achieve its own particular goal, which usually requires delivering something of value to others. Entrepreneurs try to maximize profit or minimize loss. Property owners try to get the highest price for the sale or rent of their resources. Workers try to maximize their utility (satisfaction) by finding jobs that offer the best combination of wages, hours, fringe benefits, and working conditions. Consumers try to obtain the products they want at the lowest possible price and apportion their

GLOBAL PERSPECTIVE 2.1

Index of Economic Freedom, Selected Economies

The Index of Economic Freedom measures economic freedom using 10 broad categories such as trade policy, property rights, and government intervention, with each category containing more than 50 specific criteria. The index then ranks 157 economies according to their degree of economic freedom. A few selected rankings for 2006 are listed below.

FREE
1 Hong Kong
3 Ireland
9 United States

MOSTLY FREE
22 Belgium
33 Spain
44 France

MOSTLY UNFREE
81 Brazil
111 China
122 Russia

REPRESSED
150 Cuba
152 Venezuela
157 North Korea

Source: Heritage Foundation (**www.heritage.org**) and *The Wall Street Journal.*

expenditures to maximize their utility. The motive of self-interest gives direction and consistency to what might otherwise be a chaotic economy.

Competition

The market system depends on **competition** among economic units. The basis of this competition is freedom of choice exercised in pursuit of a monetary return. Very broadly defined, competition requires:

- Two or more buyers and two or more sellers acting independently in a particular product or resource market. (Usually there are many more than two buyers or sellers.)
- Freedom of sellers and buyers to enter or leave markets, on the basis of their economic self-interest.

Competition among buyers and sellers diffuses economic power within the businesses and households that make up the economy. When there are many buyers and sellers acting independently in a market, no single buyer or seller can dictate the price of the product or resource because others can undercut that price.

Competition also implies that producers can enter or leave an industry; no insurmountable barriers prevent an industry's expanding or contracting. This freedom of an industry to expand or contract provides the economy with the flexibility needed to remain efficient over time. Freedom of entry and exit enables the economy to adjust to changes in consumer tastes, technology, and resource availability.

The diffusion of economic power inherent in competition limits the potential abuse of that power. A producer that charges more than the competitive market price will lose sales to other producers. An employer who pays less than the competitive market wage rate will lose workers to other employers. A firm that fails to exploit new technology will lose profits to firms that do. Competition is the basic regulatory force in the market system.

Markets and Prices

We may wonder why an economy based on self-interest does not collapse in chaos. If consumers want breakfast cereal but businesses choose to produce running shoes and resource suppliers decide to make computer software, production would seem to be deadlocked by the apparent inconsistencies of free choices.

In reality, the millions of decisions made by households and businesses are highly coordinated with one another by markets and prices, which are key components of the market system. They give the system its ability to coordinate millions of daily economic decisions. A **market** is

an institution or mechanism that brings buyers ("demanders") and sellers ("suppliers") into contact. A market system conveys the decisions made by buyers and sellers of products and resources. The decisions made on each side of the market determine a set of product and resource prices that guide resource owners, entrepreneurs, and consumers as they make and revise their choices and pursue their self-interest.

Just as competition is the regulatory mechanism of the market system, the market system itself is the organizing and coordinating mechanism. It is an elaborate communication network through which innumerable individual free choices are recorded, summarized, and balanced. Those who respond to market signals and heed market dictates are rewarded with greater profit and income; those who do not respond to those signals and choose to ignore market dictates are penalized. Through this mechanism society decides what the economy should produce, how production can be organized efficiently, and how the fruits of production are to be distributed among the various units that make up the economy.

QUICK REVIEW 2.1

- The market system rests on the private ownership of property and on freedom of enterprise and freedom of choice.
- The market system permits consumers, resource suppliers, and businesses to pursue and further their self-interest.
- Competition diffuses economic power and limits the actions of any single seller or buyer.
- The coordinating mechanism of capitalism is a system of markets and prices.

Technology and Capital Goods

In the market system, competition, freedom of choice, self-interest, and personal reward provide the opportunity and motivation for technological advance. The monetary rewards for new products or production techniques accrue directly to the innovator. The market system therefore encourages extensive use and rapid development of complex capital goods: tools, machinery, large-scale factories, and facilities for storage, communication, transportation, and marketing.

Advanced technology and capital goods are important because the most direct methods of production are often the least efficient. The only way to avoid that inefficiency is to rely on capital goods. It would be ridiculous for a farmer to go at production with bare hands. There are huge bene-fits to be derived from creating and using such capital equipment as plows, tractors, and storage bins. The more efficient production means much more abundant outputs.

Specialization

The extent to which market economies rely on **specialization** is extraordinary. Specialization is the use of resources of an individual, firm, region, or nation to produce one or a few goods or services rather than the entire range of goods and services. Those goods and services are then exchanged for a full range of desired products. The majority of consumers produce virtually none of the goods and services they consume, and they consume little or nothing of the items they produce. The person working nine to five installing windows in Lincolns may own a Ford. Many farmers sell their milk to the local dairy and then buy butter at the local grocery store. Society learned long ago that self-sufficiency breeds inefficiency. The jack-of-all-trades may be a very colorful individual but is certainly not an efficient producer.

Division of Labor
Human specialization—called the **division of labor**—contributes to a society's output in several ways:

- *Specialization makes use of differences in ability.*

O 2.3

Specialization division of labor

Specialization enables individuals to take advantage of existing differences in their abilities and skills. If Peyton is strong, athletic, and good at throwing a football and Beyonce is beautiful, agile, and can sing, their distribution of talents can be most efficiently used if Peyton plays professional football and Beyonce records songs and gives concerts.

- *Specialization fosters learning by doing.* Even if the abilities of two people are identical, specialization may still be advantageous. By devoting time to a single task, a person is more likely to develop the skills required and to improve techniques than by working at a number of different tasks. You learn to be a good lawyer by studying and practicing law.

- *Specialization saves time.* By devoting time to a single task, a person avoids the loss of time incurred in shifting from one job to another. Also, time is saved by not "fumbling around" with a task that one is not trained to do.

For all these reasons, specialization increases the total output society derives from limited resources.

Geographic Specialization
Specialization also works on a regional and international basis. It is conceivable that oranges could be grown in Nebraska, but because of the unsuitability of the land, rainfall, and temperature, the costs would be very high. And it is conceivable that wheat could be grown in Florida, but such production would be costly for similar geographical reasons. So Nebraskans produce products—wheat in particular—for which their resources are best suited, and Floridians do the same, producing oranges and other citrus fruits. By specializing, both economies produce more than is needed locally. Then, very sensibly, Nebraskans and Floridians swap some of their surpluses—wheat for oranges, oranges for wheat.

Similarly, on an international scale, the United States specializes in producing such items as commercial aircraft and computers, which it sells abroad in exchange for video recorders from Japan, bananas from Honduras, and woven baskets from Thailand. Both human specialization and geographic specialization are needed to achieve efficiency in the use of limited resources.

Use of Money

A rather obvious characteristic of any economic system is the extensive use of money. Money performs several functions, but first and foremost it is a **medium of exchange.** It makes trade easier.

Specialization requires exchange. Exchange can, and sometimes does, occur through **barter**—swapping goods for goods, say, wheat for oranges. But barter poses serious problems because it requires a *coincidence of wants* between the buyer and the seller. In our example, we assumed that Nebraskans had excess wheat to trade and wanted oranges. And we assumed that Floridians had excess oranges to trade and wanted wheat. So an exchange occurred. But if such a coincidence of wants is missing, trade is stymied.

Suppose that Nebraska has no interest in Florida's oranges but wants potatoes from Idaho. And suppose that Idaho wants Florida's oranges but not Nebraska's wheat. And, to complicate matters, suppose that Florida wants some of Nebraska's wheat but none of Idaho's potatoes. We summarize the situation in Figure 2.1

In none of the cases shown in the figure is there a coincidence of wants. Trade by barter clearly would be difficult. Instead, people in each state use **money,** which is simply a convenient social invention to facilitate exchanges of goods and services. Historically, people have used cattle, cigarettes, shells, stones, pieces of metal, and many other commodities, with varying degrees of success, as a medium of exchange. But to serve as money, an item needs to pass only one test: It must be generally acceptable to sellers in exchange for their

FIGURE 2.1 **Money facilitates trade when wants do not coincide.** The use of money as a medium of exchange permits trade to be accomplished despite a noncoincidence of wants. (1) Nebraska trades the wheat that Florida wants for money from Floridians; (2) Nebraska trades the money it receives from Florida for the potatoes it wants from Idaho; (3) Idaho trades the money it receives from Nebraska for the oranges it wants from Florida.

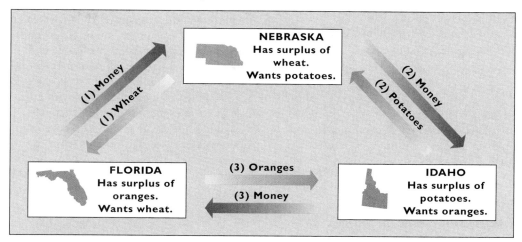

goods and services. Money is socially defined; whatever society accepts as a medium of exchange *is* money.

Most economies use pieces of paper as money. The use of paper dollars (currency) as a medium of exchange is what enables Nebraska, Florida, and Idaho to overcome their trade stalemate, as demonstrated in Figure 2.1.

On a global basis different nations have different currencies, and that complicates specialization and exchange. But markets in which currencies are bought and sold make it possible for U.S. residents, Japanese, Germans, Britons, and Mexicans, through the swapping of dollars, yen, euros, pounds, and pesos, one for another, to exchange goods and services.

Active, but Limited, Government

An active, but limited, government is the final characteristic of market systems in modern advanced industrial economies. Although a market system promotes a high degree of efficiency in the use of its resources, it has certain inherent shortcomings, called "market failures." We will discover in subsequent chapters that government can increase the overall effectiveness of the economic system in several ways.

CONSIDER THIS ...

Buy American?

Will "buying American" make Americans better off? No, says Dallas Federal Reserve economist W. Michael Cox:

A common myth is that it is better for Americans to spend their money at home than abroad. The best way to expose the fallacy of this argument is to take it to its logical extreme. If it is better for me to spend my money here than abroad, then it is even better yet to buy in Texas than in New York, better yet to buy in Dallas than in Houston ... in my own neighborhood ... within my own family ... to consume only what I can produce. Alone and poor.*

———
*"The Fruits of Free Trade," Federal Reserve Bank of Dallas, Annual Report 2002, p. 16.

QUICK REVIEW 2.2

- The market systems of modern industrial economies are characterized by extensive use of technologically advanced capital goods. Such goods help these economies achieve greater efficiency in production.
- Specialization is extensive in market systems; it enhances efficiency and output by enabling individuals, regions, and nations to produce the goods and services for which their resources are best suited.
- The use of money in market systems facilitates the exchange of goods and services that specialization requires.

Five Fundamental Questions

The key features of the market system help explain how market economies respond to five fundamental questions:

- What goods and services will be produced?
- How will the goods and services be produced?
- Who will get the goods and services?
- How will the system accommodate change?
- How will the system promote progress?

These five questions highlight the economic choices underlying the production possibilities curve discussed in Chapter 1. They reflect the reality of scarce resources in a world of unlimited wants. All economies, whether market or command, must address these five questions.

What Will Be Produced?

How will a market system decide on the specific types and quantities of goods to be produced? The simple answer is this: The goods and services produced at a continuing profit will be produced, and those produced at a continuing loss will not. Profits and losses are the difference between the total revenue (TR) a firm receives from the sale of its products and the total opportunity cost (TC) of producing those products. (For economists, economic costs include not only wage and salary payments to labor, and interest and rental payments for capital and land, but also payments to the entrepreneur for organizing and combining the other resources to produce a commodity.)

Continuing economic profit (TR > TC) in an industry results in expanded production and the movement of resources toward that industry. Existing firms grow and new firms enter. The industry expands. Continuing losses (TC > TR) in an industry leads to reduced production and the exit of resources from that industry. Some existing firms shrink in size; others go out of business. The industry contracts. In the market system, consumers are sovereign (in command). **Consumer sovereignty** is crucial in determining the types and quantities of goods produced. Consumers spend their income on the goods they are most willing and able to buy. Through these **"dollar votes"** they register their wants in the market. If the dollar votes for a certain product are great enough to create a profit, businesses will produce that product and offer it for sale. In contrast, if the dollar votes do not create sufficient revenues to cover costs, businesses will not produce the product. So the consumers are sovereign. They collectively direct resources to industries that are meeting consumer wants and away from industries that are not meeting consumer wants.

The dollar votes of consumers determine not only which industries will continue to exist but also which products will survive or fail. Only profitable industries, firms, and products survive. So firms are not as free to produce whatever products they wish as one might otherwise think. Consumers' buying decisions make the production of some products profitable and the production of other products unprofitable, thus restricting the choice of businesses in deciding what to produce. Businesses must match their production choices with consumer choices or else face losses and eventual bankruptcy.

The same holds true for resource suppliers. The employment of resources derives from the sale of the goods and services that the resources help produce. Autoworkers are employed because automobiles are sold. There are few remaining professors of early Latin because there are few

CONSIDER THIS ...

McHits and McMisses

McDonald's has introduced several new menu items over the decades. Some have been profitable "hits," while others have been "misses." Ultimately, consumers decide whether a menu item is profitable and therefore whether it stays on the McDonald's menu.

- Hulaburger (1962)—McMiss
- Filet-O-Fish (1963)—McHit
- Strawberry shortcake (1966)—McMiss
- Big Mac (1968)—McHit
- Hot apple pie (1968)—McHit
- Egg McMuffin (1975)—McHit
- Drive-thru (1975)—McHit
- Chicken McNuggets (1983)—McHit
- Extra Value Meal (1991)—McHit
- McLean Deluxe (1991)—McMiss
- Arch Deluxe (1996)—McMiss
- 55-cent special (1997)—McMiss
- Big Xtra (1999)—McHit

Source: "Polishing the Golden Arches," *Forbes,* June 15, 1998, pp. 42–43, updated.

people desiring to learn the Latin language. Resource suppliers, desiring to earn income, are not truly free to allocate their resources to the production of goods that consumers do not value highly. Consumers register their preferences in the market; producers and resource suppliers, prompted by their own self-interest, respond appropriately. **(Key Question 8)**

How Will the Goods and Services Be Produced?

What combinations of resources and technologies will be used to produce goods and services? How will the production be organized? The answer: In combinations and ways that minimize the cost per unit of output. Because competition eliminates high-cost producers, profitability requires that firms produce their output at minimum cost per unit. Achieving this least-cost production necessitates, for example, that firms use the right mix of labor and capital, given the prices and productivity of those resources. It also means locating production facilities optimally to hold down production and transportation expenses.

Least-cost production also means that firms must employ the most economically efficient technique of production in producing their output. The most efficient production technique depends on:

- The available technology, that is, the various combinations of resources that will produce the desired results.
- The prices of the needed resources.

A technique that requires just a few inputs of resources to produce a specific output may be highly inefficient economically if those resources are valued very highly in the market. Economic efficiency means obtaining a particular output of product with the least input of scarce resources, when both output and resource inputs are measured in dollars and cents. The combination of resources that will produce, say, $15 worth of bathroom soap at the lowest possible cost is the most efficient.

Suppose there are three possible techniques for producing the desired $15 worth of bars of soap. Suppose also that the quantity of each resource required by each production technique and the prices of the required resources are as shown in Table 2.1. By multiplying the required quantities of each resource by its price in each of the three techniques, we can determine the total cost of producing $15 worth of soap by means of each technique.

W 2.1

Least-cost production

Technique 2 is economically the most efficient, because it is the least costly. It enables society to obtain $15 worth of output by using a smaller amount of resources—$13 worth—than the $15 worth required by the two other techniques. Competition will dictate that producers use technique 2. Thus, the question of how goods will be produced is answered. They will be produced in a least-cost way.

A change in either technology or resource prices, however, may cause a firm to shift from the technology it is using. If the price of labor falls to $.50, technique 1 becomes more desirable than technique 2. Firms will find they can lower their costs by shifting to a technology that uses more of the resource whose price has fallen. Exercise: Would a new technique involving 1 unit of labor, 4 of land, 1 of capital, and 1 of entrepreneurial ability be preferable to the techniques listed in Table 2.1, assuming the resource prices shown there? **(Key Question 9)**

Who Will Get the Output?

The market system enters the picture in two ways when determining the distribution of total output. Generally, any product will be distributed to consumers on the basis of their ability and willingness to pay its existing market price. If the price of some product, say, a small sailboat, is $3000, then buyers who are willing and able to pay that price will "sail, sail away." Consumers who are unwilling or unable to pay the price will be "sitting on the dock of the bay."

TABLE 2.1 Three Techniques for Producing $15 Worth of Bar Soap

		Units of Resource					
		Technique 1		Technique 2		Technique 3	
Resource	Price per Unit of Resource	Units	Cost	Units	Cost	Units	Cost
Labor	$2	4	$ 8	2	$ 4	1	$ 2
Land	1	1	1	3	3	4	4
Capital	3	1	3	1	3	2	6
Entrepreneurial ability	3	1	3	1	3	1	3
Total cost of $15 worth of bar soap			$15		$13		$15

The ability to pay the prices for sailboats and other products depends on the amount of income that consumers have, along with the prices of, and preferences for, various goods. If consumers have sufficient income and want to spend their money on a particular good, they can have it. And the amount of income they have depends on (1) the quantities of the property and human resources they supply and (2) the prices those resources command in the resource market. Resource prices (wages, interest, rent, profit) are crucial in determining the size of each person's income and therefore each person's ability to buy part of the economy's output. If a lawyer earning $200 an hour and a recreational worker earning $10 an hour both work the same number of hours each year, the lawyer will be able to take possession of 20 times as much of society's output as the recreational worker that year.

How Will the System Accommodate Change?

Market systems are dynamic: Consumer preferences, technology, and supplies of resources all change. This means that the particular allocation of resources that is now the most efficient for a specific pattern of consumer tastes, range of technological alternatives, and amount of available resources will become obsolete and inefficient as consumer preferences change, new techniques of production are discovered, and resource supplies change over time. Can the market economy adjust to such changes?

Suppose consumer tastes change. For instance, assume that consumers decide they want more fruit juice and less milk than the economy currently provides. Those changes in consumer tastes will be communicated to producers through an increase in spending on fruit and a decline in spending on milk. Other things equal, prices and profits in the fruit juice industry will rise and those in the milk industry will fall. Self-interest will induce existing competitors to expand output and entice new competitors to enter the prosperous fruit industry and will in time force firms to scale down—or even exit—the depressed milk industry.

The higher prices and greater economic profit in the fruit-juice industry will not only induce that industry to expand but will also give it the revenue needed to obtain the resources essential to its growth. Higher prices and profits will permit fruit producers to attract more resources from less urgent alternative uses. The reverse occurs in the milk industry, where fewer workers and other resources are employed. These adjustments in the economy are appropriate responses to the changes in consumer tastes. This is consumer sovereignty at work.

The market system is a gigantic communications system. Through changes in prices and profits it communicates changes in such basic matters as consumer tastes and elicits appropriate responses from businesses and resource suppliers. By affecting price and profits, changes in consumer tastes direct the expansion of some industries and the contraction of others. Those adjustments are conveyed to the resource market. As expanding industries employ more resources and contracting industries employ fewer; the resulting changes in resource prices (wages and salaries, for example) and income flows guide resources from the contracting industries to the expanding industries.

This directing or guiding function of prices and profits is a core element of the market system. Without such a system, some administrative agency such as a government planning board would have to direct businesses and resources into the appropriate industries. A similar analysis shows that the system can and does adjust to other fundamental changes—for example, to changes in technology and in the prices of various resources.

How Will the System Promote Progress?

Society desires economic growth (greater output) and higher standards of living (greater income per person). How does the market system promote technological improvements and capital accumulation, both of which contribute to a higher standard of living for society?

Technological Advance The market system provides a strong incentive for technological advance and enables better products and processes to supplant inferior ones. An entrepreneur or firm that introduces a popular new product will gain revenue and economic profit at the expense of rivals. Firms that are highly profitable one year may find they are in financial trouble just a few years later.

Technological advance also includes new and improved methods that reduce production or distribution costs. By passing part of its cost reduction on to the consumer through a lower product price, the firm can increase sales and obtain economic profit at the expense of rival firms.

Moreover, the market system promotes the *rapid spread* of technological advance throughout an industry. Rival firms must follow the lead of the most innovative firm or else suffer immediate losses and eventual failure. In some cases, the result is **creative destruction:** The creation of new products and production methods completely destroys the market positions of firms that are wedded to existing products and older ways of doing business. Example: The advent of compact discs largely demolished long-play vinyl records, and MP3 and other digital technologies are now supplanting CDs.

Capital Accumulation Most technological advances require additional capital goods. The market system provides the resources necessary to produce those goods through increased dollar votes for capital goods. That is, the market system acknowledges dollar voting for capital goods as well as for consumer goods.

But who will register votes for capital goods? Answer: Entrepreneurs and owners of businesses. As receivers of profit income, they often use part of that income to purchase capital goods. Doing so yields even greater profit income in the future if the technological innovation is successful. Also, by paying interest or selling ownership shares, the entrepreneur and firm can attract some of the income of households as saving to increase their dollar votes for the production of more capital goods. **(Key Question 10)**

QUICK REVIEW 2.3

- The output mix of the market system is determined by profits, which in turn depend heavily on consumer preferences. Economic profits cause industries to expand; losses cause industries to contract.
- Competition forces industries to use the least costly production methods.
- Competitive markets reallocate resources in response to changes in consumer tastes, technological advances, and changes in availability of resources.
- In a market economy, consumer income and product prices determine how output will be distributed.
- Competitive markets create incentives for technological advance and capital accumulation, both of which contribute to increases in standards of living.

The "Invisible Hand"

In his 1776 book *The Wealth of Nations*, Adam Smith first noted that the operation of a market system creates a curious unity between private interests and social interests. Firms and resource suppliers, seeking to further their own self-interest and operating within the framework of a highly competitive market system, will simultaneously, as though guided by an **"invisible hand,"**

promote the public or social interest. For example, we have seen that in a competitive environment, businesses seek to build new and improved products to increase profits. Those enhanced products increase society's well-being. Businesses also use the least costly combination of resources to produce a specific output because doing so is in their self-interest. To act otherwise would be to forgo profit or even to risk business failure. But, at the same time, to use scarce resources in the least costly way is clearly in the social interest as well. It "frees up" resources to produce something else that society desires.

Self-interest, awakened and guided by the competitive market system, is what induces responses appropriate to the changes in society's wants. Businesses seeking to make higher profits and to avoid losses, and resource suppliers pursuing greater monetary rewards, negotiate changes in the allocation of resources and end up with the output that society wants. Competition controls or guides self-interest such that self-interest automatically and quite unintentionally furthers the best interest of society. The invisible hand ensures that when firms maximize their profits and resource suppliers maximize their incomes, these groups also help maximize society's output and income.

Of the various virtues of the market system, three merit reemphasis:

- *Efficiency* The market system promotes the efficient use of resources by guiding them into the production of the goods and services most wanted by society. It forces the use of the most efficient techniques in organizing resources for production, and it encourages the development and adoption of new and more efficient production techniques.
- *Incentives* The market system encourages skill acquisition, hard work, and innovation. Greater work skills and effort mean greater production and higher incomes, which usually translate into a higher standard of living. Similarly, the assuming of risks by entrepreneurs can result in substantial profit incomes. Successful innovations generate economic rewards.
- *Freedom* The major noneconomic argument for the market system is its emphasis on personal freedom. In contrast to central planning, the market system coordinates economic activity without coercion. The market system permits—indeed, it thrives on—freedom of enterprise and choice. Entrepreneurs and workers are free to further their own self-interest, subject to the rewards and penalties imposed by the market system itself.

The Demise of the Command Systems

Our discussion of how a market system answers the five fundamental questions provides insights on why command systems of the Soviet Union, eastern Europe, and China (prior to its market reforms) failed. Those systems encountered two insurmountable problems.

The Coordination Problem

The first difficulty was the coordination problem. The central planners had to coordinate the millions of individual decisions by consumers, resource suppliers, and businesses. Consider the setting up of a factory to produce tractors. The central planners had to establish a realistic annual production target, for example, 1000 tractors. They then had to make available all the necessary inputs—labor, machinery, electric power, steel, tires, glass, paint, transportation—for the production and delivery of those 1000 tractors.

Because the outputs of many industries serve as inputs to other industries, the failure of any single industry to achieve its output target caused a chain reaction of repercussions. For example, if iron mines, for want of machinery or labor or transportation, did not supply the steel industry with the required inputs of iron ore, the steel mills were unable to fulfill the input needs of the many industries that depended on steel. Those steel-using industries (such as tractor, automobile, and transportation) were unable to fulfill their planned production goals. Eventually the chain reaction spread to all firms that used steel as an input and from there to other input buyers or final consumers.

The coordination problem became more difficult as the economies expanded. Products and production processes grew more sophisticated, and the number of industries requiring planning increased. Planning techniques that worked for the simpler economy proved highly inadequate and inefficient for the larger economy. Bottlenecks and production stoppages became the norm, not the exception. In trying to cope, planners further suppressed product variety, focusing on one or two products in each product category.

A lack of a reliable success indicator added to the coordination problem in the Soviet Union and China (prior to its market reforms). We have seen that market economies rely on profit as a success indicator. Profit depends on consumer demand, production efficiency, and product quality. In contrast, the major success indicator for the command economies usually was a quantitative production target that the central planners assigned. Production costs, product quality, and product mix were secondary considerations. Managers and workers often sacrificed product quality and variety because they were being awarded bonuses for meeting quantitative, not qualitative, targets. If meeting production goals meant sloppy assembly work and little product variety, so be it.

It was difficult at best for planners to assign quantitative production targets without unintentionally producing distortions in output. If the plan specified a production target for producing nails in terms of *weight* (tons of nails), the enterprise made only large nails. But if it specified the target as a *quantity* (thousands of nails), the firm made all small nails, and lots of them! That is precisely what happened in the centrally planned economies.

The Incentive Problem

The command economies also faced an incentive problem. Central planners determined the output mix. When they misjudged how many automobiles, shoes, shirts, and chickens were wanted at the government-determined prices, persistent shortages and surpluses of those products arose. But as long as the managers who oversaw the production of those goods were rewarded for meeting their assigned production goals, they had no incentive to adjust production in response to the shortages and surpluses. And there were no fluctuations in prices and profitability to signal that more or less of certain products was desired. Thus, many products were unavailable or in short supply, while other products were overproduced and sat for months or years in warehouses.

The command systems of the Soviet Union and China before its market reforms also lacked entrepreneurship. Central planning did not trigger the profit motive, nor did it reward innovation and enterprise. The route for getting ahead was through participation in the political hierarchy of the Communist Party. Moving up the hierarchy meant better housing, better access to health care, and the right to shop in special stores. Meeting production targets and maneuvering through the minefields of party politics were measures of success in "business." But a definition of business success based solely on political savvy was not conducive to technological advance, which is often disruptive to existing products, production methods, and organizational structures.

O 2.4
Circular flow diagram

The Circular Flow Model

The dynamic market economy creates continuous, repetitive flows of goods and services, resources, and money. The **circular flow diagram**, shown in **Figure 2.2 (Key**

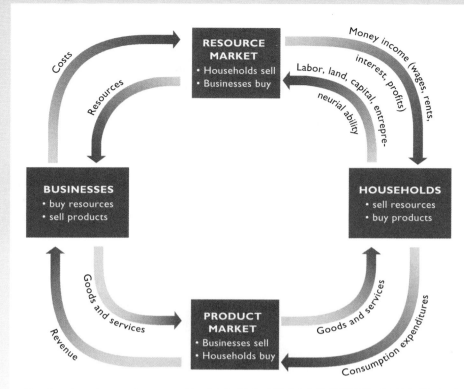

FIGURE 2.2 The circular flow diagram. Resources flow from households to businesses through the resource market, and products flow from businesses to households through the product market. Opposite these real flows are monetary flows. Households receive income from businesses (their costs) through the resource market, and businesses receive revenue from households (their expenditures) through the product market.

QUICK QUIZ 2.2

1. The resource market is the place where:
   a. households sell products and businesses buy products.
   b. businesses sell resources and households sell products.
   c. households sell resources and businesses buy resources (or the services of resources).
   d. businesses sell resources and households buy resources (or the services of resources).
2. Which of the following would be determined in the product market?
   a. a manager's salary.
   b. the price of equipment used in a bottling plant.
   c. the price of 80 acres of farmland.
   d. the price of a new pair of athletic shoes.

3. In this circular flow diagram:
   a. money flows counterclockwise.
   b. resources flow counterclockwise.
   c. goods and services flow clockwise.
   d. households are on the selling side of the product market.
4. In this circular flow diagram:
   a. households spend income in the product market.
   b. firms sell resources to households.
   c. households receive income through the product market.
   d. households produce goods.

Answers: 1. c; 2. d; 3. b; 4. a

Graph), illustrates those flows. Observe that in the diagram we group private decision makers into *businesses* and *households* and group markets into the *resource market* and the *product market*.

Resource Market

The upper half of the circular flow diagram represents the **resource market:** the place where resources or the services of resource suppliers are bought and sold. In the

resource market, households sell resources and businesses buy them. Households (that is, people) own all economic resources either directly as workers or entrepreneurs or indirectly through their ownership of business corporations. They sell their resources to businesses, which buy them because they are necessary for producing goods and services. The funds that businesses pay for resources are costs to businesses but are flows of wage, rent, interest, and profit income to the households. Productive resources

Economist Donald Boudreaux Marvels at the Way the Market System Systematically and Purposefully Arranges the World's Tens of Billions of Individual Resources.

In *The Future and Its Enemies*, Virginia Postrel notes the astonishing fact that if you thoroughly shuffle an ordinary deck of 52 playing cards, chances are practically 100 percent that the resulting arrangement of cards has never before existed. *Never.* Every time you shuffle a deck, you produce an arrangement of cards that exists for the first time in history.

The arithmetic works out that way. For a very small number of items, the number of possible arrangements is small. Three items, for example, can be arranged only six different ways. But the number of possible arrangements grows very large very quickly. The number of different ways to arrange five items is 120 . . . for ten items it's 3,628,800 . . . for fifteen items it's 1,307,674,368,000.

The number of different ways to arrange 52 items is 8.066×10^{67}. This is a *big* number. No human can comprehend its enormousness. By way of comparison, the number of possible ways to arrange a mere 20 items is 2,432,902,008,176,640,000—a number larger than the total number of seconds that have elapsed since the beginning of time ten billion years ago—and this number is Lilliputian compared to 8.066×10^{67}.

What's the significance of these facts about numbers? Consider the number of different resources available in the world—my labor, your labor, your land, oil, tungsten, cedar, coffee beans, chickens, rivers, the Empire State Building, [Microsoft] Windows, the wharves at Houston, the classrooms at Oxford, the airport at Miami, and on and on and on. No one can possibly count all of the different productive resources available for our use. But we can be sure that this number is at least in the tens of billions.

When you reflect on how incomprehensibly large is the number of ways to arrange a deck containing a mere 52 cards, the mind boggles at the number of different ways to arrange all the world's resources.

If our world were random—if resources combined together haphazardly, as if a giant took them all into his hands and tossed them down like so many [cards]—it's a virtual certainty that the resulting combination of resources would be useless. Unless this chance arrangement were quickly rearranged according to some productive logic, nothing worthwhile would be produced. We would all starve to death. Because only a tiny fraction of possible arrangements serves human ends, any arrangement will be useless if it is chosen randomly or with inadequate knowledge of how each and every resource might be productively combined with each other.

And yet, we witness all around us an arrangement of resources that's productive and serves human goals. Today's arrangement of resources might not be perfect, but it is vastly superior to most of the trillions upon trillions of other possible arrangements.

How have we managed to get one of the minuscule number of arrangements that works? The answer is private property—a social institution that encourages mutual accommodation.

Private property eliminates the possibility that resource arrangements will be random, for each resource owner chooses a course of action only if it promises rewards to the owner that exceed the rewards promised by all other available courses.

[The result] is a breathtakingly complex and productive arrangement of countless resources. This arrangement emerged over time (and is still emerging) as the result of billions upon billions of individual, daily, small decisions made by people seeking to better employ their resources and labor in ways that other people find helpful.

Source: Abridged from Donald J. Boudreaux, "Mutual Accommodation," *Ideas on Liberty*, May 2000, pp. 4–5. Reprinted with permission.

therefore flow from households to businesses, and money flows from businesses to households.

Product Market

Next consider the lower part of the diagram, which represents the **product market:** the place where goods and services produced by businesses are bought and sold. In the product market, businesses combine resources to produce and sell goods and services. Households use the (limited) income they have received from the sale of resources to buy goods and services. The monetary flow of consumer spending on goods and services yields sales revenues for businesses. Businesses compare those revenues

to their costs in determining profitability and whether or not a particular good or service should continue to be produced.

The circular flow model depicts a complex, interrelated web of decision making and economic activity involving businesses and households. For the economy, it is the circle of life. Businesses and households are both buyers and sellers. Businesses buy resources and sell products. Households buy products and sell resources. As shown in Figure 2.2, there is a counterclockwise *real flow* of economic resources and finished goods and services and a clockwise *money flow* of income and consumption expenditures.

Summary

1. The market system and the command system are the two broad types of economic systems used to address the economizing problem. In the market system (or capitalism), private individuals own most resources, and markets coordinate most economic activity. In the command system (or socialism or communism), government owns most resources, and central planners coordinate most economic activity.

2. The market system is characterized by the private ownership of resources, including capital, and the freedom of individuals to engage in economic activities of their choice to advance their material well-being. Self-interest is the driving force of such an economy, and competition functions as a regulatory or control mechanism.

3. In the market system, markets, prices, and profits organize and make effective the many millions of individual economic decisions that occur daily.

4. Specialization, use of advanced technology, and the extensive use of capital goods are common features of market systems. Functioning as a medium of exchange, money eliminates the problems of bartering and permits easy trade and greater specialization, both domestically and internationally.

5. Every economy faces five fundamental questions: (a) What goods and services will be produced? (b) How will the goods and services be produced? (c) Who will get the goods and services? (d) How will the system accommodate change? (e) How will the system promote progress?

6. The market system produces products whose production and sale yield total revenue sufficient to cover total cost. It does not produce products for which total revenue continuously falls short of total cost. Competition forces firms to use the lowest-cost production techniques.

7. Economic profit (total revenue minus total cost) indicates that an industry is prosperous and promotes its expansion. Losses signify that an industry is not prosperous and hasten its contraction.

8. Consumer sovereignty means that both businesses and resource suppliers are subject to the wants of consumers. Through their dollar votes, consumers decide on the composition of output.

9. The prices that a household receives for the resources it supplies to the economy determine that household's income. This income determines the household's claim on the economy's output. Those who have income to spend get the products produced in the market system.

10. By communicating changes in consumer tastes to entrepreneurs and resource suppliers, the market system prompts appropriate adjustments in the allocation of the economy's resources. The market system also encourages technological advance and capital accumulation, both of which raise a nation's standard of living.

11. Competition, the primary mechanism of control in the market economy, promotes a unity of self-interest and social interests. As directed by an invisible hand, competition harnesses the self-interest motives of businesses and resource supplier to further the social interest.

12. The command systems of the Soviet Union and pre-reform China met their demise because of coordination difficulties under central planning and the lack of a profit incentive. The coordination problem resulted in bottlenecks, inefficiencies, and a focus on a limited number of products. The incentive problem discouraged product improvement, new product development, and entrepreneurship.

13. The circular flow model illustrates the flows of resources and products from households to businesses and from businesses to households, along with the corresponding monetary flows. Businesses are on the buying side of the resource market and the selling side of the product market. Households are on the selling side of the resource market and the buying side of the product market.

Terms and Concepts

economic system	competition	consumer sovereignty
command system	market	dollar votes
market system	specialization	creative destruction
private property	division of labor	"invisible hand"
freedom of enterprise	medium of exchange	circular flow diagram
freedom of choice	barter	resource market
self-interest	money	product market

Study Questions

1. Contrast how a market system and a command economy try to cope with economic scarcity.

2. How does self-interest help achieve society's economic goals? Why is there such a wide variety of desired goods and services in a market system? In what way are entrepreneurs and businesses at the helm of the economy but commanded by consumers?

3. Why is private property, and the protection of property rights, so critical to the success of the market system?

4. What are the advantages of using capital in the production process? What is meant by the term "division of labor"? What are the advantages of specialization in the use of human and material resources? Explain why exchange is the necessary consequence of specialization.

5. What problem does barter entail? Indicate the economic significance of money as a medium of exchange. What is meant by the statement "We want money only to part with it"?

6. Evaluate and explain the following statements:
   a. The market system is a profit-and-loss system.
   b. Competition is the disciplinarian of the market economy.

7. In the 1990s thousands of "dot-com" companies emerged with great fanfare to take advantage of the Internet and new information technologies. A few, like Yahoo, eBay, and Amazon, have generally thrived and prospered, but many others struggled and eventually failed. Explain these varied outcomes in terms of how the market system answers the question "What goods and services will be produced?"

8. **KEY QUESTION** With current technology, suppose a firm is producing 400 loaves of banana bread daily. Also assume that the least-cost combination of resources in producing those loaves is 5 units of labor, 7 units of land, 2 units of capital, and 1 unit of entrepreneurial ability, selling at prices of $40, $60, $60, and $20, respectively. If the firm can sell these 400 loaves at $2 per unit, will it continue to produce banana bread? If this firm's situation is typical for the other makers of banana bread, will resources flow to or away from this bakery good?

9. **KEY QUESTION** Assume that a business firm finds that its profit is greatest when it produces $40 worth of product A. Suppose also that each of the three techniques shown in the table below will produce the desired output:
   a. With the resource prices shown, which technique will the firm choose? Why? Will production using that technique entail profit or losses? What will be the amount of that profit or loss? Will the industry expand or contract? When will that expansion end?
   b. Assume now that a new technique, technique 4, is developed. It combines 2 units of labor, 2 of land, 6 of capital, and 3 of entrepreneurial ability. In view of the resource prices in the table, will the firm adopt the new technique? Explain your answer.
   c. Suppose that an increase in the labor supply causes the price of labor to fall to $1.50 per unit, all other resource prices remaining unchanged. Which technique will the producer now choose? Explain.
   d. "The market system causes the economy to conserve most in the use of resources that are particularly scarce in supply. Resources that are scarcest relative to the demand for them have the highest prices. As a result, producers use these resources as sparingly as is possible." Evaluate this statement. Does your answer to part c, above, bear out this contention? Explain.

Resource	Price per Unit of Resource	Resource Units Required		
		Technique 1	Technique 2	Technique 3
Labor	$3	5	2	3
Land	4	2	4	2
Capital	2	2	4	5
Entrepreneurial ability	2	4	2	4

10. **KEY QUESTION** Some large hardware stores such as Home Depot boast of carrying as many as 20,000 different products in each store. What motivated the producers of those

individual products to make them and offer them for sale? How did the producers decide on the best combinations of resources to use? Who made those resources available, and why? Who decides whether these particular hardware products should continue to be produced and offered for sale?

11. What is meant by the term "creative destruction"? How does the emergence of MP3 (iPod) technology relate to this idea?

12. In a sentence, describe the meaning of the phrase "invisible hand."

13. In market economies, firms rarely worry about the availability of inputs to produce their products, whereas in command economies input availability is a constant concern. Why the difference?

14. Distinguish between the resource market and the product market in the circular flow model. In what way are businesses and households both sellers and buyers in this model? What are the flows in the circular flow model?

15. **LAST WORD** What explains why millions of economic resources tend to get arranged logically and productively rather than haphazardly and unproductively?

Web-Based Questions

1. **DIAMONDS—INTERESTED IN BUYING ONE?** Go to the Internet auction site eBay at **www.ebay.com** and select the category Jewelry and Watches and then Loose Diamonds and Gemstones. How many loose diamonds are for sale at the moment? Note the wide array of sizes and prices of the diamonds. In what sense is there competition among the sellers in these markets? How does that competition influence prices? In what sense is there competition among buyers? How does that competition influence prices?

2. **BARTER AND THE IRS** Bartering occurs when goods or services are exchanged without the exchange of money. For some, barter's popularity is that it enables them to avoid paying taxes to the government. How might such avoidance occur? Does the Internet Revenue Service (IRS), **www.irs.ustreas.gov/,** treat barter as taxable or nontaxable income? (Type "barter" in the site's search tool.) How is the value of a barter transaction determined? What are some IRS barter examples? What does the IRS require of the members of so-called barter exchanges?

3

IN THIS CHAPTER YOU WILL LEARN:

- What demand is and what affects it.
- What supply is and what affects it.
- How supply and demand together determine market equilibrium.
- How changes in supply and demand affect equilibrium prices and quantities.
- What government-set prices are and how they can cause product surpluses and shortages.

Demand, Supply, and Market Equilibrium

According to an old joke, if you teach a parrot to say "demand and supply," you have an economist. There is an element of truth in this quip. The tools of demand and supply can take us far in understanding how individual markets work.

O 3.1

Demand and supply

FIGURE 3.1 **An individual buyer's demand for corn.** Because price and quantity demanded are inversely related, an individual's demand schedule graphs as a downsloping curve such as *D*. Other things equal, consumers will buy more of a product as its price declines and less of the product as its price rises. (Here and in later figures, *P* stands for price and *Q* stands for quantity demanded or supplied.)

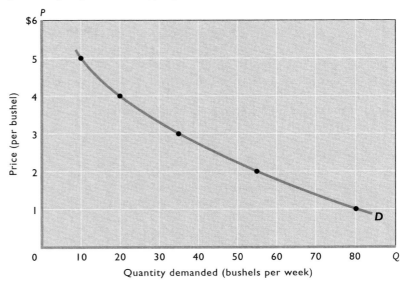

Demand for Corn	
Price per Bushel	**Quantity Demanded per Week**
$5	10
4	20
3	35
2	55
1	80

Markets

Markets bring together buyers ("demanders") and sellers ("suppliers"), and they exist in many forms. The corner gas station, an e-commerce site, the local music store, a farmer's roadside stand—all are familiar markets. The New York Stock Exchange and the Chicago Board of Trade are markets where buyers and sellers of stocks and bonds and farm commodities from all over the world communicate with one another to buy and sell. Auctioneers bring together potential buyers and sellers of art, livestock, used farm equipment, and, sometimes, real estate. In labor markets, new college graduates "sell" and employers "buy" specific labor services.

Some markets are local; others are national or international. Some are highly personal, involving face-to-face contact between demander and supplier; others are faceless, with buyer and seller never seeing or knowing each other.

To keep things simple, we will focus in this chapter on markets consisting of large numbers of independently acting buyers and sellers of standardized products. These are the highly competitive markets such as a central grain exchange, a stock market, or a market for foreign currencies in which the price is "discovered" through the interacting decisions of buyers and sellers. All such markets involve demand, supply, price, and quantity.

Demand

Demand is a schedule or a curve that shows the various amounts of a product that consumers are willing and able to purchase at each of a series of possible prices during a specified period of time.[1] Demand shows the quantities of a product that will be purchased at various possible prices, *other things equal*. Demand can easily be shown in table form. The table in Figure 3.1 is a hypothetical **demand schedule** for a *single consumer* purchasing bushels of corn.

The table reveals the relationship between the various prices of corn and the quantity of corn a particular consumer would be willing and able to purchase at each of these prices. We say "willing and able" because willingness alone is not effective in the market. You may be willing to buy a plasma television set, but if that willingness is not backed by the necessary dollars, it will not be effective and, therefore, will not be reflected in the market. In the table in Figure 3.1, if the price of corn were $5 per bushel, our consumer would be willing and able to buy 10 bushels per week; if it were $4, the consumer would be willing and able to buy 20 bushels per week; and so forth.

The table does not tell us which of the five possible prices will actually exist in the corn market. That depends

---

[1]This definition obviously is worded to apply to product markets. To adjust it to apply to resource markets, substitute the word "resource" for "product" and the word "businesses" for "consumers."

on demand and supply. Demand is simply a statement of a buyer's plans, or intentions, with respect to the purchase of a product.

To be meaningful, the quantities demanded at each price must relate to a specific period—a day, a week, a month. Saying "A consumer will buy 10 bushels of corn at $5 per bushel" is meaningless. Saying "A consumer will buy 10 bushels of corn per week at $5 per bushel" is meaningful. Unless a specific time period is stated, we do not know whether the demand for a product is large or small.

Law of Demand

O 3.2
Law of demand

A fundamental characteristic of demand is this: All else equal, as price falls, the quantity demanded rises, and as price rises, the quantity demanded falls. In short, there is a negative or *inverse* relationship between price and quantity demanded. Economists call this inverse relationship the **law of demand.**

The other-things-equal assumption is critical here. Many factors other than the price of the product being considered affect the amount purchased. For example, the quantity of Nikes purchased will depend not only on the price of Nikes but also on the prices of such substitutes as Reeboks, Adidas, and New Balances. The law of demand in this case says that fewer Nikes will be purchased if the price of Nikes rises and if the prices of Reeboks, Adidas, and New Balances all remain constant. In short, if the *relative price* of Nikes rises, fewer Nikes will be bought. However, if the price of Nikes and the prices of all other competing shoes increase by some amount—say, $5—consumers might buy more, less, or the same amount of Nikes.

Why the inverse relationship between price and quantity demanded? Let's look at three explanations, beginning with the simplest one:

- The law of demand is consistent with common sense. People ordinarily *do* buy more of a product at a low price than at a high price. Price is an obstacle that deters consumers from buying. The higher that obstacle, the less of a product they will buy; the lower the price obstacle, the more they will buy. The fact that businesses have "sales" is evidence of their belief in the law of demand.

O 3.3
Diminishing marginal utility

- In any specific time period, each buyer of a product will derive less satisfaction (or benefit, or utility) from each successive unit of the product consumed. The second Big Mac will yield less satisfaction to the consumer than the first, and the third still less than

the second. That is, consumption is subject to **diminishing marginal utility.** And because successive units of a particular product yield less and less marginal utility, consumers will buy additional units only if the price of those units is progressively reduced.

- We can also explain the law of demand in terms of income and substitution effects. The **income effect** indicates that a lower price increases the purchasing power of a buyer's money income, enabling the buyer to purchase more of the product than before. A higher price has the opposite effect. The **substitution effect** suggests that at a lower price buyers have the incentive to substitute what is now a less expensive product for similar products that are now *relatively* more expensive. The product whose price has fallen is now "a better deal" relative to the other products.

O 3.4
Income and substitution effects

For example, a decline in the price of chicken will increase the purchasing power of consumer incomes, enabling people to buy more chicken (the income effect). At a lower price, chicken is relatively more attractive and consumers tend to substitute it for pork, lamb, beef, and fish (the substitution effect). The income and substitution effects combine to make consumers able and willing to buy more of a product at a low price than at a high price.

The Demand Curve

The inverse relationship between price and quantity demanded for any product can be represented on a simple graph, in which, by convention, we measure *quantity demanded* on the horizontal axis and *price* on the vertical axis. In the graph in Figure 3.1 we have plotted the five price-quantity data points listed in the accompanying table and connected the points with a smooth curve, labeled *D*. Such a curve is called a **demand curve.** Its downward slope reflects the law of demand—people buy more of a product, service, or resource as its price falls. The relationship between price and quantity demanded is inverse (or negative).

The table and graph in Figure 3.1 on the previous page contain exactly the same data and reflect the same relationship between price and quantity demanded. But the graph shows that relationship more simply and clearly than a table or a description in words.

Market Demand

So far, we have concentrated on just one consumer. But competition requires that more than one buyer be present in each market. By adding the quantities demanded by all

TABLE 3.1 Market Demand for Corn, Three Buyers

Price per Bushel	Quantity Demanded			Total Quantity Demanded per Week
	Joe	Jen	Jay	
$5	10 +	12 +	8 =	30
4	20 +	23 +	17 =	60
3	35 +	39 +	26 =	100
2	55 +	60 +	39 =	154
1	80 +	87 +	54 =	221

consumers at each of the various possible prices, we can get from *individual* demand to *market* demand. If there are just three buyers in the market, as represented in Table 3.1, it is relatively easy to determine the total quantity demanded at each price. Figure 3.2 shows the graphical summing procedure: At each price we add the individual quantities demanded to obtain the total quantity demanded at that price; we then plot the price and the total quantity demanded as one point on the market demand curve.

Competition, of course, ordinarily entails many more than three buyers of a product. To avoid hundreds or thousands or millions of additions, we suppose that all the buyers in a market are willing and able to buy the same amounts at each of the possible prices. Then we just multiply those amounts by the number of buyers to obtain the market demand. That is how we arrived at curve D_1 in Figure 3.3 for a market of 200 corn buyers, each with a demand as shown in the table in Figure 3.1. Table 3.2 shows the calculations.

In constructing a demand curve such as D_1 in Figure 3.3, economists assume that price is the most important influence on the amount of any product purchased. But economists know that other factors can and do affect purchases. These factors, called **determinants of demand,** are assumed to be constant when a demand curve like D_1 is drawn. They are the "other things equal" in the

relationship between price and quantity demanded. When any of these determinants changes, the demand curve will shift to the right or left. For this reason, determinants of demand are sometimes referred to as *demand shifters*.

The basic determinants of demand are (1) consumers' tastes (preferences), (2) the number of buyers in the market, (3) consumers' incomes, (4) the prices of related goods, and (5) consumer expectations.

Change in Demand
A change in one or more of the determinants of demand will change the demand data (the demand schedule) in Table 3.2 and therefore the location of the demand curve in Figure 3.3. A change in the demand schedule or, graphically, a shift in the demand curve is called a *change in demand*.

If consumers desire to buy more corn at each possible price than is reflected in column 4 in Table 3.2, that *increase in demand* is shown as a shift of the demand curve to the right, say, from D_1 to D_2. Conversely, a *decrease in demand* occurs when consumers buy less corn at each possible price than is indicated in column 4, Table 3.2. The leftward shift of the demand curve from D_1 to D_3 in Figure 3.3 shows that situation.

Now let's see how changes in each determinant affect demand.

Tastes A favorable change in consumer tastes (preferences) for a product—a change that makes the product more desirable—means that more of it will be demanded at each price. Demand will increase; the demand curve will shift rightward. An unfavorable change in consumer preferences will decrease demand, shifting the demand curve to the left.

New products may affect consumer tastes; for example, the introduction of digital cameras greatly decreased the demand for film cameras. Consumers' concern over the health hazards of cholesterol and obesity have increased

FIGURE 3.2 Market demand for corn, three buyers. We establish the market demand curve D by adding horizontally the individual demand curves (D_1, D_2, and D_3) of all the consumers in the market. At the price of $3, for example, the three individual curves yield a total quantity demanded of 100 bushels.

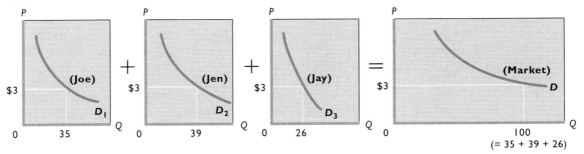

FIGURE 3.3 Changes in the demand for corn. A change in one or more of the determinants of demand causes a change in demand. An increase in demand is shown as a shift of the demand curve to the right, as from D_1 to D_2. A decrease in demand is shown as a shift of the demand curve to the left, as from D_1 to D_3. These changes in demand are to be distinguished from a change in quantity demanded, which is caused by a change in the price of the product, as shown by a movement from, say, point a to point b on fixed demand curve D_1.

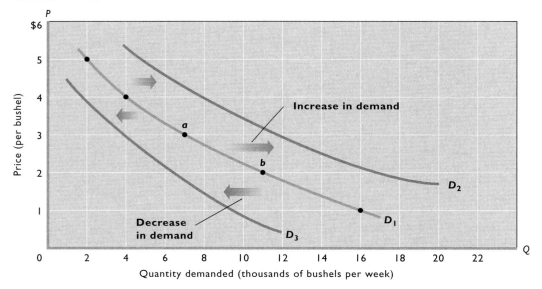

the demand for broccoli, low-calorie beverages, and fresh fruit while decreasing the demand for beef, veal, eggs, and whole milk. Over the past several years, the demand for coffee drinks and bottled water has greatly increased, driven by a change in tastes. So, too, has the demand for DVDs and MP3 players.

Number of Buyers An increase in the number of buyers in a market is likely to increase product demand; a decrease in the number of buyers will probably decrease demand. For example, the rising number of older persons in the United States in recent years has increased the demand for motor homes, medical care, and retirement communities. Large-scale immigration from Mexico has greatly increased the demand for a range of goods and services in the Southwest, including Mexican food products in local grocery stores. Improvements in communications have given financial markets international range and have thus increased the demand for stocks and bonds. International trade agreements have reduced foreign trade barriers to American farm commodities, increasing the number of buyers and therefore the demand for those products.

In contrast, the out-migration from many small rural communities has reduced the population and thus the demand for housing, home appliances, and auto repair in those towns.

Income How changes in income affect demand is a more complex matter. For most products, a rise in income causes an increase in demand. Consumers typically buy more steaks, furniture, and electronic equipment as their incomes increase. Conversely, the demand for such products declines as their incomes fall. Products whose demand varies *directly* with money income are called *superior goods*, or **normal goods.**

Although most products are normal goods, there are some exceptions. As incomes increase beyond some point, the demand for used clothing, retread tires, and third-hand automobiles may decrease, because the higher incomes enable consumers to buy new versions of those products. Rising incomes may also decrease the demand for soy-enhanced hamburger. Similarly, rising incomes may cause the demand for charcoal grills to decline as wealthier consumers

TABLE 3.2 Market Demand for Corn, 200 Buyers

(1) Price per Bushel	(2) Quantity Demanded per Week, Single Buyer		(3) Number of Buyers in the Market		(4) Total Quantity Demanded per Week
$5	10	×	200	=	2,000
4	20	×	200	=	4,000
3	35	×	200	=	7,000
2	55	×	200	=	11,000
1	80	×	200	=	16,000

switch to gas grills. Goods whose demand varies *inversely* with money income are called **inferior goods.**

Prices of Related Goods

A change in the price of a related good may either increase or decrease the demand for a product, depending on whether the related good is a substitute or a complement:

* A **substitute good** is one that can be used in place of another good.
* A **complementary good** is one that is used together with another good.

Substitutes

Leather jackets and fleece jackets are substitute goods or, simply, *substitutes.* When two products are substitutes, an increase in the price of one will increase the demand for the other. Conversely, a decrease in the price of one will decrease the demand for the other. For example, when the prices of leather jackets rise, consumers will buy fewer leather jackets and increase their demand for fleece jackets. When the price of Colgate toothpaste declines, the demand for Crest decreases. So it is with other product pairs such as Nikes and Reeboks, Budweiser and Miller beer, or Chevrolets and Fords. They are *substitutes in consumption.*

Complements

Because complementary goods (or, simply, *complements*) are used together, they are typically demanded jointly. Examples include computers and software, cell phones and cellular service, and snowboards and lift tickets. If the price of a complement (for example, lettuce) goes up, the demand for the related good (salad dressing) will decline. Conversely, if the price of a complement (for example, tuition) falls, the demand for a related good (textbooks) will increase.

Unrelated Goods

The vast majority of goods are not related to one another and are called *independent goods.* Examples are butter and golf balls, potatoes and automobiles, and bananas and wristwatches. A change in the price of one has little or no effect on the demand for the other.

Consumer Expectations

Changes in consumer expectations may shift demand. A newly formed expectation of higher future prices may cause consumers to buy now in order to "beat" the anticipated price rises, thus increasing current demand. That is often what happens in so-called hot real estate markets. Buyers rush in because they think the price of new homes will continue to escalate rapidly. Some buyers fear being "priced out of the market" and therefore not obtaining the home they desire. Other buyers—speculators—believe they will be able to sell the houses later at a higher price. Whichever their motivation, these buyers increase the demand for houses.

Similarly, a change in expectations concerning future income may prompt consumers to change their current spending. For example, first-round NFL draft choices may splurge on new luxury cars in anticipation of a lucrative professional football contract. Or workers who become fearful of losing their jobs may reduce their demand for, say, vacation travel.

In summary, an *increase* in demand—the decision by consumers to buy larger quantities of a product at each possible price—may be caused by:

* A favorable change in consumer tastes.
* An increase in the number of buyers.
* Rising incomes if the product is a normal good.
* Falling incomes if the product is an inferior good.
* An increase in the price of a substitute good.
* A decrease in the price of a complementary good.
* A new consumer expectation that either prices or income will be higher in the future.

You should "reverse" these generalizations to explain a *decrease* in demand. Table 3.3 provides additional illustrations of the determinants of demand. **(Key Question 3)**

Changes in Quantity Demanded

A *change in demand* must not be confused with a *change in quantity demanded.* A **change in demand** is a shift of the demand curve to the right (an increase in demand) or to the left (a decrease in demand). It occurs because the consumer's state of mind about purchasing the product has been altered in response to a change in one or more of

TABLE 3.3 Determinants of Demand: Factors That Shift the Demand Curve

Determinant	Examples
Change in buyer tastes	Physical fitness rises in popularity, increasing the demand for jogging shoes and bicycles; patriotism rises, increasing the demand for flags.
Change in number of buyers	A decline in the birthrate reduces the demand for children's toys.
Change in income	A rise in incomes increases the demand for normal goods such as restaurant meals, sports tickets, and necklaces while reducing the demand for inferior goods such as cabbage, turnips, and inexpensive wine.
Change in the prices of related goods	A reduction in airfares reduces the demand for bus transportation (substitute goods); a decline in the price of DVD players increases the demand for DVD movies (complementary goods).
Change in consumer expectations	Inclement weather in South America creates an expectation of higher future prices of coffee beans, thereby increasing today's demand for coffee beans.

the determinants of demand. Recall that "demand" is a schedule or a curve; therefore, a "change in demand" means a change in the schedule and a shift of the curve.

In contrast, a **change in quantity demanded** is a movement from one point to another point—from one price-quantity combination to another—on a fixed demand schedule or demand curve. The cause of such a change is an increase or decrease in the price of the product under consideration. In Table 3.2, for example, a decline in the price of corn from $5 to $4 will increase the quantity of corn demanded from 2000 to 4000 bushels.

In Figure 3.3 the shift of the demand curve D_1 to either D_2 or D_3 is a change in demand. But the movement from point a to point b on curve D_1 represents a change in quantity demanded: Demand has not changed; it is the entire curve, and it remains fixed in place.

QUICK REVIEW 3.1

- Demand is a schedule or a curve showing the amount of a product that buyers are willing and able to purchase, in a particular time period, at each possible price in a series of prices.
- The law of demand states that, other things equal, the quantity of a good purchased varies inversely with its price.
- The demand curve shifts because of changes in (a) consumer tastes, (b) the number of buyers in the market, (c) consumer income, (d) the prices of substitute or complementary goods, and (e) consumer expectations.
- A change in demand is a shift of the demand curve; a change in quantity demanded is a movement from one point to another on a fixed demand curve.

Supply

Supply is a schedule or curve showing the various amounts of a product that producers are willing and able to make available for sale at each of a series of possible prices during a specific period.[2] The table in Figure 3.4 is a hypothetical **supply schedule** for a single producer of corn. It shows the quantities of corn that will be supplied at various prices, other things equal.

Law of Supply

The table in Figure 3.4 shows a positive or direct relationship that prevails between price and quantity supplied. As price rises, the quantity supplied rises; as price falls, the quantity supplied falls. This relationship is called the **law**

[2]This definition is worded to apply to product markets. To adjust it to apply to resource markets, substitute "resource" for "product" and "owners" for "producers."

of supply. A supply schedule tells us that firms will produce and offer for sale more of their product at a high price than at a low price. This, again, is basically common sense.

Price is an obstacle from the standpoint of the consumer, who is on the paying end. The higher the price, the less the consumer will buy. But the supplier is on the receiving end of the product's price. To a supplier, price represents *revenue*, which serves as an incentive to produce and sell a product. The higher the price, the greater this incentive and the greater the quantity supplied.

Consider a farmer who can shift resources among alternative products. As price moves up, as shown in the table in Figure 3.4, the farmer finds it profitable to take land out of wheat, oats, and soybean production and put it into corn. And the higher corn prices enable the farmer to cover the increased costs associated with more intensive cultivation and the use of more seed, fertilizer, and pesticides. The overall result is more corn.

Now consider a manufacturer. Beyond some quantity of production, manufacturers usually encounter increasing *marginal cost*—the added cost of producing one more unit of output. Certain productive resources—in particular, the firm's plant and machinery—cannot be expanded quickly, so the firm uses more of other resources, such as labor, to produce more output. But as labor becomes more abundant relative to the fixed plant and equipment, the additional workers have relatively less space and access to equipment. For example, the added workers may have to wait to gain access to machines. As a result, each added worker produces less added output, and the marginal cost of successive units of output rises accordingly. The firm will not produce the more costly units unless it receives a higher price for them. Again, price and quantity supplied are directly related.

The Supply Curve

As with demand, it is convenient to represent individual supply graphically. In Figure 3.4, curve S is the **supply curve** that corresponds with the price-quantity supplied data in the accompanying table. The upward slope of the curve reflects the law of supply—producers offer more of a good, service, or resource for sale as its price rises. The relationship between price and quantity supplied is positive, or direct.

Market Supply

Market supply is derived from individual supply in exactly the same way that market demand is derived from individual demand. We sum the quantities supplied by each producer at each price. That is, we obtain the market supply curve by "horizontally adding" the supply curves of the individual producers. The price-quantity supplied data

FIGURE 3.4 An individual producer's supply of corn. Because price and quantity supplied are directly related, the supply curve for an individual producer graphs as an upsloping curve. Other things equal, producers will offer more of a product for sale as its price rises and less of the product for sale as its price falls.

Supply of Corn	
Price per Bushel	Quantity Supplied per Week
$5	60
4	50
3	35
2	20
1	5

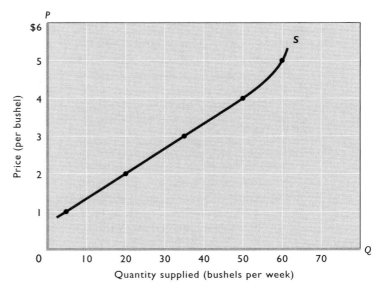

in Table 3.4 are for the many suppliers in the market, each willing to supply corn. Curve S_1 in Figure 3.5 is a graph of the market supply data. Note that the values of the axes in Figure 3.5 are the same as those used in our graph of market demand (Figure 3.3), except the change from "quantity demanded" to "quantity supplied" on the horizontal axis.

Determinants of Supply

In constructing a supply curve, we assume that price is the most significant influence on the quantity supplied of any product. But other factors (the "other things equal") can and do affect supply. The supply curve is drawn on the assumption that these other things are fixed and do not change. If one of them does change, a *change in supply* will occur, meaning that the entire supply curve will shift.

The basic **determinants of supply** are (1) resource prices, (2) technology, (3) taxes and subsidies, (4) prices of other goods, (5) producer expectations, and (6) the number of sellers in the market. A change in any one or more of these determinants of supply, or *supply shifters*, will move the supply curve for a product either right or left. A shift to the *right*, as from S_1 to S_2 in Figure 3.5, signifies an *increase* in supply: Producers supply larger quantities of the product at each possible price. A shift to the *left*, as from S_1 to S_3, indicates a *decrease* in supply: Producers offer less output at each price.

Changes in Supply

Let's consider how changes in each of the determinants affect supply. The key idea is that costs are a major factor underlying supply curves; anything that affects costs (other than changes in output itself) usually shifts the supply curve.

Resource Prices The prices of the resources used in the production process help determine the costs of production incurred by firms. Higher *resource* prices raise production costs and, assuming a particular *product* price, squeeze profits. That reduction in profits reduces the incentive for firms to supply output at each product price. For example, an increase in the prices of sand, crushed rock, and Portland cement will increase the cost of producing concrete and reduce its supply.

In contrast, lower *resource* prices reduce production costs and increase profits. So when resource prices fall, firms supply greater output at each product price. For example, a decrease in the price of flat-panel glass will increase the supply of big-screen television sets.

TABLE 3.4 Market Supply of Corn, 200 Producers

(1) Price per Bushel	(2) Quantity Supplied per Week, Single Producer		(3) Number of Sellers in the Market		(4) Total Quantity Supplied per Week
$5	60	×	200	=	12,000
4	50	×	200	=	10,000
3	35	×	200	=	7,000
2	20	×	200	=	4,000
1	5	×	200	=	1,000

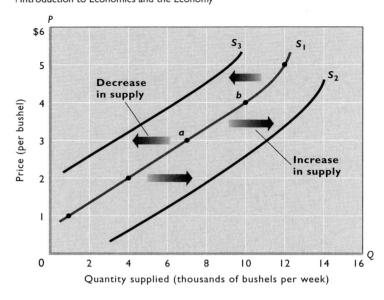

FIGURE 3.5 Changes in the supply of corn. A change in one or more of the determinants of supply causes a change in supply. An increase in supply is shown as a rightward shift of the supply curve, as from S_1 to S_2. A decrease in supply is depicted as a leftward shift of the curve, as from S_1 to S_3. In contrast, a change in the *quantity supplied* is caused by a change in the product's price and is shown by a movement from one point to another, as from *b* to *a* on fixed supply curve S_1.

Technology Improvements in technology (techniques of production) enable firms to produce units of output with fewer resources. Because resources are costly, using fewer of them lowers production costs and increases supply. Example: Technological advances in producing flat-panel computer monitors have greatly reduced their cost. Thus, manufacturers will now offer more such monitors than previously at the various prices; the supply of flat-panel monitors has increased.

Taxes and Subsidies Businesses treat most taxes as costs. An increase in sales or property taxes will increase production costs and reduce supply. In contrast, subsidies are "taxes in reverse." If the government subsidizes the production of a good, it in effect lowers the producers' costs and increases supply.

Prices of Other Goods Firms that produce a particular product, say, soccer balls, can sometimes use their plant and equipment to produce alternative goods, say, basketballs and volleyballs. The higher prices of these "other goods" may entice soccer ball producers to switch production to those other goods in order to increase profits. This *substitution in production* results in a decline in the supply of soccer balls. Alternatively, when the prices of basketballs and volleyballs decline relative to the price of soccer balls, producers of those goods may decide to produce more soccer balls instead, increasing their supply.

Producer Expectations Changes in expectations about the future price of a product may affect the producer's current willingness to supply that product. It is difficult, however, to generalize about how a new expectation of higher prices affects the present supply of a product. Farmers anticipating a higher wheat price in the future might withhold some of their current wheat harvest from the market, thereby causing a decrease in the current supply of wheat. In contrast, in many types of manufacturing industries, newly formed expectations that price will increase may induce firms to add another shift of workers or to expand their production facilities, causing current supply to increase.

Number of Sellers Other things equal, the larger the number of suppliers, the greater the market supply. As more firms enter an industry, the supply curve shifts to the right. Conversely, the smaller the number of firms in the industry, the less the market supply. This means that as firms leave an industry, the supply curve shifts to the left. Example: The United States and Canada have imposed restrictions on haddock fishing to replenish dwindling stocks. As part of that policy, the Federal government has bought the boats of some of the haddock fishers as a way of putting them out of business and decreasing the catch. The result has been a decline in the market supply of haddock.

Table 3.5 is a checklist of the determinants of supply, along with further illustrations. **(Key Question 6)**

Changes in Quantity Supplied

The distinction between a *change in supply* and a *change in quantity supplied* parallels the distinction between a change in demand and a change in quantity demanded.

TABLE 3.5 Determinants of Supply: Factors That Shift the Supply Curve

Determinant	Examples
Change in resource prices	A decrease in the price of microchips increases the supply of computers; an increase in the price of crude oil reduces the supply of gasoline.
Change in technology	The development of more effective wireless technology increases the supply of cell phones.
Changes in taxes and subsidies	An increase in the excise tax on cigarettes reduces the supply of cigarettes; a decline in subsidies to state universities reduces the supply of higher education.
Change in prices of other goods	An increase in the price of cucumbers decreases the supply of watermelons.
Change in producer expectations	An expectation of a substantial rise in future log prices decreases the supply of logs today.
Change in number of suppliers	An increase in the number of tatoo parlors increases the supply of tatoos; the formation of women's professional basketball leagues increases the supply of women's professional basketball games.

Because supply is a schedule or curve, a **change in supply** means a change in the schedule and a shift of the curve. An increase in supply shifts the curve to the right; a decrease in supply shifts it to the left. The cause of a change in supply is a change in one or more of the determinants of supply.

In contrast, a **change in quantity supplied** is a movement from one point to another on a fixed supply curve. The cause of such a movement is a change in the price of the specific product being considered.

Consider supply curve S_1 in Figure 3.5. A decline in the price of corn from \$4 to \$3 decreases the quantity of corn supplied per week from 10,000 to 7000 bushels. This movement from point *b* to point *a* along S_1 is a change in quantity supplied, not a change in supply. Supply is the full schedule of prices and quantities shown, and this schedule does not change when the price of corn changes.

QUICK REVIEW 3.2

- A supply schedule or curve shows that, other things equal, the quantity of a good supplied varies directly with its price.
- The supply curve shifts because of changes in (a) resource prices, (b) technology, (c) taxes or subsidies, (d) prices of other goods, (e) expectations of future prices, and (f) the number of suppliers.
- A change in supply is a shift of the supply curve; a change in quantity supplied is a movement from one point to another on a fixed supply curve.

Market Equilibrium

With our understanding of demand and supply, we can now show how the decisions of buyers of corn interact with the decisions of sellers to determine the equilibrium price and quantity of corn. In Table 3.6, columns 1 and 2 repeat the market supply of corn (from Table 3.4), and columns 2 and 3 repeat the market demand for corn (from Table 3.2). We assume this is a competitive market so that neither buyers nor sellers can set the price.

Equilibrium Price and Quantity

We are looking for the equilibrium price and equilibrium quantity. The **equilibrium price** (or *market-clearing price*)

G 3.1

Supply and demand

is the price where the intentions of buyers and sellers match. It is the price where quantity demanded equals quantity supplied. Table 3.6 reveals that at \$3, *and only at that price*, the number of bushels of corn that sellers wish to sell (7000) is identical to the number consumers want to buy (also 7000). At \$3 and 7000 bushels of corn, there is neither a shortage nor a surplus of corn. So 7000 bushels of corn in the **equilibrium quantity:** the quantity demanded and quantity supplied at the equilibrium price in a competitive market.

Graphically, the equilibrium price is indicated by the intersection of the supply curve and the demand curve in **Figure 3.6 (Key Graph).** (The horizontal axis now measures both quantity demanded and quantity supplied.) With neither a shortage nor a surplus at \$3, the market is in equilibrium, meaning "in balance" or "at rest."

Competition among buyers and among sellers drives the price to the equilibrium price; once there, it remains unless it is subsequently disturbed by changes in demand or supply (shifts of the curves). To better understand the

TABLE 3.6 Market Supply of and Demand for Corn

(1) Total Quantity Supplied per Week	(2) Price per Bushel	(3) Total Quantity Demanded per Week	(4) Surplus (+) or Shortage (−)*
12,000	\$5	2,000	+10,000 ↓
10,000	4	4,000	+6,000 ↓
7,000	*3*	*7,000*	*0*
4,000	2	11,000	−7,000 ↑
1,000	1	16,000	−15,000 ↑

*Arrows indicate the effect on price.

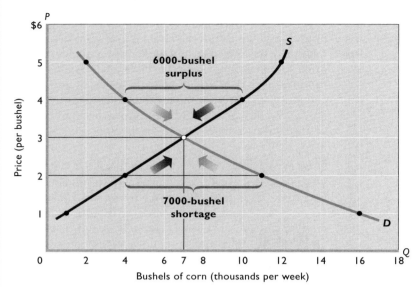

FIGURE 3.6 Equilibrium price and quantity. The intersection of the downsloping demand curve D and the upsloping supply curve S indicates the equilibrium price and quantity, here $3 and 7000 bushels of corn. The shortages of corn at below-equilibrium prices (for example, 7000 bushels at $2) drive up price. The higher prices increase the quantity supplied and reduce the quantity demanded until equilibrium is achieved. The surpluses caused by above-equilibrium prices (for example, 6000 bushels at $4) push price down. As price drops, the quantity demanded rises and the quantity supplied falls until equilibrium is established. At the equilibrium price and quantity, there are neither shortages nor surpluses of corn.

QUICK QUIZ 3.6

1. Demand curve D is downsloping because:
   a. producers offer less of a product for sale as the price of the product falls.
   b. lower prices of a product create income and substitution effects that lead consumers to purchase more of it.
   c. the larger the number of buyers in a market, the lower the product price.
   d. price and quantity demanded are directly (positively) related.
2. Supply curve S:
   a. reflects an inverse (negative) relationship between price and quantity supplied.
   b. reflects a direct (positive) relationship between price and quantity supplied.
   c. depicts the collective behavior of buyers in this market.

   d. shows that producers will offer more of a product for sale at a low product price than at a high product price.
3. At the $3 price:
   a. quantity supplied exceeds quantity demanded.
   b. quantity demanded exceeds quantity supplied.
   c. the product is abundant and a surplus exists.
   d. there is no pressure on price to rise or fall.
4. At price $5 in this market:
   a. there will be a shortage of 10,000 units.
   b. there will be a surplus of 10,000 units.
   c. quantity demanded will be 12,000 units.
   d. quantity demanded will equal quantity supplied.

Answers: 1. b; 2. b; 3. d; 4. b

uniqueness of the equilibrium price, let's consider other prices. At any above-equilibrium price, quantity supplied exceeds quantity demanded. For example, at the $4 price, sellers will offer 10,000 bushels of corn, but buyers will purchase only 4000. The $4 price encourages sellers to offer lots of corn but discourages many consumers from buying it. The result is a **surplus** (or *excess supply*) of 6000 bushels. If corn sellers produced them all, they would find themselves with 6000 unsold bushels of corn.

Surpluses drive prices down. Even if the $4 price existed temporarily, it could not persist. The large surplus would prompt competing sellers to lower the price to en-

courage buyers to take the surplus off their hands. As the price fell, the incentive to produce corn would decline and the incentive for consumers to buy corn would increase. As shown in Figure 3.6, the market would move to its equilibrium at $3.

Any price below the $3 equilibrium price would create a shortage; quantity demanded would exceed quantity supplied. Consider a $2 price, for example. We see in column 4 of Table 3.6 and in Figure 3.6 that quantity demanded exceeds quantity supplied at that price. The result is a **shortage** (or *excess demand*) of 7000 bushels of corn. The $2 price discourages sellers from devoting resources to corn and encourages consumers to desire more bushels than are available. The $2 price cannot persist as the equilibrium price. Many consumers who want to buy corn at this price will not obtain it. They will express a willingness to pay more than $2 to get corn. Competition among

CONSIDER THIS ...

Ticket Scalping: A Bum Rap!

Ticket prices for athletic events and musical concerts are usually set far in advance of the events. Sometimes the original ticket price is too low to be the equilibrium price. Lines form at the ticket window, and a severe shortage of tickets occurs at the printed price. What happens next? Buyers who are willing to pay more than the original price bid up the equilibrium price in resale ticket markets. The price rockets upward.

Tickets sometimes get resold for much greater amounts than the original price—market transactions known as "scalping." For example, an original buyer may resell a $75 ticket to a concert for $200, $250, or more. Reporters sometimes denounce scalpers for "ripping off" buyers by charging "exorbitant" prices.

But is scalping really a rip-off? We must first recognize that such ticket resales are voluntary transactions. If both buyer and seller did not expect to gain from the exchange, it would not occur! The seller must value the $200 more than seeing the event, and the buyer must value seeing the event at $200 or more. So there are no losers or victims here: Both buyer and seller benefit from the transaction. The scalping market simply redistributes assets (game or concert tickets) from those who would rather have the money (the other things money can buy) to those who would rather have the tickets.

Does scalping impose losses or injury on the sponsors of the event? If the sponsors are injured, it is because they initially priced tickets below the equilibrium level. Perhaps they did this to create a long waiting line and the attendant news media publicity. Alternatively, they may have had a genuine desire to keep tickets affordable for lower-income, ardent fans. In either case, the event sponsors suffer an opportunity cost in the form of less ticket revenue than they might have otherwise received. But such losses are self-inflicted and separate and distinct from the fact that some tickets are later resold at a higher price.

So is ticket scalping undesirable? Not on economic grounds! It is an entirely voluntary activity that benefits both sellers and buyers.

these buyers will drive up the price, eventually to the $3 equilibrium level. Unless disrupted by changes of supply or demand, this $3 price of corn will continue to prevail.

Rationing Function of Prices

The ability of the competitive forces of supply and demand to establish a price at which selling and buying decisions are consistent is called the rationing function of prices. In our case, the equilibrium price of $3 clears the market, leaving no burdensome surplus for sellers and no inconvenient shortage for potential buyers. And it is the combination of freely made individual decisions that sets this market-clearing price. In effect, the market outcome says that all buyers who are willing and able to pay $3 for a bushel of corn will obtain it; all buyers who cannot or will not pay $3 will go without corn. Similarly, all producers who are willing and able to offer corn for sale at $3 a bushel will sell it; all producers who cannot or will not sell for $3 per bushel will not sell their product. **(Key Question 8)**

Efficient Allocation

A competitive market such as that we have described not only rations goods to consumers but also allocates society's resources efficiently to the particular product. Competition among corn producers forces them to use the best technology and right mix of productive resources. Otherwise, their costs will be too high relative to the market price and they will be unprofitable. The result is **productive efficiency:** the production of any particular good in the least costly way. When society produces corn at the lowest achievable per-unit cost, it is expending the least-valued combination of resources to produce that product and therefore is making available more-valued resources to produce other desired goods. Suppose society has only $100 worth of resources available. If it can produce a bushel of corn using $3 of those resources, then it will have available $97 of resources remaining to produce other goods. This is clearly better than producing the corn for $5 and having only $95 of resources available for the alternative uses.

Competitive markets also produce **allocative efficiency:** the *particular mix* of goods and services most highly valued by society (minimum-cost production assumed). For example, society wants land suitable for growing corn used for that purpose, not to grow dandelions. It wants high-quality mineral water to be used for bottled water, not for gigantic blocks of refrigeration ice. It wants MP3 players (such as iPods), not cassette players and tapes. Moreover, society does not want to devote all its resources to corn, bottled water, and MP3 players. It wants to assign some resources to wheat, gasoline, and cell phones. Competitive markets make those allocatively efficient assignments.

The equilibrium price and quantity in competitive markets usually produce an assignment of resources that is "right" from an economic perspective. Demand essentially reflects the marginal benefit (MB) of the good, based on the utility received. Supply reflects the marginal cost (MC) of producing the good. The market ensures that firms produce all units of goods for which MB exceeds MC and no units for which MC exceeds MB. At the intersection of the demand and supply curves, MB equals MC and allocative efficiency results. As economists say, there is neither an "underallocaton of resources" nor an "overallocation of resources" to the product.

Changes in Supply, Demand, and Equilibrium

We know that demand might change because of fluctuations in consumer tastes or incomes, changes in consumer expectations, or variations in the prices of related goods. Supply might change in response to changes in resource prices, technology, or taxes. What effects will such changes in supply and demand have on equilibrium price and quantity?

Changes in Demand Suppose that the supply of some good (for example, potatoes) is constant and demand increases, as shown in Figure 3.7a. As a result, the new intersection of the supply and demand curves is at higher values on both the price and the quantity axes. Clearly, an increase in demand raises both equilibrium price and equilibrium quantity. Conversely, a decrease in demand, such as that shown in Figure 3.7b, reduces both equilibrium price and equilibrium quantity. (The value of graphical analysis is now apparent: We need not fumble with columns of figures to determine the outcomes; we need only compare the new and the old points of intersection on the graph.)

Changes in Supply What happens if the demand for some good (for example, lettuce) is constant but supply increases, as in Figure 3.7c? The new intersection of supply and demand is located at a lower equilibrium price but at a higher equilibrium quantity. An increase in supply reduces equilibrium price but increases equilibrium quantity. In contrast, if supply decreases, as in Figure 3.7d, the equilibrium price rises while the equilibrium quantity declines.

Complex Cases When both supply and demand change, the effect is a combination of the individual effects.

Supply Increase; Demand Decrease What effect will a supply increase and a demand decrease for some good (for example, apples) have on equilibrium price? Both changes decrease price, so the net result is a price drop greater than that resulting from either change alone.

What about equilibrium quantity? Here the effects of the changes in supply and demand are opposed: the increase in supply increases equilibrium quantity, but the decrease in demand reduces it. The direction of the change in quantity depends on the relative sizes of the changes in supply and demand. If the increase in supply is larger than the decrease in demand, the equilibrium quantity will increase. But if the decrease in demand is greater than the increase in supply, the equilibrium quantity will decrease.

Supply Decrease; Demand Increase A decrease in supply and an increase in demand for some good (for example, gasoline) both increase price. Their combined effect is an increase in equilibrium price greater than that caused by either change separately. But their effect on equilibrium quantity is again indeterminate, depending on the relative sizes of the changes in supply and demand. If the decrease in supply is larger than the increase in demand, the equilibrium quantity will decrease. In contrast, if the increase in demand is greater than the decrease in supply, the equilibrium quantity will increase.

Supply Increase; Demand Increase What if supply and demand both increase for some good (for example, cell phones)? A supply increase drops equilibrium price, while a demand increase boosts it. If the increase in supply is greater than the increase in demand, the equilibrium price will fall. If the opposite holds, the equilibrium price will rise.

The effect on equilibrium quantity is certain: The increases in supply and in demand each raise equilibrium quantity. Therefore, the equilibrium quantity will increase by an amount greater than that caused by either change alone.

Supply Decrease; Demand Decrease What about decreases in both supply and demand for some good (for example, fur coats)? If the decrease in supply is greater than the decrease in demand, equilibrium price will rise. If the reverse is true, equilibrium price will fall. Because decreases in supply and in demand each reduce equilibrium quantity, we can be sure that equilibrium quantity will fall.

FIGURE 3.7 **Changes in demand and supply and the effects on price and quantity.** The increase in demand from D_1 to D_2 in (a) increases both equilibrium price and equilibrium quantity. The decrease in demand from D_1 to D_2 in (b) decreases both equilibrium price and equilibrium quantity. The increase in supply from S_1 to S_2 in (c) decreases equilibrium price and increases equilibrium quantity. The decline in supply from S_1 to S_2 in (d) increases equilibrium price and decreases equilibrium quantity. The boxes in the top right corners summarize the respective changes and outcomes. The upward arrows in the boxes signify increases in demand (D), supply (S), equilibrium price (P), and equilibrium quantity (Q); the downward arrows signify decreases in these items.

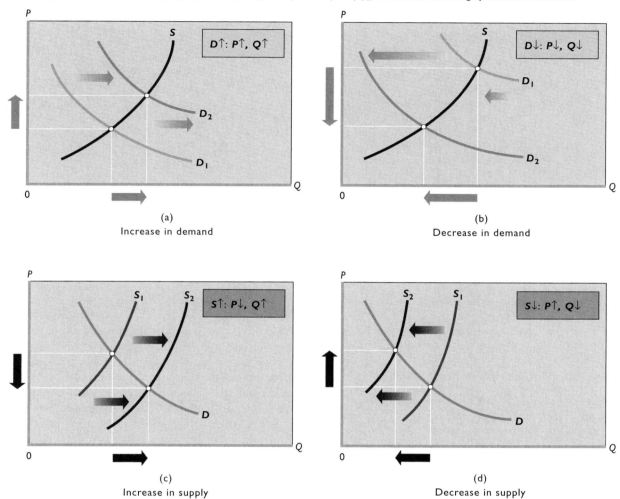

(a) Increase in demand

(b) Decrease in demand

(c) Increase in supply

(d) Decrease in supply

Table 3.7 summarizes these four cases. To understand them fully, you should draw supply and demand diagrams for each case to confirm the effects listed in this table.

TABLE 3.7 **Effects of Changes in Both Supply and Demand**

Change in Supply	Change in Demand	Effect on Equilibrium Price	Effect on Equilibrium Quantity
1. Increase	Decrease	Decrease	Indeterminate
2. Decrease	Increase	Increase	Indeterminate
3. Increase	Increase	Indeterminate	Increase
4. Decrease	Decrease	Indeterminate	Decrease

Special cases arise when a decrease in demand and a decrease in supply, or an increase in demand and an increase in supply, exactly cancel out. In both cases, the net effect on equilibrium price will be zero; price will not change. **(Key Question 9)**

Application: Government-Set Prices

Prices in most markets are free to rise or fall to their equilibrium levels, no matter how high or low those levels might be. However, government sometimes concludes that supply and demand will produce prices that are

CONSIDER THIS ...

Salsa and Coffee Beans

If you forget the other-things-equal assumption, you can encounter situations that *seem* to be in conflict with the laws of demand and supply. For example, suppose salsa manufacturers sell 1 million bottles of salsa at $4 a bottle in 1 year; 2 million bottles at $5 in the next year; and 3 million at $6 in the year thereafter. Price and quantity purchased vary directly, and these data seem to be at odds with the law of demand. But there is no conflict here; the data do not refute the law of demand. The catch is that the law of demand's other-things-equal assumption has been violated over the 3 years in the example. Specifically, because of changing tastes and rising incomes, the demand for salsa has increased sharply, as in Figure 3.7a. The result is higher prices *and* larger quantities purchased.

Another example: The price of coffee beans occasionally shoots upward at the same time that the quantity of coffee beans harvested declines. These events seemingly contradict the direct relationship between price and quantity denoted by supply. The catch again is that the other-things-equal assumption underlying the upsloping supply curve is violated. Poor coffee harvests decrease supply, as in Figure 3.7d, increasing the equilibrium price of coffee and reducing the equilibrium quantity.

The laws of demand and supply are not refuted by observations of price and quantity made over periods of time in which either demand or supply changes.

unfairly high for buyers or unfairly low for sellers. So government may place legal limits on how high or low a price or prices may go. Is that a good idea?

Price Ceilings on Gasoline

A **price ceiling** sets the maximum legal price a seller may charge for a product or service. A price at or below the ceiling is legal; a price above it is not. The rationale for establishing price ceilings (or ceiling prices) on specific products is that they purportedly enable consumers to obtain some "essential" good or service that they could not afford at the equilibrium price. Examples are rent controls and usury laws, which specify maximum "prices" in the forms of rent and interest that can be charged to borrowers.

FIGURE 3.8 A price ceiling. A price ceiling is a maximum legal price such as P_c. When the ceiling price is below the equilibrium price, a persistent product shortage results. Here that shortage is shown by the horizontal distance between Q_d and Q_s.

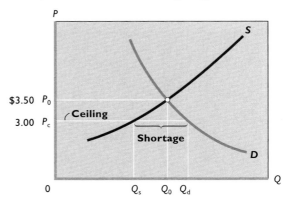

Graphical Analysis
We can easily show the effects of price ceilings graphically. Suppose that rapidly rising world income boosts the purchase of automobiles and shifts the demand for gasoline to the right so that the equilibrium or market price reaches $3.50 per gallon, shown as P_0 in Figure 3.8. The rapidly rising price of gasoline greatly burdens low- and moderate-income households, which pressure government to "do something." To keep gasoline affordable for these households, the government imposes a ceiling price P_c of $3 per gallon. To impact the market, a price ceiling must be below the equilibrium price. A ceiling price of $4, for example, would have had no immediate effect on the gasoline market.

What are the effects of this $3 ceiling price? The rationing ability of the free market is rendered ineffective. Because the ceiling price P_c is below the market-clearing price P_0, there is a lasting shortage of gasoline. The quantity of gasoline demanded at P_c is Q_d and the quantity supplied is only Q_s; a persistent excess demand or shortage of amount $Q_d - Q_s$ occurs.

The price ceiling P_c prevents the usual market adjustment in which competition among buyers bids up price, inducing more production and rationing some buyers out of the market. That process would continue until the shortage disappeared at the equilibrium price and quantity, P_0 and Q_0.

By preventing these market adjustments from occurring, the price ceiling poses problems born of the market disequilibrium.

Rationing Problem
How will the available supply Q_s be apportioned among buyers who want the greater amount Q_d? Should gasoline be distributed on a first-come, first-served basis, that is, to those willing and able to get in

line the soonest and stay in line? Or should gas stations distribute it on the basis of favoritism? Since an unregulated shortage does not lead to an equitable distribution of gasoline, the government must establish some formal system for rationing it to consumers. One option is to issue ration coupons, which authorize bearers to purchase a fixed amount of gasoline per month. The rationing system would entail first the printing of coupons for Q_s gallons of gasoline and then the equitable distribution of the coupons among consumers so that the wealthy family of four and the poor family of four both receive the same number of coupons.

Black Markets But ration coupons would not prevent a second problem from arising. The demand curve in Figure 3.8 reveals that many buyers are willing to pay more than the ceiling price P_c. And, of course, it is more profitable for gasoline stations to sell at prices above the ceiling. Thus, despite a sizable enforcement bureaucracy that would have to accompany the price controls, *black markets* in which gasoline is illegally bought and sold at prices above the legal limits will flourish. Counterfeiting of ration coupons will also be a problem. And since the price of gasoline is now "set by government," government might face political pressure to set the price even lower.

Rent Controls

About 200 cities in the United States, including New York City, Boston, and San Francisco, have at one time or another enacted rent controls: maximum rents established by law (or, more recently, have set maximum rent increases for existing tenants). Such laws are well intended. Their goals are to protect low-income families from escalating rents caused by perceived housing shortages and to make housing more affordable to the poor.

What have been the actual economic effects? On the demand side, it is true that as long as rents are below equilibrium, more families are willing to consume rental housing; the quantity of rental housing demanded increases at the lower price. But a large problem occurs on the supply side. Price controls make it less attractive for landlords to offer housing on the rental market. In the short run, owners may sell their rental units or convert them to condominiums. In the long run, low rents make it unprofitable for owners to repair or renovate their rental units. (Rent controls are one cause of the many abandoned apartment buildings found in larger cities.) Also, insurance companies, pension funds, and other potential new investors in housing will find it more profitable to invest in office buildings, shopping malls, or motels, where rents are not controlled.

In brief, rent controls distort market signals and thus resources are misallocated: Too few resources are allocated to rental housing, and too many to alternative uses. Ironically, although rent controls are often legislated to lessen the effects of perceived housing shortages, controls in fact are a primary cause of such shortages. For that reason, most American cities either have abandoned or are in the process of dismantling rent controls.

Price Floors on Wheat

A **price floor** is a minimum price fixed by the government. A price at or above the price floor is legal; a price below it is not. Price floors above equilibrium prices are usually invoked when society feels that the free functioning of the market system has not provided a sufficient income for certain groups of resource suppliers or producers. Supported prices for agricultural products and current minimum wages are two examples of price (or wage) floors. Let's look at the former.

Suppose the equilibrium price for wheat is $2 per bushel and, because of that low price, many farmers have extremely low incomes. The government decides to help out by establishing a legal price floor or price support of $3 per bushel.

What will be the effects? At any price above the equilibrium price, quantity supplied will exceed quantity demanded—that is, there will be a persistent excess supply or surplus of the product. Farmers will be willing to produce and offer for sale more than private buyers are willing to purchase at the price floor. As we saw with a price ceiling, an imposed legal price disrupts the rationing ability of the free market.

Graphical Analysis Figure 3.9 illustrates the effect of a price floor graphically. Suppose that S and D are the supply and demand curves for wheat. Equilibrium price and quantity are P_0 and Q_0, respectively. If the government imposes a price floor of P_f, farmers will produce Q_s but private buyers will purchase only Q_d. The surplus is the excess of Q_s over Q_d.

The government may cope with the surplus resulting from a price floor in two ways:

- It can restrict supply (for example, by instituting acreage allotments by which farmers agree to take a certain amount of land out of production) or increase demand (for example, by researching new uses for the product involved). These actions may reduce the difference between the equilibrium price and the price floor and that way reduce the size of the resulting surplus.
- If these efforts are not wholly successful, then the government must purchase the surplus output at the $3 price (thereby subsidizing farmers) and store or otherwise dispose of it.

A Legal Market for Human Organs?

A Legal Market Might Eliminate the Present Shortage of Human Organs for Transplant. But There Are Many Serious Objections to "Turning Human Body Parts into Commodities" for Purchase and Sale.

It has become increasingly commonplace in medicine to transplant kidneys, lungs, livers, eye corneas, pancreases, and hearts from deceased individuals to those whose organs have failed or are failing. But surgeons and many of their patients face a growing problem: There are shortages of donated organs available for transplant. Not everyone who needs a transplant can get one. In 2005 there were 89,000 Americans on the waiting list for transplants. Indeed, an inadequate supply of donated organs causes an estimated 4000 deaths in the United States each year.

Why Shortages? Seldom do we hear of shortages of desired goods in market economies. What is different about organs for transplant? One difference is that no legal market exists for human organs. To understand this situation, observe the demand curve

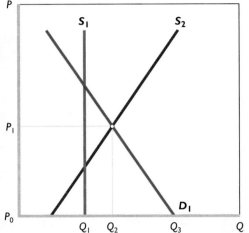

D_1 and supply curve S_1 in the accompanying figure. The downward slope of the demand curve tells us that if there were a market for human organs, the quantity of organs demanded would be greater at lower prices than at higher prices. Vertical supply curve S_1 represents the fixed quantity of human organs now donated via consent before death. Because the price of these donated organs is in effect zero, quantity demanded Q_3 exceeds quantity supplied Q_1. The shortage of $Q_3 - Q_1$ is rationed through a waiting list of those in medical need of transplants. Many people die while still on the waiting list.

Use of a Market A market for human organs would increase the incentive to donate organs. Such a market might work like this: An individual might specify in a legal document that he or she is willing to sell one or more usable human organs upon death or near-death. The person could specify where the money from the sale would go, for example, to family, a church, an educational institution, or a charity. Firms would then emerge to purchase organs and resell them where needed for profit. Under such

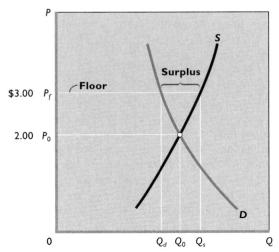

FIGURE 3.9 A price floor. A price floor is a minimum legal price such as P_f. When the price floor is above the equilibrium price, a persistent product surplus results. Here that shortage is shown by the horizontal distance between Q_s and Q_d.

Additional Consequences Price floors such as P_f in Figure 3.9 not only disrupt the rationing ability of prices but distort resource allocation. Without the price floor, the $2 equilibrium price of wheat would cause financial losses and force high-cost wheat producers to plant other crops or abandon farming altogether. But the $3 price floor allows them to continue to grow wheat and remain farmers. So society devotes too many of its scarce resources to wheat production and too few to producing other, more valuable, goods and services. It fails to achieve allocative efficiency.

That's not all. Consumers of wheat-based products pay higher prices because of the price floor. Taxpayers pay higher taxes to finance the government's purchase of the surplus. Also, the price floor causes potential environmental damage by encouraging wheat farmers to bring hilly, erosion-prone "marginal land" into production. The higher price also prompts imports of wheat. But, since such imports would increase the quantity of wheat supa system, the supply curve of usable organs would take on the normal upward slope of typical supply curves. The higher the expected price of an organ, the greater the number of people who would be willing to have their organs sold at death. Suppose that the supply curve is S_2 in the figure. At the equilibrium price P_1, the number of organs made available for transplant (Q_2) would equal the number purchased for transplant (also Q_2). In this generalized case, the shortage of organs would be eliminated and, of particular importance, the number of organs available for transplanting would rise from Q_1 to Q_2. This means more lives would be saved and enhanced than under the present donor system.

Objections In view of this positive outcome, why is there no such market for human organs? Critics of market-based solutions have two main objections. The first is a moral objection: Critics feel that turning human organs into commodities commercializes human beings and diminishes the special nature of human life. They say there is something unseemly about selling and buying body organs as if they were bushels of wheat or ounces of gold. (There

is, however, a market for blood!) Moreover, critics note that the market would ration the available organs (as represented by Q_2 in the figure) to people who either can afford them (at P_1) or have health insurance for transplants. The poor and uninsured would be left out.

Second, a health-cost objection suggests that a market for body organs would greatly increase the cost of health care. Rather than obtaining freely donated (although "too few") body organs, patients or their insurance companies would have to pay market prices for them, further increasing the cost of medical care.

Rebuttal Supporters of market-based solutions to organ shortages point out that the laws against selling organs are simply driving the market underground. Worldwide, an estimated $1 billion-per-year illegal market in human organs has emerged. As in other illegal markets, the unscrupulous tend to thrive. This fact is dramatized by the accompanying photo, in which four Pakistani villagers show off their scars after they each sold a kidney to pay off debt. Supporters say that legalization of the market for human organs would increase organ supply from legal sources, drive down the price of organs, and reduce the abuses such as those now taking place in illegal markets.

G 3.2

Price floors and ceilings

plied and thus undermine the price floor, the government needs to erect tariffs (taxes on imports) to keep the foreign wheat out. Such tariffs usually prompt other countries to retaliate with their own tariffs against U.S. agricultural or manufacturing exports.

So it is easy to see why economists "sound the alarm" when politicians advocate imposing price ceilings or price floors such as price controls, rent controls, interest-rate lids, or agricultural price supports. In all these cases, good intentions lead to bad economic outcomes. Government-controlled prices cause shortages or surpluses, distort resource allocation, and produce negative side effects. **(Key Question 14)**

QUICK REVIEW 3.3

- In competitive markets, prices adjust to the equilibrium level at which quantity demanded equals quantity supplied.
- The equilibrium price and quantity are those indicated by the intersection of the supply and demand curves for any product or resource.
- An increase in demand increases equilibrium price and quantity; a decrease in demand decreases equilibrium price and quantity.
- An increase in supply reduces equilibrium price but increases equilibrium quantity; a decrease in supply increases equilibrium price but reduces equilibrium quantity.
- Over time, equilibrium price and quantity may change in directions that seem at odds with the laws of demand and supply because the other-things-equal assumption is violated.
- Government-controlled prices in the form of ceilings and floors stifle the rationing function of prices, distort resource allocations, and cause negative side effects.

Summary

1. Demand is a schedule or curve representing the willingness of buyers in a specific period to purchase a particular product at each of various prices. The law of demand implies that consumers will buy more of a product at a low price than at a high price. So, other things equal, the relationship between price and quantity demanded is negative or inverse and is graphed as a downsloping curve.

2. Market demand curves are found by adding horizontally the demand curves of the many individual consumers in the market.

3. Changes in one or more of the determinants of demand (consumer tastes, the number of buyers in the market, the money incomes of consumers, the prices of related goods, and consumer expectations) shift the market demand curve. A shift to the right is an increase in demand; a shift to the left is a decrease in demand. A change in demand is different from a change in the quantity demanded, the latter being a movement from one point to another point on a fixed demand curve because of a change in the product's price.

4. Supply is a schedule or curve showing the amounts of a product that producers are willing to offer in the market at each possible price during a specific period. The law of supply states that, other things equal, producers will offer more of a product at a high price than at a low price. Thus, the relationship between price and quantity supplied is positive or direct, and supply is graphed as an upsloping curve.

5. The market supply curve is the horizontal summation of the supply curves of the individual producers of the product.

6. Changes in one or more of the determinants of supply (resource prices, production techniques, taxes or subsidies, the prices of other goods, producer expectations, or the number of sellers in the market) shift the supply curve of a product. A shift to the right is an increase in supply; a shift to the left is a decrease in supply. In contrast, a change in the price of the product being considered causes a change in the quantity

supplied, which is shown as a movement from one point to another point on a fixed supply curve.

7. The equilibrium price and quantity are established at the intersection of the supply and demand curves. The interaction of market demand and market supply adjusts the price to the point at which the quantities demanded and supplied are equal. This is the equilibrium price. The corresponding quantity is the equilibrium quantity.

8. The ability of market forces to synchronize selling and buying decisions to eliminate potential surpluses and shortages is known as the rationing function of prices. The equilibrium quantity in competitive markets reflects both productive efficiency (least-cost production) and allocative efficiency (the right amount of the product relative to other products).

9. A change in either demand or supply changes the equilibrium price and quantity. Increases in demand raise both equilibrium price and equilibrium quantity; decreases in demand lower both equilibrium price and equilibrium quantity. Increases in supply lower equilibrium price and raise equilibrium quantity; decreases in supply raise equilibrium price and lower equilibrium quantity.

10. Simultaneous changes in demand and supply affect equilibrium price and quantity in various ways, depending on their direction and relative magnitudes (see Table 3.7).

11. A price ceiling is a maximum price set by government and is designed to help consumers. Effective price ceilings produce persistent product shortages, and if an equitable distribution of the product is sought, government must ration the product to consumers.

12. A price floor is a minimum price set by government and is designed to aid producers. Effective price floors lead to persistent product surpluses; the government must either purchase the product or eliminate the surplus by imposing restrictions on production or increasing private demand.

13. Legally fixed prices stifle the rationing function of prices and distort the allocation of resources.

Terms and Concepts

demand	substitute good	change in quantity supplied
demand schedule	complementary good	equilibrium price
law of demand	change in demand	equilibrium quantity
diminishing marginal utility	change in quantity demanded	surplus
income effect	supply	shortage
substitution effect	supply schedule	productive efficiency
demand curve	law of supply	allocative efficiency
determinants of demand	supply curve	price ceiling
normal goods	determinants of supply	price floor
inferior goods	change in supply	

Study Questions

1. Explain the law of demand. Why does a demand curve slope downward? How is a market demand curve derived from individual demand curves?

2. What are the determinants of demand? What happens to the demand curve when any of these determinants change? Distinguish between a change in demand and a change in the quantity demanded, noting the cause(s) of each.

3. **KEY QUESTION** What effect will each of the following have on the demand for small automobiles such as the Mini Cooper and Smart car?
   a. Small automobiles become more fashionable.
   b. The price of large automobiles rises (with the price of small autos remaining the same).
   c. Income declines and small autos are an inferior good.
   d. Consumers anticipate that the price of small autos will greatly come down in the near future.
   e. The price of gasoline substantially drops.

4. Explain the law of supply. Why does the supply curve slope upward? How is the market supply curve derived from the supply curves of individual producers?

5. What are the determinants of supply? What happens to the supply curve when any of these determinants changes? Distinguish between a change in supply and a change in the quantity supplied, noting the cause(s) of each.

6. **KEY QUESTION** What effect will each of the following have on the supply of *auto* tires?
   a. A technological advance in the methods of producing tires.
   b. A decline in the number of firms in the tire industry.
   c. An increase in the prices of rubber used in the production of tires.
   d. The expectation that the equilibrium price of auto tires will be lower in the future than currently.
   e. A decline in the price of the large tires used for semi trucks and earth-hauling rigs (with no change in the price of auto tires).
   f. The levying of a per-unit tax on each auto tire sold.
   g. The granting of a 50-cent-per-unit subsidy for each auto tire produced.

7. "In the corn market, demand often exceeds supply and supply sometimes exceeds demand." "The price of corn rises and falls in response to changes in supply and demand." In which of these two statements are the terms "supply" and "demand" used correctly? Explain.

8. **KEY QUESTION** Suppose the total demand for wheat and the total supply of wheat per month in the Kansas City grain market are as shown in the accompanying table.
   a. What is the equilibrium price? What is the equilibrium quantity? Fill in the surplus-shortage column and use it to explain why your answers are correct.
   b. Graph the demand for wheat and the supply of wheat. Be sure to label the axes of your graph correctly. Label equilibrium price *P* and equilibrium quantity *Q*.

Thousands of Bushels Demanded	Price per Bushel	Thousands of Bushels Supplied	Surplus (+) or Shortage (−)
85	$3.40	72	_____
80	3.70	73	_____
75	4.00	75	_____
70	4.30	77	_____
65	4.60	79	_____
60	4.90	81	_____

   c. Why will $3.40 not be the equilibrium price in this market? Why not $4.90? "Surpluses drive prices up; shortages drive them down." Do you agree?

9. **KEY QUESTION** How will each of the following changes in demand and/or supply affect equilibrium price and equilibrium quantity in a competitive market; that is, do price and quantity rise, fall, or remain unchanged, or are the answers indeterminate because they depend on the magnitudes of the shifts? Use supply and demand diagrams to verify your answers.
   a. Supply decreases and demand is constant.
   b. Demand decreases and supply is constant.
   c. Supply increases and demand is constant.
   d. Demand increases and supply increases.
   e. Demand increases and supply is constant.
   f. Supply increases and demand decreases.
   g. Demand increases and supply decreases.
   h. Demand decreases and supply decreases.

10. In 2001 an outbreak of foot-and-mouth disease in Europe led to the burning of millions of cattle carcasses. What impact do you think this had on the supply of cattle hides, hide prices, the supply of leather goods, and the price of leather goods?

11. Use two market diagrams to explain how an increase in state subsidies to public colleges might affect tuition and enrollments in both public and private colleges.

12. Critically evaluate: "In comparing the two equilibrium positions in Figure 3.7b, I note that a smaller amount is actually demanded at a lower price. This refutes the law of demand."

13. For each stock in the stock market, the number of shares sold daily equals the number of shares purchased. That is, the quantity of each firm's shares demanded equals the quantity supplied. So, if this equality always occurs, why do the prices of stock shares ever change?

14. **KEY QUESTION** Refer to the table in question 8. Suppose that the government establishes a price ceiling of $3.70 for wheat. What might prompt the government to establish this price ceiling? Explain carefully the main effects. Demonstrate your answer graphically. Next, suppose that the government establishes a price floor of $4.60 for wheat. What

will be the main effects of this price floor? Demonstrate your answer graphically.

15. What do economists mean when they say that "price floors and ceilings stifle the rationing function of prices and distort resource allocation"?

16. **ADVANCED ANALYSIS** Assume that demand for a commodity is represented by the equation $P = 10 - .2Q_d$ and supply by the equation $P = 2 + .2Q_s$, where Q_d and Q_s are quantity demanded and quantity supplied, respectively, and P is price. Using the equilibrium condition $Q_s = Q_d$, solve the equations to determine equilibrium price. Now determine equilibrium quantity. Graph the two equations to substantiate your answers.

17. **LAST WORD** What is the current overall number of American candidates waiting for an organ transplant? (For the answer, visit the United Network for Organ Sharing Web site, **www.unos.org.**) For what transplant organ is the waiting list the longest? (Select "Data" and "At a glance.") Do you favor the establishment of a legal market for transplant organs? Why or why not?

Web-Based Questions

1. **FARM COMMODITY PRICES—SUPPLY AND DEMAND IN ACTION** The U.S. Department of Agriculture, **www.nass. usda.gov/,** publishes charts on the prices of farm products. Go to the USDA home page and select "Find charts and maps" and then "Agricultural Prices." Choose three farm products and determine whether their prices (as measured by "prices received by farmers") have generally increased, decreased, or stayed the same over the past 3 years. In which of the three cases, if any, do you think that supply has increased more rapidly than demand? In which of the three cases, if any, do you think that demand has increased more rapidly than supply? Explain your reasoning.

2. **CHANGES IN DEMAND—BABY DIAPERS AND RETIRE- MENT VILLAGES** Other things equal, an increase in the number of buyers for a product or service will increase demand. Baby diapers and retirement villages are two products designed for different population groups. The U.S. Census Bureau Web site, **www.census.gov/ipc/www/ idbpyr.html,** provides population pyramids (graphs that show the distribution of population by age and sex) for countries for 2000, 2025, and 2050. View the population pyramids for Mexico, Japan, and the United States. Which country do you think will have the greatest percentage increase in demand for baby diapers between 2000 and 2050? For retirement villages? Which country do you think will have the greatest absolute increase in demand for baby diapers? For retirement villages?

4

IN THIS CHAPTER YOU WILL LEARN:

- Important facts about U.S. households and U.S. businesses.

- Why the corporate form of business organization dominates sales and profits.

- The problem that arises when corporate owners (principals) and their managers (agents) have different interests.

- About the economic role of government in the economy.

- The categories of government spending and the sources of government revenues.

The U.S. Economy: Private and Public Sectors

We now move from the general characteristics of the market economy, including the role of supply and demand, to specific information about the world's largest economy. Each year, the value of U.S. output exceeds that of Japan, Germany, the United Kingdom, and France—combined! For descriptive convenience, we will divide the economy into two sectors: the *private sector,* which includes *households* and *businesses,* and the *public sector,* or simply *government.*

Households as Income Receivers

The U.S. economy currently has about 113 million households. These households consist of one or more persons occupying a housing unit and are both the ultimate suppliers of all economic resources *and* the major spenders in the economy. We can categorize the income received by households by how it was earned and by how it was divided among households.

The Functional Distribution of Income

The **functional distribution of income** indicates how the nation's earned income is apportioned among wages, rents, interest, and profits, that is, according to the function performed by the income receiver. Wages are paid to labor; rents and interest are paid to owners of property resources; and profits are paid to the owners of corporations and unincorporated businesses.

Figure 4.1 shows the functional distribution of U.S. income earned in 2005. The largest source of income for households is the wages and salaries paid to workers. Notice that the bulk of total U.S. income (71 percent) goes to labor, not to capital. Proprietors' income—the income of doctors, lawyers, small-business owners, farmers, and owners of other unincorporated enterprises—also has a

"wage" element. Some of this income is payment for one's own labor, and some of it is profit from one's own business.

The other three types of income are self-evident: Some households own corporate stock and receive dividend incomes on their holdings. Many households also own bonds and savings accounts that yield interest income. And some households receive rental income by providing buildings and natural resources (including land) to businesses and other individuals.

The Personal Distribution of Income

The **personal distribution of income** indicates how the nation's money income is divided among individual households. In Figure 4.2 households are divided into five numerically equal groups or quintiles; the heights of the bars show the percentage of total income received by each group. In 2004 the poorest 20 percent of all households received 3.4 percent of total personal income, and the richest 20 percent received 50.1 percent. Clearly there is considerable inequality in the personal distribution of U.S. income. **(Key Question 2)**

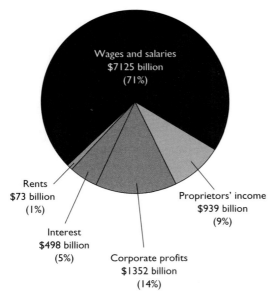

FIGURE 4.1 The functional distribution of U.S. income, 2005. Seventy-one percent of U.S. income is received as wages and salaries. Income to property owners—corporate profit, interest, and rents—accounts for about 20 percent of total income.

Source: Bureau of Economic Analysis.

FIGURE 4.2 The personal distribution of income among U.S. households, 2004. Personal income is unequally distributed in the United States, with the top 20 percent of households receiving about one-half of the total income. In an equal distribution, all five vertical bars would be as high as the horizontal line drawn at 20 percent; then each 20 percent of families would receive 20 percent of the nation's total income.

Numbers do not add to 100 percent due to rounding.

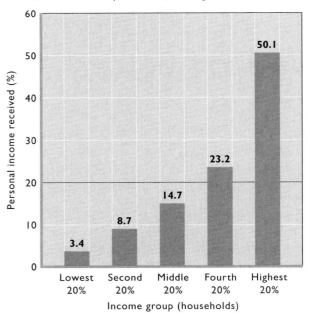

Source: Bureau of the Census.

FIGURE 4.3 **The disposition of household income, 2005.** Households apportion their income among taxes, saving, and consumption, with most going to consumption. (The way income is defined in this figure differs slightly from that used in Figure 4.1, accounting for the quantitative discrepancies between the "total income" amounts in the two figures.)

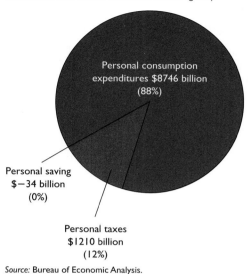

Source: Bureau of Economic Analysis.

Households as Spenders

How do households dispose of their income? Part of it flows to government as taxes, and the rest is divided between personal savings and personal consumption expenditures. In 2005, households disposed of their total personal income as shown in Figure 4.3.

Personal Taxes

U.S. households paid $1210 billion in personal taxes in 2005, or 12 percent of their $9922 billion of income. Personal taxes, of which the personal income tax is the major component, have risen in relative terms since the Second World War. In 1941, households paid just 3 percent of their total income in personal taxes.

Personal Saving

Economists define "saving" as that part of after-tax income that is not spent; hence, households have just two choices about what to do with their income after taxes—use it to consume, or save it. Saving is the portion of income that is not paid in taxes or used to purchase consumer goods but instead flows into bank accounts, insurance policies, bonds and stocks, mutual funds, and other financial assets.

U.S. households typically save about 3 percent of their income each year. Reasons for saving center on *security* and *speculation*. Households save to provide a nest egg for coping with unforeseen contingencies (sickness, accident,

and unemployment), for retirement from the workforce, to finance the education of children, or simply for financial security. They may also channel part of their income to purchase stocks, speculating that their investments will increase in value.

The desire to save is not enough in itself, however. You must be able to save, and that depends on the size of your income. If your income is low, you may not be able to save any money at all. If your income is very, very low you may *dissave*—that is, spend more than your after-tax income. You do this by borrowing or by digging into savings you may have accumulated in years when your income was higher.

Both saving and consumption vary directly with income; as households garner more income, they usually save more and consume more. In fact, the top 10 percent of income receivers account for most of the personal saving in the U.S. economy.

As Figure 4.3 implies, 2005 was a highly unusual year for personal saving. It was a negative $34 billion. The sum of personal consumption and personal taxes exceeded household income in 2005. This atypical situation resulted from heavy borrowing by Americans to buy houses, to "tap" equity in their homes, and to finance purchases of imported goods.

Personal Consumption Expenditures

As Figure 4.3 shows, more than 88 percent of the total income of households flows back into the business sector as personal consumption expenditures—money spent on consumer goods.

Figure 4.4 shows how consumers divide their expenditures among durable goods, nondurable goods, and services.

FIGURE 4.4 **The composition of consumer expenditures, 2005.** Consumers divide their spending among durable goods (goods that have expected lives of 3 years or more), nondurable goods, and services. About 59 percent of consumer spending is for services.

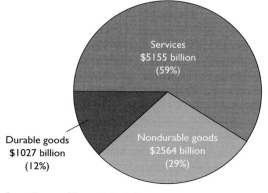

Source: Bureau of Economic Analysis.

Twelve percent of consumer expenditures are on **durable goods**—products that have expected lives of 3 years or more. Such goods include automobiles, furniture, and personal computers. Another 29 percent of consumer expenditures are on **nondurable goods**—products that have lives of less than 3 years. Included are such goods as food, clothing, and gasoline. About 59 percent of consumer expenditures are on **services**—the work done for consumers by lawyers, barbers, doctors, lodging personnel, and so on. This high percentage is the reason that the United States is often referred to as a *service-oriented economy*.

QUICK REVIEW 4.1

- The functional distribution of income indicates how income is apportioned among wages, rents, interest, and profits; the personal distribution of income indicates how income is divided among families.
- Wages and salaries are the major component of the functional distribution of income. The personal distribution of income reveals considerable inequality.
- Nearly 90 percent of household income is consumed; the rest is saved or paid in taxes.
- Consumer spending is directed to durable goods, nondurable goods, and services, with nearly 60 percent going to services.

The Business Population

Businesses constitute the second major part of the private sector. It will be useful to distinguish among a plant, a firm, and an industry:

- A **plant** is a physical establishment—a factory, farm, mine, store, or warehouse—that performs one or more functions in fabricating and distributing goods and services.
- A **firm** is a business organization that owns and operates plants. Some firms operate only one plant, but many own and operate several.
- An **industry** is a group of firms that produce the same, or similar, products.

The organizational structures of firms are often complex and varied. *Multiplant firms* may be organized horizontally, with several plants performing much the same function. Examples are the multiple bottling plants of Coca-Cola and the many individual Wal-Mart stores. Firms also may be *vertically integrated*, meaning they own plants that perform different functions in the various stages of the production process. For example, oil companies such as Shell own oil fields, refineries, and retail gasoline stations. Some firms are *conglomerates*, so named because they have plants that produce products in several industries. For example,

Pfizer makes not only prescription medicines (Lipitor, Viagra) but also chewing gum (Trident, Dentyne), razors (Schick), cough drops (Halls), breath mints (Clorets, Certs), and antacids (Rolaids).

Legal Forms of Businesses

The business population is extremely diverse, ranging from giant corporations such as ExxonMobil, with 2005 sales of $328 billion and thousands of employees, to neighborhood specialty shops with one or two employees and sales of only $200 to $300 per day. There are three major legal forms of businesses:

- A **sole proprietorship** is a business owned and operated by one person. Usually, the proprietor (the owner) personally supervises its operation.
- The **partnership** form of business organization is a natural outgrowth of the sole proprietorship. In a partnership, two or more individuals (the partners) agree to own and operate a business together. Usually they pool their financial resources and business skills. Consequently, they share the risks and the profits or losses.
- A **corporation** is a legal creation that can acquire resources, own assets, produce and sell products, incur debts, extend credit, sue and be sued, and perform the functions of any other type of enterprise. A corporation is distinct and separate from the individual stockholders who own it. Hired managers run most corporations.

Figure 4.5a shows how the business population is distributed among the three major forms. About 72 percent of U.S. firms are sole proprietorships. These firms are so numerous mainly because they are easy to set up and organize. The proprietor is one's own boss and has substantial freedom of action. Partnerships constitute 8 percent of all U.S. business enterprises. The other 20 percent are corporations.

But as Figure 4.5b shows, sole proprietorships account for only 5 percent of total sales (output value) and partnerships only 11 percent. The remainder—an amazing 84 percent—accrues to corporations.

Advantages of Corporations

Certain advantages of the corporate form of business enterprise have catapulted it into a dominant sales and profit position in the United States. The corporation is by far the most effective form of business organization for raising money to finance the expansion of its facilities and capabilities. The corporation employs unique methods of finance—the selling of stocks (equity financing) and bonds

FIGURE 4.5 **The business population and shares of domestic output.** (a) Sole proprietorships dominate the business population numerically, but (b) corporations account for about 84 percent of total sales (output).

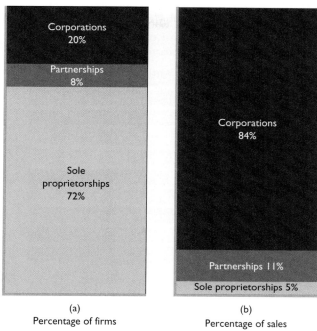

| (a) | (b) |
| Percentage of firms | Percentage of sales |

Source: U.S. Census Bureau, **www.census.gov.** Latest data.

(debt financing)—that enable it to pool the financial resources of large numbers of people.

A common **stock** represents a share in the ownership of a corporation. The purchaser of a stock certificate has the right to vote for corporate officers and to share in dividends. If you buy 1000 of the 100,000 shares issued by OutTell, Inc., then you own 1 percent of the company, are entitled to 1 percent of any dividends declared by the board of directors, and control 1 percent of the votes in the annual election of corporate officials.

In contrast, a corporate **bond** does not bestow any corporate ownership on the purchaser. A bond purchaser is simply lending money to a corporation. A bond is an IOU, in acknowledgment of a loan, whereby the corporation promises to pay the holder a fixed amount set forth on the bond at some specified future date and other fixed amounts (interest payments) every year up to the bond's maturity date. For example, you might purchase a 10-year OutTell bond with a face value of $1000 and a 5 percent rate of interest. This means that in exchange for your $1000, OT promises you a $50 interest payment for each of the next 10 years and then repays your $1000 principal at the end of that period.

Financing through sales of stocks and bonds also provides other advantages to those who purchase these *corporate securities.* An individual investor can spread risks by buying the securities of several corporations. And it is usually easy for holders of corporate securities to sell their holdings. Organized stock exchanges and bond markets simplify the transfer of securities from sellers to buyers. This "ease of sale" increases the willingness of savers to make financial investments in corporate securities. Besides, corporations have easier access to bank credit than do other types of business organizations. Corporations are better risks and are more likely to become profitable clients of banks.

Corporations provide **limited liability** to owners (stockholders), who risk only what they paid for their stock. Their personal assets are not at stake if the corporation defaults on its debts. Creditors can sue the corporation as a legal entity but cannot sue the owners of the corporation as individuals.

Because of their ability to attract financial capital, successful corporations can easily expand the scope of their operations and realize the benefits of expansion. For example, they can take advantage of mass-production technologies and division of labor. A corporation can hire specialists in production, accounting, and marketing functions and thus improve efficiency.

Unlike sole proprietorships and partnerships, the corporation has a life independent of its owners and its officers. As a legal entity, corporations are immortal. The transfer of corporate ownership through inheritance or the sale of stock does not disrupt the continuity of the corporation. Corporations have permanence that lends itself to long-range planning and growth. This permanence and growth explains why virtually all the nation's largest business enterprises are corporations.

The Principal-Agent Problem

Many of the world's corporations are extremely large. In 2005, 273 of the world's largest corporations had annual sales of more than $20 billion, and 593 firms had sales of more than $10 billion. U.S.-based ExxonMobil alone sold $328 billion of goods in 2005. Global Perspective 4.1 lists the world's 10 largest corporations, by annual sales.

But large size creates a potential problem. In sole proprietorships and partnerships, the owners of the real and financial assets of the firm enjoy direct control of those assets. But ownership of large corporations is spread over tens or hundreds of thousands of stockholders. The owners of a corporation usually do not manage it—they hire others to do so.

O 4.1

Principal-agent problem

CONSIDER THIS ...

Unprincipled Agents

In the 1990s many corporations addressed the principal-agent problem by providing a substantial part of executive pay either as shares of the firm's stock or as stock options. Stock options are contracts that allow executives or other key employees to buy shares of their employers' stock at fixed, lower prices when the stock prices rise. The intent was to align the interest of the executives and other key employees more closely with those of the broader corporate owners. By pursuing high profits and share prices, the executives would enhance their own wealth as well as that of all the stockholders.

This "solution" to the principal-agent problem had an unexpected negative side effect. It prompted a few unscrupulous executives to inflate their firms' share prices by hiding costs, overstating revenues, engaging in deceptive transactions, and, in general, exaggerating profits. These executives then sold large quantities of their inflated stock, making quick personal fortunes. In some cases, "independent" outside auditing firms turned out to be not so independent, because they held valuable consulting contracts with the firms being audited.

When the stock-market bubble of the late 1990s burst, many instances of business manipulations and fraudulent accounting were exposed. Several executives of large U.S. firms were indicted and a few large firms collapsed, among them Enron (energy trading), WorldCom (communications), and Arthur Andersen (accounting and business consulting). General stockholders of those firms were left holding severely depressed or even worthless stock.

In 2002 Congress strengthened the laws and penalties against executive misconduct. Also, corporations have improved their accounting and auditing procedures. But seemingly endless revelations of executive wrongdoings make clear that the principal-agent problem is not an easy problem to solve.

That practice can create a **principal-agent problem.** The *principals* are the stockholders who own the corporation and who hire executives as their *agents* to run the business on their behalf. But the interests of these managers (the agents) and the wishes of the owners (the principals) do not always coincide. The owners typically want maximum company profit and stock price. However, the

GLOBAL PERSPECTIVE 4.1

The World's 10 Largest Corporations

Five of the world's ten largest corporations, based on dollar revenue in 2005, were headquartered in the United States.

ExxonMobil (U.S.)	$328 billion
Wal-Mart (U.S.)	$312 billion
Shell (U.K./Netherlands)	$307 billion
BP (U.K.)	$249 billion
General Motors (U.S.)	$193 billion
Chevron (U.S.)	$185 billion
Ford Motor (U.S.)	$178 billion
DaimlerChrysler (Germany)	$177 billion
Toyota (Japan)	$173 billion
ConocoPhillips (U.S.)	$162 billion

Source: Fortune, **www.forbes.com.**

agent may want the power, prestige, and pay that often accompany control over a large enterprise, independent of its profitability and stock price.

So a conflict of interest may develop. For example, executives may build expensive office buildings, enjoy excessive perks such as corporate jets, and pay too much to acquire other corporations. Consequently, the firm's costs will be excessive, and the firm will fail to maximize profit and the stock price for the owners. **(Key Question 4)**

QUICK REVIEW 4.2

- A plant is a physical establishment that contributes to the production of goods and services; a firm is a business organization that owns and operates plants; plants may be arranged horizontally, be vertically integrated, and/or take on a conglomerate form.
- The three basic legal forms of business are the sole proprietorship, the partnership, and the corporation. While sole proprietorships make up 72 percent of all firms, corporations account for 84 percent of total sales.
- The major advantages of corporations are their ability to raise financial capital, the limited liability they bestow on owners, and their continuing life beyond the life of their owners and managers.
- The principal-agent problem is the conflict of interest that may occur when agents (executives) pursue their own objectives to the detriment of the principals' (stockholders') goals.

The Public Sector: Government's Role

The economic activities of the *public sector*—Federal, state, and local government—are extensive. We begin by discussing the economic functions of governments. What is government's role in the economy?

Providing the Legal Structure

Government provides the legal framework and the services needed for a market economy to operate effectively. The legal framework sets the legal status of business enterprises, ensures the rights of private ownership, and allows the making and enforcement of contracts. Government also establishes the legal "rules of the game" that control relationships among businesses, resource suppliers, and consumers. Discrete units of government referee economic relationships, seek out foul play, and impose penalties.

Government intervention is presumed to improve the allocation of resources. By supplying a medium of exchange, ensuring product quality, defining ownership rights, and enforcing contracts, the government increases the volume and safety of exchange. This widens the market and fosters greater specialization in the use of property and human resources. Such specialization promotes a more efficient allocation of resources.

Like the optimal amount of any "good," the optimal amount of regulation is that at which the marginal benefit and marginal cost are equal. Thus, there can be either too little regulation (MB exceeds MC) or too much regulation (MB is less than MC). The task is deciding on the right amount.

Maintaining Competition

Competition is the basic regulatory mechanism in the market system. It is the force that subjects producers and resource suppliers to the dictates of consumer sovereignty. With competition, buyers are the boss, the market is their agent, and businesses are their servants.

It is a different story where a single seller—a **monopoly**—controls an industry. By controlling supply, a monopolist can charge a higher-than-competitive price. Producer sovereignty then supplants consumer sovereignty. In the United States, government has attempted to control monopoly through *regulation* and through *antitrust.*

A few industries are natural monopolies—industries in which technology is such that only a single seller can achieve the lowest possible costs. In some cases government has allowed these monopolies to exist but has also created public commissions to regulate their prices and set their service standards. Examples of *regulated monopolies* are some firms that provide local electricity, telephone, and transportation services.

In nearly all markets, however, efficient production can best be attained with a high degree of competition. The Federal government has therefore enacted a series of antitrust (antimonopoly) laws, beginning with the Sherman Act of 1890, to prohibit certain monopoly abuses and, if necessary, break monopolists up into competing firms. Under these laws, for example, in 2000 Microsoft was found guilty of monopolizing the market for operating systems for personal computers. Rather than breaking up Microsoft, however, the government imposed a series of prohibitions and requirements that collectively limited Microsoft's ability to engage in anticompetitive actions.

Redistributing Income

The market system is impersonal and may distribute income more inequitably than society desires. It yields very large incomes to those whose labor, by virtue of inherent ability and acquired education and skills, command high wages. Similarly, those who, through hard work or inheritance, possess valuable capital and land, receive large property incomes.

But many other members of society have less productive ability, have received only modest amounts of education and training, and have accumulated or inherited no property resources. Moreover, some of the aged, the physically and mentally disabled, and the poorly educated earn small incomes or, like the unemployed, no income at all. Thus society chooses to redistribute a part of total income through a variety of government policies and programs. They are:

- *Transfer payments* *Transfer payments*, for example, in the form of welfare checks and food stamps, provide relief to the destitute, the dependent, the disabled, and older citizens; unemployment compensation payments provide aid to the unemployed.
- *Market intervention* Government also alters the distribution of income through *market intervention*, that is, by acting to modify the prices that are or would be established by market forces. Providing farmers with above-market prices for their output and requiring that firms pay minimum wages are illustrations of government interventions designed to raise the income of specific groups.
- *Taxation* Since the 1930s, government has used the personal income tax to take a larger proportion of the income of the rich than of the poor, thus narrowing the after-tax income difference between high-income and low-income earners.

The *extent* to which government should redistribute income is subject to lively debate. Redistribution involves both benefits and costs. The alleged benefits are greater "fairness," or "economic justice"; the alleged costs are reduced incentives to work, save, invest, and produce, and therefore a loss of total output and income.

Reallocating Resources

Market failure occurs when the competitive market system (1) produces the "wrong" amounts of certain goods and services or (2) fails to allocate any resources whatsoever to the production of certain goods and services whose output is economically justified. The first type of failure results from what economists call *externalities* or *spillovers*, and the second type involves *public goods*. Both kinds of market failure can be corrected by government action.

Externalities

When we say that competitive markets automatically bring about the efficient use of resources, we assume that all the benefits and costs for each product are fully reflected in the market demand and supply curves. That is not always the case. In some markets certain benefits or costs may escape the buyer or seller.

O 4.2
Externalities

An **externality** occurs when some of the costs or the benefits of a good are passed on to or "spill over to" someone other than the immediate buyer or seller. Such spillovers are called externalities, because they are benefits or costs that accrue to some third party that is *external* to the market transaction.

Negative Externalities

Production or consumption costs inflicted on a third party without compensation are called **negative externalities.** Environmental pollution is an example. When a chemical manufacturer or a meat-packing plant dumps its wastes into a lake or river, swimmers, fishers, and boaters—and perhaps those who drink the water—suffer external costs. When a petroleum refinery pollutes the air with smoke or a paper mill creates obnoxious odors, the community experiences external costs for which it is not compensated.

What are the economic effects? Recall that costs determine the position of the firm's supply curve. When a firm avoids some costs by polluting, its supply curve lies farther to the right than it does when the firm bears the full costs of production. As a result, the price of the product is too low and the output of the product is too large to achieve allocative efficiency. A market failure occurs in the form of an overallocation of resources to the production of the good.

Correcting for Negative Externalities

Government can do two things to correct the overallocation of resources. Both solutions are designed to internalize external costs, that is, to make the offending firm pay the costs rather than shift them to others:

- *Legislation* In cases of air and water pollution, the most direct action is legislation prohibiting or limiting the pollution. Such legislation forces potential polluters to pay for the proper disposal of industrial wastes—here, by installing smoke-abatement equipment or water-purification facilities. The idea is to force potential offenders, under the threat of legal action, to bear *all* the costs associated with production.

- *Specific taxes* A less direct action is based on the fact that taxes are a cost and therefore a determinant of a firm's supply curve. Government might levy a *specific tax*—that is, a tax confined to a particular product—on each unit of the polluting firm's output. The amount of this tax would roughly equal the estimated amount of the negative externality arising from the production of each unit of output. Through this tax, government would pass back to the offending firm a cost equivalent to the spillover cost the firm is avoiding. This would shift the firm's supply curve to the left, reducing equilibrium output and eliminating the overallocation of resources.

Positive Externalities

Sometimes externalities appear as benefits to other producers or consumers. These uncompensated spillovers accruing to third parties or the community at large are called **positive externalities.** Immunization against measles and polio results in direct benefits to the immediate consumer of those vaccines. But it also results in widespread substantial external benefits to the entire community.

Education is another example of positive externalities. Education benefits individual consumers: Better-educated people generally achieve higher incomes than less well educated people. But education also provides benefits to society, in the form of a more versatile and more productive labor force, on the one hand, and smaller outlays for crime prevention, law enforcement, and welfare programs, on the other.

External benefits mean that the market demand curve, which reflects only private benefits, understates total benefits. The demand curve for the product lies farther to the left than it would if the market took all benefits into account. As a result, a smaller amount of the product will be produced, or, alternatively, there will be an *underallocation* of resources to the product—again a market failure.

Correcting for Positive Externalities How might the underallocation of resources associated with spillover benefits be corrected? The answer is either to subsidize consumers (to increase demand), to subsidize producers (to increase supply), or, in the extreme, to have government produce the product:

- *Subsidize consumers* To correct the underallocation of resources to higher education, the U.S. government provides low-interest loans to students so that they can afford more education. Those loans increase the demand for higher education.

- *Subsidize suppliers* In some cases government finds it more convenient and administratively simpler to correct an underallocation by subsidizing suppliers. For example, in higher education, state governments provide substantial portions of the budgets of public colleges and universities. Such subsidies lower the costs of producing higher education and increase its supply. Publicly subsidized immunization programs, hospitals, and medical research are other examples.

- ***Provide goods via government*** A third policy option may be appropriate where positive externalities are extremely large: Government may finance or, in the extreme, own and operate the industry that is involved. Examples are the U.S. Postal Service and Federal aircraft control systems.

Public Goods and Services

Certain goods called *private goods* are produced through the competitive market system. Examples are the wide variety of items sold in stores. Private goods have two characteristics—*rivalry* and *excludability*. "Rivalry" means that when one person buys and consumes a product, it is not available for purchase and consumption by another person. What Joan gets, Jane cannot have. *Excludability* means that buyers who are willing and able to pay the market price for the product obtain its benefits, but those unable or unwilling to pay that price do not. This characteristic enables profitable production by a private firm.

Certain other goods and services called **public goods** have the opposite characteristics—*nonrivalry* and *nonexcludability*. Everyone can simultaneously obtain the benefit from a public good such as a global positioning system, national defense, street lighting, and environmental protection. One person's benefit does not reduce the benefit available to others. More important, there is no effective way of excluding individuals from the benefit of the good once it comes into existence. The inability to exclude creates a **free-rider problem,** in which people can receive benefits from a public good without contributing to its costs. The free-rider problem makes the good unprofitable to provide by a private firm.

An example of a public good is the war on terrorism (which includes homeland defense and recent military actions abroad). This public good is thought to be economically justified by the majority of Americans because the benefits are perceived as exceeding the costs. Once the war efforts are undertaken, however, the benefits accrue to all Americans (nonrivalry). And there is no practical way to exclude any American from receiving those benefits (nonexcluability).

No private firm will undertake the war on terrorism because the benefits cannot be profitably sold (due to the free-rider problem). So here we have a service that yields substantial benefits but to which the market system will not allocate sufficient resources. Like national defense in general, the pursuit of the war on terrorism is a public good. Society signals its desire for such goods by voting for particular political candidates who support their provision. Because of the free-rider problem, the public sector provides these goods and finances them through compulsory charges in the form of taxes.

Quasi-Public Goods

Government provides many goods that fit the economist's definition of a public good. However, it also provides other goods and services that could be produced and delivered in such a way that exclusion would be possible. Such goods, called **quasi-public goods,** include education, streets and highways, police and fire protection, libraries and museums, preventive medicine, and sewage disposal. They could all be priced and provided by private firms through the market system. But, as we noted earlier, because they all have substantial positive externalities, they would be underproduced by the market system. Therefore, government often provides them to avoid the underallocation of resources that would otherwise occur.

The Reallocation Process

How are resources reallocated from the production of private goods to the production of public and quasi-public goods? If the resources of the economy are fully employed, government must free up resources from the production of private goods and make them available for producing public and quasi-public goods. It does so by reducing private demand for them. And it does that by levying taxes on households and businesses, taking some of their income out of the circular flow. With lower incomes and hence less purchasing power, households and businesses must curtail their consumption and investment spending. As a result, the private

CONSIDER THIS ...

Street Entertainers

Street entertainers are often found in tourist areas of major cities. Some entertainers are highly creative and talented; others "need more practice." But, regardless of talent level, these entertainers illuminate the concepts of free riders and public goods.

Most street entertainers have a hard time earning a living from their activities (unless event organizers pay them) because they have no way of excluding nonpayers from the benefits of their entertainment. They essentially are providing public, not private, goods and must rely on voluntary payments.

The result is a significant free-rider problem. Only a few in the audience put money in the container or instrument case, and many who do so contribute only token amounts. The rest are free riders who obtain the benefits of the street entertainment and retain their money for purchases that *they* initiate.

Street entertainers are acutely aware of the free-rider problem, and some have found creative ways to lessen it. For example, some entertainers involve the audience directly in the act. This usually creates a greater sense of audience willingness (or obligation) to contribute money at the end of the performance.

"Pay for performance" is another creative approach to lessening the free-rider problem. A good example is the street entertainer painted up to look like a statue. When people drop coins into the container, the "statue" makes a slight movement. The greater the contributions, the greater the movement. But these human "statues" still face a free-rider problem: Nonpayers also get to enjoy the acts.

Finally, because talented street entertainers create a festive street environment, cities or retailers sometimes hire them to perform. The "free entertainment" attracts crowds of shoppers, who buy goods from nearby retailers. In these instances the cities or retailers use tax revenue or commercial funds to pay the entertainers, in the former case validating them as public goods.

demand for goods and services declines, as does the private demand for resources. So by diverting purchasing power from private spenders to government, taxes remove resources from private use.

Government then spends the tax proceeds to provide public and quasi-public goods and services. Taxation releases resources from the production of private consumer goods (food, clothing, television sets) and private investment goods (printing presses, boxcars, warehouses). Government shifts those resources to the production of public and quasi-public goods (post offices, submarines, parks), changing the composition of the economy's total output. **(Key Questions 9 and 10)**

Promoting Stability

An economy's level of output depends on its level of total spending relative to its production capacity. When the level of total spending matches the economy's production capacity, human and property resources are fully employed and prices in general are stable. But sometimes total spending is either inadequate or excessive and the result is either unemployment or inflation. Government promotes stability by addressing these two problems:

- **Unemployment** When private sector spending is too low, government may try to augment it so that total spending—private plus public—is sufficient to achieve full employment. It does this by increasing government spending or by lowering taxes to stimulate private spending. Also, the nation's central bank (Federal Reserve in the United States) often takes actions to lower interest rates, thereby stimulating private borrowing and spending.

- **Inflation** Inflation is a general increase in the level of prices. Prices of goods and services rise when spenders try to buy more than the economy's capacity to produce. When total spending is excessive and becomes inflationary, government may try to reduce total spending by cutting its own expenditures or by raising taxes to curtail private spending. The nation's central bank may also take actions to increase interest rates to reduce private borrowing and spending.

Government's Role: A Qualification

Government does not have an easy task in performing the aforementioned economic functions. In a democracy, government undertakes its economic role in the context of politics. To serve the public, politicians need to get elected. To stay elected, officials (presidents, senators, representatives, mayors, council members, school board members) need to satisfy their particular constituencies. At best the political realities complicate government's role in the economy; at worst, they produce undesirable economic outcomes.

In the political context, overregulation can occur in some cases; underregulation, in others. Income can be redistributed to such an extent that incentives to work, save, and invest suffer. Some public goods and quasi-public goods can be produced not because their benefits exceed their costs but because their benefits accrue to firms located in states served by powerful elected officials. Inefficiency can easily creep into government activities because of the lack of a profit incentive to hold down costs. Policies to correct negative externalities can be politically blocked by the very parties that are producing the spillovers. In short, the economic role of government, although critical to a well-functioning economy, is not always perfectly carried out.

QUICK REVIEW 4.3

- Government enhances the operation of the market system by providing an appropriate legal foundation and promoting competition.
- Transfer payments, direct market intervention, and taxation are among the ways in which government can lessen income inequality.
- Government can correct for the overallocation of resources associated with negative externalities through legislation or taxes; it can offset the underallocation of resources associated with positive externalities by granting government subsidies.
- Government provides certain public goods for which there is nonrivalry in consumption and nonexcludability of benefits; government also provides many quasi-public goods because of their large external benefits.
- To try to stabilize the economy, the government can adjust its spending and tax revenues and the nation's central bank can take monetary actions that lower or increase interest rates.

The Circular Flow Revisited

In Figure 4.6 we integrate government into the circular flow model first shown in Figure 2.2. Here flows (1) through (4) are the same as the corresponding flows in that figure. Flows (1) and (2) show business expenditures for the resources provided by households. These expenditures are costs to businesses but represent wage, rent, interest, and profit income to households. Flows (3) and (4) show household expenditures for the goods and services produced by businesses.

Now consider what happens when we add government. Flows (5) through (8) illustrate that government makes purchases in both product and resource markets. Flows (5) and (6) represent government purchases of such products as paper, computers, and military hardware from private businesses. Flows (7) and (8) represent government purchases of resources. The Federal government employs and pays salaries to members of Congress, the armed

forces, Justice Department lawyers, meat inspectors, and so on. State and local governments hire and pay teachers, bus drivers, police, and firefighters. The Federal government might also lease or purchase land to expand a military base, and a city might buy land on which to build a new elementary school.

Government then provides public goods and services to both households and businesses, as shown by flows (9) and (10). To finance those public goods and services, businesses and households are required to pay taxes, as shown by flows (11) and (12). These flows are labeled as *net* taxes to indicate that they also include "taxes in reverse" in the form of transfer payments to households and subsidies to businesses. Thus, flow (11) entails various subsidies to farmers, shipbuilders, and airlines as well as income, sales, and excise taxes paid by businesses to government. Most subsidies to business are "concealed" in the form of low-interest loans, loan guarantees, tax concessions, or public facilities provided at prices below their cost. Similarly, flow (12) includes both taxes (personal income taxes, payroll taxes) collected by government directly from households and transfer payments such as welfare payments and Social Security benefits paid by government.

Government Finance

How large is the U.S. public sector? What are the main expenditure categories of Federal, state, and local governments? How are these expenditures financed?

Government Purchases and Transfers

We can get an idea of the size of government's economic role by examining government purchases of goods and services and government transfer payments. There is a significant difference between these two kinds of outlays:

- **Government purchases** are *exhaustive;* the products purchased directly absorb (require the use of) resources and are part of the domestic output. For example, the purchase of a missile absorbs the labor of physicists and engineers along with steel, explosives, and a host of other inputs.
- **Transfer payments** are *nonexhaustive;* they do not directly absorb resources or create output. Social Security benefits, welfare payments, veterans' benefits, and unemployment compensation are examples of transfer payments. Their key characteristic is that recipients make no current contribution to domestic output in return for them.

FIGURE 4.6 **The circular flow and the public sector.** Government buys products from the product market and employs resources from the resource market to provide public goods and services to households and businesses. Government finances its expenditures through the net taxes (taxes minus transfer payments) it receives from households and businesses.

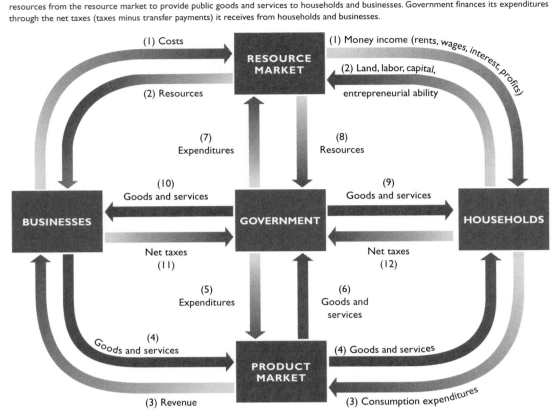

Federal, state, and local governments spent $3876 billion in 2005. Of that total, government purchases were $2360 billion and government transfers were $1516 billion. Figure 4.7 shows these amounts as percentages of U.S. domestic output for 2005 and compares them to percentages for 1960. Government purchases have declined from about 22 to 19 percent of output since 1960. But transfer payments have more than doubled as a percentage of output—from 5 percent in 1960 to 12 percent in 2005. Relative to U.S. output, total government spending is thus higher today than it was 45 years ago. This means that the tax revenues required to finance government expenditures are also higher. Today, government spending and the tax revenues needed to finance it are about 31 percent of U.S. output.

In 2006 the so-called Tax Freedom Day in the United States was April 26. On that day the average worker had earned enough (from the start of the year) to pay his or her share of the taxes required to finance government spending for the year. Tax Freedom Day arrives even

FIGURE 4.7 **Government purchases, transfers, and total spending as percentages of U.S. output, 1960 and 2005.** Government purchases have declined as a percentage of U.S. output since 1960. Transfer payments, however, have increased, so total government spending (purchases plus transfers) is now 31 percent of U.S. output.

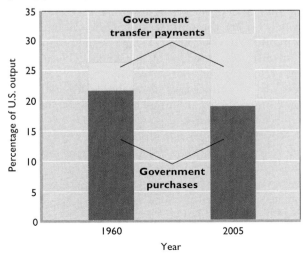

GLOBAL PERSPECTIVE 4.2

Total Tax Revenue as a Percentage of Total Output, Selected Nations

The percentage of tax revenues to total output is one measure of a country's tax burden. Among the world's industrialized nations, South Korea, Japan, the United States, and Australia have the lowest tax burdens.

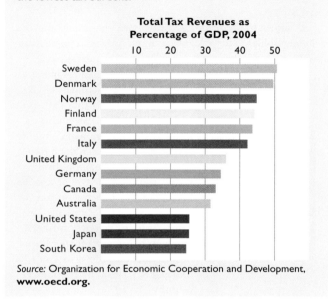

Total Tax Revenues as Percentage of GDP, 2004

Source: Organization for Economic Cooperation and Development, **www.oecd.org.**

Federal Finance

Now let's look separately at each of the Federal, state, and local units of government in the United States and compare their expenditures and taxes. Figure 4.8 tells the story for the Federal government.

Federal Expenditures

Four areas of Federal spending stand out: (1) pensions and income security, (2) national defense, (3) health, and (4) interest on the public debt. The *pensions and income security* category includes the many income-maintenance programs for the aged, persons with disabilities or handicaps, the unemployed, the retired, and families with no breadwinner. This category—dominated by the $432 billion annual Social Security program—accounts for 35 percent of total Federal expenditures. (This chapter's Last Word examines the impact of the aging U.S. population on the future financing of this area of Federal spending.) *National defense* accounts for about 20 percent of the Federal budget, underscoring the high cost of military preparedness. *Health* reflects the cost of government health programs for the retired (Medicare) and poor (Medicaid). *Interest on the public debt* is high because the public debt itself is large.

Federal Tax Revenues

The revenue side of Figure 4.8 shows that the personal income tax, payroll taxes, and the corporate income tax are the basic revenue sources, accounting respectively for 43, 37, and 13 cents of each dollar collected.

later in several other countries, as implied in Global Perspective 4.2.

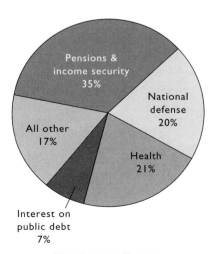

Total expenditures: $2472 billion

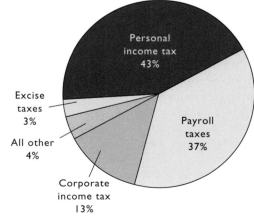

Total tax revenues: $2154 billion

Source: U.S. Office of Management and Budget.

FIGURE 4.8 Federal expenditures and tax revenues, 2005. Federal expenditures are dominated by spending for pensions and income security, health, and national defense. A full 84 percent of Federal tax revenue is derived from just two sources: the personal income tax and payroll taxes. The $318 billion difference between expenditures and revenues reflects a budget deficit.

There Is a Severe Long-Run Shortfall in Social Security Funding because of Growing Payments to Retiring Baby Boomers.

The Social Security program (excluding Medicare) has grown from less than one-half of 1 percent of U.S. GDP in 1950 to 4.2 percent of GDP today. That percentage is projected to grow to 6.2 percent of GDP in 2030 and slightly higher thereafter.

The $432 billion Social Security program is largely an annual "pay-as-you-go" plan, meaning that most of the current revenues from the 12.4 percent Social Security tax (the rate when the 2.9 percent Medicare tax is excluded) are paid out to current Social Security retirees. In anticipation of the large benefits owed to the baby boomers when they retire, however, the Social Security Administration has been placing an excess of current revenues over current payouts into a trust fund consisting of U.S. Treasury securities. But the accumulation of money in the Social Security trust fund will be greatly inadequate for paying the retirement benefits promised to all future retirees.

In 2017 Social Security retirement revenues will fall below Social Security retirement benefits and the system will begin

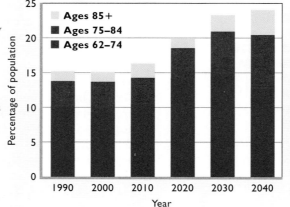

dipping into the trust fund to make up the difference. The trust fund will be exhausted in 2040, after which the promised retirement benefits will immediately exceed the Social Security tax revenues by an estimated 35 percent annually, rising to 43 percent annually in 2080. The Federal government faces a several-trillion-dollar shortfall of long-run revenues for funding Social Security.

As shown in the accompanying figure, the problem is one of demographics. The percentage of the American population age 62 or older will rise substantially over the next several decades, with the greatest increases for those age 75 and older. High fertility rates during the "baby boom" (1946–1964), declining birthrates thereafter, and rising life expectancies have combined to produce an aging population. In the future, more people will be receiving Social Security benefits for longer periods and each person's benefits will be paid for by fewer workers. The number of workers per Social Security beneficiary was 5:1 in 1960. Today it is 3:1, and by 2040 it will be only 2:1.

There is no easy way to restore long-run balance to Social Security funding. Either benefits must be reduced or revenues must be increased. The Social Security Administration concludes that bringing projected Social Security revenues and

Personal Income Tax

The **personal income tax** is the kingpin of the Federal tax system and merits special comment. This tax is levied on *taxable income*, that is, on the incomes of households and unincorporated businesses after certain exemptions ($3300 for each household member) and deductions (business expenses, charitable contributions, home mortgage interest payments, certain state and local taxes) are taken into account.

The Federal personal income tax is a *progressive tax*, meaning that people with higher incomes pay a larger percentage of their incomes as taxes than do people with lower incomes. The progressivity is achieved by applying higher tax rates to successive layers or brackets of income.

Columns 1 and 2 in Table 4.1 show the mechanics of the income tax for a married couple filing a joint return in

TABLE 4.1 Federal Personal Income Tax Rates, 2006*

(1) Total Taxable Income	(2) Marginal Tax Rate, %	(3) Total Tax on Highest Income In Bracket	(4) Average Tax Rate on Highest Income in Bracket, % (3) ÷ (1)
$1–$15,100	10.0	$ 1510	10.0
$15,101–$61,300	15.0	8440	13.8
$61,301–$123,700	25.0	24,040	19.4
$123,701–$188,450	28.0	42,170	22.4
$188,451–$336,550	33.0	91,043	27.1
Over $336,550	35.0		

*For a married couple filing a joint return.

payments into balance over the next 75 years would require a 13 percent permanent reduction in Social Security benefits, a 16 percent permanent increase in tax revenues, or some combination of the two.*

Several ideas have been offered to improve the financial outlook of Social Security. One idea is to boost the trust fund by investing all or part of it in corporate stocks and bonds. The Federal government would own the stock investments, and an appointed panel would oversee the direction of those investments. The presumed higher returns on the investments relative to the lower returns on U.S. securities would stretch out the life of the trust fund. Nevertheless, a substantial increase in the payroll tax would still be needed to cover the shortfalls after the trust fund is exhausted.

Another option is to increase the payroll tax immediately—perhaps by as much as 1.5 percentage points—and allocate the new revenues to individual accounts. Government would own the accumulations in the accounts, but individuals could direct their investments to a restricted list of broad stock or bond funds. When they retire, recipients could convert these individual account balances to annuities—securities paying monthly payments for life. That annuity income would supplement reduced monthly benefits from the pay-as-you-go system when the trust fund is exhausted.

A different route is to place half the payroll tax into accounts that individuals, not the government, would own, maintain, and bequeath. Individuals could invest these funds in bank certificates of deposit or in approved stock and bond funds and draw upon the accounts when they reach retirement age. A flat monthly benefit would supplement the accumulations in the private accounts. The personal security accounts would be phased in over time, so those individuals now receiving or about to receive Social Security benefits would continue to receive benefits.

These general ideas do not exhaust the possible reforms since the variations on each plan are nearly endless. Reaching consensus on Social Security reform will be difficult because every citizen has a direct economic stake in the outcome. Nevertheless, society will eventually need to confront the problem of trillions of dollars of unfunded Social Security liabilities.

---

*Social Security Board of Trustees. "Status of the Social Security and Medicare Programs: A Summary of the 2006 Annual Reports." **www.ssa.gov.**

†Medicare (the health insurance that accompanies Social Security) is also severely underfunded. To bring projected Medicare revenues and expenditures into long-run balance would require an immediate increase in the Medicare payroll tax by 121 percent, a 51 percent reduction of Medicare payments from their projected levels, or some combination of each. The total unfunded liabilities of Social Security and Medicare were $10 trillion in 2005.

2006. Note that a 10 percent tax rate applies to all taxable income up to $15,100 and a 15 percent rate applies to additional income up to $61,300. The rates on additional layers of income then go up to 25, 28, 33, and 35 percent.

The tax rates shown in column 2 in Table 4.1 are marginal tax rates. A **marginal tax rate** is the rate at which the tax is paid on each *additional* unit of taxable income. Thus, if a couple's taxable income is $80,000, they will pay the marginal rate of 10 percent on each dollar from $1 to $15,100, 15 percent on each dollar from $15,101 to $61,300, and 25 percent on each dollar from $61,301 to $80,000. You should confirm that their total income tax is $13,115.

The marginal tax rates in column 2 overstate the personal income tax bite because the rising rates in that col-

W 4.1

Taxes and progressivity

umn apply only to the income within each successive tax bracket. To get a better idea of the tax burden, we must consider average tax rates. The **average tax rate** is the total tax paid divided by total taxable income. The couple in our previous example is in the 25 percent tax bracket because they pay a top marginal tax rate of 25 percent on the highest dollar of their income. But their *average* tax rate is 16.4 percent (= $13,115/$80,000).

A tax whose average rate rises as income increases is a progressive tax. Such a tax claims both a larger absolute amount and a larger proportion of income as income rises. Thus we can say that the Federal personal income tax is progressive. **(Key Question 15)**

Payroll Taxes Social Security contributions are **payroll taxes**—taxes based on wages and salaries—used to finance two compulsory Federal programs for retired workers: Social Security (an income-enhancement program) and Medicare (which pays for medical services). Employers and employees pay these taxes equally. Improvements in, and extensions of, the Social Security programs, plus growth of the labor force, have resulted in significant increases in these payroll taxes in recent years. In 2006, employees and employers each paid 7.65 percent on the first $94,200 of an employee's annual earnings and 1.45 percent on all additional earnings.

Corporate Income Tax The Federal government also taxes corporate income. The **corporate income tax** is levied on a corporation's profit—the difference between its total revenue and its total expenses. For almost all corporations, the tax rate is 35 percent.

Excise Taxes Taxes on commodities or on purchases take the form of **sales and excise taxes.** The difference between the two is mainly one of coverage. Sales taxes fall on a wide range of products, whereas excises are levied individually on a small, select list of commodities. As Figure 4.8 suggests, the Federal government collects excise taxes (on the sale of such commodities as alcoholic beverages, tobacco, and gasoline) but does not levy a general sales tax; sales taxes are the primary revenue source of most state governments.

State and Local Finance

State and local governments have different mixes of revenues and expenditures than the Federal government has.

State Finances

The primary source of tax revenue for state governments is sales and excise taxes, which account for about 48 percent of all their tax revenue. State personal income taxes, which have much lower rates than the Federal income tax, are the second most important source of state tax revenue. They bring in about 34 percent of total state tax revenue. Corporate income taxes and license fees account for most of the remainder of state tax revenue.

Education expenditures account for about 35 percent of all state spending. State expenditures on public welfare are next in relative weight, at about 28 percent of the total. States also spend heavily on health and hospitals (7 percent), highway maintenance and construction (7 percent), and public safety (4 percent). That leaves about 19 percent of all state spending for a variety of other purposes.

These tax and expenditure percentages combine data from all the states, so they reveal little about the finances of individual states. States vary significantly in the taxes levied. Thus, although personal income taxes are a major source of revenue for all state governments combined, seven states do not levy a personal income tax. Also, there are great variations in the sizes of tax revenues and disbursements among the states, both in the aggregate and as percentages of personal income.

Thirty-nine states augment their tax revenues with state-run lotteries to help close the gap between their tax receipts and expenditures. Individual states also receive large intergovernmental grants from the Federal government. In fact, about 28 percent of their total revenue is in that form. States also take in revenue from miscellaneous sources such as state-owned utilities and liquor stores.

Local Finances

The local levels of government include counties, municipalities, townships, and school districts as well as cities and towns. Local governments obtain about 73 percent of their tax revenue from **property taxes.** Sales and excise taxes contribute about 17 percent of all local government tax revenue.

About 44 percent of local government expenditures go to education. Welfare, health, and hospitals (12 percent); public safety (11 percent); housing, parks, and sewerage (8 percent); and streets and highways (5 percent) are also major spending categories.

The tax revenues of local government cover less than one-half of their expenditures. The remaining revenue comes from intergovernmental grants from the Federal and state governments. Also, local governments receive considerable amounts of proprietary income, for example, revenue from government-owned utilities providing water, electricity, natural gas, and transportation.

QUICK REVIEW 4.4

- Government purchases account for about 19 percent of U.S. output; the addition of transfers increases government spending to about 31 percent of domestic output.
- Income security and national defense are the main categories of Federal spending; personal income, payroll, and corporate income taxes are the primary sources of Federal revenue.
- States rely on sales and excise taxes for revenue; their spending is largely for education and public welfare.
- Education is the main expenditure for local governments, most of whose revenue comes from property taxes.

Summary

1. The functional distribution of income shows how society's total income is divided among wages, rents, interest, and profit; the personal distribution of income shows how total income is divided among individual households.

2. Households use all their income to pay personal taxes, for saving, and to buy consumer goods. Nearly 60 percent of their consumption expenditures are for services.

3. Sole proprietorships are firms owned and usually operated by single individuals. Partnerships are firms owned and usually operated by just a handful of individuals. Corporations—the dominant form of business organization—are legal entities, distinct and separate from the individuals who own them. They often have thousands, or even millions, of owners—the stockholders.

4. Corporations finance their operations and purchases of new plant and equipment partly through the issuance of stocks and bonds. Stocks are ownership shares of a corporation, and bonds are promises to repay a loan, usually at a set rate of interest.

5. A principal-agent problem may occur in corporations when the agents (managers) hired to represent the interest of the principals (stockholders) pursue their own objectives to the detriment of the objectives of the principals.

6. Government improves the operation of the market system by (a) providing an appropriate legal and social framework and (b) acting to maintain competition.

7. Government alters the distribution of income through the tax-transfer system and through market intervention.

8. Externalities, or spillovers, cause the equilibrium output of certain goods to vary from the socially efficient output. Negative externalities result in an overallocation of resources, which can be corrected by legislation or by specific taxes. Positive externalities are accompanied by an underallocation of resources, which can be corrected by government subsidies to consumers or producers.

9. Only government is willing to provide public goods, which can be consumed by all simultaneously (nonrivalry) and entail benefits from which nonpaying consumers (free riders) cannot be excluded (nonexcludability). Because doing so is not profitable, private firms will not produce public goods. Quasi-public goods have some of the characteristics of public goods and some of the characteristics of private goods; government provides them because the private sector would underallocate resources to their production.

10. To try to stabilize the economy, the government adjusts its spending and taxes, and the nation's central bank (the Federal Reserve in the United States) uses monetary actions to alter interest rates.

11. Government purchases exhaust (use up or absorb) resources; transfer payments do not. Government purchases have declined from about 22 percent of domestic output in 1960 to 19 percent today. Transfer payments, however, have grown significantly. Total government spending now amounts to about 31 percent of domestic output.

12. The main categories of Federal spending are pensions and income security, national defense, health, and interest on the public debt; Federal revenues come primarily from personal income taxes, payroll taxes, and corporate income taxes.

13. States derive their revenue primarily from sales and excise taxes and personal income taxes; major state expenditures go to education, public welfare, health and hospitals, and highways. Local communities derive most of their revenue from property taxes; education is their most important expenditure.

14. State and local tax revenues are supplemented by sizable revenue grants from the Federal government.

Terms and Concepts

functional distribution of income

personal distribution of income

durable goods

nondurable goods

services

plant

firm

industry

sole proprietorship

partnership

corporation

stock

bond

limited liability

principal-agent problem

monopoly

externality

negative externalities

positive externalities

public goods

free-rider problem

quasi-public goods

government purchases

transfer payments

personal income tax

marginal tax rate

average tax rate

payroll taxes

corporate income tax

sales and excise taxes

property taxes

Study Questions

1. Distinguish between the functional distribution and personal distribution of income. Which is being referred to in each of the following statements? "The combined share of wage income and proprietary income has remained remarkably stable at about 80 percent since the Second World War." "The relative income of the richest households is higher today than in 1970."

2. **KEY QUESTION** Assume that the five residents of Econoville receive incomes of $50, $75, $125, $250, and $500. Present the resulting distribution of income as a graph similar to Figure 4.2. Compare the incomes of the lowest fifth and the highest fifth of the income receivers.

3. Distinguish between a plant, a firm, and an industry. Contrast a vertically integrated firm, a horizontally integrated firm, and a conglomerate. Cite an example of a horizontally integrated firm from which you have recently made a purchase.

4. **KEY QUESTION** What are the three major legal forms of business organization? Which form is the most prevalent in terms of numbers? Why do you think that is so? Which form is dominant in terms of total sales? What major advantages of this form of business organization gave rise to its dominance?

5. What is the principal-agent problem as it relates to managers and stockholders? How did firms try to solve it in the 1990s? In what way did the "solution" backfire on some firms?

6. Identify and briefly describe the main economic functions of government. What function do you think is the most controversial? Explain why.

7. What divergences arise between equilibrium output and efficient output when (a) negative externalities and (b) positive externalities are present? How might government correct these divergences? Cite an example (other than the text examples) of an external cost and an external benefit.

8. Explain why zoning laws, which allow certain land uses only in specific locations, might be justified in dealing with a problem of negative externalities. Explain why tax breaks to businesses that set up in areas of high unemployment might be justified in view of positive externalities. Explain why excise taxes on beer might be justified in dealing with a problem of external costs.

9. **KEY QUESTION** What are the two characteristics of public goods? Explain the significance of each for public provision as opposed to private provision. What is the free-rider problem as it relates to public goods? Is U.S. border patrol a public good or a private good? Why? How about satellite TV? Explain.

10. **KEY QUESTION** Draw a production possibilities curve with public goods on the vertical axis and private goods on the horizontal axis. Assuming the economy is initially operating *on the curve*, indicate how the production of public goods might be increased. How might the output of public goods be increased if the economy is initially operating at a point *inside the curve?*

11. Use the distinction between the characteristics of private and public goods to determine whether the following should be produced through the market system or provided by government: (a) French fries, (b) airport screening, (c) court systems, (d) mail delivery, and (e) medical care. State why you answered as you did in each case.

12. Use the circular flow diagram to show how each of the following government actions simultaneously affects the allocation of resources and the distribution of income:
    a. The construction of a new high school.
    b. A 2-percentage-point reduction of the corporate income tax.
    c. An expansion of preschool programs for disadvantaged children.
    d. The levying of an excise tax on polluters.

13. What do economists mean when they say government purchases are "exhaustive" expenditures whereas government transfer payments are "nonexhaustive" expenditures? Cite an example of a government purchase and a government transfer payment.

14. What is the most important source of revenue and the major type of expenditure at the Federal level? At the state level? At the local level?

15. **KEY QUESTION** Suppose in Fiscalville there is no tax on the first $10,000 of income, but a 20 percent tax on earnings between $10,000 and $20,000 and a 30 percent tax on income between $20,000 and $30,000. Any income above $30,000 is taxed at 40 percent. If your income is $50,000, how much will you pay in taxes? Determine your marginal and average tax rates. Is this a progressive tax? Explain.

16. **LAST WORD** What do economists mean when they refer to Social Security as a pay-as-you-go plan? What is the Social Security trust fund? What is the nature of the long-run fiscal imbalance in the Social Security retirement system? What are the broad options for addressing this problem?

Web-Based Questions

1. **PERSONAL DISTRIBUTION OF INCOME—WHAT IS THE TREND?** Visit the U.S. Census Bureau Web site at **www.census.gov/hhes/income/midclass/index.html** and select Data Highlights. Since 1970, how has the share of aggregate household income received by the lowest and highest income quintiles (fifths) changed?

2. **STATE TAXES AND EXPENDITURES PER CAPITA—WHERE DOES YOUR STATE RANK?** Go to the Census Bureau site, **www.census.gov/govs/www/state.html,** and find the table that ranks the states by tax revenue and expenditures per capita for the latest year. Where does your home state rank in each category? Where does the state in which you are attending college, if different, rank? Speculate as to why a large gap separates the high-ranking and low-ranking states.

5

IN THIS CHAPTER YOU WILL LEARN:

- Some key facts about U.S. international trade.
- About comparative advantage, specialization, and international trade.
- How exchange rates are determined in currency markets.
- How and why government sometimes interferes with free international trade.
- The role played by free-trade zones and the World Trade Organization (WTO) in promoting international trade.

The United States in the Global Economy

Backpackers in the wilderness like to think they are "leaving the world behind," but, like Atlas, they carry the world on their shoulders. Much of their equipment is imported—knives from Switzerland, rain gear from South Korea, cameras from Japan, aluminum pots from England, sleeping bags from China, and compasses from Finland. Moreover, they may have driven to the trailheads in Japanese-made Toyotas or German-made BMWs, sipping coffee from Brazil or snacking on bananas from Honduras.

International trade and the global economy affect all of us daily, whether we are hiking in the wilderness, driving our cars, listening to music, or working at our jobs. We cannot "leave the world behind." We are enmeshed in a global web of economic relationships—trading of goods and services, multinational corporations, cooperative ventures among the world's firms, and ties among the world's financial markets. That web is so complex that it is difficult to determine just what is—or isn't—an American product. A Finnish company owns Wilson sporting goods; a Swiss company owns Gerber baby food; and a South African corporation owns Miller Brewing. The Chrysler PT Cruiser is assembled in Mexico. Many "U.S." products such as Boeing aircraft contain numerous components from abroad, and, conversely, many "foreign" products such as Airbus planes contain numerous U.S.-produced parts.

International Linkages

Several economic flows link the U.S. economy and the economies of other nations. As identified in Figure 5.1, these flows are:

- *Goods and services flows* or simply *trade flows* The United States exports goods and services to other nations and imports goods and services from them.
- *Capital and labor flows* or simply *resource flows* U.S. firms establish production facilities—new capital—in foreign countries, and foreign firms establish production facilities in the United States. Labor also moves between nations. Each year many foreigners immigrate to the United States and some Americans move to other nations.
- *Information and technology flows* The United States transmits information to other nations about U.S. products, prices, interest rates, and investment opportunities and receives such information from abroad. Firms in other countries use technology created in the United States, and U.S. businesses incorporate technology developed abroad.
- *Financial flows* Money is transferred between the United States and other countries for several purposes, for example, paying for imports, buying foreign assets, paying interest on debt, and providing foreign aid.

The United States and World Trade

Our main goal in this chapter is to examine trade flows and the financial flows that pay for them. What is the extent and pattern of international trade, and how much has that trade grown? Who are the major participants?

Volume and Pattern

Table 5.1 suggests the importance of world trade for selected countries. Many countries, with restricted resources and limited domestic markets, cannot efficiently produce the variety of goods their citizens want. So they must import goods from other nations. That, in turn, means that they must export, or sell abroad, some of their own products. For such countries, exports may run from 25 to 50 percent or more of their gross domestic product (GDP)—the market value of all goods and services produced in an economy. Other countries, the United States, for example, have rich and diversified resource bases and large internal markets. Although the total volume of trade is huge in the United States, it constitutes a smaller percentage of GDP than it does in a number of other nations.

Volume For the United States and for the world as a whole the volume of international trade has been increasing

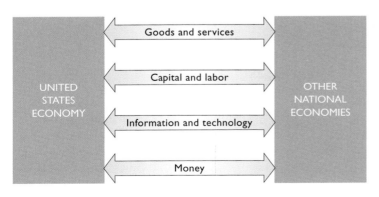

FIGURE 5.1 International linkages. The U.S. economy is intertwined with other national economies through goods and services flows (trade flows), capital and labor flows (resource flows), information and technology flows, and financial flows.

TABLE 5.1 **Exports of Goods and Services as a Percentage of GDP, Selected Countries, 2005**

Country	Exports as Percentage of GDP
Belgium	87
Netherlands	71
South Korea	44
Germany	40
Canada	38
New Zealand	28
Italy	27
France	26
United Kingdom	26
Spain	25
Japan	13
United States	11

Source: Derived by authors from IMF, *International Financial Statistics,* 2006.

both absolutely and relative to their GDPs. A comparison of the boxed data in Figure 5.2 reveals substantial growth in the dollar amount of U.S. exports and imports over the past several decades. The graph shows the rapid growth of U.S. exports and imports of goods and services as percentages of GDP. On a national income account basis, U.S.

exports and imports were 11 and 16 percent of GDP, respectively, in 2005.

Even so, the United States now accounts for a diminished percentage of total world trade. In 1950, it supplied about one-third of the world's total exports, compared with about one-eighth today. World trade has increased more rapidly for other nations than it has for the United States. But in terms of absolute volumes of imports and exports, the United States is still the world's leading trading nation.

Dependence The United States is almost entirely dependent on other countries for bananas, cocoa, coffee, spices, tea, raw silk, nickel, tin, natural rubber, and diamonds. Imported goods compete with U.S. goods in many of our domestic markets: Japanese cameras and cars, French and Italian wines, and Swiss and Austrian snow skis are a few examples. Even the "great American pastime" of baseball relies heavily on imported gloves and baseballs.

Of course, world trade is a two-way street. Many U.S. industries rely on foreign markets. Almost all segments of U.S. agriculture rely on sales abroad; for example, exports of rice, wheat, cotton, and tobacco vary from one-fourth to more than one-half of the total output of those crops. The U.S. computer, chemical, semiconductor, aircraft,

FIGURE 5.2 **U.S. trade as percentage of GDP.** U.S. imports and exports have increased in volume and have greatly increased as a percentage of GDP since 1975.

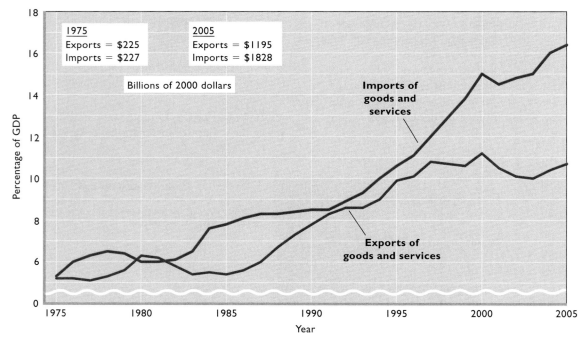

Source: Bureau of Economic Analysis. Data are compiled by the authors from the national income accounts and are adjusted for inflation (2000 dollars).

TABLE 5.2 Principal U.S. Exports and Imports of Goods, 2005 (in Billions of Dollars)

Exports	Amount	Imports	Amount
Chemicals	$68.6	Petroleum	$251.6
Consumer durables	53.5	Automobiles	123.7
Agricultural products	52.9	Household appliances	97.1
Semiconductors	47.2	Computers	93.3
Computers	45.5	Metals	83.8
Generating equipment	33.2	Clothing	79.1
Automobiles	30.4	Consumer electronics	47.3
Aircraft	29.1	Generating equipment	43.1
Medical	27.6	Semiconductors	37.1
Telecommunications	25.6	Telecommunications	25.8

Source: Consolidated by authors from Department of Commerce data.

automobile, machine tool, and coal industries, among many others, sell significant portions of their output in international markets. Table 5.2 shows some of the major commodity exports and imports of the United States.

Trade Patterns The following facts will give you an overview of U.S. international trade:

- A *trade deficit* occurs when imports exceed exports. The United States has a trade deficit in goods. In 2005, U.S. imports of goods exceeded U.S. exports of goods by $782 billion.
- A *trade surplus* occurs when exports exceed imports. The United States has a trade surplus in services (such as transportation services and financial services). In 2005, U.S. exports of services exceeded U.S. imports of services by $58 billion.

- The United States imports some of the same categories of goods that it exports, specifically, automobiles, computers, semiconductors, and telecommunications equipment (see Table 5.2).
- As Table 5.3 shows, about half of U.S. export and import trade is with other industrially advanced countries. The remainder is with developing countries, including members of the Organization of Petroleum Exporting Countries (OPEC).
- Canada is the United States' most important trading partner quantitatively. In 2005, 24 percent of U.S. exported goods were sold to Canadians, who in turn provided 17 percent of the U.S. imports of goods (see Table 5.3).
- The United States has sizable trade deficits with China and Japan. In 2005, U.S. imported goods from

TABLE 5.3 U.S. Exports and Imports of Goods by Area, 2005*

Exports to	Value, Billions of Dollars	Percentage of Total	Imports from	Value Billions of Dollars	Percentage of Total
Industrial countries	$483	54	Industrial countries	$ 770	46
Canada	$212	24	Canada	$291	17
Japan	53	6	Japan	138	8
European Union	183	20	Western Europe	308	18
Australia	15	2	Australia	7	1
Other	20	2	Other	26	2
Developing countries	410	46	Developing countries	904	54
Mexico	120	13	Mexico	171	10
China	42	5	China	244	15
OPEC countries	31	4	OPEC countries	125	7
Other	217	24	Other	364	22
Total	$893	100	Total	$1674	100

*Data are on an international transactions (balance of payments) basis and exclude military shipments.
Source: Survey of Current Business, April 2006.

China exceeded exported goods to China by $202 billion, and U.S. imported goods from Japan exceeded U.S. exported goods to Japan by $85 billion (see Table 5.3).

- The U.S. dependence on foreign oil is reflected in its trade with members of OPEC. In 2005, the United States imported $125 billion of goods (mainly oil) from OPEC members, while exporting $31 billion of goods to those countries (see Table 5.3).
- In terms of volume, the most significant U.S. export of *services* is airline transportation provided by U.S. carriers for foreign passengers.

Financial Linkages International trade requires complex financial linkages among nations. How does a nation such as the United States obtain more goods from others than it provides to them? How does the United States finance its trade deficits, such as its 2005 goods and services deficit of $724 billion (= + $58 billion in services − $782 billion in goods) in 2005? The answer is by either borrowing from foreigners or selling real assets (for example, factories, real estate) to them. The United States is the world's largest borrower of foreign funds. Moreover, nations with which the United States has large trade deficits, such as Japan, often "recycle their excess dollars" by buying U.S. real assets.

Rapid Trade Growth

Several factors have propelled the rapid growth of international trade since the Second World War.

Transportation Technology

High transportation costs are a barrier to any type of trade, particularly among traders who are distant from one another. But improvements in transportation have shrunk the globe and have fostered world trade. Airplanes now transport low-weight, high-value items such as diamonds and semiconductors swiftly from one nation to another. We now routinely transport oil in massive tankers, significantly lowering the cost of transportation per barrel. Grain is loaded onto oceangoing ships at modern, efficient grain silos at Great Lakes and coastal ports. Natural gas flows through large-diameter pipelines from exporting to importing countries—for instance, from Russia to Germany and from Canada to the United States.

Communications Technology

Dramatic improvements in communications technology have also advanced world trade. Computers, the Internet, telephones, and fax (facsimile) machines now directly link traders around the world, enabling exporters to access overseas markets and to carry out trade deals. A distributor in

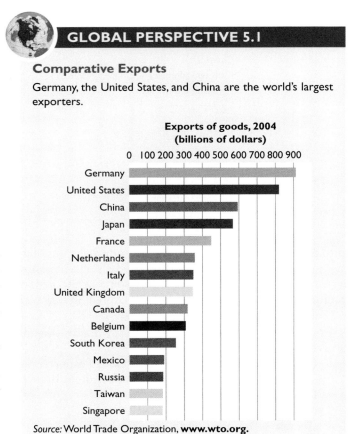

GLOBAL PERSPECTIVE 5.1

Comparative Exports

Germany, the United States, and China are the world's largest exporters.

Exports of goods, 2004 (billions of dollars)

0 100 200 300 400 500 600 700 800 900

Germany
United States
China
Japan
France
Netherlands
Italy
United Kingdom
Canada
Belgium
South Korea
Mexico
Russia
Taiwan
Singapore

Source: World Trade Organization, **www.wto.org.**

New York can get a price quote on 1000 woven baskets in Thailand as quickly as a quotation on 1000 laptop computers in Texas. Money moves around the world in the blink of an eye. Exchange rates, stock prices, and interest rates flash onto computer screens nearly simultaneously in Los Angeles, London, and Lisbon.

General Decline in Tariffs *Tariffs* are excise taxes (duties) on imported products. They have had their ups and downs over the years, but since 1940 they have generally fallen. A glance ahead to Figure 5.5, page 96, shows that U.S. tariffs as a percentage of imports (on which duties are levied) are now about 5 percent, down from 37 percent in 1940. Many nations still maintain barriers to free trade, but, on average, tariffs have fallen significantly, thus increasing international trade.

Participants in International Trade

All the nations of the world participate to some extent in international trade.

United States, Japan, and Western Europe As Global Perspective 5.1 indicates, the top participants in world trade by total volume are Germany, the United States, China, and Japan. In 2004 those four nations had combined exports of $2.9 trillion. Along with Germany, other western European nations such as France, Britain, and Italy are major exporters and importers. The United States, Japan, and the western European nations also form the heart of the world's financial system and provide headquarters for most of the world's large **multinational corporations**—firms that have sizable production and distribution activities in other countries. Examples of such firms are Unilever (Netherlands), Nestlé (Switzerland), Coca-Cola (United States), Bayer Chemicals (Germany), and Mitsubishi (Japan).

New Participants Important new participants have arrived on the world trade scene. China, with its increased reliance on the market system and its reintegration of Hong Kong, is a major trader. Since China initiated reforms in 1978, its annual growth of output has averaged 9 percent (compared with about 3 percent in the United States). At this remarkable rate, China's total output nearly doubles every 8 years! An upsurge of exports and imports has accompanied that economic growth. In 1990 Chinese exports were about $60 billion. In 2005 they were nearly $762 billion, with about one-fifth of China's exports going to the United States. Also, China has been attracting substantial foreign investment ($60 billion in 2005 and more than $1 trillion since 1990). In fact, China has become the number-one destination of foreign investment in the world.

Other Asian economies are also active traders. In particular, Singapore, South Korea, and Taiwan are major exporters and importers. Although these three economies experienced economic difficulties in the 1990s, their combined exports exceed those of France, Britain, or Italy. Other economies of southeast Asia, particularly Malaysia and Indonesia, also have expanded their international trade.

Other changes in world trade patterns have resulted from the collapse of communism in eastern Europe and the former Soviet Union. Before that collapse, the eastern European nations of Poland, Hungary, Czechoslovakia, and East Germany traded mainly with the Soviet Union and such political allies as North Korea and Cuba. Today, East Germany is reunited with West Germany, and Poland, Hungary, and the Czech Republic have established new trade relationships with western Europe and the United States.

Russia itself has initiated far-reaching market reforms, including widespread privatization of industry, and has made major trade deals with firms around the globe. Although its transition to capitalism has been far from smooth, Russia may one day be a major trading nation. Other former Soviet republics—now independent nations—such as Estonia and Azerbaijan also have opened their economies to international trade and finance.

QUICK REVIEW 5.1

- Four main categories of economic flows link nations: goods and services flows, capital and labor flows, information and technology flows, and financial flows.
- World trade has increased globally and nationally. In terms of volume, the United States is the world's leading international trader. But with exports and imports of only about 11 to 16 percent of GDP, the United States is not as dependent on international trade as some other nations.
- Advances in transportation and communications technology and declines in tariffs have all helped expand world trade.
- The United States, China, Japan, and the western European nations dominate world trade. Recent new traders are the Asian economies of Singapore, South Korea, and Taiwan; the eastern European nations; and the former Soviet states.

Specialization and Comparative Advantage

Given the presence of an *open economy*—one that includes the international sector—the United States produces more of certain goods (exports) and fewer of other goods (imports) than it would otherwise. Thus U.S. labor and other resources are shifted toward export industries and away from import industries. For example, the United States uses more resources to make commercial aircraft and to grow wheat and less to make autos and clothing. So we ask: "Do shifts of resources like these make economic sense? Do they enhance U.S. total output and thus the U.S. standard of living?"

The answers are affirmative. Specialization and international trade increase the productivity of a nation's resources and allow for greater total output than would otherwise be possible. This idea is not new. Adam Smith had this to say in 1776:

> It is the maxim of every prudent master of a family, never to attempt to make at home what it will cost him more to make than to buy. The taylor does not attempt to make his own shoes, but buys them of the shoemaker. The shoemaker does not attempt to make his own clothes, but employs a taylor. The farmer attempts to make neither the one nor the other, but employs those different artificers....
>
> What is prudence in the conduct of every private family, can scarce be folly in that of a great kingdom. If a foreign

TABLE 5.4 Mexico's Production Possibilities Table (in Tons)

Product	Production Alternatives				
	A	B	C	D	E
Avocados	0	20	24	40	60
Soybeans	15	10	9	5	0

TABLE 5.5 U.S. Production Possibilities Table (in Tons)

Product	Production Alternatives				
	R	S	T	U	V
Avocados	0	30	33	60	90
Soybeans	30	20	19	10	0

country can supply us with a commodity cheaper than we can make it, better buy it of them with some part of the produce of our own industry, employed in a way in which we have some advantage.[1]

Nations specialize and trade for the same reasons as individuals: Specialization and exchange result in greater overall output and income.

In the early 1800s British economist David Ricardo expanded on Smith's idea by observing that it pays for a person or a country to specialize and trade even if some potential trading partner is more productive in *all* economic activities. We demonstrate Ricardo's basic principle in the Consider This box to the right. You should read it before plunging into the more elaborate analysis of comparative advantage.

Comparative Advantage: Production Possibilities Analysis

The simple example in the Consider This box shows that specialization is economically desirable because it results in more efficient production. Now let's put specialization into the context of trading nations and use the familiar concept of the production possibilities table for our analysis.

Assumptions and Comparative Costs Suppose the production possibilities for one product in Mexico and for one product in the United States are as shown in Tables 5.4 and 5.5. Both tables reflect constant costs. Each country must give up a constant amount of one product to secure a certain increment of the other product. (This assumption simplifies our discussion without impairing the validity of our conclusions. Later we will allow for increasing costs.)

Also for simplicity, suppose that the labor forces in the United States and Mexico are of equal size. If the United States and Mexico use their entire (equal-size) labor forces to produce avocados, the United States can produce 90 tons compared with Mexico's 60 tons. Similarly, the United States can produce 30 tons of soybeans compared to Mexico's 15 tons. So output per worker in the United States exceeds that in Mexico in producing both goods,

[1]Adam Smith, *The Wealth of Nations* (New York: Modern Library, 1937), p. 424. (Originally published in 1776.)

perhaps because of better technology. The United States has an *absolute advantage* (relative to Mexico) in producing either soybeans or avocados.

But gains from specialization and trade between the United States and Mexico are possible even under these

CONSIDER THIS ...

A CPA and House Painter

Suppose that Madison, a certified public accountant (CPA), is a swifter painter than Mason, the professional painter she is thinking of hiring. Also assume that Madison can earn $50 per hour as an accountant but would have to pay Mason $15 per hour. And suppose that Madison would need 30 hours to paint her house but Mason would need 40 hours.

Should Madison take time from her accounting to paint her own house, or should she hire the painter? Madison's opportunity cost of painting her house is $1500 (= 30 hours of sacrificed CPA time × $50 per CPA hour). The cost of hiring Mason is only $600 (= 40 hours of painting × $15 per hour of painting). Although Madison is better at both accounting and painting, she will get her house painted at lower cost by specializing in accounting and using some of her earnings from accounting to hire a house painter.

Similarly, Mason can reduce his cost of obtaining accounting services by specializing in painting and using some of his income to hire Madison to prepare his income tax forms. Suppose Mason would need 10 hours to prepare his tax return, while Madison could handle the task in 2 hours. Mason would sacrifice $150 of income (= 10 hours of painting time × $15 per hour) to do something he could hire Madison to do for $100 (= 2 hours of CPA time × $50 per CPA hour). By using Madison to prepare his tax return, Mason lowers the cost of getting his tax return prepared.

What is true for our CPA and house painter is also true for nations. Specializing enables nations to reduce the cost of obtaining the goods and services they desire.

circumstances. Specialization and trade are mutually "profitable" to the two nations if the comparative costs of producing the two products *within* the two nations differ. What are the comparative costs of avocados and soybeans in Mexico? By comparing production alternatives A and B in Table 5.4, we see that 5 tons of soybeans (= 15 − 10) must be sacrificed to produce 20 tons of avocados (= 20 − 0). Or, more simply, in Mexico it costs 1 ton of soybeans (S) to produce 4 tons of avocados (A); that is, 1S ≡ 4A. (The "≡" sign simply signifies "equivalent to.") Because we assumed constant costs, this domestic opportunity cost will not change as Mexico expands the output of either product. This is evident from production possibilities B and C, where we see that 4 more tons of avocados (= 24 − 20) cost 1 unit of soybeans (= 10 − 9).

Similarly, in Table 5.5, comparing U.S. production alternatives R and S reveals that in the United States it costs 10 tons of soybeans (= 30 − 20) to obtain 30 tons of avocados (= 30 − 0). That is, the domestic comparative-cost ratio for the two products in the United States is 1S ≡ 3A. Comparing production alternatives S and T reinforces this conclusion: an extra 3 tons of avocados (= 33 − 30) comes at the sacrifice of 1 ton of soybeans (= 20 − 19).

The comparative costs of the two products within the two nations are obviously different. Economists say that the United States has a domestic comparative advantage or, simply, a **comparative advantage** over Mexico in soybeans. The United States must forgo only 3 tons of avocados to get 1 ton of soybeans, but Mexico must forgo 4 tons of avocados to get 1 ton of soybeans. In terms of domestic opportunity costs, soybeans are relatively cheaper in the United States. A nation has a comparative advantage in some product when it can produce that product at a lower domestic opportunity cost than can a potential trading partner. Mexico, in contrast, has a comparative advantage in avocados. While 1 ton of avocados costs $\frac{1}{3}$ ton of soybeans in the United States, it costs only $\frac{1}{4}$ ton of soybeans in Mexico. Comparatively speaking, avocados are cheaper in Mexico. We summarize the situation in Table 5.6. Be sure to give it a close look.

Because of these differences in domestic opportunity costs, if both nations specialize, each according to its comparative advantage, each can achieve a larger total output with the same total input of resources. Together they will be using their scarce resources more efficiently.

O 5.1
Absolute and comparative advantage

Terms of Trade

The United States can shift production between soybeans and avocados at the rate of 1S for 3A. Thus, the United States would specialize in soybeans

TABLE 5.6 Comparative-Advantage Example: A Summary

Soybeans	Avocados
Mexico: Must give up 4 tons of avocados to get 1 ton of soybeans	**Mexico:** Must give up $\frac{1}{4}$ ton of soybeans to get 1 ton of avocados
United States: Must give up 3 tons of avocados to get 1 ton of soybeans	**United States:** Must give up $\frac{1}{3}$ ton of soybeans to get 1 ton of avocados
Comparative advantage: United States	**Comparative advantage:** Mexico

only if it could obtain *more than* 3 tons of avocados for 1 ton of soybeans by trading with Mexico. Similarly, Mexico can shift production at the rate of 4A for 1S. So it would be advantageous to Mexico to specialize in avocados if it could get 1 ton of soybeans for *less than* 4 tons of avocados.

Suppose that through negotiation the two nations agree on an exchange rate of 1 ton of soybeans for $3\frac{1}{2}$ tons of avocados. These **terms of trade** are mutually beneficial to both countries, since each can "do better" through such trade than through domestic production alone. The United States can get $3\frac{1}{2}$ tons of avocados by sending 1 ton of soybeans to Mexico, while it can get only 3 tons of avocados by shifting its own resources domestically from soybeans to avocados. Mexico can obtain 1 ton of soybeans at a lower cost of $3\frac{1}{2}$ tons of avocados through trade with the United States, compared to the cost of 4 tons if Mexico produced the ton of soybeans itself.

Gains from Specialization and Trade

Let's pinpoint the gains in total output from specialization and trade. Suppose that, before specialization and trade, production alternative C in Table 5.4 and alternative T in 5.5 were the optimal product mixes for the two countries. That is, Mexico preferred 24 tons of avocados and 9 tons of soybeans (Table 5.4) and the United States preferred 33 tons of avocados and 19 tons of soybeans (Table 5.5) to all other available domestic alternatives. These outputs are shown in column 1 in Table 5.7.

Now assume that both nations specialize according to their comparative advantage, with Mexico producing 60 tons of avocados and no soybeans (alternative E) and the United States producing no avocados and 30 tons of soybeans (alternative R). These outputs are shown in column 2 in Table 5.7. Using our 1S ≡ $3\frac{1}{2}$A terms of trade, assume that Mexico exchanges 35 tons of avocados for 10 tons of U.S. soybeans. Column 3 in Table 5.7 shows the quantities exchanged in this trade, with a minus sign indicating exports and a plus sign indicating imports. As shown in column 4, after the trade Mexico has 25 tons of avocados and

TABLE 5.7 Specialization According to Comparative Advantage and the Gains from Trade (in Tons)

Country	(1) Outputs before Specialization	(2) Outputs after Specialization	(3) Amounts Traded	(4) Outputs Available after Trade	(5) Gains from Specialization and Trade (4) − (1)
Mexico	24 avocados	60 avocados	−35 avocados	25 avocados	1 avocados
	9 soybeans	0 soybeans	+10 soybeans	10 soybeans	1 soybeans
United States	33 avocados	0 avocados	+35 avocados	35 avocados	2 avocados
	19 soybeans	30 soybeans	−10 soybeans	20 soybeans	1 soybeans

10 tons of soybeans, while the United States has 35 tons of avocados and 20 tons of soybeans. Compared with their optimum product mixes before specialization and trade (column 1), *both* nations now enjoy more avocados and more soybeans! Specifically, Mexico has gained 1 ton of avocados and 1 ton of soybeans. The United States has gained 2 tons of avocados and 1 ton of soybeans. These gains are shown in column 5.

Specialization based on comparative advantage improves global resource allocation. The same total inputs of world resources and technology result in a larger global output. If Mexico and the United States allocate all their resources to avocados and soybeans, respectively, the same total inputs of resources can produce more output between them, indicating that resources are being allocated more efficiently.

Through specialization and international trade a nation can overcome the production constraints imposed by its domestic production possibilities table and curve. Our discussion of Tables 5.4, 5.5, and 5.7 has shown just how this is done. The domestic production possibilities data (Tables 5.4 and 5.5) of the two countries have not changed, meaning that neither nation's production possibilities curve has shifted. But specialization and trade mean that citizens of both countries can enjoy increased consumption (column 5 of Table 5.7). **(Key Question 4)**

W 5.1

Gains from specialization

The Foreign Exchange Market

Buyers and sellers, whether individuals, firms, or nations, use money to buy products or to pay for the use of resources. Within the domestic economy, prices are stated in terms of the domestic currency and buyers use that currency to purchase domestic products. In Mexico, for example, buyers have pesos, and that is what sellers want.

International markets are different. Sellers set their prices in terms of their domestic currencies, but buyers often possess entirely different currencies. How many

dollars does it take to buy a truckload of Mexican avocados selling for 3000 pesos, a German automobile selling for 50,000 euros, or a Japanese motorcycle priced at 300,000 yen? Producers in Mexico, Germany, and Japan want payment in pesos, euros, and yen, respectively, so that they can pay their wages, rent, interest, dividends, and taxes.

A **foreign exchange market,** a market in which various national currencies are exchanged for one another, serves this need. The equilibrium prices in such currency markets are called **exchange rates.** An exchange rate is the rate at which the currency of one nation can be exchanged for the currency of another nation. (See Global Perspective 5.2.)

The market price or exchange rate of a nation's currency is an unusual price; it links all domestic prices with all foreign prices. Exchange rates enable consumers in one

GLOBAL PERSPECTIVE 5.2

Exchange Rates: Foreign Currency per U.S. Dollar

The amount of foreign currency that a dollar will buy varies greatly from nation to nation and fluctuates in response to supply and demand changes in the foreign exchange market. The amounts shown here are for March 2006.

$1 Will Buy

44.3 Indian rupees
.57 British pounds
1.16 Canadian dollars
10.7 Mexican pesos
1.31 Swiss francs
.83 European euros
117 Japanese yen
975 South Korean won
7.8 Swedish kronors

country to translate prices of foreign goods into units of their own currency: They need only multiply the foreign product price by the exchange rate. If the U.S. dollar–yen exchange rate is $.01 (1 cent) per yen, a Sony television set priced at ¥20,000 will cost $200 (= 20,000 × $.01) in the United States. If the exchange rate rises to $.02 (2 cents) per yen, the television will cost $400 (= 20,000 × $.02) in the United States. Similarly, all other Japanese products would double in price to U.S. buyers in response to the altered exchange rate.

Dollar-Yen Market

How does the foreign exchange market work? Let's look briefly at the market for dollars and yen. U.S. firms exporting goods to Japan want payment in dollars, not yen; but the Japanese importers of those U.S. goods possess yen, not dollars. So the Japanese importers supply their yen in exchange for dollars in the foreign exchange market. At the same time, there are U.S. importers of Japanese goods who need to pay the Japanese exporters in yen, not dollars. These importers go to the foreign exchange market as demanders of yen. We then have a market in which the "price" is in dollars and the "product" is yen.

G 5.1
Exchange rates

Figure 5.3 shows the supply of yen (by Japanese importers) and the demand for yen (by U.S. importers). The intersection of demand curve D_y and supply curve S_y establishes the equilibrium dollar price of yen.

FIGURE 5.3 The market for yen. U.S. imports from Japan create a demand D_y for yen, while U.S. exports to Japan (Japan's imports) create a supply S_y of yen. The dollar price of 1 yen—the exchange rate—is determined at the intersection of the supply and demand curves. In this case the equilibrium price is $.01, meaning that 1 cent will buy 1 yen.

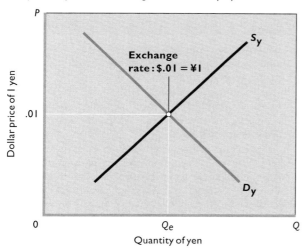

Here the equilibrium price of 1 yen—the dollar-yen exchange rate—is 1 cent per yen, or $.01 = ¥1. At this price, the market for yen clears; there is neither a shortage nor a surplus of yen. The equilibrium $.01 price of 1 yen means

that $1 will buy 100 yen or ¥100 worth of Japanese goods. Conversely, 100 yen will buy $1 worth of U.S. goods.

Changing Rates: Depreciation and Appreciation

What might cause the exchange rate to change? The determinants of the demand for and supply of yen are similar to the determinants of demand and supply for almost any product. In the United States, several things might increase the demand for—and therefore the dollar price of—yen. Incomes might rise in the United States, enabling residents to buy not only more domestic goods but also more Sony televisions, Nikon cameras, and Nissan automobiles from Japan. So people in the United States would need more yen, and the demand for yen would increase. Or a change in people's tastes might enhance their preferences for Japanese goods. When gas prices soared in the 1970s, many auto buyers in the United States shifted their demand from gas-guzzling domestic cars to gas-efficient Japanese compact cars. The result was an increased demand for yen.

The point is that an increase in the U.S. demand for Japanese goods will increase the demand for yen and raise the dollar price of yen. Suppose the dollar price of yen rises from $.01 = ¥1 to $.02 = ¥1. When the dollar price of yen increases, we say a **depreciation** of the dollar relative to the yen has occurred. It then takes more dollars (pennies in this case) to buy a single yen. Alternatively stated, the *international value of the dollar* has declined. A depreciated dollar buys fewer yen and therefore fewer Japanese goods; the yen and all Japanese goods have become more expensive to U.S. buyers. Result: Consumers in the United States shift their expenditures from Japanese goods to now less expensive American goods. The Ford Taurus becomes relatively more attractive than the Honda Accord to U.S. consumers. Conversely, because each yen buys more dollars—that is, because the international value of the yen has increased—U.S. goods become cheaper to people in Japan and U.S. exports to Japan rise.

If the opposite event occurred—if the Japanese demanded more U.S. goods—then they would supply more yen to pay for these goods. The increase in the supply of yen relative to the demand for yen would decrease the equilibrium price of yen in the foreign exchange market. For example, the dollar price of yen might decline from $.01 = ¥1 to $.005 = ¥1. A decrease in the dollar price of yen is called an **appreciation** of the dollar relative to the yen. It means that the international value of the dollar has increased. It then takes fewer dollars (or pennies) to buy a single yen; the dollar is worth more because it can purchase more yen and therefore more Japanese goods. Each

FIGURE 5.4 **Currency appreciation and depreciation.** Suppose the dollar price of a certain foreign currency rises (as illustrated by the upper left arrow). That means the international value of the dollar depreciates (upper right arrow). It also means that the foreign currency price of the dollar has declined (lower left arrow) and that the international value of the foreign currency has appreciated (lower right arrow).

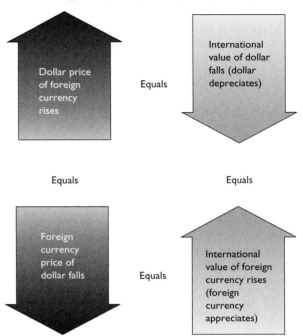

Sony PlayStation becomes less expensive in terms of dollars, so people in the United States purchase more of them. In general, U.S. imports rise. Meanwhile, because it takes more yen to get a dollar, U.S. exports to Japan fall.

Figure 5.4 summarizes these currency relationships. **(Key Question 6)**

QUICK REVIEW 5.2

- A country has a comparative advantage when it can produce a product at a lower domestic opportunity cost than a potential trading partner can.
- Specialization based on comparative advantage increases the total output available for nations that trade with one another.
- The foreign exchange market is a market in which national currencies are exchanged.
- An appreciation of the dollar is an increase in the international value of the dollar relative to the currency of some other nation; after appreciation a dollar buys more units of that currency. A depreciation of the dollar is a decrease in the international value of the dollar relative to some other currency; after depreciation a dollar buys fewer units of that currency.

Government and Trade

If people and nations benefit from specialization and international exchange, why do governments sometimes try to restrict the free flow of imports or encourage exports? What kinds of world trade barriers can governments erect, and why would they do so?

Trade Impediments and Subsidies

There are four means by which governments commonly interfere with free trade:

- **Protective tariffs** are excise taxes or duties placed on imported goods. Protective tariffs are designed to shield domestic producers from foreign competition. They impede free trade by causing a rise in the prices of imported goods, thereby shifting demand toward domestic products. An excise tax on imported shoes, for example, would make domestically produced shoes more attractive to consumers.

- **Import quotas** are limits on the quantities or total value of specific items that may be imported. Once a quota is "filled," further imports of that product are choked off. Import quotas are more effective than tariffs in retarding international commerce. With a tariff, a product can go on being imported in large quantities; with an import quota, however, all imports are prohibited once the quota is filled.

- **Nontariff barriers** (and, implicitly, *nonquota* barriers) include onerous licensing requirements, unreasonable standards pertaining to product quality, or simply bureaucratic red tape in customs procedures. Some nations require that importers of foreign goods obtain licenses and then restrict the number of licenses issued. Although many nations carefully inspect imported agricultural products to prevent the introduction of potentially harmful insects, some countries use lengthy inspections to impede imports.

- **Export subsidies** consist of government payments to domestic producers of export goods. By reducing production costs, the subsidies enable producers to charge lower prices and thus to sell more exports in world markets. Two examples: Some European governments have heavily subsidized Airbus Industries, a European firm that produces commercial aircraft, to help Airbus compete against the American firm Boeing. The United States and other nations have subsidized domestic farmers to boost the domestic food supply. Such subsidies have lowered the market price of food and have artificially lowered export prices on agricultural produce.

Why Government Trade Interventions?

In view of the benefits of free trade, what accounts for the impulse to impede imports and boost exports through government policy? There are several reasons—some legitimate, most not.

Misunderstanding the Gains from Trade   It is a commonly accepted myth that the greatest benefit to be derived from international trade is greater domestic employment in the export sector. This suggests that exports are "good" because they increase domestic employment, whereas imports are "bad" because they deprive people of jobs at home. Actually, the true benefit created by international trade is the overall increase in output obtained through specialization and exchange. A nation can fully employ its resources, including labor, with or without international trade. International trade, however, enables society to use its resources in ways that increase its total output and therefore its overall well-being.

A nation does not need international trade to operate *on* its production possibilities curve. A closed (nontrading) national economy can have full employment without international trade. However, through world trade an economy can reach a point of consumption *beyond* its domestic production possibilities curve. The gain from trade is the extra output obtained from abroad—the imports obtained for less cost than the cost if they were produced at home.

Political Considerations   While a nation as a whole gains from trade, trade may harm particular domestic industries and particular groups of resource suppliers. In our earlier comparative-advantage example, specialization and trade adversely affected the U.S. avocado industry and the Mexican soybean industry. Those industries might seek to preserve their economic positions by persuading their respective governments to protect them from imports—perhaps through tariffs or import quotas.

Those who directly benefit from import protection are few in number but have much at stake. Thus, they have a strong incentive to pursue political activity to achieve their aims. However, the overall cost of tariffs and quotas typically greatly exceeds the benefits. It is not uncommon to find that it costs the public $200,000 or more a year to protect a domestic job that pays less than one-fourth that amount. Moreover, because these costs are buried in the price of goods and spread out over millions of citizens, the cost born by each individual citizen is quite small. In the political arena, the voice of the relatively few producers demanding *protectionism* is loud and constant, whereas the voice of those footing the bill is soft or nonexistent.

Indeed, the public may be won over by the apparent plausibility ("Cut imports and prevent domestic unemployment") and the patriotic ring ("Buy American!") of the protectionist arguments. The alleged benefits of tariffs are immediate and clear-cut to the public, but the adverse effects cited by economists are obscure and dispersed over the entire economy. When political deal making is added in—"You back tariffs for the apparel industry in my state, and I'll back tariffs on the auto industry in your state"—the outcome can be a network of protective tariffs, import quotas, and export subsidies.

Costs to Society

Tariffs and quotas benefit domestic producers of the protected products, but they harm domestic consumers, who must pay higher than world prices for the protected goods. They also hurt domestic firms that use the protected goods as inputs in their production processes. For example, a tariff on imported steel would boost the price of steel girders, thus hurting firms that construct large buildings. Also, tariffs and quotas reduce competition in the protected industries. With less competition from foreign producers, domestic firms may be slow to design and implement cost-saving production methods and introduce new or improved products.

Multilateral Trade Agreements and Free-Trade Zones

When one nation enacts barriers against imports, the nations whose exports suffer may retaliate with trade barriers of their own. In such a *trade war*, escalating tariffs choke world trade and reduce everyone's economic well-being. The **Smoot-Hawley Tariff Act** of 1930 is a classic example. Although that act was meant to reduce imports and stimulate U.S. production, the high tariffs it authorized prompted adversely affected nations to retaliate with tariffs equally high. International trade fell, lowering the output and income of all nations. Economic historians generally agree that the Smoot-Hawley Tariff Act was a contributing cause of the Great Depression. Aware of that fact, nations have worked to lower tariffs worldwide. Their pursuit of free trade has been aided by powerful domestic interest groups: Exporters of goods and services, importers of foreign components used in "domestic" products, and domestic sellers of imported products all strongly support lower tariffs.

Figure 5.5 makes clear that while the United States has been a high-tariff nation over much of its history, U.S. tariffs have generally declined during the past half-century.

FIGURE 5.5 U.S. tariff rates, 1860–2005. Historically, U.S. tariff rates have fluctuated. But beginning with the Reciprocal Trade Agreements Act of 1934, the trend has been downward.

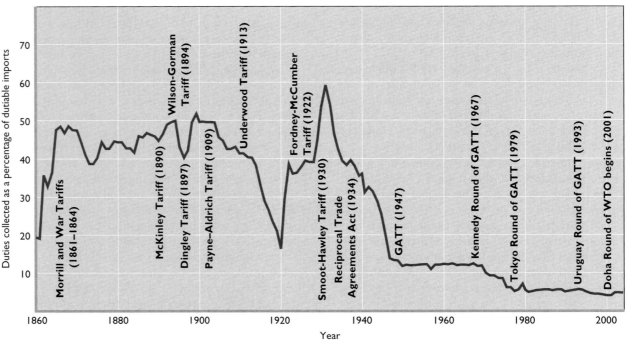

Source: U.S. Department of Commerce data.

Reciprocal Trade Agreements Act

The **Reciprocal Trade Agreements Act** of 1934 started the downward trend of tariffs. Aimed at reducing tariffs, this act had two main features:

- *Negotiating authority* It authorized the president to negotiate with foreign nations agreements that would reduce existing U.S. tariffs by up to 50 percent. Those reductions were contingent on the actions other nations took to lower tariffs on U.S. exports.

- *Generalized reductions* The specific tariff reductions negotiated between the United States and any particular nation were generalized through **most-favored-nation clauses**, which often accompany such agreements. These clauses stipulate that any subsequently reduced U.S. tariffs, resulting from negotiation with any other nation, would apply equally to any nation that signed the original agreement. So if the United States negotiates a reduction in tariffs on wristwatches with, say, France, the lower U.S. tariffs on imported French watches also apply to the imports of the other nations having most-favored-nation status, say, Japan and Switzerland. This way, the reductions in U.S. tariffs automatically apply to many nations.

General Agreement on Tariffs and Trade

The Reciprocal Trade Agreements Act provided only bilateral (between two nations) negotiations. Its approach was broadened in 1947 when 23 nations, including the United States, signed the **General Agreement on Tariffs and Trade (GATT).** GATT was based on three principles: (1) equal, nondiscriminatory trade treatment for all member nations, (2) the reduction of tariffs by multilateral negotiation, and (3) the elimination of import quotas. Basically, GATT provided a forum for the negotiation of reduced trade barriers on a multilateral basis among nations.

Since the Second World War, member nations have completed eight "rounds" of GATT negotiations to reduce trade barriers. The eighth round of negotiations began in Uruguay in 1986. After 7 years of complex discussions, in 1993 the 128 member nations reached a new agreement. The *Uruguay Round* agreement took effect on January 1, 1995, and its provisions were phased in through 2005.

Under this agreement, tariffs on thousands of products were eliminated or reduced, with overall tariffs dropping by 33 percent. The agreement also liberalized government rules that in the past impeded the global market for such services as advertising, legal services, tourist services, and financial services. Quotas on imported textiles and apparel were phased out and replaced with tariffs. Other provisions reduced agricultural subsidies paid to farmers and protected intellectual property (patents, trademarks, copyrights) against piracy.

World Trade Organization

The Uruguay Round agreement established the **World Trade Organization (WTO)** as GATT's successor. Some 149 nations belong to the WTO, with China being one of the latest entrants. The WTO oversees trade agreements reached by the member nations and rules on trade disputes among them. It also provides forums for further rounds of trade negotiations. The ninth and latest round of negotiations—the **Doha Round**—was launched in Doha, Qatar, in late 2001. (The trade rounds occur over several years in several venues but are named after the city or country of origination.) The negotiations are aimed at further reducing tariffs and quotas, as well as agricultural subsidies that distort trade. One of this chapter's Web-based questions asks you to update the progress of the Doha Round.

GATT and the WTO have been positive forces in the trend toward liberalized world trade. The trade rules agreed upon by the member nations provide a strong and necessary bulwark against the protectionism called for by the special-interest groups in the various nations.

For that reason and others, the WTO is controversial. Critics are concerned that rules crafted to expand international trade and investment enable firms to circumvent national laws that protect workers and the environment. What good are minimum-wage laws, worker safety laws, collective bargaining rights, and environmental laws if firms can easily shift their production to nations that have weaker laws or consumers can buy goods produced in those countries?

Proponents of the WTO respond that labor and environmental protections should be pursued directly in nations that have low standards and via international organizations other than the WTO. These issues should not be linked to the process of trade liberalization, which confers widespread economic benefits across nations. Moreover, say proponents of the WTO, many environmental and labor concerns are greatly overblown. Most world trade is among advanced industrial countries, not between them and countries that have lower environmental and labor standards. Moreover, the free flow of goods and resources raises output and income in the developing nations. Historically, such increases in living standards have eventually resulted in stronger, not weaker, protections for the environment and for workers.

The European Union

Countries have also sought to reduce tariffs by creating regional *free-trade zones*—also called *trade blocs*. The most dramatic example is the **European Union (EU)**, formerly called the European Economic Community. Initiated in 1958 as the Common Market, in 2003 the EU comprised 15 European nations—France, Germany, United Kingdom, Italy, Belgium, the Netherlands, Luxembourg, Denmark, Ireland, Greece, Spain, Portugal, Austria, Finland, and Sweden. In 2004, the EU expanded by 10 additional European countries—Poland, Hungary, Czech Republic, Slovakia, Lithuania, Latvia, Estonia, Slovenia, Malta, and Cyprus.

The EU Trade Bloc

The EU has abolished tariffs and import quotas on nearly all products traded among the participating nations and established a common system of tariffs applicable to all goods received from nations outside the EU. It has also liberalized the movement of capital and labor within the EU and has created common policies in other economic matters of joint concern, such as agriculture, transportation, and business practices. The EU is now a strong **trade bloc:** a group of countries having common identity, economic interests, and trade rules.

EU integration has achieved for Europe what the U.S. constitutional prohibition on tariffs by individual states has achieved for the United States: increased regional specialization, greater productivity, greater output, and faster economic growth. The free flow of goods and services has created large markets for EU industries. The resulting economies of large-scale production have enabled these industries to achieve much lower costs than they could have achieved in their small, single-nation markets.

The effects of EU success on nonmember nations, such as the United States, have been mixed. A peaceful and increasingly prosperous EU makes its members better customers for U.S. exports. But U.S. firms and other nonmember firms have been faced with tariffs and other barriers that make it difficult for them to compete against firms within the EU trade bloc. For example, autos produced in Germany and sold in Spain or France face no tariffs, whereas U.S. and Japanese autos exported to EU countries do. This puts U.S. and Japanese firms at a serious disadvantage.

By giving preferences to countries within their free-trade zone, trade blocs such as the EU tend to reduce their members' trade with non-bloc members. Thus, the world loses some of the benefits of a completely open global trading system. Eliminating that disadvantage has been one of the motivations for liberalizing global trade through the World Trade Organization. Those liberalizations apply equally to all nations that belong to the WTO.

The Euro

One of the most significant accomplishments of the EU was the establishment of the so-called Euro Zone in the early 2000s. In 2006, 12 members of the EU used the **euro** as a common currency. Great Britain, Denmark, and Sweden have opted out of the common currency, at least for now. But gone are French francs, German marks, Italian liras, and other national currencies within the Euro Zone.

Economists expect the euro to raise the standard of living of the Euro Zone members over time. By ending the inconvenience and expense of exchanging currencies, the euro will enhance the free flow of goods, services, and resources among the Euro Zone members. It will also enable consumers and businesses to comparison shop for outputs and inputs, and this will increase competition, reduce prices, and lower costs.

North American Free Trade Agreement

In 1993 Canada, Mexico, and the United States formed a major trade bloc. The **North American Free Trade Agreement (NAFTA)** established a free-trade zone that has about the same combined output as the EU but encompasses a much larger geographic area. NAFTA has greatly reduced tariffs and other trade barriers between Canada, Mexico, and the United States and will eliminate them entirely by 2008.

Critics of NAFTA feared that it would cause a massive loss of U.S. jobs as firms moved to Mexico to take advantage of lower wages and weaker regulations on pollution and workplace safety. Also, there was concern that Japan and South Korea would build plants in Mexico and transport goods tariff-free to the United States, further hurting U.S. firms and workers.

In retrospect, critics were much too pessimistic. Since the passage of NAFTA in 1993, employment in the United States has increased by 21 million workers and the unemployment rate has declined from 6.9 to 5.1 percent. Increased trade among Canada, Mexico, and the United States has enhanced the standard of living in all three countries. **(Key Question 10)**

QUICK REVIEW 5.3

- Governments curtail imports and promote exports through protective tariffs, import quotas, nontariff barriers, and export subsidies.
- The General Agreement on Tariffs and Trade (GATT) established multinational reductions in tariffs and import quotas. The Uruguay Round of GATT (1993) reduced tariffs worldwide, liberalized international trade in services, strengthened protections for intellectual property, and reduced agricultural subsidies.
- The World Trade Organization (WTO)—GATT's successor—rules on trade disputes and provides forums for negotiations on further rounds of trade liberalization. The current round is called the Doha Round.
- The European Union (EU) and the North American Free Trade Agreement (NAFTA) have reduced internal trade barriers among their members by establishing large free-trade zones. Of the 25 EU members (as of 2006), 12 now have a common currency—the euro.

Global Competition

Globalization—the integration of industry, commerce, communication, travel, and culture among the world's nations—is one of the major trends of our time. (See Global Perspective 5.3 for a list of the top 12 globalized nations, according to one set of criteria.) There is a lively debate internationally as to whether globalization is a positive or negative force. Those who support globalization focus on the improvements to general standards of living that it brings. Those who oppose it express concerns about its impacts on the environment, unionized workers, and the poor. (We discuss this issue in detail in a later Last Word.)

One thing about globalization is certain and relevant to our present discussion: It has brought intense competition both within the United States and across the globe. In the United States, imports have gained major shares of many markets, including those for cars, steel, lumber, car tires, clothing, sporting goods, electronics, and toys. Nevertheless, hundreds of U.S. firms have prospered in the global marketplace. Such firms as Boeing, McDonald's, Intel, Coca-Cola, Microsoft, Monsanto, Procter & Gamble, and Caterpillar have continued to retain high market shares at home and have dramatically expanded their sales abroad. Of course, not all firms have been successful. Some have not been able to compete, because their international competitors make higher-quality products, have lower production costs, or both.

Is the heightened competition that accompanies the global economy a good thing? Although some domestic

GLOBAL PERSPECTIVE 5.3

The Top 12 Globalized Nations, 2005

Foreign Policy magazine publishes an annual list of the worlds' most globalized nations, based on 13 key indicators such as foreign trade, cross-border travel, Internet use, and international investment flows. Here is the magazine's list, in descending order, for 2005.

1. Singapore
2. Ireland
3. Switzerland
4. United States
5. Netherlands
6. Canada
7. Denmark
8. Sweden
9. Austria
10. Finland
11. New Zealand
12. United Kingdom

Source: A. T. Kearney, *Foreign Policy,* **www.foreignpolicy.com** and **www.atkearney.com.**

producers *do* get hurt and their workers must find employment elsewhere, foreign competition clearly benefits consumers and society in general. Imports break down the monopoly power of existing firms, thereby lowering product prices and providing consumers with a greater variety of goods. Foreign competition also forces domestic producers to become more efficient and to improve product quality; that has already happened in several U.S. industries, including steel and autos. Most U.S. firms can and do compete quite successfully in the global marketplace.

What about the U.S. firms that cannot compete successfully in open markets? The unfortunate reality is that they must sell off production facilities, scale back their operations, and try to develop new products. If they remain unprofitable despite their best efforts, they will need to go out of business. Persistent economic losses mean that scarce resources are not being used efficiently. Shifting those resources to alternative, profitable uses will increase total U.S. output. It will be far less expensive for the United States to provide training and, if necessary, relocation assistance to laid-off workers than to try to protect these jobs from foreign competition.

Petition of the Candlemakers, 1845

French Economist Frédéric Bastiat (1801–1850) Devastated the Proponents of Protectionism by Satirically Extending Their Reasoning to Its Logical and Absurd Conclusions.

Petition of the Manufacturers of Candles, Waxlights, Lamps, Candlesticks, Street Lamps, Snuffers, Extinguishers, and of the Producers of Oil Tallow, Rosin, Alcohol, and, Generally, of Everything Connected with Lighting.

TO MESSIEURS THE MEMBERS OF THE CHAMBER OF DEPUTIES.

Gentlemen—You are on the right road. You reject abstract theories, and have little consideration for cheapness and plenty. Your chief care is the interest of the producer. You desire to emancipate him from external competition, and reserve the national market for national industry.

We are about to offer you an admirable opportunity of applying your—what shall we call it? your theory? No; nothing is more deceptive than theory; your doctrine? your system? your principle? but you dislike doctrines, you abhor systems, and as for principles, you deny that there are any in social economy: we shall say, then, your practice, your practice without theory and without principle.

We are suffering from the intolerable competition of a foreign rival, placed, it would seem, in a condition so far superior to ours for the production of light, that he absolutely inundates our national market with it at a price fabulously reduced. The moment he shows himself, our trade leaves us—all consumers apply to him; and a branch of native industry, having countless ramifications, is all at once rendered completely stagnant. This rival . . . is no other than the Sun.

What we pray for is, that it may please you to pass a law ordering the shutting up of all windows, skylights, dormer windows, outside and inside shutters, curtains, blinds, bull's-eyes; in a word, of all openings, holes, chinks, clefts, and fissures, by or through which the light of the sun has been in use to enter houses, to the prejudice of the meritorious manufacturers with which we flatter ourselves we have accommodated our country,—a country which, in gratitude, ought not to abandon us now to a strife so unequal.

If you shut up as much as possible all access to natural light, and create a demand for artificial light, which of our French manufacturers will not be encouraged by it?

If more tallow is consumed, then there must be more oxen and sheep; and, consequently, we shall behold the multiplication of artificial meadows, meat, wool, hides, and, above all, manure, which is the basis and foundation of all agricultural wealth.

The same remark applies to navigation. Thousands of vessels will proceed to the whale fishery; and, in a short time, we shall possess a navy capable of maintaining the honor of France, and gratifying the patriotic aspirations of your petitioners, the undersigned candlemakers and others.

Only have the goodness to reflect, Gentlemen, and you will be convinced that there is, perhaps, no Frenchman, from the wealthy coalmaster to the humblest vender of lucifer matches, whose lot will not be ameliorated by the success of this our petition.

Source: Frédéric Bastiat, *Economic Sophisms* (Edinburgh: Oliver and Boyd, Tweeddale Court, 1873), pp. 49–53, abridged.

Summary

1. Goods and services flows, capital and labor flows, information and technology flows, and financial flows link the United States and other countries.

2. International trade is growing in importance globally and for the United States. World trade is significant to the United States in two respects: (a) The absolute volumes of U.S. imports and exports exceed those of any other single nation. (b) The United States is completely dependent on trade for certain commodities and materials that cannot be obtained domestically.

3. Principal U.S. exports include chemicals, consumer durables, agricultural products, semiconductors, and computers. Principal imports include oil, automobiles, household appliances, computers, and metals. Quantitatively, Canada is the United States' most important trading partner.

4. Global trade has been greatly facilitated by (a) improvements in transportation technology, (b) improvements in communications technology, and (c) general declines in tariffs. Although the United States, Japan, and the western European nations dominate the global economy, the total volume of trade has been increased by the contributions of several new trade participants. They include the Asian economies of Singapore, South Korea, Taiwan, and China (including Hong Kong), the eastern European countries (such as the Czech Republic, Hungary, and Poland), and the newly independent countries of the former Soviet Union (such as Estonia, Ukraine, and Azerbaijan).

5. Specialization based on comparative advantage enables nations to achieve higher standards of living through trade with other countries. A trading partner should specialize in products and services for which its domestic opportunity costs are lowest. The terms of trade must be such that both nations can obtain more of some product via trade than they could obtain by producing it at home.

6. The foreign exchange market sets exchange rates between currencies. Each nation's imports create a supply of its own currency and a demand for foreign currencies. The resulting supply-demand equilibrium sets the exchange rate that links the currencies of all nations. Depreciation of a nation's currency reduces its imports and increases its exports; appreciation increases its imports and reduces its exports.

7. Governments influence trade flows through (a) protective tariffs, (b) quotas, (c) nontariff barriers, and (d) export subsidies. Such impediments to free trade result from misunderstandings about the advantages of free trade and from political considerations. By artificially increasing product prices, trade barriers cost U.S. consumers billions of dollars annually.

8. The Reciprocal Trade Agreements Act of 1934 marked the beginning of a trend toward lower U.S. tariffs. Most-favored-nation status allows a nation to export goods into the United States at the United States' lowest tariff level, then or at any later time.

9. In 1947 the General Agreement on Tariffs and Trade (GATT) was formed to encourage nondiscriminatory treatment for all member nations, to reduce tariffs, and to eliminate import quotas. The Uruguay Round of GATT negotiations (1993) reduced tariffs and quotas, liberalized trade in services, reduced agricultural subsidies, reduced pirating of intellectual property, and phased out quotas on textiles.

10. GATT's successor, the World Trade Organization (WTO), has 149 member nations. It implements WTO agreements, rules on trade disputes between members, and provides forums for continued discussions on trade liberalization. The latest round of trade negotiations—the Doha Round—began in late 2001 and as of mid-2006 was still in progress.

11. Free-trade zones (trade blocs) liberalize trade within regions but may at the same time impede trade with non-bloc members. Two examples of free-trade arrangements are the 25-member European Union (EU) and the North American Free Trade Agreement (NAFTA), comprising Canada, Mexico, and the United States. Twelve of the EU nations have abandoned their national currencies for a common currency called the euro.

12. The global economy has created intense foreign competition in many U.S. product markets, but most U.S. firms are able to compete well both at home and globally.

Terms and Concepts

multinational corporations

comparative advantage

terms of trade

foreign exchange market

exchange rates

depreciation

appreciation

protective tariffs

import quotas

nontariff barriers

export subsidies

Smoot-Hawley Tariff Act

Reciprocal Trade
    Agreements Act

most-favored-nation clauses

General Agreement on Tariffs and
    Trade (GATT)

World Trade Organization (WTO)

Doha Round

European Union (EU)

trade bloc

euro

North American Free Trade Agreement
    (NAFTA)

Study Questions

1. Describe the four major economic flows that link the United States with other nations. Provide a specific example to illustrate each flow. Explain the relationships between the top and bottom flows in Figure 5.1.

2. How important is international trade to the U.S. economy? In terms of volume, does the United States trade more with the industrially advanced economies or with developing economies? What country is the United States' most important trading partner, quantitatively?

3. What factors account for the rapid growth of world trade since the Second World War? Who are the major players in international trade today? Besides Japan, what other Asian nations play significant roles in international trade?

4. **KEY QUESTION** The following are production possibilities tables for China and the United States. Assume that before specialization and trade the optimal product mix for China is alternative B and for the United States is alternative U.

China Production Possibilities						
Product	A	B	C	D	E	F
Apparel (in thousands)	30	24	18	12	6	0
Chemicals (in tons)	0	6	12	18	24	30

U.S. Production Possibilities						
Product	R	S	T	U	V	W
Apparel (in thousands)	10	8	6	4	2	0
Chemicals (in tons)	0	4	8	12	16	20

   a. Are comparative-cost conditions such that the two areas should specialize? If so, what product should each produce?

   b. What is the total gain in apparel and chemical output that would result from such specialization?

   c. What are the limits of the terms of trade? Suppose actual terms of trade are 1 unit of apparel for $1\frac{1}{2}$ units of chemicals and that 4 units of apparel are exchanged for 6 units of chemicals. What are the gains from specialization and trade for each nation?

   d. Explain why this illustration allows you to conclude that specialization according to comparative advantage results in more efficient use of world resources.

5. Suppose that the comparative-cost ratios of two products— baby formula and tuna fish—are as follows in the hypothetical nations of Canswicki and Tunata:

   Canswicki: 1 can baby formula ≡ 2 cans tuna fish

   Tunata: 1 can baby formula ≡ 4 cans tuna fish

   In what product should each nation specialize? Explain why terms of trade of 1 can baby formula ≡ $2\frac{1}{2}$ cans tuna fish would be acceptable to both nations.

6. **KEY QUESTION** True or False? "U.S. exports create a demand for foreign currencies; foreign imports of U.S. goods create a supply of foreign currencies." Explain. Would a decline in U.S. consumer income or a weakening of U.S. preferences for foreign products cause the dollar to depreciate or to appreciate? Other things equal, what would be the effects of that depreciation or appreciation on U.S. exports and imports?

7. If the European euro were to decline in value (depreciate) in the foreign exchange market, would it be easier or harder for the French to sell their wine in the United States? Suppose you were planning a trip to Paris. How would depreciation of the euro change the dollar cost of your trip?

8. True or False? "An increase in the American dollar price of the South Korean won implies that the South Korean won has depreciated in value." Explain.

9. What measures do governments take to promote exports and restrict imports? Who benefits and who loses from protectionist policies? What is the net outcome for society?

10. **KEY QUESTION** Identify and state the significance of each of the following: (a) WTO; (b) EU; (c) euro; (d) NAFTA. What commonality do they share?

11. Explain: "Free-trade zones such as the EU and NAFTA lead a double life: They can promote free trade among members, but they pose serious trade obstacles for nonmembers." Do you think the net effects of trade blocs are good or bad for world trade? Why? How do the efforts of the WTO relate to these trade blocs?

12. Speculate as to why some U.S. firms strongly support trade liberalization while other U.S. firms favor protectionism. Speculate as to why some U.S. labor unions strongly support trade liberalization while other U.S. labor unions strongly oppose it.

13. What is the Doha Round and why is it so-named? How does it relate to the WTO? How does it relate to the Uruguay Round?

14. **LAST WORD** What point is Bastiat trying to make in his imaginary petition of the candlemakers?

Web-Based Questions

1. **TRADE BALANCES WITH PARTNER COUNTRIES** The U.S. Census Bureau, at **www.census.gov/foreign-trade/statistics,** lists the top trading partners of the United States (imports and exports added together) as well as the top 10 countries with which the United States has a trade surplus and a trade deficit. Using the current year-to-date data, compare the top 10 deficit and surplus countries with the top 10 trading partners. Are deficit and surplus countries equally represented in the top 10 trading partners list, or does one group dominate the list? The top 10 trading partners represent what percent of U.S. imports and what percent of U.S. exports?

2. **FOREIGN EXCHANGE RATES—THE YEN FOR DOLLARS** The Federal Reserve System Web site, **www.federalreserve.gov/releases/H10/hist/,** provides historical foreign-exchange-rate data for a wide variety of currencies. Look at the data for the Japanese yen from 1995 to the present. Assume that you were in Tokyo every New Year's from January 1, 2000, to this year and bought a *bento* (box lunch) for 1000 yen each year. Convert this amount to dollars using the yen-dollar exchange rate for each January since 2000, and plot the dollar price of the *bento* over time. Has the dollar appreciated or depreciated against the yen? What was the least amount in dollars that your box lunch cost? The most?

3. **THE DOHA ROUND—WHAT IS THE CURRENT STATUS?** Determine and briefly summarize the current status of the Doha Round of trade negotiations by accessing the World Trade Organization site, **www.wto.org.** Is the round still in progress or has it been concluded with an agreement? If the former, when and where was the latest ministerial meeting? If the latter, what are the main features of the agreement?

6

Measuring Domestic Output and National Income

IN THIS CHAPTER YOU WILL LEARN:

- **How gross domestic product (GDP) is defined and measured.**
- **The relationships among GDP, net domestic product, national income, personal income, and disposable income.**
- **The nature and function of a GDP price index.**
- **The difference between nominal GDP and real GDP.**
- **Some limitations of the GDP measure.**

"Disposable Income Flat." "Personal Consumption Surges." "Investment Spending Stagnates." "GDP Up 4 Percent." These headlines, typical of those in *The Wall Street Journal*, give knowledgeable readers valuable information on the state of the economy. This chapter will help you interpret such headlines and understand the stories reported under them. Specifically, it will help you become familiar with the vocabulary and methods of national income accounting. Also, the terms and ideas that you encounter in this chapter will provide a needed foundation for the macroeconomic analysis found in subsequent chapters.

Assessing the Economy's Performance

National income accounting measures the economy's overall performance. It does for the economy as a whole what private accounting does for the individual firm or for the individual household.

A business firm measures its flows of income and expenditures regularly—usually every 3 months or once a year. With that information in hand, the firm can gauge its economic health. If things are going well and profits are good, the accounting data can be used to explain that success. Were costs down? Was output up? Have market prices risen? If things are going badly and profits are poor, the firm may be able to identify the reason by studying the record over several accounting periods. All this information helps the firm's managers plot their future strategy.

National income accounting operates in much the same way for the economy as a whole. The Bureau of Economic Analysis (BEA, an agency of the Commerce Department) compiles the National Income and Product Accounts (NIPA) for the U.S. economy. This accounting enables economists and policymakers to:

- Assess the health of the economy by comparing levels of production at regular intervals.
- Track the long-run course of the economy to see whether it has grown, been constant, or declined.
- Formulate policies that will safeguard and improve the economy's health.

Gross Domestic Product

The primary measure of the economy's performance is its annual total output of goods and services or, as it is called, its *aggregate output*. Aggregate output is labeled **gross domestic product (GDP):** the total market value of all final goods and services produced in a given year. GDP includes all goods and services produced by either citizen-supplied or foreign-supplied resources employed within the country. The U.S. GDP includes the market value of Fords produced by an American-owned factory in Michigan and the market value of Hondas produced by a Japanese-owned factory in Ohio.

A Monetary Measure

If the economy produces three sofas and two computers in year 1 and two sofas and three computers in year 2, in which year is output greater? We can't answer that question until we attach a price tag to each of the two products to indicate how society evaluates their relative worth.

TABLE 6.1 Comparing Heterogeneous Output by Using Money Prices

Year	Annual Output	Market Value
1	3 sofas and 2 computers	3 at $500 + 2 at $2000 = $5500
2	2 sofas and 3 computers	2 at $500 + 3 at $2000 = $7000

That's what GDP does. It is a *monetary measure*. Without such a measure we would have no way of comparing the relative values of the vast number of goods and services produced in different years. In Table 6.1 the price of sofas is $500 and the price of computers is $2000. GDP would gauge the output of year 2 ($7000) as greater than the output of year 1 ($5500), because society places a higher monetary value on the output of year 2. Society is willing to pay $1500 more for the combination of goods produced in year 2 than for the combination of goods produced in year 1.

Avoiding Multiple Counting

To measure aggregate output accurately, all goods and services produced in a particular year must be counted once and only once. Because most products go through a series of production stages before they reach the market, some of their components are bought and sold many times. To avoid counting those components each time, GDP includes only the market value of *final goods* and ignores *intermediate goods* altogether.

Intermediate goods are goods and services that are purchased for resale or for further processing or manufacturing. **Final goods** are goods and services that are purchased for final use by the consumer, not for resale or for further processing or manufacturing.

Why is the value of final goods included in GDP but the value of intermediate goods excluded? Because the value of final goods already includes the value of all the intermediate goods that were used in producing them. Including the value of intermediate goods would amount to **multiple counting,** and that would distort the value of GDP.

To see why, suppose that five stages are needed to manufacture a wool suit and get it to the consumer—the final user. Table 6.2 shows that firm A, a sheep ranch, sells $120 worth of wool to firm B, a wool processor. Firm A pays out the $120 in wages, rent, interest, and profit. Firm B processes the wool and sells it to firm C, a suit manufacturer, for $180. What does firm B do with the $180 it receives? It pays $120 to firm A for the wool and uses the remaining $60 to pay wages, rent, interest, and profit for the resources used in processing the wool. Firm C, the

TABLE 6.2 **Value Added in a Five-Stage Production Process**

(1) Stage of Production	(2) Sales Value of Materials or Product	(3) Value Added
	$ 0	
Firm A, sheep ranch	120	$120 (= $120 − $ 0)
Firm B, wool processor	180	60 (= 180 − 120)
Firm C, suit manufacturer	220	40 (= 220 − 180)
Firm D, clothing wholesaler	270	50 (= 270 − 220)
Firm E, retail clothier	**350**	80 (= 350 − 270)
Total sales values	$1140	
Value added (total income)		**$350**

manufacturer, sells the suit to firm D, a wholesaler, which sells it to firm E, a retailer. Then at last a consumer, the final user, comes in and buys the suit for $350.

How much of these amounts should we include in GDP to account for the production of the suit? Just $350, the value of the final product. The $350 includes all the intermediate transactions leading up to the product's final sale. Including the sum of all the intermediate sales, $1140, in GDP would amount to multiple counting. The production and sale of the final suit generated just $350 of output, not $1140.

Alternatively, we could avoid multiple counting by measuring and cumulating only the *value added* at each stage. **Value added** is the market value of a firm's output *less* the value of the inputs the firm has bought from others. At each stage, the difference between what a firm pays for a product and what it receives from selling the product is paid out as wages, rent, interest, and profit. Column 3 of Table 6.2 shows that the value added by firm B is $60, the difference between the $180 value of its output and the $120 it paid for the input from firm A. We find the total value of the suit by adding together all the values added by the five firms. Similarly, by calculating and summing the values added to all the goods and services produced by all firms in the economy, we can find the market value of the economy's total output—its GDP.

GDP Excludes Nonproduction Transactions

Although many monetary transactions in the economy involve final goods and services, many others do not. Those nonproduction transactions must be excluded from GDP because they have nothing to do with the generation of final goods. *Nonproduction transactions* are of two types: purely financial transactions and second-hand sales.

Financial Transactions Purely financial transactions include the following:

- *Public transfer payments* These are the social security payments, welfare payments, and veterans' payments that the government makes directly to households. Since the recipients contribute nothing to *current production* in return, to include such payments in GDP would be to overstate the year's output.

- *Private transfer payments* Such payments include, for example, the money that parents give children or the cash gifts given at Christmas time. They produce no output. They simply transfer funds from one private individual to another and consequently do not enter into GDP.

- *Stock market transactions* The buying and selling of stocks (and bonds) is just a matter of swapping bits of paper. Stock market transactions create nothing in the way of current production and are not included in GDP. Payments for the services of a security broker *are* included, however, because those services do contribute to current output.

Secondhand Sales Secondhand sales contribute nothing to current production and for that reason are excluded from GDP. Suppose you sell your 1965 Ford Mustang to a friend; that transaction would be ignored in reckoning this year's GDP because it generates no current production. The same would be true if you sold a brand-new Mustang to a neighbor a week after you purchased it. **(Key Question 3)**

Two Ways of Looking at GDP: Spending and Income

Let's look again at how the market value of total output—or of any single unit of total output—is measured. Given the data listed in Table 6.2, how can we measure the market value of a suit?

One way is to see how much the final user paid for it. That will tell us the market value of the final product. Or we can add up the entire wage, rental, interest, and profit incomes that were created in producing the suit. The second approach is the value-added technique used in Table 6.2.

The final-product approach and the value-added approach are two ways of looking at the same thing. What is spent on making a product is income to those who helped make it. If $350 is spent on manufacturing a suit, then $350 is the total income derived from its production.

We can look at GDP in the same two ways. We can view GDP as the sum of all the money spent in buying it. That is the *output approach*, or **expenditures approach.** Or we can view GDP in terms of the income derived or created from producing it. That is the *earnings* or *allocations approach*, or the **income approach.**

As illustrated in Figure 6.1, we can determine GDP for a particular year either by adding up all that was spent to buy total output or by adding up all the money that was derived as income from its production. Buying (spending money) and selling (receiving income) are two aspects of the same transaction. On the expenditures side of GDP, all final goods produced by the economy are bought either by three domestic sectors (households, businesses, and government) or by foreign buyers. On the income side (once certain statistical adjustments are made), the total receipts acquired from the sale of that total output are allocated to the suppliers of resources as wage, rent, interest, and profit income.

The Expenditures Approach

To determine GDP using the expenditures approach, we add up all the spending on final goods and services that has taken place throughout the year. National income accountants use precise terms for the types of spending listed on the left side of Figure 6.1.

Personal Consumption Expenditures (*C*)

What we have called "consumption expenditures by households," the national income accountants call **personal consumption expenditures.** That term covers all expenditures by households on *durable consumer goods* (automobiles, refrigerators, video recorders), *nondurable consumer goods* (bread, milk, vitamins, pencils, toothpaste), and *consumer expenditures for services* (of lawyers, doctors, mechanics, barbers). The accountants use the symbol *C* to designate this component of GDP.

Gross Private Domestic Investment (I_g)

Under the heading **gross private domestic investment,** the accountants include the following items:
- All final purchases of machinery, equipment, and tools by business enterprises.
- All construction.
- Changes in inventories.

FIGURE 6.1 The expenditures and income approaches to GDP. There are two general approaches to measuring gross domestic product. We can determine GDP as the value of output by summing all expenditures on that output. Alternatively, with some modifications, we can determine GDP by adding up all the components of income arising from the production of that output.

Expenditures, or output, approach

Consumption expenditures by households
plus
Investment expenditures by businesses
plus
Government purchases of goods and services
plus
Expenditures by foreigners

= GDP =

Income, or allocations, approach

Wages
plus
Rents
plus
Interest
plus
Profits
plus
Statistical adjustments

Notice that this list, except for the first item, includes more than we have meant by "investment" so far. The second item includes residential construction as well as the construction of new factories, warehouses, and stores. Why do the accountants regard residential construction as investment rather than consumption? Because apartment buildings and houses, like factories and stores, earn income when they are rented or leased. Owner-occupied houses are treated as investment goods because they *could be* rented to bring in an income return. So the national income accountants treat all residential construction as investment. Finally, increases in inventories (unsold goods) are considered to be investment because they represent, in effect, "unconsumed output." For economists, all new output that is not consumed is, by definition, capital. An increase in inventories is an addition (although perhaps temporary) to the stock of capital goods, and such additions are precisely how we define investment.

Positive and Negative Changes in Inventories

We need to look at changes in inventories more closely. Inventories can either increase or decrease over some period. Suppose they increased by $10 billion between December 31, 2004, and December 31, 2005. That means the economy produced $10 billion more output than was purchased in 2005. We need to count all output produced in 2005 as part of that year's GDP, even though some of it remained unsold at the end of the year. This is accomplished by including the $10 billion increase in inventories as investment in 2005. That way the expenditures in 2005 will correctly measure the output produced that year.

Alternatively, suppose that inventories decreased by $10 billion in 2005. This "drawing down of inventories" means that the economy sold $10 billion more of output in 2005 than it produced that year. It did this by selling goods produced in prior years—goods already counted as GDP in those years. Unless corrected, expenditures in 2005 will overstate GDP for 2005. So in 2005 we consider the $10 billion decline in inventories as "negative investment" and subtract it from total investment that year. Thus, expenditures in 2005 will correctly measure the output produced in 2005.

Noninvestment Transactions

So much for what investment is. You also need to know what it isn't. Investment does *not* include the transfer of paper assets (stocks, bonds) or the resale of tangible assets (houses, jewelry, boats). Such transactions merely transfer the ownership of existing assets. Investment has to do with the creation of *new* capital assets—assets that create jobs and income. The mere transfer (sale) of claims to existing capital goods does not create new capital.

Gross Investment versus Net Investment

As we have seen, the category gross private domestic investment includes (1) all final purchases of machinery, equipment, and tools; (2) all construction; and (3) changes in inventories. The words "private" and "domestic" mean that we are speaking of spending by private businesses, not by government (public) agencies, and that the investment is taking place inside the country, not abroad.

The word "gross" means that we are referring to *all* investment goods—both those that replace machinery, equipment, and buildings that were used up (worn out or made obsolete) in producing the current year's output and any net additions to the economy's stock of capital. Gross investment includes investment in replacement capital *and* in added capital.

In contrast, **net private domestic investment** includes *only* investment in the form of added capital. The amount of capital that is used up over the course of a year is called *depreciation*. So

$$\text{Net investment} = \text{gross investment} - \text{depreciation}$$

In typical years, gross investment exceeds depreciation. Thus net investment is positive and the nation's stock of capital rises by the amount of net investment. As illustrated in Figure 6.2, the stock of capital at the end of the year exceeds the stock of capital at the beginning of the year by the amount of net investment.

Gross investment need not always exceed depreciation, however. When gross investment and depreciation *are equal*, net investment is zero and there is no change in the size of the capital stock. When gross investment *is less than* depreciation, net investment is negative. The economy then is *disinvesting*—using up more capital than it is producing—and the nation's stock of capital shrinks. That happened in the Great Depression of the 1930s.

National income accountants use the symbol I for private domestic investment spending, along with the subscript g to signify gross investment. They use the subscript n to signify net investment. But it is gross investment, I_g, that they use in determining GDP.

Government Purchases (*G*)

The third category of expenditures in the national income accounts is **government purchases,** officially labeled "government consumption expenditures and gross investment." These expenditures have two components: (1) expenditures for goods and services that government consumes in providing public services and (2) expenditures for *social capital* such as schools and highways, which have long lifetimes. Government purchases (Federal, state, and

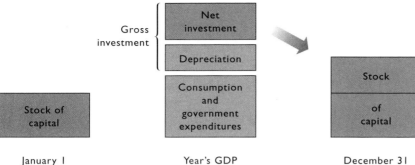

January 1   Year's GDP   December 31

FIGURE 6.2 Gross investment, depreciation, net investment, and the stock of capital. When gross investment exceeds depreciation during a year, net investment occurs. This net investment expands the stock of private capital from the beginning of the year to the end of the year by the amount of the net investment. Other things equal, the economy's production capacity expands.

local) include all government expenditures on final goods and all direct purchases of resources, including labor. It

CONSIDER THIS ...

Stock Answers about Flows

An analogy of a reservoir is helpful in thinking about a nation's capital stock, investment, and depreciation. Picture a reservoir that has water flowing in from a river and flowing out from an outlet after it passes through turbines. The volume of water in the reservoir *at any particular point in time* is a "stock." In contrast, the inflow from the river and outflow from the outlet are "flows."

The volume or stock of water in the reservoir will rise if the weekly inflow exceeds the weekly outflow. It will fall if the inflow is less than the outflow. And it will remain constant if the two flows are equal.

Now let's apply this analogy to the stock of capital, gross investment, and depreciation. The stock of capital is the total capital in place at any point in time and is analogous to the level of water in the reservoir. Changes in this capital stock over some period, for example, 1 year, depend on *gross investment* and *depreciation*. Gross investment (analogous to the reservoir inflow) is an addition of capital goods and therefore adds to the stock of capital, while depreciation (analogous to the reservoir outflow) is the using up of capital and thus subtracts from the capital stock. The capital stock increases when gross investment exceeds depreciation, declines when gross investment is less than depreciation, and remains the same when gross investment and depreciation are equal.

Alternatively, the stock of capital increases when *net investment* (gross investment *minus* depreciation) is positive. When net investment is negative, the stock of capital declines, and when net investment is zero, the stock of capital remains constant.

does *not* include government transfer payments, because, as we have seen, they merely transfer government receipts to certain households and generate no production of any sort. National income accountants use the symbol G to signify government purchases.

Net Exports (X_n)

International trade transactions are a significant item in national income accounting. We know that GDP records all spending on goods and services produced in the United States, including spending on U.S. output by people abroad. So we must include the value of exports when we are using the expenditures approach to determine GDP.

At the same time, we know that Americans spend a great deal of money on imports—goods and services produced abroad. That spending shows up in other nations' GDP. We must subtract the value of imports from U.S. spending to avoid overstating total production in the United States.

Rather than add exports and then subtract imports, national income accountants use "exports less imports," or **net exports.** We designate exports as X, imports as M, and net exports as X_n:

Net exports (X_n) = exports (X) − imports (M)

Table 6.3 shows that in 2005 Americans spent $727 billion more on imports than foreigners spent on U.S. exports. That is, net exports in 2005 were a *minus* $727 billion.

Putting It All Together: GDP = $C + I_g + G + X_n$

Taken together, these four categories of expenditures provide a measure of the market value of a given year's total output—its GDP. For the United States in 2005 (Table 6.3),

GDP = $8746 + 2105 + 2363 − 727 = $12,487 billion

TABLE 6.3 **Accounting Statement for the U.S. Economy, 2005 (in Billions)**

Receipts: Expenditures Approach		Allocations: Income Approach*	
Personal consumption expenditures (C)	$ 8746	Compensation of employees	$ 7125
Gross private domestic investment (I_g)	2105	Rents	73
Government purchases (G)	2363	Interest	498
Net exports (X_n)	−727	Proprietors' income	939
		Corporate profits	1352
		Taxes on production and imports	917
		National income†	**$10,904**
		Net foreign factor income	−34
		Statistical discrepancy	43
		Consumption of fixed capital	1574
Gross domestic product	**$12,487**	*Gross domestic product*	**$12,487**

*Some of the items in this column combine related categories that appear in the more detailed accounts.

†In the 2003 comprehensive revision of the NIPA, the Bureau of Economic Analysis redefined national income to include government revenue from taxes on production and imports. Previously, it had been excluded.

Global Perspective 6.1 lists the GDPs of several countries. The values of GDP are converted to dollars using international exchange rates.

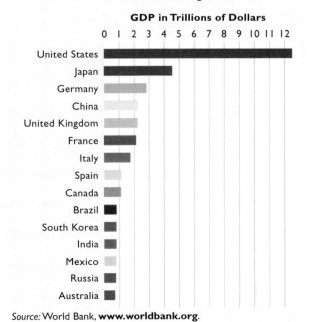

GLOBAL PERSPECTIVE 6.1

Comparative GDPs in Trillions of Dollars, Selected Nations, 2005

The United States, Japan, and Germany have the world's highest GDPs. The GDP data charted below have been converted to U.S. dollars via international exchange rates.

GDP in Trillions of Dollars

Source: World Bank, **www.worldbank.org.**

The Income Approach

Table 6.3 shows how 2005's expenditures of $12,487 billion were allocated as income to those responsible for producing the output. It would be simple if we could say that the entire amount flowed back to them in the form of wages, rent, interest, and profit. But we have to make a few adjustments to balance the expenditures and income sides of the account. We look first at the items that make up *national income*, shown on the right side of the table. Then we turn to the adjustments.

Compensation of Employees

By far the largest share of national income—$7125 billion—was paid as wages and salaries by business and government to their employees. That figure also includes wage and salary supplements, in particular, payments by employers into social insurance and into a variety of private pension, health, and welfare funds for workers.

Rents

Rents consist of the income received by the households and businesses that supply property resources. They include the monthly payments tenants make to landlords and the lease payments corporations pay for the use of office space. The figure used in the national accounts is *net* rent—gross rental income minus depreciation of the rental property.

Interest

Interest consists of the money paid by private businesses to the suppliers of money capital. It also includes such items as the interest households receive on savings deposits, certificates of deposit (CDs), and corporate bonds.

Proprietors' Income

What we have loosely termed "profits" is broken down by the national income accountants into two accounts: proprietors' income, which consists of the net income of sole proprietorships, partnerships, and other unincorporated businesses; and corporate profits. Proprietors' income flows to the proprietors.

Corporate Profits

Corporate profits are the earnings of owners of corporations. National income accountants subdivide corporate profits into three categories:

- *Corporate income taxes* These taxes are levied on corporations' net earnings and flow to the government.
- *Dividends* These are the part of corporate profits that are paid to the corporate stockholders and thus flow to households—the ultimate owners of all corporations.
- *Undistributed corporate profits* These are monies saved by corporations to be invested later in new plants and equipment. They are also called *retained earnings*.

Taxes on Production and Imports

The account called **taxes on production and imports** includes general sales taxes, excise taxes, business property taxes, license fees, and customs duties. Why do national income accountants add these indirect business taxes to wages, rent, interest, and profits in determining national income (they didn't prior to 2003!)? The answer is "mainly for accounting convenience." Assume that a firm produces a product that sells for $1. The production and sale of that product create $1 of wage, rent, interest, and profit income. But now suppose that the government imposes a 5 percent sales tax on all products sold at retail. The retailer adds the $.05 tax to the price of the product and shifts it along to consumers. But only $1 of the $1.05 consumer expenditures becomes wage, rent, interest, and profit income. So the national income accountants add the $.05 to the $1.00 in order to match up the $1.05 of expenditures on one side of the accounting ledger with the $1.05 of receipts (earned income plus taxes on production and imports). They make this kind of adjustment for the entire economy.

From National Income to GDP

The sum of employee compensation, rents, interest, proprietors' income, corporate profits, and taxes on production and imports yields **national income**—all the income that flows to American-supplied resources, whether here or abroad, plus taxes on production and imports. But notice that the figure for national income shown in Table 6.3— $10,904 billion—is less than GDP as reckoned by the expenditures approach shown on the left side of the table. The two sides of the accounting statement are brought into balance by adding three items to national income.

Net Foreign Factor Income First, we need to make a slight adjustment in "national" income versus "domestic" income. National income includes the total income of Americans, whether it was earned in the United States or abroad. But GDP is a measure of *domestic* output—total output produced within the United States regardless of the nationality of those who provide the resources. So in moving from national income to GDP, we must consider the income Americans gain from supplying resources abroad and the income that foreigners gain by supplying resources in the United States. In 2005, American-owned resources earned $34 billion more abroad than foreign-owned resources earned in the United States. That difference is called *net foreign factor income*. Because it is earnings of Americans, it is included in U.S. national income. But this income is not part of domestic income because it reflects earnings from output produced in some other nation. Thus, we subtract net foreign factor income from U.S. national income to stay on the correct path to use the income approach to determine the value of U.S. *domestic* output (output produced within the U.S. borders).

Statistical Discrepancy NIPA accountants add a statistical discrepancy to national income to make the income approach match the outcome of the expenditures approach. In 2005 that discrepancy was $43 billion.

Consumption of Fixed Capital Finally, we must recognize that the useful lives of private capital equipment (such as bakery ovens or automobile assembly lines) extend far beyond the year in which they were produced. To avoid understating profit and income in the year of purchase and to avoid overstating profit and income in succeeding years, the cost of such capital must be allocated over its lifetime. The amount allocated is an estimate of how much of the capital is being used up each year. It is called *depreciation*. A bookkeeping entry, the depreciation allowance results in a more accurate statement of profit and income for the economy each year. Social capital, such as courthouses and bridges, also requires a depreciation allowance in the national income accounts.

The huge depreciation charge made against private and social capital each year is called **consumption of fixed capital** because it is the allowance for capital that has been "consumed" in producing the year's GDP. It is the portion of GDP that is set aside to pay for the ultimate replacement of those capital goods.

The money allocated to consumption of fixed capital (the depreciation allowance) is a cost of production and thus included in the gross value of output. But this money is not available for other purposes, and, unlike other costs of production, it does not add to anyone's income. So it is not included in national income. We must therefore add it to national income to achieve balance with the economy's expenditures, as in Table 6.3.

Table 6.3 summarizes the expenditures approach and income approach to GDP. The left side shows what the U.S. economy produced in 2005 and what was spent to purchase it. The right side shows how those expenditures, when appropriately adjusted, were allocated as income.

QUICK REVIEW 6.1

- Gross domestic product (GDP) is a measure of the total market value of all final goods and services produced by the economy in a given year.
- The expenditures approach to GDP sums the total spending on final goods and services: GDP = $C + I_g + G + X_n$.
- The economy's stock of private capital expands when net investment is positive; stays constant when net investment is zero; and declines when net investment is negative.
- The income approach to GDP sums compensation to employees, rent, interest, proprietors' income, corporate profits, and taxes on production and imports to obtain national income, and then subtracts net foreign factor income and adds a statistical discrepancy and consumption of fixed capital to obtain GDP.

Other National Accounts

Several other national accounts provide additional useful information about the economy's performance. We can derive these accounts by making various adjustments to GDP.

Net Domestic Product

As a measure of total output, GDP does not make allowances for replacing the capital goods used up in each year's production. As a result, it does not tell us how much new output was available for consumption and for additions to the stock of capital. To determine that, we must subtract from GDP the capital that was consumed in producing the GDP and that had to be replaced. That is, we need to sub-

tract consumption of fixed capital (depreciation) from GDP. The result is a measure of **net domestic product (NDP):**

$$NDP = GDP - \text{consumption of fixed capital} \text{ (depreciation)}$$

For the United States in 2005:

	Billions
Gross domestic product	$12,487
Consumption of fixed capital	−1574
Net domestic product	$10,913

NDP is simply GDP adjusted for depreciation. It measures the total annual output that the entire economy—households, businesses, government, and foreigners—can consume without impairing its capacity to produce in ensuing years.

National Income

Sometimes it is useful to know how much Americans earned for their contributions of land, labor, capital, and entrepreneurial talent. Recall that U.S. national income (NI) includes all income earned through the use of American-owned resources, whether they are located at home or abroad. It also includes taxes on production and imports. To derive NI from NDP, we must subtract the aforementioned statistical discrepancy from NDP and add net foreign factor income, since the latter is income earned by Americans.

For the United States in 2005:

	Billions
Net domestic product	$10,913
Statistical discrepancy	−43
Net foreign factor income	34
National income	$10,904

We know, too, that we can calculate national income through the income approach by simply adding up employee compensation, rent, interest, proprietors' income, corporate profit, and taxes on production and imports.

Personal Income

Personal income (PI) includes all income received whether earned or unearned. It is likely to differ from national income (income earned) because some income earned—taxes on production and imports, Social Security taxes (payroll taxes), corporate income taxes, and undistributed corporate profits—is not received by households. Conversely, some income received—such as Social Security payments, unemployment compensation payments, welfare payments, disability and education payments to veterans, and private pension payments—is not earned. These transfer payments must be added to obtain PI.

In moving from national income to personal income, we must subtract the income that is earned but not received and add the income that is received but not earned. For the United States in 2005:

	Billions
National income	$10,904
Taxes on production and imports	−917
Social Security contributions	−871
Corporate income taxes	−378
Undistributed corporate profits	−460
Transfer payments	+1970*
Personal income	$10,248

*Includes a statistical discrepancy.

Disposable Income

W 6.1

Measuring output and income

Disposable income (DI) is personal income less personal taxes. Personal taxes include personal income taxes, personal property taxes, and inheritance taxes. Disposable income is the amount of income that households have left over after paying their personal taxes. They are free to divide that income between consumption (C) and saving (S):

$$DI = C + S$$

For the United States in 2005:

	Billions
Personal income	$10,248
Personal taxes	−1210
Disposable income	$ 9038

Table 6.4 summarizes the relationships among GDP, NDP, NI, PI, and DI. **(Key Question 8)**

The Circular Flow Revisited

Figure 6.3 is an elaborate flow diagram that shows the economy's four main sectors along with the flows of expenditures and allocations that determine GDP, NDP, NI, and PI. The orange arrows represent the spending flows—$C + I_g + G + X_n$—that together measure gross domestic product. To the right of the GDP rectangle are green arrows

TABLE 6.4 The Relationships between GDP, NDP, NI, PI, and DI in the United States, 2005*

	Billions
Gross domestic product (GDP)	$12,487
Consumption of fixed capital	−1574
Net domestic product (NDP)	$10,913
Statistical discrepancy	−43
Net foreign factor income	34
National income (NI)†	$10,904
Taxes on production and imports	−917
Social Security contributions	−871
Corporate income taxes	−378
Undistributed corporate profits	−460
Transfer payments	+1970
Personal income (PI)	$10,248
Personal taxes	−1210
Disposable income (DI)	$ 9038

*Some of the items combine related categories that appear in the more detailed accounts.

†In the 2003 comprehensive revision of the NIPA, the Bureau of Economic Analysis redefined national income to include revenue from taxes on production and imports. Previously, it had excluded these indirect business taxes.

that show first the allocations of GDP and then the adjustments needed to derive NDP, NI, PI, and DI.

The diagram illustrates the adjustments necessary to determine each of the national income accounts. For example, net domestic product is smaller than GDP because consumption of fixed capital flows away from GDP in determining NDP. Also, disposable income is smaller than personal income because personal taxes flow away from PI (to government) in deriving DI.

Note the three domestic sectors of the economy: households, government, and businesses. The household sector has an inflow of disposable income and outflows of consumption spending and saving. The government sector has an inflow of revenue in the form of types of taxes and an outflow of government disbursements in the form of purchases and transfers. The business sector has inflows of three major sources of funds for business investment and an outflow of investment expenditures.

Finally, note the foreign sector (all other countries) in the flow diagram. Spending by foreigners on U.S. exports adds to U.S. GDP, but some of U.S. consumption, government, and investment expenditures buy imported products. The flow from foreign markets shows that we handle this complication by calculating net exports (U.S. exports minus U.S. imports). The net export flow may be a positive or negative amount, adding to or subtracting from U.S. GDP.

FIGURE 6.3 U.S. domestic output and the flows of expenditure and income. This figure is an elaborate circular flow diagram that fits the expenditures and allocations sides of GDP to one another. The expenditures flows are shown in orange; the allocations or income flows are shown in green. You should trace through the income and expenditures flows, relating them to the five basic national income accounting measures.

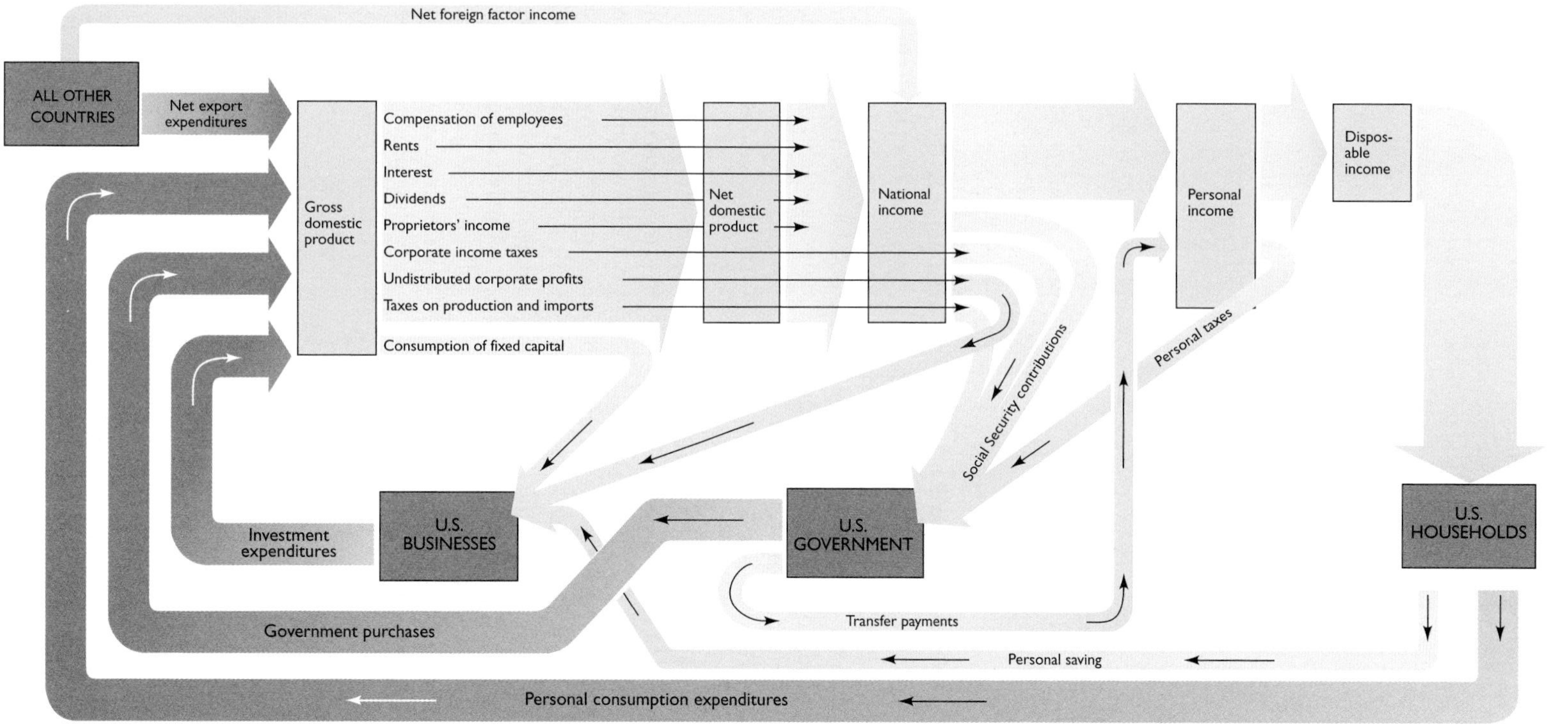

Figure 6.3 shows that flows of expenditures and income are part of a continuous, repetitive process. Cause and effect are intermingled: Expenditures create income, and from this income arise expenditures, which again flow to resource owners as income.

Nominal GDP versus Real GDP

Recall that GDP is a measure of the market or money value of all final goods and services produced by the economy in a given year. We use money or nominal values as a common denominator in order to sum that heterogeneous output into a meaningful total. But that creates a problem: How can we compare the market values of GDP from year to year if the value of money itself changes in response to inflation (rising prices) or deflation (falling prices)? After all, we determine the value of GDP by multiplying total output by market prices.

Whether there is a 5 percent increase in output with no change in prices or a 5 percent increase in prices with no change in output, the change in the value of GDP will be the same. And yet it is the *quantity* of goods that get produced and distributed to households that affects our standard of living, not the price of the goods. The hamburger that sold for $2 in 2000 yields the same satisfaction as an identical hamburger that sold for 50 cents in 1970.

The way around this problem is to *deflate* GDP when prices rise and to *inflate* GDP when prices fall. These adjustments give us a measure of GDP for various years as if the value of the dollar had always been the same as it was in some reference year. A GDP based on the prices that prevailed when the output was produced is called unadjusted GDP, or **nominal GDP.** A GDP that has been deflated or inflated to reflect changes in the price level is called adjusted GDP, or **real GDP.**

Adjustment Process in a One-Product Economy

There are two ways we can adjust nominal GDP to reflect price changes. For simplicity, let's assume that the economy produces only one good, pizza, in the amounts indicated in Table 6.5 for years 1, 2, and 3. Suppose that we gather revenue data directly from the financial reports of the pizza businesses to measure nominal GDP in various years. After completing our effort, we will have determined nominal GDP for each year, as shown in column 4 of Table 6.5. We will have no way of knowing to what extent changes in price and/or changes in quantity of output have accounted for the increases or decreases in nominal GDP that we observe.

GDP Price Index How can we determine real GDP in our pizza economy? One way is to assemble data on the price changes that occurred over various years (column 2) and use them to establish an overall price index for the entire period. Then we can use the index in each year to adjust nominal GDP to real GDP for that year.

A **price index** is a measure of the price of a specified collection of goods and services, called a "market basket," in a given year as compared to the price of an identical (or highly similar) collection of goods and services in a

TABLE 6.5 Calculating Real GDP (Base Year = Year 1)

Year	(1) Units of Output	(2) Price of Pizza per Unit	(3) Price Index (Year 1 = 100)	(4) Unadjusted, or Nominal, GDP, (1) × (2)	(5) Adjusted, or Real, GDP
1	5	$10	100	$ 50	$50
2	7	20	200	140	70
3	8	25	250	200	80
4	10	30	—	—	—
5	11	28	—	—	—

reference year. That point of reference, or benchmark, is known as the base period or base year. More formally,

$$\begin{array}{c} \text{Price} \\ \text{index} \\ \text{in given} \\ \text{year} \end{array} = \dfrac{\begin{array}{c}\text{price of market basket}\\ \text{in specific year}\end{array}}{\begin{array}{c}\text{price of same market}\\ \text{basket in base year}\end{array}} \times 100 \quad (1)$$

By convention, the price ratio between a given year and the base year is multiplied by 100 to facilitate computation. For example, a price ratio of 2/1 (= 2) is expressed as a price index of 200. A price ratio of 1/3 (= .33) is expressed as a price index of 33.

In our pizza-only example, of course, our market basket consists of only one product. Column 2 of Table 6.5 reveals that the price of pizza was $10 in year 1, $20 in year 2, $25 in year 3, and so on. Let's select year 1 as our base year. Now we can express the successive prices of the contents of our market basket in, say, years 2 and 3 as compared to the price of the market basket in year 1:

$$\text{Price index, year 2} = \frac{\$20}{\$10} \times 100 = 200$$

$$\text{Price index, year 3} = \frac{\$25}{\$10} \times 100 = 250$$

For year 1 the index has to be 100, since that year and the base year are identical.

The index numbers tell us that the price of pizza rose from year 1 to year 2 by 100 percent {= [(200 − 100)/100] × 100} and from year 1 to year 3 by 150 percent {= [(250 − 100)/100] × 100}.

Dividing Nominal GDP by the Price Index

We can now use the index numbers shown in column 3 to deflate the nominal GDP figures in column 4. The simplest and most direct method of deflating is to express the index numbers as hundredths—in decimal form—and then to divide them into corresponding nominal GDP. That gives us real GDP:

$$\text{Real GDP} = \frac{\text{nominal GDP}}{\text{price index (in hundredths)}} \quad (2)$$

Column 5 shows the results. These figures for real GDP

W 6.2

Real GDP and price indexes

measure the market value of the output of pizza in years 1, 2, and 3 as if the price of pizza had been a constant $10 throughout the 3-year period. In short, real GDP reveals the market value of each year's output measured in terms of dollars that have the same purchasing power as dollars had in the base year.

O 6.1

GDP price index

To test your understanding, extend Table 6.5 to years 4 and 5, using equations 1 and 2. Then run through the entire deflating procedure, using year 3 as the base period. This time you will have to inflate some of the nominal GDP data, using the same procedure as we used in the examples.

An Alternative Method

Another way to establish real GDP is to gather separate data on physical outputs (as in column 1) and their prices (as in column 2) of Table 6.5. We could then determine the market value of outputs in successive years *if the base-year price ($10) had prevailed*. In year 2, the 7 units of pizza would have a value of $70 (= 7 units × $10). As column 5 confirms, that $70 worth of output is year 2's real GDP. Similarly, we could determine the real GDP for year 3 by multiplying the 8 units of output that year by the $10 price in the base year.

Once we have determined real GDP through this method, we can identify the price index for a given year simply by dividing the nominal GDP by the real GDP for that year:

$$\begin{array}{c}\text{Price index}\\ \text{(in hundredths)}\end{array} = \frac{\text{nominal GDP}}{\text{real GDP}} \quad (3)$$

Example: In year 2 we get a price index of 200—or, in hundredths, 2.00—which equals the nominal GDP of $140 divided by the real GDP of $70. Note that equation 3 is simply a rearrangement of equation 2. Table 6.6 summarizes the two methods of determining real GDP in our single-good economy. **(Key Question 11)**

Real-World Considerations and Data

In the real world of many goods and services, of course, determining GDP and constructing a reliable price index are far more complex matters than in our pizza-only

TABLE 6.6 Steps for Deriving Real GDP from Nominal GDP

Method 1

1. Find nominal GDP for each year.
2. Compute a GDP price index.
3. Divide each year's nominal GDP by that year's price index (in hundredths) to determine real GDP.

Method 2

1. Break down nominal GDP into physical quantities of output and prices for each year.
2. Find real GDP for each year by determining the dollar amount that each year's physical output would have sold for if base-year prices had prevailed. (The GDP price index can then be found by dividing nominal GDP by real GDP.)

TABLE 6.7 Nominal GDP, Real GDP, and GDP Price Index, Selected Years

(1) Year	(2) Nominal GDP, Billions of $	(3) Real GDP, Billions of $	(4) GDP Price Index (2000 = 100)
1980	2789.5	5161.7	____
1985	4220.3	6053.7	69.7
1990	5803.1	_____	81.6
2000	9817.0	9817.0	100.0
2003	10,971.2	_____	106.3
2005	12,487.1	11,134.8	112.1

Source: Bureau of Economic Analysis, **www.bea.doc.gov.**

economy. The government accountants must assign a "weight" to each of several categories of goods and services based on the relative proportion of each category in total output. They update the weights annually as expenditure patterns change and roll the base year forward year by year using a moving average of expenditure patterns. The GDP price index used in the United States is called the *chain-type annual-weights price index*—which hints at its complexity. We spare you the details.

Table 6.7 shows some of the real-world relationships between nominal GDP, real GDP, and the GDP price index. Here the reference year is 2000, where the value of the index is set at 100. Because the price level has been rising over the long run, the pre-2000 values of real GDP (column 3) are higher than the nominal values of GDP for those years (column 2). This upward adjustment acknowledges that prices were lower in the years before 2000, and thus nominal GDP understated the real output of those years in 2000 prices and must be inflated to show the correct relationship to other years.

Conversely, the rising price level of the post-2000 years caused nominal GDP figures for those years to overstate real output. So the statisticians deflate those figures to determine what real GDP would have been in other years if 2000 prices had prevailed. Doing so reveals that real GDP has been less than nominal GDP since 2000.

By inflating the nominal pre-2000 GDP data and deflating the post-2000 data, government accountants determine annual real GDP, which can then be compared with the real GDP of any other year in the series of years. So the real GDP values in column 3 are directly comparable with one another.

Once we have determined nominal GDP and real GDP, we can fashion the price index. And once we have determined nominal GDP and the price index, we can calculate real GDP. Example: Nominal GDP in 2005 was $12,487.1

billion and real GDP was $11,134.8 billion. So the price level in 2005 was 112.1 (= $12,487.1/$11,134.8 × 100), or 12.1 percent higher than in 2000. If we knew the nominal GDP and the price level only, we could find the real GDP for 2005 by dividing the nominal GDP of $12,487.1 by the 2005 price index, expressed in hundredths (1.1214).

To test your understanding of the relationships between nominal GDP, real GDP, and the price level, determine the values of the price index for 1980 in Table 6.7 and determine real GDP for 1990 and 2003. We have left those figures out on purpose. **(Key Question 12)**

QUICK REVIEW 6.3

- Nominal GDP is output valued at current prices. Real GDP is output valued at constant base-year prices.
- The GDP price index compares the price (market value) of all the goods and services included in GDP in a given year to the price of the same market basket in a reference year.
- Nominal GDP can be transformed into real GDP by dividing the nominal GDP by the GDP price index expressed in hundredths.

Shortcomings of GDP

GDP is a reasonably accurate and highly useful measure of how well or how poorly the economy is performing. But it has several shortcomings as a measure of both total output and well-being (total utility).

Nonmarket Activities

Certain productive activities do not take place in any market—the services of homemakers, for example, and the labor of carpenters who repair their own homes. Such activities never show up in GDP, which measures only the *market value* of output. Consequently, GDP understates a nation's total output. There is one exception: The portion of farmers' output that farmers consume themselves *is* estimated and included in GDP.

Leisure

The average workweek (excluding overtime) in the United States has declined since the beginning of the 1900s—from about 53 hours to about 35 hours. Moreover, the greater frequency of paid vacations, holidays, and leave time has shortened the work year itself. This increase in leisure time has clearly had a positive effect on overall well-being. But our system of national income accounting understates well-being by ignoring leisure's value. Nor does the system accommodate the satisfaction—the "psychic income"—that many people derive from their work.

Improved Product Quality

Because GDP is a quantitative measure rather than a qualitative measure, it fails to capture the full value of improvements in product quality. There is a very real difference in quality between a $200 cell phone purchased today and a cell phone that cost the same amount just a decade ago. Today's cell phone is digital and has greater memory capacity, a viewing screen, and enhanced capabilities.

Obviously quality improvement has a great effect on economic well-being, as does the quantity of goods produced. Although the BEA adjusts GDP for quality improvement for selected items, the vast majority of such improvement for the entire range of goods and services does not get reflected in GDP.

The Underground Economy

Embedded in our economy is a flourishing, productive underground sector. Some of the people who conduct business there are gamblers, smugglers, prostitutes, "fences" of stolen goods, drug growers, and drug dealers. They have good reason to conceal their incomes.

Most participants in the underground economy, however, engage in perfectly legal activities but choose illegally not to report their full incomes to the Internal Revenue Service (IRS). A bell captain at a hotel may report just a portion of the tips received from customers. Storekeepers may report only a portion of their sales receipts. Workers who want to hold on to their unemployment compensation benefits may take an "off-the-books" or "cash-only" job. A brick mason may agree to rebuild a neighbor's fireplace in exchange for the neighbor's repairing his boat engine. The value of none of these transactions shows up in GDP.

The value of underground transactions is estimated to be about 8 percent of the recorded GDP in the United States. That would mean that GDP in 2005 was understated by about $1 trillion. Global Perspective 6.2 shows estimates of the relative sizes of underground economies in selected nations.

GDP and the Environment

The growth of GDP is inevitably accompanied by "gross domestic by-products," including dirty air and polluted water, toxic waste, congestion, and noise. The social costs of the negative by-products reduce our economic well-being. And since those costs are not deducted from

GLOBAL PERSPECTIVE 6.2

The Underground Economy as a Percentage of GDP, Selected Nations

Underground economies vary in size worldwide. Three factors that help explain the variation are (1) the extent and complexity of regulation, (2) the type and degree of taxation, and (3) the effectiveness of law enforcement.

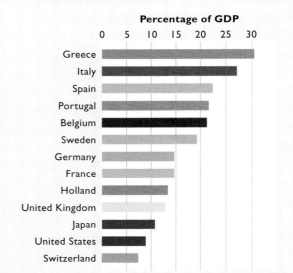

Source: Friedrich Schneider and Dominik H. Enste, "Shadow Economies: Size, Causes, and Consequences," *Journal of Economic Literature,* March 2000, p. 104.

total output, GDP overstates our national well-being. Ironically, when money is spent to clean up pollution and reduce congestion, those expenses are added to the GDP!

Composition and Distribution of Output

The composition of output is undoubtedly important for well-being. But GDP does not tell us whether the mix of goods and services is enriching or potentially detrimental to society. GDP assigns equal weight to an assault rifle and a set of encyclopedias, as long as both sell for the same price. Moreover, GDP reveals nothing about the way output is distributed. Does 90 percent of the output go to 10 percent of the households, for example, or is the output more evenly distributed? The distribution of output may make a big difference for society's overall well-being.

The Bureau of Economic Analysis (BEA), an Agency of the Department of Commerce, Compiles the NIPA Tables. Where Does It Get the Actual Data?

Discussions of national income accounting often leave the impression that the data for the National Income and Product Accounts magically appear from some mysterious place. Let's take a tour to see where economists get their data.

Consumption The BEA derives the data for the consumption component of the GDP accounts from four main sources:

- The Census Bureau's *Retail Trade Survey*, which gains sales information from a sample of 22,000 firms.
- The Census Bureau's *Survey of Manufacturers*, which gathers information on shipments of consumer goods from 50,000 establishments.
- The Census Bureau's *Service Survey*, which collects sales data from 30,000 service businesses.
- Industry trade sources. For example, data on auto sales and aircraft are collected directly from auto and aircraft manufacturers.

Investment The sources of the data for the investment component of GDP include:

- All the sources above used to determine consumption. Purchases of capital goods are separated from purchases of consumer goods. For example, estimates of investment in equipment and software are based on manufacturers' shipments reported in the *Survey of Manufacturers*, the *Service Survey*, and industry sources.
- Census construction surveys. The Census Bureau's *Housing Starts Survey* and *Housing Sales Survey* produce the data used to measure the amount of housing construction, and

the *Construction Progress Reporting Survey* is the source of data on nonresidential construction. The BEA determines changes in business inventories through the *Retail Trade Survey*, the *Wholesale Trade Survey* (of 7100 wholesale firms), and the *Survey of Manufacturing*.

Government Purchases The data for government purchases (officially "government consumption and investment expenditures") are obtained through the following sources:

- The U.S. Office of Personnel Management, which collects data on wages and benefits, broken out by the private and public sector. Wages and benefits of government employees are the single largest "purchase" by Federal, state, and local government.
- The previously mentioned Census Bureau's construction surveys, which break out private and public sector construction expenditures.
- The Census Bureau's *Survey of Government Finance*, which provides data on government consumption and investment expenditures.

Net Exports The BEA determines net exports through two main sources:

- The U.S. Customs Service, which collects data on exports and imports of goods.
- BEA surveys of potential domestic exporters and importers of services, which collect data on exports and imports of services.

So there you have it. Not so magical after all!

Source: Based on Joseph A. Ritter, "Feeding the National Accounts," Federal Reserve Bank of St. Louis *Review*, March–April 2000, pp. 11–20. For those interested, this article also provides information on the sources of data for the income side of the national accounts.

Noneconomic Sources of Well-Being

Finally, the connection between GDP and well-being is problematic for another reason. Just as a household's income does not measure its total happiness, a nation's GDP does not measure its total well-being. Many things could make a society better off without necessarily raising GDP: a reduction of crime and violence, peaceful relations with other countries, people's greater civility toward one another, better understanding between parents and children, and a reduction of drug and alcohol abuse.

Summary

1. Gross domestic product (GDP), a basic measure of an economy's economic performance, is the market value of all final goods and services produced within the borders of a nation in a year.

2. Intermediate goods, nonproduction transactions, and secondhand sales are purposely excluded in calculating GDP.

3. GDP may be calculated by summing total expenditures on all final output or by summing the income derived from the production of that output.

4. By the expenditures approach, GDP is determined by adding consumer purchases of goods and services, gross investment spending by businesses, government purchases, and net exports: $GDP = C + I_g + G + X_n$.

5. Gross investment is divided into (a) replacement investment (required to maintain the nation's stock of capital at its existing level) and (b) net investment (the net increase in the stock of capital). In most years, net investment is positive and therefore the economy's stock of capital and production capacity increase.

6. By the income or allocations approach, GDP is calculated as the sum of compensation to employees, rents, interest, proprietors' income, corporate profits, taxes on production and imports *minus* net foreign factor income, *plus* a statistical discrepancy and consumption of fixed capital.

7. Other national accounts are derived from GDP. Net domestic product (NDP) is GDP less the consumption of fixed capital. National income (NI) is total income earned by a nation's resource suppliers plus taxes on production and imports; it is found by subtracting a statistical discrepancy from NDP and adding net foreign factor income to NDP. Personal income (PI) is the total income paid to households prior to any allowance for personal taxes. Disposable income (DI) is personal income after personal taxes have been paid. DI measures the amount of income available to households to consume or save.

8. Price indexes are computed by dividing the price of a specific collection or market basket of output in a particular period by the price of the same market basket in a base period and multiplying the result (the quotient) by 100. The GDP price index is used to adjust nominal GDP for inflation or deflation and thereby obtain real GDP.

9. Nominal (current-dollar) GDP measures each year's output valued in terms of the prices prevailing in that year. Real (constant-dollar) GDP measures each year's output in terms of the prices that prevailed in a selected base year. Because real GDP is adjusted for price-level changes, differences in real GDP are due only to differences in production activity.

10. GDP is a reasonably accurate and very useful indicator of a nation's economic performance, but it has its limitations. It fails to account for nonmarket and illegal transactions, changes in leisure and in product quality, the composition and distribution of output, and the environmental effects of production. The link between GDP and well-being is tenuous.

Terms and Concepts

national income accounting	personal consumption expenditures (*C*)	net domestic product (NDP)
gross domestic product (GDP)	gross private domestic investment (*I*$_g$)	personal income (PI)
intermediate goods	net private domestic investment	disposable income (DI)
final goods	government purchases (*G*)	nominal GDP
multiple counting	net exports (*X*$_n$)	real GDP
value added	taxes on production and imports	price index
expenditures approach	national income	
income approach	consumption of fixed capital	

Study Questions

1. In what ways are national income statistics useful?

2. Explain why an economy's output, in essence, is also its income.

3. **KEY QUESTION** Why do economists include only final goods in measuring GDP for a particular year? Why don't they include the value of the stocks and bonds bought and sold? Why don't they include the value of the used furniture bought and sold?

4. What is the difference between gross private domestic investment and net private domestic investment? If you were to determine net domestic product (NDP) through the expenditures approach, which of these two measures of investment spending would be appropriate? Explain.

5. Why are changes in inventories included as part of investment spending? Suppose inventories declined by $1 billion during 2006. How would this affect the size of gross private domestic investment and gross domestic product in 2006? Explain.

6. Use the concepts of gross investment and net investment to distinguish between an economy that has a rising stock of capital and one that has a falling stock of capital. "In 1933 net private domestic investment was minus $6 billion. This means that in that particular year the economy produced no capital goods at all." Do you agree? Why or why not? Explain: "Though net investment can be positive, negative, or zero, it is quite impossible for gross investment to be less than zero."

7. Define net exports. Explain how U.S. exports and imports each affect domestic production. Suppose foreigners spend $7 billion on U.S. exports in a specific year and Americans spend $5 billion on imports from abroad in the same year. What is the amount of the United States' net exports? Explain how net exports might be a negative amount.

8. **KEY QUESTION** Below is a list of domestic output and national income figures for a certain year. All figures are in billions. The questions that follow ask you to determine the major national income measures by both the expenditures and the income approaches. The results you obtain with the different methods should be the same.

Personal consumption expenditures	$245
Net foreign factor income	4
Transfer payments	12
Rents	14
Statistical discrepancy	−8
Consumption of fixed capital (depreciation)	27
Social Security contributions	20
Interest	13
Proprietors' income	33
Net exports	11
Dividends	16

Compensation of employees	223
Taxes on production and imports	18
Undistributed corporate profits	21
Personal taxes	26
Corporate income taxes	19
Corporate profits	56
Government purchases	72
Net private domestic investment	33
Personal saving	20

a. Using the above data, determine GDP by both the expenditures and the income approaches. Then determine NDP.

b. Now determine NI in two ways: first, by making the required additions or subtractions from NDP; and second, by adding up the types of income and taxes that make up NI.

c. Adjust NI (from part *b*) as required to obtain PI.

d. Adjust PI (from part *c*) as required to obtain DI.

9. Using the following national income accounting data, compute (*a*) GDP, (*b*) NDP, and (*c*) NI. All figures are in billions.

Compensation of employees	$194.2
U.S. exports of goods and services	17.8
Consumption of fixed capital	11.8
Government purchases	59.4
Taxes on production and imports	14.4
Net private domestic investment	52.1
Transfer payments	13.9
U.S. imports of goods and services	16.5
Personal taxes	40.5
Net foreign factor income	2.2
Personal consumption expenditures	219.1
Statistical discrepancy	0

10. Why do national income accountants compare the market value of the total outputs in various years rather than actual physical volumes of production? What problem is posed by any comparison over time of the market values of various total outputs? How is this problem resolved?

11. **KEY QUESTION** Suppose that in 1984 the total output in a single-good economy was 7000 buckets of chicken. Also suppose that in 1984 each bucket of chicken was priced at $10. Finally, assume that in 2000 the price per bucket of chicken was $16 and that 22,000 buckets were produced. Determine the GDP price index for 1984, using 2000 as the base year. By what percentage did the price level, as measured by this index, rise between 1984 and 2000? Use the two methods listed in Table 6.6 to determine real GDP for 1984 and 2000.

12. **KEY QUESTION** The following table shows nominal GDP and an appropriate price index for a group of selected years. Compute real GDP. Indicate in each calculation whether you are inflating or deflating the nominal GDP data.

Year	Nominal GDP, Billions	Price Index (2000 = 100)	Real GDP, Billions
1964	$ 663.6	22.13	$_____
1974	1500.0	34.73	$_____
1984	3933.2	67.66	$_____
1994	7072.2	90.26	$_____
2004	11,734,3	109.10	$_____

13. Which of the following are included in this year's GDP? Explain your answer in each case.
   a. Interest on an AT&T corporate bond.
   b. Social Security payments received by a retired factory worker.
   c. The unpaid services of a family member in painting the family home.
   d. The income of a dentist.
   e. The money received by Smith when she sells her economics textbook to a book buyer.
   f. The monthly allowance a college student receives from home.
   g. Rent received on a two-bedroom apartment.
   h. The money received by Josh when he resells his current-year-model Honda automobile to Kim.
   i. The publication of a college textbook.
   j. A 2-hour decrease in the length of the workweek.
   k. The purchase of an AT&T corporate bond.
   l. A $2 billion increase in business inventories.
   m. The purchase of 100 shares of GM common stock.
   n. The purchase of an insurance policy.

14. **LAST WORD** What government agency compiles the U.S. NIPA tables? In what U.S. department is it located? Of the several specific sources of information, name one source for each of the four components of GDP: consumption, investment, government purchases, and net exports.

Web-Based Questions

1. **UPDATE THE KEY NATIONAL INCOME AND PRODUCT ACCOUNT NUMBERS** Go to the Bureau of Economic Analysis Web site, **www.bea.gov,** and access the BEA interactively by selecting National Income and Product Account Tables. Select Frequently Requested NIPA Tables, and find Table 1.1 on GDP. Update the data in the left column of the text's Table 6.3, using the latest available quarterly data. Search the full list of NIPA tables to find the latest reported data for national income (NI), personal income (PI), and disposable income (DI). Update the data in the text's Table 6.4 for these three items. By what percentages are GDP, NI, PI, and DI higher (or lower) than the numbers in the table?

2. **NOMINAL GDP AND REAL GDP—BOTH UP?** Visit the Bureau of Economic Analysis Web site, **www.bea.gov**, and access the BEA interactively by selecting National Income and Product Account Tables. Select Frequently Requested NIPA Tables, and use Tables 1.1 and 1.2 to identify the GDP (nominal GDP) and real GDP for the past four quarters. Why was nominal GDP greater than real GDP in each of those quarters? What were the percentage changes in nominal GDP and real GDP for the most recent quarter? What accounts for the difference?

3. **GDPs IN THE AMERICAS—HOW DO NATIONS COMPARE?** Visit the World Bank Web site, **www.worldbank.org,** and type "GDP" in the search space. Find the latest data for total GDP (not PPP GDP) for the North and South America countries listed. Arrange the countries by highest to lowest GDPs, and express their GDPs as ratios of U.S. GDP. What general conclusion can you draw from your ratios?

7

Introduction to Economic Growth and Instability

Between 1996 and 2000, real GDP in the United States expanded briskly and the price level rose only slowly. The economy experienced neither significant unemployment nor inflation. Some observers felt that the United States had entered a "new era" in which the business cycle was dead. But that wishful thinking came to an end in March 2001, when the economy entered its ninth recession since 1950. Since 1970, real GDP has declined in the United States in five periods: 1973–1975, 1980, 1981–1982, 1990–1991, and 2001.

Although the U.S. economy has experienced remarkable economic growth over time, high unemployment or inflation has sometimes been a problem. For example, between March 2001 and December 2001, unemployment rose by 2.2 million workers. The U.S. rate of inflation was 13.5 percent in 1980 and 5.4 percent in 1990. Further, other nations have suffered high unemployment rates or inflation rates in recent years. For example, the unemployment rate in Germany reached 10.7 percent in 2005. The inflation rate was 585 percent in Zimbabwe in 2005.

In this chapter we provide an introductory look at the trend of real GDP growth in the United States and the macroeconomic instability that has occasionally accompanied it. Our specific topics are economic growth, the business cycle, unemployment, and inflation.

Economic Growth

Economists define and measure **economic growth** as either:

- An increase in real GDP occurring over some time period.
- An increase in real GDP per capita occurring over some time period.

With either definition, economic growth is calculated as a percentage rate of growth per quarter (3-month period) or per year. For the first definition, for example, real GDP in the United States was $10,755.7 billion in 2004 and $11,134.8 billion in 2005. So the rate of economic growth in the United States for 2005 was 3.5 percent {= [$11,134.8 billion − $10,755.7 billion)/$10,755.7 bilion] × 100}.

The second definition takes into consideration the size of the population. **Real GDP per capita** (or per capita output) is found by dividing real GDP by the size of the population. The resulting number is then compared in percentage terms with that of the previous period. For example, in the United States real GDP was $10,755.7 billion in 2004 and population was 293.9 million. So that year real U.S. GDP per capita was $36,596. In 2005, real per capita GDP rose to $37,536. So the rate of growth of GDP per capita for 2005 was 2.6 percent {= [$37,536 − $36,596/$36,596] × 100}.

For measuring expansion of military potential or political preeminence, the growth of real GDP is more useful. Unless specified otherwise, growth rates reported in the news and by international agencies use this definition of economic growth. For comparing living standards, however, the second definition is superior. While China's GDP in 2004 was $1938 billion compared with Denmark's $220 billion, Denmark's real GDP per capita was $40,750 compared with China's meager $1500. And in some cases growth of real GDP can be misleading. Madagascar's real GDP grew at a rate of 1.7 percent per year from 1990–2004. But over the same period its annual population growth was 2.9 percent, resulting in a decline in real GDP per capita of roughly 1.2 percent per year. **(Key Question 2)**

Growth as a Goal

Growth is a widely held economic goal. The expansion of total output relative to population results in rising real wages and incomes and thus higher standards of living. An economy that is experiencing economic growth is better able to meet people's wants and resolve socioeconomic problems. Rising real wages and income provide richer opportunities to individuals and families—a vacation trip, a personal computer, a higher education—without sacrificing other opportunities and pleasures. A growing economy can undertake new programs to alleviate poverty embrace diversity, cultivate the arts, and protect the environment without impairing existing levels of consumption, investment, and public goods production.

In short, *growth lessens the burden of scarcity*. A growing economy, unlike a static economy, can consume more today while increasing its capacity to produce more in the future. By easing the burden of scarcity—by relaxing society's constraints on production—economic growth enables a nation to attain its economic goals more readily and to undertake new endeavors that require the use of goods and services to be accomplished.

Arithmetic of Growth

Why do economists pay so much attention to small changes in the rate of economic growth? Because those changes really matter! For the United States, with a current real GDP of about $12.5 trillion, the difference between a 3 percent and a 4 percent rate of growth is about $125 billion of output each year. For a poor country, a difference of one-half of a percentage point in the rate of growth may mean the difference between starvation and mere hunger.

The mathematical approximation called the **rule of 70** provides a quantitative grasp of the effect of economic growth. It tells us that we can find the number of years it will take for some measure to double, given its annual percentage increase, by dividing that percentage increase into the number 70. So

$$\text{Approximate number of years required to double real GDP} = \frac{70}{\text{annual percentage rate of growth}}$$

Examples: A 3 percent annual rate of growth will double real GDP in about 23 (= 70 ÷ 3) years. Growth of 8 percent per year will double real GDP in about 9 (= 70 ÷ 8) years. The rule of 70 is applicable generally. For example, it works for estimating how long it will take the price level or a savings account to double at various percentage rates of inflation or interest. When compounded over many years, an apparently small difference in the rate of growth thus becomes highly significant. Suppose China and Italy have identical GDPs, but China grows at an 8 percent yearly rate, while Italy grows at 2 percent. China's GDP would double in about 9 years, while Italy's GDP would double in 35 years.

W 7.1

GDP growth

Main Sources of Growth

Society can increase its real output and income in two fundamental ways: (1) by increasing its inputs of resources, and (2) by increasing the productivity of those inputs. Other things equal, increases in land, labor, capital, and entrepreneurial resources yield additional output. But economic growth also occurs through increases in **productivity**—measured broadly as real output per unit of input. Productivity rises when the health, training, education, and motivation of workers are improved; when workers have more and better machinery and natural resources with which to work; when production is better organized and managed; and when labor is reallocated from less efficient industries to more efficient industries. About one-third of U.S. growth comes from more inputs. The remaining two-thirds results from improved productivity.

Growth in the United States

Table 7.1 gives an overview of economic growth in the United States over past periods. Column 2 reveals strong growth as measured by increases in real GDP. Note that between 1950 and 2005 real GDP increased about 6 fold. But the U.S. population also increased. Nevertheless, in column 4 we find that real GDP per capita rose more than threefold over these years.

What has been the *rate* of U.S. growth? Real GDP grew at an annual rate of about 3.5 percent between 1950 and 2005. Real GDP per capita increased 2.3 percent per year over that time. But we must qualify these raw numbers in several ways:

- **Improved products and services** Since the numbers in Table 7.1 do not fully account for the improvements in products and services, they understate the

TABLE 7.1 Real GDP and Per Capita Real GDP, Selected Years, 1950–2005

(1) Year	(2) Real GDP, Billions of 2000 $	(3) Population, Millions	(4) Real Per Capita GDP, 2000 $ (2) ÷ (3)
1950	$ 1773.3	152	$11,666
1960	2501.8	181	13,822
1970	3771.9	205	18,400
1980	5161.7	228	22,639
1990	7112.7	250	28,451
2000	9817.0	267	36,768
2005	11,134.8	297	37,491

Source: Data are from the Bureau of Economic Analysis, **www.bea.doc.gov**, and the U.S. Census Bureau, **www.census.gov**.

growth of economic well-being. Such purely quantitative data do not fully compare an era of iceboxes and LPs with an era of refrigerators and CDs.

- **Added leisure** The increases in real GDP and per capita GDP identified in Table 7.1 were accomplished despite increases in leisure. The standard workweek, once 50 hours, is now about 35 hours (excluding overtime hours). Again the raw growth numbers understate the gain in economic well-being.

- **Other impacts** These measures of growth do not account for any effects growth may have had on the environment and the quality of life. If growth debases the physical environment and creates a stressful work environment, the bare growth numbers will overstate the gains in well-being that result from growth. On the other hand, if growth leads to stronger environmental protections and greater human security, these numbers will understate the gains in well-being.

Relative Growth Rates

Viewed from the perspective of the last half-century, economic growth in the United States lagged behind that in Japan, Germany, Italy, Canada, and France. Japan's annual growth rate, in fact, averaged twice that of the United States. But more recent economic growth is quite another matter. As shown in Global Perspective 7.1, in the late 1990s the U.S. growth rate exceeded those in several other industrial countries, including Japan and Germany. After stalling in 2001, the U.S. growth rate again climbed above the rates in those nations.

Average Annual Growth Rates, 1997–2005, Selected Nations

Between 1997 and 2005, economic growth in the United States generally was greater than that in several other major countries.

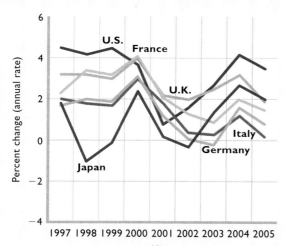

Source: Economic Report of the President, 2006.

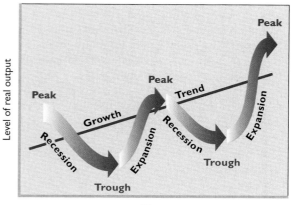

FIGURE 7.1 The business cycle. Economists distinguish four phases of the business cycle; the duration and strength of each phase may vary.

- A **recession** is a period of decline in total output, income, and employment. This downturn, which lasts 6 months or more, is marked by the widespread contraction of business activity in many sectors of the economy. Along with declines in real GDP, significant increases in unemployment occur. Table 7.2 documents the 10 recessions in the United States since 1950.

- In the **trough** of the recession or depression, output and employment "bottom out" at their lowest levels. The trough phase may be either short-lived or quite long.

- A recession is usually followed by a recovery and **expansion,** a period in which real GDP, income, and employment rise. At some point, the economy again

The Business Cycle

We have seen that the long-run trend of the U.S. economy is one of economic growth. But growth has been interrupted by periods of economic instability usually associated with **business cycles.** Business cycles are alternating rises and declines in the level of economic activity, sometime over several years. Individual cycles (one "up" followed by one "down") vary substantially in duration and intensity.

O 7.1
Business cycles

Phases of the Business Cycle

Figure 7.1 shows the four phases of a generalized business cycle:

- At a **peak,** such as the middle peak shown in Figure 7.1, business activity has reached a temporary maximum. Here the economy is near or at full employment and the level of real output is at or very close to the economy's capacity. The price level is likely to rise during this phase.

TABLE 7.2 U.S. Recessions since 1950

Period	Duration, Months	Depth (Decline in Real Output)
1953–54	10	−3.7%
1957–58	8	−3.9
1960–61	10	−1.6
1969–70	11	−1.0
1973–75	16	−4.9
1980	6	−2.3
1981–82	16	−3.3
1990–91	8	−1.8
2001	8	−0.5

Source: Economic Report of the President, 1993, updated.

approaches full employment. If spending then expands more rapidly than does production capacity, prices of nearly all goods and services will rise. In other words, inflation will occur.

Although business cycles all pass through the same phases, they vary greatly in duration and intensity. Many economists prefer to talk of business "fluctuations" rather than cycles because cycles imply regularity while fluctuations do not. The Great Depression of the 1930s resulted in a 40 percent decline in real GDP over a 3-year period in the United States and seriously impaired business activity for a decade. By comparison, more recent U.S. recessions, detailed in Table 7.2, were relatively mild in both intensity and duration.

Recessions, of course, occur in other countries, too. At one time or another during the past 10 years Argentina, Brazil, Colombia, Japan, Indonesia, Mexico, Germany, and South Korea experienced recessions.

Causation: A First Glance

Economists have suggested many theories to explain fluctuations in business activity. Some say that momentous innovations, such as the railroad, the automobile, synthetic fibers, and microchips, have great impact on investment and consumption spending and therefore on output, employment, and the price level. Such major innovations occur irregularly and thus contribute to the variability of economic activity.

Some economists see major changes in productivity as causes of business cycles. When productivity expands, the economy booms; when productivity falls, the economy recedes. Still others view the business cycle as a purely monetary phenomenon. When government creates too much money, they say, an inflationary boom occurs. Too little money triggers a decline in output and employment and, eventually, in the price level.

Most economists, however, believe that the immediate cause of cyclical changes in the levels of real output and employment is changes in the level of total spending. In a market economy, businesses produce goods or services only if they can sell them at a profit. If total spending sinks, many businesses find that producing their current volume of goods and services is no longer profitable. As a consequence, output, employment, and incomes all fall. When the level of spending rises, an increase in production becomes profitable, and output, employment, and incomes will rise accordingly. Once the economy nears full employment, however, further gains in real output become more difficult to achieve. Continued increases

in spending may raise the price level as consumers bid for the limited amount of goods available.

We have seen that the long-run growth trend of the U.S. economy is one of expansion. Note that the stylized cycle in Figure 7.1 is drawn against a trend of economic growth.

Cyclical Impact: Durables and Nondurables

Although the business cycle is felt everywhere in the economy, it affects different segments in different ways and to different degrees.

Firms and industries producing *capital goods* (for example, housing, commercial buildings, heavy equipment, and farm implements) and *consumer durables* (for example, automobiles, personal computers, refrigerators) are affected most by the business cycle. Within limits, firms can postpone the purchase of capital goods. As the economy recedes, producers frequently delay the purchase of new equipment and the construction of new plants. The business outlook simply does not warrant increases in the stock of capital goods. In good times, capital goods are usually replaced before they depreciate completely. But when recession strikes, firms patch up their old equipment and make do. As a result, investment in capital goods declines sharply. Firms that have excess plant capacity may not even bother to replace all the capital that is depreciating. For them, net investment may be negative. The pattern is much the same for consumer durables such as automobiles and major appliances. When recession occurs and households must trim their budgets, purchases of these goods are often deferred. Families repair their old cars and appliances rather than buy new ones, and the firms producing these products suffer. (Of course, producers of capital goods and consumer durables also benefit most from expansions.)

In contrast, *service* industries and industries that produce *nondurable consumer goods* are somewhat insulated from the most severe effects of recession. People find it difficult to cut back on needed medical and legal services, for example. And a recession actually helps some service firms, such as pawnbrokers and law firms that specialize in bankruptcies. Nor are the purchases of many nondurable goods such as food and clothing easy to postpone. The quantity and quality of purchases of nondurables will decline, but not so much as will purchases of capital goods and consumer durables. **(Key Question 4)**

- Economic growth can be measured as (a) an increase in real GDP over time or (b) an increase in real GDP per capita over time.
- Real GDP in the United States has grown at an average annual rate of about 3.5 percent since 1950; real GDP per capita has grown at roughly a 2.3 percent annual rate over that same period.
- The typical business cycle goes through four phases: peak, recession, trough, and expansion.
- During recession, industries that produce capital goods and consumer durables normally suffer greater output and employment declines than do service and nondurable consumer goods industries.

Unemployment

The twin problems that arise from the business cycle are unemployment and inflation. Let's look at unemployment first.

Measurement of Unemployment

The U.S. Bureau of Labor Statistics (BLS) conducts a nationwide random survey of some 60,000 households each month to determine who is employed and who is not employed. In a series of questions it asks which members of the household are working, unemployed and looking for work, not looking for work, and so on. From the answers it determines an unemployment rate for the entire nation.

Figure 7.2 helps explain the mathematics. The BLS divides the total U.S. population into three groups. One group is made up of people under 16 years of age and people who are institutionalized, for example, in mental hospitals or correctional institutions. Such people are not considered potential members of the labor force.

A second group, labeled "Not in labor force," is composed of adults who are potential workers but are not employed and are not seeking work. For example, they are homemakers, full-time students, or retirees.

The third group is the **labor force,** which constituted about 50 percent of the total population in 2005. The labor force consists of people who are able and willing to work. Both those who are employed and those who are unemployed but actively seeking work are counted as being in the labor force. The **unemployment rate** is the percentage of the labor force unemployed:

$$\text{Unemployment rate} = \frac{\text{unemployed}}{\text{labor force}} \times 100$$

FIGURE 7.2 **The labor force, employment, and unemployment, 2005.** The labor force consists of persons 16 years of age or older who are not in institutions and who are (1) employed or (2) unemployed but seeking employment.

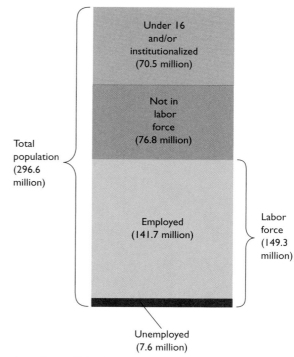

Source: Bureau of Labor Statistics, **www.bls.gov** (civilian labor force data, which excludes military employment).

The statistics included in Figure 7.2 show that in 2005 the unemployment rate averaged

$$\frac{7,591,000}{149,320,000} \times 100 = 5.1\%$$

W 7.2

Unemployment rate

Unemployment rates for selected years appear on the inside covers of this book.

Despite the use of scientific sampling and interviewing techniques, the data collected in this survey are subject to criticism:

- *Part-time employment* The BLS lists all part-time workers as fully employed. In 2005 about 28 million people worked part-time as a result of personal choice. But another 4.4 million part-time workers either wanted to work full-time and could not find suitable full-time work or worked fewer hours because of a temporary slack in consumer demand. These last two groups were, in effect, partially employed and partially unemployed. By counting them as fully employed, say critics, the official BLS data understate the unemployment rate.

- *Discouraged workers* You must be actively seeking work in order to be counted as unemployed. An unemployed individual who is not actively seeking employment is classified as "not in the labor force." The problem is that many workers, after unsuccessfully seeking employment for a time, become discouraged and drop out of the labor force. The number of such **discouraged workers** was 436,000 in 2005. By not counting discouraged workers as unemployed, say critics, the official BLS data understate the unemployment problem. **(Key Question 6)**

Types of Unemployment

There are three *types* of unemployment: frictional, structural, and cyclical.

Frictional Unemployment

At any given time some workers are "between jobs." Some of them will be moving voluntarily from one job to another. Others will have been fired and will be seeking reemployment. Still others will have been laid off temporarily because of seasonal demand. In addition to those between jobs, many young workers will be searching for their first jobs.

As these unemployed people find jobs or are called back from temporary layoffs, other job seekers and laid-off workers will replace them in the "unemployment pool." So even though the workers who are unemployed for such reasons change from month to month, this type of unemployment persists.

Economists use the term **frictional unemployment**—consisting of *search unemployment* and *wait unemployment*—for workers who are either searching for jobs or waiting to take jobs in the near future. The word "frictional" implies that the labor market does not operate perfectly and instantaneously (without friction) in matching workers and jobs.

Frictional unemployment is inevitable and, at least in part, desirable. Many workers who are voluntarily between jobs are moving from low-paying, low-productivity jobs to higher-paying, higher-productivity positions. That means greater income for the workers, a better allocation of labor resources, and a larger real GDP for the economy.

Structural Unemployment

Frictional unemployment blurs into a category called **structural unemployment.** Here, economists use "structural" in the sense of "compositional." Changes over time in consumer demand and in technology alter the "structure" of the total demand for labor, both occupationally and geographically.

Occupationally, the demand for certain skills (for example, sewing clothes or working on farms) may decline or even vanish. The demand for other skills (for example, designing software or maintaining computer systems) will intensify. Unemployment results because the composition of the labor force does not respond immediately or completely to the new structure of job opportunities. Workers who find that their skills and experience have become obsolete or unneeded thus find that they have no marketable talents. They are structurally unemployed until they adapt or develop skills that employers want.

Geographically, the demand for labor also changes over time. An example: migration of industry and thus of employment opportunities from the Snow Belt to the Sun Belt over the past few decades. Another example is the movement of jobs from inner-city factories to suburban industrial parks. As job opportunities shift from one place to another, some workers become structurally unemployed.

The distinction between frictional and structural unemployment is hazy at best. The key difference is that *frictionally* unemployed workers have salable skills and either live in areas where jobs exist or are able to move to areas where they do. *Structurally* unemployed workers find it hard to obtain new jobs without retraining, gaining additional education, or relocating. Frictional unemployment is short-term; structural unemployment is more likely to be long-term and consequently more serious.

Cyclical Unemployment

Unemployment that is caused by a decline in total spending is called **cyclical unemployment** and typically begins in the recession phase of the business cycle. As the demand for goods and services decreases, employment falls and unemployment rises. Cyclical unemployment results from insufficient demand for goods and services. The 25 percent unemployment rate in the depth of the Great Depression in 1933 reflected mainly cyclical unemployment, as did significant parts of the 9.7 percent unemployment rate in 1982, the 7.5 percent rate in 1992, and the 5.8 percent rate in 2002.

Cyclical unemployment is a very serious problem when it occurs. We will say more about its high costs later, but first we need to define "full employment."

Definition of Full Employment

Because frictional and structural unemployment is largely unavoidable in a dynamic economy, *full employment* is something less than 100 percent employment of the labor force. Economists say that the economy is "fully employed" when it is experiencing only frictional and structural unemployment. That is, full employment occurs when there is no cyclical unemployment.

Economists describe the unemployment rate that is consistent with full employment as the **full-employment rate of unemployment,** or the **natural rate of**

unemployment (NRU). At the NRU, the economy is said to be producing its **potential output.** This is the real GDP that occurs when the economy is "fully employed."

The NRU occurs when the number of *job seekers* equals the number of *job vacancies.* Even when labor markets are in balance, however, the NRU is some positive percentage because it takes time for frictionally unemployed job seekers to find open jobs they can fill. Also, it takes time for the structurally unemployed to achieve the skills and geographic relocation needed for reemployment.

"Natural" does not mean, however, that the economy will always operate at this rate and thus realize its potential output. When cyclical unemployment occurs, the economy has much more unemployment than that which would occur at the NRU. Moreover, the economy can operate for a while at an unemployment rate *below* the NRU. At times, the demand for labor may be so great that firms take a stronger initiative to hire and train the structurally unemployed. Also, some homemakers, teenagers, college students, and retirees who were casually looking for just the right part-time or full-time jobs may quickly find them. Thus the unemployment rate temporarily falls below the natural rate.

Also, the NRU can vary over time. In the 1980s, the NRU was about 6 percent. Today, it is 4 to 5 percent. Why the decline?

- The growing proportion of younger workers in the labor force has declined as the baby-boom generation has aged. The labor force now has a larger proportion of middle-aged workers, who traditionally have lower unemployment rates.
- The growth of temporary-help agencies and the improved information resulting from the Internet have lowered the NRU by enabling workers to find jobs more quickly.
- The work requirements under the new welfare laws have moved many people from the ranks of the unemployed to the ranks of the employed.
- The doubling of the U.S. prison population since 1985 has removed relatively high unemployment individuals from the labor force and thus lowered the overall unemployment rate.

A decade ago, a 4 to 5 percent rate of unemployment would have reflected excessive spending, an unbalanced labor market, and rising inflation; today, the same rate is consistent with a balanced labor market and a stable, low rate of inflation.

Economic Cost of Unemployment

Unemployment that is excessive involves great economic and social costs.

GDP Gap and Okun's Law The basic economic cost of unemployment is forgone output. When the economy fails to create enough jobs for all who are able and willing to work, potential production of goods and services is irretrievably lost. In terms of Chapter 1's analysis, unemployment above the natural rate means that society is operating at some point inside its production possibilities curve. Economists call this sacrifice of output a **GDP gap**—the difference between actual and potential GDP. That is:

$$\text{GDP gap} = \text{actual GDP} - \text{potential GDP}$$

The GDP gap can be either negative (actual GDP < potential GDP) or positive (actual GDP > potential GDP). In the case of unemployment above the natural rate, it is negative because actual GDP falls short of potential GDP.

Potential GDP is determined by assuming that the natural rate of unemployment prevails. The growth of potential GDP is simply projected forward on the basis of the economy's "normal" growth rate of real GDP. Figure 7.3 shows the GDP gap for recent years in the United States. It also indicates the close correlation between the actual unemployment rate (Figure 7.3b) and the GDP gap (Figure 7.3a). The higher the unemployment rate, the larger is the GDP gap.

Macroeconomist Arthur Okun was the first to quantify the relationship between the unemployment rate and the GDP gap. On the basis of recent estimates, **Okun's law** indicates that for every 1 percentage point by which

W 7.3
Okun's law

the actual unemployment rate exceeds the natural rate, a negative GDP gap of about 2 percent occurs. With this information, we can calculate the absolute loss of output associated with any above-natural unemployment rate. For example, in 1992 the unemployment rate was 7.4 percent, or 1.4 percentage points above the 6.0 percent natural rate of unemployment then existing. Multiplying this 1.4 percent by Okun's 2 indicates that 1992's GDP gap was 2.8 percent of potential GDP (in real terms). By applying this 2.8 percent loss to 1992's potential GDP of $7337 billion, we find that the economy sacrificed $205 billion of real output because the natural rate of unemployment was not achieved. **(Key Question 8)**

As you can see in Figure 7.3, sometimes the economy's actual output will exceed its potential or full-employment output. Figure 7.3 reveals that an economic expansion in 1999 and 2000, for example, caused actual GDP to exceed potential GDP in those years. There was a positive GDP gap in 1999 and 2000. Actual GDP for a time can exceed potential GDP, but positive GDP gaps create inflationary pressures and cannot be sustained indefinitely.

FIGURE 7.3 Actual and potential GDP and the unemployment rate. (a) The difference between actual and potential GDP is the GDP gap. A negative GDP gap measures the output the economy sacrifices when actual GDP falls short of potential GDP. A positive GDP gap indicates that actual GDP is above potential GDP. (b) A high unemployment rate means a large GDP gap (negative), and a low unemployment rate means a small or even positive GDP gap.

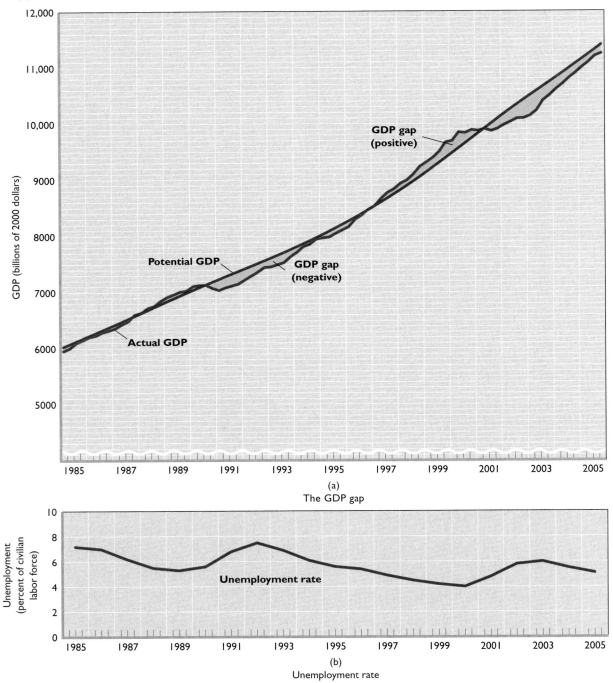

(a)
The GDP gap

(b)
Unemployment rate

Source: Data are from the Congressional Budget Office, **www.cbo.gov/,** and Bureau of Economic Analysis, **www.bea.gov.**

Unequal Burdens An increase in the unemployment rate from 5 to, say, 7 or 8 percent might be more tolerable to society if every worker's hours of work and wage income were reduced proportionally. But this is not the case. Part of the burden of unemployment is that its cost is unequally distributed.

Table 7.3 examines unemployment rates for various labor market groups for 2 years. The 2001 recession pushed the 2002 unemployment rate to 5.8 percent. In 1999, the economy achieved full employment, with a 4.2 percent unemployment rate. By observing the large variance in unemployment rates for the different groups within each year and comparing the rates between the 2 years, we can generalize as follows:

- **Occupation** Workers in lower-skilled occupations (for example, laborers) have higher unemployment rates than workers in higher-skilled occupations (for

TABLE 7.3 Unemployment Rates by Demographic Group: Recession (2002) and Full Employment (1999)*

Demographic Group	Unemployment Rate 2002	1999
Overall	5.8%	4.2%
Occupation:		
Managerial and professional	3.1	1.9
Operators, fabricators, and laborers	8.9	6.3
Age:		
16–19	16.5	13.9
African-American, 16–19	29.8	27.9
White, 16–19	14.5	12.0
Male, 20+	5.3	3.5
Female, 20+	5.1	3.8
Race and ethnicity:		
African-American	10.2	8.0
Hispanic	7.5	6.4
White	5.1	3.7
Gender:		
Women	5.6	4.3
Men	5.9	4.2
Education:†		
Less than high school diploma	8.4	6.0
High school diploma only	5.3	3.5
College degree or more	2.9	1.8
Duration:		
15 or more weeks	2.0	1.1

*Civilian labor-force data. In 2002 the economy was suffering the lingering unemployment effects of the 2001 recession.

†People age 25 or over.

Source: Economic Report of the President; Employment and Earnings; Census Bureau, **www.census.gov.**

example, professionals). Lower-skilled workers have more and longer spells of structural unemployment than higher-skilled workers. They also are less likely to be self-employed than are higher-skilled workers. Moreover, lower-skilled workers usually bear the brunt of recessions. Businesses generally retain most of their higher-skilled workers, in whom they have invested the expense of training.

- **Age** Teenagers have much higher unemployment rates than adults. Teenagers have lower skill levels, quit their jobs more frequently, are more frequently "fired," and have less geographic mobility than adults. Many unemployed teenagers are new in the labor market, searching for their first jobs. Male African-American teenagers, in particular, have very high unemployment rates.
- **Race and ethnicity** The unemployment rate for African-Americans and Hispanics is higher than that for whites. The causes of the higher rates include lower rates of educational attainment, greater concentration in lower-skilled occupations, and discrimination in the labor market. In general, the unemployment rate for African-Americans is twice that of whites.
- **Gender** The unemployment rates for men and women are very similar.
- **Education** Less educated workers, on average, have higher unemployment rates than workers with more education. Less education is usually associated with lower-skilled, less permanent jobs, more time between jobs, and jobs that are more vulnerable to cyclical layoff.
- **Duration** The number of persons unemployed for long periods—15 weeks or more—as a percentage of the labor force is much lower than the overall unemployment rate. But that percentage rises significantly during recessions.

Noneconomic Costs

Severe cyclical unemployment is more than an economic malady; it is a social catastrophe. Depression means idleness. And idleness means loss of skills, loss of self-respect, plummeting morale, family disintegration, and sociopolitical unrest. Widespread joblessness increases poverty, heightens racial and ethnic tensions, and reduces hope for material advancement.

History demonstrates that severe unemployment can lead to rapid and sometimes violent social and political change. Witness Hitler's ascent to power against a background of unemployment in Germany. Furthermore, relatively high unemployment among some racial and ethnic minorities has contributed to the unrest and violence that has periodically plagued some cities in the United States and abroad. At the individual level, research links increases in suicide, homicide, fatal heart attacks and strokes, and mental illness to high unemployment.

International Comparisons

Unemployment rates differ greatly among nations at any given time. One reason is that nations have different natural rates of unemployment. Another is that nations may be in different phases of their business cycles. Global Perspective 7.2 shows unemployment rates for five industrialized nations in recent years. Between 1995 and 2005, the U.S. unemployment rate was considerably lower than the rates in Italy, France, and Germany.

QUICK REVIEW 7.2

- Unemployment is of three general types: frictional, structural, and cyclical.
- The natural unemployment rate (frictional plus structural) is presently 4 to 5 percent in the United States.
- A positive GDP gap occurs when actual GDP exceeds potential GDP; a negative GDP gap occurs when actual GDP falls short of potential GDP.
- Society loses real GDP when cyclical unemployment occurs; according to Okun's law, for each 1 percentage point of unemployment above the natural rate, the U.S. economy suffers a 2 percent decline in real GDP below its potential GDP.
- Lower-skilled workers, teenagers, African-Americans and Hispanics, and less educated workers bear a disproportionate burden of unemployment.

Inflation

We now turn to inflation, another aspect of macroeconomic instability. The problems inflation poses are subtler than those posed by unemployment.

Meaning of Inflation

Inflation is a rise in the general level of prices. When inflation occurs, each dollar of income will buy fewer goods and services than before. Inflation reduces the "purchasing power" of money. But inflation does not mean that *all* prices are rising. Even during periods of rapid inflation, some prices may be relatively constant while others are falling. For example, although the United States experienced high rates of inflation in the 1970s and early 1980s, the prices of video recorders, digital watches, and personal computers declined.

CONSIDER THIS ...

Why Is the Unemployment Rate in Europe So High?

Several European economies have had exceptionally high unemployment rates recently. For example, based on U.S. measurement concepts, the percentage unemployment rate in 2005 in France was 9.7 percent; in Germany, 9.7 percent; in Spain, 9.6 percent; and in Italy, 7.8 percent. Those numbers compare very unfavorably with the 5.1 percent in the United States that year. Furthermore, the high European unemployment rates do not appear to be cyclical. Even during business cycle peaks, the unemployment rates are roughly twice those in the United States. Unemployment rates are particularly high for European youth. For example, the unemployment rate for 20- to 24-year-olds in France was 20 percent in 2005 (compared to 8.8 percent in the United States).

The causes of high unemployment rates in these countries are complex, but European economists generally point to government policies and union contracts that have increased the business costs of hiring workers and have reduced the individual cost of being unemployed. Examples: High legal minimum wages have discouraged employers from hiring low-skilled workers. Generous welfare benefits and unemployment benefits have encouraged absenteeism, led to high job turnover, and weakened incentives for people to take available jobs.

Restrictions on firing of workers have made firms leery of adding workers during expansions. Short work weeks mandated by government or negotiated by unions have limited the ability of employers to spread their recruitment and training costs over a longer number of hours. Paid vacations and holidays of 30 to 40 days per year have boosted the cost of hiring workers. Also, high employer costs of pension and other benefits have discouraged hiring.

Attempts to make labor market more flexible in France, Germany, Italy, and Spain have met with stiff political resistance—including large rallies and protests. The direction of future employment policy is unclear, but economists do not expect the high rates of unemployment in these nations to decline anytime soon.

Measurement of Inflation

The main measure of inflation in the United States is the **Consumer Price Index (CPI),** compiled by the Bureau of Labor Statistics (BLS). The government uses this index

The rate of inflation for a certain year (say, 2005) is found by comparing, in percentage terms, that year's index with the index in the previous year. For example, the CPI was 195.3 in 2005, up from 188.9 in 2004. So the rate of inflation for 2005 is calculated as follows:

$$\text{Rate of inflation} = \frac{195.3 - 188.9}{188.9} \times 100 = 3.4\%$$

Recall that the mathematical approximation called the *rule of 70* tells us that we can find the number of years it will take for some measure to double, given its annual percentage increase, by dividing that percentage increase into the number 70. So a 3 percent annual rate of inflation will double the price level in about 23 (= 70 ÷ 3) years. Inflation of 8 percent per year will double the price level in about 9 (= 70 ÷ 8) years. **(Key Question 11)**

Facts of Inflation

Figure 7.4 shows the annual rates of inflation in the United States between 1960 and 2005. Observe that inflation reached double-digit rates in the 1970s and early 1980s but has since declined and has been relatively mild recently.

In recent years U.S. inflation has been neither unusually high nor low relative to inflation in several other industrial countries (see Global Perspective 7.3). Some nations (not shown) have had double-digit or even higher

GLOBAL PERSPECTIVE 7.2

Unemployment Rates in Five Industrial Nations, 1995–2005

Compared with Italy, France, and Germany, the United States had a relatively low unemployment rate in recent years.

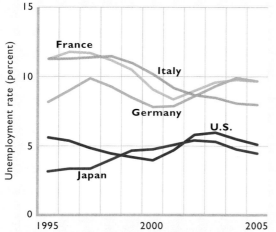

Source: Bureau of Labor Statistics, **www.bls.gov.** Based on U.S. unemployment concepts.

to report inflation rates each month and each year. It also uses the CPI to adjust Social Security benefits and income tax brackets for inflation. The CPI reports the price of a "market basket" of some 300 consumer goods and services that presumably are purchased by a typical urban consumer. (The GDP price index of Chapter 6 is a much broader measure of inflation since it includes not only consumer goods and services but also capital goods, goods and services purchased by government, and goods and services that enter world trade.)

The composition of the market basket for the CPI is based on spending patterns of urban consumers in a specific period, presently 2001–2002. The BLS updates the composition of the market basket every 2 years so that it reflects the most recent patterns of consumer purchases and captures the inflation that consumers are currently experiencing. The BLS arbitrarily sets the CPI equal to 100 for 1982–1984. So the CPI for any particular year is found as follows:

$$\text{CPI} = \frac{\substack{\text{price of the most recent market} \\ \text{basket in the particular year}}}{\substack{\text{price estimate of the same market} \\ \text{basket in 1982–1984}}} \times 100$$

GLOBAL PERSPECTIVE 7.3

Inflation Rates in Five Industrial Nations, 1995–2005

Inflation rates in the United States in recent years were neither extraordinarily high nor extraordinarily low relative to rates in other industrial nations.

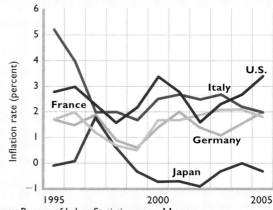

Source: Bureau of Labor Statistics, **www.bls.gov.**

FIGURE 7.4 Annual inflation rates in the United States, 1960–2005. The major periods of inflation in the United States in the past 40 years were in the 1970s and 1980s.

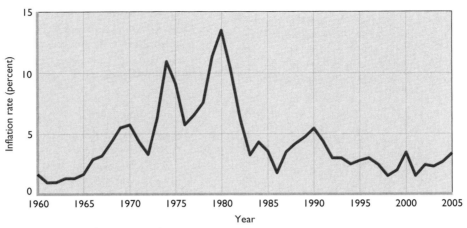

Source: Bureau of Labor Statistics, **stats.bls.gov**

annual rates of inflation in recent years. In 2005, for example, the annual inflation rate in Iraq was 40 percent; in Liberia, 15 percent; and in Azerbaijan, 12 percent. Recall from the chapter opener that inflation was 585 percent in Zimbabwe that year. For 2006, Zimbabwe's inflation rate is expected to reach 1000 percent!

Types of Inflation

Economists sometimes distinguish between two types of inflation: *demand-pull inflation* and *cost-push inflation*.

Demand-Pull Inflation

Usually, changes in the price level are caused by an excess of total spending beyond the economy's capacity to produce. Where inflation is rapid and sustained, the cause invariably is an overissuance of money by the central bank (the Federal Reserve in the United States). When resources are already fully employed, the business sector cannot respond to excess demand by expanding output. So the excess demand bids up the prices of the limited output, producing **demand-pull inflation.** The essence of this type of inflation is "too much spending chasing too few goods."

Cost-Push Inflation

Inflation may also arise on the supply, or cost, side of the economy. During some periods in U.S. economic history, including the mid-1970s, the price level increased even though total spending was not excessive. These were periods when output and employment were both *declining* (evidence that total spending was not excessive) while the general price level was *rising*.

The theory of **cost-push inflation** explains rising prices in terms of factors that raise **per-unit production costs** at each level of spending. A per-unit production cost is the average cost of a particular level of output. This average cost is found by dividing the total cost of all resource inputs by the amount of output produced. That is,

$$\text{Per-unit production cost} = \frac{\text{total input cost}}{\text{unit of output}}$$

Rising per-unit production costs squeeze profits and reduce the amount of output firms are willing to supply at the existing price level. As a result, the economy's supply of goods and services declines and the price level rises. In this scenario, costs are *pushing* the price level upward, whereas in demand-pull inflation demand is *pulling* it upward.

The major source of cost-push inflation has been so-called *supply shocks*. Specifically, abrupt increases in the costs of raw materials or energy inputs have on occasion driven up per-unit production costs and thus product prices. The rocketing prices of imported oil in 1973–1974 and again in 1979–1980 are good illustrations. As energy prices surged upward during these periods, the costs of producing and transporting virtually every product in the economy rose. Rapid cost-push inflation ensued.

Complexities

The real world is more complex than the distinction between demand-pull and cost-push inflation suggests. It is

Clipping Coins

Some interesting early episodes of demand-pull inflation occurred in Europe during the ninth to the fifteenth centuries under feudalism. In that economic system *lords* (or *princes*) ruled individual fiefdoms and their *vassals* (or *peasants*) worked the fields. The peasants initially paid parts of their harvest as taxes to the princes. Later, when the princes began issuing "coins of the realm," peasants began paying their taxes with gold coins.

Some princes soon discovered a way to transfer purchasing power from their vassals to themselves without explicitly increasing taxes. As coins came into the treasury, princes clipped off parts of the gold coins, making them slightly smaller. From the clippings they minted new coins and used them to buy more goods for themselves.

This practice of clipping coins was a subtle form of taxation. The quantity of goods being produced in the fiefdom remained the same, but the number of gold coins increased. With "too much money chasing too few goods," inflation occurred. Each gold coin earned by the peasants therefore had less purchasing power than previously because prices were higher. The increase of the money supply shifted purchasing power away from the peasants and toward the princes just as surely as if the princes had increased taxation of the peasants.

In more recent eras some dictators have simply printed money to buy more goods for themselves, their relatives, and their key loyalists. These dictators, too, have levied hidden taxes on their population by creating inflation.

The moral of the story is quite simple: A society that values price-level stability should not entrust the control of its money supply to people who benefit from inflation.

difficult to distinguish between demand-pull inflation and cost-push inflation unless the original source of inflation is known. For example, suppose a significant increase in total spending occurs in a fully employed economy, causing demand-pull inflation. But as the demand-pull stimulus works its way through various product and resource markets, individual firms find their wage costs, material costs, and fuel prices rising. From their perspective they must raise their prices because production costs (someone else's prices) have risen. Although this inflation is clearly demand-pull in origin, it may mistakenly appear to be cost-push inflation to business firms and to government.

Without proper identification of the source of the inflation, government and the Federal Reserve may be slow to undertake policies to reduce excessive total spending.

Another complexity is that cost-push inflation and demand-pull inflation differ in their sustainability. Demand-pull inflation will continue as long as there is excess total spending. Cost-push inflation is automatically self-limiting; it will die out by itself. Increased per-unit costs will reduce supply, and this means lower real output and employment. Those decreases will constrain further per-unit cost increases. In other words, cost-push inflation generates a recession. And in a recession, households and businesses concentrate on keeping their resources employed, not on pushing up the prices of those resources.

- Inflation is a rising general level of prices and is measured as a percentage change in a price index such as the CPI.
- For the past several years, the U.S. inflation rate has been within the middle range of the rates of other advanced industrial nations and far below the rates experienced by some nations.
- Demand-pull inflation occurs when total spending exceeds the economy's ability to provide goods and services at the existing price level; total spending *pulls* the price level upward.
- Cost-push inflation occurs when factors such as rapid increases in the prices of imported raw materials drive up per-unit production costs at each level of output; higher costs *push* the price level upward.

Redistribution Effects of Inflation

Inflation hurts some people, leaves others unaffected, and actually helps still others. That is, inflation redistributes real income from some people to others. Who gets hurt? Who benefits? Before we can answer, we need some terminology.

Nominal and Real Income There is a difference between money (or nominal) income and real income. **Nominal income** is the number of dollars received as wages, rent, interest, or profits. **Real income** is a measure of the amount of goods and services nominal income can buy; it is the purchasing power of nominal income, or income adjusted for inflation. That is,

$$\text{Real income} = \frac{\text{nominal income}}{\text{price index (in hundredths)}}$$

Inflation need not alter an economy's overall real income—its total purchasing power. It is evident from the above equation that real income will remain the same when nominal income rises at the same percentage rate as does the price index.

But when inflation occurs, not everyone's nominal income rises at the same pace as the price level. Therein lies the potential for redistribution of real income from some to others. If the change in the price level differs from the change in a person's nominal income, his or her real income will be affected. The following rule tells us approximately by how much real income will change:

$$\begin{array}{ccc} \text{Percentage} & \text{percentage} & \text{percentage} \\ \text{change in} \cong & \text{change in} & - \text{change in} \\ \text{real income} & \text{nominal income} & \text{price level} \end{array}$$

W 7.4
Nominal and real income

For example, suppose that the price level rises by 6 percent in some period. If Bob's nominal income rises by 6 percent, his real income will *remain unchanged.* But if his nominal income instead rises by 10 percent, his real income will *increase* by about 4 percent. And if Bob's nominal income rises by only 2 percent, his real income will *decline* by about 4 percent.[1]

Anticipations The redistribution effects of inflation depend on whether or not it is expected. With fully expected or **anticipated inflation,** an income receiver may be able to avoid or lessen the adverse effects of inflation on real income. The generalizations that follow assume **unanticipated inflation**—inflation whose full extent was not expected.

Who Is Hurt by Inflation?

Unanticipated inflation hurts fixed-income recipients, savers, and creditors. It redistributes real income away from them and toward others.

Fixed-Income Receivers People whose incomes are fixed see their real incomes fall when inflation occurs.

---

[1]A more precise calculation uses our equation for real income. In our first illustration above, if nominal income rises by 10 percent from $100 to $110 and the price level (index) rises by 6 percent from 100 to 106, then real income has increased as follows:

$$\frac{\$110}{1.06} = \$103.77$$

The 4 percent increase in real income shown by the simple formula in the text is a reasonable approximation of the 3.77 percent yielded by our more precise formula.

The classic case is the elderly couple living on a private pension or annuity that provides a fixed amount of nominal income each month. They may have retired in, say, 1990 on what appeared to be an adequate pension. However, by 2005 they would have discovered that inflation had cut the purchasing power of that pension—their real income—by one-third.

Similarly, landlords who receive lease payments of fixed dollar amounts will be hurt by inflation as they receive dollars of declining value over time. Likewise, public sector workers whose incomes are dictated by fixed pay schedules may suffer from inflation. The fixed "steps" (the upward yearly increases) in their pay schedules may not keep up with inflation. Minimum-wage workers and families living on fixed welfare incomes will also be hurt by inflation.

Savers Unanticipated inflation hurts savers. As prices rise, the real value, or purchasing power, of an accumulation of savings deteriorates. Paper assets such as savings accounts, insurance policies, and annuities that were once adequate to meet rainy-day contingencies or provide for a comfortable retirement decline in real value during inflation. The simplest case is the person who hoards money as a cash balance. A $1000 cash balance would have lost one-half its real value between 1982 and 2005. Of course, most forms of savings earn interest. But the value of savings will still decline if the rate of inflation exceeds the rate of interest.

Example: A household may save $1000 in a certificate of deposit (CD) in a commercial bank or savings and loan association at 6 percent annual interest. But if inflation is 13 percent (as it was in 1980), the real value or purchasing power of that $1000 will be cut to about $938 by the end of the year. Although the saver will receive $1060 (equal to $1000 plus $60 of interest), deflating that $1060 for 13 percent inflation means that its real value is only about $938 (= $1060 ÷ 1.13).

Creditors Unanticipated inflation harms creditors (lenders). Suppose Chase Bank lends Bob $1000, to be repaid in 2 years. If in that time the price level doubles, the $1000 that Bob repays will have only half the purchasing power of the $1000 he borrowed. True, if we ignore interest charges, the same number of dollars will be repaid as was borrowed. But because of inflation, each of those dollars will buy only half as much as it did when the loan was negotiated. As prices go up, the value of the dollar goes down. So the borrower pays back less valuable dollars than those received from the lender. The owners of Chase Bank suffer a loss of real income.

Who Is Unaffected or Helped by Inflation?

Some people are unaffected by inflation and others are actually helped by it. For the second group, inflation redistributes real income toward them and away from others.

Flexible-Income Receivers
People who have flexible incomes may escape inflation's harm or even benefit from it. For example, individuals who derive their incomes solely from Social Security are largely unaffected by inflation because Social Security payments are *indexed* to the CPI. Benefits automatically increase when the CPI increases, preventing erosion of benefits from inflation. Some union workers also get automatic **cost-of-living adjustments (COLAs)** in their pay when the CPI rises, although such increases rarely equal the full percentage rise in inflation.

Some flexible-income receivers and all borrowers are helped by unanticipated inflation. The strong product demand and labor shortages implied by rapid demand-pull inflation may cause some nominal incomes to spurt ahead of the price level, thereby enhancing real incomes. For some, the 3 percent increase in nominal income that occurs when inflation is 2 percent may become a 7 percent increase when inflation is 5 percent. As an example, property owners faced with an inflation-induced real estate boom may be able to boost flexible rents more rapidly than the rate of inflation. Also, some business owners may benefit from inflation. If product prices rise faster than resource prices, business revenues will increase more rapidly than costs. In those cases, the growth rate of profit incomes will outpace the rate of inflation.

Debtors
Unanticipated inflation benefits debtors (borrowers). In our earlier example, Chase Bank's loss of real income from inflation is Bob's gain of real income. Debtor Bob borrows "dear" dollars but, because of inflation, pays back the principal and interest with "cheap" dollars whose purchasing power has been eroded by inflation. Real income is redistributed away from the owners of Chase Bank toward borrowers such as Bob.

The Federal government, which had amassed $7.9 trillion of public debt through 2005 has also benefited from inflation. Historically, the Federal government regularly paid off its loans by taking out new ones. Inflation permitted the Treasury to pay off its loans with dollars of less purchasing power than the dollars originally borrowed. Nominal national income and therefore tax collections rise with inflation; the amount of public debt owed does not. Thus, inflation reduces the real burden of the public debt to the Federal government.

Anticipated Inflation

The redistribution effects of inflation are less severe or are eliminated altogether if people anticipate inflation and can adjust their nominal incomes to reflect the expected price-level rises. The prolonged inflation that began in the late 1960s prompted many labor unions in the 1970s to insist on labor contracts with cost-of-living adjustment clauses.

Similarly, if inflation is anticipated, the redistribution of income from lender to borrower may be altered. Suppose a lender (perhaps a commercial bank or a savings and loan institution) and a borrower (a household) both agree that 5 percent is a fair rate of interest on a 1-year loan provided the price level is stable. But assume that inflation has been occurring and is expected to be 6 percent over the next year. If the bank lends the household $100 at 5 percent interest, the bank will be paid back $105 at the end of the year. But if 6 percent inflation does occur during that year, the purchasing power of the $105 will have been reduced to about $99. The lender will, in effect, have paid the borrower $1 for the use of the lender's money for a year.

The lender can avoid this subsidy by charging an *inflation premium*—that is, by raising the interest rate by 6 percent, the amount of the anticipated inflation. By charging 11 percent, the lender will receive back $111 at the end of the year. Adjusted for the 6 percent inflation, that amount will have the purchasing power of today's $105. The result then will be a mutually agreeable transfer of purchasing power from borrower to lender of $5, or 5 percent, for the use of $100 for 1 year. Financial institutions have also developed variable-interest-rate mortgages to protect themselves from the adverse effects of inflation. (Incidentally, this example points out that, rather than being a *cause* of inflation, high nominal interest rates are a *consequence* of inflation.)

Our example reveals the difference between the real rate of interest and the nominal rate of interest. The **real interest rate** is the percentage increase in *purchasing power* that the borrower pays the lender. In our example the real interest rate is 5 percent. The **nominal interest rate** is the percentage increase in *money* that the borrower pays the lender, including that resulting from the built-in expectation of inflation, if any. In equation form:

O 7.2

Real interest rates

$$\text{Nominal interest rate} = \text{real interest rate} + \text{inflation premium (the expected rate of inflation)}$$

FIGURE 7.5 The inflation premium and nominal and real interest rates. The inflation premium—the expected rate of inflation—gets built into the nominal interest rate. Here, the nominal interest rate of 11 percent comprises the real interest rate of 5 percent plus the inflation premium of 6 percent.

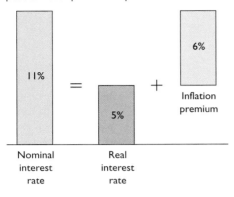

As illustrated in Figure 7.5, the nominal interest rate in our example is 11 percent.

Addenda

We end our discussion of the redistribution effects of inflation by making three final points:

- *Deflation* The effects of unanticipated **deflation**—declines in the price level—are the reverse of those of inflation. People with fixed nominal incomes will find their real incomes enhanced. Creditors will benefit at the expense of debtors. And savers will discover that the purchasing power of their savings has grown because of the falling prices.

- *Mixed effects* A person who is an income earner, a holder of financial assets, and an owner of real assets simultaneously will probably find that the redistribution impact of inflation is cushioned. If the person owns fixed-value monetary assets (savings accounts, bonds, and insurance policies), inflation will lessen their real value. But that same inflation may increase the real value of any property assets (a house, land) that the person owns. In short, many individuals are simultaneously hurt and benefited by inflation. All these effects must be considered before we can conclude that any particular person's net position is better or worse because of inflation.

- *Arbitrariness* The redistribution effects of inflation occur regardless of society's goals and values. Inflation lacks a social conscience and takes from some and

gives to others, whether they are rich, poor, young, old, healthy, or infirm.

Does Inflation Affect Output?

Thus far, our discussion has focused on how inflation redistributes a given level of total real income. But inflation may also affect an economy's level of real output (and thus its level of real income). The direction and significance of this effect on output depends on the type of inflation and its severity.

Cost-Push Inflation and Real Output

Recall that abrupt and unexpected rises in key resource prices such as oil can sufficiently drive up overall production costs to cause cost-push inflation. As prices rise, the quantity of goods and services demanded falls. So firms respond by producing less output, and unemployment goes up.

Economic events of the 1970s provide an example of how inflation can reduce real output. In late 1973 the Organization of Petroleum Exporting Countries (OPEC), by exerting its market power, managed to quadruple the price of oil. The cost-push inflationary effects generated rapid price-level increases in the 1973–1975 period. At the same time, the U.S. unemployment rate rose from slightly less than 5 percent in 1973 to 8.5 percent in 1975. Similar outcomes occurred in 1979–1980 in response to a second OPEC oil supply shock.

In short, cost-push inflation reduces real output. It redistributes a decreased level of real income.

Demand-Pull Inflation and Real Output

Economists do not fully agree on the effects of mild inflation (less than 3 percent) on real output. One perspective is that even low levels of inflation reduce real output, because inflation diverts time and effort toward activities designed to hedge against inflation. Examples:

- Businesses must incur the cost of changing thousands of prices on their shelves and in their computers simply to reflect inflation.
- Households and businesses must spend considerable time and effort obtaining the information they need to distinguish between real and nominal values such as prices, wages, and interest rates.
- To limit the loss of purchasing power from inflation, people try to limit the amount of money they hold in their billfolds and checking accounts at any one time and instead put more money into interest-bearing accounts and stock and bond funds. But cash and checks are needed in even greater amounts to buy the higher-priced goods and services. So more frequent trips, phone calls, or Internet visits to financial institutions are required to transfer funds to checking accounts and billfolds, when needed.

Without inflation, these uses of resources, time, and effort would not be needed, and they could be diverted toward producing more valuable goods and services. Proponents of "zero inflation" bolster their case by pointing to cross-country studies that indicate that lower rates of inflation are associated with higher rates of economic growth. Even mild inflation, say these economists, is detrimental to economic growth.

In contrast, other economists point out that full employment and economic growth depend on strong levels of total spending. Such spending creates high profits, strong demand for labor, and a powerful incentive for firms to expand their plants and equipment. In this view, the mild inflation that is a by-product of strong spending is a small price to pay for full employment and continued economic growth. Moreover, a little inflation may have positive effects because it makes it easier for firms to adjust real wages downward when the demands for their products fall. With mild inflation, firms can reduce real wages by holding nominal wages steady. With zero inflation firms would need to cut nominal wages to reduce real wages. Such cuts in nominal wages are highly visible and may cause considerable worker resistance and labor strife.

Finally, defenders of mild inflation say that it is much better for an economy to err on the side of strong spending, full employment, economic growth, and mild inflation than on the side of weak spending, unemployment, recession, and deflation.

Hyperinflation

All economists agree that **hyperinflation,** which is extraordinarily rapid inflation, can have a devastating impact on real output and employment.

As prices shoot up sharply and unevenly during hyperinflation, people begin to anticipate even more rapid inflation and normal economic relationships are disrupted. Business owners do not know what to charge for their products. Consumers do not know what to pay. Resource suppliers want to be paid with actual output, rather than with rapidly depreciating money. Creditors avoid debtors to keep them from repaying their debts with cheap money. Money eventually becomes almost worthless and ceases to do its job as a medium of exchange. Businesses, anticipating further price increases, may find that hoarding both materials and finished products is profitable. Individual savers may decide to buy nonproductive wealth—jewels, gold, and other precious metals, real estate, and so forth—rather than providing funds that can be borrowed to purchase capital equipment. The economy may be thrown into a state of barter, and production and exchange drop further. The net result is economic collapse and, often, political chaos.

Examples of hyperinflation are Germany after the First World War and Japan after the Second World War. In Germany, "prices increased so rapidly that waiters changed the prices on the menu several times during the course of a lunch. Sometimes customers had to pay double the price listed on the menu when they ordered."[2] In postwar Japan, in 1947 "fisherman and farmers . . . used scales to weigh currency and change, rather than bothering to count it."[3]

There are also more recent examples: Between June 1986 and March 1991 the cumulative inflation in Nicaragua was 11,895,866,143 percent. From November 1993 to December 1994 the cumulative inflation rate in the Democratic Republic of Congo was 69,502 percent. From February 1993 to January 1994 the cumulative inflation rate in Serbia was 156,312,790 percent.[4]

Such dramatic hyperinflations are almost invariably the consequence of highly imprudent expansions of the money supply by government. The rocketing money supply produces frenzied total spending and severe demand-pull inflation.

---

[2]Theodore Morgan, *Income and Employment*, 2nd ed. (Englewood Cliffs, N.J.: Prentice-Hall, 1952), p. 361.
[3]Raburn M. Williams, *Inflation! Money, Jobs, and Politicians* (Arlington Heights, Ill.: AHM Publishing, 1980), p. 2.
[4]Stanley Fischer, Ratna Sahay, and Carlos Végh, "Modern Hyper- and High Inflations," *Journal of Economic Literature*, September 2002, p. 840.

The Stock Market and the Economy

How, If at All, Do Changes in Stock Prices Relate to Macroeconomic Instability?

Every day, the individual stocks (ownership shares) of thousands of corporations are bought and sold in the stock market. The owners of the individual stocks receive dividends—a portion of the firm's profit. Supply and demand in the stock market determine the price of each firm's stock, with individual stock prices generally rising and falling in concert with the collective expectations for each firm's profits. Greater profits normally result in higher dividends to the stock owners, and, in anticipation of higher dividends, people are willing to pay a higher price for the stock.

The media closely monitor and report stock market averages such as the Dow Jones Industrial Average (DJIA)—the weighted-average price of the stocks of 30 major U.S. industrial firms. It is common for these price averages to change over time or even to rise or fall sharply during a single day. On "Black Monday," October 19, 1987, the DJIA fell by 20 percent. A sharp drop in stock prices also occurred in October 1997, mainly in response to rapid declines in stock prices in Hong Kong and other southeast Asia stock markets. In contrast, the stock market averages rose spectacularly in 1998 and 1999, with the DJIA rising 16 and 25 percent in those two years. In 2002, the DJIA fell 17 percent. In 2003, it rose by 25 percent.

The volatility of the stock market raises this question: Do changes in stock price averages and thus stock market wealth cause macroeconomic instability? Linkages between the stock market and the economy might lead us to answer "yes." Consider a sharp increase in stock prices. Feeling wealthier, stock owners respond by increasing their spending (the *wealth effect*). Firms react by increasing their purchases of new capital goods, because they can finance such purchases through issuing new shares of high-valued stock (the *investment effect*). Of course, sharp declines in stock prices would produce the opposite results.

Studies find that changes in stock prices do affect consumption and investment but that these consumption and investment impacts are relatively weak. For example, a 10 percent sustained increase in stock market values in 1 year is associated with a 4 percent increase in consumption spending over the next 3 years. The investment response is even weaker. So typical day-to-day and year-to-year changes in stock market values have little impact on the macroeconomy.

In contrast, *stock market bubbles* can be detrimental to an economy. Such bubbles are huge run-ups of overall stock prices, caused by excessive optimism and frenzied buying. The rising stock values are unsupported by realistic prospects of the future strength of the economy and the firms operating in it. Rather than slowly decompress, such bubbles may burst and cause harm to the economy. The free fall of stock values, if long-lasting, causes reverse wealth effects. The stock market crash may also create an overall pessimism about the economy that undermines consumption and investment spending even further.

A related question: Even though typical changes in stock prices do not cause recession or inflation, might they predict such maladies? That is, since stock market values are based on expected profits, wouldn't we expect rapid changes in stock price averages to forecast changes in future business conditions? Indeed, stock prices often do fall prior to recessions and rise prior to expansions. For this reason stock prices are among a group of 10 variables that constitute an index of leading indicators (Last Word, Chapter 11). Such an index may provide a useful clue to the future direction of the economy. But taken alone, stock market prices are not a reliable predictor of changes in GDP. Stock prices have fallen rapidly in some instances with no recession following. Black Monday itself did not produce a recession during the following 2 years. In other instances, recessions have occurred with no prior decline in stock market prices.

Summary

1. Economic growth may be defined as either (a) an increase of real GDP over time or (b) an increase in real GDP per capita over time. Growth lessens the burden of scarcity and provides increases in real GDP that can be used to resolve socioeconomic problems. Since 1950, real GDP growth in the United States has been about 3.5 percent annually; real GDP per capita has grown at about a 2.3 percent annual rate.

2. The United States and other industrial economies have gone through periods of fluctuations in real GDP, employment, and the price level. Although they have certain phases in common—peak, recession, trough, expansion—business cycles vary greatly in duration and intensity.

3. Although economists explain the business cycle in terms of such causal factors as major innovations, political events, and money creation, they generally agree that changes in the level of total spending are the immediate causes of fluctuating real output and employment.

4. The business cycle affects all sectors of the economy, though in varying ways and degrees. The cycle has greater effects on output and employment in the capital goods and durable consumer goods industries than in the services and nondurable goods industries.

5. Economists distinguish between frictional, structural, and cyclical unemployment. The full-employment or natural rate of unemployment, which is made up of frictional and structural unemployment, is currently between 4 and 5 percent. The presence of part-time and discouraged workers makes it difficult to measure unemployment accurately.

6. The GDP gap, which can be either a positive or a negative value, is found by subtracting potential GDP from actual GDP. The economic cost of unemployment, as measured by the GDP gap, consists of the goods and services forgone by society when its resources are involuntarily idle. Okun's law suggests that every 1-percentage-point increase in unemployment above the natural rate causes an additional 2 percent negative GDP gap.

7. Inflation is a rise in the general price level and is measured in the United States by the Consumer Price Index (CPI). When inflation occurs, each dollar of income will buy fewer goods and services than before. That is, inflation reduces the purchasing power of money.

8. Unemployment rates and inflation rates vary widely globally. Unemployment rates differ because nations have different natural rates of unemployment and often are in different phases of their business cycles. Inflation and unemployment rates in the United States recently have been in the middle to low range compared with rates in other industrial nations.

9. Economists discern both demand-pull and cost-push (supply-side) inflation. Demand-pull inflation results from an excess of total spending relative to the economy's capacity to produce. The main source of cost-push inflation is abrupt and rapid increases in the prices of key resources. These supply shocks push up per-unit production costs and ultimately raise the prices of consumer goods.

10. Unanticipated inflation arbitrarily redistributes real income at the expense of fixed-income receivers, creditors, and savers. If inflation is anticipated, individuals and businesses may be able to take steps to lessen or eliminate adverse redistribution effects.

11. When inflation is anticipated, lenders add an inflation premium to the interest rate charged on loans. The nominal interest rate thus reflects the real interest rate plus the inflation premium (the expected rate of inflation).

12. Cost-push inflation reduces real output and employment. Proponents of zero inflation argue that even mild demand-pull inflation (1 to 3 percent) reduces the economy's real output. Other economists say that mild inflation may be a necessary by-product of the high and growing spending that produces high levels of output, full employment, and economic growth.

13. Hyperinflation, caused by highly imprudent expansions of the money supply, may undermine the monetary system and cause severe declines in real output.

Terms and Concepts

economic growth	expansion	natural rate of unemployment (NRU)
real GDP per capita	labor force	potential output
rule of 70	unemployment rate	GDP gap
productivity	discouraged workers	Okun's law
business cycles	frictional unemployment	inflation
peak	structural unemployment	Consumer Price Index (CPI)
recession	cyclical unemployment	demand-pull inflation
trough	full-employment rate of unemployment	cost-push inflation

per-unit production costs	unanticipated inflation	nominal interest rate
nominal income	cost-of-living adjustments (COLAs)	deflation
real income	real interest rate	hyperinflation
anticipated inflation		

Study Questions

1. Why is economic growth important? Why could the difference between a 2.5 percent and a 3 percent annual growth rate be of great significance over several decades?

2. **KEY QUESTION** Suppose an economy's real GDP is $30,000 in year 1 and $31,200 in year 2. What is the growth rate of its real GDP? Assume that population is 100 in year 1 and 102 in year 2. What is the growth rate of GDP per capita?

3. Briefly describe the growth record of the United States. Compare the rates of growth of real GDP and real GDP per capita, explaining any differences. Compare the average growth rates of Japan and the United States between 1997 and 2005. To what extent might growth rates understate or overstate economic well-being?

4. **KEY QUESTION** What are the four phases of the business cycle? How long do business cycles last? How do seasonal variations and long-run trends complicate measurement of the business cycle? Why does the business cycle affect output and employment in capital goods industries and consumer durable goods industries more severely than in industries producing consumer nondurables?

5. What factors make it difficult to determine the unemployment rate? Why is it difficult to distinguish between frictional, structural, and cyclical unemployment? Why is unemployment an economic problem? What are the consequences of a negative GDP gap? What are the noneconomic effects of unemployment?

6. **KEY QUESTION** Use the following data to calculate (*a*) the size of the labor force and (*b*) the official unemployment rate: total population, 500; population under 16 years of age or institutionalized, 120; not in labor force, 150; unemployed, 23; part-time workers looking for full-time jobs, 10.

7. Since the United States has an unemployment compensation program that provides income for those out of work, why should we worry about unemployment?

8. **KEY QUESTION** Assume that in a particular year the natural rate of unemployment is 5 percent and the actual rate of unemployment is 9 percent. Use Okun's law to determine the size of the GDP gap in percentage-point terms. If the potential GDP is $500 billion in that year, how much output is being forgone because of cyclical unemployment?

9. Explain how an increase in your nominal income and a decrease in your real income might occur simultaneously. Who loses from inflation? Who loses from unemployment? If you had to choose between (*a*) full employment with a 6 percent annual rate of inflation and (*b*) price stability with an 8 percent unemployment rate, which would you choose? Why?

10. What is the Consumer Price Index (CPI) and how is it determined each month? How does the Bureau of Labor Statistics calculate the rate of inflation from one year to the next? What effect does inflation have on the purchasing power of a dollar? How does it explain differences between nominal and real interest rates? How does deflation differ from inflation?

11. **KEY QUESTION** If the CPI was 110 last year and is 121 this year, what is this year's rate of inflation? What is the "rule of 70"? How long would it take for the price level to double if inflation persisted at (*a*) 2, (*b*) 5, and (*c*) 10 percent per year?

12. Distinguish between demand-pull inflation and cost-push inflation. Which of the two types is most likely to be associated with a negative GDP gap? Which with a positive GDP gap, in which actual GDP exceeds potential GDP?

13. Explain how hyperinflation might lead to a severe decline in total output.

14. Evaluate as accurately as you can how each of the following individuals would be affected by unanticipated inflation of 10 percent per year:

   a. A pensioned railroad worker.

   b. A department-store clerk.

   c. A unionized automobile assembly-line worker.

   d. A heavily indebted farmer.

   e. A retired business executive whose current income comes entirely from interest on government bonds.

   f. The owner of an independent small-town department store.

15. **LAST WORD** Suppose that stock prices were to fall by 10 percent in the stock market. All else equal, would the lower stock prices be likely to cause a decrease in real GDP? How might they predict a decline in real GDP?

Web-Based Questions

1. **WHAT IS THE CURRENT U.S. UNEMPLOYMENT RATE?** Visit the Bureau of Labor Statistics Web Site, **www.bls. gov/news.release/empsit.toc.htm,** and select Employment Situation Summary. What month (and year) is summarized? What was the unemployment rate for that month? How does that rate compare with the rate in the previous month? What were the unemployment rates for adult men, adult women, teenagers, blacks, Hispanics, and whites? How did these rates compare with those a month earlier?

2. **WHAT IS THE CURRENT U.S. INFLATION RATE?** Visit the Bureau of Labor Statistics Web Site, **www.bls.gov/ news.release/cpi.toc.htm,** and select Consumer Price Index Summary. What month (and year) is summarized? What was the CPI-U for the month? What was the rate of inflation (change in the CPI-U) for the month? How does that rate of inflation compare with the rate for the previous month? Which two categories of goods or services had the greatest price increases for the month? Which two had the lowest price increases (or greatest price decreases) for the month?

8

IN THIS CHAPTER YOU WILL LEARN:

- **How changes in income affect consumption (and saving).**

- **About factors other than income that can affect consumption.**

- **How changes in real interest rates affect investment.**

- **About factors other than the real interest rate that can affect investment.**

- **Why changes in investment increase or decrease real GDP by a multiple amount.**

Basic Macroeconomic Relationships*

In Chapter 7 we described economic growth, the business cycle, recession, and inflation. Our eventual goal is to build economic models to explain those occurrences and assess the current status of the economy. This chapter begins that process by examining basic relationships between several economic aggregates. (Recall that to economists "aggregate" means "total" or "combined.") Specifically, this chapter looks at the relationships between:

- income and consumption (and income and saving).
- the interest rate and investment.
- changes in spending and changes in output.

*Note to the Instructor: If you wish to bypass the aggregate expenditures model covered in full in Chapter 9, assigning the present chapter will provide a seamless transition to the AD-AS model of Chapter 10 and the chapters beyond. If you want to cover the aggregate expenditure model, this present chapter provides the necessary building blocks.

What explains the trends in consumption (consumer spending) and saving reported in the news? How do changes in interest rates affect investment? How can initial changes in spending ultimately produce multiplied changes in GDP?

The Income-Consumption and Income-Saving Relationships

The other-things-equal relationship between an economy's income and consumption is one of the best-established relationships in macroeconomics. In examining that relationship, we are also exploring the relationship between income and saving. Recall that economists define *personal saving* as "not spending" or "that part of disposable (after-tax) income not consumed." Saving (S) equals disposable income (DI) *minus* consumption (C).

Many factors determine the nation's levels of consumption and saving, but the most significant is disposable income. Consider some recent historical data for the United States. In Figure 8.1 each dot represents consump-

tion and disposable income for 1 year since 1983. The line *C* that is loosely fitted to these points shows that consumption is directly (positively) related to disposable income; moreover, households spend most of their income.

But we can say more. The **45° (degree) line** is a reference line. Because it bisects the 90° angle formed by the two axes of the graph, each point on it is equidistant from the two axes. At each point on the 45° line, consumption would equal disposable income, or C = DI. Therefore, the vertical distance between the 45° line and any point on the horizontal axis measures either consumption *or* disposable income. If we let it measure disposable income, the vertical distance between it and the consumption line labeled *C* represents the amount of saving (S) in that year. Saving is the amount by which actual

FIGURE 8.1 Consumption and disposable income, 1983–2005. Each dot in this figure shows consumption and disposable income in a specific year. The line C, which generalizes the relationship between consumption and disposable income, indicates a direct relationship and shows that households consume most of their incomes. In the unusual year 2005, they consumed more than their income.

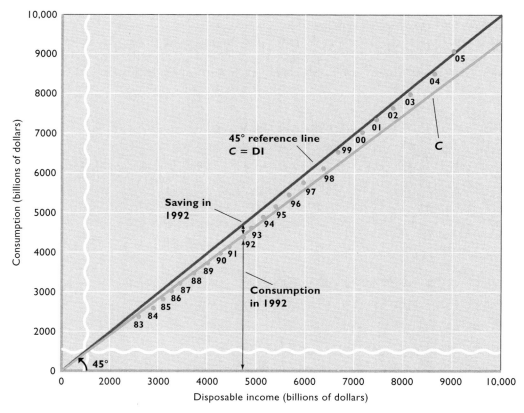

147

consumption in any year falls short of the 45° line—($S =$ DI − C). For example, in 1992 disposable income was $4751 billion and consumption was $4385 billion, so saving was $366 billion. Observe that the vertical distance between the 45° line and line C increases as we move rightward along the horizontal axis and decreases as we move leftward. Like consumption, saving typically varies directly with the level of disposable income. That historical pattern, however, has temporarily broken down in recent years.

The Consumption Schedule

The dots in Figure 8.1 represent historical data—the actual amounts of DI, C, and S in the United States over a period of years. But, for analytical purposes, we need a schedule showing the various amounts that households would *plan* to consume at each of the various levels of disposable income that might prevail at some specific time. Columns 1 and 2 of Table 8.1, represented in **Figure 8.2a (Key Graph),** show the hypothetical consumption schedule that we require. This **consumption schedule** (or "consumption function") reflects the direct consumption–disposable income relationship suggested by the data in Figure 8.1, and it is consistent with many household budget studies. In the aggregate, households increase their spending as their disposable income rises and spend a larger proportion of a small disposable income than of a large disposable income.

O 8.1

Income-consumption relationship

The Saving Schedule

It is relatively easy to derive a **saving schedule** (or "saving function"). Because saving equals disposable income less consumption ($S =$ DI − C), we need only subtract consumption (Table 8.1, column 2) from disposable income (column 1) to find the amount saved (column 3) at each DI. Thus, columns 1 and 3 in Table 8.1 are the saving schedule, represented in Figure 8.2b. The graph shows that there is a direct relationship between saving and DI but that saving is a smaller proportion of a small DI than of a large DI. If households consume a smaller and smaller proportion of DI as DI increases, then they must be saving a larger and larger proportion.

Remembering that at each point on the 45° line consumption equals DI, we see that *dissaving* (consuming in excess of after-tax income) will occur at relatively low DIs. For example, at $370 billion (row 1, Table 8.1), consumption is $375 billion. Households can consume more than their incomes by liquidating (selling for cash) accumulated wealth or by borrowing. Graphically, dissaving is shown as the vertical distance of the consumption schedule above the 45° line or as the vertical distance of the saving schedule below the horizontal axis. We have marked the dissaving at the $370 billion level of income in Figure 8.2a and 8.2b. Both vertical distances measure the $5 billion of dissaving that occurs at $370 billion of income.

In our example, the **break-even income** is $390 billion (row 2). This is the income level at which households plan to consume their entire incomes ($C =$ DI). Graphically, the consumption schedule cuts the 45° line, and the

TABLE 8.1 Consumption and Saving Schedules (in Billions) and Propensities to Consume and Save

(1) Level of Output and Income (GDP = DI)	(2) Consumption (C)	(3) Saving (S), (1) − (2)	(4) Average Propensity to Consume (APC), (2)/(1)	(5) Average Propensity to Save (APS), (3)/(1)	(6) Marginal Propensity to Consume (MPC), Δ(2)/Δ(1)*	(7) Marginal Propensity to Save (MPS), Δ(3)/Δ(1)*
(1) $370	$375	$−5	1.01	−.01		
					.75	.25
(2) 390	390	0	1.00	.00		
					.75	.25
(3) 410	405	5	.99	.01		
					.75	.25
(4) 430	420	10	.98	.02		
					.75	.25
(5) 450	435	15	.97	.03		
					.75	.25
(6) 470	450	20	.96	.04		
					.75	.25
(7) 490	465	25	.95	.05		
					.75	.25
(8) 510	480	30	.94	.06		
					.75	.25
(9) 530	495	35	.93	.07		
					.75	.25
(10) 550	510	40	.93	.07		

*The Greek letter Δ, delta, means "the change in."

keygraph

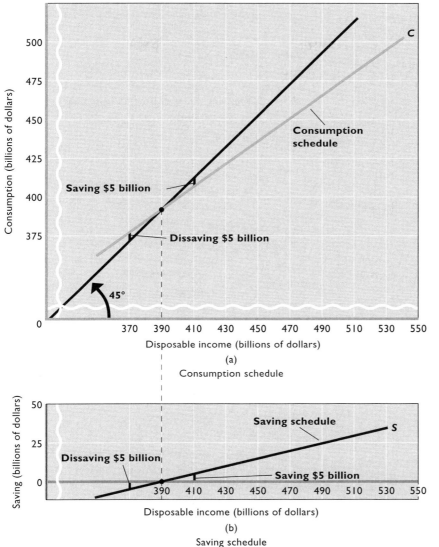

FIGURE 8.2 (a) Consumption and (b) saving schedules. The two parts of this figure show the income-consumption and income-saving relationships in Table 8.1 graphically. The saving schedule in (b) is found by subtracting the consumption schedule in (a) vertically from the 45° line. Consumption equals disposable income (and saving thus equals zero) at $390 billion for these hypothetical data.

(a)
Consumption schedule

(b)
Saving schedule

QUICK QUIZ 8.2

1. The slope of the consumption schedule in this figure is .75. Thus the:
   a. slope of the saving schedule is 1.33.
   b. marginal propensity to consume is .75.
   c. average propensity to consume is .25.
   d. slope of the saving schedule is also .75.
2. In this figure, when consumption is a positive amount, saving:
   a. must be a negative amount.
   b. must also be a positive amount.
   c. can be either a positive or a negative amount.
   d. is zero.

3. In this figure:
   a. the marginal propensity to consume is constant at all levels of income.
   b. the marginal propensity to save rises as disposable income rises.
   c. consumption is inversely (negatively) related to disposable income.
   d. saving is inversely (negatively) related to disposable income.
4. When consumption equals disposable income:
   a. the marginal propensity to consume is zero.
   b. the average propensity to consume is zero.
   c. consumption and saving must be equal.
   d. saving must be zero.

Answers: 1. b; 2. c; 3. a; 4. d

149

saving schedule cuts the horizontal axis (saving is zero) at the break-even income level.

At all higher incomes, households plan to save part of their incomes. Graphically, the vertical distance between the consumption schedule and the 45° line measures this saving (see Figure 8.2a), as does the vertical distance between the saving schedule and the horizontal axis (see Figure 8.2b). For example, at the $410 billion level of income (row 3), both these distances indicate $5 billion of saving.

Average and Marginal Propensities

Columns 4 to 7 in Table 8.1 show additional characteristics of the consumption and saving schedules.

APC and APS
The fraction, or percentage, of total income that is consumed is the **average propensity to consume (APC)**. The fraction of total income that is saved is the **average propensity to save (APS)**. That is,

$$APC = \frac{consumption}{income}$$

and

$$APS = \frac{saving}{income}$$

For example, at $470 billion of income (row 6) in Table 8.1, the APC is $\frac{450}{470} = \frac{45}{47}$ or about 96 percent, while the APS is $\frac{20}{470} = \frac{2}{47}$, or about 4 percent. Columns 4 and 5 in Table 8.1 show the APC and APS at each of the 10 levels of DI; note in the table that the APC falls and the APS rises as DI increases, as was implied in our previous comments.

Because disposable income is either consumed or saved, the fraction of any DI consumed plus the fraction saved (not consumed) must exhaust that income. Mathematically, APC + APS = 1 at any level of disposable income, as columns 4 and 5 in Table 8.1 illustrate.

Global Perspective 8.1 shows APCs for several countries.

MPC and MPS
The fact that households consume a certain proportion of a particular total income, for example, $\frac{45}{47}$ of a $470 billion disposable income, does not guarantee they will consume the same proportion of any *change* in income they might receive. The proportion, or fraction, of any change in income consumed is called the **marginal propensity to consume (MPC)**, "marginal" meaning "extra" or "a change in." Equivalently, the MPC is the ratio of a change in consumption to a change in the

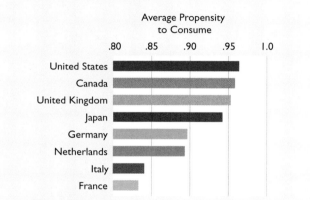
income that caused the consumption change:

$$MPS = \frac{change\ in\ saving}{change\ in\ income}$$

Similarly, the fraction of any change in income saved is the **marginal propensity to save (MPS)**. The MPS is the ratio of a change in saving to the change in income that brought it about:

$$MPS = \frac{change\ in\ saving}{change\ in\ income}$$

If disposable income is $470 billion (row 6 horizontally in Table 8.1) and household income rises by $20 billion to $490 billion (row 7), households will consume $\frac{15}{20}$, or $\frac{3}{4}$, and save $\frac{5}{20}$, or $\frac{1}{4}$, of that increase in income. In other words, the MPC is $\frac{3}{4}$ or .75, and the MPS is $\frac{1}{4}$ or .25, as shown in columns 6 and 7.

The sum of the MPC and the MPS for any change in disposable income must always be 1. Consuming or saving out of extra income is an either-or proposition; the fraction of any change in income not consumed is, by definition, saved. Therefore, the fraction consumed (MPC) plus the fraction saved (MPS) must exhaust the whole change in income:

$$MPC + MPS = 1$$

In our example, .75 plus .25 equals 1.

MPC and MPS as Slopes The MPC is the numerical value of the slope of the consumption schedule,

W 8.1

Consumption and saving

and the MPS is the numerical value of the slope of the saving schedule. We know from the appendix to Chapter 1 that the slope of any line is the ratio of the vertical change to the horizontal change occasioned in moving from one point to another on that line.

Figure 8.3 measures the slopes of the consumption and saving lines, using enlarged portions of Figure 8.2a and 8.2b. Observe that consumption changes by $15 billion (the vertical change) for each $20 billion change in disposable income (the horizontal change). The slope of the consumption line is thus .75 (= $15/$20), which is the value of the MPC. Saving changes by $5 billion (shown as the vertical change) for every $20 billion change in disposable income (shown as the horizontal change). The slope of the

saving line therefore is .25 (= $5/$20), which is the value of the MPS. **(Key Question 5)**

Nonincome Determinants of Consumption and Saving

The amount of disposable income is the basic determinant of the amounts households will consume and save. But certain determinants other than income might prompt households to consume more or less at each possible level of income and thereby change the locations of the consumption and saving schedules. Those other determinants are wealth, expectations, interest rates, and indebtedness.

Wealth
The amount that households spend and save from current income depends partly on the value of the existing wealth they have already accumulated. By "wealth" we mean the value of both real assets (for example, houses, land) and financial assets (for example, cash, savings accounts, stocks, bonds, pensions) that households own. Households save to accumulate wealth. When events boost the value of existing wealth, households increase their spending and reduce their saving. This so-called **wealth effect** shifts the consumption schedule upward and the saving schedule downward. Examples: In the late 1990s, skyrocketing U.S. stock values expanded the value of household wealth. Predictably, households spent more and saved less. In contrast, a modest "reverse wealth effect" occurred in 2000 and 2001, when stock prices sharply fell.

Expectations
Household expectations about future prices and income may affect current spending and saving. For example, expectations of rising prices tomorrow may trigger more spending and less saving today. Thus, the current consumption schedule shifts up and the current saving schedule shifts down. Or expectations of a recession and thus lower income in the future may lead households to reduce consumption and save more today. If so, the consumption schedule will shift down and the saving schedule will shift up.

Real Interest Rates
When real interest rates (those adjusted for inflation) fall, households tend to borrow more, consume more, and save less. A lower interest rate, for example, induces consumers to purchase automobiles and other goods bought on credit. A lower interest rate also diminishes the incentive to save because of the reduced interest "payment" to the saver. These effects on consumption and saving, however, are very modest. They mainly shift consumption toward some products (those

FIGURE 8.3 The marginal propensity to consume and the marginal propensity to save. The MPC is the slope (ΔC/ΔDI) of the consumption schedule, and the MPS is the slope (ΔS/ΔDI) of the saving schedule. The Greek letter delta (Δ) means "the change in."

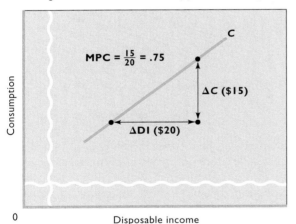

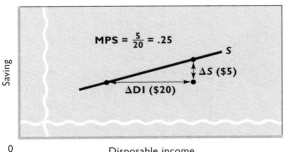

bought on credit) and away from others. At best, lower interest rates shift the consumption schedule slightly upward and the saving schedule slightly downward. Higher interest rates do the opposite.

Household Debt   In drawing a particular consumption schedule, household debt as a percentage of DI is held constant. But when consumers as a group increase their household debt, they can increase current consumption at each level of DI. Increased borrowing shifts the consumption schedule upward. In contrast, reduced borrowing shifts the consumption schedule downward.

Other Important Considerations

There are several additional important points regarding the consumption and saving schedules:

*   **Switch to real GDP**   When developing macroeconomic models, economists change their focus from the relationship between consumption (and saving) and *disposable income* to the relationship between consumption (and saving) and *real domestic output (real GDP)*. This modification is reflected in Figure 8.4a and 8.4b, where the horizontal axes measure real GDP.

*   **Changes along schedules**   The movement from one point to another on a consumption schedule (for example, from *a* to *b* on C_0 in Figure 8.4a) is a *change in the amount consumed* and is solely caused by a change in real GDP. On the other hand, an upward or downward shift of the entire schedule, for example, a shift from C_0 to C_1 or C_2 in Figure 8.4a, is caused by changes in any one or more of the *nonincome* determinants of consumption just discussed.

    A similar distinction in terminology applies to the saving schedule in Figure 8.4b.

*   **Schedule shifts**   Changes in wealth, expectations, interest rates, and household debt will shift the consumption schedule in one direction and the saving schedule in the opposite direction. If households decide to consume more at each possible level of real GDP, they want to save less, and vice versa. (Even when they spend more by borrowing, they are, in effect, reducing their current saving by the amount borrowed.) Graphically, if the consumption schedule shifts upward from C_0 to C_1 in Figure 8.4a, the saving schedule shifts downward, from S_0 to S_1 in Figure 8-4b. Similarly, a downward shift of the consumption schedule from C_0 to C_2 means an upward shift of the saving schedule from S_0 to S_2.

*   **Taxation**   In contrast, a change in taxes shifts the consumption and saving schedules in the same direction. Taxes are paid partly at the expense of consumption

FIGURE 8.4 Shifts in the (a) consumption and (b) saving schedules.   Normally, if households consume more at each level of real GDP, they are necessarily saving less. Graphically this means that an upward shift of the consumption schedule (C_0 to C_1) entails a downward shift of the saving schedule (S_0 to S_1). If households consume less at each level of real GDP, they are saving more. A downward shift of the consumption schedule (C_0 to C_2) is reflected in an upward shift of the saving schedule (S_0 to S_2). This pattern breaks down, however, when taxes change; then the consumption and saving schedules move in the *same* direction—opposite to the direction of the tax change.

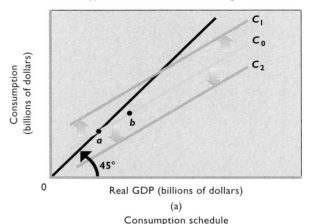

(a)
Consumption schedule

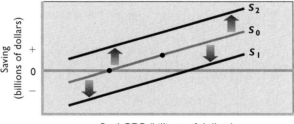

(b)
Saving schedule

and partly at the expense of saving. So an increase in taxes will reduce both consumption and saving, shifting the consumption schedule in Figure 8.4a and the saving schedule in Figure 8.4b downward. Conversely, households will partly consume and partly save any decrease in taxes. Both the consumption schedule and saving schedule will shift upward.

*   **Stability**   The consumption and saving schedules usually are relatively stable unless altered by major tax increases or decreases. Their stability may be because consumption-saving decisions are strongly influenced by long-term considerations such as saving to meet emergencies or saving for retirement. It may also be because changes in the nonincome determinants frequently work in opposite directions and therefore may be self-canceling.

G 8.1

Consumption and saving schedules

CONSIDER THIS ...

What Wealth Effect?

The consumption schedule is relatively stable even during rather extraordinary times. Between March 2000 and July 2002, the U.S. stock market lost a staggering $3.7 trillion of value (yes, trillion). Yet consumption spending was greater at the end of that period than at the beginning. How can that be? Why didn't a "reverse wealth effect" reduce consumption?

There are a number of reasons. Of greatest importance, the amount of consumption spending in the economy depends mainly on the *flow* of income, not the *stock* of wealth. Disposable income (DI) in the United States is about $8 trillion annually and consumers spend a large portion of it. Even though there was a mild recession in 2001, DI and consumption spending were both greater in July 2002 than in March 2000. Second, the Federal government cut personal income tax rates during this period and that bolstered consumption spending. Third, household wealth did not fall by the full amount of the $3.7 trillion stock market loss because the value of houses increased dramatically over this period. Finally, lower interest rates during this period enabled many households to refinance their mortgages, reduce monthly loan payments, and increase their current consumption.

For all these offsetting reasons, the general consumption-income relationship of Figure 8.2 held true in the face of the extraordinary loss of stock market value.

The Interest-Rate–Investment Relationship

In our consideration of major macro relationships, we next turn to the relationship between the real interest rate and investment. Recall that investment consists of expenditures on new plants, capital equipment, machinery, inventories, and so on. The investment decision is a marginal-benefit–marginal-cost decision: The marginal benefit from investment is the expected rate of return businesses hope to realize. The marginal cost is the interest rate that must be paid for borrowed funds. We will see that businesses will invest in all projects for which the expected rate of return exceeds the interest rate. Expected returns (profits) and the interest rate therefore are the two basic determinants of investment spending.

Expected Rate of Return

Investment spending is guided by the profit motive; businesses buy capital goods only when they think such purchases will be profitable. Suppose the owner of a small cabinetmaking shop is considering whether to invest in a new sanding machine that costs $1000 and has a useful life of only 1 year. (Extending the life of the machine beyond 1 year complicates the economic decision but does not change the fundamental analysis. We discuss the valuation of returns beyond 1 year in Internet Chapter 14 W.) The new machine will increase the firm's output and sales revenue. Suppose the net expected revenue from the machine (that is, after such operating costs as power, lumber, labor, and certain taxes have been subtracted) is $1100. Then, after the $1000 cost of the machine is subtracted from the net expected revenue of $1100, the firm will have an expected profit of $100. Dividing this $100 profit by the $1000 cost of the machine, we find that the **expected rate of return**, r, on the machine is 10 percent (= $100/$1000). It is important to note that this is an *expected* rate of return, not a *guaranteed* rate of return. The investment may or may not generate revenue and therefore profit as anticipated. Investment involves risk.

The Real Interest Rate

One important cost associated with investing that our example has ignored is interest, which is the financial cost of borrowing the $1000 of *money* "capital" to purchase the $1000 of *real* capital (the sanding machine).

The interest cost of the investment is computed by multiplying the interest rate, i, by the $1000 borrowed to buy the machine. If the interest rate is, say, 7 percent, the total interest cost will be $70. This compares favorably with the net expected return of $100, which produced the 10 percent expected rate of return. If the investment works out as expected, it will add $30 to the firm's profit. We can generalize as follows: If the expected rate of return (10 percent) exceeds the interest rate (here, 7 percent), the investment should be undertaken. The firm expects the investment to be profitable. But if the interest rate (say, 12 percent) exceeds the expected rate of return (10 percent), the investment should not be undertaken. The firm expects the investment to be unprofitable. The firm should undertake all investment projects it thinks will be profitable. That means it should invest up to the point where $r = i$, because then it has undertaken all investment for which r exceeds i.

This guideline applies even if a firm finances the investment internally out of funds saved from past profit rather than borrowing the funds. The role of the interest rate in the investment decision does not change. When the firm uses money from savings to invest in the sander, it incurs an opportunity cost because it forgoes the interest income it could have earned by lending the funds to someone else. That interest cost, converted to percentage terms, needs to be weighed against the expected rate of return.

The *real* rate of interest, rather than the *nominal* rate, is crucial in making investment decisions. Recall from Chapter 7 that the nominal interest rate is expressed in dollars of current value, while the real interest rate is stated in dollars of constant or inflation-adjusted value. Recall that the real interest rate is the nominal rate less the rate of inflation. In our sanding machine illustration our implicit assumption of a constant price level ensures that all our data, including the interest rate, are in real terms.

But what if inflation *is* occurring? Suppose a $1000 investment is expected to yield a real (inflation-adjusted) rate of return of 10 percent and the nominal interest rate is 15 percent. At first, we would say the investment would be unprofitable. But assume there is ongoing inflation of 10 percent per year. This means the investing firm will pay back dollars with approximately 10 percent less in purchasing power. While the nominal interest rate is 15 percent, the real rate is only 5 percent (= 15 percent − 10 percent). By comparing this 5 percent real interest rate with the 10 percent expected real rate of return, we find that the investment is potentially profitable and should be undertaken. **(Key Question 7)**

Investment Demand Curve

We now move from a single firm's investment decision to total demand for investment goods by the entire business sector. Assume that every firm has estimated the expected rates of return from all investment projects and has recorded those data. We can cumulate (successively sum) these data by asking: How many dollars' worth of investment projects have an expected rate of return of, say,

TABLE 8.2 Rates of Expected Return and Investment

Expected Rate of Return (r)	Cumulative Amount of Investment Having This Rate of Return or Higher, Billions per Year
16%	$ 0
14	5
12	10
10	15
8	20
6	25
4	30
2	35
0	40

16 percent or more? How many have 14 percent or more? How many have 12 percent or more? And so on.

Suppose no prospective investments yield an expected return of 16 percent or more. But suppose there are $5 billion of investment opportunities with expected rates of return between 14 and 16 percent; an additional $5 billion yielding between 12 and 14 percent; still an additional $5 billion yielding between 10 and 12 percent; and an additional $5 billion in each successive 2 percent range of yield down to and including the 0 to 2 percent range.

To cumulate these figures for each rate of return, r, we add the amounts of investment that will yield each particular rate of return r or higher. This provides the data in Table 8.2, shown graphically in **Figure 8.5 (Key Graph)**. In Table 8.2 the number opposite 12 percent, for example, means there are $10 billion of investment opportunities that will yield an expected rate of return of 12 percent or more. The $10 billion includes the $5 billion of investment expected to yield a return of 14 percent or more plus the $5 billion expected to yield between 12 and 14 percent.

We know from our example of the sanding machine that an investment project will be undertaken if its expected rate of return, r, exceeds the real interest rate, i. Let's first suppose i is 12 percent. Businesses will undertake all investments for which r exceeds 12 percent. That is, they will invest until the 12 percent rate of return equals the 12 percent interest rate. Figure 8.5 reveals that $10 billion of investment spending will be undertaken at a 12 percent interest rate; that means $10 billion of investment projects have an expected rate of return of 12 percent or more.

Put another way: At a financial "price" of 12 percent, $10 billion of investment goods will be demanded. If the interest rate is lower, say, 8 percent, the amount of investment for which r equals or exceeds i is $20 billion. Thus, firms will demand $20 billion of investment goods at an

keygraph

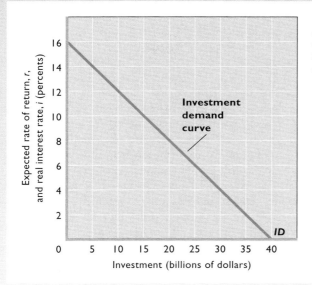

FIGURE 8.5 **The investment demand curve.** The investment demand curve is constructed by arraying all potential investment projects in descending order of their expected rates of return. The curve slopes downward, reflecting an inverse relationship between the real interest rate (the financial "price" of each dollar of investing) and the quantity of investment demanded.

QUICK QUIZ 8.5

1. The investment demand curve:
   a. reflects a direct (positive) relationship between the real interest rate and investment.
   b. reflects an inverse (negative) relationship between the real interest rate and investment.
   c. shifts to the right when the real interest rate rises.
   d. shifts to the left when the real interest rate rises.
2. In this figure:
   a. greater cumulative amounts of investment are associated with lower expected rates of return on investment.
   b. lesser cumulative amounts of investment are associated with lower expected rates of return on investment.
   c. higher interest rates are associated with higher expected rates of return on investment, and therefore greater amounts of investment.
   d. interest rates and investment move in the same direction.

3. In this figure, if the real interest rate falls from 6 to 4 percent:
   a. investment will increase from 0 to $30 billion.
   b. investment will decrease by $5 billion.
   c. the expected rate of return will rise by $5 billion.
   d. investment will increase from $25 billion to $30 billion.
4. In this figure, investment will be:
   a. zero if the real interest rate is zero.
   b. $40 billion if the real interest rate is 16 percent.
   c. $30 billion if the real interest rate is 4 percent.
   d. $20 billion if the real interest rate is 12 percent.

Answers: 1. b; 2. a; 3. d; 4. c

8 percent real interest rate. At 6 percent, they will demand $25 billion of investment goods.

By applying the marginal-benefit–marginal-cost rule that investment projects should be undertaken up to the point where $r = i$, we see that we can add the real interest rate to the vertical axis in Figure 8.5. The curve in Figure 8.5 not only shows rates of return; it shows the quantity of investment demanded at each "price" i (interest rate) of investment. The vertical axis in Figure 8.5 shows the various possible real interest

O 8.2

Interest-rate–investment relationship

rates, and the horizontal axis shows the corresponding quantities of investment demanded. The inverse (downsloping) relationship between the interest rate (price) and dollar quantity of investment demanded conforms to the law of demand discussed in Chapter 3. The curve *ID* in Figure 8.5 is the economy's **investment demand curve.** It shows the amount of investment forthcoming at each real interest rate. The level of investment depends on the expected rate of return and the real interest rate. (**Key Question 8**)

G 8.2

Investment demand curve

155

Shifts of the Investment Demand Curve

Figure 8.5 shows the relationship between the interest rate and the amount of investment demanded, other things equal. When other things change, the investment demand curve shifts. In general, any factor that leads businesses collectively to expect greater rates of return on their investments increases investment demand. That factor shifts the investment demand curve to the right, as from ID_0 to ID_1 in Figure 8.6. Any factor that leads businesses collectively to expect lower rates of return on their investments shifts the curve to the left, as from ID_0 to ID_2. What are those non-interest-rate determinants of investment demand?

Acquisition, Maintenance, and Operating Costs
The initial costs of capital goods, and the estimated costs of operating and maintaining those goods, affect the expected rate of return on investment. When these costs rise, the expected rate of return from prospective investment projects falls and the investment demand curve shifts to the left. Example: Higher electricity costs associated with operating tools and machinery shifts the investment demand curve to the left. Lower costs, in contrast, shift it to the right.

Business Taxes
When government is considered, firms look to expected returns *after taxes* in making their investment decisions. An increase in business taxes lowers the expected profitability of investments and shifts the investment demand curve to the left; a reduction of business taxes shifts it to the right.

Technological Change
Technological progress—the development of new products, improvements in existing products, and the creation of new machinery and production processes—stimulates investment. The development of a more efficient machine, for example, lowers production costs or improves product quality and increases the expected rate of return from investing in the machine. Profitable new products (cholesterol medications, Internet services, high-resolution televisions, cellular phones, and so on) induce a flurry of investment as businesses tool up for expanded production. A rapid rate of technological progress shifts the investment demand curve to the right.

Stock of Capital Goods on Hand
The stock of capital goods on hand, relative to output and sales, influences investment decisions by firms. When the economy is overstocked with production facilities and when firms have excessive inventories of finished goods, the expected rate of return on new investment declines. Firms with excess production capacity have little incentive to invest in new capital. Therefore, less investment is forthcoming at each real interest rate; the investment demand curve shifts leftward.

When the economy is understocked with production facilities and when firms are selling their output as fast as they can produce it, the expected rate of return on new investment increases and the investment demand curve shifts rightward.

Expectations
We noted that business investment is based on expected returns (expected additions to profit). Most capital goods are durable, with a life expectancy of 10 or 20 years. Thus, the expected rate of return on capital investment depends on the firm's expectations of future sales, future operating costs, and future profitability of the product that the capital helps produce. These expectations are based on forecasts of future business conditions as well as on such elusive and difficult-to-predict factors as changes in the domestic political climate, international relations, population growth, and consumer tastes. If executives become more optimistic about future sales, costs, and profits, the investment demand curve will shift to the right; a pessimistic outlook will shift the curve to the left.

Global Perspective 8.2 compares investment spending relative to GDP for several nations in a recent year.

FIGURE 8.6 Shifts of the investment demand curve. Increases in investment demand are shown as rightward shifts of the investment demand curve; decreases in investment demand are shown as leftward shifts of the investment demand curve.

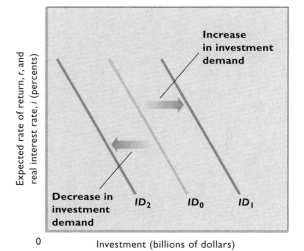

GLOBAL PERSPECTIVE 8.2

Gross Investment Expenditures as a Percentage of GDP, Selected Nations

As a percentage of GDP, investment varies widely by nation. These differences, of course, can change from year to year.

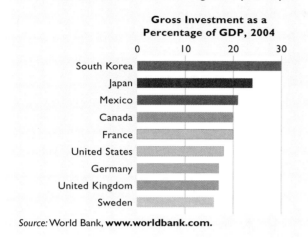

Source: World Bank, **www.worldbank.com.**

Domestic real interest rates and investment demand determine the levels of investment relative to GDP.

Instability of Investment

In contrast to consumption, investment is unstable; it rises and falls quite often. Investment, in fact, is the most volatile component of total spending. Figure 8.7 shows just how volatile investment in the United States has been. Note that its swings are much greater than those of GDP.

Several factors explain the variability of investement.

Durability Because of their durability, capital goods have an indefinite useful life. Within limits, purchases of capital goods are discretionary and therefore can be postponed. Firms can scrap or replace older equipment and buildings, or they can patch them up and use them for a few more years. Optimism about the future may prompt firms to replace their older facilities and such modernizing will call for a high level of investment. A less optimistic view, however, may lead to smaller amounts of investment as firms repair older facilities and keep them in use.

Irregularity of Innovation We know that technological progress is a major determinant of investment. New products and processes stimulate investment. But history suggests that major innovations such as railroads, electricity, automobiles, fiber optics, and computers occur quite irregularly. When they do happen, they induce a

FIGURE 8.7 The volatility of investment. Annual percentage changes in investment spending are often several times greater than the percentage changes in GDP. (Data are in real terms.)

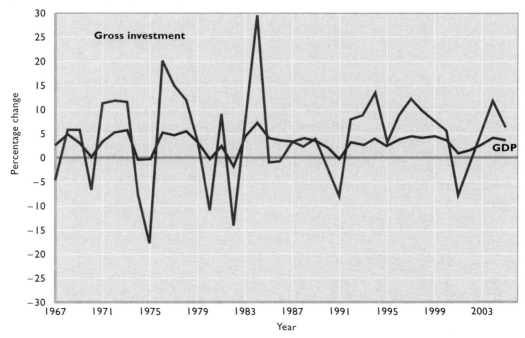

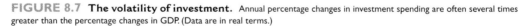

vast upsurge or "wave" of investment spending that in time recedes.

A contemporary example is the widespread acceptance of the personal computer and Internet, which has caused a wave of investment in those industries and in many related industries such as computer software and electronic commerce. Some time in the future, this surge of investment undoubtedly will level off.

Variability of Profits The expectation of future profitability is influenced to some degree by the size of current profits. Current profits, however, are themselves highly variable. Thus, the variability of profits contributes to the volatile nature of the incentive to invest.

The instability of profits may cause investment fluctuations in a second way. Profits are a major source of funds for business investment. U.S. businesses sometimes prefer this internal source of financing to increases in external debt or stock issue.

In short, expanding profits give firms both greater incentives and greater means to invest; declining profits have the reverse effects. The fact that actual profits are variable thus adds doubly to the instability of investment.

Variability of Expectations Firms tend to project current business conditions into the future. But their expectations can change quickly when some event suggests a significant possible change in future business conditions. Changes in exchange rates, changes in the outlook for international peace, court decisions in key labor or antitrust cases, legislative actions, changes in trade barriers, changes in governmental economic policies, and a host of similar considerations may cause substantial shifts in business expectations.

The stock market can influence business expectations because firms look to it as one of several indicators of society's overall confidence in future business conditions. Rising stock prices tend to signify public confidence in the business future, while falling stock prices may imply a lack of confidence. The stock market, however, is quite speculative. Some participants buy when stock prices begin to rise and sell as soon as prices begin to fall. This behavior can magnify what otherwise would be modest changes in stock prices. By creating swings in optimism and pessimism, the stock market may add to the instability of investment spending.

For all these reasons, changes in investment cause most of the fluctuations in output and employment. In terms of Figures 8.5 and 8.6, we would represent volatility of investment as occasional and substantial shifts in the investment demand curve.

The Multiplier Effect*

A final basic relationship that requires discussion is the relationship between changes in spending and changes in real GDP. Assuming the economy has room to expand, there is a direct relationship between these two aggregates. More spending results in higher GDP; less spending results in a lower GDP. But there is much more to this relationship. A change in spending, say, investment, ultimately changes output and income by more than the initial change in investment spending. That surprising result is called the *multiplier effect*: a change in a component of total spending leads to a larger change in GDP. The **multiplier** determines how much larger that change will be; it is the ratio of a change in GDP to the initial change in spending (in this case, investment). Stated generally,

$$\text{Multiplier} = \frac{\text{change in real GDP}}{\text{initial change in spending}}$$

By rearranging this equation, we can also say that

Change in GDP = multiplier × initial change in spending

So if investment in an economy rises by $30 billion and GDP increases by $90 billion as a result, we then know from our first equation that the multiplier is 3 (= $90/30).

Note these three points about the multiplier:

- The "initial change in spending" is usually associated with investment spending because of investment's volatility. But changes in consumption (unrelated to changes in income), net exports, and government purchases also lead to the multiplier effect.
- The "initial change in spending" associated with investment spending results from a change in the real interest rate and/or a shift of the investment demand curve.

---

*Instructors who cover the full aggregate expenditures (AE) model (Chapter 9) rather than moving directly to aggregate demand and aggregate supply (Chapter 10) may choose to defer this discussion until after the analysis of equilibrium real GDP.

- Implicit in the preceding point is that the multiplier works in both directions. An increase in initial spending may create a multiple increase in GDP, and a decrease in spending may be multiplied into a larger decrease in GDP.

Rationale

The multiplier effect follows from two facts. First, the economy supports repetitive, continuous flows of expenditures and income through which dollars spent by Smith are received as income by Chin and then spent by Chin and received as income by Gonzales, and so on. (This chapter's Last Word presents this idea in a humorous way.) Second, any change in income will vary both consumption and saving in the same direction as, and by a fraction of, the change in income.

It follows that an initial change in spending will set off a spending chain throughout the economy. That chain of spending, although of diminishing importance at each successive step, will cumulate to a multiple change in GDP. Initial changes in spending produce magnified changes in output and income.

Table 8.3 illustrates the rationale underlying the multiplier effect. Suppose that a $5 billion increase in investment spending occurs. We assume that the MPC is .75 and the MPS is .25.

The initial $5 billion increase in investment generates an equal amount of wage, rent, interest, and profit income, because spending and receiving income are two sides of the same transaction. How much consumption will be induced by this $5 billion increase in the incomes of households? We find the answer by applying the marginal propensity to consume of .75 to this change in income. Thus, the $5 billion increase in income initially raises consumption by $3.75 (= .75 × $5) billion and saving by $1.25 (= .25 × $5) billion, as shown in columns 2 and 3 in Table 8.3.

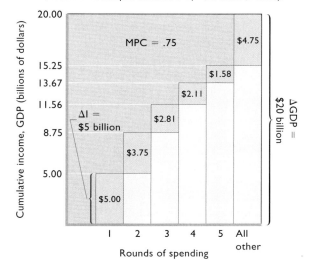

FIGURE 8.8 The multiplier process (MPC = .75). An initial change in investment spending of $5 billion creates an equal $5 billion of new income in round 1. Households spend $3.75 (= .75 × $5) billion of this new income, creating $3.75 of added income in round 2. Of this $3.75 of new income, households spend $2.81 (= .75 × $3.75) billion, and income rises by that amount in round 3. Such income increments over the entire process get successively smaller but eventually produce a total change of income and GDP of $20 billion. The multiplier therefore is 4 (= $20 billion/$5 billion).

Other households receive as income (second round) the $3.75 billion of consumption spending. Those households consume .75 of this $3.75 billion, or $2.81 billion, and save .25 of it, or $.94 billion. The $2.81 billion that is consumed flows to still other households as income to be spent or saved (third round). And the process continues, with the added consumption and income becoming less in each round. The process ends when there is no more additional income to spend.

Figure 8.8 shows several rounds of the multiplier process of Table 8.3 graphically. As shown by rounds 1 to 5, each round adds a smaller and smaller blue block to national income and GDP. The process, of course, continues

TABLE 8.3 The Multiplier: A Tabular Illustration (in Billions)

	(1) Change in Income	(2) Change in Consumption (MPC = .75)	(3) Change in Saving (MPS = .25)
Increase in investment of **$5.00**	$5.00	$ 3.75	$1.25
Second round	3.75	2.81	.94
Third round	2.81	2.11	.70
Fourth round	2.11	1.58	.53
Fifth round	1.58	1.19	.39
All other rounds	4.75	3.56	1.19
Total	**$20.00**	$15.00	$5.00

Squaring the Economic Circle

Humorist Art Buchwald Examines the Multiplier

WASHINGTON—The recession hit so fast that nobody knows exactly how it happened. One day we were the land of milk and honey and the next day we were the land of sour cream and food stamps.

This is one explanation.

Hofberger, the Ford salesman in Tomcat, Va., a suburb of Washington, called up Littleton, of Littleton Menswear & Haberdashery, and said, "Good news, the new Fords have just come in and I've put one aside for you and your wife."

Littleton said, "I can't, Hofberger, my wife and I are getting a divorce."

"I'm sorry," Littleton said, "but I can't afford a new car this year. After I settle with my wife, I'll be lucky to buy a bicycle."

Hofberger hung up. His phone rang a few minutes later.

"This is Bedcheck the painter," the voice on the other end said. "When do you want us to start painting your house?"

"I changed my mind," said Hofberger, "I'm not going to paint the house."

"But I ordered the paint," Bedcheck said. "Why did you change your mind?"

"Because Littleton is getting a divorce and he can't afford a new car."

That evening when Bedcheck came home his wife said, "The new color television set arrived from Gladstone's TV Shop."

"Take it back," Bedcheck told his wife.

"Why?" she demanded.

"Because Hofberger isn't going to have his house painted now that the Littletons are getting a divorce."

The next day Mrs. Bedcheck dragged the TV set in its carton back to Gladstone. "We don't want it."

Gladstone's face dropped. He immediately called his travel agent, Sandstorm. "You know that trip you had scheduled for me to the Virgin Islands?"

"Right, the tickets are all written up."

"Cancel it. I can't go. Bedcheck just sent back the color TV set because Hofberger didn't sell a car to Littleton because they're going to get a divorce and she wants all his money."

Sandstorm tore up the airline tickets and went over to see his banker, Gripsholm. "I can't pay back the loan this month because Gladstone isn't going to the Virgin Islands."

Gripsholm was furious. When Rudemaker came in to borrow money for a new kitchen he needed for his restaurant, Gripsholm turned him down cold. "How can I loan you money when Sandstorm hasn't repaid the money he borrowed?"

Rudemaker called up the contractor, Eagleton, and said he couldn't put in a new kitchen. Eagleton laid off eight men.

Meanwhile, Ford announced it was giving a rebate on its new models. Hofberger called up Littleton immediately. "Good news," he said, "even if you are getting a divorce, you can afford a new car."

"I'm not getting a divorce," Littleton said. "It was all a misunderstanding and we've made up."

"That's great," Hofberger said. "Now you can buy the Ford."

"No way," said Littleton. "My business has been so lousy I don't know why I keep the doors open."

"I didn't realize that," Hofberger said.

"Do you realize I haven't seen Bedcheck, Gladstone, Sandstorm, Gripsholm, Rudemaker or Eagleton for more than a month? How can I stay in business if they don't patronize my store?"

Source: Art Buchwald, "Squaring the Economic Circle," *Cleveland Plain Dealer*, Feb. 22, 1975. Reprinted by permission.

beyond the five rounds shown (for convenience we have simply cumulated the subsequent declining blocks into a single block labeled "All other"). The accumulation of the additional income in each round—the sum of the blue blocks—is the total change in income or GDP resulting from the initial $5 billion change in spending. Because the spending and respending effects of the increase in investment diminish with each successive round of spending, the cumulative increase in output and income eventually ends. In this case, the ending occurs when $20 billion of additional income accumulates. Thus, the multiplier is 4 (= $20 billion/$5 billion).

The Multiplier and the Marginal Propensities

You may have sensed from Table 8.3 that the fractions of an increase in income consumed (MPC) and saved (MPS) determine the cumulative respending effects of any initial change in spending and therefore determine the size of the multiplier. The MPC and the multiplier are directly related and the MPS and the multiplier are inversely related. The precise formulas are as shown in the next two equations:

$$\text{Multiplier} = \frac{1}{1 - \text{MPC}}$$

Recall, too, that MPC + MPS = 1. Therefore MPS = 1 − MPC, which means we can also write the multiplier formula as

$$\text{Multiplier} = \frac{1}{\text{MPS}}$$

This latter formula is a quick way to determine the multiplier. All you need to know is the MPS.

The smaller the fraction of any change in income saved, the greater the respending at each round and, therefore, the greater the multiplier. When the MPS is .25, as in our example, the multiplier is 4. If the MPS were .2, the multiplier would be 5. If the MPS were .33, the multiplier would be 3. Let's see why.

Suppose the MPS is .2 and businesses increase investment by $5 billion. In the first round of Table 8.3, consumption will rise by $4 billion (= MPC of .8 × $5 billion) rather than by $3.75 billion because saving will increase by $1 billion (= MPS of .2 × $5 billion) rather than $1.25 billion. The greater rise in consumption in round 1 will produce a greater increase in income in round 2. The same will be true for all successive rounds. If we worked through all rounds of the multiplier, we would find that the process ends when income has cumulatively increased by $25 billion, not the $20 billion

shown in the table. When the MPS is .2 rather than .25, the multiplier is 5 (= $25 billion/$5 billion) as opposed to 4 (= $20 billion/$5 billion.)

If the MPS were .33 rather than .25, the successive increases in consumption and income would be less than those in Table 8.3. We would discover that the process ended with a $15 billion increase in income rather than the $20 billion shown. When the MPS is .33, the multiplier is 3 (= $15 billion/$5 billion). The mathematics works such that the multiplier is equal to the reciprocal of the MPS. The reciprocal of any number is the quotient you obtain by dividing 1 by that number.

A large MPC (small MPS) means the succeeding rounds of consumption spending shown in Figure 8.8 diminish slowly and thereby cumulate to a large change in income. Conversely, a small MPC (a large MPS) causes the increases in consumption to decline quickly, so the cumulative change in income is small. The relationship between the MPC (and thus the MPS) and the multiplier is summarized in Figure 8.9.

W 8.2

Multiplier effect

FIGURE 8.9 The MPC and the multiplier. The larger the MPC (the smaller the MPS), the greater the size of the multiplier.

MPC	Multiplier
.9	10
.8	5
.75	4
.67	3
.5	2

QUICK REVIEW 8.3

- The multiplier effect reveals that an initial change in spending can cause a larger change in domestic income and output. The multiplier is the factor by which the initial change is magnified: multiplier = change in real GDP/initial change in spending.
- The higher the marginal propensity to consume (the lower the marginal propensity to save), the larger the multiplier: multiplier = 1/(1 − MPC) or 1/MPS.

How Large Is the Actual Multiplier Effect?

The multiplier we have just described is based on simplifying assumptions. Consumption of domestic output rises by the increases in income minus the increases in saving. But in reality, consumption of domestic output increases in each round by a lesser amount than implied by the MPS alone. In addition to saving, households use some of the extra income in each round to purchase additional goods from abroad (imports) and pay additional taxes. Buying imports and paying taxes drains off some of the additional consumption spending (on domestic output) created by the increases in income. So the multiplier effect is reduced and the 1/MPS formula for the multiplier overstates the actual outcome. To correct that problem, we would need to change the multiplier equation to read "1 divided by the fraction of the change in income that is not spent on domestic output." Also, we will find in later chapters that an increase in spending may be partly dissipated as inflation rather than realized fully as an increase in real GDP. That, too, reduces the size of the multiplier effect. The Council of Economic Advisers, which advises the U.S. president on economic matters, has estimated that the actual multiplier effect for the United States is about 2. So keep in mind throughout later discussions that the actual multiplier is less than the multipliers in our simple examples. **(Key Question 9)**

Summary

1. Other things equal, there is a direct (positive) relationship between income and consumption and income and saving. The consumption and saving schedules show the various amounts that households intend to consume and save at the various income and output levels, assuming a fixed price level.

2. The *average* propensities to consume and save show the fractions of any total income that are consumed and saved; APC + APS = 1. The *marginal* propensities to consume and save show the fractions of any change in total income that are consumed and saved; MPC + MPS = 1.

3. The locations of the consumption and saving schedules (as they relate to real GDP) are determined by (a) the amount of wealth owned by households, (b) expectations of future prices and incomes, (c) real interest rates, (d) household debt, and (e) tax levels. The consumption and saving schedules are relatively stable.

4. The immediate determinants of investment are (a) the expected rate of return and (b) the real rate of interest. The economy's investment demand curve is found by cumulating investment projects, arraying them in descending order according to their expected rates of return, graphing the result, and applying the rule that investment should be undertaken up to the point at which the real interest rate, i, equals the expected rate of return, r. The investment demand curve reveals an inverse (negative) relationship between the interest rate and the level of aggregate investment.

5. Shifts of the investment demand curve can occur as the result of changes in (a) the acquisition, maintenance, and operating costs of capital goods, (b) business taxes, (c) technology, (d) the stocks of capital goods on hand, and (e) expectations.

6. Either changes in interest rates or shifts of the investment demand curve can change the level of investment.

7. The durability of capital goods, the irregular occurrence of major innovations, profit volatility, and the variability of expectations all contribute to the instability of investment spending.

8. Through the multiplier effect, an increase in investment spending (or consumption spending, government purchases, or net export spending) ripples through the economy, ultimately creating a magnified increase in real GDP. The multiplier is the ultimate change in GDP divided by the initiating change in investment or some other component of spending.

9. The multiplier is equal to the reciprocal of the marginal propensity to save: The greater is the marginal propensity to save, the smaller is the multiplier. Also, the greater is the marginal propensity to consume, the larger is the multiplier.

10. Economists estimate that the actual multiplier effect in the U.S. economy is about 2, which is less than the multiplier in the text examples.

Terms and Concepts

45° (degree) line	average propensity to consume (APC)	wealth effect
consumption schedule	average propensity to save (APS)	expected rate of return
saving schedule	marginal propensity to consume (MPC)	investment demand curve
break-even income	marginal propensity to save (MPS)	multiplier

Study Questions

1. Very briefly summarize the relationships shown by (*a*) the consumption schedule, (*b*) the saving schedule, (*c*) the investment demand curve, and (*d*) the multiplier effect. Which of these relationships are direct (positive) relationships and which are inverse (negative) relationships? Why are consumption and saving in the United States greater today than they were a decade ago?

2. Precisely how do the APC and the MPC differ? Why must the sum of the MPC and the MPS equal 1? What are the basic determinants of the consumption and saving schedules? Of your personal level of consumption?

3. Explain how each of the following will affect the consumption and saving schedules (as they relate to GDP) or the investment schedule, other things equal:
   a. A large increase in the value of real estate, including private houses.
   b. A decline in the real interest rate.
   c. A sharp, sustained decline in stock prices.
   d. An increase in the rate of population growth.
   e. The development of a cheaper method of manufacturing computer chips.
   f. A sizable increase in the retirement age for collecting Social Security benefits.
   g. An increase in the Federal personal income tax.

4. Explain why an upward shift of the consumption schedule typically involves an equal downshift of the saving schedule. What is the exception to this relationship?

5. **KEY QUESTION** Complete the following table:
   a. Show the consumption and saving schedules graphically.
   b. Find the break-even level of income. Explain how it is possible for households to dissave at very low income levels.
   c. If the proportion of total income consumed (APC) decreases and the proportion saved (APS) increases as income rises, explain both verbally and graphically how the MPC and MPS can be constant at various levels of income.

6. What are the basic determinants of investment? Explain the relationship between the real interest rate and the level of investment. Why is investment spending unstable? How is it possible for investment spending to increase even in a period in which the real interest rate rises?

7. **KEY QUESTION** Suppose a handbill publisher can buy a new duplicating machine for $500 and the duplicator has a 1-year life. The machine is expected to contribute $550 to the year's net revenue. What is the expected rate of return? If the real interest rate at which funds can be borrowed to purchase the machine is 8 percent, will the publisher choose to invest in the machine? Explain.

8. **KEY QUESTION** Assume there are no investment projects in the economy that yield an expected rate of return of 25 percent or more. But suppose there are $10 billion of investment projects yielding expected returns of between 20 and 25 percent; another $10 billion yielding between 15 and 20 percent; another $10 billion between 10 and 15 percent; and so forth. Cumulate these data and present them graphically, putting the expected rate of return on the vertical axis and the amount of investment on the horizontal axis. What will be the equilibrium level of aggregate investment if the real interest rate is (*a*) 15 percent, (*b*) 10 percent, and (*c*) 5 percent? Explain why this curve is the investment demand curve.

9. **KEY QUESTION** What is the multiplier effect? What relationship does the MPC bear to the size of the multiplier? The MPS? What will the multiplier be when the MPS is 0, .4, .6, and 1? What will it be when the MPC is 1, .90, .67, .50, and 0? How much of a change in GDP will result if firms increase their level of investment by $8 billion and the MPC is .80? If the MPC is .67?

10. Why is the actual multiplier for the U.S. economy less than the multiplier in this chapter's simple examples?

11. **ADVANCED ANALYSIS** Linear equations for the consumption and saving schedules take the general form $C = a + bY$

Level of Output and Income (GDP = DI)	Consumption	Saving	APC	APS	MPC	MPS
$240	$	$−4	___	___		
260		0	___	___	___	___
280		4	___	___	___	___
300		8	___	___	___	___
320		12	___	___	___	___
340		16	___	___	___	___
360		20	___	___	___	___
380		24	___	___	___	___
400		28	___	___	___	___

and $S = -a + (1 - b)Y$, where C, S, and Y are consumption, saving, and national income, respectively. The constant a represents the vertical intercept, and b represents the slope of the consumption schedule.

a. Use the following data to substitute numerical values for a and b in the consumption and saving equations:

b. What is the economic meaning of b? Of $(1 - b)$?

National Income (Y)	Consumption (C)
$ 0	$ 80
100	140
200	200
300	260
400	320

c. Suppose that the amount of saving that occurs at each level of national income falls by $20 but that the values of b and $(1 - b)$ remain unchanged. Restate the saving and consumption equations for the new numerical values, and cite a factor that might have caused the change.

12. **ADVANCED ANALYSIS** Suppose that the linear equation for consumption in a hypothetical economy is $C = 40 + .8Y$. Also suppose that income (Y) is $400. Determine (a) the marginal propensity to consume, (b) the marginal propensity to save, (c) the level of consumption, (d) the average propensity to consume, (e) the level of saving, and (f) the average propensity to save.

13. **LAST WORD** What is the central economic idea humorously illustrated in Art Buchwald's piece, "Squaring the Economic Circle"? How does the central idea relate to recessions, on the one hand, and vigorous expansions, on the other?

Web-Based Questions

1. **THE BEIGE BOOK AND CURRENT CONSUMER SPENDING** Go to the Federal Reserve Web site, **federalreserve.gov,** and select About the Fed and then Federal Reserve Districts and Banks. Find your Federal Reserve District. Next, return to the Fed home page and select Monetary Policy and then Beige Book. What is the Beige Book? Locate the current Beige Book report and compare consumer spending for the entire U.S. economy with consumer spending in your Federal Reserve District. What are the economic strengths and weaknesses in both? Are retailers reporting that recent sales have met their expectations? What are their expectations for the future?

2. **INVESTMENT INSTABILITY—CHANGES IN REAL PRIVATE NONRESIDENTIAL FIXED INVESTMENT** The Bureau of Economic Analysis provides data for real private nonresidential fixed investment in table form at **www.bea.gov.** Access the BEA interactively and select National Income and Product Account Tables. Find Table 5.4, "Private Fixed Investment by Type." Has recent real private nonresidential fixed investment been volatile (as measured by percentage change from previous quarters)? Which is the largest component of this type of investment, (a) structures or (b) equipment and software? Which of these two components has been more volatile? How do recent quarterly percentage changes compare with the previous years' changes? Looking at the investment data, what investment forecast would you make for the forthcoming year?

9

IN THIS CHAPTER YOU WILL LEARN:

- **How economists combine consumption and investment to depict an aggregate expenditures schedule for a private closed economy.**

- **The three characteristics of the equilibrium level of real GDP in a private closed economy: aggregate expenditures = output; saving = investment; and no unplanned changes in inventories.**

- **How changes in equilibrium real GDP can occur and how those changes relate to the multiplier.**

- **How economists integrate the international sector (exports and imports) and the public sector (government expenditures and taxes) into the aggregate expenditures model.**

- **About the nature and causes of "recessionary expenditure gaps" and "inflationary expenditure gaps."**

The Aggregate Expenditures Model

O 9.1

Aggregate
expenditures
model

Two of the most critical questions in macroeconomics are: (1) What determines the level of GDP, given a nation's production capacity? (2) What causes real GDP to rise in one period and to fall in another? To answer these questions we construct the aggregate expenditures model, which has its origins in 1936 in the writings of British economist John Maynard Keynes (pronounced "Caines"). The basic premise of the aggregate expenditures model—also known as the "Keynesian cross" model—is that the amount of goods and services produced and therefore the level of employment depend directly on the level of aggregate expenditures (total spending). Businesses will produce only a level of output that they think they can profitably sell. They will idle their workers and machinery when there are no markets for their goods and services. When aggregate expenditures fall, total output and employment decrease; when aggregate expenditures rise, total output and employment increase.

Simplifications

Let's first look at aggregate expenditures and equilibrium GDP in a *private closed economy*—one without international trade or government. Then we will "open" the "closed" economy to exports and imports and also convert our "private" economy to a more realistic "mixed" economy that includes government purchases (or, more loosely, "government spending") and taxes.

Until we introduce taxes into the model, we will assume that real GDP equals disposable income (DI). If $500 billion of output is produced as GDP, households will receive exactly $500 billion of disposable income to consume or to save. And, unless specified otherwise, we will assume the economy has excess production capacity and unemployed labor. Thus, an increase in aggregate expenditures will increase real output and employment but not raise the price level.

Consumption and Investment Schedules

In the private closed economy, the two components of aggregate expenditures are consumption, C, and gross investment, I_g. Because we examined the *consumption schedule* (Figure 8.2a) in the previous chapter, there is no need to repeat that analysis here. But to add the investment decisions of businesses to the consumption plans of households, we need to construct an investment schedule showing the amounts business firms collectively intend to invest—their **planned investment**—at each possible level of GDP. Such a schedule represents the investment plans of businesses in the same way the consumption schedule represents the consumption plans of households. In developing the investment schedule, we will assume that this planned investment is independent of the level of current disposable income or real output.

Suppose the investment demand curve is as shown in Figure 9.1a and the current real interest rate is 8 percent. This means that firms will spend $20 billion on investment goods. Our assumption tells us that this $20 billion of investment will occur at both low and high levels of GDP. The line I_g in Figure 9.1b shows this graphically; it is the economy's **investment schedule.** You should not confuse this investment schedule I_g with the investment demand curve *ID* in Figure 9.1a. The investment schedule shows the amount of investment forthcoming at each level of GDP. As indicated in Figure 9.1b, the interest rate and investment demand curve together determine this amount ($20 billion). Table 9.1 shows the investment schedule in tabular form. Note that investment (I_g) in column 2 is $20 billion at all levels of real GDP.

FIGURE 9.1 **(a) The investment demand curve and (b) the investment schedule.** (a) The level of investment spending (here, $20 billion) is determined by the real interest rate (here, 8 percent) together with the investment demand curve *ID*. (b) The investment schedule I_g relates the amount of investment ($20 billion) determined in (a) to the various levels of GDP.

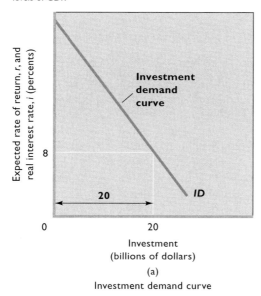

(a)
Investment demand curve

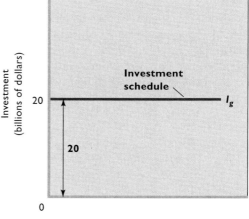

(b)
Investment schedule

TABLE 9.1 The Investment Schedule (in Billions)

(1) Level of Real Output and Income	(2) Investment (I_g)
$370	$20
390	20
410	20
430	20
450	20
470	20
490	20
510	20
530	20
550	20

Equilibrium GDP: $C + Ig = $ GDP

Now let's combine the consumption schedule of Chapter 8 and the investment schedule here to explain the equilibrium levels of output, income, and employment in the private closed economy.

Tabular Analysis

Columns 2 through 5 in Table 9.2 repeat the consumption and saving schedules of Table 8.1 and the investment schedule of Table 9.1.

Real Domestic Output
Column 2 in Table 9.2 lists the various possible levels of total output—of real GDP—that the private sector might produce. Producers are willing to offer any of these 10 levels of output if they

can expect to receive an identical level of income from the sale of that output. For example, firms will produce $370 billion of output, incurring $370 billion of costs (wages, rents, interest, and normal profit costs) only if they believe they can sell that output for $370 billion. Firms will offer $390 billion of output if they think they can sell that output for $390 billion. And so it is for all the other possible levels of output.

Aggregate Expenditures
In the private closed economy of Table 9.2, aggregate expenditures consist of consumption (column 3) plus investment (column 5). Their sum is shown in column 6, which with column 2 makes up the **aggregate expenditures schedule** for the private closed economy. This schedule shows the amount $(C + I_g)$ that will be spent at each possible output or income level.

At this point we are working with *planned investment*—the data in column 5, Table 9.2. These data show the amounts firms plan or intend to invest, not the amounts they actually will invest if there are unplanned changes in inventories. More about that shortly.

Equilibrium GDP
Of the 10 possible levels of GDP in Table 9.2, which is the equilibrium level? Which total output is the economy capable of sustaining?

The equilibrium output is that output whose production creates total spending just sufficient to purchase that output. So the equilibrium level of GDP is the level at which the total quantity of goods produced (GDP) equals the total quantity of goods purchased $(C + I_g)$. If you look at the domestic output levels in column 2 and the aggregate expenditures levels in column 6, you will see that this

TABLE 9.2 Determination of the Equilibrium Levels of Employment, Output, and Income: A Closed Private Economy

(1) Possible Levels of Employment, Millions	(2) Real Domestic Output (and Income) (GDP = DI),* Billions	(3) Consumption (C), Billions	(4) Saving (S), Billions	(5) Investment (I_g), Billions	(6) Aggregate Expenditures ($C + I_g$), Billions	(7) Unplanned Changes in Inventories, (+ or −)	(8) Tendency of Employment, Output, and Income
(1) 40	$370	$375	$−5	$20	$395	$−25	Increase
(2) 45	390	390	0	20	410	−20	Increase
(3) 50	410	405	5	20	425	−15	Increase
(4) 55	430	420	10	20	440	−10	Increase
(5) 60	450	435	15	20	455	−5	Increase
(6) **65**	**470**	**450**	**20**	**20**	**470**	**0**	**Equilibrium**
(7) 70	490	465	25	20	485	+5	Decrease
(8) 75	510	480	30	20	500	+10	Decrease
(9) 80	530	495	35	20	515	+15	Decrease
(10) 85	550	510	40	20	530	+20	Decrease

*If depreciation and net foreign factor income are zero, government is ignored and it is assumed that all saving occurs in the household sector of the economy. GDP as a measure of domestic output is equal to NI, PI, and DI. This means that households receive a DI equal to the value of total output.

equality exists only at $470 billion of GDP (row 6). That is the only output at which the economy is willing to spend precisely the amount needed to move that output off the shelves. At $470 billion of GDP, the annual rates of production and spending are in balance. There is no overproduction, which would result in a piling up of unsold goods and consequently cutbacks in the production rate. Nor is there an excess of total spending, which would draw down inventories of goods and prompt increases in the rate of production. In short, there is no reason for businesses to alter this rate of production; $470 billion is the **equilibrium GDP.**

Disequilibrium No level of GDP other than the equilibrium level of GDP can be sustained. At levels of GDP *below* equilibrium, the economy wants to spend at higher levels than the levels of GDP the economy is producing. If, for example, firms produced $410 billion of GDP (row 3 in Table 9.2), they would find it would yield $405 billion in consumer spending. Supplemented by $20 billion of planned investment, aggregate expenditures $(C + I_g)$ would be $425 billion, as shown in column 6. The economy would provide an annual rate of spending more than sufficient to purchase the $410 billion of annual production. Because buyers would be taking goods off the shelves faster than firms could produce them, an unplanned decline in business inventories of $15 billion would occur (column 7) if this situation continued. But businesses can adjust to such an imbalance between aggregate expenditures and real output by stepping up production. Greater output will increase employment and total income. This process will continue until the equilibrium level of GDP is reached ($470 billion).

The reverse is true at all levels of GDP *above* the $470 billion equilibrium level. Businesses will find that these total outputs fail to generate the spending needed to clear the shelves of goods. Being unable to recover their costs, businesses will cut back on production. To illustrate: At the $510 billion output (row 8), business managers would find spending is insufficient to permit the sale of all that output. Of the $510 billion of income that this output creates, $480 billion would be received back by businesses as consumption spending. Though supplemented by $20 billion of planned investment spending, total expenditures ($500 billion) would still be $10 billion below the $510 billion quantity produced. If this imbalance persisted, $10 billion of inventories would pile up (column 7). But businesses can adjust to this unintended accumulation of unsold goods by cutting back on the rate of production. The resulting

W 9.1

Equilibrium GDP

decline in output would mean fewer jobs and a decline in total income.

Graphical Analysis

We can demonstrate the same analysis graphically. In **Figure 9.2 (Key Graph)** the 45° line developed in Chapter 8 now takes on increased significance. Recall that at any point on this line, the value of what is being measured on the horizontal axis (here, GDP) is equal to the value of what is being measured on the vertical axis (here, aggregate expenditures, or $C + I_g$). Having discovered in our tabular analysis that the equilibrium level of domestic output is determined where $C + I_g$ equals GDP, we can say that the 45° line in Figure 9.2 is a graphical statement of that equilibrium condition.

Now we must graph the aggregate expenditures schedule onto Figure 9.2. To do this, we duplicate the consumption schedule C in Figure 8.2a and add to it vertically the constant $20 billion amount of investment I_g from Figure 9.1b. This $20 billion is the amount we assumed firms plan to invest at all levels of GDP. Or, more directly, we can plot the $C + I_g$ data in column 6, Table 9.2.

Observe in Figure 9.2 that the aggregate expenditures line $C + I_g$ shows that total spending rises with income and output (GDP), but not as much as income rises. That is true because the marginal propensity to consume—the slope of line C—is less than 1. A part of any increase in income will be saved rather than spent. And because the aggregate expenditures line $C + I_g$ is parallel to the consumption line C, the slope of the aggregate expenditures line also equals the MPC for the economy and is less than 1. For our particular data, aggregate expenditures rise by $15 billion for every $20 billion increase in real output and income because $5 billion of each $20 billion increment is saved. Therefore, the slope of the aggregate expenditures line is .75 $(= \Delta\$15/\Delta\$20)$.

The equilibrium level of GDP is determined by the intersection of the aggregate expenditures schedule and the 45° line. This intersection locates the only point at which aggregate expenditures (on the vertical axis) are equal to GDP (on the horizontal axis). Because Figure 9.2 is based on the data in Table 9.2, we once again find that equilibrium output is $470 billion. Observe that consumption at this output is $450 billion and investment is $20 billion.

It is evident from Figure 9.2 that no levels of GDP *above* the equilibrium level are sustainable because at those levels $C + I_g$ falls short of GDP. Graphically, the aggregate expenditures schedule lies below the 45° line in those situations. At the $510 billion GDP level, for example, $C + I_g$ is only $500 billion. This underspending causes inventories to rise, prompting firms to readjust production downward in the direction of the $470 billion output level.

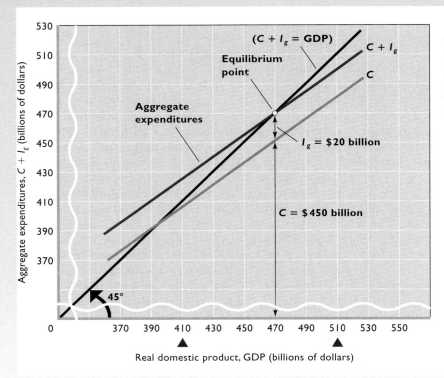

FIGURE 9.2 **Equilibrium GDP.** The aggregate expenditures schedule, $C + I_g$, is determined by adding the investment schedule I_g to the upsloping consumption schedule C. Since investment is assumed to be the same at each level of GDP, the vertical distances between C and $C + I_g$ do not change. Equilibrium GDP is determined where the aggregate expenditures schedule intersects the 45° line, in this case at $470 billion.

QUICK QUIZ 9.2

1. In this figure, the slope of the aggregate expenditures schedule $C + I_g$:
   a. increases as real GDP increases.
   b. falls as real GDP increases.
   c. is constant and equals the MPC.
   d. is constant and equals the MPS.

2. At all points on the 45° line:
   a. equilibrium GDP is possible.
   b. aggregate expenditures exceed real GDP.
   c. consumption exceeds investment.
   d. aggregate expenditures are less than real GDP.

3. The $490 billion level of real GDP is not at equilibrium because:
   a. investment exceeds consumption.
   b. consumption exceeds investment.
   c. planned $C + I_g$ exceeds real GDP.
   d. planned $C + I_g$ is less than real GDP.

4. The $430 billion level of real GDP is not at equilibrium because:
   a. investment exceeds consumption.
   b. consumption exceeds investment.
   c. planned $C + I_g$ exceeds real GDP.
   d. planned $C + I_g$ is less than real GDP.

Answers: 1. c; 2. a; 3. d; 4. c

Conversely, at levels of GDP *below* $470 billion, the economy wants to spend in excess of what businesses are producing. Then $C + I_g$ exceeds total output. Graphically, the aggregate expenditures schedule lies above the 45° line. At the $410 billion GDP level, for example, $C + I_g$ totals $425 billion. This excess spending causes inventories to fall below their planned level, prompting firms to raise production toward the $470 billion GDP. Unless there is some change in the location of the

G 9.1

Equilibrium GDP

aggregate expenditures line, the $470 billion level of GDP will be sustained indefinitely.

Other Features of Equilibrium GDP

We have seen that $C + I_g = $ GDP at equilibrium in the private closed economy. A closer look at Table 9.2 reveals two more characteristics of equilibrium GDP:

• Saving and planned investment are equal.
• There are no unplanned changes in inventories.

Saving Equals Planned Investment

As shown by row 6 in Table 9.2, saving and planned investment are both $20 billion at the $470 billion equilibrium level of GDP.

Saving is a **leakage** or withdrawal of spending from the income-expenditures stream. Saving is what causes consumption to be less than total output or GDP. Because of saving, consumption by itself is insufficient to remove domestic output from the shelves, apparently setting the stage for a decline in total output.

However, firms do not intend to sell their entire output to consumers. Some of that output will be capital goods sold to other businesses. Investment—the purchases of capital goods—is therefore an **injection** of spending into the income-expenditures stream. As an adjunct to consumption, investment is thus a potential replacement for the leakage of saving.

If the leakage of saving at a certain level of GDP exceeds the injection of investment, then $C + I_g$ will be less than GDP and that level of GDP cannot be sustained. Any GDP for which saving exceeds investment is an above-equilibrium GDP. Consider GDP of $510 billion (row 8 in Table 9.2). Households will save $30 billion, but firms will plan to invest only $20 billion. This $10 billion excess of saving over planned investment will reduce total spending to $10 billion below the value of total output. Specifically, aggregate expenditures will be $500 billion while real GDP is $510 billion. This spending deficiency will reduce real GDP.

Conversely, if the injection of investment exceeds the leakage of saving, then $C + I_g$ will be greater than GDP and drive GDP upward. Any GDP for which investment exceeds saving is a below-equilibrium GDP. For example, at a GDP of $410 billion (row 3) households will save only $5 billion, but firms will invest $20 billion. So investment exceeds saving by $15 billion. The small leakage of saving at this relatively low GDP level is more than compensated for by the larger injection of investment spending. That causes $C + I_g$ to exceed GDP and drives GDP higher.

Only where $S = I_g$—where the leakage of saving of $20 billion is exactly offset by the injection of planned investment of $20 billion—will aggregate expenditures ($C + I_g$) equal real output (GDP). That $C + I_g$ = GDP equality is what defines the equilibrium GDP. **(Key Question 2)**

No Unplanned Changes in Inventories

As part of their investment plans, firms may decide to increase or decrease their inventories. But, as confirmed in line 6 of Table 9.2, there are no **unplanned changes in inventories** at equilibrium GDP. This fact, along with $C + I_g$ = GDP, and $S = I$, is a characteristic of equilibrium GDP in the private closed economy.

Unplanned changes in inventories play a major role in achieving equilibrium GDP. Consider, as an example, the $490 billion *above-equilibrium* GDP shown in row 7 of Table 9.2. What happens if firms produce that output, thinking they can sell it? Households save $25 billion of their $490 billion DI, so consumption is only $465 billion. Planned investment (column 5) is $20 billion. So aggregate expenditures ($C + I_g$) are $485 billion and sales fall short of production by $5 billion. Firms retain that extra $5 billion of goods as an unplanned increase in inventories (column 7). It results from the failure of total spending to remove total output from the shelves.

Because changes in inventories are a part of investment, we note that *actual investment* is $25 billion. It consists of $20 billion of planned investment *plus* the $5 billion unplanned increase in inventories. Actual investment equals the saving of $25 billion, even though saving exceeds planned investment by $5 billion. Because firms cannot earn profits by accumulating unwanted inventories, the $5 billion unplanned increase in inventories will prompt them to cut back employment and production. GDP will fall to its equilibrium level of $470 billion, at which unplanned changes in inventories are zero.

Now look at the *below-equilibrium* $450 billion output (row 5, Table 9.2). Because households save only $15 billion of their $450 billion DI, consumption is $435 billion. Planned investment by firms is $20 billion, so aggregate expenditures are $455 billion. Sales exceed production by $5 billion. This is so only because a $5 billion unplanned decrease in business inventories has occurred. Firms must *disinvest* $5 billion in inventories (column 7). Note again that actual investment is $15 billion ($20 billion planned *minus* the $5 billion decline in inventory investment) and is equal to saving of $15 billion, even though planned investment exceeds saving by $5 billion. The unplanned decline in inventories, resulting from the excess of sales over production, will encourage firms to expand production. GDP will rise to $470 billion, at which unplanned changes in inventories are zero.

When economists say differences between investment and saving can occur and bring about changes in equilibrium GDP, they are referring to planned investment and saving. Equilibrium occurs only when planned investment and saving are equal. But when unplanned changes in inventories are considered, investment and saving are always equal, regardless of the level of GDP. That is true because actual investment consists of planned investment and unplanned investment (unplanned changes in inventories). Unplanned changes in inventories act as a balancing item that equates the actual amounts saved and invested in any period.

Changes in Equilibrium GDP and the Multiplier

In the private closed economy, the equilibrium GDP will change in response to changes in either the investment schedule or the consumption schedule. Because changes in the investment schedule usually are the main source of instability, we will direct our attention toward them.

Figure 9.3 shows the effect of changes in investment spending on the equilibrium real GDP. Suppose that the expected rate of return on investment rises or that the real interest rate falls such that investment spending increases by $5 billion. That would be shown as an upward shift of the investment schedule in Figure 9.1b. In Figure 9.3, the $5 billion increase of investment spending will increase aggregate expenditures from $(C + I_g)_0$ to $(C + I_g)_1$ and raise equilibrium real GDP from $470 billion to $490 billion.

If the expected rate of return on investment decreases or if the real interest rate rises, investment spending will decline by, say, $5 billion. That would be shown as a downward shift of the investment schedule in Figure 9.1b and a downward shift of the aggregate expenditures schedule from $(C + I_g)_0$ to $(C + I_g)_2$ in Figure 9.3. Equilibrium GDP will fall from $470 billion to $450 billion.

In our examples, a $5 billion change in investment spending leads to a $20 billion change in output and income. So the *multiplier* is 4 (= $20/$5). The MPS is .25, meaning that for every $1 billion of new income, $.25 billion of new saving occurs. Therefore, $20 billion of new income is needed to generate $5 billion of new saving. Once that increase in income and saving occurs, the economy is back in equilibrium—$C + I_g$ = GDP; saving and investment are equal; and there are no unplanned changes in inventories. You can see, then, that the multiplier process is an integral part of the aggregate expenditures model. (A brief review of Table 8.3 and Figure 8.8 will be helpful at this point.)

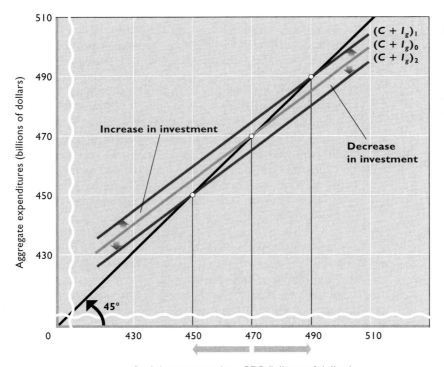

FIGURE 9.3 Changes in the equilibrium GDP caused by shifts in the aggregate expenditures schedule and the investment schedule. An upward shift of the aggregate expenditures schedule from $(C + I_g)_0$ to $(C + I_g)_1$ will increase the equilibrium GDP. Conversely, a downward shift from $(C + I_g)_0$ to $(C + I_g)_2$ will lower the equilibrium GDP. The extent of the changes in equilibrium GDP will depend on the size of the multiplier, which in this case is 4 (=20/5).

Real domestic product, GDP (billions of dollars)

Adding International Trade

We next move from a closed economy to an open economy that incorporates exports (X) and imports (M). Our focus will be on **net exports** (exports minus imports), which may be either positive or negative.

Net Exports and Aggregate Expenditures

Like consumption and investment, exports create domestic production, income, and employment for a nation. Although U.S. goods and services produced for export are sent abroad, foreign spending on those goods and services increases production and creates jobs and incomes in the United States. We must therefore include exports as a component of each nation's aggregate expenditures.

Conversely, when an economy is open to international trade, it will spend part of its income on imports—goods and services produced abroad. To avoid overstating the value of domestic production, we must subtract from total spending the amount spent on imported goods because such spending generates production and income abroad. In measuring aggregate expenditures for domestic goods and services, we must subtract expenditures on imports.

In short, for a private closed economy, aggregate expenditures are $C + I_g$. But for an open economy, aggregate expenditures are $C + I_g + (X - M)$. Or, recalling that net exports (X_n) equal $(X - M)$, we can say that aggregate expenditures for a private open economy are $C + I_g + X_n$.

The Net Export Schedule

A net export schedule lists the amount of net exports that will occur at each level of GDP. Table 9.3 shows two possible net export schedules for the hypothetical economy represented in Table 9.2. In net export schedule X_{n1} (columns 1 and 2), exports exceed imports by $5 billion at each level of GDP. Perhaps exports are $15 billion while imports are $10 billion. In schedule X_{n2} (columns 1 and 3), imports are $5 billion higher than exports. Perhaps imports are $20 billion while exports are $15 billion. To simplify our discussion, we assume in both schedules that net exports are independent of GDP.[1]

Figure 9.4b represents the two net export schedules in Table 9.3. Schedule X_{n1} is above the horizontal axis and depicts positive net exports of $5 billion at all levels of GDP.

---

[1]In reality, although our exports depend on foreign incomes and are thus independent of U.S. GDP, our imports do vary directly with our own domestic national income. Just as our domestic consumption varies directly with our GDP, so do our purchases of foreign goods. As our GDP rises, U.S. households buy not only more Pontiacs and more Pepsi but also more Porsches and more Perrier. However, for now we will ignore the complications of the positive relationship between imports and U.S. GDP.

TABLE 9.3 Two Net Export Schedules (in Billions)

(1) Level of GDP	(2) Net Exports, X_{n1} (X > M)	(3) Net Exports, X_{n2} (X < M)
$370	$+5	$−5
390	+5	−5
410	+5	−5
430	+5	−5
450	+5	−5
470	+5	−5
490	+5	−5
510	+5	−5
530	+5	−5
550	+5	−5

Schedule X_{n2}, which is below the horizontal axis, shows negative net exports of $5 billion at all levels of GDP.

Net Exports and Equilibrium GDP

The aggregate expenditures schedule labeled $C + I_g$ in Figure 9.4a reflects the private closed economy. It shows the combined consumption and gross investment expenditures occurring at each level of GDP. With no foreign sector, the equilibrium GDP is $470 billion.

But in the private open economy net exports can be either positive or negative. Let's see how each of the net export schedules in Figure 9.4b affects equilibrium GDP.

Positive Net Exports Suppose the net export schedule is X_{n1}. The $5 billion of additional net export expenditures by the rest of the world is accounted for by adding that $5 billion to the $C + I_g$ schedule in Figure 9.4a. Aggregate expenditures at each level of GDP are then $5 billion higher than $C + I_g$ alone. The aggregate expenditures schedule for the open economy thus becomes $C + I_g + X_{n1}$. In this case, international trade increases equilibrium GDP from $470 billion in the private closed economy to $490 billion in the private open economy.

Generalization: Other things equal, positive net exports increase aggregate expenditures and GDP beyond what they would be in a closed economy. Exports reduce the stock of available goods in an economy because some of an economy's output is sent abroad. But exports boost an economy's real GDP by increasing expenditures on domestically produced output. Adding net exports of $5 billion has increased GDP by $20 billion, in this case implying a multiplier of 4.

Negative Net Exports Conversely, suppose that net exports are a negative $5 billion as shown by X_{n2} in Figure 9.4b. This means that our hypothetical economy is

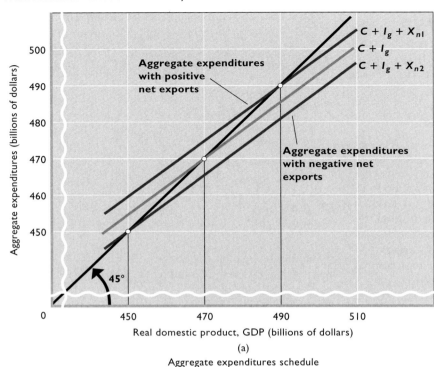

Aggregate expenditures with positive net exports

Aggregate expenditures with negative net exports

$C + I_g + X_{n1}$
$C + I_g$
$C + I_g + X_{n2}$

45°

Real domestic product, GDP (billions of dollars)

(a)
Aggregate expenditures schedule

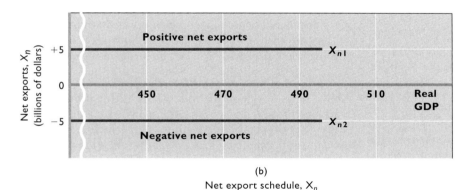

Positive net exports

X_{n1}

Real GDP

Negative net exports

X_{n2}

(b)
Net export schedule, X_n

FIGURE 9.4 Net exports and equilibrium GDP. Positive net exports such as shown by the net export schedule X_{n1} in (b) elevate the aggregate expenditures schedule in (a) from the closed-economy level of $C + I_g$ to the open-economy level of $C + I_g + X_{n1}$. Negative net exports such as depicted by the net export schedule X_{n2} in (b) lower the aggregate expenditures schedule in (a) from the closed-economy level of $C + I_g$ to the open-economy level of $C + I_g + X_{n2}$.

importing $5 billion more of goods than it is exporting. The aggregate expenditures schedule shown as $C + I_g$ in Figure 9.4a therefore overstates the expenditures on domestic output at each level of GDP. We must reduce the sum of expenditures by the $5 billion net amount spent on imported goods. We do that by subtracting the $5 billion of net imports from $C + I_g$.

The relevant aggregate expenditures schedule in Figure 9.4a becomes $C + I_g + X_{n2}$ and equilibrium GDP falls from $470 billion to $450 billion. Again, a change in net exports of $5 billion has produced a fourfold change in GDP, reminding us that the multiplier in this example is 4.

This gives us a corollary to our first generalization: Other things equal, negative net exports reduce aggregate expenditures and GDP below what they would be in a closed economy. Imports add to the stock of goods available in the economy, but they diminish real GDP by reducing expenditures on domestically produced products.

Our generalizations of the effects of net exports on GDP mean that a decline in X_n—a decrease in exports or an increase in imports—reduces aggregate expenditures and contracts a nation's GDP. Conversely, an increase in X_n—the result of either an increase in exports or a decrease in imports—increases aggregate expenditures and expands GDP.

GLOBAL PERSPECTIVE 9.1

Net Exports of Goods, Selected Nations, 2004

Some nations, such as Germany and Japan, have positive net exports, other countries, such as the United States and the United Kingdom, have negative net exports.

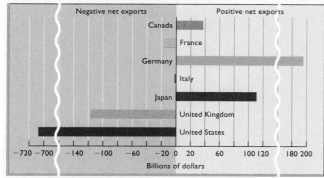

Source: World Trade Organization. **www.wto.org.**

As is shown in Global Perspective 9.1, net exports vary greatly among the major industrial nations. **(Key Question 9)**

International Economic Linkages

Our analysis of net exports and real GDP suggests how circumstances or policies abroad can affect U.S. GDP.

Prosperity Abroad

A rising level of real output and income among U.S. foreign trading partners enables the United States to sell more goods abroad, thus raising U.S. net exports and increasing its real GDP (assuming initially there is excess capacity). There is good reason for Americans to be interested in the prosperity of our trading partners. Their good fortune enables them to buy more of our exports, increasing our income and enabling us in turn to buy more foreign imports. These lower-price imported goods are the ultimate benefit of international trade. Prosperity abroad transfers some of that prosperity to Americans.

Tariffs

Suppose foreign trading partners impose high tariffs on U.S. goods to reduce their imports from the United States and thus increase production in their economies. Their imports, however, are U.S. exports. So when they restrict their imports to stimulate *their* economies, they are reducing U.S. exports and depressing *our* economy. We are likely to retaliate by imposing tariffs on their products. If so, their exports to us will decline and their net exports may fall. It is not clear, then, whether tariffs increase or decrease a nation's net exports. In the Great Depression of the

1930s various nations, including the United States, imposed trade barriers as a way of reducing domestic unemployment. But rounds of retaliation simply throttled world trade, worsened the Depression, and increased unemployment.

Exchange Rates

Depreciation of the dollar relative to other currencies (discussed in Chapter 5) enables people abroad to obtain more dollars with each unit of their own currencies. The price of U.S. goods in terms of those currencies will fall, stimulating purchases of U.S. exports. Also, U.S. customers will find they need more dollars to buy foreign goods and, consequently, will reduce their spending on imports. The increased exports and decreased imports will increase U.S. net exports and thus expand the nation's GDP.

Whether depreciation of the dollar will actually raise real GDP or produce inflation depends on the initial position of the economy relative to its full-employment output. If the economy is operating below its full-employment level, depreciation of the dollar and the resulting rise in net exports will increase aggregate expenditures and thus expand real GDP. But if the economy is already fully employed, the increase in net exports and aggregate expenditures will cause demand-pull inflation. Because resources are already fully employed, the increased spending cannot expand real output; but it can and does increase the prices of the existing output.

This last example has been cast only in terms of depreciation of the dollar. You should think through the impact that appreciation of the dollar would have on net exports and equilibrium GDP.

QUICK REVIEW 9.2

- Positive net exports increase aggregate expenditures relative to the closed economy and, other things equal, increase equilibrium GDP.
- Negative net exports decrease aggregate expenditures relative to the closed economy and, other things equal, reduce equilibrium GDP.
- In the open economy changes in (a) prosperity abroad, (b) tariffs, and (c) exchange rates can affect U.S. net exports and therefore U.S. aggregate expenditures and equilibrium GDP.

Adding the Public Sector

Our final step in constructing the full aggregate expenditures model is to move the analysis from a private (no-government) open economy to an economy with a public sector (sometimes called a "mixed economy"). This means adding government purchases and taxes to the model.

For simplicity, we will assume that government purchases are independent of the level of GDP and do not alter the consumption and investment schedules. Also, government's net tax revenues—total tax revenues less "negative taxes" in the form of transfer payments—are derived entirely from personal taxes. Finally, a fixed amount of taxes is collected regardless of the level of GDP.

Government Purchases and Equilibrium GDP

Suppose the government decides to purchase $20 billion of goods and services regardless of the level of GDP and tax collections.

Tabular Example Table 9.4 shows the impact of this purchase on the equilibrium GDP. Columns 1 through 4 are carried over from Table 9.2 for the private closed economy, in which the equilibrium GDP was $470 billion. The only new items are exports and imports in column 5 and government purchases in column 6. (Observe in column 5 that net exports are zero.) As shown in column 7, the addition of government purchases to private spending $(C + I_g + X_n)$ yields a new, higher level of aggregate expenditures $(C + I_g + X_n + G)$. Comparing columns 1 and 7, we find that aggregate expenditures and real output are equal at a higher level of GDP. Without government purchases, equilibrium GDP was $470 billion (row 6); *with* government purchases, aggregate expenditures and real output are equal at $550 billion (row 10). Increases in public spending, like increases in private spending, shift the aggregate expenditures schedule upward and produce a higher equilibrium GDP.

Note, too, that government spending is subject to the multiplier. A $20 billion increase in government purchases has increased equilibrium GDP by $80 billion (from $470 billion to $550 billion). The multiplier in this example is 4.

This $20 billion increase in government spending is *not* financed by increased taxes. Shortly, we will demonstrate that increased taxes *reduce* equilibrium GDP.

Graphical Analysis In Figure 9.5, we vertically add $20 billion of government purchases, G, to the level of private spending, $C + I_g + X_n$. That added $20 billion raises the aggregate expenditures schedule (private plus public) to $C + I_g + X_n + G$, resulting in an $80 billion increase in equilibrium GDP, from $470 to $550 billion.

A decline in government purchases G will lower the aggregate expenditures schedule in Figure 9.5 and result in a multiplied decline in the equilibrium GDP. Verify in Table 9.4 that if government purchases were to decline from $20 billion to $10 billion, the equilibrium GDP would fall by $40 billion.

Taxation and Equilibrium GDP

The government not only spends but also collects taxes. Suppose it imposes a **lump-sum tax,** which is a tax of a constant amount or, more precisely, a tax yielding the same amount of tax revenue at each level of GDP. Let's assume this tax is $20 billion, so that the government obtains $20 billion of tax revenue at each level of GDP regardless of the level of government purchases.

TABLE 9.4 The Impact of Government Purchases on Equilibrium GDP

(1) Real Domestic Output and Income (GDP = DI), Billions	(2) Consumption (C), Billions	(3) Savings (S), Billions	(4) Investment (I_g), Billions	(5) Net Exports (X_n), Billions		(6) Government Purchases (G), Billions	(7) Aggregate Expenditures ($C + I_g + X_n + G$), Billions (2) + (4) + (5) + (6)
				Exports (X)	Imports (M)		
(1) $370	$375	$−5	$20	$10	$10	$20	$415
(2) 390	390	0	20	10	10	20	430
(3) 410	405	5	20	10	10	20	445
(4) 430	420	10	20	10	10	20	460
(5) 450	435	15	20	10	10	20	475
(6) 470	450	20	20	10	10	20	490
(7) 490	465	25	20	10	10	20	505
(8) 510	480	30	20	10	10	20	520
(9) 530	495	35	20	10	10	20	535
(10) *550*	*510*	*40*	*20*	*10*	*10*	*20*	*550*

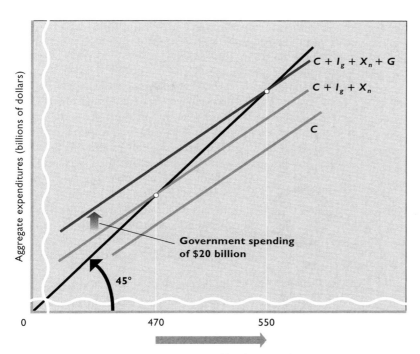

FIGURE 9.5 Government spending and equilibrium GDP. The addition of government expenditures of G to our analysis raises the aggregate expenditures ($C + I_g + X_n + G$) schedule and increases the equilibrium level of GDP, as would an increase in C, I_g or X_n.

Tabular Example In Table 9.5, which continues our example, we find taxes in column 2, and we see in column 3 that disposable (after-tax) income is lower than GDP (column 1) by the $20 billion amount of the tax. Because households use disposable income both to consume and to save, the tax lowers both consumption and saving. The MPC and MPS tell us how much consumption and saving will decline as a result of the $20 billion in taxes. Because the MPC is .75, the government tax collection of $20 billion will reduce consumption by $15 billion (= .75 × $20 billion). Since the MPS is .25, saving will drop by $5 billion (= .25 × $20 billion).

Columns 4 and 5 in Table 9.5 list the amounts of consumption and saving *at each level of GDP*. Note they are $15 billion and $5 billion smaller than those in Table 9.4. Taxes reduce disposable income relative to GDP

TABLE 9.5 Determination of the Equilibrium Levels of Employment, Output, and Income: Private and Public Sectors

(1) Real Domestic Output and Income (GDP = NI = PI), Billions	(2) Taxes (T), Billions	(3) Disposable Income (DI), Billions, (1) − (2)	(4) Consumption (C_a), Billions	(5) Saving (S_a), Billions (3)−(4)	(6) Investment (I_g), Billions	(7) Net Exports (X_n), Billions Exports (X)	(7) Imports (M)	(8) Government Purchases (G), Billions	(9) Aggregate Expenditures ($C_a + I_g + X_n + G$), Billions, (4) + (6) + (7) + (8)
(1) $370	$20	$350	$360	$−10	$20	$10	$10	$20	$400
(2) 390	20	370	375	−5	20	10	10	20	415
(3) 410	20	390	390	0	20	10	10	20	430
(4) 430	20	410	405	5	20	10	10	20	445
(5) 450	20	430	420	10	20	10	10	20	460
(6) 470	20	450	435	15	20	10	10	20	475
(7) **490**	**20**	**470**	**450**	**20**	**20**	**10**	**10**	**20**	**490**
(8) 510	20	490	465	25	20	10	10	20	505
(9) 530	20	510	480	30	20	10	10	20	520
(10) 550	20	530	495	35	20	10	10	20	535

by the amount of the taxes. This decline in DI reduces both consumption and saving at each level of GDP. The MPC and the MPS determine the declines in C and S.

To find the effect of taxes on equilibrium GDP, we calculate aggregate expenditures again, as shown in column 9, Table 9.5. Aggregate spending is $15 billion less at each level of GDP than it was in Table 9.4. The reason is that after-tax consumption, designated by C_a, is $15 billion less at each level of GDP. A comparison of real output and aggregate expenditures in columns 1 and 9 shows that the aggregate amounts produced and purchased are equal only at $490 billion of GDP (row 7). The $20 billion lump-sum tax has reduced equilibrium GDP by $60 billion, from $550 billion (row 10, Table 9.3) to $490 billion (row 7, Table 9.4).

Graphical Analysis

In Figure 9.6 the $20 billion increase in taxes shows up as a $15 (not $20) billion decline in the aggregate expenditures ($C_a + I_g + X_n + G$) schedule. This decline in the schedule results solely from a decline in the consumption C component of aggregate expenditures. The equilibrium GDP falls from $550 billion to $490 billion because of this tax-caused drop in consumption. With no change in government expenditures, tax increases lower the aggregate expenditures schedule relative to the 45° line and reduce the equilibrium GDP.

In contrast to our previous case, a *decrease* in existing taxes will raise the aggregate expenditures schedule in Figure 9.6 as a result of an increase in consumption at all GDP levels. You should confirm that a tax reduction of

$10 billion (from the present $20 billion to $10 billion) would increase the equilibrium GDP from $490 billion to $520 billion. **(Key Question 12)**

Differential Impacts

You may have noted that equal changes in G and T do not have equivalent impacts on GDP. The $20 billion increase in G in our illustration, subject to the multiplier of 4, produced an $80 billion increase in real GDP. But the $20 billion increase in taxes reduced GDP by only $60 billion. Given an MPC of .75, the tax increase of $20 billion reduced consumption by only $15 billion (not $20 billion) because saving also fell by $5 billion. Subjecting the $15 billion decline in consumption to the multiplier of 4, we find the tax increase of $20 billion reduced GDP by $60 billion (not $80 billion).

W 9.2

Complete aggregate expenditures model

Table 9.5 and Figure 9.6 constitute the complete aggregate expenditures model for an open economy with government. When total spending equals total production, the economy's output is in equilibrium. In the open mixed economy, equilibrium GDP occurs where

$$C_a + I_g + X_n + G = \text{GDP}$$

Injections, Leakages, and Unplanned Changes in Inventories

The related characteristics of equilibrium noted for the private closed economy also apply to the full model. Injections into the income-

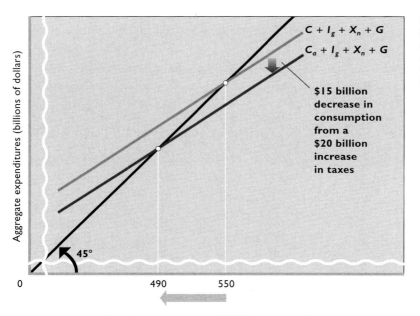

FIGURE 9.6 **Taxes and equilibrium GDP.** If the MPC is .75, the $20 billion of taxes will lower the consumption schedule by $15 billion and cause a $60 billion decline in the equilibrium GDP. In the open economy with government, equilibrium GDP occurs where C_a (after-tax income) $+ I_g + X_n + G = $ GDP. Here that equilibrium is $490 billion.

Figure labels:
$C + I_g + X_n + G$
$C_a + I_g + X_n + G$

$15 billion decrease in consumption from a $20 billion increase in taxes

45°

Aggregate expenditures (billions of dollars)

Real domestic product, GDP (billions of dollars)

0   490   550

expenditures stream equal leakages from the income stream. For the private closed economy, $S = I_g$. For the expanded economy, imports and taxes are added leakages. Saving, importing, and paying taxes are all uses of income that subtract from potential consumption. Consumption will now be less than GDP—creating a potential spending gap—in the amount of after-tax saving (S_a), imports (M), and taxes (T). But exports (X) and government purchases (G), along with investment (I_g), are injections into the income-expenditures stream. At the equilibrium GDP, the sum of the leakages equals the sum of injections. In symbols:

$$S_a + M + T = I_g + X + G$$

You should use the data in Table 9.5 to confirm this equality between leakages and injections at the equilibrium GDP of $490 billion. Also, substantiate that a lack of such equality exists at all other possible levels of GDP.

Although not directly shown in Table 9.5, the equilibrium characteristic of "no unplanned changes in inventories" will also be fulfilled at the $490 billion GDP. Because aggregate expenditures equal GDP, all the goods and services produced will be purchased. There will be no unplanned increase in inventories, so firms will have no incentive to reduce their employment and production. Nor will they experience an unplanned decline in their inventories, which would prompt them to expand their employment and output in order to replenish their inventories.

G 9.2
Changes in GDP

Equilibrium versus Full-Employment GDP

Now let's use the complete aggregate expenditures model to evaluate the equilibrium GDP. The $490 billion equilibrium GDP in our complete analysis may or may not provide full employment. Indeed, we have assumed thus far that the economy is operating at less-than-full employment. The economy, we will see, need not always produce full employment and price-level stability. We will also see that the economy can produce full-employment GDP even while experiencing large negative net exports.

Recessionary Expenditure Gap

Suppose in **Figure 9.7 (Key Graph),** panel (a), that the full-employment level of GDP is $510 billion and the aggregate expenditures schedule is AE_1. (For simplicity, we will now dispense with the $C_a + I_g + X_n + G$ labeling.) This schedule intersects the 45° line to the left of the

economy's full-employment output, so the economy's equilibrium GDP of $490 billion is $20 billion short of its full-employment output of $510 billion. According to column 1 in Table 9.2, total employment at the full-employment GDP is 75 million workers. But the economy depicted in Figure 9.7a is employing only 70 million workers; 5 million available workers are not employed. For that reason, the economy is sacrificing $20 billion of output.

A **recessionary expenditure gap** is the amount by which aggregate expenditures *at the full-employment GDP* fall short of those required to achieve the full-employment GDP. Insufficient total spending contracts or depresses the economy. Table 9.5 shows that at the full-employment level of $510 billion (column 1), the corresponding level of aggregate expenditures is only $505 billion (column 9). The recessionary expenditure gap is thus $5 billion, the amount by which the aggregate expenditures curve would have to shift upward to realize equilibrium at the full-employment GDP. Graphically, the recessionary expenditure gap is the *vertical* distance (measured at the full-employment GDP) by which the actual aggregate expenditures schedule AE_1 lies below the hypothetical full-employment aggregate expenditures schedule AE_0. In Figure 9.7a, this recessionary expenditure gap is $5 billion. Because the multiplier is 4, there is a $20 billion differential (the recessionary expenditure gap of $5 billion times the multiplier of 4) between the equilibrium GDP and the full-employment GDP. This $20 billion difference is a negative *GDP gap*—an idea we first developed when discussing cyclical unemployment in Chapter 7.

Inflationary Expenditure Gap

An **inflationary expenditure gap** is the amount by which an economy's aggregate expenditures *at the full-employment GDP* exceed those just necessary to achieve the full-employment GDP. In Figure 9.7b, there is a $5 billion inflationary expenditure gap at the $510 billion full-employment GDP. This is shown by the vertical distance between the actual aggregate expenditures schedule AE_2 and the hypothetical schedule AE_0, which would be just sufficient to achieve the $510 billion full-employment GDP. Thus, the inflationary expenditure gap is the amount by which the aggregate expenditures schedule would have to shift downward to realize equilibrium at the full-employment GDP.

The effect of this inflationary expenditure gap is that the excessive spending will pull up output prices. Since businesses cannot respond to the $5 billion in excessive spending by expanding their real output,

W 9.3
Expenditure gaps

keygraph

FIGURE 9.7 Recessionary and inflationary expenditure gaps. The equilibrium and full-employment GDPs may not coincide. (a) A recessionary expenditure gap is the amount by which aggregate expenditures at the full-employment GDP fall short of those needed to achieve the full-employment GDP. Here, the $5 billion recessionary expenditure gap causes a $20 billion negative GDP gap. (b) An inflationary expenditure gap is the amount by which aggregate expenditures at the full-employment GDP exceed those just sufficient to achieve the full-employment GDP. Here, the inflationary expenditure gap is $5 billion; this overspending produces demand-pull inflation.

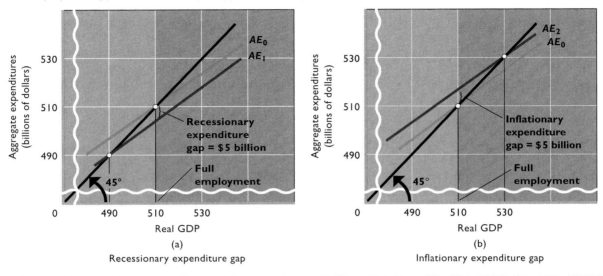

(a)
Recessionary expenditure gap

(b)
Inflationary expenditure gap

QUICK QUIZ 9.7

1. In the economy depicted:
   a. the MPS is .50.
   b. the MPC is .75.
   c. the full-employment level of real GDP is $530 billion.
   d. nominal GDP always equals real GDP.
2. The inflationary expenditure gap depicted will cause:
   a. demand-pull inflation.
   b. cost-push inflation.
   c. cyclical unemployment.
   d. frictional unemployment.
3. The recessionary expenditure gap depicted will cause:
   a. demand-pull inflation.
   b. cost-push inflation.

   c. cyclical unemployment.
   d. frictional unemployment.
4. In the economy depicted, the $5 billion inflationary expenditure gap:
   a. expands real GDP to $530 billion.
   b. leaves real GDP at $510 billion but causes inflation.
   c. could be remedied by equal $5 billion increases in taxes and government spending.
   d. implies that real GDP exceeds nominal GDP.

Answers: 1. b; 2. a; 3. c; 4. b

demand-pull inflation will occur. Nominal GDP will rise because of a higher price level, but real GDP will not. Excessive total spending causes inflation. **(Key Question 13)**

Application: The U.S. Recession of 2001

The U.S. economy grew briskly in the last half of the 1990s, with real GDP expanding at about 4 percent annually and the unemployment rate averaging roughly

4.5 percent. The economic boom and low rates of unemployment, however, did not spark inflation, as had been the case in prior business cycles. Exceptionally strong productivity growth in the late 1990s increased the economy's production capacity and enabled aggregate expenditures to expand without causing inflation. In terms of Figure 9.7b, it was as if the full-employment level of real GDP expanded from $510 billion to $530 billion at the same time the aggregate expenditures curve rose from AE_0 to AE_2. So the inflationary expenditure gap of $5 billion never materialized. Between 1995 and 1999, inflation averaged less than 2.5 percent annually.

But the booming economy of the second half of the 1990s produced notable excesses. A large number of ill-conceived Internet-related firms were born, attracting billions of investment dollars. Investment spending surged throughout the economy and eventually added too much production capacity. A stock market "bubble" developed as stock market investing became a national pastime. Consumers increased their household debt to expand their consumption. Some unscrupulous executives engaged in fraudulent business practices to further their own personal interests.

The boom ended in the early 2000s. Hundreds of Internet-related start-up firms folded. Many firms, particularly those in telecommunications and aircraft manufacturing, began to experience severe overcapacity. The stock market bubble burst, erasing billions of dollars of "paper" wealth. Firms significantly reduced their investment spending because of lower estimates of rates of return. In March 2001 aggregate expenditures declined sufficiently to push the economy into its ninth recession since 1950. The unemployment rate rose from 4.2 percent in February 2001 to 5.8 percent in December 2001. In terms of Figure 9.7a, a recessionary expenditure gap emerged. The terrorist attacks of September 11, 2001, damaged consumer confidence and prolonged the recession through 2001. In 2002 the economy resumed economic growth, but the unemployment rate remained a stubbornly high 6 percent at the end of 2002. Even so, the recession of 2001 was relatively mild by historical standards and in view of the unusual set of circumstances.

Application: U.S. Inflation in the Late 1980s

The United States has not had an episode of rising inflation since the late 1980s. During that period, however, a sizable U.S. inflationary expenditure gap developed. As the economy moved beyond its full-employment output between 1986 and 1990, the price level rose at an increasing rate. Specifically, the annual rate of inflation increased from 1.9 percent in 1986 to 3.6 percent in 1987 to 4.1 percent in 1988 to 4.8 percent in 1989. In terms of Figure 9.7b, the aggregate expenditures schedule moved upward from year to year and increased the expenditure inflationary gap. The gap closed as the expansion came to an end. In 1990–1991 a recessionary gap emerged. Inflation fell to 3 percent immediately after the recession of 1990–1991 and remained at or below 3 percent throughout the 1990s.

Application: Full-Employment Output, with Large Negative Net Exports

In 2005 the United States had negative net exports of $632 billion in real (2000) dollar terms, yet its actual (real) GDP of $11,135 billion roughly matched its potential (real) GDP of $11,274. The economy experienced neither a recessionary expenditure gap nor an inflationary expenditure gap. It was fully employed, with an unemployment rate of 5.1 percent.

How could this outcome be? Doesn't the aggregate expenditure model suggest that large negative net exports reduce aggregate expenditures and therefore decrease equilibrium GDP, presumably to below its potential level? That undesirable outcome is possible, *other things equal*. But in 2005 large domestic consumption, investment, and government expenditures fully made up for the $632 billion of negative net exports. In 2005, U.S. consumers spent (in real terms) $7858 billion—an amount that exceeded their total after-tax income! Businesses invested $1921 billion, even though total U.S. saving was negative. The Federal government spent $1988 billion, financing more than one-fourth of that amount through borrowing.

Negative net exports—even large ones—do not preclude achieving full-employment output. Aggregate expenditures in total were sufficient in 2005 to purchase the potential output, with no unplanned changes in inventories. The $C_a + I_g + G$ expenditures were financed, in part, by foreigners whose large trade surpluses with the United States left them with equally large quantities of U.S. dollars. People and business abroad willingly lent many of those dollars to the United States in anticipation of high returns. That foreign lending in turn helped finance the high U.S. domestic spending.

QUICK REVIEW 9.3

- Government purchases shift the aggregate expenditures schedule upward and raise the equilibrium GDP.
- Taxes reduce disposable income, lower consumption spending and saving, shift the aggregate expenditures schedule downward, and reduce the equilibrium GDP.
- A recessionary expenditure gap is the amount by which an economy's aggregate expenditures schedule must shift upward to achieve the full-employment GDP; an inflationary expenditure gap is the amount by which the economy's aggregate expenditures schedule must shift downward to eliminate demand-pull inflation and still achieve the full-employment GDP.

Last *Word*

Say's Law, the Great Depression, and Keynes

The Aggregate Expenditure Theory Emerged as a Critique of Classical Economics and as a Response to the Great Depression.

Until the Great Depression of the 1930s, many prominent economists, including David Ricardo (1772–1823) and John Stuart Mill (1806–1873), believed that the market system would ensure full employment of an economy's resources. These so-called *classical economists* acknowledged that now and then abnormal circumstances such as wars, political upheavals, droughts, speculative crises, and gold rushes would occur, deflecting the economy from full-employment status. But when such deviations occurred, the economy would automatically adjust and soon return to full-employment output. For example, a slump in output and employment would result in lower prices, wages, and interest rates, which in turn would increase consumer spending, employment, and investment spending. Any excess supply of goods and workers would soon be eliminated.

Classical macroeconomists denied that the level of spending in an economy could be too low to bring about the purchase of the entire full-employment output. They based their denial of inadequate spending in part on *Say's law*, attributed to the nineteenth-century French economist J. B. Say (1767–1832). This law is the disarmingly simple idea that the very act of producing goods generates income equal to the value of the goods produced. The production of any output automatically provides the income needed to buy that output. More succinctly stated, *supply creates its own demand.*

Say's law can best be understood in terms of a barter economy. A woodworker, for example, produces or supplies furniture as a means of buying or demanding the food and clothing produced by other workers. The woodworker's supply of furniture is the income that he will "spend" to satisfy his demand for other goods. The goods he buys (demands) will have a total

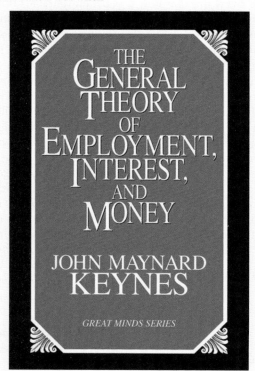

value exactly equal to the goods he produces (supplies). And so it is for other producers and for the entire economy. Demand must be the same as supply!

Assuming that the composition of output is in accord with consumer preferences, all markets would be cleared of their outputs. It would seem that all firms need to do to sell a full-employment output is to produce that level of output. Say's law guarantees there will be sufficient spending to purchase it all.

O 9.2
Say's law

The Great Depression of the 1930s called into question the theory that supply creates its own demand (Say's law). In the United States, real GDP declined by 40 percent and the unemployment rate rocketed to nearly 25 percent. Other nations experienced similar impacts. And cyclical unemployment lingered for a decade. An obvious inconsistency exists between a theory that says that unemployment is virtually impossible and the actual occurrence of a 10-year siege of substantial unemployment.

In 1936 British economist John Maynard Keynes (1883–1946) explained why cyclical unemployment could occur in a market economy. In his *General Theory of Employment, Interest, and Money*, Keynes attacked the foundations of classical theory and developed the ideas underlying the aggregate expenditures model. Keynes disputed Say's law, pointing out that not all income need be spent in the same period that it is produced. Investment spending, in particular, is volatile, said Keynes. A substantial decline in investment will lead to insufficient total spending. Unsold goods will accumulate in producers' warehouses, and producers will respond by reducing their output and discharging workers. A recession or depression will result, and widespread cyclical unemployment will occur. Moreover, said Keynes, recessions or depressions are not likely to correct themselves. In contrast to the more laissez-faire view of the classical economists, Keynes argued that government should play an active role in stabilizing the economy.

Limitations of the Model

This chapter's analysis demonstrates the power of the aggregate expenditures model to explain how the economy works, how recessions or depressions can occur, and how demand-pull inflation can arise. But this model has five well-known limitations:

- *It does not show price-level changes.* The model can account for demand-pull inflation, as in Figure 9.7b, but it does not indicate how much the price level will rise when aggregate expenditures are excessive relative to the economy's capacity. The aggregate expenditures model has no way of measuring the rate of inflation.

- *It ignores premature demand-pull inflation.* Mild demand-pull inflation can occur before an economy reaches its full-employment level of output. The aggregate expenditures model does not explain why that can happen.

- *It limits real GDP to the full-employment level of output.* For a time an actual economy can expand beyond its full-employment real GDP. The aggregate expenditures model does not allow for that possibility.

- *It does not deal with cost-push inflation.* We know from Chapter 7 that there are two general types of inflation: demand-pull inflation and cost-push inflation. The aggregate expenditures model does not address cost-push inflation.

- *It does not allow for "self-correction."* In reality, the economy contains some internal features that, given enough time, may correct a recessionary expenditure gap or an inflationary expenditure gap. The aggregate expenditures model does not contain those features.

In subsequent chapters we remedy these limitations while preserving the many valuable insights of the aggregate expenditures model.

Summary

1. For a private closed economy the equilibrium level of GDP occurs when aggregate expenditures and real output are equal or, graphically, where the $C + I_g$ line intersects the 45° line. At any GDP greater than equilibrium GDP, real output will exceed aggregate spending, resulting in unplanned investment in inventories and eventual declines in output and income (GDP). At any below-equilibrium GDP, aggregate expenditures will exceed real output, resulting in unplanned disinvestment in inventories and eventual increases in GDP.

2. At equilibrium GDP, the amount households save (leakages) and the amount businesses plan to invest (injections) are equal. Any excess of saving over planned investment will cause a shortage of total spending, forcing GDP to fall. Any excess of planned investment over saving will cause an excess of total spending, inducing GDP to rise. The change in GDP will in both cases correct the discrepancy between saving and planned investment.

3. At equilibrium GDP, there are no unplanned changes in inventories. When aggregate expenditures diverge from real GDP, an unplanned change in inventories occurs. Unplanned increases in inventories are followed by a cutback in production and a decline of real GDP. Unplanned decreases in inventories result in an increase in production and a rise of GDP.

4. Actual investment consists of planned investment plus unplanned changes in inventories and is always equal to saving.

5. A shift in the investment schedule (caused by changes in expected rates of return or changes in interest rates) shifts the aggregate expenditures curve and causes a new equilibrium level of real GDP. Real GDP changes by more than the amount of the initial change in investment. This multiplier effect ($\Delta GDP/\Delta I_g$) accompanies both increases and decreases in aggregate expenditures and also applies to changes in net exports (X_n) and government purchases (G).

6. The net export schedule in the model of the open economy relates net exports (exports minus imports) to levels of real GDP. For simplicity, we assume that the level of net exports is the same at all levels of real GDP.

7. Positive net exports increase aggregate expenditures to a higher level than they would if the economy were "closed" to international trade. Negative net exports decrease aggregate expenditures relative to those in a closed economy, decreasing equilibrium real GDP by a multiple of their amount. Increases in exports or decreases in imports have an expansionary effect on real GDP, while decreases in exports or increases in imports have a contractionary effect.

8. Government purchases in the model of the mixed economy shift the aggregate expenditures schedule upward and raise GDP.

9. Taxation reduces disposable income, lowers consumption and saving, shifts the aggregate expenditures curve downward, and reduces equilibrium GDP.

10. In the complete aggregate expenditures model, equilibrium GDP occurs where $C_a + I_g + X_n + G = GDP$. At the equilibrium GDP, *leakages* of after-tax saving (S_a), imports (M), and taxes (T) equal *injections* of investment (I_g), exports (X), and government purchases (G): $S_a + M + T = I_g + X_n + G$. Also, there are no unplanned changes in inventories.

11. The equilibrium GDP and the full-employment GDP may differ. A recessionary expenditure gap is the amount by which aggregate expenditures at the full-employment GDP fall short of those needed to achieve the full-employment GDP. This gap produces a negative GDP gap (actual GDP minus potential GDP). An inflationary expenditure gap is the amount by which aggregate expenditures at the full-employment GDP exceed those just sufficient to achieve the full-employment GDP. This gap causes demand-pull inflation.

12. The aggregate expenditures model provides many insights into the macroeconomy, but it does not (a) show price-level changes, (b) account for premature demand-pull inflation, (c) allow for real GDP to temporarily expand beyond the full-employment output, (d) account for cost-push inflation, or (e) allow for partial or full "self-correction" from a recessionary expenditure gap or an inflationary expenditure gap.

Terms and Concepts

planned investment	leakage	lump-sum tax
investment schedule	injection	recessionary expenditure gap
aggregate expenditures schedule	unplanned changes in inventories	inflationary expenditure gap
equilibrium GDP	net exports	

Study Questions

1. What is an investment schedule and how does it differ from an investment demand curve?

2. **KEY QUESTION** Assuming the level of investment is $16 billion and independent of the level of total output, complete the accompanying table and determine the equilibrium levels of output and employment in this private closed economy. What are the sizes of the MPC and MPS?

Possible Levels of Employment, Millions	Real Domestic Output (GDP = DI), Billions	Consumption, Billions	Saving, Billions
40	$240	$244	$ _____
45	260	260	_____
50	280	276	_____
55	300	292	_____
60	320	308	_____
65	340	324	_____
70	360	340	_____
75	380	356	_____
80	400	372	_____

3. Using the consumption and saving data in question 2 and assuming investment is $16 billion, what are saving and planned investment at the $380 billion level of domestic output? What are saving and actual investment at that level? What are saving and planned investment at the $300 billion level of domestic output? What are the levels of saving and

actual investment? Use the concept of unplanned investment to explain adjustments toward equilibrium from both the $380 billion and the $300 billion levels of domestic output.

4. Why is saving called a *leakage*? Why is planned investment called an *injection*? Why must saving equal planned investment at equilibrium GDP in the private closed economy? Are unplanned changes in inventories rising, falling, or constant at equilibrium GDP? Explain.

5. What effect will each of the changes listed in Study Question 3 of Chapter 8 have on the equilibrium level of GDP in the private closed economy? Explain your answers.

6. By how much will GDP change if firms increase their investment by $8 billion and the MPC is .80? If the MPC is .67?

7. Depict graphically the aggregate expenditures model for a private closed economy. Now show a decrease in the aggregate expenditures schedule and explain why the decline in real GDP in your diagram is greater than the initial decline in aggregate expenditures. What would be the ratio of a decline in real GDP to the initial drop in aggregate expenditures if the slope of your aggregate expenditures schedule was .8?

8. Suppose that a certain country has an MPC of .9 and a real GDP of $400 billion. If its investment spending decreases by $4 billion, what will be its new level of real GDP?

9. **KEY QUESTION** The data in columns 1 and 2 in the accompanying table are for a private closed economy:
   a. Use columns 1 and 2 to determine the equilibrium GDP for this hypothetical economy.
   b. Now open up this economy to international trade by including the export and import figures of columns 3

(1) Real Domestic Output (GDP = DI), Billions	(2) Aggregate Expenditures, Private Closed Economy, Billions	(3) Exports, Billions	(4) Imports, Billions	(5) Net Exports, Billions	(6) Aggregate Expenditures, Private Open Economy, Billions
$200	$240	$20	$30	$ _____	$ _____
250	280	20	30	_____	_____
300	320	20	30	_____	_____
350	360	20	30	_____	_____
400	400	20	30	_____	_____
450	440	20	30	_____	_____
500	480	20	30	_____	_____
550	520	20	30	_____	_____

and 4. Fill in columns 5 and 6 and determine the equilibrium GDP for the open economy. Explain why this equilibrium GDP differs from that of the closed economy.

c. Given the original $20 billion level of exports, what would be net exports and the equilibrium GDP if imports were $10 billion greater at each level of GDP?

d. What is the multiplier in this example?

10. Assume that, without taxes, the consumption schedule of an economy is as follows:

GDP, Billions	Consumption, Billions
$100	$120
200	200
300	280
400	360
500	440
600	520
700	600

a. Graph this consumption schedule and determine the MPC.

b. Assume now that a lump-sum tax is imposed such that the government collects $10 billion in taxes at all levels of GDP. Graph the resulting consumption schedule, and compare the MPC and the multiplier with those of the pretax consumption schedule.

11. Explain graphically the determination of equilibrium GDP for a private economy through the aggregate expenditures model. Now add government purchases (any amount you choose) to your graph, showing its impact on equilibrium GDP. Finally, add taxation (any amount of lump-sum tax that you choose) to your graph and show its effect on equilibrium GDP. Looking at your graph, determine whether equilibrium GDP has increased, decreased, or stayed the same given the sizes of the government purchases and taxes that you selected.

12. **KEY QUESTION** Refer to columns 1 and 6 in the table for question 9. Incorporate government into the table by assuming that it plans to tax and spend $20 billion at each possible level of GDP. Also assume that the tax is a personal tax and that government spending does not induce a shift in the private aggregate expenditures schedule. Compute and explain the change in equilibrium GDP caused by the addition of government.

13. **KEY QUESTION** Refer to the table below in answering the questions that follow:

a. If full employment in this economy is 130 million, will there be an inflationary expenditure gap or a recessionary expenditure gap? What will be the consequence of this gap? By how much would aggregate expenditures in column 3 have to change at each level of GDP to eliminate the inflationary expenditure gap or the recessionary expenditure gap? Explain. What is the multiplier in this example?

b. Will there be an inflationary expenditure gap or a recessionary expenditure gap if the full-employment level of output is $500 billion? Explain the consequences. By how much would aggregate expenditures in column 3 have to change at each level of GDP to eliminate the gap? What is the multiplier in this example?

c. Assuming that investment, net exports, and government expenditures do not change with changes in real GDP, what are the sizes of the MPC, the MPS, and the multiplier?

(1) Possible Levels of Employment, Millions	(2) Real Domestic Output, Billions	(3) Aggregate Expenditures $(C_a + I_g + X_n + G)$, Billions
90	$500	$520
100	550	560
110	600	600
120	650	640
130	700	680

14. **ADVANCED ANALYSIS** Assume that the consumption schedule for a private open economy is such that consumption $C = 50 + 0.8Y$. Assume further that planned investment I_g and net exports X_n are independent of the level of real GDP and constant at $I_g = 30$ and $X_n = 10$. Recall also that, in equilibrium, the real output produced (Y) is equal to aggregate expenditures: $Y = C + I_g + X_n$.
   a. Calculate the equilibrium level of income or real GDP for this economy.
   b. What happens to equilibrium Y if I_g changes to 10? What does this outcome reveal about the size of the multiplier?
15. Answer the following questions, which relate to the aggregate expenditures model:

a. If C_a is \$100, I_g is \$50, X_n is −\$10, and G is \$30, what is the economy's equilibrium GDP?
b. If real GDP in an economy is currently \$200, C_a is \$100, I_g is \$50, X_n is −\$10, and G is \$30, will the economy's real GDP rise, fall, or stay the same?
c. Suppose that full-employment (and full-capacity) output in an economy is \$200. If C_a is \$150, I_g is \$50, X_n is −\$10, and G is \$30, what will be the macroeconomic result?

16. **LAST WORD** What is Say's law? How does it relate to the view held by classical economists that the economy generally will operate at a position on its production possibilities curve (Chapter 1)? Use production possibilities analysis to demonstrate Keynes' view on this matter.

Web-Based Questions

1. **THE MULTIPLIER—CALCULATING HYPOTHETICAL CHANGES IN GDP** Go to the Bureau of Economic Analysis at **www.bea.gov,** and use the BEA interactivity feature to select National Income and Product Account Tables. Then find Table 1.1, which contains the most recent values for GDP = $C_a + I_g + G + (X − M)$. Assume that the MPC is .75 and that, for each of the following, the values of the initial variables are those you just discovered. Determine the new value of GDP if, other things equal, (a) investment increased by 5 percent, (b) imports increased by 5 percent while exports increased by 5 percent, (c) consumption increased by 5 percent, and (d) government spending increased by 5 percent. Which of the changes, (a) through (d), caused the greatest change in GDP in absolute dollars?

2. **GDP GAP AND EXPENDITURE GAP** The St. Louis Federal Reserve Bank at **www.research.stlouisfed.org/fred2** provides data on both real GDP (chained 2000 dollars) and real potential GDP for the United States. Both sets of data are located as links under "Gross Domestic Product and Components." What was potential GDP for the third quarter of 2001? What was the actual level of real GDP for that quarter? What was the size difference between the two—the negative GDP gap? If the multiplier was 2 in that period, what was the size of the economy's recessionary expenditure gap?

Aggregate Demand and Aggregate Supply

In early 2000, Alan Greenspan, then chair of the Federal Reserve, made the following statement:

Through the so-called wealth effect, [recent stock market gains] have tended to foster increases in aggregate demand beyond the increases in supply. It is this imbalance . . . that contains the potential seeds of rising inflationary . . . pressures that could undermine the current expansion. Our goal [at the Federal Reserve] is to extend the expansion by containing its imbalances and avoiding the very recession that would complete the business cycle.[1]

Although the Federal Reserve held inflation in check, it did not accomplish its goal of extending the decade-long economic expansion. In March 2001 the U.S. economy experienced a recession and the

---

[1]Alan Greenspan, speech to the New York Economics Club, Jan. 13, 2000.

expansionary phase of the business cycle ended. Recovery and economic expansion resumed in 2002 and picked up considerable strength in 2003, 2004, and 2005.

We will say more about recession and expansion later. Our immediate focus is the terminology in the Greenspan quotation, which is precisely the language of the **aggregate demand–aggregate supply model (AD-AS model).** The AD-AS model—the subject of this chapter—enables us to analyze changes in real GDP and the price level simultaneously. The AD-AS model therefore provides keen insights on inflation, recession, unemployment, and economic growth. In later chapters, we will see that it also explains the logic of macroeconomic stabilization policies, such as those implied by Greenspan.

Aggregate Demand

Aggregate demand is a schedule or curve that shows the amounts of real output (real GDP) that buyers collectively desire to purchase at each possible price level. The relationship between the price level (as measured by the GDP price index) and the amount of real GDP demanded is inverse or negative: When the price level rises, the quantity of real GDP demanded decreases; when the price level falls, the quantity of real GDP demanded increases.

Aggregate Demand Curve

The inverse relationship between the price level and real GDP is shown in Figure 10.1, where the aggregate demand curve AD slopes downward, as does the demand curve for an individual product.

Why the downward slope? The explanation is *not* the same as that for why the demand for a single product slopes downward. That explanation centered on the

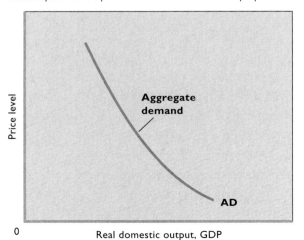

FIGURE 10.1 **The aggregate demand curve.** The downsloping aggregate demand curve AD indicates an inverse (or negative) relationship between the price level and the amount of real output purchased.

income effect and the substitution effect. When the price of an *individual* product falls, the consumer's (constant) nominal income allows a larger purchase of the product (the income effect). And, as price falls, the consumer wants to buy more of the product because it becomes relatively less expensive than other goods (the substitution effect).

But these explanations do not work for aggregates. In Figure 10.1, when the economy moves down its aggregate demand curve, it moves to a lower general price level. But our circular flow model tells us that when consumers pay lower prices for goods and services, less nominal income flows to resource suppliers in the form of wages, rents, interest, and profits. As a result, a decline in the price level does not necessarily mean an increase in the nominal income of the economy as a whole. Thus, a decline in the price level need not produce an income effect, where more output is purchased because lower prices leave buyers with greater real income.

Similarly, in Figure 10.1 prices in general are falling as we move down the aggregate demand curve, so the rationale for the substitution effect (where more of a specific product is purchased because it becomes cheaper relative to all other products) is not applicable. There is no *overall* substitution effect among domestically produced goods when the price level falls.

If the conventional substitution and income effects do not explain the downward slope of the aggregate demand curve, what does? That explanation rests on three effects of a price-level change.

Real-Balances Effect A change in the price level produces a **real-balances effect.** Here is how it works: A higher price level reduces the real value or purchasing power of the public's accumulated savings balances. In particular, the real value of assets with fixed money values, such as savings accounts or bonds, diminishes. Because a higher price level erodes the purchasing power of such assets, the public is poorer in real terms and will reduce its

O 10.1
Real-balances
effect

spending. A household might buy a new car or a plasma TV if the purchasing power of its financial asset balances is, say, $50,000. But if inflation erodes the purchasing power of its asset balances to $30,000, the household may defer its purchase. So a higher price level means less consumption spending.

Interest-Rate Effect The aggregate demand curve also slopes downward because of the **interest-rate effect.** When we draw an aggregate demand curve, we assume that the supply of money in the economy is fixed. But when the price level rises, consumers need more money for purchases and businesses need more money to meet their payrolls and to buy other resources. A $10 bill will do when the price of an item is $10, but a $10 bill plus a $1 bill is needed when the item costs $11. In short, a higher price level increases the demand for money. So, given a fixed supply of money, an increase in money demand will drive up the price paid for its use. That price is the interest rate.

Higher interest rates curtail investment spending and interest-sensitive consumption spending. Firms that expect a 6 percent rate of return on a potential purchase of capital will find that investment potentially profitable when the interest rate is, say, 5 percent. But the investment will be unprofitable and will not be made when the interest rate has risen to 7 percent. Similarly, consumers may decide not to purchase a new house or new automobile when the interest rate on loans goes up. So, by increasing the demand for money and consequently the interest rate, a higher price level reduces the amount of real output demanded.

Foreign Purchases Effect The final reason why the aggregate demand curve slopes downward is the **foreign purchases effect.** When the U.S. price level rises relative to foreign price levels (and exchange rates do not respond quickly or completely), foreigners buy fewer U.S. goods and Americans buy more foreign goods. Therefore, U.S. exports fall and U.S. imports rise. In short, the rise in the price level reduces the quantity of U.S. goods demanded as net exports.

These three effects, of course, work in the opposite direction for a decline in the price level. Then the quantity demanded of consumption goods, investment goods, and net exports rises.

Changes in Aggregate Demand

Other things equal, a change in the price level will change the amount of aggregate spending and therefore change the amount of real GDP demanded by the economy.

Movements along a fixed aggregate demand curve represent these changes in real GDP. However, if one or more of those "other things" change, the entire aggregate demand curve will shift. We call these other things **determinants of aggregate demand** or, less formally, *aggregate demand shifters.* They are listed in Figure 10.2.

Changes in aggregate demand involve two components:
- A change in one of the determinants of aggregate demand that directly changes the amount of real GDP demanded.
- A multiplier effect that produces a greater ultimate change in aggregate demand than the initiating change in spending.

In Figure 10.2, the full rightward shift of the curve from AD_1 to AD_2 shows an increase in aggregate demand, separated into these two components. The horizontal distance between AD_1 and the broken curve to its right illustrates an initial increase in spending, say, $5 billion of added investment. If the economy's MPC is .75, for example, then the simple multiplier is 4. So the aggregate demand curve shifts rightward from AD_1 to AD_2—four times the distance between AD_1 and the broken line. The multiplier process magnifies the initial change in spending into successive rounds of new consumption spending. After the shift, $20 billion (= $5 × 4) of additional real goods and services are demanded at each price level.

Similarly, the leftward shift of the curve from AD_1 to AD_3 shows a decrease in aggregate demand, the lesser amount of real GDP demanded at each price level. It also involves the initial decline in spending (shown as the horizontal distance between AD_1 and the dashed line to its left), followed by multiplied declines in consumption spending and the ultimate leftward shift to AD_3.

Let's examine each of the determinants of aggregate demand listed in Figure 10.2.

Consumer Spending

Even when the U.S. price level is constant, domestic consumers may alter their purchases of U.S.-produced real output. If those consumers decide to buy more output at each price level, the aggregate demand curve will shift to the right, as from AD_1 to AD_2 in Figure 10.2. If they decide to buy less output, the aggregate demand curve will shift to the left, as from AD_1 to AD_3.

Several factors other than a change in the price level may change consumer spending and therefore shift the aggregate demand curve. As Figure 10.2 shows, those factors are real consumer wealth, consumer expectations, household debt, and taxes. Because our discussion here parallels that of Chapter 8, we will be brief.

FIGURE 10.2 Changes in aggregate demand. A change in one or more of the listed determinants of aggregate demand will shift the aggregate demand curve. The rightward shift from AD$_1$ to AD$_2$ represents an increase in aggregate demand; the leftward shift from AD$_1$ to AD$_3$ shows a decrease in aggregate demand. The vertical distances between AD$_1$ and the dashed lines represent the initial changes in spending. Through the multiplier effect, that spending produces the full shifts of the curves.

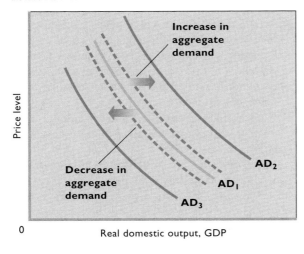

Determinants of Aggregate Demand: Factors that Shift the Aggregate Demand Curve
1. Change in consumer spending
a. Consumer wealth
b. Consumer expectations
c. Household debt
d. Taxes
2. Change in investment spending
a. Interest rates
b. Expected returns
• Expected future business conditions
• Technology
• Degree of excess capacity
• Business taxes
3. Change in government spending
4. Change in net export spending
a. National income abroad
b. Exchange rates

Consumer Wealth Consumer wealth includes both financial assets such as stocks and bonds and physical assets such as houses and land. A sharp increase in the real value of consumer wealth (for example, because of a rise in stock market values) prompts people to save less and buy more products. The resulting increase in consumer spending—called the *wealth effect*—will shift the aggregate demand curve to the right. In contrast, a major decrease in the real value of consumer wealth at each price level will reduce consumption spending (a negative wealth effect) and thus shift the aggregate demand curve to the left.

Consumer Expectations Changes in expectations about the future may alter consumer spending. When people expect their future real incomes to rise, they tend to spend more of their current incomes. Thus current consumption spending increases (current saving falls), and the aggregate demand curve shifts to the right. Similarly, a widely held expectation of surging inflation in the near future may increase aggregate demand today because consumers will want to buy products before their prices escalate. Conversely, expectations of lower future income or lower future prices may reduce current consumption and shift the aggregate demand curve to the left.

Household Debt An existing aggregate demand curve assumes a constant level of household debt. Increased household debt enables consumers collectively to increase their consumption spending. That shifts the aggregate demand curve to the right. Alternatively, when consumers reduce their household debt, both consumption spending and aggregate demand decline.

Personal Taxes A reduction in personal income tax rates raises take-home income and increases consumer purchases at each possible price level. Tax cuts shift the aggregate demand curve to the right. Tax increases reduce consumption spending and shift the curve to the left.

Investment Spending

Investment spending (the purchase of capital goods) is a second major determinant of aggregate demand. A decline in investment spending at each price level will shift the aggregate demand curve to the left. An increase in investment spending will shift it to the right. In Chapter 8 we saw that investment spending depends on the real interest rate and the expected return from the investment.

Real Interest Rates Other things equal, an increase in real interest rates will lower investment spending and reduce aggregate demand. We are not referring here to the "interest-rate effect" resulting from a change in the price level. Instead, we are identifying a change in the real interest rate resulting from, say, a change in the nation's money supply. An increase in the money supply lowers the interest rate, thereby increasing investment and aggregate demand. A decrease in the money supply raises the interest rate, reducing investment and decreasing aggregate demand.

Expected Returns

Higher expected returns on investment projects will increase the demand for capital goods and shift the aggregate demand curve to the right. Alternatively, declines in expected returns will decrease investment and shift the curve to the left. Expected returns, in turn, are influenced by several factors:

- **Expectations about future business conditions** If firms are optimistic about future business conditions, they are more likely to forecast high rates of return on current investment and therefore may invest more today. On the other hand, if they think the economy will deteriorate in the future, they will forecast low rates of return and perhaps will invest less today.
- **Technology** New and improved technologies enhance expected returns on investment and thus increase aggregate demand. For example, recent advances in microbiology have motivated pharmaceutical companies to establish new labs and production facilities.
- **Degree of excess capacity** A rise in excess capacity—unused capital—will reduce the expected return on new investment and hence decrease aggregate demand. Other things equal, firms operating factories at well below capacity have little incentive to build new factories. But when firms discover that their excess capacity is dwindling or has completely disappeared, their expected returns on new investment in factories and capital equipment rise. Thus, they increase their investment spending, and the aggregate demand curve shifts to the right.
- **Business taxes** An increase in business taxes will reduce after-tax profits from capital investment and lower expected returns. So investment and aggregate demand will decline. A decrease in business taxes will have the opposite effects.

The variability of interest rates and expected returns makes investment highly volatile. In contrast to consumption, investment spending rises and falls often, independent of changes in total income. Investment, in fact, is the least stable component of aggregate demand.

Government Spending

Government purchases are the third determinant of aggregate demand. An increase in government purchases (for example, more military equipment) will shift the aggregate demand curve to the right, as long as tax collections and interest rates do not change as a result. In contrast, a reduction in government spending (for example, fewer transportation projects) will shift the curve to the left.

Net Export Spending

The final determinant of aggregate demand is net export spending. Other things equal, higher U.S. *exports* mean an increased foreign demand for U.S. goods. So a rise in net exports (higher exports relative to imports) shifts the aggregate demand curve to the right. In contrast, a decrease in U.S. net exports shifts the aggregate demand curve leftward. (These changes in net exports are *not* those prompted by a change in the U.S. price level—those associated with the foreign purchases effect. The changes here explain shifts of the curve, not movements along the curve.)

What might cause net exports to change, other than the price level? Two possibilities are changes in national income abroad and changes in exchange rates.

National Income Abroad

Rising national income abroad encourages foreigners to buy more products, some of which are made in the United States. U.S. net exports thus rise, and the U.S. aggregate demand curve shifts to the right. Declines in national income abroad do the opposite: They reduce U.S. net exports and shift the U.S. aggregate demand curve to the left.

Exchange Rates

Change in the dollar's exchange rate—the price of foreign currencies in terms of the U.S. dollar—may affect U.S. exports and therefore aggregate demand. Suppose the dollar depreciates in terms of the euro (meaning the euro appreciates in terms of the dollar). The new, relatively lower value of dollars and higher value of euros enables European consumers to obtain more dollars with each euro. From their perspective, U.S. goods are now less expensive; it takes fewer euros to obtain them. So European consumers buy more U.S. goods, and U.S. exports rise. But American consumers can now obtain fewer euros for each dollar. Because they must pay more dollars to buy European goods, Americans reduce their imports. U.S. exports rise and U.S. imports fall. Conclusion: Dollar depreciation increases net exports (imports go down; exports go up) and therefore increases aggregate demand.

Dollar appreciation has the opposite effects: Net exports fall (imports go up; exports go down) and aggregate demand declines.

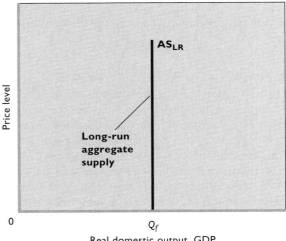

FIGURE 10.3 Aggregate supply in the long run. The long-run aggregate supply curve AS_{LR} is vertical at the full-employment level of real GDP (Q_f) because in the long run wages and other input prices rise and fall to match changes in the price level. So price-level changes do not affect firms' profits and thus they create no incentive for firms to alter their output.

Aggregate Supply

Aggregate supply is a schedule or curve showing the level of real domestic output that firms will produce at each price level. The production responses of firms to changes in the price level differ in the *long run*, which in macroeconomics is a period in which nominal wages (and other resource prices) match changes in the price level, and the *short run*, a period in which nominal wages (and other resource prices) do not respond to price-level changes. So the long and short runs vary by degree of wage adjustment, not by a set length of time such as 1 month, 1 year, or 3 years.

Aggregate Supply in the Long Run

In the long run, the aggregate supply curve is vertical at the economy's full-employment output (or its potential output), as represented by AS_{LR} in Figure 10.3. When changes in wages respond completely to changes in the price level, those price-level changes do not alter the amount of real GDP produced and offered for sale.

Consider a one-firm economy in which the firm's owners must receive a real profit of $20 in order to produce the full-employment output of 100 units. The real reward the owner receives, not the level of prices, is what really counts. Assume the owner's only input (aside from entrepreneurial talent) is 10 units of hired labor at $8 per worker, for a total wage cost of $80. Also, assume that the 100 units of output sell for $1 per unit, so total

revenue is $100. The firm's nominal profit is $20 (= $100 − $80), and using the $1 price to designate the base-price index of 100, its real profit is also $20 (= $20/1.00). Well and good; the full-employment output is produced.

Next, suppose the price level doubles. Would the owner earn more than the $20 of real profit and therefore boost production beyond the 100-unit full-employment output? The answer is no, given the assumption that nominal wages and the price level rise by the same amount, as is true in the long run. Once the product price has doubled to $2, total revenue will be $200 (= 100 × $2). But the cost of 10 units of labor will double from $80 to $160 because the wage rate rises from $8 to $16. Nominal profit thus increases to $40 (= $200 − $160). What about real profit? By dividing the nominal profit of $40 by the new price index of 200 (expressed as a decimal), we obtain real profit of $20 (= $40/2.00). Because real profit does not change, the firm will not alter its production. Because the firm's output is the economy's output, real GDP will remain at its full-employment level.

In the long run, wages and other input prices rise or fall to match changes in the price level. Changes in the price level therefore do not change real profit, and there is no change in real output. As shown in Figure 10.3, the **long-run aggregate supply curve** is vertical at the economy's potential output (or full-employment output).

Aggregate Supply in the Short Run

In reality, nominal wages do not immediately adjust to changes in the price level and perfect adjustment may take several months or even a number of years. Reconsider our previous one-firm economy. If the $8 nominal wage for each of the 10 workers is unresponsive to the price-level change, the doubling of the price level will boost total revenue from $100 to $200 but leave total cost unchanged at $80. Nominal profit will rise from $20 (= $100 − $80) to $120 (= $200 − $80). Dividing that $120 profit by the new price index of 200 (= 2.0 in hundredths), we find that the real profit is now $60. The rise in the real reward from $20 to $60 prompts the firm (economy) to produce more output. Conversely, price-level declines reduce real profits and cause the firm (economy) to reduce its output. So, in the short run, there is a direct or positive relationship between the price level and real output.

The **short-run aggregate supply curve** is upsloping, as shown in Figure 10.4. A rise in the price level increases real output; a fall in the price level reduces it. Per-unit production costs underlie the aggregate supply curve. Recall from Chapter 7 that

$$\text{Per-unit production cost} = \frac{\text{total input cost}}{\text{units of output}}$$

FIGURE 10.4 The aggregate supply curve (short run). The upsloping aggregate supply curve AS indicates a direct (or positive) relationship between the price level and the amount of real output that firms will offer for sale. The AS curve is relatively flat below the full-employment output because unemployed resources and unused capacity allow firms to respond to price-level rises with large increases in real output. It is relatively steep beyond the full-employment output because resource shortages and capacity limitations make it difficult to expand real output as the price level rises.

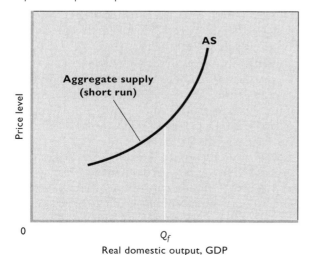

The per-unit production cost of any specific level of output establishes that output's price level because the price level must cover all the costs of production, including profit "costs."

As the economy expands in the short run, per-unit production costs generally rise because of reduced efficiency. But the extent of that rise depends on where the economy is operating relative to its capacity. The aggregate supply curve in Figure 10.4 is relatively flat at outputs below the full-employment output Q_f and relatively steep at outputs above it. Why the difference?

When the economy is operating below its full-employment output, it has large amounts of unused machinery and equipment and unemployed workers. Firms can put these idle human and property resources back to work with little upward pressure on per-unit production costs. And as output expands, few if any shortages of inputs or production bottlenecks will arise to raise per-unit production costs.

When the economy is operating beyond its full-employment output, the vast majority of its available resources are already employed. Adding more workers to a relatively fixed number of highly used capital resources such as plant and equipment creates congestion in the workplace and reduces the efficiency (on average) of workers. Adding more capital, given the limited number of available workers, leaves equipment idle and reduces the efficiency of capital. Adding more land resources when capital and labor are highly constrained reduces the efficiency of land resources. Under these circumstances, total output rises less rapidly than total input cost. So per-unit production costs increase.

Our focus in the remainder of this chapter, the rest of Part 3, and all of Part 4 is on short-run aggregate supply, such as that shown in Figure 10.4. Unless stated otherwise, all references to "aggregate supply" are to aggregate supply in the short run. We will bring long-run aggregate supply prominently back into the analysis in Part 5, when we discuss long-run wage adjustments and economic growth.

Changes in Aggregate Supply

An existing aggregate supply curve identifies the relationship between the price level and real output, other things equal. But when one or more of these other things change, the curve itself shifts. The rightward shift of the curve from AS_1 to AS_2 in Figure 10.5 represents an increase in aggregate supply, indicating that firms are willing to produce and sell more real output at each price level. The leftward shift of the curve from AS_1 to AS_3 represents a

FIGURE 10.5 Changes in aggregate supply. A change in one or more of the listed determinants of aggregate supply will shift the aggregate supply curve. The rightward shift of the aggregate supply curve from AS₁ to AS₂ represents an increase in aggregate supply; the leftward shift of the curve from AS₁ to AS₃ shows a decrease in aggregate supply.

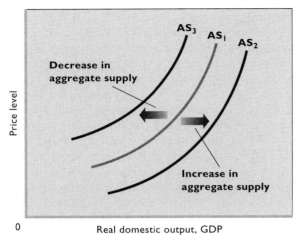

Determinants of Aggregate Supply: Factors That Shift the Aggregate Supply Curve

1. Change in input prices
   a. Domestic resource prices
   b. Prices of imported resources
   c. Market power
2. Change in productivity
3. Change in legal-institutional environment
   a. Business taxes and subsidies
   b. Government regulations

decrease in aggregate supply. At each price level, firms produce less output than before.

Figure 10.5 lists the other things that cause a shift of the aggregate supply curve. Called the **determinants of aggregate supply** or *aggregate supply shifters*, they collectively position the aggregate supply curve and shift the curve when they change. Changes in these determinants raise or lower per-unit production costs *at each price level (or each level of output)*. These changes in per-unit production cost affect profits, thereby leading firms to alter the amount of output they are willing to produce *at each price level*. For example, firms may collectively offer $9 trillion of real output at a price level of 1.0 (100 in index value), rather than $8.8 trillion. Or they may offer $7.5 trillion rather than $8 trillion. The point is that when one of the determinants listed in Figure 10.5 changes, the aggregate supply curve shifts to the right or left. Changes that reduce per-unit production costs shift the aggregate supply curve to the right, as from AS₁ to AS₂; changes that increase per-unit production costs shift it to the left, as from AS₁ to AS₃. When per-unit production costs change for reasons other than changes in real output, the aggregate supply curve shifts.

The aggregate supply determinants listed in Figure 10.5 require more discussion.

Input Prices

Input or resource prices—to be distinguished from the output prices that make up the price level—are a major ingredient of per-unit production costs and therefore a key determinant of aggregate supply. These resources can either be domestic or imported.

Domestic Resource Prices Wages and salaries make up about 75 percent of all business costs. Other things equal, decreases in wages reduce per-unit production costs. So the aggregate supply curve shifts to the right. Increases in wages shift the curve to the left. Examples:

- Labor supply increases because of substantial immigration. Wages and per-unit production costs fall, shifting the AS curve to the right.
- Labor supply decreases because of a rapid rise in pension income and early retirements. Wage rates and per-unit production costs rise, shifting the AS curve to the left.

Similarly, the aggregate supply curve shifts when the prices of land and capital inputs change. Examples:

- The price of machinery and equipment falls because of declines in the prices of steel and electronic components. Per-unit production costs decline, and the AS curve shifts to the right.
- Land resources expand through discoveries of mineral deposits, irrigation of land, or technical innovations that transform "nonresources" (say, vast desert lands) into valuable resources (productive lands). The price of land declines, per-unit production costs fall, and the AS curve shifts to the right.

Prices of Imported Resources Just as foreign demand for U.S. goods contributes to U.S. aggregate demand, resources imported from abroad (such as oil, tin, and copper) add to U.S. aggregate supply. Added supplies of resources—whether domestic or imported—typically reduce per-unit production costs. A decrease in the price of imported resources increases U.S. aggregate supply, while an increase in their price reduces U.S. aggregate supply.

Exchange-rate fluctuations are one factor that may alter the price of imported resources. Suppose that the dollar appreciates, enabling U.S. firms to obtain more foreign currency with each dollar. This means that domestic producers face a lower *dollar* price of imported resources. U.S. firms will respond by increasing their imports of foreign resources, thereby lowering their per-unit production costs at each level of output. Falling per-unit production costs will shift the U.S. aggregate supply curve to the right.

A depreciation of the dollar will have the opposite set of effects.

Market Power
A change in the degree of market power—the ability to set prices above competitive levels—held by sellers of major inputs also can affect input prices and aggregate supply. An example is the fluctuating market power held by the Organization of Petroleum Exporting Countries (OPEC) over the past several decades. The 10-fold increase in the price of oil that OPEC achieved during the 1970s drove up per-unit production costs and jolted the U.S. aggregate supply curve leftward. Then a steep reduction in OPEC's market power during the mid-1980s resulted in a sharp decline in oil prices and a rightward shift of the U.S. aggregate supply curve. In 1999 OPEC temporarily reasserted its market power, raising oil prices and therefore per-unit production costs for some U.S. producers (for example, airlines and truckers).

Productivity
The second major determinant of aggregate supply is **productivity,** which is a measure of the relationship between a nation's level of real output and the amount of resources used to produce that output. Productivity is a measure of average real output, or of real output per unit of input:

$$\text{Productivity} = \frac{\text{total output}}{\text{total inputs}}$$

An increase in productivity enables the economy to obtain more real output from its limited resources. It does this by reducing the per-unit cost of output (per-unit production cost). Suppose, for example, that real output is 10 units, that 5 units of input are needed to produce that quantity, and that the price of each input unit is $2. Then

$$\text{Productivity} = \frac{\text{total output}}{\text{total inputs}} = \frac{10}{5} = 2$$

and

$$\text{Per-unit production cost} = \frac{\text{total input cost}}{\text{total output}}$$

$$= \frac{\$2 \times 5}{10} = \$1$$

Note that we obtain the total input cost by multiplying the unit input cost by the number of inputs used.

Now suppose productivity increases so that real output doubles to 20 units, while the price and quantity of the input remain constant at $2 and 5 units. Using the above equations, we see that productivity rises from 2 to 4 and that the per-unit production cost of the output falls from $1 to $.50. The doubled productivity has reduced the per-unit production cost by half.

By reducing the per-unit production cost, an increase in productivity shifts the aggregate supply curve to the right. The main source of productivity advance is improved production technology, often embodied within new plant and equipment that replaces old plant and equipment. Other sources of productivity increases are a better-educated and -trained workforce, improved forms of business enterprises, and the reallocation of labor resources from lower- to higher-productivity uses.

Much rarer, decreases in productivity increase per-unit production costs and therefore reduce aggregate supply (shift the curve to the left).

Legal-Institutional Environment
Changes in the legal-institutional setting in which businesses operate are the final determinant of aggregate supply. Such changes may alter the per-unit costs of output and, if so, shift the aggregate supply curve. Two changes of this type are (1) changes in taxes and subsidies and (2) changes in the extent of regulation.

Business Taxes and Subsidies
Higher business taxes, such as sales, excise, and payroll taxes, increase per-unit costs and reduce short-run aggregate supply in much the same way as a wage increase does. An increase in such taxes paid by businesses will increase per-unit production costs and shift aggregate supply to the left.

Similarly, a business subsidy—a payment or tax break by government to producers—lowers production costs and increases short-run aggregate supply. For example, the Federal government subsidizes firms that blend ethanol (derived from corn) with gasoline to increase the U.S.

gasoline supply. This reduces the per-unit production cost of making blended gasoline. To the extent that this and other subsidies are successful, the aggregate supply curve shifts rightward.

Government Regulation   It is usually costly for businesses to comply with government regulations. More regulation therefore tends to increase per-unit production costs and shift the aggregate supply curve to the left. "Supply-side" proponents of deregulation of the economy have argued forcefully that, by increasing efficiency and reducing the paperwork associated with complex regulations, deregulation will reduce per-unit costs and shift the aggregate supply curve to the right. Other economists are less certain. Deregulation that results in accounting manipulations, monopolization, and business failures is likely to shift the AS curve to the left rather than to the right.

QUICK REVIEW 10.2

- The long-run aggregate supply curve is vertical because, given sufficient time, wages and other input prices rise and fall to match price-level changes; because price-level changes do not change real rewards, they do not change production decisions.

- The short-run aggregate supply curve (or simply the "aggregate supply curve") is upward-sloping because wages and other input prices do not immediately adjust to changes in price levels. The curve's upward slope reflects rising per-unit production costs as output expands.

- By altering per-unit production costs independent of changes in the level of output, changes in one or more of the determinants of aggregate supply (Figure 10.5) shift the aggregate supply curve.

- An increase in short-run aggregate supply is shown as a rightward shift of the aggregate supply curve; a decrease is shown as a leftward shift of the curve.

Equilibrium and Changes in Equilibrium

Of all the possible combinations of price levels and levels of real GDP, which combination will the economy gravitate toward, at least in the short run? **Figure 10.6 (Key Graph)** and its accompanying table provide the answer. Equilibrium occurs at the price level that equalizes the amounts of real output demanded and supplied. The intersection of the aggregate demand curve AD and the aggregate supply curve AS establishes the economy's **equilibrium price level** and **equilibrium real output.** So aggregate demand and aggregate supply jointly establish the price level and level of real GDP.

In Figure 10.6 the equilibrium price level and level of real output are 100 and $510 billion, respectively. To illustrate why, suppose the price level is 92 rather than 100. We see from the table that the lower price level will encourage businesses to produce real output of $502 billion. This is shown by point a on the AS curve in the graph. But, as revealed by the table and point b on the aggregate demand curve, buyers will want to purchase $514 billion of real output at price level 92. Competition among buyers to purchase the lesser available real output of $502 billion will eliminate the $12 billion (= $514 billion − $502 billion) shortage and pull up the price level to 100.

G 10.1

Aggregate demand–aggregate supply

As the table and graph show, the rise in the price level from 92 to 100 encourages producers to increase their real output from $502 billion to $510 billion and causes buyers to scale back their purchases from $514 billion to $510 billion. When equality occurs between the amounts of real output produced and purchased, as it does at price level 100, the economy has achieved equilibrium (here, at $510 billion of real GDP).

Now let's apply the AD-AS model to various situations that can confront the economy. For simplicity we will use P and Q symbols, rather than actual numbers. Remember that these symbols represent price index values and amounts of real GDP.

Increases in AD: Demand-Pull Inflation

Suppose the economy is operating at its full-employment output and businesses and government decide to increase their spending—actions that shift the aggregate demand curve to the right. Our list of determinants of aggregate demand (Figure 10.2) provides several reasons why this shift might occur. Perhaps firms boost their investment spending because they anticipate higher future profits from investments in new capital. Those profits are predicated on having new equipment and facilities that incorporate a number of new technologies. And perhaps government increases spending to expand national defense.

As shown by the rise in the price level from P_1 to P_2 in Figure 10.7, the increase in aggregate demand beyond the full-employment level of output causes inflation. This is *demand-pull inflation*, because the price level is being pulled up by the increase in aggregate demand. Also, observe that the increase in demand expands real output from Q_f to Q_1. The distance between Q_1 and Q_f is a positive GDP gap. Actual GDP exceeds potential GDP.

keygraph

FIGURE 10.6 **The equilibrium price level and equilibrium real GDP.** The intersection of the aggregate demand curve and the aggregate supply curve determines the economy's equilibrium price level. At the equilibrium price level of 100 (in index-value terms) the $510 billion of real output demanded matches the $510 billion of real output supplied. So the equilibrium GDP is $510 billion.

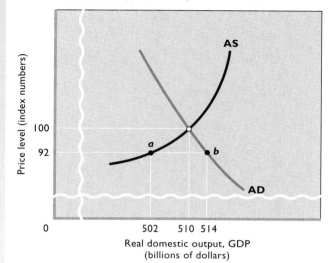

Real Output Demanded (Billions)	Price Level (Index Number)	Real Output Supplied (Billions)
$506	108	$513
508	104	512
510	*100*	*510*
512	96	507
514	92	502

QUICK QUIZ 10.6

1. The AD curve slopes downward because:
   a. per-unit production costs fall as real GDP increases.
   b. the income and substitution effects are at work.
   c. changes in the determinants of AD alter the amounts of real GDP demanded at each price level.
   d. decreases in the price level give rise to real-balances effects, interest-rate effects, and foreign purchases effects that increase the amounts of real GDP demanded.

2. The AS curve slopes upward because:
   a. per-unit production costs rise as real GDP expands toward and beyond its full-employment level.
   b. the income and substitution effects are at work.
   c. changes in the determinants of AS alter the amounts of real GDP supplied at each price level.
   d. increases in the price level give rise to real-balances effects, interest-rate effects, and foreign purchases effects that increase the amounts of real GDP supplied.

3. At price level 92:
   a. a GDP surplus of $12 billion occurs that drives the price level up to 100.
   b. a GDP shortage of $12 billion occurs that drives the price level up to 100.
   c. the aggregate amount of real GDP demanded is less than the aggregate amount of GDP supplied.
   d. the economy is operating beyond its capacity to produce.

4. Suppose real output demanded rises by $4 billion at each price level. The new equilibrium price level will be:
   a. 108.
   b. 104.
   c. 96.
   d. 92.

Answers: 1. d; 2. a; 3. b; 4. b

The classic American example of demand-pull inflation occurred in the late 1960s. The escalation of the war in Vietnam resulted in a 40 percent increase in defense spending between 1965 and 1967 and another 15 percent increase in 1968. The rise in government spending, imposed on an already growing economy, shifted the economy's aggregate demand curve to the right, producing the worst inflation in two decades. Actual GDP exceeded potential GDP, and inflation jumped from 1.6 percent in 1965 to 5.7 percent by 1970. (**Key Question 4**)

A careful examination of Figure 10.7 reveals an interesting point concerning the multiplier effect. The increase in aggregate demand from AD_1 to AD_2 increases real output only to Q_1, not to Q_2, because part of the increase in aggregate demand is absorbed as inflation as the price level rises from P_1 to P_2. Had the price level remained at P_1, the shift of aggregate demand from AD_1 to AD_2 would have

197

FIGURE 10.7 **An increase in aggregate demand that causes demand-pull inflation.** The increase of aggregate demand from AD_1 to AD_2 causes demand-pull inflation, shown as the rise in the price level from P_1 to P_2. It also causes a positive GDP gap of Q_1 minus Q_f. The rise of the price level reduces the size of the multiplier effect. If the price level had remained at P_1, the increase in aggregate demand from AD_1 to AD_2 would increase output from Q_f to Q_2 and the multiplier would have been at full strength. But because of the increase in the price level, real output increases only from Q_f to Q_1 and the multiplier effect is reduced.

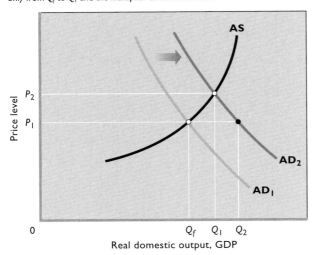

FIGURE 10.8 **A decrease in aggregate demand that causes a recession.** If the price level is downwardly inflexible at P_1, a decline of aggregate demand from AD_1 to AD_2 will move the economy leftward from a to b along the horizontal broken-line segment and reduce real GDP from Q_f to Q_1. Idle production capacity, cyclical unemployment, and a negative GDP gap (of Q_1 minus Q_f) will result. If the price level is flexible downward, the decline in aggregate demand will move the economy depicted from a to c.

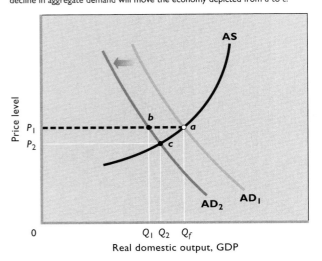

increased real output to Q_2. The full-strength multiplier effect of Chapters 8 and 9 would have occurred. But in Figure 10.7 inflation reduced the increase in real output—and thus the multiplier effect—by about one-half. For any initial increase in aggregate demand, the resulting increase in real output will be smaller the greater is the increase in the price level. Price-level rises weaken the realized multiplier effect.

Decreases in AD: Recession and Cyclical Unemployment

Decreases in aggregate demand describe the opposite end of the business cycle: recession and cyclical unemployment (rather than above-full employment and demand-pull inflation). For example, in 2000 investment spending substantially declined because of an overexpansion of capital during the second half of the 1990s. In Figure 10.8 we show the resulting decline in aggregate demand as a leftward shift from AD_1 to AD_2.

But now we add an important twist to the analysis. What goes up—the price level—does not always go down. *Deflation*—a decline in the price level—is a rarity in the American economy. Suppose, for example, that the economy represented by Figure 10.8 moves from a to b, rather than from a to c. The outcome is a decline of real output from Q_f to Q_1, with *no* change in the price level. In this

case, it is as if the aggregate supply curve in Figure 10.8 is horizontal at P_1, to the left of Q_f, as indicated by the dashed line. This decline of real output from Q_f to Q_1 constitutes a *recession*, and since fewer workers are needed to produce the lower output, *cyclical unemployment* arises. The distance between Q_1 and Q_f is a negative GDP gap—the amount by which actual output falls short of potential output.

Close inspection of Figure 10.8 also reveals that without a fall in the price level, the multiplier is at full strength. With the price level stuck at P_1, real GDP decreases by $Q_f - Q_1$, which matches the full leftward shift of the AD curve. The multiplier of Chapter 8 and Chapter 9 is at full strength when changes in aggregate demand occur along what, in effect, is a horizontal segment of the AS curve. This full-strength multiplier would also exist for an increase in aggregate demand from AD_2 to AD_1 along this broken line, since none of the increase in output would be dissipated as inflation. We will say more about that in Chapter 11.

All recent recessions in the United States have mimicked the "GDP gap but no deflation" scenario shown in Figure 10.8. Consider the recession of 2001, which resulted from a significant decline in investment spending. Because of the resulting decline in aggregate demand, GDP fell short of potential GDP by an average $67 billion for each of the last quarters of the year. Between February 2001 and December 2001, unemployment increased by 1.8 million workers, and the nation's unemployment rate rose from

4.2 percent to 5.8 percent. Although the rate of inflation fell—an outcome called *disinflation*—the price level did not decline. That is, deflation did not occur.

Real output takes the brunt of declines in aggregate demand in the U.S. economy because the price level tends to be inflexible in a downward direction. There are numerous reasons for this.

- *Fear of price wars* Some large firms may be concerned that if they reduce their prices, rivals not only will match their price cuts but may retaliate by making even deeper cuts. An initial price cut may touch off an unwanted *price war:* successively deeper and deeper rounds of price cuts. In such a situation, each firm eventually ends up with far less profit or higher losses than would be the case if each had simply maintained its prices. For this reason, each firm may resist making the initial price cut, choosing instead to reduce production and lay off workers.

- *Menu costs* Firms that think a recession will be relatively short lived may be reluctant to cut their prices. One reason is what economists metaphorically call **menu costs,** named after their most obvious example: the cost of printing new menus when a restaurant decides to reduce its prices. But lowering prices also creates other costs. Additional costs derive from (1) estimating the magnitude and duration of the shift in demand to determine whether prices should be lowered, (2) repricing items held in inventory, (3) printing and mailing new catalogs, and (4) communicating new prices to customers, perhaps through advertising. When menu costs are present, firms may choose to avoid them by retaining current prices. That is, they may wait to see if the decline in aggregate demand is permanent.

- *Wage contracts* Firms rarely profit from cutting their product prices if they cannot also cut their wage rates. Wages are usually inflexible downward because large parts of the labor force work under contracts prohibiting wage cuts for the duration of the contract. (Collective bargaining agreements in major industries frequently run for 3 years.) Similarly, the wages and salaries of nonunion workers are usually adjusted once a year, rather than quarterly or monthly.

- *Morale, effort, and productivity* Wage inflexibility downward is reinforced by the reluctance of many employers to reduce wage rates. Some current wages may be so-called **efficiency wages**—wages that elicit maximum work effort and thus minimize labor costs per unit of output. If worker productivity (output per hour of work) remains constant, lower wages *do* reduce labor costs per unit of output. But lower wages

O 10.2
Efficiency wage

might impair worker morale and work effort, thereby reducing productivity. Considered alone, lower productivity raises labor costs per unit of output because less output is produced. If the higher labor costs resulting from reduced productivity exceed the cost savings from the lower wage, then wage cuts will increase rather than reduce labor costs per unit of output. In such situations, firms will resist lowering wages when they are faced with a decline in aggregate demand.

- *Minimum wage* The minimum wage imposes a legal floor under the wages of the least skilled workers. Firms paying those wages cannot reduce that wage rate when aggregate demand declines.

But a major "caution" is needed here: Although most economists agree that prices and wages tend to be inflexible downward in the short run, price and wages are more flexible than in the past. Intense foreign competition and the declining power of unions in the United States have undermined the ability of workers and firms to resist price and wage cuts when faced with falling aggregate demand. This increased flexibility may be one reason the recession of 2001 was relatively mild. The U.S. auto manufacturers, for example, maintained output in the face of falling demand by offering zero-interest loans on auto purchases. This, in effect, was a disguised price cut. But our description in Figure 10.8 remains valid. In the 2001 recession, the overall price level did not decline although output fell by .5 percent and unemployment rose by 1.8 million workers.

Decreases in AS: Cost-Push Inflation

Suppose that a major terrorist attack on oil facilities severely disrupts world oil supplies and drives up oil prices by, say, 300 percent. Higher energy prices would spread through the economy, driving up production and distribution costs on a wide variety of goods. The U.S. aggregate supply curve would shift to the left, say, from AS_1 to AS_2 in Figure 10.9. The resulting increase in the price level would be *cost-push inflation.*

The effects of a leftward shift in aggregate supply are doubly bad. When aggregate supply shifts from AS_1 to AS_2, the economy moves from *a* to *b*. The price level rises from P_1 to P_2 and real output declines from Q_f to Q_1. Along with the cost-push inflation, a recession (and negative GDP gap) occurs. That is exactly what happened in the United States in the mid-1970s when the price of oil rocketed upward. Then, oil expenditures were about 10 percent of U.S. GDP, compared to only 3 percent

CONSIDER THIS ...

Ratchet Effect

A *ratchet analogy* is a good way to think about effects of changes in aggregate demand on the price level. A ratchet is a tool or mechanism such as a winch, car jack, or socket wrench that cranks a wheel forward but does not allow it to go backward. Properly set, each allows the operator to move an object (boat, car, or nut) in one direction while preventing it from moving in the opposite direction.

Product prices, wage rates, and per-unit production costs are highly flexible upward when aggregate demand increases along the aggregate supply curve. In the United States, the price level has increased in 55 of the 56 years since 1950.

But when aggregate demand decreases, product prices, wage rates, and per-unit production costs are inflexible downward. The U.S. price level has declined in only a single year (1955) since 1950, even though aggregate demand and real output have declined in a number of years.

In terms of our analogy, increases in aggregate demand ratchet the U.S. price level upward. Once in place, the higher price level remains until it is ratcheted up again. The higher price level tends to remain even with declines in aggregate demand.

today. So, as indicated in this chapter's Last Word, the U. S. economy is now less vulnerable to cost-push inflation arising from such "aggregate supply shocks."

Increases in AS: Full Employment with Price-Level Stability

Between 1996 and 2000, the United States experienced a combination of full employment, strong economic growth, and very low inflation. Specifically, the unemployment rate fell to 4 percent and real GDP grew nearly 4 percent annually, *without igniting inflation*. At first thought, this "macroeconomic bliss" seems to be incompatible with the AD-AS model. The aggregate supply curve suggests that increases in aggregate demand that are sufficient for over-full employment will raise the price level (see Figure 10.7). Higher inflation, so it would seem, is the inevitable price paid for expanding output beyond the full-employment level.

But inflation remained very mild in the late 1990s. Figure 10.10 helps explain why. Let's first suppose that aggregate demand increased from AD_1 to AD_2 along aggregate supply curve AS_1. Taken alone, that increase in aggregate demand would move the economy from *a* to *b*. Real output would rise from full-employment output Q_1 to beyond-full-employment output Q_2. The economy would experience inflation, as shown by the increase in the price level from P_1 to P_3. Such inflation had occurred at the end

FIGURE 10.10 Growth, full employment, and relative price stability. Normally, an increase in aggregate demand from AD_1 to AD_2 would move the economy from *a* to *b* along AS_1. Real output would expand to Q_2, and inflation would result (P_1 to P_3). But in the late 1990s, significant increases in productivity shifted the aggregate supply curve, as from AS_1 to AS_2. The economy moved from *a* to *c* rather than from *a* to *b*. It experienced strong economic growth (Q_1 to Q_3), full employment, and only very mild inflation (P_1 to P_2) before receding in March 2001.

FIGURE 10.9 A decrease in aggregate supply that causes cost-push inflation. A leftward shift of aggregate supply from AS_1 to AS_2 raises the price level from P_1 to P_2 and produces cost-push inflation. Real output declines and a negative GDP gap (of Q_1 minus Q_f) occurs.

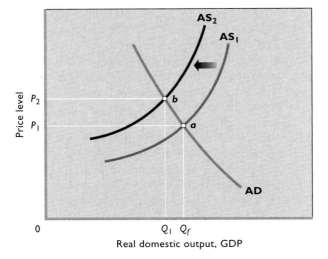

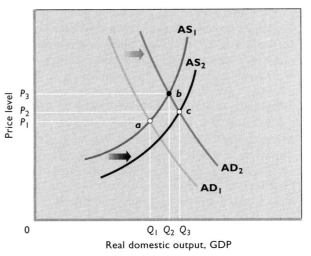

Has the Impact of Oil Prices Diminished?

Significant Changes in Oil Prices Historically Have Shifted the Aggregate Supply Curve and Greatly Affected the U.S. Economy. Have the Effects of Such Changes Weakened?

The United States has experienced several aggregate supply shocks— abrupt shifts of the aggregate supply curve—caused by significant changes in oil prices. In the mid-1970s the price of oil rose from $4 to $12 per barrel, and then again in the late 1970s it increased to $24 per barrel and eventually to $35. These oil price increases shifted the aggregate supply curve leftward, causing rapid cost-push inflation and ultimately rising unemployment and a negative GDP gap.

In the late 1980s and through most of the 1990s oil prices fell, sinking to a low of $11 per barrel in late 1998. This decline created a positive aggregate supply shock beneficial to the U.S. economy. But in response to those low oil prices, in late 1999 OPEC teamed with Mexico, Norway, and Russia to restrict oil output and thus boost prices. That action, along with a rapidly growing international demand for oil, sent oil prices upward once again. By March 2000 the price of a barrel of oil reached $34, before settling back to about $25 to $28 in 2001 and 2002.

Some economists feared that the rising price of oil would increase energy prices by so much that the U.S. aggregate supply curve would shift to the left, creating cost-push inflation. But inflation in the United States remained modest.

Then came a greater test: A "perfect storm"—continuing conflict in Iraq, the rising demand for oil in India and China, a pickup of economic growth in several industrial nations, disruption of oil production by hurricanes, and concern about political developments in Venezuela—pushed the price of oil to over $60 a barrel in 2005. (You can find the current daily price of oil at OPEC's Web site, **www.opec.org.**) The U.S. inflation rate rose in 2005, but *core inflation* (the inflation rate after subtracting changes in the prices of food and energy) remained steady. Why have rises in oil prices lost their inflationary punch?

In the early 2000s, other determinants of aggregate supply swamped the potential inflationary impacts of the oil price increases. Lower production costs resulting from rapid productivity advance and lower input prices from global competition more than compensated for the rise in oil prices. Put simply, aggregate supply did not decline as it had in earlier periods.

Perhaps of greater importance, oil prices are a less significant factor in the U.S. economy than they were in the 1970s. Prior to 1980, changes in oil prices greatly affected core inflation in the United States. But since 1980 they have had very little effect on core inflation.[*] The main reason has been a significant decline in the amount of oil and gas used in producing each dollar of U.S. output. In 2005 producing a dollar of real GDP required about 7000 Btus of oil and gas, compared to 14,000 Btus in 1970. Part of this decline resulted from new production techniques spawned by the higher oil and energy prices. But equally important has been the changing relative composition of the GDP, away from larger, heavier items (such as earth-moving equipment) that are energy-intensive to make and transport and toward smaller, lighter items (such as microchips and software). Experts on energy economics estimate that the U.S. economy is about 33 percent less sensitive to oil price fluctuations than it was in the early 1980s and 50 percent less sensitive than in the mid-1970s.[†]

A final reason why changes in oil prices seem to have lost their inflationary punch is that the Federal Reserve has become more vigilant and adept at maintaining price stability through monetary policy The Fed did not let the oil price increases of 1999–2000 become generalized as core inflation. It remains to be seen whether it can do the same with the dramatic rise in oil prices from the "perfect storm" of 2005. (We will discuss monetary policy in depth in Chapter 14.)

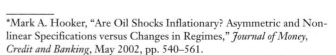

[*]Mark A. Hooker, "Are Oil Shocks Inflationary? Asymmetric and Nonlinear Specifications versus Changes in Regimes," *Journal of Money, Credit and Banking*, May 2002, pp. 540–561.
[†]Stephen P. A. Brown and Mine K. Yücel, "Oil Prices and the Economy," Federal Reserve Bank of Dallas *Southwest Economy*, July–August 2000, pp. 1–6.

of previous vigorous expansions of aggregate demand, including the expansion of the late 1980s.

Between 1990 and 2000, however, larger-than-usual increases in productivity occurred because of a burst of new technology relating to computers, the Internet, inventory management systems, electronic commerce, and so on. We represent this higher-than-usual productivity growth as the rightward shift from AS_1 to AS_2 in Figure 10.10. The relevant aggregate demand and aggregate supply curves thus became AD_2 and AS_2, not AD_2 and AS_1. Instead of moving from a to b, the economy moved from a to c. Real output increased from Q_1 to Q_3, and the price level rose only modestly (from P_1 to P_2). The shift of the aggregate supply curve from AS_1 to AS_2 accommodated the rapid increase in aggregate demand and kept inflation mild. This remarkable combination of rapid productivity growth, rapid real GDP growth, full employment, and relative price-level stability led some observers to proclaim that the United States was experiencing a "new era" or a New Economy.

But in 2001 the New Economy came face-to-face with the old economic principles. Aggregate demand declined because of a substantial fall in investment spending, and in March 2001 the economy experienced a recession. The terrorist attacks of September 11, 2001, further dampened private spending and prolonged the recession throughout 2001. The unemployment rate rose from 4.2 percent in January 2001 to 6 percent in December 2002.

Throughout 2001 the Federal Reserve lowered interest rates to try to halt the recession and promote recovery. Those Fed actions, along with Federal tax cuts, increased military spending, and strong demand for new housing, helped spur recovery. The economy haltingly resumed its economic growth in 2002 and 2003 and then expanded rapidly in 2004 and 2005.

We will examine stabilization policies, such as those carried out by the Federal government and the Federal Reserve, in chapters that follow. We will also discuss what remains of the New Economy thesis in more detail. (**Key Questions 5, 6, and 7**)

QUICK REVIEW 10.3

- The equilibrium price level and amount of real output are determined at the intersection of the aggregate demand curve and the aggregate supply curve.
- Increases in aggregate demand beyond the full-employment level of real GDP cause demand-pull inflation.
- Decreases in aggregate demand cause recessions and cyclical unemployment, partly because the price level and wages tend to be inflexible in a downward direction.
- Decreases in aggregate supply cause cost-push inflation.
- Full employment, high economic growth, and price stability are compatible with one another if productivity-driven increases in aggregate supply are sufficient to balance growing aggregate demand.

Summary

1. The aggregate demand–aggregate supply model (AD-AS model) is a variable-price model that enables analysis of simultaneous changes of real GDP and the price level.

2. The aggregate demand curve shows the level of real output that the economy will purchase at each price level.

3. The aggregate demand curve is downsloping because of the real-balances effect, the interest-rate effect, and the foreign purchases effect. The real-balances effect indicates that inflation reduces the real value or purchasing power of fixed-value financial assets held by households, causing cutbacks in consumer spending. The interest-rate effect means that, with a specific supply of money, a higher price level increases the demand for money, thereby raising the interest rate and reducing investment purchases. The foreign purchases effect suggests that an increase in one country's price level relative to the price levels in other countries reduces the net export component of that nation's aggregate demand.

4. The determinants of aggregate demand consist of spending by domestic consumers, by businesses, by government, and by foreign buyers. Changes in the factors listed in

Figure 10.2 alter the spending by these groups and shift the aggregate demand curve. The extent of the shift is determined by the size of the initial change in spending and the strength of the economy's multiplier.

5. The aggregate supply curve shows the levels of real output that businesses will produce at various possible price levels. The long-run aggregate supply curve assumes that nominal wages and other input prices fully match any change in the price level. The curve is vertical at the full-employment output.

6. The short-run aggregate supply curve (or simply "aggregate supply curve") assumes nominal wages and other input prices do not respond to price-level changes. The aggregate supply curve is generally upsloping because per-unit production costs, and hence the prices that firms must receive, rise as real output expands. The aggregate supply curve is relatively steep to the right of the full-employment output and relatively flat to the left of it.

7. Figure 10.5 lists the determinants of aggregate supply: input prices, productivity, and the legal-institutional environment. A change in any one of these factors will change per-unit

production costs at each level of output and therefore will shift the aggregate supply curve.

8. The intersection of the aggregate demand and aggregate supply curves determines an economy's equilibrium price level and real GDP. At the intersection, the quantity of real GDP demanded equals the quantity of real GDP supplied.

9. Increases in aggregate demand to the right of the full-employment output cause inflation and positive GDP gaps (actual GDP exceeds potential GDP). An upsloping aggregate supply curve weakens the multiplier effect of an increase in aggregate demand because a portion of the increase in aggregate demand is dissipated in inflation.

10. Shifts of the aggregate demand curve to the left of the full employment output cause recession, negative GDP gaps, and cyclical unemployment. The price level may not fall during recessions because of downwardly inflexible prices and wages. This inflexibility results from fear of price wars, menu costs, wage contracts, efficiency wages, and minimum wages. When the price level is fixed, full multiplier effects occur along what, in essence, is a horizontal portion of the aggregate supply curve.

11. Leftward shifts of the aggregate supply curve reflect increases in per-unit production costs and cause cost-push inflation, with accompanying negative GDP gaps.

12. Rightward shifts of the aggregate supply curve, caused by large improvements in productivity, help explain the simultaneous achievement of full employment, economic growth, and price stability that occurred in the United States between 1996 and 2000. The recession of 2001, however, ended the expansionary phase of the business cycle.

Terms and Concepts

aggregate demand–aggregate supply (AD-AS) model

aggregate demand

real-balances effect

interest-rate effect

foreign purchases effect

determinants of aggregate demand

aggregate supply

long-run aggregate supply curve

short-run aggregate supply curve

determinants of aggregate supply

productivity

equilibrium price level

equilibrium real output

menu costs

efficiency wages

Study Questions

1. Why is the aggregate demand curve downsloping? Specify how your explanation differs from the explanation for the downsloping demand curve for a single product. What role does the multiplier play in shifts of the aggregate demand curve?

2. Distinguish between "real-balances effect" and "wealth effect," as the terms are used in this chapter. How does each relate to the aggregate demand curve?

3. Why is the long-run aggregate supply curve vertical? Explain the shape of the short-run aggregate supply curve. Why is the short-run curve relatively flat to the left of the full-employment output and relatively steep to the right?

4. **KEY QUESTION** Suppose that the aggregate demand and supply schedules for a hypothetical economy are as shown below:

Amount of Real GDP Demanded, Billions	Price Level (Price Index)	Amount of Real GDP Supplied, Billions
$100	300	$450
200	250	400
300	200	300
400	150	200
500	100	100

a. Use these sets of data to graph the aggregate demand and aggregate supply curves. What is the equilibrium price level and the equilibrium level of real output in this hypothetical economy? Is the equilibrium real output also necessarily the full-employment real output? Explain.

b. Why will a price level of 150 not be an equilibrium price level in this economy? Why not 250?

c. Suppose that buyers desire to purchase $200 billion of extra real output at each price level. Sketch in the new aggregate demand curve as AD_1. What factors might cause this change in aggregate demand? What is the new equilibrium price level and level of real output?

5. **KEY QUESTION** Suppose that a hypothetical economy has the following relationship between its real output and the input quantities necessary for producing that output:

Input Quantity	Real GDP
150.0	$400
112.5	300
75.0	200

a. What is productivity in this economy?

b. What is the per-unit cost of production if the price of each input unit is $2?

c. Assume that the input price increases from $2 to $3 with no accompanying change in productivity. What is the new per-unit cost of production? In what direction would the $1 increase in input price push the economy's aggregate supply curve? What effect would this shift of aggregate supply have on the price level and the level of real output?

d. Suppose that the increase in input price does not occur but, instead, that productivity increases by 100 percent. What would be the new per-unit cost of production? What effect would this change in per-unit production cost have on the economy's aggregate supply curve? What effect would this shift of aggregate supply have on the price level and the level of real output?

6. **KEY QUESTION** What effects would each of the following have on aggregate demand or aggregate supply? In each case use a diagram to show the expected effects on the equilibrium price level and the level of real output. Assume all other things remain constant.

a. A widespread fear of depression on the part of consumers.

b. A $2 increase in the excise tax on a pack of cigarettes.

c. A reduction in interest rates at each price level.

d. A major increase in Federal spending for health care.

e. The expectation of rapid inflation.

f. The complete disintegration of OPEC, causing oil prices to fall by one-half.

g. A 10 percent reduction in personal income tax rates.

h. A sizable increase in labor productivity (with no change in nominal wages).

i. A 12 percent increase in nominal wages (with no change in productivity).

j. Depreciation in the international value of the dollar.

7. **KEY QUESTION** Assume that (a) the price level is flexible upward but not downward and (b) the economy is currently operating at its full-employment output. Other things equal, how will each of the following affect the equilibrium price level and equilibrium level of real output in the short run?

a. An increase in aggregate demand.

b. A decrease in aggregate supply, with no change in aggregate demand.

c. Equal increases in aggregate demand and aggregate supply.

d. A decrease in aggregate demand.

e. An increase in aggregate demand that exceeds an increase in aggregate supply.

8. Explain how an upsloping aggregate supply curve weakens the realized multiplier effect.

9. Why does a reduction in aggregate demand reduce real output, rather than the price level? Why might a full-strength multiplier apply to a decrease in aggregate demand?

10. Explain: "Unemployment can be caused by a decrease of aggregate demand or a decrease of aggregate supply." In each case, specify the price-level outcomes.

11. Use shifts of the AD and AS curves to explain (a) the U.S. experience of strong economic growth, full employment, and price stability in the late 1990s and early 2000s and (b) how a strong negative wealth effect from, say, a precipitous drop in the stock market could cause a recession even though productivity is surging.

12. In early 2001 investment spending sharply declined in the United States. In the 2 months following the September 11, 2001, attacks on the United States, consumption also declined. Use AD-AS analysis to show the two impacts on real GDP.

13. **LAST WORD** Go to the OPEC Web site, **www.opec.org**, and find the current "OPEC basket price" of oil. By clicking on that amount, you will find the annual prices of oil for the past 5 years. By what percentage is the current price higher or lower than 5 years ago? Next, go to the Bureau of Economic Analysis Web site, **www.bea.gov,** and use the interactive feature to find U.S. real GDP for the past years. By what percentage is real GDP higher or lower than it was 5 years ago? What if, anything, can you conclude about the relationship between the price of oil and the level of real GDP in the United States?

Web-Based Questions

1. **FEELING WEALTHIER; SPENDING MORE?** Access the Bureau of Economic Analysis Web site, **www.bea.gov,** interactively via the National Income and Product Account Tables. From Table 1.2 find the annual levels of real GDP and real consumption for 1996 and 1999. Did consumption increase more rapidly or less rapidly in percentage terms than real GDP? At **http://dowjones.com** in sequence select Dow Jones Industrial Average, Index Data, and Historical Values to find the level of the DJI on June 1, 1996, and June 1, 1999. What was the percentage change in the DJI over that period? How might that change help explain your findings about the growth of consumption versus real GDP between 1996 and 1999?

2. **THE RECESSION OF 2001—WHICH COMPONENT OF AD DECLINED THE MOST?** Use the interactive feature of the Bureau of Economic Analysis Web site, **www.bea.gov,** to access the National Income and Product Account Tables. From Table 1.2 find the levels of real GDP, personal consumption expenditures (C), gross private investment (I_g), net exports (X_n), and government consumption expenditures and gross investment (G) in the first and third quarters of 2001. By what percentage did real GDP decline over this period? Which of the four broad components of aggregate demand decreased by the largest percentage amount?

The Relationship of the Aggregate Demand Curve to the Aggregate Expenditures Model*

The aggregate demand curve of this chapter and the aggregate expenditures model of Chapter 9 are intricately related.

Derivation of the Aggregate Demand Curve from the Aggregate Expenditures Model

We can directly connect the downward-sloping aggregate demand curve to the aggregate expenditures model by relating various possible price levels to corresponding equilibrium GDPs. In Figure 1 we have stacked the aggregate expenditures model (Figure 1a) and the aggregate demand curve (Figure 1b) vertically. This is possible because the horizontal axes of both models measure real GDP. Now let's derive the AD curve in three distinct steps. (Throughout this discussion, keep in mind that price level P_1 is lower than price level P_2, which is lower than price level P_3.)

- First suppose that the economy's price level is P_1 and its aggregate expenditures schedule is AE_1, the top schedule in Figure 1a. The equilibrium GDP is then Q_1 at point 1. So in Figure 1b we can plot the equilibrium real output Q_1 and the corresponding price level P_1. This gives us one point 1' in Figure 1b.

- Now assume the price level rises from P_1 to P_2. Other things equal, this higher price level will (1) decrease the value of real balances (wealth), decreasing consumption expenditures; (2) increase the interest rate, reducing investment and interest-sensitive consumption expenditures; and (3) increase imports and decrease exports, reducing net export expenditures. The aggregate expenditures schedule will fall from AE_1 to, say, AE_2 in

Figure 1a, giving us equilibrium Q_2 at point 2. In Figure 1b we plot this new price-level–real-output combination, P_2 and Q_2, as point 2'.

FIGURE 1 Deriving the aggregate demand curve from the expenditures-output model. (a) Rising price levels from P_1 to P_2 to P_3 shift the aggregate expenditures curve downward from AE_1 to AE_2 to AE_3 and reduce real GDP from Q_1 to Q_2 to Q_3. (b) The aggregate demand curve AD is derived by plotting the successively lower real GDPs from the upper graph against the P_1, P_2, and P_3 price levels.

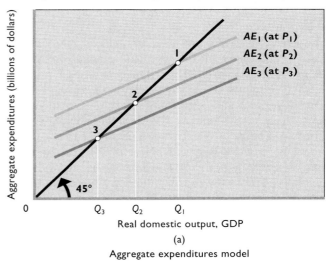

(a)
Aggregate expenditures model

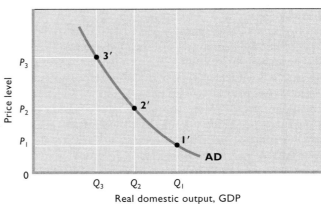

(b)
Aggregate demand–aggregate supply model

---

*This appendix presumes knowledge of the aggregate expenditures model discussed in Chapter 9 and should be skipped if Chapter 9 was not assigned.

- Finally, suppose the price level rises from P_2 to P_3. The value of real balances falls, the interest rate rises, exports fall, and imports rise. Consequently, the consumption, investment, and net export schedules fall, shifting the aggregate expenditures schedule downward from AE_2 to AE_3, which gives us equilibrium Q_3 at point 3. In Figure 1b, this enables us to locate point 3′, where the price level is P_3 and real output is Q_3.

In summary, increases in the economy's price level will successively shift its aggregate expenditures schedule downward and will reduce real GDP. The resulting price-level–real-GDP combinations will yield various points such as 1′, 2′, and 3′ in Figure 1b. Together, such points locate the downward-sloping aggregate demand curve for the economy.

Aggregate Demand Shifts and the Aggregate Expenditures Model

The determinants of aggregate demand listed in Figure 10.2 are the components of the aggregate expenditures model discussed in Chapter 9. When there is a change in one of the determinants of aggregate demand, the aggregate expenditures schedule shifts upward or downward. We can easily link such shifts of the aggregate expenditures schedule to shifts of the aggregate demand curve.

Let's suppose that the price level is constant. In Figure 2 we begin with the aggregate expenditures schedule at AE_1 in the top diagram, yielding real output of Q_1. Assume now that investment increases in response to more optimistic business expectations, so the aggregate expenditures schedule rises from AE_1 to AE_2. (The notation "at P_1" reminds us that the price level is assumed constant.) The result will be a multiplied increase in real output from Q_1 to Q_2.

In Figure 2b the increase in investment spending is reflected in the horizontal distance between AD_1 and the broken curve to its right. The immediate effect of the increase in investment is an increase in aggregate demand by the exact amount of the new spending. But then the multiplier process magnifies the initial increase in investment into successive rounds of consumption spending and an ultimate multiplied increase in aggregate demand from AD_1 to AD_2. Equilibrium real output rises from Q_1 to Q_2, the same multiplied increase in real GDP as that in the top graph. The initial increase in investment in the

FIGURE 2 Shifts in the aggregate expenditures schedule and in the aggregate demand curve. (a) A change in some determinant of consumption, investment, or net exports (other than the price level) shifts the aggregate expenditures schedule upward from AE_1 to AE_2. The multiplier increases real output from Q_1 to Q_2. (b) The counterpart of this change is an initial rightward shift of the aggregate demand curve by the amount of initial new spending (from AD_1 to the broken curve). This leads to a multiplied rightward shift of the curve to AD_2, which is just sufficient to show the same increase of real output as that in the aggregate expenditures model.

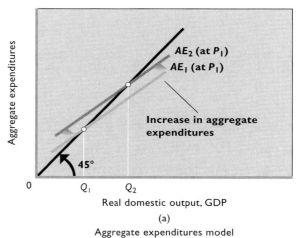

(a)
Aggregate expenditures model

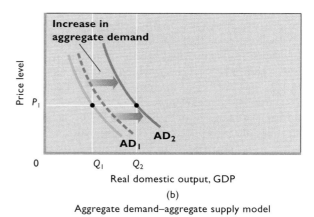

(b)
Aggregate demand–aggregate supply model

top graph has shifted the AD curve in the lower graph by a horizontal distance equal to the change in investment times the multiplier. This particular change in real GDP is still associated with the constant price level P_1. To generalize,

$$\text{Shift of AD curve} = \text{initial change in spending} \times \text{multiplier}$$

Appendix Summary

1. A change in the price level alters the location of the aggregate expenditures schedule through the real-balances, interest-rate, and foreign purchases effects. The aggregate demand curve is derived from the aggregate expenditures model by allowing the price level to change and observing the effect on the aggregate expenditures schedule and thus on equilibrium GDP.

2. With the price level held constant, increases in consumption, investment, government, and net export expenditures shift the aggregate expenditures schedule upward and the aggregate demand curve to the right. Decreases in these spending components produce the opposite effects.

Appendix Study Questions

1. Explain carefully: "A change in the price level shifts the aggregate expenditures curve but not the aggregate demand curve."

2. Suppose that the price level is constant and that investment decreases sharply. How would you show this decrease in the aggregate expenditures model? What would be the outcome for real GDP? How would you show this fall in investment in the aggregate demand–aggregate supply model, assuming the economy is operating in what, in effect, is a horizontal section of the aggregate supply curve?

11

Fiscal Policy, Deficits, and Debt

In the previous chapter we saw that an excessive increase in aggregate demand can cause demand-pull inflation and that a significant decline in aggregate demand can cause recession and cyclical unemployment. For these reasons, the Federal government sometimes uses budgetary actions to try to "stimulate the economy" or "rein in inflation." Such countercyclical **fiscal policy** consists of deliberate changes in government spending and tax collections designed to achieve full employment, control inflation, and encourage economic growth. (The adjective "fiscal" simply means "financial.")

O 11.1
Fiscal policy

We begin this chapter by examining the logic behind fiscal policy, its current status, and its limitations. Then we examine a closely related topic: the U.S. public debt.

Fiscal Policy and the AD-AS Model

The fiscal policy defined above is *discretionary* (or "active"). It is often initiated on the advice of the president's **Council of Economic Advisers (CEA),** a group of three economists appointed by the president to provide expertise and assistance on economic matters. Discretionary changes in government spending and taxes are *at the option* of the Federal government. They do not occur automatically. Changes that occur without congressional action are *nondiscretionary* (or "passive" or "automatic"), and we will examine them later in this chapter.

Expansionary Fiscal Policy

When recession occurs, an **expansionary fiscal policy** may be in order. Consider Figure 11.1, where we suppose that a sharp decline in investment spending has shifted the economy's aggregate demand curve to the left from AD_1 to AD_2. (Disregard the arrows and dashed downsloping line for now.) The cause of the recession may be that profit expectations on investment projects have dimmed, curtailing investment spending and reducing aggregate demand.

Suppose the economy's potential or full-employment output is $510 billion in Figure 11.1. If the price level is inflexible downward at P_1, the broken horizontal line in effect becomes the relevant aggregate supply curve. The aggregate demand curve moves leftward and reduces real GDP from $510 billion to $490 billion. A negative GDP gap of $20 billion (= $490 billion − $510 billion) arises. An increase in unemployment accompanies this negative GDP gap because fewer workers are needed to produce

the reduced output. In short, the economy depicted is suffering both recession and cyclical unemployment.

What fiscal policy should the Federal government adopt to try to stimulate the economy? It has three main options: (1) Increase government spending, (2) reduce taxes, or (3) use some combination of the two. If the Federal budget is balanced at the outset, expansionary fiscal policy will create a government **budget deficit**—government spending in excess of tax revenues.

Increased Government Spending Other things equal, a sufficient increase in government spending will shift an economy's aggregate demand curve to the right, from AD_2 to AD_1 in Figure 11.1. To see why, suppose that the recession prompts the government to initiate $5 billion of new spending on highways, education, and health care. We represent this new $5 billion of government spending as the horizontal distance between AD_2 and the dashed line immediately to its right. At each price level, the amount of real output that is demanded is now $5 billion greater than that demanded before the expansion of government spending.

But the initial increase in aggregate demand is not the end of the story. Through the multiplier effect, the aggregate demand curve shifts to AD_1, a distance that exceeds that represented by the originating $5 billion increase in government purchases. This greater shift occurs because the multiplier process magnifies the initial change in spending into successive rounds of new consumption spending. If the economy's MPC is .75, then the simple multiplier is 4. So the aggregate demand curve shifts rightward by four times the distance between AD_2 and the broken line. Because this *particular* increase in aggregate

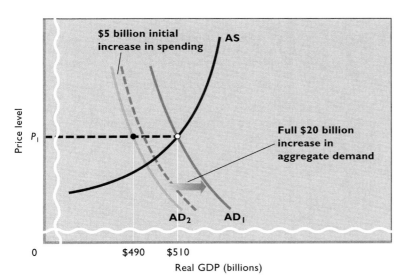

FIGURE 11.1 Expansionary fiscal policy. Expansionary fiscal policy uses increases in government spending or tax cuts to push the economy out of recession. In an economy with an MPC of .75, a $5 billion increase in government spending or a $6.67 billion decrease in personal taxes (producing a $5 billion initial increase in consumption) expands aggregate demand from AD_2 to the downsloping dashed curve. The multiplier then magnifies this initial increase in spending to AD_1. So real GDP rises along the horizontal broken aggregate supply segment by $20 billion.

demand occurs along the horizontal broken-line segment of aggregate supply, real output rises by the full extent of the multiplier. Observe that real output rises to $510 billion, up $20 billion from its recessionary level of $490 billion. Concurrently, unemployment falls as firms increase their employment to the full-employment level that existed before the recession.

Tax Reductions Alternatively, the government could reduce taxes to shift the aggregate demand curve rightward, as from AD_2 to AD_1. Suppose the government cuts personal income taxes by $6.67 billion, which increases disposable income by the same amount. Consumption will rise by $5 billion (= MPC of .75 × $6.67 billion), and saving will go up by $1.67 billion (= MPS of .25 × $6.67 billion). In this case the horizontal distance between AD_2 and the dashed downsloping line in Figure 11.1 represents only the $5 billion initial increase in consumption spending. Again, we call it "initial" consumption spending because the multiplier process yields successive rounds of increased consumption spending. The aggregate demand curve eventually shifts rightward by four times the $5 billion initial increase in consumption produced by the tax cut. Real GDP rises by $20 billion, from $490 billion to $510 billion, implying a multiplier of 4. Employment increases accordingly.

You may have noted that a tax cut must be somewhat larger than the proposed increase in government spending if it is to achieve the same amount of rightward shift in the aggregate demand curve. This is because part of a tax reduction increases saving, rather than consumption. To increase initial consumption by a specific amount, the government must reduce taxes by more than that amount. With an MPC of .75, taxes must fall by $6.67 billion for $5 billion of new consumption to be forthcoming, because

$1.67 billion is saved (not consumed). If the MPC had instead been, say, .6, an $8.33 billion reduction in tax collections would have been necessary to increase initial consumption by $5 billion. The smaller the MPC, the greater the tax cut needed to accomplish a specific initial increase in consumption and a specific shift in the aggregate demand curve.

Combined Government Spending Increases and Tax Reductions The government may combine spending increases and tax cuts to produce the desired initial increase in spending and the eventual increase in aggregate demand and real GDP. In the economy depicted in Figure 11.1, the government might increase its spending by $1.25 billion while reducing taxes by $5 billion. As an exercise, you should explain why this combination will produce the targeted $5 billion initial increase in new spending.

If you were assigned Chapter 9, think through these three fiscal policy options in terms of the recessionary-expenditure-gap analysis associated with the aggregate expenditures model (Figure 9.7). And recall from the appendix to Chapter 10 that rightward shifts of the aggregate demand curve relate directly to upward shifts of the aggregate expenditures schedule. **(Key Question 2)**

Contractionary Fiscal Policy

When demand-pull inflation occurs, a restrictive or **contractionary fiscal policy** may help control it. Look at Figure 11.2, where the full-employment level of real GDP is $510 billion. Suppose a sharp increase in investment and net export spending shifts the aggregate demand curve from AD_3 to AD_4. (Ignore the downsloping dashed line for now.) The outcomes are demand-pull inflation, as shown by the rise of the price level from P_1 to P_2, and a positive GDP gap of $12 billion (= $522 billion − $510 billion).

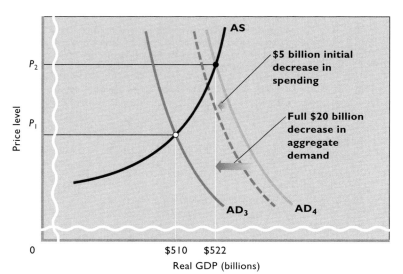

FIGURE 11.2 Contractionary fiscal policy.
Contractionary fiscal policy uses decreases in government spending or increases in taxes to reduce demand-pull inflation. In an economy with an MPC of .75, a $5 billion decline in government spending or a $6.67 billion increase in taxes (producing a $5 billion initial decrease in consumption) shifts the aggregate demand curve from AD_4 to the dashed line. The multiplier effect then shifts the curve farther leftward to AD_3. The overall decrease in aggregate demand halts the demand-pull inflation.

$5 billion initial decrease in spending

Full $20 billion decrease in aggregate demand

Price level

P_2

P_1

0

$510 $522

Real GDP (billions)

AS

AD_3 AD_4

If the government looks to fiscal policy to control this inflation, its options are the opposite of those used to combat recession. It can (1) decrease government spending, (2) raise taxes, or (3) use some combination of those two policies. When the economy faces demand-pull inflation, fiscal policy should move toward a government **budget surplus**—tax revenues in excess of government spending.

Decreased Government Spending

Reduced government spending shifts the aggregate demand curve leftward to control demand-pull inflation. In Figure 11.2, the horizontal distance between AD₄ and the dashed line to its left represents a $5 billion reduction in government spending. Once the multiplier process is complete, this spending cut will have shifted the aggregate demand curve leftward from AD₄ all the way to AD₃. If the price level were downwardly flexible, the price level would return to P_1, where it was before demand-pull inflation occurred. That is, deflation would occur.

Unfortunately, the actual economy is not as simple and tidy as Figure 11.2 suggests. Increases in aggregate demand that expand real output beyond the full-employment level of output tend to ratchet the price level upward, but declines in aggregate demand do not seem to push the price level downward. So stopping inflation is a matter of halting the rise of the price level, not trying to lower it to the previous level. Demand-pull inflation usually is experienced as a continual rightward shifting of the aggregate demand curve. Contractionary fiscal policy is designed to stop a further shift, not to restore a lower price level. Successful fiscal policy eliminates a continuing positive (and thus inflationary) GDP gap and prevents the price level from continuing its inflationary rise. Nevertheless, Figure 11.2 displays the basic principle: Reductions in government expenditures can be used as a fiscal policy action to tame demand-pull inflation.

Increased Taxes

Just as government can use tax cuts to increase consumption spending, it can use tax *increases* to *reduce* consumption spending. If the economy in Figure 11.2 has an MPC of .75, the government must raise taxes by $6.67 billion to reduce consumption by $5 billion. The $6.67 billion tax reduces saving by $1.67 billion (= the MPS of .25 × $6.67 billion). This $1.67 billion reduction in saving, by definition, is not a reduction in spending. But the $6.67 billion tax increase also reduces consumption spending by $5 billion (= the MPC of .75 × $6.67 billion), as shown by the distance between AD₄ and the dashed line to its left in Figure 11.2. After the multiplier process is complete, aggregate demand will have shifted leftward by $20 billion at each price level (= multiplier of 4 × $5 billion) and the demand-pull inflation will have been controlled.

Combined Government Spending Decreases and Tax Increases

The government may choose to combine spending decreases and tax increases in order to reduce aggregate demand and check inflation. To check your

G 11.1

Fiscal policy

understanding, determine why a $2 billion decline in government spending with a $4 billion increase in taxes would shift the aggregate demand curve from AD₄ to AD₃.

Also, if you were assigned Chapter 9, explain the three fiscal policy options for fighting inflation by referring to the inflationary-expenditure-gap concept developed with the aggregate expenditures model (Figure 9.8). And recall from the appendix to Chapter 10 that leftward shifts of the aggregate demand curve are associated with downshifts of the aggregate expenditures schedule. **(Key Question 3)**

Policy Options: *G* or *T*?

Which is preferable as a means of eliminating recession and inflation? The use of government spending or the use of taxes? The answer depends largely on one's view as to whether the government is too large or too small.

Economists who believe there are many unmet social and infrastructure needs usually recommend that government spending be increased during recessions. In times of demand-pull inflation, they usually recommend tax increases. Both actions either expand or preserve the size of government.

Economists who think that the government is too large and inefficient usually advocate tax cuts during recessions and cuts in government spending during times of demand-pull inflation. Both actions either restrain the growth of government or reduce its size.

The point is that discretionary fiscal policy designed to stabilize the economy can be associated with either an expanding government or a contracting government.

QUICK REVIEW 11.1

- Discretionary fiscal policy is the purposeful change of government expenditures and tax collections by government to promote full employment, price stability, and economic growth.
- The government uses expansionary fiscal policy to shift the aggregate demand curve rightward in order to expand real output. This policy entails increases in government spending, reductions in taxes, or some combination of the two.
- The government uses contractionary fiscal policy to shift the aggregate demand curve leftward (or to restrain its rightward shift) in an effort to halt demand-pull inflation. This policy entails reductions in government spending, tax increases, or some combination of the two.

Built-In Stability

To some degree, government tax revenues change automatically over the course of the business cycle and in ways that stabilize the economy. This automatic response, or built-in stability, constitutes nondiscretionary (or "passive" or "automatic") budgetary policy and results from the makeup of most tax systems. We did not include this built-in stability in our discussion of fiscal policy because we implicitly assumed that the same amount of tax revenue was being collected at each level of GDP. But the actual U.S. tax system is such that *net tax revenues* vary directly with GDP. (Net taxes are tax revenues less transfers and subsidies. From here on, we will use the simpler "taxes" to mean "net taxes.")

Virtually any tax will yield more tax revenue as GDP rises. In particular, personal income taxes have progressive rates and thus generate more-than-proportionate increases in tax revenues as GDP expands. Furthermore, as GDP rises and more goods and services are purchased, revenues from corporate income taxes and from sales taxes and excise taxes also increase. And, similarly, revenues from payroll taxes rise as economic expansion creates more jobs. Conversely, when GDP declines, tax receipts from all these sources also decline.

Transfer payments (or "negative taxes") behave in the opposite way from tax revenues. Unemployment compensation payments and welfare payments decrease during economic expansion and increase during economic contraction.

Automatic or Built-In Stabilizers

A **built-in stabilizer** is anything that increases the government's budget deficit (or reduces its budget surplus) during a recession and increases its budget surplus (or reduces its budget deficit) during an expansion without requiring explicit action by policymakers. As Figure 11.3 reveals, this is precisely what the U.S. tax system does. Government expenditures *G* are fixed and assumed to be independent of the level of GDP. Congress decides on a particular level of spending, but it does not determine the magnitude of tax revenues. Instead, it establishes tax rates, and the tax revenues then vary directly with the level of GDP that the economy achieves. Line *T* represents that direct relationship between tax revenues and GDP.

Economic Importance
The economic importance of the direct relationship between tax receipts and GDP becomes apparent when we consider that:

• Taxes reduce spending and aggregate demand.
• Reductions in spending are desirable when the economy is moving toward inflation, whereas increases in spending are desirable when the economy is slumping.

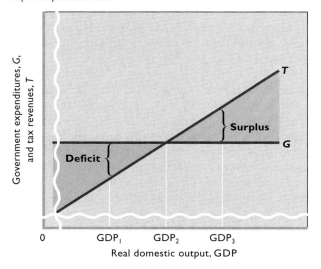

FIGURE 11.3 Built-in stability. Tax revenues *T* vary directly with GDP, and government spending *G* is assumed to be independent of GDP. As GDP falls in a recession, deficits occur automatically and help alleviate the recession. As GDP rises during expansion, surpluses occur automatically and help offset possible inflation.

As shown in Figure 11.3, tax revenues automatically increase as GDP rises during prosperity, and since taxes reduce household and business spending, they restrain the economic expansion. That is, as the economy moves toward a higher GDP, tax revenues automatically rise and move the budget from deficit toward surplus. In Figure 11.3, observe that the high and perhaps inflationary income level GDP_3 automatically generates a contractionary budget surplus.

Conversely, as GDP falls during recession, tax revenues automatically decline, increasing spending and cushioning the economic contraction. With a falling GDP, tax receipts decline and move the government's budget from surplus toward deficit. In Figure 11.3, the low level of income GDP_1 will automatically yield an expansionary budget deficit.

Tax Progressivity   Figure 11.3 reveals that the size of the automatic budget deficits or surpluses—and therefore built-in stability—depends on the responsiveness of tax revenues to changes in GDP. If tax revenues change sharply as GDP changes, the slope of line *T* in the figure will be steep and the vertical distances between *T* and *G* (the deficits or surpluses) will be large. If tax revenues change very little when GDP changes, the slope will be gentle and built-in stability will be low.

The steepness of *T* in Figure 11.3 depends on the tax system itself. In a **progressive tax system,** the average tax rate (= tax revenue/GDP) rises with GDP. In a

proportional tax system, the average tax rate remains constant as GDP rises. In a **regressive tax system,** the average tax rate falls as GDP rises. The progressive tax system has the steepest tax line T of the three. However, tax revenues will rise with GDP under both the progressive and the proportional tax systems, and they may rise, fall, or stay the same under a regressive tax system. The main point is this: The more progressive the tax system, the greater the economy's built-in stability.

The built-in stability provided by the U.S. tax system has reduced the severity of business fluctuations, perhaps by as much as 8 to 10 percent of the change in GDP that otherwise would have occurred.[1] But built-in stabilizers can only diminish, not eliminate, swings in real GDP. Discretionary fiscal policy (changes in tax rates and expenditures) or monetary policy (central bank–caused changes in interest rates) may be needed to correct recession or inflation of any appreciable magnitude.

Evaluating Fiscal Policy

How can we determine whether discretionary fiscal policy is expansionary, neutral, or contractionary in a particular period? We cannot simply examine changes in the actual budget deficits or surpluses, because those changes may reflect automatic changes in tax revenues that accompany changes in GDP, not changes in discretionary fiscal policy. Moreover, the strength of any deliberate change in government spending or taxes depends on how large it is relative to the size of the economy. So, in evaluating the status of fiscal policy, we must adjust deficits and surpluses to eliminate automatic changes in tax revenues and compare the sizes of the adjusted budget deficits (or surpluses) to the levels of potential GDP.

Standardized Budget

Economists use the **standardized budget** (also called the *full-employment budget*) to adjust the actual Federal budget deficits and surpluses to eliminate the automatic changes in tax revenues. The standardized budget measures what the Federal budget deficit or surplus would be with existing tax rates and government spending levels if the economy had achieved its full-employment level of GDP (its potential output) in each year. The idea essentially is to compare *actual* government expenditures for each year with the tax revenues *that would have occurred* in that year if the economy had achieved full-employment GDP. That

procedure removes budget deficits or surpluses that arise simply because of changes in GDP and thus tell us nothing about changes in discretionary fiscal policy.

Consider Figure 11.4a, where line G represents government expenditures and line T represents tax revenues. In full-employment year 1, government expenditures of $500 billion equal tax revenues of $500 billion, as indicated by the intersection of lines G and T at point a. The standardized budget deficit in year 1 is zero—government expenditures equal the tax revenues forthcoming at the full-employment output GDP_1. Obviously, the full-employment deficit *as a percentage of potential GDP* is also zero.

Now suppose that a recession occurs and GDP falls from GDP_1 to GDP_2, as shown in Figure 11.4a. Let's also assume that the government takes no discretionary action, so lines G and T remain as shown in the figure. Tax revenues automatically fall to $450 billion (point c) at GDP_2, while government spending remains unaltered at $500 billion (point b). A $50 billion budget deficit (represented by distance bc) arises. But this **cyclical deficit** is simply a by-product of the economy's slide into recession, not the result of discretionary fiscal actions by the government. We would be wrong to conclude from this deficit that the government is engaging in an expansionary fiscal policy.

That fact is highlighted when we consider the standardized budget deficit for year 2 in Figure 11.4a. The $500 billion of government expenditures in year 2 is shown by b on line G. And, as shown by a on line T, $500 billion of tax revenues would have occurred if the economy had achieved its full-employment GDP. Because both b and a represent $500 billion, the standardized budget deficit in year 2 is zero, as is this deficit as a percentage of potential GDP. Since the standardized deficits are zero in both years, we know that government did not change its discretionary fiscal policy, even though a recession occurred and an actual deficit of $50 billion resulted.

Next, consider Figure 11.4b. Suppose that real output declined from full-employment GDP_3 to GDP_4. But also suppose that the Federal government responded to the recession by reducing tax rates in year 4, as represented by the downward shift of the tax line from T_1 to T_2. What has happened to the size of the standardized deficit? Government expenditures in year 4 are $500 billion, as shown by e. We compare that amount with the $475 billion of tax revenues that would occur if the economy achieved its full-employment GDP. That is, we compare position e on line G with position h on line T_2. The $25 billion of tax revenues by which e exceeds h is the standardized budget deficit for year 4. As a percentage of potential GDP, the

[1]Alan J. Auerbach and Daniel Feenberg, "The Significance of Federal Taxes as Automatic Stabilizers," *Journal of Economic Perspectives*, Summer 2000, p. 54.

FIGURE 11.4 **Standardized deficits.** (a) In the left-hand graph the standardized deficit is zero at the full-employment output GDP$_1$. But it is also zero at the recessionary output GDP$_2$, because the $500 billion of government expenditures at GDP$_2$ equals the $500 billion of tax revenues that would be forthcoming at the full-employment GDP$_1$. There has been no change in fiscal policy. (b) In the right-hand graph, discretionary fiscal policy, as reflected in the downward shift of the tax line from T_1 to T_2, has increased the standardized budget deficit from zero in year 3 to $25 billion in year 4. This is found by comparing the $500 billion of government spending in year 4 with the $475 billion of taxes that would accrue at the full-employment GDP$_3$. Such a rise in the standardized deficit (as a percentage of potential GDP) identifies an expansionary fiscal policy.

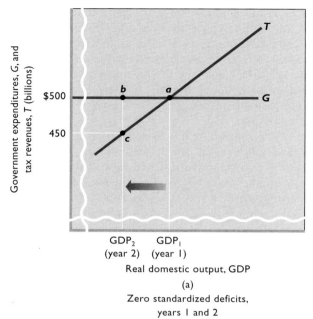

(a)
Zero standardized deficits,
years 1 and 2

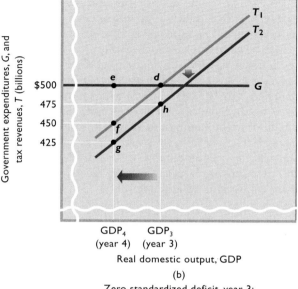

(b)
Zero standardized deficit, year 3;
$25 billion full-employment deficit, year 4

standardized budget deficit has increased from zero in year 3 (before the tax-rate cut) to some positive percent [= ($25 billion/GDP$_3$) × 100] in year 4. This increase in the relative size of the full-employment deficit between the two years reveals that fiscal policy is *expansionary*.

In contrast, if we observed a standardized deficit (as a percentage of potential GDP) of zero in one year, followed by a standardized budget surplus in the next, we could conclude that fiscal policy is contractionary. Because the standardized budget adjusts for automatic changes in tax revenues, the increase in the standardized budget surplus reveals that government either decreased its spending (G) or increased tax rates such that tax revenues (T) increased. These changes in G and T are precisely the discretionary actions that we have identified as elements of a *contractionary* fiscal policy.

Recent U.S. Fiscal Policy

Table 11.1 lists the actual Federal budget deficits and surpluses (column 2) and the standardized deficits and surpluses (column 3), as percentages of actual and potential GDP, respectively, for recent years. Observe that the standardized deficits are generally smaller than the actual deficits. This is because the actual deficits include cyclical

TABLE 11.1 **Federal Deficits (−) and Surpluses (+) as Percentages of GDP, 1990–2005**

(1) Year	(2) Actual Deficit − or Surplus +	(3) Standardized Deficit − or Surplus +*
1990	−3.9%	−2.2%
1991	−4.4	−2.5
1992	−4.5	−2.9
1993	−3.8	−2.9
1994	−2.9	−2.1
1995	−2.2	−2.0
1996	−1.4	−1.2
1997	−0.3	−1.0
1998	+0.8	−0.4
1999	+1.4	+0.1
2000	+2.5	+1.1
2001	+1.3	+1.1
2002	−1.5	−1.1
2003	−3.4	−2.7
2004	−3.5	−2.4
2005	−2.6	−1.8

*As a percentage of potential GDP.

Source: Congressional Budget Office, **www.cbo.gov.**

deficits, whereas the standardized deficits do not. The latter deficits provide the information needed to assess discretionary fiscal policy.

Column 3 shows that fiscal policy was expansionary in the early 1990s. Consider 1992, for example. From the table we see that the actual budget deficit was 4.5 percent of GDP and the standardized budget deficit was 2.9 percent of potential GDP. The economy was recovering from the 1990–1991 recession, so tax revenues were relatively low. But even if the economy were at full employment in 1992, with the greater tax revenues that would imply, the Federal budget would have been in deficit by 2.9 percent. And that percentage was greater than the deficits in the prior 2 years. So the standardized budget deficit in 1992 clearly reflected expansionary fiscal policy.

But the large standardized budget deficits were projected to continue even when the economy fully recovered from the 1990–1991 recession. The concern was that the large actual and standardized deficits would cause high interest rates, low levels of investment, and slow economic growth. In 1993 the Clinton administration and Congress increased personal income and corporate income tax rates to prevent these potential outcomes. Observe from column 3 of Table 11.1 that the standardized budget deficits shrunk each year and eventually gave way to surpluses in 1999, 2000, and 2001.

On the basis of projections that actual budget surpluses would accumulate to as much as $5 trillion between 2000 and 2010, the Bush administration and Congress passed a major tax reduction package in 2001. The tax cuts went into effect over a number of years. For example, the cuts reduced tax liabilities by an estimated $44 billion in 2001 and $52 billion in 2002. In terms of fiscal policy, the timing was good since the economy entered a recession in March 2001 and absorbed a second economic blow from the terrorist attacks on September 11, 2001. The government greatly increased its spending on war abroad and homeland security. Also, in March 2002 Congress passed a "recession-relief" bill that extended unemployment compensation benefits and offered business tax relief. That legislation was specifically designed to inject $51 billion into the economy in 2002 and another $71 billion over the following 2 years.

As seen in Table 11.1, the standardized budget moved from a *surplus* of 1.1 percent of potential GDP in 2000 to a *deficit* of 1.1 percent in 2002. Clearly, fiscal policy had turned expansionary. Nevertheless, the economy remained very sluggish in 2003. In June of that year, Congress again cut taxes, this time by an enormous $350 billion over several years. Specifically, the tax legislation accelerated the reduction of marginal tax rates already scheduled for future years

GLOBAL PERSPECTIVE 11.1

Standardized Budget Deficits or Surpluses as a Percentage of Potential GDP, Selected Nations

In 2005 some nations had standardized budget surpluses, while others had standardized budget deficits. These surpluses and deficits varied as a percentage of each nation's potential GDP. Generally, the surpluses represented contractionary fiscal policy and the deficits expansionary fiscal policy.

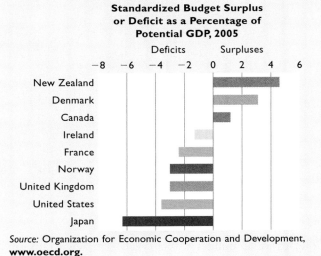

Source: Organization for Economic Cooperation and Development, **www.oecd.org.**

and slashed tax rates on income from dividends and capital gains. It also increased tax breaks for families and small businesses. This tax package increased the standardized budget deficit as a percentage of potential GDP to –2.7 percent in 2003. The purpose of this expansionary fiscal policy was to prevent another recession, reduce unemployment, and increase economic growth. **(Key Question 6)**

Global Perspective 11.1 shows the extent of the standardized deficits or surpluses of a number of countries in a recent year.

Budget Deficits and Projections

Figure 11.5 shows the absolute magnitudes of recent U.S. budget surpluses and deficits. It also shows the projected future deficits or surpluses as published by the Congressional Budget Office (CBO). The United States has been experiencing large budget deficits that are expected to continue for several years. But projected deficits and surpluses are subject to swift change, as government alters its fiscal policy and the GDP growth accelerates or slows. So we suggest that you update this figure by going to the

FIGURE 11.5 Federal budget deficits and surpluses, actual and projected, fiscal years 1992–2012 (in billions of nominal dollars). The annual budget deficits of 1992 through 1997 gave way to budget surpluses from 1998 through 2001. Deficits reappeared in 2002 and are projected to continue through 2011.

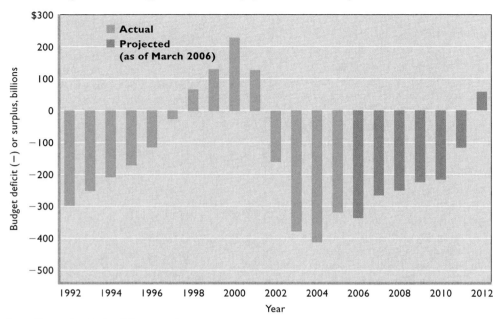

Source: Congressional Budget Office, **www.cbo.gov.**

Congressional Budget Office Web site, **www.cbo.gov**, and selecting Current Budget Projections and then CBO's Baseline Budget Projections. The relevant numbers are in the row Surplus (+) or Deficit (−).

Social Security Considerations

The surpluses and deficits in Figure 11.5 include all tax revenues, even those obligated for future Social Security payments. Recall from the Last Word in Chapter 4 that Social Security is basically a "pay-as-you-go plan" in which the mandated benefits paid out each year are financed by the payroll tax revenues received each year. But current tax rates now bring in more revenue than current payouts, in partial preparation for the opposite circumstance when the baby boomers retire in the next one or two decades. The Federal government saves the excess revenues by purchasing U.S. securities and holding them in the Social Security trust fund.

Some economists argue that these present Social Security surpluses ($175 billion in 2005) should be subtracted from Federal government revenue when calculating present Federal deficits. Because these surpluses represent future government obligations on a dollar-for-dollar basis, they should not be considered revenue offsets to current government spending. Without the Social Security sur-

pluses, the total public debt in 2005 would be $523 billion rather than the $318 billion shown.

Problems, Criticisms, and Complications

Economists recognize that governments may encounter a number of significant problems in enacting and applying fiscal policy.

Problems of Timing

Several problems of timing may arise in connection with fiscal policy:

- *Recognition lag* The recognition lag is the time between the beginning of recession or inflation and the certain awareness that it is actually happening. This lag arises because of the difficulty in predicting the future course of economic activity. Although forecasting tools such as the index of leading indicators (see this chapter's Last Word) provide clues to the direction of the economy, the economy may be 4 or 6 months into a recession or inflation before that fact appears in relevant statistics and is acknowledged. Meanwhile, the economic downslide or the inflation may become more serious than it would have if the situation had been identified and acted on sooner.

- *Administrative lag* The wheels of democratic government turn slowly. There will typically be a significant lag between the time the need for fiscal action is recognized and the time action is taken. Following the terrorist attacks of September 11, 2001, the U.S. Congress was stalemated for 5 months before passing a compromise economic stimulus law in March 2002. (In contrast, the Federal Reserve began lowering interest rates the week after the attacks.)

- *Operational lag* A lag also occurs between the time fiscal action is taken and the time that action affects output, employment, or the price level. Although changes in tax rates can be put into effect relatively quickly, government spending on public works—new dams, interstate highways, and so on—requires long planning periods and even longer periods of construction. Such spending is of questionable use in offsetting short (for example, 6- to 12-month) periods of recession. Consequently, discretionary fiscal policy has increasingly relied on tax changes rather than on changes in spending as its main tool.

Political Considerations

Fiscal policy is conducted in a political arena. That reality not only may slow the enactment of fiscal policy but also may create the potential for political considerations swamping economic considerations in its formulation. It is a human trait to rationalize actions and policies that are in one's self-interest. Politicians are very human—they want to get reelected. A strong economy at election time will certainly help them. So they may favor large tax cuts under the guise of expansionary fiscal policy even though that policy is economically inappropriate. Similarly, they may rationalize increased government spending on popular items such as farm subsidies, health care, highways, education, and homeland security.

At the extreme, elected officials and political parties might collectively "hijack" fiscal policy for political purposes, cause inappropriate changes in aggregate demand, and thereby cause (rather than avert) economic fluctuations. They may stimulate the economy using expansionary fiscal policy before elections and use contractionary fiscal policy to dampen excessive aggregate demand after the election. In short, elected officials may cause so-called **political business cycles.** Such scenarios are difficult to document and prove, but there is little doubt that political considerations weigh heavily in the formulation of fiscal policy. The question is how often, if ever, do those political considerations run counter to "sound economics."

Future Policy Reversals

Fiscal policy may fail to achieve its intended objectives if households expect future reversals of policy. Consider a tax cut, for example. If taxpayers believe the tax reduction is temporary, they may save a large portion of their tax saving, reasoning that rates will return to their previous level in the future. At that time, they can draw on this extra saving to maintain their consumption. So a tax reduction thought to be temporary may not increase present consumption spending and aggregate demand by as much as our simple model (Figure 11.1) suggests.

The opposite may be true for a tax increase. If taxpayers think it is temporary, they may reduce their saving to pay the tax while maintaining their present consumption. They may reason they can restore their saving when the tax rate again falls. So the tax increase may not reduce current consumption and aggregate demand by as much as the policymakers desired.

To the extent that this so-called *consumption smoothing* occurs over time, fiscal policy will lose some of its strength. The lesson is that tax-rate changes that households view as permanent are more likely to alter consumption and aggregate demand than tax changes they view as temporary.

Offsetting State and Local Finance

The fiscal policies of state and local governments are frequently *pro-cyclical*, meaning that they worsen rather than correct recession or inflation. Unlike the Federal government, most state and local governments face constitutional or other legal requirements to balance their budgets. Like households and private businesses, state and local governments increase their expenditures during prosperity and cut them during recession. During the Great Depression of the 1930s, most of the increase in Federal spending was offset by decreases in state and local spending. During and immediately following the recession of 2001, many state and local governments had to increase tax rates, impose new taxes, and reduce spending to offset lower tax revenues resulting from the reduced personal income and spending of their citizens.

Crowding-Out Effect

Another potential flaw of fiscal policy is the so-called **crowding-out effect:** An expansionary fiscal policy (deficit spending) may increase the interest rate and reduce private spending, thereby weakening or canceling the stimulus of the expansionary policy.

O 11.2
Crowding out

Suppose the economy is in recession and government enacts a discretionary fiscal policy in the form of increased government spending. Also suppose that the monetary authorities hold the supply of money constant. To finance its budget deficit, the government borrows funds in the money market. The resulting increase in the demand for money raises the price paid for borrowing money: the interest rate. Because investment spending varies inversely with the interest rate, some investment will be choked off or crowded out. (Some interest-sensitive consumption spending such as purchases of automobiles on credit may also be crowded out.)

Nearly all economists agree that a budget deficit is inappropriate when the economy has achieved full employment. Such a deficit will surely crowd out some private investment. But economists disagree on whether crowding out exists under all circumstances. Many believe that little crowding out will occur when fiscal policy is used to move the economy from recession. The added amount of government financing resulting from typical budget deficits is small compared to the total amount of private and public financing occurring in the money market. Therefore, interest rates are not likely to be greatly affected. Moreover, both increased government spending and increased consumption spending resulting from tax cuts may improve the profit expectations of businesses. The greater expected returns on private investment may encourage more of it. Thus, private investment need not fall, even though interest rates do rise. (We will soon see that the financing of the entire public debt, as opposed to the financing of new debt from annual deficits, is more likely to raise interest rates.)

Current Thinking on Fiscal Policy

Where do these complications leave us as to the advisability and effectiveness of discretionary fiscal policy? In view of the complications and uncertain outcomes of fiscal policy, some economists argue that it is better not to engage in it at all. Those holding that view point to the superiority of monetary policy (changes in interest rates engineered by the Federal Reserve) as a stabilizing device or believe that most economic fluctuations tend to be mild and self-correcting.

But most economists believe that fiscal policy remains an important, useful policy lever in the government's macroeconomic toolkit. The current popular view is that fiscal policy can help push the economy in a particular direction but cannot fine-tune it to a precise macroeconomic outcome. Mainstream economists generally agree that monetary policy is the best month-to-month stabilization tool for the U.S. economy. If monetary policy is doing its job, the government should maintain a relatively neutral fiscal policy, with a standardized budget deficit or surplus of no more than 2 percent of potential GDP. It should hold major discretionary fiscal policy in reserve to help counter situations where recession threatens to be deep and long-lasting or where inflation threatens to escalate rapidly despite the efforts of the Federal Reserve to stabilize the economy.

Finally, economists agree that proposed fiscal policy should be evaluated for its potential positive and negative impacts on long-run productivity growth. The short-run policy tools used for conducting active fiscal policy often have long-run impacts. Countercyclical fiscal policy should be shaped to strengthen, or at least not impede, the growth of long-run aggregate supply (shown as a rightward shift of the long-run aggregate supply curve in Figure 10.3). For example, a tax cut might be structured to enhance work effort, strengthen investment, and encourage innovation. Alternatively, an increase in government spending might center on preplanned projects for public capital (highways, mass transit, ports, airports), which are complementary to private investment and thus support long-term economic growth. **(Key Question 8)**

QUICK REVIEW 11.2

- Automatic changes in net taxes (taxes minus transfers) add a degree of built-in stability to the economy.
- The standardized budget compares government spending to the tax revenues that would accrue if there were full employment; changes in standardized budget deficits or surpluses (as percentages of potential GDP) reveal whether fiscal policy is expansionary, neutral, or contractionary.
- Standardized budget deficits are distinct from cyclical deficits, which simply reflect declines in tax revenues resulting from reduced GDP.
- Time lags, political problems, expectations, and state and local finances complicate fiscal policy.
- The crowding-out effect indicates that an expansionary fiscal policy may increase the interest rate and reduce investment spending.

The Public Debt

The national or **public debt** is essentially the total accumulation of the deficits (minus the surpluses) the Federal government has incurred through time. These deficits have emerged mainly because of war financing, recessions, and fiscal policy. Lack of political will by Congress has also contributed to the size of the debt. In 2005 the total public debt was $7.96 trillion—$3.9 trillion held by the public and $4.06 trillion held by Federal Agencies and the Federal Reserve. (You can find the size of the public debt, to the penny, at the Web site of the Department of Treasury, Bureau of the Public Debt, at **www.publicdebt.treas.gov/opd/opdpenny.htm.**)

Ownership

The total public debt of nearly $8 trillion represents the total amount of money owed by the Federal government to the holders of **U.S. securities:** financial instruments issued by the Federal government to borrow money to finance expenditures that exceed tax revenues. These U.S. securities (loan instruments) are of four types: Treasury bills (short-term securities), Treasury notes (medium-term securities), Treasury bonds (long-term securities), and U.S. saving bonds (long-term, nonmarketable bonds).

Figure 11.6 shows that the public held 49 percent of the Federal debt in 2005 and that Federal government agencies and the Federal Reserve (the U.S. central bank)

held the other 51 percent. In this case the "public" consists of individuals here and abroad, state and local governments, and U.S. financial institutions. Foreigners held about 25 percent of the total debt in 2005. So, most of the debt is held internally, not externally. Americans owe three-fourths of the debt to Americans.

Debt and GDP

A simple statement of the absolute size of the debt ignores the fact that the wealth and productive ability of the U.S. economy is also vast. A wealthy, highly productive nation can incur and carry a large public debt more easily than a poor nation can. A more meaningful measure of the public debt relates it to an economy's GDP. Figure 11.7 shows the relative size of the Federal debt held by the public (as opposed to the Federal Reserve and Federal agencies) over time. This percentage—31.4 percent in 2005—has increased since 2001, but remains well below the percentages in the 1990s.

International Comparisons

As shown in Global Perspective 11.2, it is not uncommon for countries to have public debts. The numbers shown are government debts held by the public, as a percentage of GDP.

FIGURE 11.6 Ownership of the total public debt, 2005. The total public debt can be divided into the proportion held by the public (49 percent) and the proportion held by Federal agencies and the Federal Reserve System (51 percent). Of the total debt, 25 percent is foreign-owned.

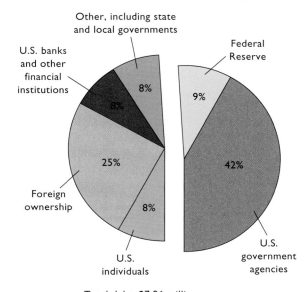

Source: U.S. Treasury, **www.fms.treas.gov/bulletin.**

FIGURE 11.7 Federal debt held by the public as a percentage of GDP, 1970–2005. As a percentage of GDP, the Federal debt held by the public (held outside the Federal Reserve and Federal government agencies) increased sharply over the 1980–1995 period and declined significantly between 1995 and 2001. Since 2001, the percentage has gone up again, but remains lower than it was in the 1990s.

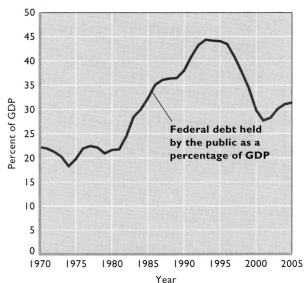

GLOBAL PERSPECTIVE 11.2

Publicly Held Debt: International Comparisons

Although the United States has the world's largest public debt, a number of other nations have larger debts as percentages of their GDPs.

Public Sector Debt as Percentage of GDP, 2005

Italy	
Belgium	
Japan	
Germany	
France	
United States	
Hungary	
Netherlands	
United Kingdom	
Spain	
Canada	
Poland	

0 20 40 60 80 100 120

Source: Organization for Economic Cooperation and Development, **www.oecd.org/.**

Interest Charges

Many economists conclude that the primary burden of the debt is the annual interest charge accruing on the bonds sold to finance the debt. In 2005 interest on the total public debt was $184 billion, which is now the fourth-largest item in the Federal budget (behind income security, national defense, and health).

Interest payments were 1.5 percent of GDP in 2005. That percentage reflects the level of taxation (the average tax rate) required to pay the interest on the public debt. That is, in 2005 the Federal government had to collect taxes equal to 1.5 percent of GDP to service the total public debt. Thanks to relatively low costs of borrowing, this percentage was down from 3.2 percent in 1990 and 2.3 percent in 2000.

False Concerns

You may wonder if the large public debt might bankrupt the United States or at least place a tremendous burden on your children and grandchildren. Fortunately, these are false concerns. People were wondering the same things 50 years ago!

Bankruptcy

The large U.S. public debt does not threaten to bankrupt the Federal government, leaving it unable to meet its financial obligations. There are two main reasons: refinancing and taxation.

Refinancing The public debt is easily refinanced. As portions of the debt come due on maturing Treasury bills, notes, and bonds each month, the government does not cut expenditures or raise taxes to provide the funds required. Rather, it refinances the debt by selling new bonds and using the proceeds to pay holders of the maturing bonds. The new bonds are in strong demand, because lenders can obtain a relatively good interest return with no risk of default by the Federal government.

Taxation The Federal government has the constitutional authority to levy and collect taxes. A tax increase is a government option for gaining sufficient revenue to pay interest and principal on the public debt. Financially distressed private households and corporations cannot extract themselves from their financial difficulties by taxing the public. If their incomes or sales revenues fall short of their expenses, they can indeed go bankrupt. But the Federal government does have the option to impose new taxes or increase existing tax rates if necessary to finance its debt.

Burdening Future Generations

In 2005 public debt per capita was $26,834. Was each child born in 2005 handed a $26,834 bill from the Federal government? Not really. The public debt does not impose as much of a burden on future generations as commonly thought.

The United States owes a substantial portion of the public debt to itself. U.S. citizens and institutions (banks, businesses, insurance companies, governmental agencies, and trust funds) own about 74 percent of the U.S. government securities. Although that part of the public debt is a liability to Americans (as taxpayers), it is simultaneously an asset to Americans (as holders of Treasury bills, Treasury notes, Treasury bonds, and U.S. savings bonds).

To eliminate the American-owned part of the public debt would require a gigantic transfer payment from Americans to Americans. Taxpayers would pay higher taxes, and holders of the debt would receive an equal amount for their U.S. securities. Purchasing power in the United States would not change. Only the repayment of the 25 percent of the public debt owned by foreigners would negatively impact U.S. purchasing power.

The public debt increased sharply during the Second World War. But the decision to finance military purchases through the sale of government bonds did not shift the economic burden of the war to future generations. The economic cost of the Second World War consisted of the civilian goods society had to forgo in shifting scarce resources to war goods production (recall production possibilities analysis). Regardless of whether society financed this reallocation through higher taxes or through borrowing, the real economic burden of the war would have been the same. That burden was borne almost entirely by those who lived during the war. They were the ones who did without a multitude of consumer goods to enable the United States to arm itself and its allies. The next generation inherited the debt from the war but also an equal amount of government bonds. It also inherited the enormous benefits from the victory—namely, preserved political and economic systems at home and the "export" of those systems to Germany, Italy, and Japan. Those outcomes enhanced postwar U.S. economic growth and helped raise the standard of living of future generations of Americans.

Substantive Issues

Although the preceding issues relating to the public debt are false concerns, a number of substantive issues are not. Economists, however, attach varying degrees of importance to them.

Income Distribution

The distribution of ownership of government securities is highly uneven. Some people own much more than the $26,834-per-person portion of government securities; other people own less or none at all. In general, the ownership of the public debt is concentrated among wealthier groups, who own a large percentage of all stocks and bonds. Because the overall Federal tax system is only slightly progressive, payment of interest on the public debt mildly increases income inequality. Income is transferred from people who, on average, have lower incomes to the higher-income bondholders. If greater income equality is one of society's goals, then this redistribution is undesirable.

Incentives

The current public debt necessitates annual interest payments of $184 billion. With no increase in the size of the debt, that interest charge must be paid out of tax revenues. Higher taxes may dampen incentives to bear risk, to innovate, to invest, and to work. So, in this indirect way, a large public debt may impair economic growth.

Foreign-Owned Public Debt

The 25 percent of the U.S. debt held by citizens and institutions of foreign countries *is* an economic burden to Americans. Because we do not owe that portion of the debt "to ourselves," the payment of interest and principal on this **external public debt** enables foreigners to buy some of our output. In return for the benefits derived from the borrowed funds, the United States transfers goods and services to foreign lenders. Of course, Americans also own debt issued by foreign governments, so payment of principal and interest by those governments transfers some of their goods and services to Americans. **(Key Question 10)**

Crowding-Out Effect Revisited

A potentially more serious problem is the financing (and continual refinancing) of the large public debt, which can transfer a real economic burden to future generations by passing on to them a smaller stock of capital goods. This possibility involves the previously discussed crowding-out effect: the idea that public borrowing drives up real interest rates, which reduces private investment spending. If the amount of current investment crowded out is extensive, future generations will inherit an economy with a smaller production capacity and, other things equal, a lower standard of living.

A Graphical Look at Crowding Out We

know from Chapter 8 that the real interest rate is inversely related to the amount of investment spending. When graphed, that relationship is shown as a downward-sloping investment demand curve, such as either ID_1 or ID_2 in Figure 11.8. Let's first consider curve ID_1. (Ignore curve ID_2 for now.) Suppose that government borrowing increases the real interest rate from 6 percent to 10 percent. Investment spending will then fall from $25 billion to $15 billion, as shown by the economy's move from *a* to *b*. That is, the financing of the debt will compete with the financing of private investment projects and crowd out

FIGURE 11.8 The investment demand curve and the crowding-out effect. If the investment demand curve (ID_1) is fixed, the increase in the interest rate from 6 percent to 10 percent caused by financing a large public debt will move the economy from a to b and crowd out $10 billion of private investment and decrease the size of the capital stock inherited by future generations. However, if the public goods enabled by the debt improve the investment prospects of businesses, the private investment demand curve will shift rightward, as from ID_1 to ID_2. That shift may offset the crowding-out effect wholly or in part. In this case, it moves the economy from a to c.

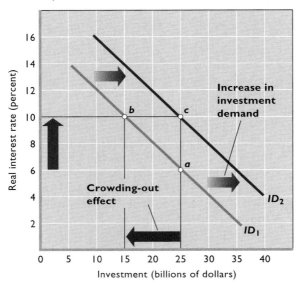

financing through debt, the stock of public capital passed on to future generations may be higher than otherwise. That greater stock of public capital may offset the diminished stock of private capital resulting from the crowding-out effect, leaving overall production capacity unimpaired.

So-called public-private complementarities are a second factor that could reduce the crowding out effect. Some public and private investments are complementary. Thus, the public investment financed through the debt could spur some private-sector investment by increasing its expected rate of return. For example, a Federal building in a city may encourage private investment in the form of nearby office buildings, shops, and restaurants. Through its complementary effect, the spending on public capital may shift the private investment demand curve to the right, as from ID_1 to ID_2 in Figure 11.8. Even though the government borrowing boosts the interest rate from 6 percent to 10 percent, total private investment need not fall. In the case shown as the move from a to c in Figure 11.8, it remains at $25 billion. Of course, the increase in investment demand might be smaller than that shown. If it were smaller, the crowding-out effect would not be fully offset. But the point is that an increase in private investment demand may counter the decline in investment that would otherwise result from the higher interest rate. **(Key Question 13)**

$10 billion of private investment. So the stock of private capital handed down to future generations will be $10 billion less than it would have been without the need to finance the public debt.

Public Investments and Public-Private Complementarities

But even with crowding out, two factors could partly or fully offset the net economic burden shifted to future generations. First, just as private goods may involve either consumption or investment, so it is with public goods. Part of the government spending enabled by the public debt is for public investment outlays (for example, highways, mass transit systems, and electric power facilities) and "human capital" (for example, investments in education, job training, and health). Like private expenditures on machinery and equipment, those **public investments** increase the economy's future production capacity. Because of the

One of Several Tools Policymakers Use to Forecast the Future Direction of Real GDP Is a Monthly Index of 10 Variables That in the Past Have Provided Advance Notice of Changes in GDP.

The Conference Board's *index of leading indicators* has historically reached a peak or a trough in advance of corresponding turns in the business cycle.* Thus changes in this composite index of 10 economic variables provide a clue to the future direction of the economy. Such advance warning helps policymakers formulate appropriate macroeconomic policy.

Here is how each of the 10 components of the index would change if it were predicting a decline in real GDP. The opposite changes would forecast a rise in real GDP.

1. *Average workweek* Decreases in the length of the average workweek of production workers in manufacturing foretell declines in future manufacturing output and possible declines in real GDP.

2. *Initial claims for unemployment insurance* Higher first-time claims for unemployment insurance are associated with falling employment and subsequently sagging real GDP.

3. *New orders for consumer goods* Decreases in the number of orders received by manufacturers for consumer goods portend reduced future production—a decline in real GDP.

4. *Vendor performance* Somewhat ironically, better on-time delivery by sellers of inputs indicates slackening business demand for final output and potentially falling real GDP.

5. *New orders for capital goods* A drop in orders for capital equipment and other investment goods implies reduced future spending by businesses and thus reduced aggregate demand and lower real GDP.

6. *Building permits for houses* Decreases in the number of building permits issued for new homes imply future declines in investment and therefore the possibility that real GDP will fall.

7. *Stock prices* Declines in stock prices often are reflections of expected declines in corporate sales and profits. Also, lower stock prices diminish consumer wealth, leading to possible cutbacks in consumer spending. Lower stock prices also make it less attractive for firms to issue new shares of stock as a way of raising funds for investment. Thus, declines in stock prices can mean declines in future aggregate demand and real GDP.

8. *Money supply* Decreases in the nation's money supply are associated with falling real GDP.

9. *Interest-rate spread* Increases in short-term nominal interest rates typically reflect monetary policies designed to slow the economy. Such policies have much less effect on long-term interest rates, which usually are higher than short-term rates. So a smaller difference between short-term interest rates and long-term interest rates suggests restrictive monetary policies and potentially a future decline in GDP.

10. *Consumer expectations* Less favorable consumer attitudes about future economic conditions, measured by an index of consumer expectations, foreshadow lower consumption spending and potential future declines in GDP.

None of these factors alone consistently predicts the future course of the economy. It is not unusual in any month, for example, for one or two of the indicators to be decreasing while the other indicators are increasing. Rather, changes in the composite of the 10 components are what in the past have provided advance notice of a change in the direction of GDP. The rule of thumb is that three successive monthly declines or increases in the index indicate the economy will soon turn in that same direction.

Although the composite index has correctly signaled business fluctuations on numerous occasions, it has not been infallible. At times the index has provided false warnings of recessions that never happened. In other instances, recessions have so closely followed the downturn in the index that policymakers have not had sufficient time to make use of the "early" warning. Moreover, changing structural features of the economy have, on occasion, rendered the existing index obsolete and necessitated its revision.

Given these caveats, the index of leading indicators can best be thought of as a useful but not totally reliable signaling device that authorities must employ with considerable caution in formulating macroeconomic policy.

---

*The Conference Board is a private, nonprofit research and business membership group, with more than 2700 corporate and other members in 60 nations. See **www.conferenceboard.org**.

Summary

1. Fiscal policy consists of deliberate changes in government spending, taxes, or some combination of both to promote full employment, price-level stability, and economic growth. Fiscal policy requires increases in government spending, decreases in taxes, or both—a budget deficit—to increase aggregate demand and push an economy from a recession. Decreases in government spending, increases in taxes, or both—a budget surplus—are appropriate fiscal policy for dealing with demand-pull inflation.

2. Built-in stability arises from net tax revenues, which vary directly with the level of GDP. During recession, the Federal budget automatically moves toward a stabilizing deficit; during expansion, the budget automatically moves toward an anti-inflationary surplus. Built-in stability lessens, but does not fully correct, undesired changes in the real GDP.

3. The standardized budget measures the Federal budget deficit or surplus that would occur if the economy operated at full employment throughout the year. Cyclical deficits or surpluses are those that result from changes in GDP. Changes in the standardized deficit or surplus provide meaningful information as to whether the government's fiscal policy is expansionary, neutral, or contractionary. Changes in the actual budget deficit or surplus do not, since such deficits or surpluses can include cyclical deficits or surpluses.

4. Certain problems complicate the enactment and implementation of fiscal policy. They include (a) timing problems associated with recognition, administrative, and operational lags; (b) the potential for misuse of fiscal policy for political rather than economic purposes; (c) the fact that state and local finances tend to be pro-cyclical; (d) potential ineffectiveness if households expect future policy reversals; and (e) the possibility of fiscal policy crowding out private investment.

5. Most economists believe that fiscal policy can help move the economy in a desired direction but cannot reliably be used to fine-tune the economy to a position of price stability and full employment. Nevertheless, fiscal policy is a valuable backup tool for aiding monetary policy in fighting significant recession or inflation.

6. The large Federal budget deficits of the 1980s and early 1990s prompted Congress in 1993 to increase tax rates and limit government spending. As a result of these policies, along with a very rapid and prolonged economic expansion, the deficits dwindled to $22 billion in 1997. Large budget surpluses occurred in 1999, 2000, and 2001. In 2001 the Congressional Budget Office projected that $5 trillion of annual budget surpluses would accumulate between 2000 and 2010.

7. In 2001 the Bush administration and Congress chose to reduce marginal tax rates and phase out the Federal estate tax. A recession occurred in 2001, the stock market crashed, and Federal spending for the war on terrorism rocketed. The Federal budget swung from a surplus of $127 billion in 2001 to a deficit of $158 billion in 2002. In 2003 the Bush administration and Congress accelerated the tax reductions scheduled under the 2001 tax law and cut tax rates on capital gains and dividends. The purposes were to stimulate a sluggish economy. In 2005 the budget deficit was $318 billion and deficits are projected to continue through 2011 before surpluses again reemerge.

8. The public debt is the total accumulation of the government's deficits (minus surpluses) over time and consists of Treasury bills, Treasury notes, Treasury bonds, and U.S. savings bonds. In 2005 the U.S. public debt was nearly $8 trillion, or $26,834 per person. The public (which here includes banks and state and local governments) holds 49 percent of that Federal debt; the Federal Reserve and Federal agencies hold the other 51 percent. Foreigners hold 25 percent of the Federal debt. Interest payments as a percentage of GDP were about 1.5 percent in 2005. This is down from 3.2 percent in 1990.

9. The concern that a large public debt may bankrupt the government is a false worry because (a) the debt needs only to be refinanced rather than refunded and (b) the Federal government has the power to increase taxes to make interest payments on the debt.

10. In general, the public debt is not a vehicle for shifting economic burdens to future generations. Americans inherit not only most of the public debt (a liability) but also most of the U.S. securities (an asset) that finance the debt.

11. More substantive problems associated with public debt include the following: (a) Payment of interest on the debt may increase income inequality. (b) Interest payments on the debt require higher taxes, which may impair incentives. (c) Paying interest or principal on the portion of the debt held by foreigners means a transfer of real output abroad. (d) Government borrowing to refinance or pay interest on the debt may increase interest rates and crowd out private investment spending, leaving future generations with a smaller stock of capital than they would have otherwise.

12. The increase in investment in public capital that may result from debt financing may partly or wholly offset the crowding-out effect of the public debt on private investment. Also, the added public investment may stimulate private investment, where the two are complements.

Terms and Concepts

fiscal policy	built-in stabilizer	political business cycle
Council of Economic Advisers (CEA)	progressive tax system	crowding-out effect
expansionary fiscal policy	proportional tax system	public debt
budget deficit	regressive tax system	U.S. securities
contractionary fiscal policy	standardized budget	external public debt
budget surplus	cyclical deficit	public investments

Study Questions

1. What is the role of the Council of Economic Advisers (CEA) as it relates to fiscal policy? Class assignment: Determine the names and educational backgrounds of the present members of the CEA.

2. **KEY QUESTION** Assume that a hypothetical economy with an MPC of .8 is experiencing severe recession. By how much would government spending have to increase to shift the aggregate demand curve rightward by $25 billion? How large a tax cut would be needed to achieve the same increase in aggregate demand? Why the difference? Determine one possible combination of government spending increases and tax decreases that would accomplish the same goal.

3. **KEY QUESTION** What are government's fiscal policy options for ending severe demand-pull inflation? Use the aggregate demand–aggregate supply model to show the impact of these policies on the price level. Which of these fiscal options do you think might be favored by a person who wants to preserve the size of government? A person who thinks the public sector is too large?

4. (For students who were assigned Chapter 9) Use the aggregate expenditures model to show how government fiscal policy could eliminate either a recessionary expenditure gap or an inflationary expenditure gap (Figure 9.7). Explain how equal-size increases in G and T could eliminate a recessionary gap and how equal-size decreases in G and T could eliminate an inflationary gap.

5. Explain how built-in (or automatic) stabilizers work. What are the differences between proportional, progressive, and regressive tax systems as they relate to an economy's built-in stability?

6. **KEY QUESTION** Define the standardized budget, explain its significance, and state why it may differ from the actual budget. Suppose the full-employment, noninflationary level of real output is GDP_3 (not GDP_2) in the economy depicted in Figure 11.3. If the economy is operating at GDP_2, instead of GDP_3, what is the status of its standardized budget? The status of its current fiscal policy? What change in fiscal policy would you recommend? How would you accomplish that in terms of the G and T lines in the figure?

7. Some politicians have suggested that the United States enact a constitutional amendment requiring that the Federal government balance its budget annually. Explain why such an amendment, if strictly enforced, would force the government to enact a contractionary fiscal policy whenever the economy experienced a severe recession.

8. **KEY QUESTION** Briefly state and evaluate the problem of time lags in enacting and applying fiscal policy. Explain the idea of a political business cycle. How might expectations of a near-term policy reversal weaken fiscal policy based on changes in tax rates? What is the crowding-out effect, and why might it be relevant to fiscal policy? In view of your answers, explain the following statement: "Although fiscal policy clearly is useful in combating the extremes of severe recession and demand-pull inflation, it is impossible to use fiscal policy to fine-tune the economy to the full-employment, noninflationary level of real GDP and keep the economy there indefinitely."

9. **ADVANCED ANALYSIS** (For students who were assigned Chapter 9) Assume that, without taxes, the consumption schedule for an economy is as shown below:

GDP, Billions	Consumption, Billions
$100	$120
200	200
300	280
400	360
500	440
600	520
700	600

a. Graph this consumption schedule, and determine the size of the MPC.

b. Assume that a lump-sum (regressive) tax of $10 billion is imposed at all levels of GDP. Calculate the tax rate at each level of GDP. Graph the resulting consumption schedule, and compare the MPC and the multiplier with those of the pretax consumption schedule.

c. Now suppose a proportional tax with a 10 percent tax rate is imposed instead of the regressive tax. Calculate and graph the new consumption schedule, and note the MPC and the multiplier.

d. Finally, impose a progressive tax such that the tax rate is 0 percent when GDP is $100, 5 percent at $200, 10 percent at $300, 15 percent at $400, and so forth. Determine and graph the new consumption schedule, noting the effect of this tax system on the MPC and the multiplier.

e. Explain why proportional and progressive taxes contribute to greater economic stability, while a regressive tax does not. Demonstrate, using a graph similar to Figure 11.3.

10. **KEY QUESTION** How do economists distinguish between the absolute and relative sizes of the public debt? Why is the distinction important? Distinguish between refinancing the debt and retiring the debt. How does an internally held public debt differ from an externally held public debt? Contrast the effects of retiring an internally held debt and retiring an externally held debt.

11. True or false? If false, explain why.
    a. The total public debt is more relevant to an economy than the public debt as percentage of GDP.
    b. An internally held public debt is like a debt of the left hand owed to the right hand.

c. The Federal Reserve and Federal government agencies hold more than three-fourths of the public debt.

d. The portion of the U.S. debt held by the public (and not by government entities) was larger as a percentage of GDP in 2005 than it was in 1995.

e. In recent years, Social Security payments to retirees have exceeded Social Security tax revenues from workers and their employers.

12. Why might economists be quite concerned if the annual interest payments on the debt sharply increased as a percentage of GDP?

13. **KEY QUESTION** Trace the cause-and-effect chain through which financing and refinancing of the public debt might affect real interest rates, private investment, the stock of capital, and economic growth. How might investment in public capital and complementarities between public capital and private capital alter the outcome of the cause-effect chain?

14. What would happen to the stated sizes of Federal budget deficits or surpluses if the current annual additions or subtractions from the Social Security trust fund were excluded?

15. What is the index of leading economic indicators, and how does it relate to discretionary fiscal policy?

Web-Based Questions

1. **LEADING ECONOMIC INDICATORS—HOW GOES THE ECONOMY?** The Conference Board, at **www.conference-board.org/**, tracks the leading economic indicators. Check the summary of the index of leading indicators and its individual components for the latest month. Is the index up or down? Which specific components are up, and which are down? What has been the trend of the composite index over the past 3 months?

2. **TEXT TABLE 11.1, COLUMN 3—WHAT ARE THE LATEST NUMBERS?** Go to the Congressional Budget Office Web site, **www.cbo.gov**, and select Historical Budget Data. Find the historical data for the actual budget deficit or surplus (total). Update column 2 of text Table 11.1. Next, find the historical data for the standardized (full-employment) budget deficit or surplus as a percentage of potential GDP. Update column 3 of Table 11.1. Is fiscal policy more expansionary or less expansionary than it was in 2005?

12

IN THIS CHAPTER YOU WILL LEARN:

- **About the functions of money and the components of the U.S. money supply.**
- **What "backs" the money supply, making us willing to accept it as payment.**
- **The makeup of the Federal Reserve and the U.S. banking system.**
- **The functions and responsibilities of the Federal Reserve.**

Money and Banking

Money is a fascinating aspect of the economy:

> Money bewitches people. They fret for it, and they sweat for it. They devise most ingenious ways to get it, and most ingenuous ways to get rid of it. Money is the only commodity that is good for nothing but to be gotten rid of. It will not feed you, clothe you, shelter you, or amuse you unless you spend it or invest it. It imparts value only in parting. People will do almost anything for money, and money will do almost anything for people. Money is a captivating, circulating, masquerading puzzle.[1]

In this chapter and the two chapters that follow we want to unmask the critical role of money and the monetary system in the economy. When the monetary system is working properly, it provides

[1]Federal Reserve Bank of Philadelphia, "Creeping Inflation," *Business Review*, August 1957, p. 3.

the lifeblood of the circular flows of income and expenditure. A well-operating monetary system helps the economy achieve both full employment and the efficient use of resources. A malfunctioning monetary system creates severe fluctuations in the economy's levels of output, employment, and prices and distorts the allocation of resources.

The Functions of Money

Just what is money? There is an old saying that "money *is* what money *does*." In a general sense, anything that performs the functions of money *is* money. Here are those functions:

- *Medium of exchange* First and foremost, money is a **medium of exchange** that is usable for buying and selling goods and services. A bakery worker does not want to be paid 200 bagels per week. Nor does the bakery owner want to receive, say, halibut in exchange for bagels. Money, however, is readily acceptable as payment. As we saw in Chapter 2, money is a social invention with which resource suppliers and producers can be paid and that can be used to buy any of the full range of items available in the marketplace. As a medium of exchange, money allows society to escape the complications of barter. And because it provides a convenient way of exchanging goods, money enables society to gain the advantages of geographic and human specialization.

- *Unit of account* Money is also a **unit of account.** Society uses monetary units—dollars, in the United States—as a yardstick for measuring the relative worth of a wide variety of goods, services, and resources. Just as we measure distance in miles or kilometers, we gauge the value of goods in dollars.

   With money as an acceptable unit of account, the price of each item need be stated only in terms of the monetary unit. We need not state the price of cows in terms of corn, crayons, and cranberries. Money aids rational decision making by enabling buyers and sellers to easily compare the prices of various goods, services, and resources. It also permits us to define debt obligations, determine taxes owed, and calculate the nation's GDP.

- *Store of value* Money also serves as a **store of value** that enables people to transfer purchasing power from the present to the future. People normally do not spend all their incomes on the day they receive them. In order to buy things later, they store some of their wealth as money. The money you place in a safe or a checking account will still be available to you a few weeks or months from now. Money is often the preferred store of value for short periods because it is the

most liquid (spendable) of all assets. People can obtain their money nearly instantly and can immediately use it to buy goods or take advantage of financial investment opportunities. When inflation is nonexistent or mild, holding money is a relatively risk-free way to store your wealth for later use.

The Components of the Money Supply

Money is a "stock" of some item or group of items (unlike income, for example, which is a "flow"). Societies have used many items as money, including whales' teeth, circular stones, elephant-tail bristles, gold coins, furs, and pieces of paper. Anything that is widely accepted as a medium of exchange can serve as money. In the United States, certain debts of government and of financial institutions are used as money, as you will see.

Money Definition *M*1

The narrowest definition of the U.S. money supply is called ***M*1.** It consists of:

- Currency (coins and paper money) in the hands of the public.
- All checkable deposits (all deposits in commercial banks and "thrift" or savings institutions on which checks of any size can be drawn).[2]

Government and government agencies supply coins and paper money. Commercial banks ("banks") and savings institutions ("thrifts") provide checkable deposits. Figure 12.1a shows the amounts of each category of money in the *M*1 money supply.

Currency: Coins + Paper Money From copper pennies to gold-colored dollars, coins are the "small change" of our money supply. All coins in circulation in the United States are **token money.** This means that the

---

[2]In the ensuing discussion, we do not discuss several of the quantitatively less significant components of the definitions of money in order to avoid a maze of details. For example, traveler's checks are included in the *M*1 money supply. The statistical appendix of any recent *Federal Reserve Bulletin* provides more comprehensive definitions.

FIGURE 12.1 **Components of money supply *M*1 and money supply *M*2, in the United States.** (a) *M*1 is a narrow definition of the money supply that includes currency (in circulation) and checkable deposits. (b) *M*2 is a broader definition that includes *M*1 along with several other relatively liquid account balances.

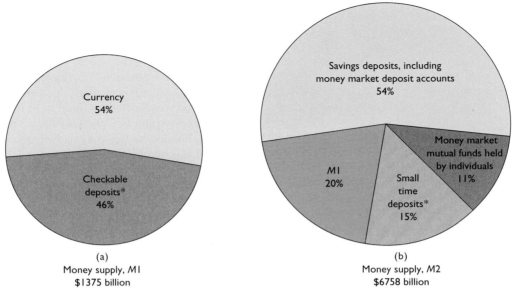

(a)
Money supply, *M*1
$1375 billion

(b)
Money supply, *M*2
$6758 billion

*These categories include other, quantitatively smaller components such as traveler's checks.

Source: Federal Reserve System, **www.federalreserve.gov.** Data are for February 2006.

intrinsic value, or the value of the metal contained in the coin itself, is less than the face value of the coin. This is to prevent people from melting down the coins for sale as a "commodity," in this case, the metal. If 50-cent pieces each contained 75 cents' worth of silver metal, it would be profitable to melt them and sell the metal. The 50-cent pieces would disappear from circulation.

Most of the nation's currency is paper money. This "folding currency" consists of **Federal Reserve Notes,** issued by the Federal Reserve System (the U.S. central bank) with the authorization of Congress. Every bill carries the phrase "Federal Reserve Note" on its face.

Figure 12.1a shows that currency (coins and paper money) constitutes 54 percent of the *M*1 money supply in the United States.

Checkable Deposits The safety and convenience of checks has made **checkable deposits** a large component of the *M*1 money supply. You would not think of stuffing $4896 in bills in an envelope and dropping it in a mailbox to pay a debt. But writing and mailing a check for a large sum is commonplace. The person cashing a check must endorse it (sign it on the reverse side); the writer of the check subsequently receives a record of the cashed check as a receipt attesting to the fulfillment of the obligation. Similarly, because the writing of a check requires endorsement, the theft or loss of your checkbook is not nearly as calamitous as losing an identical amount of currency. Finally, it is more convenient

to write a check than to transport and count out a large sum of currency. For all these reasons, checkable deposits (checkbook money) are a large component of the stock of money in the United States. About 46 percent of *M*1 is in the form of checkable deposits, on which checks can be drawn.

It might seem strange that checking account balances are regarded as part of the money supply. But the reason is clear: Checks are nothing more than a way to transfer the ownership of deposits in banks and other financial institutions and are generally acceptable as a medium of exchange. Although checks are less generally accepted than currency for small purchases, for major purchases most sellers willingly accept checks as payment. Moreover, people can convert checkable deposits into paper money and coins on demand; checks drawn on those deposits are thus the equivalent of currency.

To summarize:

$$\text{Money, } M1 = \text{currency} + \text{checkable deposits}$$

Institutions That Offer Checkable Deposits
In the United States, a variety of financial institutions allow customers to write checks in any amount on the funds they have deposited. **Commercial banks** are the primary depository institutions. They accept the deposits of households and businesses, keep the money safe until it is demanded via checks, and in the meantime use it to make available a wide variety of loans. Commercial bank loans provide short-term

financial capital to businesses, and they finance consumer purchases of automobiles and other durable goods.

Savings and loan associations (S&Ls), mutual savings banks, and credit unions supplement the commercial banks and are known collectively as savings or **thrift institutions,** or simply "thrifts." *Savings and loan associations* and *mutual savings banks* accept the deposits of households and businesses and then use the funds to finance housing mortgages and to provide other loans. *Credit unions* accept deposits from and lend to "members," who usually are a group of people who work for the same company.

The checkable deposits of banks and thrifts are known variously as demand deposits, NOW (negotiable order of withdrawal) accounts, ATS (automatic transfer service) accounts, and share draft accounts. Their commonality is that depositors can write checks on them whenever, and in whatever amount, they choose.

A Qualification We must qualify our discussion in an important way. Currency and checkable deposits owned by the government (the U.S. Treasury) and by Federal Reserve Banks, commercial banks, or other financial institutions are *excluded* from $M1$ and other measures of the money supply.

A paper dollar in the hands of, say, Emma Buck obviously constitutes just $1 of the money supply. But if we counted dollars held by banks as part of the money supply, the same $1 would count for $2 when it was deposited in a bank. It would count for a $1 checkable deposit owned by Buck and also for $1 of currency resting in the bank's till or vault. By excluding currency resting in banks in determining the total money supply, we avoid this problem of double counting.

Excluding government financial holdings from the money supply allows for better assessment of the amount of money available to firms and households for potential spending. That amount of money and potential spending is of keen interest to the Federal Reserve in conducting its monetary policy (a topic we cover in detail in Chapter 14).

Money Definition *M2*

A second and broader definition of money includes $M1$ plus several near-monies. **Near-monies** are certain highly liquid financial assets that do not function directly or fully as a medium of exchange but can be readily converted into currency or checkable deposits. There are three categories of near-monies included in the $M2$ definition of money:

- *Savings deposits, including money market deposit accounts* A depositor can easily withdraw funds from a **savings account** at a bank or thrift or simply request that the funds be transferred from a savings account to a checkable account. A person can also withdraw funds from a **money market deposit**

account (MMDA), which is an interest-bearing account containing a variety of interest-bearing short-term securities. MMDAs, however, have a minimum-balance requirement and a limit on how often a person can withdraw funds.

- *Small (less than $100,000) time deposits* Funds from **time deposits** become available at their maturity. For example, a person can convert a 6-month time deposit ("certificate of deposit," or "CD") to currency without penalty 6 months or more after it has been deposited. In return for this withdrawal limitation, the financial institution pays a higher interest rate on such deposits than it does on its MMDAs. Also, a person can "cash in" a CD at any time but must pay a severe penalty.

- *Money market mutual funds held by individuals* By making a telephone call, using the Internet, or writing a check for $500 or more, a depositor can redeem shares in a **money market mutual fund (MMMF)** offered by a mutual fund company. Such companies use the combined funds of individual shareholders to buy interest-bearing short-term credit instruments such as certificates of deposit and U.S. government securities. Then they can offer interest on the MMMF accounts of the shareholders (depositors) who jointly own those financial assets. The MMMFs in $M2$ include only the MMMF accounts held by individuals, not by businesses and other institutions.

All three categories of near-monies imply substantial liquidity. Thus, in equation form,

$$\text{Money, } M2 = \begin{array}{l} M1 + \text{savings deposits,} \\ \text{including MMDAs} + \text{small} \\ \text{(less than \$100,000) time deposits} \\ + \text{MMMFs held by individuals} \end{array}$$

In summary, $M2$ includes the immediate medium-of-exchange items (currency and checkable deposits) that constitute $M1$ plus certain near-monies that can be easily converted into currency and checkable deposits. In Figure 12.1b we see that the addition of all these items yields an $M2$ money supply that is about five times larger than the narrower $M1$ money supply.

Money Definition *MZM*

There are other definitions of money, each including or excluding various categories of near-money. One definition of increasing importance is MZM (money zero maturity), reported by the Federal Reserve Bank of St. Louis. MZM focuses exclusively on monetary balances that are immediately available, at zero cost, for household and business transactions. Economists make two adjustments to $M2$ to obtain MZM. They

- Subtract small time deposits because the maturity (time length until repayment) on deposits is 6 months, 1 year, or some other length beyond instant (zero) maturity. Withdrawal prior to maturity requires the payment of a substantial financial penalty.

- Add money market mutual fund (MMMF) balances owned by businesses. Businesses can write checks on these MMMFs and can move funds to checkable deposits from them without penalty. Like the MMMFs held by individuals, the MMMFs held by businesses are immediately available for purchases.

In equation form,

$$\text{Money } MZM = \begin{array}{c} M2 - \text{small (\$100,000 or less)} \\ \text{time deposits} + \text{MMMFs held} \\ \text{by businesses} \end{array}$$

The advantage of the MZM definition is that it includes the main items—currency, checkable deposits, MMDAs, and MMMFs—used on a daily basis to buy goods, services, and resources. It excludes time deposits, which are normally used for saving rather than for immediate transactions. In February 2006 MZM was $6934 billion, slightly larger than M2 of $6758 billion.

Each of the three definitions of money is useful. The narrowest definition, M1, is easiest to understand and is often cited. But economists generally use the broader measures M2 and MZM to measure the nation's money supply. Unless stated otherwise, we will dispense with the M1, M2, and MZM distinctions in our subsequent analysis and simply designate the supply of money as M_s. Keep in mind that the M1 components of the money supply—currency and checkable deposits—are base items in the broader M2 and MZM definitions. Monetary actions that increase currency and checkable deposits also increase M2 and MZM, or simply M_s. **(Key Question 4)**

QUICK REVIEW 12.1

- Money serves as a medium of exchange, a unit of account, and a store of value.
- The narrow M1 definition of money includes currency held by the public plus checkable deposits in commercial banks and thrift institutions.
- Thrift institutions as well as commercial banks offer accounts on which checks can be written.
- The M2 definition of money includes M1 plus savings deposits, including money market deposit accounts, small (less than $100,000) time deposits, and money market mutual fund balances held by individuals.
- Money supply MZM (money zero maturity) adjusts M2 by subtracting small (less than $100,000) time deposits and adding money market mutual fund balances held by businesses.

CONSIDER THIS . . .

Are Credit Cards Money?

You may wonder why we have ignored credit cards such as Visa and MasterCard in our discussion of how the money supply is defined. After all, credit cards are a convenient way to buy things and account for about 25% of the dollar value of all transactions in the United States. The answer is that a credit card is not money. Rather, it is a convenient means of obtaining a short-term loan from the financial institution that issued the card.

What happens when you purchase an item with a credit card? The bank that issued the card will reimburse the store, charging it a transaction fee, and later you will reimburse the bank. Rather than reduce your cash or checking account with each purchase, you bunch your payments once a month. You may have to pay an annual fee for the services provided, and if you pay the bank in installments, you will pay a sizable interest charge on the loan. Credit cards are merely a means of deferring or postponing payment for a short period. Your checking account balance that you use to pay your credit card bill *is* money; the credit card is *not* money.*

Although credit cards are not money, they allow individuals and businesses to "economize" in the use of money. Credit cards enable people to hold less currency in their billfolds and, prior to payment due dates, fewer checkable deposits in their bank accounts. Credit cards also help people coordinate the timing of their expenditures with their receipt of income.

*A bank debit card, however, is very similar to a check in your checkbook. Unlike a purchase with a credit card, a purchase with a debit card creates a direct "debit" (a subtraction) from your checking account balance. That checking account balance is money—it is part of M1.

What "Backs" the Money Supply?

The money supply in the United States essentially is "backed" (guaranteed) by government's ability to keep the value of money relatively stable. Nothing more!

Money as Debt

The major components of the money supply—paper money and checkable deposits—are debts, or promises to pay. In the United States, paper money is the circulating debt of the Federal Reserve Banks. Checkable deposits are the debts of commercial banks and thrift institutions.

Paper currency and checkable deposits have no intrinsic value. A $5 bill is just an inscribed piece of paper. A checkable deposit is merely a bookkeeping entry. And coins, we know, have less intrinsic value than their face value. Nor will government redeem the paper money you hold for anything tangible, such as gold. In effect, the government has chosen to "manage" the nation's money supply. Its monetary authorities attempt to provide the amount of money needed for the particular volume of business activity that will promote full employment, price-level stability, and economic growth.

Nearly all today's economists agree that managing the money supply is more sensible than linking it to gold or to some other commodity whose supply might change arbitrarily and capriciously. A large increase in the nation's gold stock as the result of a new gold discovery might increase the money supply too rapidly and thereby trigger rapid inflation. Or a long-lasting decline in gold production might reduce the money supply to the point where recession and unemployment resulted.

In short, people cannot convert paper money into a fixed amount of gold or any other precious commodity. Money is exchangeable only for paper money. If you ask the government to redeem $5 of your paper money, it will swap one paper $5 bill for another bearing a different serial number. That is all you can get. Similarly, checkable deposits can be redeemed not for gold but only for paper money, which, as we have just seen, the government will not redeem for anything tangible.

Value of Money

So why are currency and checkable deposits money, whereas, say, Monopoly (the game) money is not? What gives a $20 bill or a $100 checking account entry its value? The answer to these questions has three parts.

Acceptability
Currency and checkable deposits are money because people accept them as money. By virtue of long-standing business practice, currency and checkable deposits perform the basic function of money: They are acceptable as a medium of exchange. We accept paper money in exchange because we are confident it will be exchangeable for real goods, services, and resources when we spend it.

Legal Tender
Our confidence in the acceptability of paper money is strengthened because government has designated currency as **legal tender.** Specifically, each bill contains the statement "This note is legal tender for all debts, public and private." That means paper money is a valid and legal means of payment of debt. (But private firms and government are not mandated to accept cash. It is not illegal for them to specify payment in noncash forms such as checks, cashier's checks, money orders, or credit cards.)

The general acceptance of paper currency in exchange is more important than the government's decree that money is legal tender, however. The government has never decreed checks to be legal tender, and yet they serve as such in many of the economy's exchanges of goods, services, and resources. But it is true that government agencies—the Federal Deposit Insurance Corporation (FDIC) and the National Credit Union Administration (NCUA)—insure individual deposits of up to $100,000 at commercial banks and thrifts. That fact enhances our willingness to use checkable deposits as a medium of exchange.

Relative Scarcity
The value of money, like the economic value of anything else, depends on its supply and demand. Money derives its value from its scarcity relative to its utility (its want-satisfying power). The utility of money lies in its capacity to be exchanged for goods and services, now or in the future. The economy's demand for money thus depends on the total dollar volume of transactions in any period plus the amount of money individuals and businesses want to hold for future transactions. With a reasonably constant demand for money, the supply of money will determine the domestic value or "purchasing power" of the monetary unit (dollar, yen, peso, or whatever).

Money and Prices

The purchasing power of money is the amount of goods and services a unit of money will buy. When money rapidly loses its purchasing power, it loses its role as money.

The Purchasing Power of the Dollar
The amount a dollar will buy varies inversely with the price level; that is, a reciprocal relationship exists between the general price level and the purchasing power of the dollar. When the consumer price index or "cost-of-living" index goes up, the value of the dollar goes down, and vice versa. Higher prices lower the value of the dollar, because more dollars are needed to buy a particular amount of goods, services, or resources. For example, if the price level doubles, the value of the dollar declines by one-half, or 50 percent.

Conversely, lower prices increase the purchasing power of the dollar, because fewer dollars are needed to obtain a specific quantity of goods and services. If the price level falls by, say, one-half, or 50 percent, the purchasing power of the dollar doubles.

In equation form, the relationship looks like this:

$$\$V = 1/P$$

To find the value of the dollar V, divide 1 by the price level P expressed as an index number (in hundredths). If the price level is 1, then the value of the dollar is 1. If the price level rises to, say, 1.20, V falls to .833; a 20 percent increase in the price level reduces the value of the dollar by 16.67 percent. Check your understanding of this reciprocal relationship by determining the value of V and its percentage rise when P falls by 20 percent from $1 to .80. **(Key Question 6)**

Inflation and Acceptability

In Chapter 7 we noted situations in which a nation's currency became worthless and unacceptable in exchange. They were circumstances in which the government issued so many pieces of paper currency that the purchasing power of each of those units of money was almost totally undermined. The infamous post–World War I inflation in Germany is an example. In December 1919 there were about 50 billion marks in circulation. Four years later there were 496,585,345,900 billion marks in circulation! The result? The German mark in 1923 was worth an infinitesimal fraction of its 1919 value.[3]

Runaway inflation may significantly depreciate the value of money between the time it is received and the time it is spent. Rapid declines in the value of a currency may cause it to cease being used as a medium of exchange. Businesses and households may refuse to accept paper money in exchange because they do not want to bear the loss in its value that will occur while it is in their possession. (All this despite the fact that the government says that paper currency is legal tender!) Without an acceptable domestic medium of exchange, the economy may simply revert to barter. Alternatively, more stable currencies such as the U.S. dollar or European euro may come into widespread use. At the extreme, a country may adopt a foreign currency as its own official currency as a way to counter hyperinflation.

Similarly, people will use money as a store of value only as long as there is no sizable deterioration in the value of that money because of inflation. And an economy can effectively employ money as a unit of account only when its purchasing power is relatively stable. A monetary yardstick that no longer measures a yard (in terms of purchasing power) does not permit buyers and sellers to establish the terms of trade clearly. When the value of the dollar is declining rapidly, sellers will not know what to charge, and buyers will not know what to pay, for goods and services.

---

[3]Frank G. Graham, *Exchange, Prices and Production in Hyperinflation Germany, 1920-1923* (Princeton, N.J.: Princeton University Press, 1930), p. 13.

Stabilizing Money's Purchasing Power

Rapidly rising price levels (rapid inflation) and the consequent erosion of the purchasing power of money typically result from imprudent economic policies. Stabilization of the purchasing power of a nation's money requires stabilization of the nation's price level. Such price-level stability (2–3 percent annual inflation) mainly necessitates intelligent management or regulation of the nation's money supply and interest rates *(monetary policy)*. It also requires appropriate *fiscal policy* supportive of the efforts of the nation's monetary authorities to hold down inflation. In the United States, a combination of legislation, government policy, and social practice inhibits imprudent expansion of the money supply that might jeopardize money's purchasing power. The critical role of the U.S. monetary authorities (the Federal Reserve) in maintaining the purchasing power of the dollar is the subject of Chapter 14. For now simply note that they make available a particular quantity of money, such as *M2* in Figure 12.1, and can change that amount through their policy tools.

QUICK REVIEW 12.2

- In the United States, all money consists essentially of the debts of government, commercial banks, and thrift institutions.
- These debts efficiently perform the functions of money as long as their value, or purchasing power, is relatively stable.
- The value of money is rooted not in specified quantities of precious metals but in the amount of goods, services, and resources that money will purchase.
- The value of the dollar (its domestic purchasing power) is inversely related to the price level.
- Government's responsibility in stabilizing the purchasing power of the monetary unit calls for (a) effective control over the supply of money by the monetary authorities and (b) the application of appropriate fiscal policies by the president and Congress.

The Federal Reserve and the Banking System

In the United States, the "monetary authorities" we have been referring to are the members of the Board of Governors of the **Federal Reserve System** (the "Fed"). As shown in Figure 12.2, the Board directs the activities of the 12 Federal Reserve Banks, which in turn control the lending activity of the nation's banks and thrift institutions.

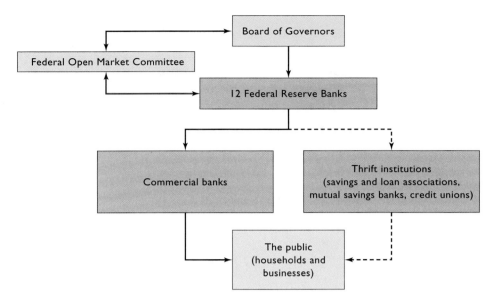

FIGURE 12.2 Framework of the Federal Reserve System and its relationship to the public. With the aid of the Federal Open Market Committee, the Board of Governors makes the basic policy decisions that provide monetary control of the U.S. money and banking systems. The 12 Federal Reserve Banks implement these decisions.

Historical Background

Early in the twentieth century, Congress decided that centralization and public control were essential for an efficient banking system. Decentralized, unregulated banking had fostered the inconvenience and confusion of numerous private bank notes being used as currency. It had also resulted in occasional episodes of monetary mismanagement such that the money supply was inappropriate to the needs of the economy. Sometimes "too much" money precipitated rapid inflation; other times "too little money" stunted the economy's growth by hindering the production and exchange of goods and services. No single entity was charged with creating and implementing nationally consistent banking policies.

An unusually acute banking crisis in 1907 motivated Congress to appoint the National Monetary Commission to study the monetary and banking problems of the economy and to outline a course of action for Congress. The result was the Federal Reserve Act of 1913.

Let's examine the various parts of the Federal Reserve System and their relationship to one another.

Board of Governors

The central authority of the U.S. money and banking system is the **Board of Governors** of the Federal Reserve System. The U.S. president, with the confirmation of the Senate, appoints the seven Board members. Terms are 14 years and staggered so that one member is replaced every 2 years. In addition, new members are appointed when resignations occur. The president selects the chairperson and vice-chairperson of the Board from among the members. Those officers serve 4-year terms and can be reappointed to new 4-year terms by the president. The long-term appointments provide the Board with continuity, experienced membership, and independence from political pressures that could result in inflation.

The 12 Federal Reserve Banks

The 12 **Federal Reserve Banks,** which blend private and public control, collectively serve as the nation's "central bank." These banks also serve as bankers' banks.

Central Bank Most nations have a single central bank—for example, Britain's Bank of England or Japan's Bank of Japan. The United States' central bank consists of 12 banks whose policies are coordinated by the Fed's Board of Governors. The 12 Federal Reserve Banks accommodate the geographic size and economic diversity of the United States and the nation's large number of commercial banks and thrifts.

Figure 12.3 locates the 12 Federal Reserve Banks and indicates the district that each serves. These banks implement the basic policy of the Board of Governors.

Quasi-Public Banks The 12 Federal Reserve Banks are quasi-public banks, which blend private ownership and public control. Each Federal Reserve Bank is owned by the private commercial banks in its district.

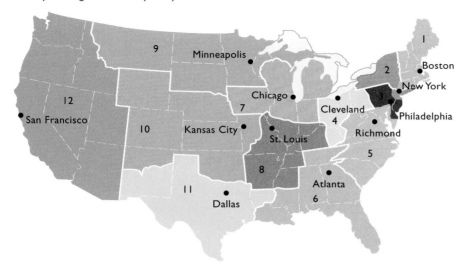

FIGURE 12.3 **The 12 Federal Reserve Districts.** The Federal Reserve System divides the United States into 12 districts, each having one central bank and in some instances one or more branches of the central bank. Hawaii and Alaska are included in the twelfth district.

Source: Federal Reserve Bulletin.

(Federally chartered banks are required to purchase shares of stock in the Federal Reserve Bank in their district.) But the Board of Governors, a government body, sets the basic policies that the Federal Reserve Banks pursue.

Despite their private ownership, the Federal Reserve Banks are in practice public institutions. Unlike private firms, they are not motivated by profit. The policies they follow are designed by the Board of Governors to promote the well-being of the economy as a whole. Thus, the activities of the Federal Reserve Banks are frequently at odds with the profit motive.[4] Also, the Federal Reserve Banks do not compete with commercial banks. In general, they do not deal with the public; rather, they interact with the government and commercial banks and thrifts.

Bankers' Banks The Federal Reserve Banks are "bankers' banks." They perform essentially the same functions for banks and thrifts as those institutions perform for the public. Just as banks and thrifts accept the deposits of and make loans to the public, so the central banks accept the deposits of and make loans to banks and thrifts. Normally, these loans average only about $150 million a day. But in emergency circumstances the Federal Reserve Banks become the "lender of last resort" to the banking system and can lend out as much as needed to

ensure that banks and thrifts can meet their cash obligations. On the day after terrorists attacked the United States on September 11, 2001, the Fed lent $45 *billion* to U.S. banks and thrifts. The Fed wanted to make sure that the destruction and disruption in New York City and the Washington, D.C., area did not precipitate a nationwide banking crisis.

But the Federal Reserve Banks have a third function, which banks and thrifts do not perform: They issue currency. Congress has authorized the Federal Reserve Banks to put into circulation Federal Reserve Notes, which constitute the economy's paper money supply. **(Key Question 8)**

FOMC

The **Federal Open Market Committee (FOMC)** aids the Board of Governors in conducting monetary policy. The FOMC is made up of 12 individuals:

- The seven members of the Board of Governors.
- The president of the New York Federal Reserve Bank.
- Four of the remaining presidents of Federal Reserve Banks on a 1-year rotating basis.

The FOMC meets regularly to direct the purchase and sale of government securities (bills, notes, bonds) in the open market in which such securities are bought and sold on a daily basis. We will find in Chapter 14 that the purpose of these aptly named *open-market operations* is to control the nation's money supply and influence interest rates. The Federal Reserve Bank in New York City conducts most of the Fed's open-market operations.

---

[4]Although it is not their goal, the Federal Reserve Banks have actually operated profitably, largely as a result of the Treasury debts they hold. Part of the profit is used to pay 6 percent annual dividends to the commercial banks that hold stock in the Federal Reserve Banks; the remaining profit is usually turned over to the U.S. Treasury.

Commercial Banks and Thrifts

There are about 7600 commercial banks. Roughly three-fourths are state banks. These are private banks chartered (authorized) by the individual states to operate within those states. One-fourth are private banks chartered by the Federal government to operate nationally; these are national banks. Some of the U.S. national banks are very large, ranking among the world's largest financial institutions (see Global Perspective 12.1).

The 11,400 thrift institutions—most of which are credit unions—are regulated by agencies separate and apart from the Board of Governors and the Federal Reserve Banks. For example, the operations of savings and loan associations are regulated and monitored by the Treasury Department's Office of Thrift Supervision. But the thrifts *are* subject to monetary control by the Federal Reserve System. In particular, like the banks, thrifts are required to keep a certain percentage of their checkable deposits as "reserves." In Figure 12.2 we use dashed arrows to indicate that the thrift institutions are partially subject to the control of the Board of Governors and the central banks. Decisions concerning monetary policy affect the thrifts along with the commercial banks.

GLOBAL PERSPECTIVE 12.1

The World's 12 Largest Financial Institutions

The world's 12 largest private sector financial institutions are headquartered in Europe, Japan, and the United States (2005 data).

Assets (millions of U.S. dollars)

Barclays (U.K.)
UBS (Switzerland)
Citigroup (U.S.)
ING Group (Netherlands)
Mizuho Financial (Japan)
Allianz Worldwide (Germany)
Bank of America (U.S.)
HSBC Group (U.K.)
BNP Paribas (France)
JPMorgan Chase (U.S.)
Deutsche Bank Group (Germany)
Royal Bank of Scotland (U.K.)

Source: Forbes Global 2000, **www.forbes.com.**

Fed Functions and the Money Supply

The Fed performs several functions, some of which we have already identified but they are worth repeating:

- *Issuing currency* The Federal Reserve Banks issue Federal Reserve Notes, the paper currency used in the U.S. monetary system. (The Federal Reserve Bank that issued a particular bill is identified in black in the upper left of the front of the newly designed bills. "A1," for example, identifies the Boston bank, "B2" the New York bank, and so on.)

- *Setting reserve requirements and holding reserves* The Fed sets reserve requirements, which are the fractions of checking account balances that banks must maintain as currency reserves. The central banks accept as deposits from the banks and thrifts any portion of their mandated reserves not held as vault cash.

- *Lending money to banks and thrifts* From time to time the Fed lends money to banks and thrifts and charges them an interest rate called the *discount rate*. In times of financial emergencies, the Fed serves as a lender of last resort to the U.S. banking industry.

- *Providing for check collection* The Fed provides the banking system with a means for collecting checks. If Sue writes a check on her Miami bank or thrift to Joe, who deposits it in his Dallas bank or thrift, how does the Dallas bank collect the money represented by the check drawn against the Miami bank? Answer: The Fed handles it by adjusting the reserves (deposits) of the two banks.

- *Acting as fiscal agent* The Fed acts as the fiscal agent (provider of financial services) for the Federal government. The government collects huge sums through taxation, spends equally large amounts, and sells and redeems bonds. To carry out these activities, the government uses the Fed's facilities.

- *Supervising banks* The Fed supervises the operations of banks. It makes periodic examinations to assess bank profitability, to ascertain that banks perform in accordance with the many regulations to which they are subject, and to uncover questionable practices or fraud.[5]

- *Controlling the money supply* Finally, and most important, the Fed has ultimate responsibility for

---

[5]The Fed is not alone in this task of supervision. The individual states supervise all banks that they charter. The Comptroller of the Currency supervises all national banks, and the Office of Thrift Supervision supervises all thrifts. Also, the Federal Deposit Insurance Corporation supervises all banks and thrifts whose deposits it insures.

regulating the supply of money, and this in turn enables it to influence interest rates. The major task of the Fed is to manage the money supply (and thus interest rates) according to the needs of the economy. This involves making an amount of money available that is consistent with high and rising levels of output and employment and a relatively constant price level. While all the other functions of the Fed are routine activities or have a service nature, managing the nation's money supply requires making basic, but unique, policy decisions. (We discuss those decisions in detail in Chapter 14.)

Federal Reserve Independence

Congress purposely established the Fed as an independent agency of government. The objective was to protect the Fed from political pressures so that it could effectively control the money supply and maintain price stability. Political pressures on Congress and the executive branch may at times result in inflationary fiscal policies, including tax cuts and special-interest spending. If Congress and the executive branch also controlled the nation's monetary policy, citizens and lobbying groups undoubtedly would

pressure elected officials to keep interest rates low even though at times high interest rates are necessary to reduce aggregate demand and thus control inflation. An independent monetary authority (the Fed) can take actions to increase interest rates when higher rates are needed to stem inflation. Studies show that countries that have independent central banks like the Fed have lower rates of inflation, on average, than countries that have little or no central bank independence.

Recent Developments in Money and Banking

The banking industry is undergoing a series of sweeping changes, spurred by competition from other financial institutions, the globalization of banking, and advances in information technology.

The Relative Decline of Banks and Thrifts

Banks and thrifts are just two of several types of firms that offer financial services. Table 12.1 lists the major categories of firms within the U.S. **financial services industry**

TABLE 12.1 Major U.S. Financial Institutions

Institution	Description	Examples
Commercial banks	State and national banks that provide checking and savings accounts, sell certificates of deposit, and make loans. The Federal Deposit Insurance Corporation (FDIC) insures checking and savings accounts up to $100,000.	J.P. Morgan Chase, Bank of America, Citibank, Wells Fargo
Thrifts	Savings and loan associations (S&Ls), mutual saving banks, and credit unions that offer checking and savings accounts and make loans. Historically, S&Ls made mortgage loans for houses while mutual savings banks and credit unions made small personal loans, such as automobile loans. Today, major thrifts offer the same range of banking services as commercial banks. The Federal Deposit Insurance Corporation and the National Credit Union Administration insure checking and savings deposits up to $100,000.	Washington Mutual, Golden State (owned by Citigroup), Golden West, Charter One
Insurance companies	Firms that offer policies (contracts) through which individuals pay premiums to insure against some loss, say, disability or death. In some life insurance policies and annuities, the funds are invested for the client in stocks and bonds and paid back after a specified number of years. Thus, insurance sometimes has a saving or financial-investment element.	Prudential, New York Life, Massachusetts Mutual
Mutual fund companies	Firms that pool deposits by customers to purchase stocks or bonds (or both). Customers thus indirectly own a part of a particular set of stocks or bonds, say stocks in companies expected to grow rapidly (a growth fund) or bonds issued by state governments (a municipal bond fund).	Fidelity, Putnam, Dreyfus, Kemper
Pension funds	For-profit or nonprofit institutions that collect savings from workers (or from employers on their behalf) throughout their working years and then buy stocks and bonds with the proceeds and make monthly retirement payments.	TIAA-CREF, Teamsters' Union
Securities firms	Firms that offer security advice and buy and sell stocks and bonds for clients. More generally known as *stock brokerage firms*.	Merrill Lynch, Salomon Smith Barney, Lehman Brothers, Charles Schwab

and gives examples of firms in each category. Although banks and thrifts remain the only institutions that offer checkable deposits that have no restrictions on either the number or size of checks, their shares of total financial assets (value of things owned) are declining. In 1980 banks and thrifts together held nearly 60 percent of financial assets in the United States. By 2005 that percentage had declined to about 24 percent.

Where did the declining shares of the banks and thrifts go? Pension funds, insurance firms, and particularly securities firms and mutual fund companies expanded their shares of financial assets. (Mutual fund companies offer shares of a wide array of stock and bond funds, as well as the previously mentioned money market funds.) Clearly, between 1980 and 2005, U.S. households and businesses channeled relatively more saving away from banks and thrifts and toward other financial institutions. Those other institutions generally offered higher rates of return on funds than did banks and thrifts, largely because they could participate more fully in national and international stock and bond markets.

Consolidation among Banks and Thrifts

During the past two decades, many banks have purchased bankrupt thrifts or have merged with other banks. Two examples of mergers of major banks are the mergers of Bank of America and FleetBoston Financial in 2003 and J.P. Morgan Chase and Bank One in 2004. Major savings and loans have also merged. The purpose of such mergers is to create large regional or national banks or thrifts that can compete more effectively in the financial services industry. Consolidation of traditional banking is expected to continue; there are 5200 fewer banks today than there were in 1990. Today, the seven largest U.S. banks and thrifts hold roughly one-third of total bank deposits.

Convergence of Services Provided by Financial Institutions

In 1996 Congress greatly loosened the Depression-era prohibition against banks selling stocks, bonds, and mutual funds, and it ended the prohibition altogether in the Financial Services Modernization Act of 1999. Banks, thrifts, pension companies, insurance companies, and securities firms can now merge with one another and sell each other's products. Thus, the lines between the subsets of the financial industry are beginning to blur. Many banks have acquired stock brokerage firms and, in a few cases, insurance companies. For example, Citigroup now owns Salomon Smith Barney, a large securities firm. Many large banks (for example, Wells Fargo) and pension funds (for example, TIAA-CREF) now provide mutual funds, including money market funds that pay relatively high interest and on which checks of $500 or more can be written.

The lifting of restraints against banks and thrifts should work to their advantage because they can now provide their customers with "one-stop shopping" for financial services. In general, the reform will likely intensify competition and encourage financial innovation. The downside is that financial losses in securities subsidiaries—such as could occur during a major recession—could increase the number of bank failures. Such failures might undermine confidence in the entire banking system and complicate the Fed's task of maintaining an appropriate money supply.

Globalization of Financial Markets

Another significant banking development is the increasing integration of world financial markets. Major foreign financial institutions now have operations in the United States, and U.S. financial institutions do business abroad. For example, Visa, MasterCard, and American Express offer worldwide credit card services. Moreover, U.S. mutual fund companies now offer a variety of international stock and bond funds. Globally, financial capital increasingly flows in search of the highest risk-adjusted returns. As a result, U.S. banks increasingly compete with foreign banks for both deposits and loan customers.

Recent advances in computer and communications technology are likely to speed up the trend toward international financial integration. Yet the bulk of investment in the major nations is still financed through domestic saving within each nation.

Electronic Payments

Finally, the rapid advance of new payment forms and Internet "banking" is of great significance to financial institutions and central banks. Households and businesses increasingly use **electronic payments,** not currency and checks, to buy products, pay bills, pay income taxes, transfer bank funds, and handle recurring mortgage and utility payments.

Several electronic-based means of making payments and transferring funds have pushed currency and checks aside. *Credit cards* enable us to make immediate purchases using credit established in advance with the card provider. In most cases, a swipe of the credit card makes the transaction electronically. Credit card balances can be paid via the Internet, rather than by sending a check to the card provider. *Debit cards* work much like credit cards but, since no loan is involved, more closely resemble checks. The swipe of the card authorizes an electronic payment directly to the seller from the buyer's bank account.

Other electronic payments include *Fedwire* transfers. This system, maintained by the Federal Reserve, enables banks to transfer funds to other banks. Individuals and businesses can also "wire" funds between financial institutions, domestically or internationally. Households can "send" funds or payments to businesses using *automated clearinghouse transactions* (ACHs). For example, they can make recurring utility and mortgage payments and transfer funds among financial institutions. The ACH system also allows sellers to scan checks at point of sale, convert them to ACH payments, and move the funds immediately from the buyer's checking account to the seller's checking account. Then the seller immediately hands the check back to the customer.

Some experts believe the next step will be greater use of *electronic money*, which is simply an entry in an electronic file stored in a computer. Electronic money will be deposited, or "loaded," into an account through electronic deposits of paychecks, retirement benefits, stock dividends, and other sources of income. The owner of the account will withdraw, or "unload," the money from his or her account through Internet payments to others for a wide variety of goods and services. PayPal—used by 96 million account holders in 55 countries—roughly fits this description, and is familiar to eBay users. Buyers and sellers establish accounts based on funds in checking accounts or funds available via credit cards. Customers then can securely make electronic payments or transfer funds to other holders of PayPal accounts.

In the future, the public may be able to insert so-called *smart cards* into card readers connected to their computers and load electronic money onto the card. These plastic cards contain computer chips that store information, including the amount of electronic money the consumer has loaded. When purchases or payments are made, their amounts are automatically deducted from the balance in the card's memory. Consumers will be able to transfer traditional money to their smart cards through computers or cell phones or at automatic teller machines. Thus, it will be possible for nearly all payments to be made through the Internet or a smart card.

A few general-use smart cards with embedded programmable computer chips are available in the United States, including cards issued by Visa, MasterCard, and American Express ("Blue Cards"). More common are *stored-value cards*, which facilitate purchases at the establishments that issued them. Examples are prepaid phone cards, copy-machine cards, mass-transit cards, single-store gift cards, and university meal-service cards. Like the broader smart cards, these cards are "reloadable," meaning the amounts stored on them can be increased. A number of retailers—including Kinko's, Sears, Starbucks, Walgreens, and Wal-Mart—make stored-value cards available to their customers.

QUICK REVIEW 12.3

- The Federal Reserve System consists of the Board of Governors and 12 Federal Reserve Banks.
- The 12 Federal Reserve Banks are publicly controlled central banks that deal with banks and thrifts rather than with the public.
- The Federal Reserve's major role is to regulate the supply of money in the economy.
- Recent developments in banking are the (a) relative decline in traditional banking; (b) consolidation within the banking industry; (c) convergence of services offered by banks, thrifts, insurance companies, pension funds, and mutual funds; (d) globalization of banking; and (e) widespread emergence of electronic transactions.

A Large Amount of U.S. Currency Is Circulating Abroad.

Like commercial aircraft, computer software, and movie videos, American currency has become a major U.S. "export." Russians hold about $40 billion of U.S. currency, and Argentineans hold $7 billion. The Polish government estimates that $6 billion of U.S. dollars is circulating in Poland. In all, an estimated $315 billion of U.S. currency is circulating abroad. That amounts to about 45 percent of the total U.S. currency held by the public.

Dollars leave the United States when Americans buy imports, travel in other countries, or send dollars to relatives living abroad. The United States profits when the dollars stay in other countries. It costs the government about 4 cents to print a dollar. For someone abroad to obtain that new dollar, $1 worth of resources, goods, or services must be sold to Americans. These commodities are U.S. gains. The dollar goes abroad and, assuming it stays there, presents no claim on U.S. resources or goods or services. Americans in effect make 96 cents on the dollar (= $1 gain in resources, goods, or services − the 4-cent printing cost). It's like American Express selling traveler's checks that never get cashed.

Black markets and other illegal activity undoubtedly fuel some of the demand for U.S. cash abroad. The dollar is king in covert trading in diamonds, weapons, and pirated software. Billions of cash dollars are involved in the narcotics trade. But the illegal use of dollars is only a small part of the story. The massive volume of dollars in other nations reflects a global search for monetary stability. On the basis of past experience, foreign citizens are confident that the dollar's purchasing power will remain relatively steady.

Following the collapse of the Soviet Union in the early 1990s, high rates of inflation led many Russians to abandon rubles for U.S. dollars. While the dollar retained its purchasing power in Russia, the purchasing power of the ruble plummeted.

As a result, many Russians still hold large parts of their savings in dollars today. Recently, however, some Russians have transferred some of their holdings of dollars to euros.

In Brazil, where inflation rates above 1000% annually were once common, people have long sought the stability of dollars. In the shopping districts of Beijing and Shanghai, Chinese consumers trade their domestic currency for dollars. In Bolivia half of all bank accounts are denominated in dollars. There is a thriving "dollar economy" in Vietnam, and even Cuba has partially legalized the use of U.S. dollars. The U.S. dollar is the official currency in Panama and Liberia. Immediately after the invasion of Iraq in 2003, the purchasing power of the Iraqi dinar fell dramatically because looting of banks placed many more dinars into circulation. The United States and British forces began paying Iraqi workers in U.S. dollars, and dollars in effect became the transition currency in the country.

Is there any financial risk for people who hold dollars in foreign countries? While the dollar is likely to hold its purchasing power internally in those nations, holders of dollars do face *exchange-rate risk*. If the international value of the dollar depreciates, as it did in early 2005, more dollars are needed to buy goods imported from countries other than the United States. Those goods, priced in say, euros, Swiss francs, or yen, become more expensive to holders of dollars. Offsetting that "downside risk," of course, is the "upside opportunity" of the dollar's appreciating.

There is little risk for the United States in satisfying the world's demand for dollars. If all the dollars came rushing back to the United States at once, the nation's money supply would surge, possibly causing demand-pull inflation. But there is not much chance of that happening. Overall, the global greenback is a positive economic force. It is a reliable medium of exchange, unit of account, and store of value that facilitates transactions that might not otherwise occur. Dollar holdings have helped buyers and sellers abroad overcome special monetary problems. The result has been increased output in those countries and thus greater output and income globally.

Summary

1. Anything that is accepted as (a) a medium of exchange, (b) a unit of monetary account, and (c) a store of value can be used as money.

2. There are several definitions of the money supply. $M1$ consists of currency and checkable deposits; $M2$ consists of $M1$ plus savings deposits, including money market deposit accounts, small (less than $100,000) time deposits, and money market mutual fund balances held by individuals; and MZM consists of $M2$ minus small (less than $100,000) time deposits plus money market mutual fund balances held by businesses.

3. Money represents the debts of government and institutions offering checkable deposits (commercial banks and thrift institutions) and has value because of the goods, services, and resources it will command in the market. Maintaining the purchasing power of money depends largely on the government's effectiveness in managing the money supply.

4. The U.S. banking system consists of (a) the Board of Governors of the Federal Reserve System, (b) the 12 Federal Reserve Banks, and (c) some 7600 commercial banks and 11,400 thrift institutions (mainly credit unions). The Board of Governors is the basic policymaking body for the entire banking system. The directives of the Board and the Federal Open Market Committee (FOMC) are made effective through the 12 Federal Reserve Banks, which are simultaneously (a) central banks, (b) quasi-public banks, and (c) bankers' banks.

5. The major functions of the Fed are to (a) issue Federal Reserve Notes, (b) set reserve requirements and hold reserves deposited by banks and thrifts, (c) lend money to banks and thrifts, (d) provide for the rapid collection of checks, (e) act as the fiscal agent for the Federal government, (f) supervise the operations of the banks, and (g) regulate the supply of money in the best interests of the economy.

6. The Fed is essentially an independent institution, controlled neither by the president of the United States nor by Congress. This independence shields the Fed from political pressure and allows it to raise and lower interest rates (via changes in the money supply) as needed to promote full employment, price stability, and economic growth.

7. Between 1980 and 2005, banks and thrifts lost considerable market share of the financial services industry to pension funds, insurance companies, mutual funds, and securities firms. Other recent banking developments of significance include the consolidation of the banking and thrift industry; the convergence of services offered by banks, thrifts, mutual funds, securities firms, and pension companies; the globalization of banking services; and the emergence of the Internet and electronic payments.

Terms and Concepts

medium of exchange	thrift institutions	legal tender
unit of account	near-monies	Federal Reserve System
store of value	$M2$	Board of Governors
$M1$	savings account	Federal Reserve Banks
token money	money market deposit account (MMDA)	Federal Open Market Committee (FOMC)
Federal Reserve Notes	time deposits	financial services industry
checkable deposits	money market mutual fund (MMMF)	electronic payments
commercial banks	MZM	

Study Questions

1. What are the three basic functions of money? Describe how rapid inflation can undermine money's ability to perform each of the three functions.

2. Which two of the following financial institutions offer checkable deposits included within the $M1$ money supply: mutual fund companies; insurance companies; commercial banks; securities firms; thrift institutions? Which of the following is not included in either $M1$ or $M2$: currency held by the public; checkable deposits; money market mutual fund balances; small (less than $100,000) time deposits; currency held by banks; savings deposits.

3. Explain and evaluate the following statements:
   a. The invention of money is one of the great achievements of humankind, for without it the enrichment that comes from broadening trade would have been impossible.
   b. Money is whatever society says it is.
   c. In most economies of the world, the debts of government and commercial banks are used as money.

d. People often say they would like to have more money, but what they usually mean is that they would like to have more goods and services.

e. When the price of everything goes up, it is not because everything is worth more but because the currency is worth less.

f. Any central bank can create money; the trick is to create enough, but not too much, of it.

4. **KEY QUESTION** What are the components of the *M1* money supply? What is the largest component? Which of the components of *M1* is *legal tender?* Why is the face value of a coin greater than its intrinsic value? What near-monies are included in the *M2* money supply? What distinguishes the *M2* and *MZM* money supplies?

5. What "backs" the money supply in the United States? What determines the value (domestic purchasing power) of money? How does the purchasing power of money relate to the price level? Who in the United States is responsible for maintaining money's purchasing power?

6. **KEY QUESTION** Suppose the price level and value of the dollar in year 1 are 1 and $1, respectively. If the price level rises to 1.25 in year 2, what is the new value of the dollar? If, instead, the price level falls to .50, what is the value of the dollar? What generalization can you draw from your answers?

7. How is the chairperson of the Federal Reserve System selected? Describe the relationship between the Board of Governors of the Federal Reserve System and the 12 Federal Reserve Banks. What is the composition and purpose of the Federal Open Market Committee (FOMC)?

8. **KEY QUESTION** What is meant when economists say that the Federal Reserve Banks are central banks, quasi-public banks, and bankers' banks? What are the seven basic functions of the Federal Reserve System?

9. Following are two hypothetical ways in which the Federal Reserve Board might be appointed. Would you favor either of these two methods over the present method? Why or why not?

a. Upon taking office, the U.S. president appoints seven people to the Federal Reserve Board, including a chair. Each appointee must be confirmed by a majority vote of the Senate, and each serves the same 4-year term as the president.

b. Congress selects seven members from its ranks (four from the House of Representatives and three from the Senate) to serve at its pleasure as the Board of Governors of the Federal Reserve System.

10. What are the major categories of firms that make up the U.S. financial services industry? Did the bank and thrift share of the financial services market rise, fall, or stay the same between 1980 and 2005? Are there more or fewer bank firms today than a decade ago? Why are the lines between the categories of financial firms becoming more blurred than in the past?

11. How does a debit card differ from a credit card? How does a stored-value card differ from both? Suppose that a person has a credit card, debit card, and stored-value card. Create a fictional scenario in which the person uses all three cards in the same day. Explain the person's logic for using one card rather than one of the others for each transaction. How do Fedwire and ACH transactions differ from credit card, debit card, and stored-value card transactions?

12. **LAST WORD** Over the years, the Federal Reserve Banks have printed many billions of dollars more in currency than U.S. households, businesses, and financial institutions now hold. Where is this "missing" money? Why is it there?

Web-Based Questions

1. **WHO ARE THE MEMBERS OF THE FEDERAL RESERVE BOARD?** The Federal Reserve Board Web site, **www. federalreserve.gov/BIOS/,** provides a detailed biography of the seven members of the Board of Governors. What is the composition of the Board with regard to age, gender, education, previous employment, and ethnic background? Which Board members are near the ends of their terms?

2. **CURRENCY TRIVIA** Visit the Web site of the Federal Reserve Bank of Atlanta, **www.frbatlanta.org/publica/ brochure/fundfac/money.htm,** to answer the following questions: What are the denominations of Federal Reserve Notes now being printed? What was the largest-denomination Federal Reserve Note ever printed and circulated, and when was it last printed? What are some tips for spotting counterfeit currency? When was the last silver dollar minted? What have been the largest and smallest U.S. coin denominations since the Coinage Act of 1792?.

13

IN THIS CHAPTER YOU WILL LEARN:

- Why the U.S. banking system is called a "fractional reserve" system.

- The distinction between a bank's actual reserves and its required reserves.

- How a bank can create money through granting loans.

- About the multiple expansion of loans and money by the entire banking system.

- What the monetary multiplier is and how to calculate it.

Money Creation

We have seen that the *M*1 money supply consists of currency (coins and Federal Reserve Notes) and checkable deposits and that *M*1 is a base component of broader measures of the money supply such as *M*2 and *MZM*. The U.S. Mint produces the coins and the U.S. Bureau of Engraving creates the Federal Reserve Notes. So who creates the checkable deposits? Surprisingly, it is loan officers! Although that may sound like something a congressional committee should investigate, the monetary authorities are well aware that banks and thrifts create checkable deposits. In fact, the Federal Reserve relies on these institutions to create this vital component of the nation's money supply.

The Fractional Reserve System

The United States, like most other countries today, has a **fractional reserve banking system** in which only a portion (fraction) of checkable deposits are backed up by cash in bank vaults or deposits at the central bank. Our goal is to explain this system and show how commercial banks can create checkable deposits by issuing loans. Our examples will involve commercial banks, but remember that thrift institutions also provide checkable deposits. So the analysis applies to banks and thrifts alike.

Illustrating the Idea: The Goldsmiths

Here is the history behind the idea of the fractional reserve system.

When early traders began to use gold in making transactions, they soon realized that it was both unsafe and inconvenient to carry gold and to have it weighed and assayed (judged for purity) every time they negotiated a transaction. So by the sixteenth century they had begun to deposit their gold with goldsmiths, who would store it in vaults for a fee. On receiving a gold deposit, the goldsmith would issue a receipt to the depositor. Soon people were paying for goods with goldsmiths' receipts, which served as the first kind of paper money.

At this point the goldsmiths—embryonic bankers—used a 100 percent reserve system; they backed their circulating paper money receipts fully with the gold that they held "in reserve" in their vaults. But because of the public's acceptance of the goldsmiths' receipts as paper money, the goldsmiths soon realized that owners rarely redeemed the gold they had in storage. In fact, the goldsmiths observed that the amount of gold being deposited with them in any week or month was likely to exceed the amount that was being withdrawn.

Then some clever goldsmith hit on the idea that paper "receipts" could be issued in excess of the amount of gold held. Goldsmiths would put these receipts, which were redeemable in gold, into circulation by making interest-earning loans to merchants, producers, and consumers. Borrowers were willing to accept loans in the form of gold receipts because the receipts were accepted as a medium of exchange in the marketplace.

This was the beginning of the fractional reserve system of banking, in which reserves in bank vaults are a fraction of the total money supply. If, for example, the goldsmith issued $1 million in receipts for actual gold in storage and another $1 million in receipts as loans, then the total value of paper money in circulation would be $2 million—twice the value of the gold. Gold reserves would be a fraction (one-half) of outstanding paper money.

Significant Characteristics of Fractional Reserve Banking

The goldsmith story highlights two significant characteristics of fractional reserve banking. First, banks can create money through lending. In fact, goldsmiths created money when they made loans by giving borrowers paper money that was not fully backed by gold reserves. The quantity of such money goldsmiths could create depended on the amount of reserves they deemed prudent to have available. The smaller the amount of reserves thought necessary, the larger the amount of paper money the goldsmiths could create. Today, gold is no longer used as bank reserves. Instead, the creation of checkable deposit money by banks (via their lending) is limited by the amount of *currency reserves* that the banks feel obligated, or are required by law, to keep.

A second reality is that banks operating on the basis of fractional reserves are vulnerable to "panics" or "runs." A goldsmith who issued paper money equal to twice the value of his gold reserves would be unable to convert all that paper money into gold in the event that all the holders of that money appeared at his door at the same time demanding their gold. In fact, many European and U.S. banks were once ruined by this unfortunate circumstance. However, a bank panic is highly unlikely if the banker's reserve and lending policies are prudent. Indeed, one reason why banking systems are highly regulated industries is to prevent runs on banks. This is also the reason why the United States has a system of deposit insurance, discussed in the previous chapter.

A Single Commercial Bank

To illustrate the workings of the modern fractional reserve banking system, we need to examine a commercial bank's balance sheet.

The **balance sheet** of a commercial bank (or thrift) is a statement of assets and claims on assets that summarizes the financial position of the bank at a certain time. Every balance sheet must balance; this means that the value of *assets* must equal the amount of claims against those assets. The claims shown on a balance sheet are divided into two groups: the claims of nonowners against the firm's assets, called *liabilities*, and the claims of the owners of the firm against the firm's assets, called *net worth*. A balance sheet is balanced because

$$\text{Assets} = \text{liabilities} + \text{net worth}$$

Every $1 change in assets must be offset by a $1 change in liabilities + net worth. Every $1 change in liabilities + net worth must be offset by a $1 change in assets.

Now let's work through a series of bank transactions involving balance sheets to establish how individual banks can create money.

Transaction 1: Creating a Bank

Suppose some far-sighted citizens of the town of Wahoo, Nebraska (yes, there is such a place), decide their town needs a new commercial bank to provide banking services for that growing community. Once they have secured a state or national charter for their bank, they turn to the task of selling, say, $250,000 worth of stock (equity shares) to buyers, both in and out of the community. Their efforts meet with success and the Bank of Wahoo comes into existence—at least on paper. What does its balance sheet look like at this stage?

The founders of the bank have sold $250,000 worth of shares of stock in the bank—some to themselves, some to other people. As a result, the bank now has $250,000 in cash on hand and $250,000 worth of stock shares outstanding. The cash is an asset to the bank. Cash held by a bank is sometimes called **vault cash** or till money. The shares of stock outstanding constitute an equal amount of claims that the owners have against the bank's assets. Those shares of stock constitute the net worth of the bank. The bank's balance sheet reads:

Creating a Bank Balance Sheet 1: Wahoo Bank			
Assets		Liabilities and net worth	
Cash	$250,000	Stock shares	$250,000

Each item listed in a balance sheet such as this is called an *account*.

Transaction 2: Acquiring Property and Equipment

The board of directors (who represent the bank's owners) must now get the new bank off the drawing board and make it a reality. First, property and equipment must be acquired. Suppose the directors, confident of the success of their venture, purchase a building for $220,000 and pay $20,000 for office equipment. This simple transaction changes the composition of the bank's assets. The bank now has $240,000 less in cash and $240,000 of new property assets. Using blue to denote accounts affected by each

transaction, we find that the bank's balance sheet at the end of transaction 2 appears as follows:

Acquiring Property and Equipment Balance Sheet 2: Wahoo Bank			
Assets		Liabilities and net worth	
Cash	$ 10,000	Stock shares	$250,000
Property	240,000		

Note that the balance sheet still balances, as it must.

Transaction 3: Accepting Deposits

Commercial banks have two basic functions: to accept deposits of money and to make loans. Now that the bank is operating, suppose that the citizens and businesses of Wahoo decide to deposit $100,000 in the Wahoo bank. What happens to the bank's balance sheet?

The bank receives cash, which is an asset to the bank. Suppose this money is deposited in the bank as checkable deposits (checking account entries), rather than as savings accounts or time deposits. These newly created *checkable deposits* constitute claims that the depositors have against the assets of the Wahoo bank and thus are a new liability account. The bank's balance sheet now looks like this:

Accepting Deposits Balance Sheet 3: Wahoo Bank			
Assets		Liabilities and net worth	
Cash	$110,000	Checkable deposits	$100,000
Property	240,000	Stock shares	250,000

There has been no change in the economy's total supply of money as a result of transaction 3, but a change has occurred in the composition of the money supply. Bank money, or checkable deposits, has increased by $100,000, and currency held by the public has decreased by $100,000. Currency held by a bank, you will recall, is not part of the economy's money supply.

A withdrawal of cash will reduce the bank's checkable-deposit liabilities and its holdings of cash by the amount of the withdrawal. This, too, changes the composition, but not the total supply, of money in the economy.

Transaction 4: Depositing Reserves in a Federal Reserve Bank

All commercial banks and thrift institutions that provide checkable deposits must by law keep **required reserves.** Required reserves are an amount of funds equal to a specified percentage of the bank's own deposit liabilities. A bank must keep these reserves on deposit with the Federal Reserve Bank in its district or as cash in the bank's vault. To simplify, we suppose the Bank of Wahoo keeps its required reserves entirely as deposits in the Federal Reserve Bank of its district. But remember that vault cash is counted as reserves and real-world banks keep a significant portion of their own reserves in their vaults.

The "specified percentage" of checkable-deposit liabilities that a commercial bank must keep as reserves is known as the **reserve ratio**—the ratio of the required reserves the commercial bank must keep to the bank's own outstanding checkable-deposit liabilities:

$$\text{Reserve ratio} = \frac{\text{commercial bank's required reserves}}{\text{commercial bank's checkable-deposit liabilities}}$$

If the reserve ratio is $\frac{1}{10}$, or 10 percent, the Wahoo bank, having accepted $100,000 in deposits from the public, would have to keep $10,000 as reserves. If the ratio is $\frac{1}{5}$, or 20 percent, $20,000 of reserves would be required. If $\frac{1}{2}$, or 50 percent, $50,000 would be required.

The Fed has the authority to establish and vary the reserve ratio within limits legislated by Congress. The limits now prevailing are shown in Table 13.1. The first $7.8 million of checkable deposits held by a commercial bank or thrift is exempt from reserve requirements. A 3 percent reserve is required on checkable deposits of between $7.8 million and $48.3 million. A 10 percent reserve is required on checkable deposits over $48.3 million, although the Fed can vary that percentage between 8 and 14 percent. Currently, no reserves are required against noncheckable nonpersonal (business) savings or time deposits, although up to 9 percent can be required. Also, after consultation with appropriate congressional committees, the Fed for 180 days may impose reserve requirements outside the 8–14 percent range specified in Table 13.1.

In order to simplify, we will suppose that the reserve ratio for checkable deposits in commercial banks is $\frac{1}{5}$, or 20 percent. Although 20 percent obviously is higher than the requirement really is, the figure is convenient for calculations. Because we are concerned only with checkable (spendable) deposits, we ignore reserves on noncheckable savings and time deposits. The main point is that reserve requirements are fractional, meaning that they are less than 100 percent. This point is critical in our analysis of the lending ability of the banking system.

By depositing $20,000 in the Federal Reserve Bank, the Wahoo bank will just be meeting the required 20 percent ratio between its reserves and its own deposit liabilities. We will use "reserves" to mean the funds commercial banks deposit in the Federal Reserve Banks, to distinguish those funds from the public's deposits in commercial banks.

But suppose the Wahoo bank anticipates that its holdings of checkable deposits will grow in the future. Then, instead of sending just the minimum amount, $20,000, it sends an extra $90,000, for a total of $110,000. In so doing, the bank will avoid the inconvenience of sending additional reserves to the Federal Reserve Bank each time its own checkable-deposit liabilities increase. And, as you will see, it is these extra reserves that enable banks to lend money and earn interest income.

Actually, the bank would not deposit *all* its cash in the Federal Reserve Bank. However, because (1) banks as a rule hold vault cash only in the amount of $1\frac{1}{2}$ or 2 percent of their total assets and (2) vault cash can be counted as reserves, we can assume that all the bank's cash is deposited in the Federal Reserve Bank and therefore constitutes the commercial bank's actual reserves. Then we do not need to bother adding two assets—"cash" and "deposits in the Federal Reserve Bank"—to determine "reserves."

After the Wahoo bank deposits $110,000 of reserves at the Fed, its balance sheet becomes:

TABLE 13.1 Reserve Requirements (Reserve Ratios) for Banks and Thrifts, 2006

Type of Deposit	Current Requirement	Statutory Limits
Checkable deposits:		
$0–$7.8 million	0%	3%
$7.8–$48.3 million	3	3
Over $48.3 million	10	8–14
Noncheckable nonpersonal savings and time deposits	0	0–9

Source: Federal Reserve, Regulation D, **www.federalreserve.gov**. Data are for 2006.

Depositing Reserves at the Fed
Balance Sheet 4: Wahoo Bank

Assets		Liabilities and net worth	
Cash	$ 0	Checkable	
Reserves	110,000	deposits	$100,000
Property	240,000	Stock shares	250,000

There are three things to note about this latest transaction.

Excess Reserves

A bank's **excess reserves** are found by subtracting its *required reserves* from its **actual reserves:**

Excess reserves = actual reserves − required reserves

In this case,

Actual reserves	$110,000
Required reserves	−20,000
Excess reserves	$ 90,000

The only reliable way of computing excess reserves is to multiply the bank's checkable-deposit liabilities by the reserve ratio to obtain required reserves ($100,000 × 20 percent = $20,000) and then to subtract the required reserves from the actual reserves listed on the asset side of the bank's balance sheet.

To test your understanding, compute the bank's excess reserves from balance sheet 4, assuming that the reserve ratio is (1) 10 percent, (2) $33\frac{1}{3}$ percent, and (3) 50 percent.

We will soon demonstrate that the ability of a commercial bank to make loans depends on the existence of excess reserves. Understanding this concept is crucial in seeing how the banking system creates money.

Control

You might think the basic purpose of reserves is to enhance the liquidity of a bank and protect commercial bank depositors from losses. Reserves would constitute a ready source of funds from which commercial banks could meet large, unexpected cash withdrawals by depositors.

But this reasoning breaks down under scrutiny. Although historically reserves have been seen as a source of liquidity and therefore as protection for depositors, a bank's required reserves are not great enough to meet sudden, massive cash withdrawals. If the banker's nightmare should materialize—everyone with checkable deposits appearing at once to demand those deposits in cash—the actual reserves held as vault cash or at the Federal Reserve Bank would be insufficient. The banker simply could not meet this "bank panic." Because reserves are fractional, checkable deposits may be much greater than a bank's required reserves.

So commercial bank deposits must be protected by other means. Periodic bank examinations are one way of promoting prudent commercial banking practices. Furthermore, insurance funds administered by the Federal Deposit Insurance Corporation (FDIC) and the National Credit Union Administration (NCUA) insure individual deposits in banks and thrifts up to $100,000.

If it is not the purpose of reserves to provide for commercial bank liquidity, then what is their function? *Control*

is the answer. Required reserves help the Fed control the lending ability of commercial banks. The Fed can take certain actions that either increase or decrease commercial bank reserves and affect the ability of banks to grant credit. The objective is to prevent banks from overextending or underextending bank credit. To the degree that these policies successfully influence the volume of commercial bank credit, the Fed can help the economy avoid business fluctuations. Another function of reserves is to facilitate the collection or "clearing" of checks. **(Key Question 2)**

Asset and Liability

Transaction 4 brings up another matter. Specifically, the reserves created in transaction 4 are an asset to the depositing commercial bank because they are a claim this bank has against the assets of another institution—the Federal Reserve Bank. The checkable deposit you get by depositing money in a commercial bank is an asset to you and a liability to the bank. In the same way, the reserves that a commercial bank establishes by depositing money in a bankers' bank are an asset to that bank and a liability to the Federal Reserve Bank.

Transaction 5: Clearing a Check Drawn against the Bank

Assume that Fred Bradshaw, a Wahoo farmer, deposited a substantial portion of the $100,000 in checkable deposits that the Wahoo bank received in transaction 3. Now suppose that Fred buys $50,000 of farm machinery from the Ajax Farm Implement Company of Surprise, Nebraska. Bradshaw pays for this machinery by writing a $50,000 check against his deposit in the Wahoo bank. He gives the check to the Ajax Company. What are the results?

Ajax deposits the check in its account with the Surprise bank. The Surprise bank increases Ajax's checkable deposits by $50,000 when Ajax deposits the check. Ajax is now paid in full. Bradshaw is pleased with his new machinery.

Now the Surprise bank has Bradshaw's check. This check is simply a claim against the assets of the Wahoo bank. The Surprise bank will collect this claim by sending the check (along with checks drawn on other banks) to the regional Federal Reserve Bank. Here a bank employee will clear, or collect, the check for the Surprise bank by increasing Surprise's reserve in the Federal Reserve Bank by $50,000 and decreasing the Wahoo bank's reserve by that same amount. The check is "collected" merely by making bookkeeping notations to the effect that Wahoo's claim against the Federal Reserve Bank is reduced by $50,000 and Surprise's claim is increased by $50,000.

Finally, the Federal Reserve Bank sends the cleared check back to the Wahoo bank, and for the first time the

Wahoo bank discovers that one of its depositors has drawn a check for $50,000 against his checkable deposit. Accordingly, the Wahoo bank reduces Bradshaw's checkable deposit by $50,000 and notes that the collection of this check has caused a $50,000 decline in its reserves at the Federal Reserve Bank. All the balance sheets balance: The Wahoo bank has reduced both its assets and its liabilities by $50,000. The Surprise bank has $50,000 more in assets (reserves) and in checkable deposits. Ownership of reserves at the Federal Reserve Bank has changed—with Wahoo owning $50,000 less, and Surprise owning $50,000 more—but total reserves stay the same.

Whenever a check is drawn against one bank and deposited in another bank, collection of that check will reduce both the reserves and the checkable deposits of the bank on which the check is drawn. Conversely, if a bank receives a check drawn on another bank, the bank receiving the check will, in the process of collecting it, have its reserves and deposits increased by the amount of the check. In our example, the Wahoo bank loses $50,000 in both reserves and deposits to the Surprise bank. But there is no loss of reserves or deposits for the banking system as a whole. What one bank loses, another bank gains.

If we bring all the other assets and liabilities back into the picture, the Wahoo bank's balance sheet looks like this at the end of transaction 5:

Clearing a Check Balance Sheet 5: Wahoo Bank			
Assets		Liabilities and net worth	
Reserves	$ 60,000	Checkable	
Property	240,000	deposits	$ 50,000
		Stock shares	250,000

Verify that with a 20 percent reserve requirement, the bank's excess reserves now stand at $50,000.

QUICK REVIEW 13.1

- When a bank accepts deposits of cash, the composition of the money supply is changed but the total supply of money is not directly altered.
- Commercial banks and thrifts are obliged to keep required reserves equal to a specified percentage of their own checkable-deposit liabilities as cash or on deposit with the Federal Reserve Bank of their district.
- The amount by which a bank's actual reserves exceed its required reserves is called excess reserves.
- A bank that has a check drawn and collected against it will lose to the recipient bank both reserves and deposits equal to the value of the check.

Money-Creating Transactions of a Commercial Bank

The next two transactions are crucial because they explain how a commercial bank can literally create money by making loans and how banks create money by purchasing government bonds from the public.

Transaction 6: Granting a Loan

In addition to accepting deposits, commercial banks grant loans to borrowers. What effect does lending by a commercial bank have on its balance sheet?

Suppose the Gristly Meat Packing Company of Wahoo decides it is time to expand its facilities. Suppose, too, that the company needs exactly $50,000—which just happens to be equal to the Wahoo bank's excess reserves—to finance this project.

Gristly goes to the Wahoo bank and requests a loan for this amount. The Wahoo bank knows the Gristly Company's fine reputation and financial soundness and is convinced of its ability to repay the loan. So the loan is granted. In return, the president of Gristly hands a promissory note—a fancy IOU—to the Wahoo bank. Gristly wants the convenience and safety of paying its obligations by check. So, instead of receiving a bushel basket full of currency from the bank, Gristly gets a $50,000 increase in its checkable-deposit account in the Wahoo bank.

The Wahoo bank has acquired an interest-earning asset (the promissory note, which it files under "Loans") and has created checkable deposits (a liability) to "pay" for this asset. Gristly has swapped an IOU for the right to draw an additional $50,000 worth of checks against its checkable deposit in the Wahoo bank. Both parties are pleased.

At the moment the loan is completed, the Wahoo bank's position is shown by balance sheet 6a:

When a Loan Is Negotiated Balance Sheet 6a: Wahoo Bank			
Assets		Liabilities and net worth	
Reserves	$ 60,000	Checkable	
Loans	50,000	deposits	$100,000
Property	240,000	Stock shares	250,000

All this looks simple enough. But a close examination of the Wahoo bank's balance statement reveals a startling fact: When a bank makes loans, it creates money. The president of Gristly went to the bank with something that is *not* money—her IOU—and walked out with something that *is* money—a checkable deposit.

Contrast transaction 6a with transaction 3, in which checkable deposits were created but only as a result of currency having been taken out of circulation. There was a change in the *composition* of the money supply in that situation but no change in the *total supply* of money. But when banks lend, they create checkable deposits that *are* money. By extending credit, the Wahoo bank has "monetized" an IOU. Gristly and the Wahoo bank have created and then swapped claims. The claim created by Gristly and given to the bank is not money; an individual's IOU is not acceptable as a medium of exchange. But the claim created by the bank and given to Gristly *is* money; checks drawn against a checkable deposit are acceptable as a medium of exchange.

Much of the money we use in our economy is created through the extension of credit by commercial banks. This checkable-deposit money may be thought of as "debts" of commercial banks and thrift institutions. Checkable deposits are bank debts in the sense that they are claims that banks and thrifts promise to pay "on demand."

But certain factors limit the ability of a commercial bank to create checkable deposits ("bank money") by lending. The Wahoo bank can expect the newly created checkable deposit of $50,000 to be a very active account. Gristly would not borrow $50,000 at, say, 7, 10, or 12 percent interest for the sheer joy of knowing that funds were available if needed.

Assume that Gristly awards a $50,000 building contract to the Quickbuck Construction Company of Omaha. Quickbuck, true to its name, completes the expansion promptly and is paid with a check for $50,000 drawn by Gristly against its checkable deposit in the Wahoo bank. Quickbuck, with headquarters in Omaha, does not deposit this check in the Wahoo bank but instead deposits it in the Fourth National Bank of Omaha. Fourth National now has a $50,000 claim against the Wahoo bank. The check is collected in the manner described in transaction 5. As a result, the Wahoo bank loses both reserves and deposits equal to the amount of the check; Fourth National acquires $50,000 of reserves and deposits.

In summary, assuming a check is drawn by the borrower for the entire amount of the loan ($50,000) and is given to a firm that deposits it in some other bank, the Wahoo bank's balance sheet will read as follows after the check has been cleared against it:

After a Check Is Drawn on the Loan
Balance Sheet 6b: Wahoo Bank

Assets		Liabilities and net worth	
Reserves	$ 10,000	Checkable	
Loans	50,000	deposits	$ 50,000
Property	240,000	Stock shares	250,000

After the check has been collected, the Wahoo bank just meets the required reserve ratio of 20 percent (= $10,000/$50,000). The bank has *no* excess reserves. This

poses a question: Could the Wahoo bank have lent more than $50,000—an amount greater than its excess reserves—and still have met the 20 percent reserve requirement when a check for the full amount of the loan was cleared against it? The answer is no; the bank is "fully loaned up."

W 13.1
Single bank accounting

Here is why: Suppose the Wahoo bank had lent $55,000 to the Gristly company. Collection of the check against the Wahoo bank would have lowered its reserves to $5,000 (= $60,000 − $55,000), and checkable deposits would once again stand at $50,000 (= $105,000 − $55,000). The ratio of actual reserves to checkable deposits would then be $5,000/$50,000, or only 10 percent. The Wahoo bank could thus not have lent $55,000.

By experimenting with other amounts over $50,000, you will find that the maximum amount the Wahoo bank could lend at the outset of transaction 6 is $50,000. This amount is identical to the amount of excess reserves the bank had available when the loan was negotiated.

A single commercial bank in a multibank banking system can lend only an amount equal to its initial preloan excess reserves. When it lends, the lending bank faces the possibility that checks for the entire amount of the loan will be drawn and cleared against it. If that happens, the lending bank will lose (to other banks) reserves equal to the amount it lends. So, to be safe, it limits its lending to the amount of its excess reserves.

Transaction 7: Buying Government Securities

When a commercial bank buys government bonds from the public, the effect is substantially the same as lending. New money is created.

Assume that the Wahoo bank's balance sheet initially stands as it did at the end of transaction 5. Now suppose that instead of making a $50,000 loan, the bank buys $50,000 of government securities from a securities dealer. The bank receives the interest-bearing bonds, which appear on its balance statement as the asset "Securities," and gives the dealer an increase in its checkable-deposit account. The Wahoo bank's balance sheet appears as follows:

Buying Government Securities
Balance Sheet 7: Wahoo Bank

Assets		Liabilities and net worth	
Reserves	$ 60,000	Checkable	
Securities	50,000	deposits	$100,000
Property	240,000	Stock shares	250,000

Checkable deposits, that is, the supply of money, have been increased by $50,000, as in transaction 6. Bond purchases from the public by commercial banks increase the supply of money in the same way as lending to the public does. The bank accepts government bonds (which are not money) and gives the securities dealer an increase in its checkable deposits (which *are* money).

Of course, when the securities dealer draws and clears a check for $50,000 against the Wahoo bank, the bank loses both reserves and deposits in that amount and then just meets the legal reserve requirement. Its balance sheet now reads precisely as in 6b except that "Securities" is substituted for "Loans" on the asset side.

Finally, the *selling* of government bonds to the public by a commercial bank—like the repayment of a loan—reduces the supply of money. The securities buyer pays by check, and both "Securities" and "Checkable deposits" (the latter being money) decline by the amount of the sale.

Profits, Liquidity, and the Federal Funds Market

The asset items on a commercial bank's balance sheet reflect the banker's pursuit of two conflicting goals:

- *Profit* One goal is profit. Commercial banks, like any other businesses, seek profits, which is why the bank makes loans and buys securities—the two major earning assets of commercial banks.

- *Liquidity* The other goal is safety. For a bank, safety lies in liquidity, specifically such liquid assets as cash and excess reserves. A bank must be on guard for depositors who want to transform their checkable deposits into cash. Similarly, it must guard against more checks clearing against it than are cleared in its favor, causing a net outflow of reserves. Bankers thus seek a balance between prudence and profit. The compromise is between assets that earn higher returns and highly liquid assets that earn no returns.

An interesting way in which banks can partly reconcile the goals of profit and liquidity is to lend temporary excess reserves held at the Federal Reserve Banks to other commercial banks. Normal day-to-day flows of funds to banks rarely leave all banks with their exact levels of required reserves. Also, funds held at the Federal Reserve Banks are highly liquid, but they do not draw interest. Banks therefore lend these excess reserves to other banks on an overnight basis as a way of earning additional interest without sacrificing long-term liquidity. Banks that borrow in this Federal funds market—the market for immediately available reserve balances at the Federal Reserve—do so because they are temporarily short of required reserves. The interest rate paid on these overnight loans is called the **Federal funds rate.**

We would show an overnight loan of reserves from the Surprise bank to the Wahoo bank as a decrease in reserves at the Surprise bank and an increase in reserves at the Wahoo bank. Ownership of reserves at the Federal Reserve Bank of Kansas City would change, but total reserves would not be affected. Exercise: Determine what other changes would be required on the Wahoo and Surprise banks' balance sheets as a result of the overnight loan. **(Key Questions 4 and 8)**

QUICK REVIEW 13.2

- Banks create money when they make loans; money vanishes when bank loans are repaid.
- New money is created when banks buy government bonds from the public; money disappears when banks sell government bonds to the public.
- Banks balance profitability and safety in determining their mix of earning assets and highly liquid assets.
- Banks borrow and lend temporary excess reserves on an overnight basis in the Federal funds market; the interest rate on these loans is the Federal funds rate.

The Banking System: Multiple-Deposit Expansion

Thus far we have seen that a single bank in a banking system can lend one dollar for each dollar of its excess reserves. The situation is different for all commercial banks as a group. We will find that the commercial banking system can lend—that is, can create money—by a multiple of its excess reserves. This multiple lending is accomplished even though each bank in the system can lend only "dollar for dollar" with its excess reserves.

How do these seemingly paradoxical results come about? To answer this question, we must keep our analysis uncluttered and rely on three simplifying assumptions:

- The reserve ratio for all commercial banks is 20 percent.
- Initially all banks are meeting this 20 percent reserve requirement exactly. No excess reserves exist; or, in the parlance of banking, they are "loaned up" (or "loaned out") fully in terms of the reserve requirement.
- If any bank can increase its loans as a result of acquiring excess reserves, an amount equal to those excess reserves will be lent to one borrower, who will write a check for the entire amount of the loan and give it to someone else, who will deposit the check in another bank. This third assumption means that the worst thing possible happens to every lending bank—a check for the entire amount of the loan is drawn and cleared against it in favor of another bank.

The Banking System's Lending Potential

Suppose a junkyard owner finds a $100 bill while dismantling a car that has been on the lot for years. He deposits the $100 in bank A, which adds the $100 to its reserves. We will record only changes in the balance sheets of the various commercial banks. The deposit changes bank A's balance sheet as shown by entries (a_1):

Multiple-Deposit Expansion Process			
Balance Sheet: Commercial Bank A			
Assets		Liabilities and net worth	
Reserves	$+100 ($a_1$)	Checkable	
	−80 (a_3)	deposits	$+100 ($a_1$)
Loans	+80 (a_2)		+80 (a_2)
			−80 (a_3)

Recall from transaction 3 that this $100 deposit of currency does not alter the money supply. While $100 of checkable-deposit money comes into being, it is offset by the $100 of currency no longer in the hands of the public (the junkyard owner). But bank A *has* acquired excess reserves of $80. Of the newly acquired $100 in currency, 20 percent, or $20, must be earmarked for the required reserves on the new $100 checkable deposit, and the remaining $80 goes to excess reserves. Remembering that a single commercial bank can lend only an amount equal to its excess reserves, we conclude that bank A can lend a maximum of $80. When a loan for this amount is made, bank A's loans increase by $80 and the borrower gets an $80 checkable deposit. We add these figures—entries (a_2)—to bank A's balance sheet.

But now we make our third assumption: The borrower draws a check ($80) for the entire amount of the loan, and gives it to someone who deposits it in bank B, a different bank. As we saw in transaction 6, bank A loses both reserves and deposits equal to the amount of the loan, as indicated in entries (a_3). The net result of these transactions is that bank A's reserves now stand at +$20 (= $100 − $80), loans at +$80, and checkable deposits at +$100 (= $100 + $80 − $80). When the dust has settled, bank A is just meeting the 20 percent reserve ratio.

Recalling our previous discussion, we know that bank B acquires both the reserves and the deposits that bank A has lost. Bank B's balance sheet is changed as in entries (b_1):

Multiple-Deposit Expansion Process			
Balance Sheet: Commercial Bank B			
Assets		Liabilities and net worth	
Reserves	$+80 ($b_1$)	Checkable	
	−64 (b_3)	deposits	$+80 ($b_1$)
Loans	+64 (b_2)		+64 (b_2)
			−64 (b_3)

When the borrower's check is drawn and cleared, bank A loses $80 in reserves and deposits and bank B gains $80 in reserves and deposits. But 20 percent, or $16, of bank B's new reserves must be kept as required reserves against the new $80 in checkable deposits. This means that bank B has $64 (= $80 − $16) in excess reserves. It can therefore lend $64 [entries ($b_2$)]. When the new borrower draws a check for the entire amount and deposits it in bank C, the reserves and deposits of bank B both fall by $64 [entries ($b_3$)]. As a result of these transactions, bank B's reserves now stand at +$16 (= $80 − $64), loans at +$64, and checkable deposits at +$80 (= $80 + $64 − $64). After all this, bank B is just meeting the 20 percent reserve requirement.

We are off and running again. Bank C acquires the $64 in reserves and deposits lost by bank B. Its balance sheet changes as in entries (c_1):

Multiple-Deposit Expansion Process			
Balance Sheet: Commercial Bank C			
Assets		Liabilities and net worth	
Reserves	$+64.00 ($c_1$)	Checkable	
	−51.20 (c_3)	deposits	$+64.00 ($c_1$)
Loans	+51.20 (c_2)		+51.20 (c_2)
			−51.20 (c_3)

Exactly 20 percent, or $12.80, of these new reserves will be required reserves, the remaining $51.20 being excess reserves. Hence, bank C can safely lend a maximum of $51.20. Suppose it does [entries (c_2)]. And suppose the borrower draws a check for the entire amount and gives it to someone who deposits it in another bank [entries (c_3)].

We could go ahead with this procedure by bringing banks D, E, F, G . . . , N into the picture. But we suggest that you work through the computations for banks D, E, and F to be sure you understand the procedure.

The entire analysis is summarized in Table 13.2. Data for banks D through N are supplied so that you may check your computations. Our conclusion is startling: On the basis of only $80 in excess reserves (acquired by the banking system when someone deposited $100 of currency in bank A), the entire commercial banking system is able to lend $400, the sum of the amounts in column 4. The banking system can lend excess reserves by a multiple of 5 when the reserve ratio is 20 percent. Yet each single bank in the banking system is lending only an amount equal to its own excess reserves. How do we explain this? How can the banking system lend by a multiple of its excess reserves, when each individual bank can lend only dollar for dollar with its excess reserves?

TABLE 13.2 Expansion of the Money Supply by the Commercial Banking System

Bank	(1) Acquired Reserves and Deposits	(2) Required Reserves (Reserve Ratio = .2)	(3) Excess Reserves, (1) − (2)	(4) Amount Bank Can Lend; New Money Created = (3)
Bank A	$ 100.00 (a_1)	$20.00	$80.00	$ 80.00 (a_2)
Bank B	80.00 (a_3, b_1)	16.00	64.00	64.00 (b_2)
Bank C	64.00 (b_3, c_1)	12.80	51.20	51.20 (c_2)
Bank D	51.20	10.24	40.96	40.96
Bank E	40.96	8.19	32.77	32.77
Bank F	32.77	6.55	26.21	26.21
Bank G	26.21	5.24	20.97	20.97
Bank H	20.97	4.20	16.78	16.78
Bank I	16.78	3.36	13.42	13.42
Bank J	13.42	2.68	10.74	10.74
Bank K	10.74	2.15	8.59	8.59
Bank L	8.59	1.72	6.87	6.87
Bank M	6.87	1.37	5.50	5.50
Bank N	5.50	1.10	4.40	4.40
Other banks	21.99	4.40	17.59	17.59
Total amount of money created (sum of the amounts in column 4)				**$400.00**

The answer is that reserves lost by a single bank are not lost to the banking system as a whole. The reserves lost by bank A are acquired by bank B. Those lost by B are gained by C. C loses to D, D to E, E to F, and so forth. Although reserves can be, and are, lost by individual banks in the banking system, there is no loss of reserves for the banking system as a whole.

An individual bank can safely lend only an amount equal to its excess reserves, but the commercial banking system can lend by a multiple of its excess reserves. This contrast, incidentally, is an illustration of why it is imperative that we keep the fallacy of composition (Last Word, Chapter 1) firmly in mind. Commercial banks as a group can create money by lending in a manner much different from that of the individual banks in the group.

The Monetary Multiplier

The banking system magnifies any original excess reserves into a larger amount of newly created checkable-deposit money. The *checkable-deposit multiplier,* or **monetary multiplier,** is similar in concept to the spending-income multiplier in Chapter 8. That multiplier exists because the expenditures of one household become some other household's income; the multiplier magnifies a change in initial spending into a larger change in GDP. The spending-

income multiplier is the reciprocal of the MPS (the leakage into saving that occurs at each round of spending).

Similarly, the monetary multiplier exists because the reserves and deposits lost by one bank become reserves of another bank. It magnifies excess reserves into a larger creation of checkable-deposit money. The monetary multiplier m is the reciprocal of the required reserve ratio R (the leakage into required reserves that occurs at each step in the lending process). In short,

$$\text{Monetary multiplier} = \frac{1}{\text{required reserve ratio}}$$

or, in symbols,

$$m = \frac{1}{R}$$

In this formula, m represents the maximum amount of new checkable-deposit money that can be created by a single dollar of excess reserves, given the value of R. By multiplying the excess reserves E by m, we can find the maximum amount of new checkable-deposit money, D, that can be created by the banking system. That is,

$$\text{Maximum checkable-deposit creation} = \text{excess reserves} \times \text{monetary multiplier}$$

FIGURE 13.1 The outcome of the money expansion process. A deposit of $100 of currency into a checking account creates an initial checkable deposit of $100. If the reserve ratio is 20 percent, only $20 of reserves is legally required to support the $100 checkable deposit. The $80 of excess reserves allows the banking system to create $400 of checkable deposits through making loans. The $100 of reserves supports a total of $500 of money ($100 + $400).

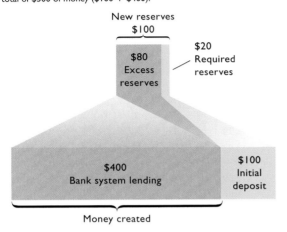

or, more simply,

$$D = E \times m$$

In our example in Table 13.2, R is .20, so m is 5 (= 1/.20). Then

$$D = \$80 \times 5 = \$400$$

Figure 13.1 depicts the final outcome of our example of a multiple-deposit expansion of the money supply. The initial deposit of $100 of currency into the bank (lower right-hand box) creates new reserves of an equal amount (upper box). With a 20 percent reserve ratio, however, only $20 of reserves are needed to "back up" this $100 checkable deposit. The excess reserves of $80 permit the creation of $400 of new checkable deposits via the making of loans, confirming a monetary multiplier of 5. The $100 of new reserves supports a total supply of money of $500, consisting of the $100 initial checkable deposit plus $400 of checkable deposits created through lending.

W 13.2

Money creation

Higher reserve ratios mean lower monetary multipliers and therefore less creation of new checkable-deposit money via loans; smaller reserve ratios mean higher monetary multipliers and thus more creation of new checkable-deposit money via loans. With a high reserve ratio, say, 50 percent, the monetary multiplier would be 2 (= 1/.5), and in our example the banking system could create only

$100 (= $50 of excess reserves × 2) of new checkable deposits. With a low reserve ratio, say, 5 percent, the monetary multiplier would be 20 (= 1/.05), and the banking system could create $1900 (= $95 of excess reserves × 20) of new checkable deposits.

You might experiment with the following two brainteasers to test your understanding of multiple credit expansion by the banking system:

- Rework the analysis in Table 13.2 (at least three or four steps of it) assuming the reserve ratio is 10 percent. What is the maximum amount of money the banking system can create upon acquiring $100 in new reserves and deposits? (The answer is not $800!)
- Suppose the banking system is loaned up and faces a 20 percent reserve ratio. Explain how it might have to reduce its outstanding loans by $400 when a $100 cash withdrawal from a checkable-deposit account forces one bank to draw down its reserves by $100.

(Key Question 13)

Reversibility: The Multiple Destruction of Money

The process we have described is reversible. Just as checkable-deposit money is created when banks make loans, checkable-deposit money is destroyed when loans are paid off. Loan repayment, in effect, sets off a process of multiple destruction of money the opposite of the multiple creation process. Because loans are both made and paid off in any period, the direction of the loans, checkable deposits, and money supply in a given period will depend on the net effect of the two processes. If the dollar amount of loans made in some period exceeds the dollar amount of loans paid off, checkable deposits will expand and the money supply will increase. But if the dollar amount of loans is less than the dollar amount of loans paid off, checkable deposits will contract and the money supply will decline.

QUICK REVIEW 13.3

- A single bank in a multibank system can safely lend (create money) by an amount equal to its excess reserves; the banking system can lend (create money) by a multiple of its excess reserves.
- The monetary multiplier is the reciprocal of the required reserve ratio; it is the multiple by which the banking system can expand the money supply for each dollar of excess reserves.
- The monetary multiplier works in both directions; it applies to money destruction from the payback of loans as well as the money creation from the making of loans.

The Bank Panics of 1930 to 1933

A Series of Bank Panics in the Early 1930s Resulted in a Multiple Contraction of the Money Supply.

In the early months of the Great Depression, before there was deposit insurance, several financially weak banks went out of business. As word spread that customers of those banks had lost their deposits, a general concern arose that something similar could happen at other banks. Depositors became frightened that their banks did not, in fact, still have all the money they had deposited. And, of course, in a fractional reserve banking system, that is the reality. Acting on their fears, people en masse tried to withdraw currency—that is, to "cash out" their accounts—from their banks. They wanted to get their money before it was all gone. Economists liken this sort of collective response to "herd" or "flock" behavior. The sudden "run on the banks" caused many previously financially sound banks to declare bankruptcy. More than 9000 banks failed within 3 years.

The massive conversion of checkable deposits to currency during 1930 to 1933 reduced the nation's money supply. This might seem strange, since a check written for "cash" reduces checkable-deposit money and increases currency in the hands of the public by the same amount. So how does the money supply decline? Our discussion of the money-creation process provides the answer, but now the story becomes one of money destruction.

Suppose that people collectively cash out $10 billion from their checking accounts. As an immediate result, checkable-deposit money declines by $10 billion, while currency held by the public increases by $10 billion. But here is the catch: Assuming a reserve ratio of 20 percent, the $10 billion of currency in the banks had been supporting $50 billion of deposit money, the $10 billion of deposits plus $40 billion created through loans. The $10 billion withdrawal of currency forces banks to reduce loans (and thus checkable-deposit money) by $40 billion to continue to meet their reserve requirement. In short, a $40 billion destruction of deposit money occurs. This is the scenario that occurred in the early years of the 1930s.

Accompanying this multiple contraction of checkable deposits was the banks' "scramble for liquidity" to try to meet further withdrawals of currency. To obtain more currency, they sold many of their holdings of government securities to the public. You know from this chapter that a bank's sale of government securities to the public, like a reduction in loans, reduces the money supply. People write checks for the securities, reducing their checkable deposits, and the bank uses the currency it obtains to meet the ongoing bank run. In short, the loss of reserves from the banking system, in conjunction with the scramble for security, reduced the amount of checkable-deposit money by far more than the increase in currency in the hands of the public. Thus, the money supply collapsed.

In 1933, President Franklin Roosevelt ended the bank panics by declaring a "national bank holiday," which closed all national banks for 1 week and resulted in the federally insured deposit program. Meanwhile, the nation's money supply had plummeted by 25 percent, the largest such drop in U.S. history. This decline in the money supply contributed to the nation's deepest and longest depression.

Today, a multiple contraction of the money supply of the 1930–1933 magnitude is unthinkable. FDIC insurance has kept individual bank failures from becoming general panics. Also, while the Fed stood idly by during the bank panics of 1930 to 1933, today it would take immediate and dramatic actions to maintain the banking system's reserves and the nation's money supply. Those actions are the subject of Chapter 14.

Summary

1. Modern banking systems are fractional reserve systems: Only a fraction of checkable deposits is backed by currency.
2. The operation of a commercial bank can be understood through its balance sheet, where assets equal liabilities plus net worth.
3. Commercial banks keep required reserves on deposit in a Federal Reserve Bank or as vault cash. These required reserves are equal to a specified percentage of the commercial bank's checkable-deposit liabilities. Excess reserves are equal to actual reserves minus required reserves.
4. Banks lose both reserves and checkable deposits when checks are drawn against them.
5. Commercial banks create money—checkable deposits, or checkable-deposit money—when they make loans. The creation of checkable deposits by bank lending is the most important source of money in the U.S. economy. Money is destroyed when lenders repay bank loans.
6. The ability of a single commercial bank to create money by lending depends on the size of its excess reserves. Generally speaking, a commercial bank can lend only an amount equal to its excess reserves. Money creation is thus limited because, in all likelihood, checks drawn by borrowers will be deposited

in other banks, causing a loss of reserves and deposits to the lending bank equal to the amount of money that it has lent.

7. Rather than making loans, banks may decide to use excess reserves to buy bonds from the public. In doing so, banks merely credit the checkable-deposit accounts of the bond sellers, thus creating checkable-deposit money. Money vanishes when banks sell bonds to the public, because bond buyers must draw down their checkable-deposit balances to pay for the bonds.

8. Banks earn interest by making loans and by purchasing bonds; they maintain liquidity by holding cash and excess reserves. Banks having temporary excess reserves often lend them overnight to banks that are short of required reserves. The interest rate paid on loans in this Federal funds market is called the Federal funds rate.

9. The commercial banking system as a whole can lend by a multiple of its excess reserves because the system as a whole cannot lose reserves. Individual banks, however, can lose reserves to other banks in the system.

10. The multiple by which the banking system can lend on the basis of each dollar of excess reserves is the reciprocal of the reserve ratio. This multiple credit expansion process is reversible.

Terms and Concepts

fractional reserve banking system	required reserves	actual reserves
balance sheet	reserve ratio	Federal funds rate
vault cash	excess reserves	monetary multiplier

Study Questions

1. Why must a balance sheet always balance? What are the major assets and claims on a commercial bank's balance sheet?
2. **KEY QUESTION** Why does the Federal Reserve require commercial banks to have reserves? Explain why reserves are an asset to commercial banks but a liability to the Federal Reserve Banks. What are excess reserves? How do you calculate the amount of excess reserves held by a bank? What is the significance of excess reserves?
3. "Whenever currency is deposited in a commercial bank, cash goes out of circulation and, as a result, the supply of money is reduced." Do you agree? Explain why or why not.
4. **KEY QUESTION** "When a commercial bank makes loans, it creates money; when loans are repaid, money is destroyed." Explain.
5. Explain why a single commercial bank can safely lend only an amount equal to its excess reserves but the commercial banking system as a whole can lend by a multiple of its excess reserves. What is the monetary multiplier, and how does it relate to the reserve ratio?
6. Assume that Jones deposits $500 in currency into her checkable-deposit account in First National Bank. A half-hour later Smith obtains a loan for $750 at this bank. By how

Assets		(1)	(2)	Liabilities and net worth		(1)	(2)
Reserves	$22,000	___	___	Checkable		___	___
Securities	38,000	___	___	deposits	$100,000		
Loans	40,000	___	___				

much and in what direction has the money supply changed? Explain.

7. Suppose the National Bank of Commerce has excess reserves of $8000 and outstanding checkable deposits of $150,000. If the reserve ratio is 20 percent, what is the size of the bank's actual reserves?

8. **KEY QUESTION** Suppose that Continental Bank has the simplified balance sheet shown on the previous page and that the reserve ratio is 20 percent:

   a. What is the maximum amount of new loans that this bank can make? Show in column 1 how the bank's balance sheet will appear after the bank has lent this additional amount.

   b. By how much has the supply of money changed? Explain.

   c. How will the bank's balance sheet appear after checks drawn for the entire amount of the new loans have been cleared against the bank? Show the new balance sheet in column 2.

   d. Answer questions a, b, and c on the assumption that the reserve ratio is 15 percent.

9. The Third National Bank has reserves of $20,000 and checkable deposits of $100,000. The reserve ratio is 20 percent. Households deposit $5000 in currency into the bank that is added to reserves. What level of excess reserves does the bank now have?

10. Suppose again that the Third National Bank has reserves of $20,000 and checkable deposits of $100,000. The reserve ratio is 20 percent. The bank now sells $5000 in securities to the Federal Reserve Bank in its district, receiving a $5000 increase in reserves in return. What level of excess reserves does the bank now have? Why does your answer differ (yes, it does!) from the answer to question 9?

11. Suppose a bank discovers that its reserves will temporarily fall slightly short of those legally required. How might it remedy this situation through the Federal funds market?

Now assume the bank finds that its reserves will be substantially and permanently deficient. What remedy is available to this bank? (Hint: Recall your answer to question 4.)

12. Suppose that Bob withdraws $100 of cash from his checking account at Security Bank and uses it to buy a camera from Joe, who deposits the $100 in his checking account in Serenity Bank. Assuming a reserve ratio of 10 percent and no initial excess reserves, determine the extent to which (a) Security Bank must reduce its loans and checkable deposits because of the cash withdrawal, (b) Serenity Bank can safely increase its loans and checkable deposits because of the cash deposit, and (c) the entire banking system, including Serenity, can increase loans and checkable deposits because of the cash deposit. Have the cash withdrawal and deposit changed the total money supply?

13. **KEY QUESTION** Suppose the simplified consolidated balance sheet shown below is for the entire commercial banking system. All figures are in billions. The reserve ratio is 25 percent.

Assets			Liabilities and net worth		
		(1)			(1)
Reserves	$ 52	____	Checkable		
Securities	48	____	deposits	$200	____
Loans	100	____			

   a. What amount of excess reserves does the commercial banking system have? What is the maximum amount the banking system might lend? Show in column 1 how the consolidated balance sheet would look after this amount has been lent. What is the monetary multiplier?

   b. Answer the questions in part a assuming the reserve ratio is 20 percent. Explain the resulting difference in the lending ability of the commercial banking system.

14. **LAST WORD** Explain how the bank panics of 1930 to 1933 produced a decline in the nation's money supply. Why are such panics highly unlikely today?

Web-Based Questions

1. **ASSETS AND LIABILITIES OF ALL COMMERCIAL BANKS IN THE UNITED STATES** The Federal Reserve, at **www.federalreserve.gov/releases/h8/Current/,** provides an aggregate balance sheet for commercial banks in the United States. Check the current release, and look in the asset column for "Loans and leases." Rank the following components of loans and leases in terms of size: commercial and industrial, real estate, consumer, security, and other. Over the past 12 months, which component has increased by the largest percentage? By the largest absolute amount? Has the

net worth (assets less liabilities) of all commercial banks in the United States increased, decreased, or remained constant during the past year?

2. **RESERVE REQUIREMENTS—ANY CHANGES TO TABLE 13.1?** Go to the Fed's Web site, **www.federalreserve.gov/,** and select "Monetary Policy." Then, in order, select Reserve Requirements and find the link to "low-reserve amounts and exemptions." Does any part of Table 13.1 need updating? If so, prepare a new, updated table.

14

IN THIS CHAPTER YOU WILL LEARN:

- How the equilibrium interest rate is determined in the market for money.
- The goals and tools of monetary policy.
- About the Federal funds rate and how the Fed controls it.
- The mechanisms by which monetary policy affects GDP and the price level.
- The effectiveness of monetary policy and its shortcomings.

Interest Rates and Monetary Policy

Some newspaper commentators have stated that the chairman of the Federal Reserve Board (previously Alan Greenspan and now Ben Bernanke) is the second most powerful person in the United States, after the U.S. president. That is undoubtedly an exaggeration because the chair has only a single vote on the 7-person Federal Reserve Board and 12-person Federal Open Market Committee. But there can be no doubt about the chair's influence, the overall importance of the Federal Reserve, and the **monetary policy** that it conducts. Such policy consists of deliberate changes in the money supply to influence interest rates and thus the total level of spending in the economy. The goal is to achieve and maintain price-level stability, full employment, and economic growth.

Interest Rates

The Fed's primary influence is on the money supply and interest rates. So we initially need to better understand the market in which interest rates are established. **Interest** is the price paid for the use of money. It is the price that borrowers need to pay lenders for transferring purchasing power to the future. It can be thought of as the amount of money that must be paid for the use of $1 for 1 year. Although there is a full cluster of U.S. interest rates that vary by purpose, size, risk, maturity, and taxability, we will simply speak of "the interest rate" unless stated otherwise.

Let's see how the interest rate is determined. Because it is a "price," we again turn to demand and supply analysis for the answer.

The Demand for Money

Why does the public want to hold some of its wealth as *money?* There are two main reasons: to make purchases with it and to hold it as an asset.

Transactions Demand, D_t People hold money because it is convenient for purchasing goods and services. Households usually are paid once a week, every 2 weeks, or monthly, whereas their expenditures are less predictable and typically more frequent. So households must have enough money on hand to buy groceries and pay mortgage and utility bills. Nor are business revenues and expenditures simultaneous. Businesses need to have money available to pay for labor, materials, power, and other inputs. The demand for money as a medium of exchange is called **transactions demand** for money.

The level of nominal GDP is the main determinant of the amount of money demanded for transactions. The larger the total money value of all goods and services exchanged in the economy, the larger the amount of money needed to negotiate those transactions. The transactions demand for money varies directly with nominal GDP. We specify *nominal* GDP because households and firms will want more money for transactions if prices rise or if real output increases. In both instances a larger dollar volume will be needed to accomplish the desired transactions.

In Figure 14.1a we graph the quantity of money demanded for transactions against the interest rate. For simplicity, let's assume that the amount demanded depends exclusively on the level of nominal GDP and is independent of the interest rate. (In reality, higher interest rates are associated with slightly lower volumes of money demanded for transactions.) Our simplifying assumption allows us to graph the transactions demand, D_t, as a vertical line. This demand curve is positioned at $100 billion, on the assumption that each dollar held for transactions purposes is spent on an average of three times per year and that nominal GDP is $300 billion. Thus the public needs $100 billion (= $300 billion/3) to purchase that GDP.

Asset Demand, D_a The second reason for holding money derives from money's function as a store of value. People may hold their financial assets in many forms, including corporate stocks, corporate or government bonds, or money. To the extent they want to hold money as an asset, there is an **asset demand** for money.

People like to hold some of their financial assets as money (apart from using it to buy goods and services) because money is the most liquid of all financial assets; it is immediately usable for purchasing other assets when opportunities arise. Money is also an attractive asset to hold when the prices of other assets such as bonds are expected to decline. For example, when the price of a bond falls, the bondholder who sells the bond prior to the payback date of the full principal will suffer a loss (called a *capital loss*). That loss will partially or fully offset the interest received on the bond. There is no such risk of capital loss in holding money.

The disadvantage of holding money as an asset is that it earns no or very little interest. Checkable deposits pay either no interest or lower interest rates than bonds. Idle currency, of course, earns no interest at all.

Knowing these advantages and disadvantages, the public must decide how much of its financial assets to hold as money, rather than other assets such as bonds. The answer depends primarily on the rate of interest. A household or a business incurs an opportunity cost when it holds money; in both cases, interest income is forgone or sacrificed. If a bond pays 6 percent interest, for example, holding $100 as cash or in a noninterest checkable account costs $6 per year of forgone income.

The amount of money demanded as an asset therefore varies inversely with the rate of interest (the opportunity cost of holding money as an asset). When the interest rate rises, being liquid and avoiding capital losses becomes more costly. The public reacts by reducing its holdings of money as an asset. When the interest rate falls, the cost of being liquid and avoiding capital losses also declines. The public therefore increases the amount of financial assets that it wants to hold as money. This inverse relationship just described is shown by D_a in Figure 14.1b.

O 14.1

Liquidity preference

Total Money Demand, D_m As shown in Figure 14.1, we find the **total demand for money** D_m, by horizontally adding the asset demand to the transactions

keygraph

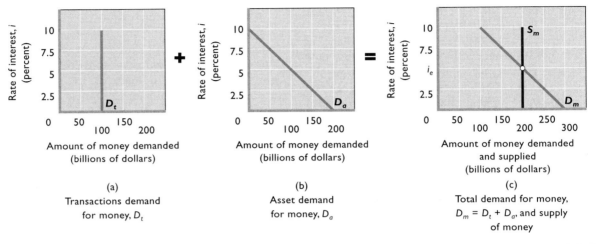

FIGURE 14.1 The demand for money, the supply of money, and the equilibrium interest rate. The total demand for money D_m is determined by horizontally adding the asset demand for money D_a to the transactions demand D_t. The transactions demand is vertical because it is assumed to depend on nominal GDP rather than on the interest rate. The asset demand varies inversely with the interest rate because of the opportunity cost involved in holding currency and checkable deposits that pay no interest or very low interest. Combining the money supply (stock) S_m with the total money demand D_m portrays the market for money and determines the equilibrium interest rate i_e.

(a) Transactions demand for money, D_t

(b) Asset demand for money, D_a

(c) Total demand for money, $D_m = D_t + D_a$, and supply of money

QUICK QUIZ 14.1

1. In this graph, at the interest rate i_e (5 percent):
   a. the amount of money demanded as an asset is $50 billion.
   b. the amount of money demanded for transactions is $200 billion.
   c. bond prices will decline.
   d. $100 billion is demanded for transactions, $100 billion is demanded as an asset, and the money supply is $200 billion.

2. In this graph, at an interest rate of 10 percent:
   a. no money will be demanded as an asset.
   b. total money demanded will be $200 billion.
   c. the Federal Reserve will supply $100 billion of money.
   d. there will be a $100 billion shortage of money.

3. Curve D_a slopes downward because:
   a. lower interest rates increase the opportunity cost of holding money.
   b. lower interest rates reduce the opportunity cost of holding money.
   c. the asset demand for money varies directly (positively) with the interest rate.
   d. the transactions-demand-for-money curve is perfectly vertical.

4. Suppose the supply of money declines to $100 billion. The equilibrium interest rate would:
   a. fall, the amount of money demanded for transactions would rise, and the amount of money demanded as an asset would decline.
   b. rise, and the amounts of money demanded both for transactions and as an asset would fall.
   c. fall, and the amounts of money demanded both for transactions and as an asset would increase.
   d. rise, the amount of money demanded for transactions would be unchanged, and the amount of money demanded as an asset would decline.

Answers: 1. d; 2. a; 3. b; 4. d

demand. The resulting downward-sloping line in Figure 14.1c represents the total amount of money the public wants to hold, both for transactions and as an asset, at each possible interest rate.

Recall that the transactions demand for money depends on the nominal GDP. A change in the nominal GDP—working through the transactions demand for money—will shift the total money demand curve. Specifically, an increase

W 14.1

Demand for money

in nominal GDP means that the public wants to hold a larger amount of money for transactions, and that extra demand will shift the total money demand curve to the right. In contrast, a decline in the nominal GDP will shift the total money demand curve to the left. As an example, suppose nominal GDP increases from $300 billion to $450 billion and the average dollar held for transactions is still spent three times per year. Then the transactions demand curve will shift from $100 billion (= $300 billion/3) to $150 billion (= $450 billion/3). The total money demand curve will then lie $50 billion farther to the right at each possible interest rate.

The Equilibrium Interest Rate

We can combine the demand for money with the supply of money to determine the equilibrium rate of interest. In Figure 14.1c the vertical line, S_m, represents the money supply. It is a vertical line because the monetary authorities and financial institutions have provided the economy with some particular stock of money. Here it is $200 billion.

Just as in a product market or a resource market, the intersection of demand and supply determines the equilibrium price in the market for money. Here, the equilibrium "price" is the interest rate (i_e)—the price that is paid for the use of money over some time period.

G 14.1

Equilibrium interest rate

Changes in the demand for money, the supply of money, or both can change the equilibrium interest rate. For reasons that will soon become apparent, we are most interested in changes in the supply of money. The important generalization is this: An increase in the supply of money will lower the equilibrium interest rate; a decrease in the supply of money will raise the equilibrium interest rate. **(Key Questions 1 and 2)**

Interest Rates and Bond Prices

Interest rates and bond prices are closely related. When the interest rate increases, bond prices fall; when the interest rate falls, bond prices rise. Why so? First understand that bonds are bought and sold in financial markets, and that the price of bonds is determined by bond demand and bond supply.

Suppose that a bond with no expiration date pays a fixed $50 annual interest and is selling for its face value of $1000. The interest yield on this bond is 5 percent:

$$\frac{\$50}{\$1000} = 5\% \text{ interest yield}$$

Now suppose the interest rate in the economy rises to $7\frac{1}{2}$ percent from 5 percent. Newly issued bonds will pay $75 per $1000 lent. Older bonds paying only $50 will not be salable at their $1000 face value. To compete with the $7\frac{1}{2}$ percent bond, the price of this bond will need to fall to $667 to remain competitive. The $50 fixed annual interest payment will then yield $7\frac{1}{2}$ percent to whoever buys the bond:

$$\frac{\$50}{\$667} = 7\frac{1}{2}\%$$

Next suppose that the interest rate falls to $2\frac{1}{2}$ percent from the original 5 percent. Newly issued bonds will pay $25 on $1000 loaned. A bond paying $50 will be highly attractive. Bond buyers will bid up its price to $2000, at which the yield will equal $2\frac{1}{2}$ percent:

W 14.2

Bond prices and interest rates

$$\frac{\$50}{\$2000} = 2\frac{1}{2}\%$$

The point is that bond prices fall when the interest rate rises and rise when the interest rate falls. There is an inverse relationship between the interest rate and bond prices. **(Key Question 3)**

QUICK REVIEW 14.1

- People demand money for transaction and asset purposes.
- The total demand for money is the sum of the transactions and asset demands; it is graphed as an inverse relationship (downward-sloping line) between the interest rate and the quantity of money demanded.
- The equilibrium interest rate is determined by money demand and supply; it occurs when people are willing to hold the exact amount of money being supplied by the monetary authorities.
- Interest rates and bond prices are inversely related.

The Consolidated Balance Sheet of the Federal Reserve Banks

With this basic understanding of interest rates we can turn to monetary policy, which relies on changes in interest rates to be effective. The 12 Federal Reserve Banks together constitute the U.S. "central bank," nicknamed the "Fed." (Global Perspective 14.1 also lists some of the other central banks in the world, along with their nicknames.)

The Fed's balance sheet helps us consider how the Fed conducts monetary policy. Table 14.1 consolidates the pertinent assets and liabilities of the 12 Federal Reserve Banks as of March 29, 2006. You will see that some of the Fed's assets and liabilities differ from those found on the balance sheet of a commercial bank.

TABLE 14.1 Consolidated Balance Sheet of the 12 Federal Reserve Banks, March 29, 2006 (in Millions)

Assets		Liabilities and Net Worth	
Securities	$758,551	Reserves of commercial banks	$ 14,923
Loans to commercial banks	19,250	Treasury deposits	4,663
All other assets	59,967	Federal Reserve Notes (outstanding)	754,567
		All other liabilities and net worth	63,615
Total	$837,768	Total	$837,768

Source: Federal Reserve Statistical Release, H.4.1, March 29, 2006, **www.federalreserve.gov/.**

GLOBAL PERSPECTIVE 14.1

Central Banks, Selected Nations

The monetary policies of the world's major central banks are often in the international news. Here are some of their official names, along with a few of their popular nicknames.

Australia: Reserve Bank of Australia (RBA)

Canada: Bank of Canada

Euro Zone: European Central Bank (ECB)

Japan: The Bank of Japan ("BOJ")

Mexico: Banco de Mexico (Mex Bank)

Russia: Central Bank of Russia

Sweden: Sveriges Riksbank

United Kingdom: Bank of England

United States: Federal Reserve System (the "Fed") (12 regional Federal Reserve Banks)

Assets

The two main assets of the Federal Reserve Banks are securities and loans to commercial banks. (Again, we will simplify by referring only to *commercial banks,* even though the analysis also applies to *thrifts*—savings and loans, mutual savings banks, and credit unions.)

Securities The securities shown in Table 14.1 are government bonds that have been purchased by the Federal Reserve Banks. They consist largely of Treasury bills (short-term securities), Treasury notes (mid-term securities), and Treasury bonds (long-term securities) issued by the U.S. government to finance past budget deficits. These securities are part of the public debt—the money borrowed by the Federal government. The Federal Reserve Banks bought these securities from commercial banks and the public through open-market operations. Although they are

an important source of interest income to the Federal Reserve Banks, they are mainly bought and sold to influence the size of commercial bank reserves and, therefore, the ability of those banks to create money by lending.

Loans to Commercial Banks For reasons that will soon become clear, commercial banks occasionally borrow from Federal Reserve Banks. The IOUs that commercial banks give these "bankers' banks" in return for loans are listed on the Federal Reserve balance sheet as "Loans to commercial banks." They are assets to the Fed because they are claims against the commercial banks. To commercial banks, of course, these loans are liabilities in that they must be repaid. Through borrowing in this way, commercial banks can increase their reserves.

Liabilities

On the liability side of the Fed's consolidated balance sheet, we find three items: reserves, Treasury deposits, and Federal Reserve Notes.

Reserves of Commercial Banks The Fed requires that the commercial banks hold reserves against their checkable deposits. When held in the Federal Reserve Banks, these reserves are listed as a liability on the Fed's balance sheet. They are assets on the books of the commercial banks, which still own them even though they are deposited at the Federal Reserve Banks.

Treasury Deposits The U.S. Treasury keeps deposits in the Federal Reserve Banks and draws checks on them to pay its obligations. To the Treasury these deposits are assets; to the Federal Reserve Banks they are liabilities. The Treasury creates and replenishes these deposits by depositing tax receipts and money borrowed from the public or from the commercial banks through the sale of bonds.

Federal Reserve Notes Outstanding As we have seen, the supply of paper money in the United States consists of Federal Reserve Notes issued by the Federal

Reserve Banks. When this money is circulating outside the Federal Reserve Banks, it constitutes claims against the assets of the Federal Reserve Banks. The Fed thus treats these notes as a liability.

Tools of Monetary Policy

O 14.2

Tools of monetary policy

With this look at the Federal Reserve Banks' consolidated balance sheet, we can now explore how the Fed can influence the money-creating abilities of the commercial banking system. The Fed has three tools of monetary control it can use to alter the reserves of commercial banks:

- Open-market operations
- The reserve ratio
- The discount rate

Open-Market Operations

Bond markets are "open" to all buyers and sellers of corporate and government bonds (securities). The Federal Reserve is the largest single holder of U.S. government securities. The U.S. government, not the Fed, issued these Treasury bills, Treasury notes, and Treasury bonds to finance past budget deficits. Over the decades, the Fed has purchased these securities from major financial institutions that buy and sell government and corporate securities for themselves or their customers.

The Fed's **open-market operations** consist of the buying of government bonds from, or the selling of government bonds to, commercial banks and the general public. (The Fed actually buys and sells the government bonds to commercial banks and the public through two dozen or so large financial firms, called "primary dealers.") Open-market operations are the Fed's most important instrument for influencing the money supply.

Buying Securities
Suppose that the Fed decides to have the Federal Reserve Banks buy government bonds. They can purchase these bonds either from commercial banks or from the public. In both cases the reserves of the commercial banks will increase.

From Commercial Banks
When Federal Reserve Banks buy government bonds *from commercial banks,*

(*a*) The commercial banks give up part of their holdings of securities (the government bonds) to the Federal Reserve Banks.

(*b*) The Federal Reserve Banks, in paying for these securities, place newly created reserves in the

accounts of the commercial banks at the Fed. (These reserves are created "out of thin air," so to speak!) The reserves of the commercial banks go up by the amount of the purchase of the securities.

We show these outcomes as (*a*) and (*b*) on the following consolidated balance sheets of the commercial banks and the Federal Reserve Banks:

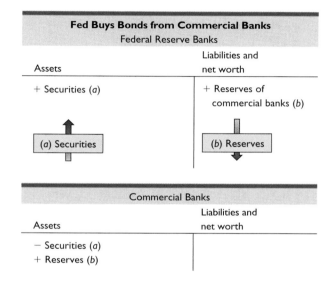

The upward arrow shows that securities have moved from the commercial banks to the Federal Reserve Banks. So we enter " − Securities" (minus securities) in the asset column of the balance sheet of the commercial banks. For the same reason, we enter " + Securities" in the asset column of the balance sheet of the Federal Reserve Banks.

The downward arrow indicates that the Federal Reserve Banks have provided reserves to the commercial banks. So we enter " + Reserves" in the asset column of the balance sheet for the commercial banks. In the liability column of the balance sheet of the Federal Reserve Banks, the plus sign indicates that although commercial bank reserves have increased, they are a liability to the Federal Reserve Banks because the reserves are owned by the commercial banks.

What is most important about this transaction is that when Federal Reserve Banks purchase securities from commercial banks, they increase the reserves in the banking system, which then increases the lending ability of the commercial banks.

From the Public
The effect on commercial bank reserves is much the same when Federal Reserve Banks purchase securities from the general public. Suppose the Gristly Meat Packing Company has government bonds

FIGURE 14.2 The Federal Reserve's purchase of bonds and the expansion of the money supply. Assuming all banks are loaded up initially, a Federal Reserve purchase of a $1000 bond from either a commercial bank or the public can increase the money supply by $5000 when the reserve ratio is 20 percent. In the left panel of the diagram, the purchase of a $1000 bond from a commercial bank creates $1000 of excess reserves that support a $5000 expansion of checkable deposits through loans. In the right panel, the purchase of a $1000 bond from the public creates a $1000 checkable deposit but only $800 of excess reserves, because $200 of reserves is required to "back up" the $1000 new checkable deposit. The commercial banks can therefore expand the money supply by only $4000 by making loans. This $4000 of checkable-deposit money plus the new checkable deposit of $1000 equals $5000 of new money.

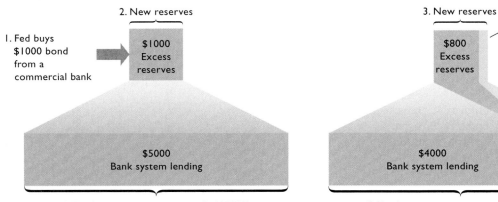

that it sells in the open market to the Federal Reserve Banks. The transaction has several elements:

(a) Gristly gives up securities to the Federal Reserve Banks and gets in payment a check drawn by the Federal Reserve Banks on themselves.

(b) Gristly promptly deposits the check in its account with the Wahoo bank.

(c) The Wahoo bank sends this check against the Federal Reserve Banks to a Federal Reserve Bank for collection. As a result, the Wahoo bank enjoys an increase in its reserves.

To keep things simple, we will dispense with showing the balance sheet changes resulting from the Fed's sale or purchase of bonds from the public. But two aspects of this transaction are particularly important. First, as with Federal Reserve purchases of securities directly from commercial banks, the purchases of securities from the public increases the lending ability of the commercial banking system. Second, the supply of money is directly increased by the Federal Reserve Banks' purchase of government bonds (aside from any expansion of the money supply that may occur from the increase in commercial bank reserves). This direct increase in the money supply has taken the form of an increased amount of checkable deposits in the economy as a result of Gristly's deposit.

The Federal Reserve Banks' purchases of securities from the commercial banking system differ slightly from their purchases of securities from the public. If we assume that all commercial banks are loaned up initially, Federal Reserve bond purchases *from commercial banks* increase the

actual reserves and excess reserves of commercial banks by the entire amount of the bond purchases. As shown in the left panel in Figure 14.2, a $1000 bond purchase from a commercial bank increases both the actual and the excess reserves of the commercial bank by $1000.

In contrast, Federal Reserve Bank purchases of bonds from the public increase actual reserves but also increase checkable deposits when the sellers place the Fed's check into their personal checking accounts. Thus, a $1000 bond purchase from the public would increase checkable deposits by $1000 and hence the actual reserves of the loaned-up banking system by the same amount. But with a 20 percent reserve ratio applied to the $1000 checkable deposit, the excess reserves of the banking system would be only $800 since $200 of the $1000 would have to be held as reserves.

However, in both transactions the end result is the same: When Federal Reserve Banks buy securities in the open market, commercial banks' reserves are increased. When the banks lend out an amount equal to their excess reserves, the nation's money supply will rise. Observe in Figure 14.2 that a $1000 purchase of bonds by the Federal Reserve results in a potential of $5000 of additional money, regardless of whether the purchase was made from commercial banks or from the general public.

W 14.3

Open-market
operations

Selling Securities As you may suspect, when the Federal Reserve Banks sell government bonds, commercial banks' reserves are reduced. Let's see why.

To Commercial Banks When the Federal Reserve Banks sell securities in the open market to commercial banks,

(a) The Federal Reserve Banks give up securities that the commercial banks acquire.

(b) The commercial banks pay for those securities by drawing checks against their deposits—that is, against their reserves—in Federal Reserve Banks. The Fed collects those checks by reducing the commercial banks' reserves accordingly.

The balance-sheet changes—again identified by (a) and (b)—appear as shown below. The reduction in commercial bank reserves is indicated by the minus signs before the appropriate entries.

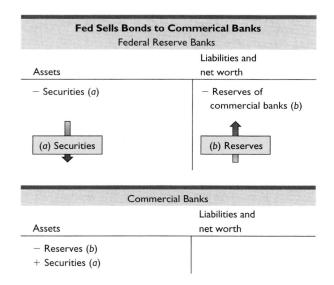

To the Public When the Federal Reserve Banks sell securities to the public, the outcome is much the same. Let's put the Gristly Company on the buying end of government bonds that the Federal Reserve Banks are selling:

(a) The Federal Reserve Banks sell government bonds to Gristly, which pays with a check drawn on the Wahoo bank.

(b) The Federal Reserve Banks clear this check against the Wahoo bank by reducing Wahoo's reserves.

(c) The Wahoo bank returns the canceled check to Gristly, reducing Gristly's checkable deposit accordingly.

Federal Reserve bond sales of $1000 to the commercial banking system reduce the system's actual and excess reserves by $1000. But a $1000 bond sale to the public reduces excess reserves by $800, because the public's checkable-deposit money is also reduced by $1000 by the sale. Since the commercial banking system's outstanding checkable deposits are reduced by $1000, banks need keep $200 less in reserves.

Whether the Fed sells bonds to the public or to commercial banks, the result is the same: When Federal Reserve Banks sell securities in the open market, commercial bank reserves are reduced. If all excess reserves are already lent out, this decline in commercial bank reserves produces a decline in the nation's money supply. In our example, a $1000 sale of government securities results in a $5000 decline in the money supply whether the sale is made to commercial banks or to the general public. You can verify this by reexamining Figure 14.2 and tracing the effects of a *sale* of a $1000 bond by the Fed either to commercial banks or to the public.

What makes commercial banks and the public willing to sell government securities to, or buy them from, Federal Reserve Banks? The answer lies in the price of bonds and their interest yields. We know that bond prices and interest rates are inversely related. When the Fed buys government bonds, the demand for them increases. Government bond prices rise, and their interest yields decline. The higher bond prices and their lower interest yields prompt banks, securities firms, and individual holders of government bonds to sell them to the Federal Reserve Banks.

When the Fed sells government bonds, the additional supply of bonds in the bond market lowers bond prices and raises their interest yields, making government bonds attractive purchases for banks and the public.

The Reserve Ratio

The Fed can also manipulate the **reserve ratio** in order to influence the ability of commercial banks to lend. Suppose a commercial bank's balance sheet shows that reserves are $5000 and checkable deposits are $20,000. If the legal reserve ratio is 20 percent (row 2, Table 14.2), the bank's required reserves are $4000. Since actual reserves are $5000, the excess reserves of this bank are $1000. On the basis of $1000 of excess reserves, this one bank can lend $1000; however, the banking system as a whole can create a maximum of $5000 of new checkable-deposit money by lending (column 7).

Raising the Reserve Ratio Now, what if the Fed raised the reserve ratio from 20 to 25 percent? (See row 3.) Required reserves would jump from $4000 to $5000, shrinking excess reserves from $1000 to zero. Raising the reserve ratio increases the amount of required reserves banks must keep. As a consequence, either banks lose excess reserves, diminishing their ability to create money by lending, or they find their reserves deficient and are forced to

TABLE 14.2 The Effects of Changes in the Reserve Ratio on the Lending Ability of Commercial Banks

(1) Reserve Ratio, %	(2) Checkable Deposits	(3) Actual Reserves	(4) Required Reserves	(5) Excess Reserves, (3) − (4)	(6) Money-Creating Potential of Single Bank, = (5)	(7) Money-Creating Potential of Banking System
(1) 10	$20,000	$5000	$2000	$ 3000	$ 3000	$30,000
(2) 20	20,000	5000	4000	1000	1000	5000
(3) 25	20,000	5000	5000	0	0	0
(4) 30	20,000	5000	6000	−1000	−1000	−3333

contract checkable deposits and therefore the money supply. In the example in Table 14.2, excess reserves are transformed into required reserves, and the money-creating potential of our single bank is reduced from $1000 to zero (column 6). Moreover, the banking system's money-creating capacity declines from $5000 to zero (column 7).

What if the Fed increases the reserve requirement to 30 percent? (See row 4.) The commercial bank, to protect itself against the prospect of failing to meet this requirement, would be forced to lower its checkable deposits and at the same time increase its reserves. To reduce its checkable deposits, the bank could let outstanding loans mature and be repaid without extending new credit. To increase reserves, the bank might sell some of its bonds, adding the proceeds to its reserves. Both actions would reduce the supply of money.

Lowering the Reserve Ratio
What would happen if the Fed lowered the reserve ratio from the original 20 percent to 10 percent? (See row 1.) In this case, required reserves would decline from $4000 to $2000, and excess reserves would jump from $1000 to $3000. The single bank's lending (money-creating) ability would increase from $1000 to $3000 (column 6), and the banking system's money-creating potential would expand from $5000 to $30,000 (column 7). Lowering the reserve ratio transforms required reserves into excess reserves and enhances the ability of banks to create new money by lending.

The examples in Table 14.2 show that a change in the reserve ratio affects the money-creating ability of the *banking system* in two ways:

- It changes the amount of excess reserves.
- It changes the size of the monetary multiplier.

For example, when the legal reserve ratio is raised from 10 to 20 percent, excess reserves are reduced from $3000 to $1000 and the checkable-deposit multiplier is reduced from 10 to 5. The money-creating potential of the banking system declines from $30,000 (= $3000 × 10) to $5000 (= $1000 × 5). Raising the reserve ratio forces banks to reduce the amount of checkable deposits they create through lending.

The Discount Rate

One of the functions of a central bank is to be a "lender of last resort." Occasionally, commercial banks have unexpected and immediate needs for additional funds. In such cases, each Federal Reserve Bank will make short-term loans to commercial banks in its district.

When a commercial bank borrows, it gives the Federal Reserve Bank a promissory note (IOU) drawn against itself and secured by acceptable collateral—typically U.S. government securities. Just as commercial banks charge interest on their loans, so too Federal Reserve Banks charge interest on loans they grant to commercial banks. The interest rate they charge is called the **discount rate.**

As a claim against the commercial bank, the borrowing bank's promissory note is an asset to the lending Federal Reserve Bank and appears on its balance sheet as "Loans to commercial banks." To the commercial bank the IOU is a liability, appearing as "Loans from the Federal Reserve Banks" on the commercial bank's balance sheet. [See entries (*a*) on the balance sheets below.]

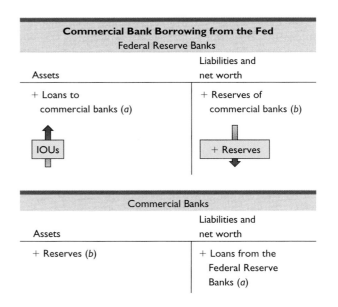

In providing the loan, the Federal Reserve Bank increases the reserves of the borrowing commercial bank. Since no required reserves need be kept against loans from Federal Reserve Banks, all new reserves acquired by borrowing from Federal Reserve Banks are excess reserves. [These changes are reflected in entries (*b*) on the balance sheets.]

In short, borrowing from the Federal Reserve Banks by commercial banks increases the reserves of the commercial banks and enhances their ability to extend credit.

The Fed has the power to set the discount rate at which commercial banks borrow from Federal Reserve Banks. From the commercial banks' point of view, the discount rate is a cost of acquiring reserves. A lowering of the discount rate encourages commercial banks to obtain additional reserves by borrowing from Federal Reserve Banks. When the commercial banks lend new reserves, the money supply increases.

An increase in the discount rate discourages commercial banks from obtaining additional reserves through borrowing from the Federal Reserve Banks. So the Fed may raise the discount rate when it wants to restrict the money supply. **(Key Question 5)**

Relative Importance

Of the three instruments of monetary control, buying and selling securities in the open market is clearly the most important. This technique has the advantage of flexibility—government securities can be purchased or sold daily in large or small amounts—and the impact on bank reserves is prompt. And, compared with reserve-requirement changes, open-market operations work subtly and less directly. Furthermore, the ability of the Federal Reserve Banks to affect commercial bank reserves through the purchase and sale of bonds is virtually unquestionable. The Federal Reserve Banks have very large holdings of government securities ($760 billion in early 2006, for example). The sale of those securities could theoretically reduce commercial bank reserves to zero.

Changing the reserve requirement is a less important instrument of monetary control, and the Fed has used this technique only sparingly. Normally, it can accomplish its monetary goals easier through open-market operations. The limited use of changes in the reserve ratio undoubtedly relates to the fact that reserves earn no interest. Consequently, raising or lowering reserve requirements has a substantial effect on bank profits. The last change in the reserve requirement was in 1992, when the Fed reduced the requirement from 12 percent to 10 percent. The main purpose was to shore up the profitability of banks and thrifts during recession rather than to increase reserves, expand the money supply, and reduce interest rates.

The discount rate has become a passive, not active, tool of monetary policy. The Fed now sets the discount rate at 1 percentage point above the Fed's targeted rate of interest on the overnight loans that commercial banks make to other commercial banks that need the funds to meet the required reserve ratio. When the interest rate on overnight loans rises or falls, the discount rate automatically rises or falls along with it. We will say more about interest rate on overnight loans next.

QUICK REVIEW 14.2

- The Fed has three main tools of monetary control, each of which works by changing the amount of reserves in the banking system: (a) conducting open-market operations (the Fed's buying and selling of government bonds to the banks and the public); (b) changing the reserve ratio (the percentage of commercial bank deposit liabilities required as reserves); and (c) changing the discount rate (the interest rate the Federal Reserve Banks charge on loans to banks and thrifts).
- Open-market operations are the Fed's monetary control mechanism of choice; the Fed rarely changes the reserve requirement and it now links the discount rate directly to the interest rate banks pay on overnight loans.

Targeting the Federal Funds Rate

The Federal Reserve focuses monetary policy on the interest rate that it can best control: the **Federal funds rate.** This is the rate of interest that banks charge one another on overnight loans made from temporary excess reserves. Recall from Chapter 13 that the Federal Reserve requires banks (and thrifts) to deposit in the regional Federal Reserve Bank a certain percentage of their checkable deposits as reserves. At the end of any business day, some banks temporarily have excess reserves (more actual reserves than required) and other banks have reserve deficiencies (fewer reserves than required). Because reserves held at the Federal Reserve Banks do not earn interest, banks desire to lend out their temporary excess reserves overnight to other banks that temporarily need them to meet their reserve requirements. The funds being lent and borrowed overnight are called "Federal funds" because they are reserves (funds) that are required by the Federal Reserve to meet reserve requirements. An equilibrium interest rate—the Federal funds rate—arises in this market for bank reserves.

Although individual banks can lend excess reserves to one another, the Federal Reserve is the only supplier of Federal funds—the currency used by banks as reserves. The Fed uses its status as a monopoly supplier of reserves

FIGURE 14.3 **Targeting the Federal funds rate** In implementing monetary policy, the Federal Reserve determines a desired Federal funds rate and then uses open-market operations (buying and selling of U.S. securities) to add or subtract bank reserves to achieve and maintain that targeted rate. In an expansionary monetary policy, the Fed increases the supply of reserves, for example, from S_{f1} to S_{f2} in this case, to move the Federal funds rate from 4 percent to 3.5 percent. In a restrictive monetary policy, it decreases the supply of reserves, say, from S_{f1} to S_{f3}. Here, the Federal fund rate rises from 4 percent to 4.5 percent.

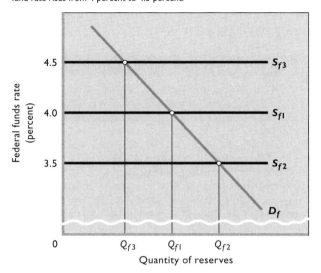

to target the specific Federal funds rate that it deems appropriate for the economy. The FOMC meets regularly to choose a desired Federal funds rate. It then directs the Federal Reserve Bank of New York to undertake open-market operations to achieve and maintain the targeted rate.

We demonstrate how this works in Figure 14.3, where we initially assume the Fed desires a 4 percent interest rate. The demand curve for Federal funds D_f is downsloping because lower interest rates give commercial banks a greater incentive to borrow Federal funds rather than reduce loans as a way to meet reserve requirements. The supply curve for Federal funds, S_{f1}, is somewhat unusual. Specifically, it is horizontal at the targeted Federal funds rate, here 4 percent. (Disregard supply curves S_{f2} and S_{f3} for now.) The Fed will use open-market operation to provide whatever level of Federal funds the banks desire to hold at the targeted 4 percent interest rate.

In this case, the Fed seeks to achieve an equilibrium Federal funds rate of 4 percent. In Figure 14.3 it is successful. Note that at the 4 percent Federal funds rate, the quantity of Federal funds supplied (Q_{f1}) equals the quantity of funds demanded (also Q_{f1}). This 4 percent Federal funds rate will remain, as long as the supply curve of Federal funds is horizontal at 4 percent. If the demand for Federal funds increases (D_f shifts to the right along S_{f1}), the Fed will use its open-market operations to increase the

availability of reserves such that the 4 percent Federal fund rate is retained. If the demand for Federal funds declines (D_f shifts to the left along S_{f1}), the Fed will withdraw reserves to keep the Federal funds rate at 4 percent.

Expansionary Monetary Policy

Suppose that the economy faces recession and unemployment. How will the Fed respond? It will initiate an **expansionary monetary policy** (or "easy money policy"). This policy will lower the interest rate to bolster borrowing and spending, which will increase aggregate demand and expand real output. The Fed's immediate step will be to announce a lower target for the Federal funds rate, say 3.5 percent instead of 4 percent. To achieve that lower rate the Fed will use open-market operations to buy bonds from banks and the public. We know from previous discussion that the purchase of bonds increases the reserves in the banking system. Alternatively, the Fed could expand reserves by lowering the reserve requirement or lowering the discount rate to achieve the same result, but we have seen that the former is rarely used and the latter is not presently used for *active* monetary policy.

The greater reserves in the banking system produce two critical results:

- The supply of Federal funds increases, lowering the Federal funds rate to the new targeted rate. We show this in Figure 14.3 as a downward shift to the horizontal supply curve from S_{f1} to S_{f2}. The equilibrium Federal funds rate falls to 3.5 percent, just as the FOMC wanted. The equilibrium quantity of reserves in the overnight market for reserves rises from Q_{f1} to Q_{f2}.

- A multiple expansion of the nation's money supply occurs (as we demonstrated in Chapter 13). Given the demand for money, the larger money supply places a downward pressure on other interest rates.

One such rate is the **prime interest rate**—the benchmark interest rate used by banks as a reference point for a wide range of interest rates charged on loans to businesses and individuals. The prime interest rate is higher than the Federal funds rate because the prime rate involves longer, more risky loans than overnight loans between banks. But the Federal funds rate and the prime interest rate closely track one another, as evident in Figure 14.4.

Restrictive Monetary Policy

The opposite monetary policy is in order for periods of rising inflation. The Fed will then undertake a **restrictive monetary policy** (or "tight money policy"). This policy will increase the interest rate in order to reduce borrowing and spending, which will curtail the expansion of aggregate

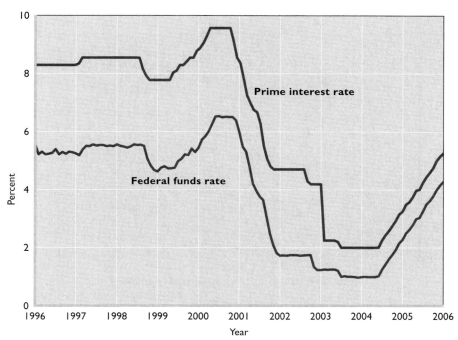

Source: Federal Reserve data, **www.federalreserve.gov/.**

FIGURE 14.4 The prime interest rate and the Federal funds rate in the United States, 1996–2006. The prime interest rate rises and falls with changes in the Federal funds rate.

demand and hold down price-level increases. The Fed's immediate step will be to announce a higher target for the Federal funds rate, say 4.5 percent instead of 4 percent. Through open-market operations, the Fed will sell bonds to the banks and the public and the sale of those bonds will absorb reserves in the banking system. Alternatively, the Fed could absorb reserves by raising the reserve requirement or raising the discount rate to achieve the same result, but we have seen that the former is rarely used and the latter is not presently used for *active* monetary policy.

The smaller reserves in the banking system produce two results opposite those discussed for an expansionary monetary policy:

- The supply of Federal funds decreases, raising the Federal funds rate to the new targeted rate. We show this in Figure 14.3 as an upward shift of the horizontal supply curve from S_{f1} to S_{f3}. The equilibrium Federal funds rate rises to 4.5 percent, just as the FOMC wanted, and the equilibrium quantity of funds in this market falls to Q_{f3}.
- A multiple contraction of the nation's money supply occurs (as demonstrated in Chapter 13). Given the demand for money, the smaller money supply places an upward pressure on other interest rates. For example, the prime interest rate rises.

CONSIDER THIS ...

The Fed as a Sponge

A good way to remember the role of the Fed in setting the Federal funds rate might be to imagine a bowl of water, with the amount of water in the bowl representing the stock of reserves in the banking system. Then think of the FOMC as having a large sponge, labeled open-market operations. When it wants to decrease the Federal funds rate, it uses the sponge—soaked with water (reserves) created by the Fed—to squeeze new reserves into the banking system bowl. It continues this process until the higher supply of reserves reduces the Federal funds rate to the Fed's desired level. If the Fed wants to increase the Federal funds rate, it uses the sponge to absorb reserves from the bowl (banking system). As the supply of reserves falls, the Federal funds rate rises to the Fed's desired level.

keygraph

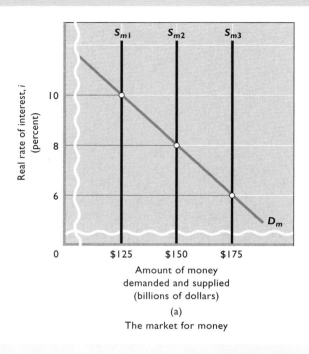

(a)

The market for money

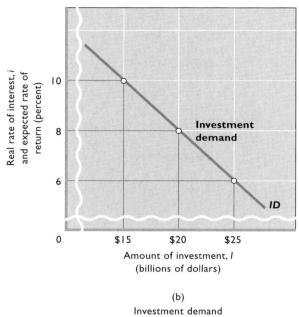

(b)

Investment demand

The Taylor Rule

The proper Federal funds rate for a certain period is a matter of policy discretion by the members of the FOMC. The FOMC does not adhere to a strict inflationary target or monetary policy rule. It targets the Federal funds rate at the level it thinks is appropriate for the underlying economic conditions. Nevertheless, the Fed appears to roughly follow a rule first established by economist John Taylor of Stanford. The **Taylor rule** assumes a 2 percent target rate of inflation and has three parts:

- If real GDP rises by 1 percent above potential GDP, the Fed should raise the Federal funds rate by $\frac{1}{2}$ a percentage point.
- If inflation rises by 1 percentage point above its

target of 2 percent, then the Fed should raise the Federal funds rate by $\frac{1}{2}$ a percentage point.
- When real GDP is equal to potential GDP and inflation is equal to its target rate of 2 percent, the Federal funds rate should remain at about 4 percent, which would imply a real interest rate of 2 percent.

These rules are reversible for situations in which the real GDP falls below potential GDP and the rate of inflation falls below 2 percent. But it is crucial to point out that the Fed has shown a clear willingness to diverge from the Taylor rule under some circumstances. One such occasion occurred when the slow recovery from the 2001 recession raised concerns about potential deflation.

W 14.4

Taylor rule

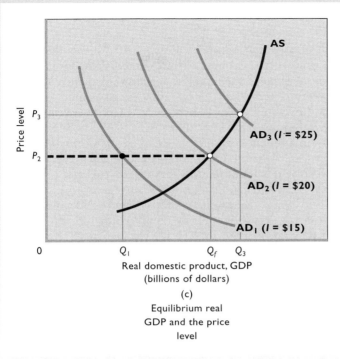

FIGURE 14.5 Monetary policy and equilibrium GDP. An expansionary monetary policy that shifts the money supply curve rightward from S_{m1} to S_{m2} lowers the interest rate from 10 to 8 percent. As a result, investment spending increases from $15 billion to $20 billion, shifting the aggregate demand curve rightward from AD_1 to AD_2, and real output rises from the recessionary level Q_1 to the full-employment level Q_f. A restrictive monetary policy that shifts the money supply curve leftward from S_{m3} to S_{m2} increases the interest rate from 6 to 8 percent. Investment spending thus falls from $25 billion to $20 billion, and the aggregate demand curve shifts leftward from AD_3 to AD_2, curtailing inflation.

d. S_{m3} to S_{m2}, a decrease in investment from $25 billion to $20 billion, and an increase in aggregate demand from AD_2 to AD_3.

3. The Federal Reserve could increase the money supply from S_{m1} to S_{m2} by:
   a. increasing the discount rate.
   b. reducing taxes.
   c. buying government securities in the open market.
   d. increasing the reserve requirement.

4. If the spending-income multiplier is 4 in the economy depicted, an increase in the money supply from $125 billion to $150 billion will:
   a. shift the aggregate demand curve rightward by $20 billion.
   b. increase real GDP by $25 billion.
   c. increase real GDP by $100 billion.
   d. shift the aggregate demand curve leftward by $5 billion.

Answers: 1. d; 2. c; 3. c; 4. a

Monetary Policy, Real GDP, and the Price Level

G 14.2

Monetary policy

We have identified and explained the tools of expansionary and contractionary monetary policy. We now want to emphasize how monetary policy affects the economy's levels of investment, aggregate demand, real GDP, and prices.

Cause-Effect Chain

The three diagrams in **Figure 14.5 (Key Graph)** will help you understand how monetary policy works toward achieving its goals.

Market for Money

Figure 14.5a represents the market for money, in which the demand curve for money and the supply curve of money are brought together. Recall that the total demand for money is made up of the transactions and asset demands.

This figure also shows three potential money supply curves, S_{m1}, S_{m2}, and S_{m3}. In each case the money supply is shown as a vertical line representing some fixed amount of money determined by the Fed. While monetary policy (specifically, the supply of money) helps determine the interest rate, the interest rate does not determine the location of the money supply curve.

The equilibrium interest rate is the rate at which the amount of money demanded and the amount supplied are equal. With money demand D_m in Figure 14.5a, if the supply of money is $125 billion ($S_{m1}$), the equilibrium interest rate is 10 percent. With a money supply of $150 billion ($S_{m2}$), the equilibrium interest rate is 8 percent; with a money supply of $175 billion ($S_{m3}$), it is 6 percent.

You know from Chapter 8 that the real, not the nominal, rate of interest is critical for investment decisions. So here we assume that Figure 14.5a portrays real interest rates.

Investment

These 10, 8, and 6 percent real interest rates are carried rightward to the investment demand curve in Figure 14.5b. This curve shows the inverse relationship between the interest rate—the cost of borrowing to invest—and the amount of investment spending. At the 10 percent interest rate it will be profitable for the nation's businesses to invest $15 billion; at 8 percent, $20 billion; at 6 percent, $25 billion.

Changes in the interest rate mainly affect the investment component of total spending, although they also affect spending on durable consumer goods (such as autos) that are purchased on credit. The impact of changing interest rates on investment spending is great because of the large cost and long-term nature of capital purchases. Capital equipment, factory buildings, and warehouses are tremendously expensive. In absolute terms, interest charges on funds borrowed for these purchases are considerable.

Similarly, the interest cost on a house purchased on a long-term contract is very large: A $\frac{1}{2}$-percentage-point change in the interest rate could amount to thousands of dollars in the total cost of a home.

In brief, the impact of changing interest rates is mainly on investment (and, through that, on aggregate demand, output, employment, and the price level). Moreover, as

Figure 14.5b shows, investment spending varies inversely with the real interest rate.

Equilibrium GDP

Figure 14.5c shows the impact of our three real interest rates and corresponding levels of investment spending on aggregate demand. As noted, aggregate demand curve AD_1 is associated with the $15 billion level of investment, AD_2 with investment of $20 billion, and AD_3 with investment of $25 billion. That is, investment spending is one of the determinants of aggregate demand. Other things equal, the greater the investment spending, the farther to the right lies the aggregate demand curve.

Suppose the money supply in Figure 14.5a is $150 billion ($S_{m2}$), producing an equilibrium interest rate of 8 percent. In Figure 14.5b we see that this 8 percent interest rate will bring forth $20 billion of investment spending. This $20 billion of investment spending joins with consumption spending, net exports, and government spending to yield aggregate demand curve AD_2 in Figure 14.5c. The equilibrium levels of real output and prices are Q_f and P_2, as determined by the intersection of AD_2 and the aggregate supply curve AS.

To test your understanding of these relationships, explain why each of the other two levels of money supply in Figure 14.5a results in a different interest rate, level of investment, aggregate demand curve, and equilibrium real output.

Effects of an Expansionary Monetary Policy

Next, suppose that the money supply is $125 billion ($S_{m1}$) in Figure 14.5a. Because the resulting real output Q_1 in Figure 14.5c is far below the full-employment output, Q_f, the economy must be experiencing recession, a negative GDP gap, and substantial unemployment. The Fed therefore should institute an expansionary monetary policy.

To increase the money supply, the Federal Reserve Banks will take some combination of the following actions: (1) Buy government securities from banks and the public in the open market, (2) lower the legal reserve ratio, and (3) lower the discount rate. The intended outcome will be an increase in excess reserves in the commercial banking system and a decline in the Federal funds rate. Because excess reserves are the basis on which commercial banks and thrifts can earn profit by lending and thus creating checkable-deposit money, the nation's money supply will rise. An increase in the money supply will lower the interest rate, increasing investment, aggregate demand, and equilibrium GDP.

TABLE 14.3 Monetary Policies for Recession and Inflation

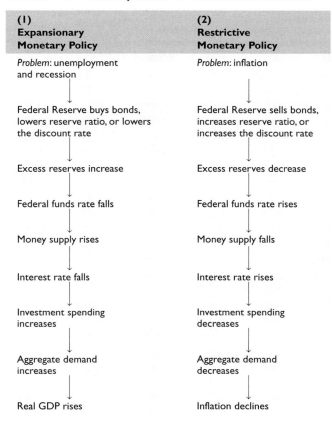

(1) Expansionary Monetary Policy	(2) Restrictive Monetary Policy
Problem: unemployment and recession	*Problem:* inflation
↓	↓
Federal Reserve buys bonds, lowers reserve ratio, or lowers the discount rate	Federal Reserve sells bonds, increases reserve ratio, or increases the discount rate
↓	↓
Excess reserves increase	Excess reserves decrease
↓	↓
Federal funds rate falls	Federal funds rate rises
↓	↓
Money supply rises	Money supply falls
↓	↓
Interest rate falls	Interest rate rises
↓	↓
Investment spending increases	Investment spending decreases
↓	↓
Aggregate demand increases	Aggregate demand decreases
↓	↓
Real GDP rises	Inflation declines

For example, an increase in the money supply from $125 billion to $150 billion ($S_{m1}$ to S_{m2}) will reduce the interest rate from 10 to 8 percent, as indicated in Figure 14.5a, and will boost investment from $15 billion to $20 billion, as shown in Figure 14.5b. This $5 billion increase in investment will shift the aggregate demand curve rightward by more than the increase in investment because of the multiplier effect. If the economy's MPC is .75, the multiplier will be 4, meaning that the $5 billion increase in investment will shift the AD curve rightward by $20 billion (= 4 × $5) at each price level. Specifically, aggregate demand will shift from AD₁ to AD₂, as shown in Figure 14.5c. This rightward shift in the aggregate demand curve will eliminate the negative GDP gap by increasing GDP from Q_1 to the full-employment GDP of Q_f.[1]

Column 1 in Table 14.3 summarizes the chain of events associated with an expansionary monetary policy.

Effects of a Restrictive Monetary Policy

Now let's assume that the money supply is $175 billion ($S_{m3}$) in Figure 14.2a. This results in an interest rate of 6 percent, investment spending of $25 billion, and aggregate demand AD₃. As you can see in Figure 14.5c, we have depicted a positive GDP gap of $Q_3 - Q_f$ and demand-pull inflation. Aggregate demand AD₃ is excessive relative to the economy's full-employment level of real output Q_f. To rein in spending, the Fed will institute a restrictive monetary money policy.

The Federal Reserve Board will direct Federal Reserve Banks to undertake some combination of the following actions: (1) Sell government securities to banks and the public in the open market, (2) increase the legal reserve ratio, and (3) increase the discount rate. Banks then will discover that their reserves are below those required and that the Federal funds rate has increased. So they will need to reduce their checkable deposits by refraining from issuing new loans as old loans are paid back. This will shrink the money supply and increase the interest rate. The higher interest rate will discourage investment, lowering aggregate demand and restraining demand-pull inflation.

If the Fed reduces the money supply from $175 billion to $150 billion ($S_{m3}$ to S_{m2} in Figure 14.5a), the interest rate will rise from 6 to 8 percent and investment will decline from $25 billion to $20 billion (Figure 14.5b). This $5 billion decrease in investment, bolstered by the multiplier process, will shift the aggregate demand curve leftward from AD₃ to AD₂. For example, if the MPC is .75, the multiplier will be 4 and the aggregate demand curve will shift leftward by $20 billion (= 4 × $5 billion of investment) at each price level. This leftward shift of the aggregate demand curve will eliminate the excessive spending and thus the demand-pull inflation. In the real world, of course, the goal will be to stop inflation—that is, to halt further increases in the price level—rather than to actually drive down the price level.[2]

Column 2 in Table 14.3 summarizes the cause-effect chain of a tight money policy.

---

[1]To keep things simple, we assume that the increase in real GDP does not increase the demand for money. In reality, the transactions demand for money would rise, slightly dampening the decline in the interest rate shown in Figure 14.5a.

[2]Again, we assume for simplicity that the decrease in nominal GDP does not feed back to reduce the demand for money and thus the interest rate. In reality, this would occur, slightly dampening the increase in the interest rate shown in Figure 14.5a.

Monetary Policy: Evaluation and Issues

Monetary policy has become the dominant component of U.S. national stabilization policy. It has two key advantages over fiscal policy:

- Speed and flexibility.
- Isolation from political pressure.

Compared with fiscal policy, monetary policy can be quickly altered. Recall that congressional deliberations may delay the application of fiscal policy for months. In contrast, the Fed can buy or sell securities from day to day and thus affect the money supply and interest rates almost immediately.

Also, because members of the Fed's Board of Governors are appointed and serve 14-year terms, they are relatively isolated from lobbying and need not worry about retaining their popularity with voters. Thus, the Board, more readily than Congress, can engage in politically unpopular policies (higher interest rates) that may be necessary for the long-term health of the economy. Moreover, monetary policy is a subtler and more politically conservative measure than fiscal policy. Changes in government spending directly affect the allocation of resources, and changes in taxes can have extensive political ramifications. Because monetary policy works more subtly, it is more politically palatable.

Recent U.S. Monetary Policy

In the early 1990s, the Fed's expansionary monetary policy helped the economy recover from the 1990–1991 recession. The expansion of GDP that began in 1992 continued through the rest of the decade. By 2000 the U.S. unemployment rate had declined to 4 percent—the lowest rate in 30 years. To counter potential inflation during that strong expansion, in 1994 and 1995, and then again in early 1997, the Fed reduced reserves in the banking system to raise the interest rate. In 1998 the Fed temporarily reversed its course and moved to a more expansionary monetary policy to make sure that the U.S. banking system had plenty of liquidity in the face of a severe financial crisis in southeast Asia. The economy continued to expand briskly, and in 1999 and 2000 the Fed, in a series of steps, boosted interest rates to make sure that inflation remained under control.

Significant inflation did not occur in the late 1990s. But in the last quarter of 2000 the economy abruptly slowed. The Fed responded by cutting interest rates by a full percentage point in two increments in January 2001. Despite these rate cuts, the economy entered a recession in March 2001. Between March 20, 2001, and August 21, 2001, the Fed cut the Federal funds rate from 5 percent to 3.5 percent in a series of steps. In the 3 months following the terrorist attacks of September 11, 2001, it lowered the Federal funds rate from 3.5 percent to 1.75 percent, and it left the rate there until it lowered it to 1.25 percent in November 2002. Partly because of the Fed's actions, the prime interest rate dropped from 9.5 percent at the end of 2000 to 4.25 percent in December 2002.

Economists generally credit the Fed's adroit use of monetary policy as one of a number of factors that helped the U.S. economy achieve and maintain the rare combination of full employment, price-level stability, and strong economic growth that occurred between 1996 and 2000. The Fed also deserves high marks for helping to keep the recession of 2001 relatively mild, particularly in view of the adverse economic impacts of the terrorist attacks of September 11, 2001, and the steep stock market drop in 2001–2002.

In 2003 the Fed left the Federal funds rate at historic lows. But as the economy began to expand robustly in 2004, the Fed engineered a series of five separate $\frac{1}{4}$-percentage-point hikes in the Federal funds rate. It continued to raise the rate throughout 2005. At the end of 2005 the rate stood at 4.25 percent. The purpose of the rate hikes was to boost the prime interest rate (7.25 percent at the end of 2005) and other interest rates to make sure that aggregate demand continued to grow at a pace consistent with low inflation. In that regard, the Fed was successful. (To see the latest direction of the targeted Federals funds rate, go to the Federal Reserve's Web site, **www.federalreserve.gov,** and select Monetary Policy and then Open Market Operations.)

Problems and Complications

Despite its recent successes in the United States, monetary policy has certain limitations and faces real-world complications.

Lags Recall that three elapses of time (lags)—a recognition lag, an administrative lag, and an operational lag—hinder the timing of fiscal policy. Monetary policy faces a similar recognition lag and also an operational lag, but it avoids the administrative lag. Because of monthly variations in economic activity and changes in the price level, the Fed may take a while to recognize that the economy is receding or the rate of inflation is rising (recognition lag). And once the Fed acts, it may take 3 to 6 months or more for interest-rate changes to have their full impacts on investment, aggregate demand, real GDP, and the price level (operational lag). These two lags thus complicate the timing of monetary policy.

Cyclical Asymmetry

Monetary policy may be highly effective in slowing expansions and controlling inflation but less reliable in pushing the economy from a severe recession. Economists say that monetary policy may suffer from **cyclical asymmetry.**

If pursued vigorously, a restrictive monetary policy could deplete commercial banking reserves to the point where banks would be forced to reduce the volume of loans. That would mean a contraction of the money supply, higher interest rates, and reduced aggregate demand. The Fed can absorb reserves and eventually achieve its goal.

But it cannot be certain of achieving its goal when it adds reserves to the banking system. An expansionary monetary policy suffers from a "You can lead a horse to water, but you can't make it drink" problem. The Fed can create excess reserves, but it cannot guarantee that the banks will actually make the added loans and thus increase the supply of money. If commercial banks seek liquidity and are unwilling to lend, the efforts of the Fed will be of little avail. Similarly, businesses can frustrate the intentions of the Fed by not borrowing excess reserves. And the public may use money paid to them through Fed sales of U.S. securities to pay off existing bank loans.

Furthermore, a severe recession may so undermine business confidence that the investment demand curve shifts to the left and frustrates an expansionary monetary policy. That is what happened in Japan in the 1990s and early 2000s. Although its central bank drove the real interest rate to 0 percent, investment spending remained low and the Japanese economy stayed mired in recession. In fact, deflation—a fall in the price level—occurred. The Japanese experience reminds us that monetary policy is not an assured cure for the business cycle.

In March 2003 some members of the Fed's Open Market Committee expressed concern about potential deflation in the United States if the economy remained weak. But the economy soon began to vigorously expand, and deflation did not occur.

"Artful Management" or "Inflation Targeting"?

Under the leadership of Alan Greenspan, the Fed and FOMC artfully managed the money supply to avoid escalating inflation, on the one hand, and deep recession and deflation, on the other. The emphasis was on "risk management" and achieving a multiple set of objectives: primarily to maintain price stability but also to smooth the business cycle, maintain high levels of employment, and promote strong economic growth. Greenspan and the FOMC used their best judgment (and, some suggest, Greenspan's personal intuition) to determine appropriate changes in monetary policy. But Greenspan retired in early 2006 and was replaced by Ben Bernanke as chairman of the Federal Reserve Board. Does Bernanke—or anyone for that matter—have Greenspan's intuition?

Some economists are concerned that this "artful management" may have been unique to Greenspan and

---

CONSIDER THIS . . .

Pushing on a String

In the late 1990s and early 2000s, the central bank of Japan used an expansionary monetary policy to reduce real interest rates to zero. Even with "interest-free" loans available, most consumers and businesses did not borrow and spend more. Japan's economy continued to sputter in and out of recession.

The Japanese circumstance illustrates the possible *asymmetry* of monetary policy, which economists have likened to "pulling versus pushing on a string." A string may be effective at pulling something back to a desirable spot, but it is ineffective at pushing it toward a desired location.

So it is with monetary policy, say some economists. Monetary policy can readily *pull* the aggregate demand curve to the left, reducing demand-pull inflation. There is no limit on how much a central bank can restrict a nation's money supply and hike interest rates. Eventually, a sufficiently restrictive monetary policy will reduce aggregate demand and inflation.

But during severe recession, participants in the economy may be highly pessimistic about the future. If so, an expansionary monetary policy may not be able to push the aggregate demand curve to the right, increasing real GDP. The central bank can produce excess reserves in the banking system by reducing the reserve ratio, lowering the discount rate, and purchasing government securities. But commercial banks may not be able to find willing borrowers for those excess reserves, no matter how low interest rates fall. Instead of borrowing and spending, consumers and businesses may be more intent on reducing debt and increasing saving in preparation for expected worse times ahead. If so, monetary policy will be ineffective. Using it under those circumstances will be much like pushing on a string.

keygraph

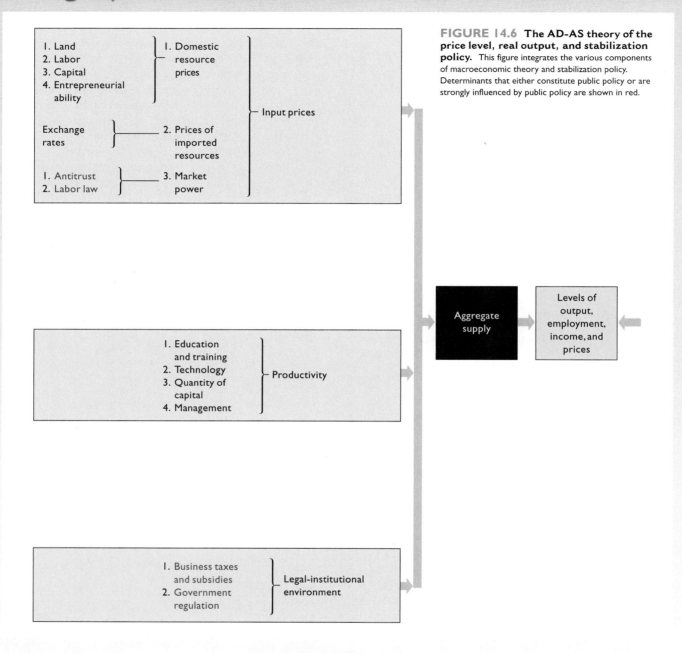

FIGURE 14.6 **The AD-AS theory of the price level, real output, and stabilization policy.** This figure integrates the various components of macroeconomic theory and stabilization policy. Determinants that either constitute public policy or are strongly influenced by public policy are shown in red.

QUICK QUIZ 14.6

1. All else equal, an increase in domestic resource availability will:
   a. increase input prices, reduce aggregate supply, and increase real output.
   b. raise labor productivity, reduce interest rates, and lower the international value of the dollar.
   c. increase net exports, increase investment, and reduce aggregate demand.
   d. reduce input prices, increase aggregate supply, and increase real output.

2. All else equal, an expansionary monetary policy during a recession will:
   a. lower the interest rate, increase investment, and reduce net exports.
   b. lower the interest rate, increase investment, and increase aggregate demand.
   c. increase the interest rate, increase investment, and reduce net exports.
   d. reduce productivity, aggregate supply, and real output.

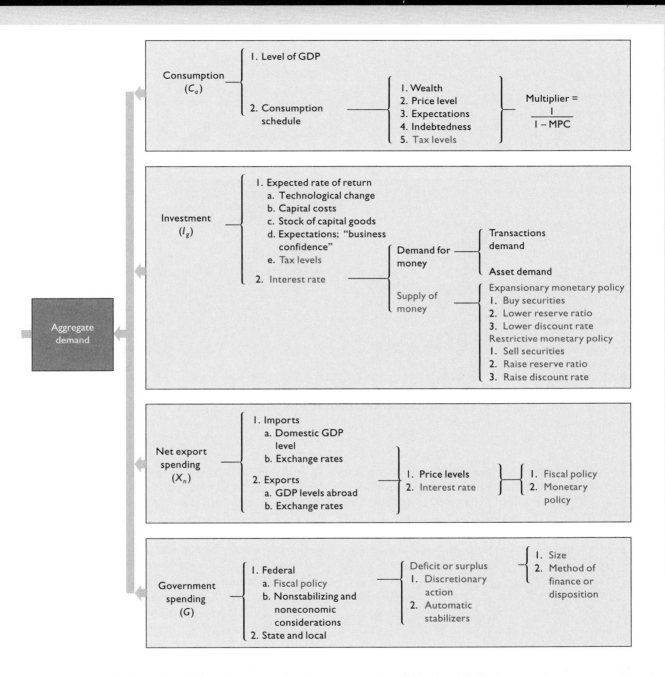

3. A personal income tax cut, combined with a reduction in corporate income and excise taxes, would:
   a. increase consumption, investment, aggregate demand, and aggregate supply.
   b. reduce productivity, raise input prices, and reduce aggregate supply.
   c. increase government spending, reduce net exports, and increase aggregate demand.
   d. increase the supply of money, reduce interest rates, increase investment, and expand real output.

4. An appreciation of the dollar would:
   a. reduce the price of imported resources, lower input prices, and increase aggregate supply.
   b. increase net exports and aggregate demand.
   c. increase aggregate supply and aggregate demand.
   d. reduce consumption, investment, net export spending, and government spending.

For the Fed, Life Is a Metaphor

The Popular Press Often Describes the Federal Reserve Board and Its Chair (Ben Bernanke) in Colorful Terms:

The Federal Reserve Board leads a very dramatic life, or so it seems when one reads journalistic accounts of its activities. It loosens or tightens reins while riding herd on a rambunctious economy, goes to the rescue of an embattled dollar, tightens spigots on credit . . . you get the picture. For the Fed, life is a metaphor.

The Fed as Mechanic The Fed sometimes must roll up its sleeves and adjust the economic machinery. The Fed spends a lot of time tightening things, loosening things, or debating about whether to tighten or loosen.

Imagine a customer taking his car into Bernanke's Garage:

Normally calm, Bernanke took one look at the car and started to sweat. This would be hard to fix—it was an economy car:

"What's the problem?" asked Bernanke.

"It's been running beautifully for over 6 years now," said the customer. "But recently it's been acting sluggish."

"These cars are tricky," said Bernanke. "We can always loosen a few screws, as long as you don't mind the side effects."

"What side effects?" asked the customer.

"Nothing at first," said Bernanke. "We won't even know if the repairs have worked for at least a year. After that, either everything will be fine, or your car will accelerate wildly and go totally out of control."

"Just as long as it doesn't stall," said the customer. "I hate that."

that someone less insightful may not be as successful. These economists, including Bernanke, say it might be beneficial to replace or combine the artful management of monetary policy with so-called **inflation targeting**— the annual statement of a target range of inflation, say, 1 to 2 percent, for the economy over some period such as 2 years. The Fed would then undertake monetary policy to achieve that goal, explaining to the public how each monetary action fits within its overall strategy. If the Fed missed its target, it would need to explain what went wrong. So inflation targeting would increase the "transparency" (openness) of monetary policy and increase Fed accountability. Several countries, including Canada, New Zealand, Sweden, and the United Kingdom, have adopted inflation targeting.

Proponents of inflation targeting say that, along with increasing transparency and accountability, it would focus the Fed on what should be its main mission: controlling inflation and keeping deflation from occurring. They say that an explicit commitment to price-level stability will create more certainty for households and firms about future product and input prices and create greater output

stability. In the advocates' view, setting and meeting an inflation target is the single best way for the Fed to achieve its important subsidiary goals of full employment and strong economic growth.

But some economists are relatively unconvinced by the arguments for inflation targeting. They say that the overall success of the countries that have adopted the policy has come at a time in which inflationary pressures, in general, have been weak. The truer test will occur under more severe economic conditions. Critics of inflation targeting say that it assigns too narrow a role for the Fed. They do not want to limit the Fed's discretion to adjust the money supply and interest rates to smooth the business cycle, independent of meeting a specific inflation target. Those who oppose inflation targeting say the recent U.S. monetary policy owes its success to adherence to sound principles of monetary policy, not simply to special intuition. In fact, the Fed has kept the rate of inflation generally lower than have the central banks in nations that use inflation targeting. In view of this overall success, ask critics, why saddle the Fed with an explicit inflation target? **(Key Question 8)**

The Fed as Warrior The Fed must fight inflation. But can it wage a protracted war? There are only seven Fed governors, including Bernanke—not a big army:

Gen. Bernanke sat in the war room plotting strategy. You never knew where the enemy would strike next—producer prices, retail sales, factory payrolls, manufacturing inventories.

Suddenly, one of his staff officers burst into the room: "Straight from the Western European front, sir—the dollar is under attack by the major industrial nations."

Bernanke whirled around toward the big campaign map. "We've got to turn back this assault!" he said.

"Yes sir. "The officer turned to go.

"Hold it!" Bernanke shouted. Suddenly, his mind reeled with conflicting data. A strong dollar was good for inflation, right? Yes, but it was bad for the trade deficit. Or was it the other way around? Attack? Retreat? Macroeconomic forces were closing in.

"Call out the Reserve!" he told the officer.

"Uh . . . we are the Reserve," the man answered.

The Fed as the Fall Guy Inflation isn't the only tough customer out there. The Fed must also withstand pressure from administration officials who are regularly described as "leaning heavily" on the Fed to ease up and relax. This always sounds vaguely threatening:

Ben Bernanke was walking down a deserted street late one night. Suddenly a couple of thugs wearing pin-stripes and wing-tips cornered him in a dark alley.

"What do you want?" Bernanke asked.

"Just relax," said one.

"How can I relax?" asked Bernanke. "I'm in a dark alley talking to thugs."

"You know what we mean," said the other. "Ease up on the Federal funds rate—or else."

"Or else what?" asked Bernanke.

"Don't make us spell it out. Let's just say that if anything unfortunate happens to the gross domestic product, I'm holding you personally responsible."

"Yeah," added the other. "A recession could get real painful."

The Fed as Cosmic Force The Fed may be a cosmic force. After all, it does satisfy the three major criteria—power, mystery, and a New York office. Some observers even believe the Fed can control the stock market, either by action, symbolic action, anticipated action, or non-action. But saner heads realize this is ridiculous—the market has always been controlled by sunspots.

I wish we could get rid of all these romantic ideas about the Federal Reserve. If you want to talk about the Fed, keep it simple. Just say the Fed is worried about the money. This is something we all can relate to.

Source: Paul Hellman, "Greenspan and the Feds: Captains Courageous," *The Wall Street Journal*, Jan. 31, 1991, p. 18. Reprinted with permission of *The Wall Street Journal*, © 1990 Dow Jones & Company, Inc. All rights reserved. Updated by text authors.

QUICK REVIEW 14.4

- The Fed is engaging in an expansionary monetary policy when it increases the money supply to reduce interest rates and increase investment spending and real GDP; it is engaging in a restrictive monetary policy when it reduces the money supply to increase interest rates and reduce investment spending and inflation.
- The main strengths of monetary policy are (a) speed and flexibility and (b) political acceptability; its main weaknesses are (a) time lags and (b) potential ineffectiveness during severe recession.
- The Fed's "artful management" of monetary policy has been highly successful in recent years, but some economists contend that this approach should be replaced or combined with explicit inflation targeting.

The "Big Picture"

Figure 14.6 (Key Graph) on pages 276 and 277 brings together the analytical and policy aspects of macroeconomics discussed in this and the eight preceding chapters.

This "big picture" shows how the many concepts and principles discussed relate to one another and how they constitute a coherent theory of the price level and real output in a market economy.

Study this diagram and you will see that the levels of output, employment, income, and prices all result from the interaction of aggregate supply and aggregate demand. The items shown in red relate to public policy.

Summary

1. The goal of monetary policy is to help the economy achieve price stability, full employment, and economic growth.

2. The total demand for money consists of the transactions demand and asset demand for money. The amount of money demanded for transactions varies directly with the nominal GDP; the amount of money demanded as an asset varies directly with the interest rate. The market for money combines the total demand for money with the money supply to determine equilibrium interest rates.

3. Interest rates and bond prices are inversely related.

4. The three available instruments of monetary policy are (a) open-market operations, (b) the reserve ratio, and (c) the discount rate.

5. The Federal funds rate is the interest rate that banks charge one another for overnight loans of reserves. The prime interest rate is the benchmark rate that banks use as a reference rate for a wide range of interest rates on short-term loans to businesses and individuals.

6. The Fed adjusts the Federal funds rate to a level appropriate for economic conditions. In an expansionary monetary policy, it purchases securities from commercial banks and the general public to inject reserves into the banking system. This lowers the Federal funds rate to the targeted level and also reduces other interest rates (such as the prime rate). In a restrictive monetary policy, the Fed sells securities to commercial banks and the general public via open-market operations. Consequently, reserves are removed from the banking system, and the Federal funds rate and other interest rates rise.

7. Monetary policy affects the economy through a complex cause-effect chain: (a) Policy decisions affect commercial bank reserves; (b) changes in reserves affect the money supply; (c) changes in the money supply alter the interest rate; (d) changes in the interest rate affect investment; (e) changes in investment affect aggregate demand; (f) changes in aggregate demand affect the equilibrium real GDP and the price level. Table 14.3 draws together all the basic ideas relevant to the use of monetary policy.

8. The advantages of monetary policy include its flexibility and political acceptability. In the recent past, the Fed has adroitly used monetary policy to hold inflation in check as the economy boomed, to limit the depth of the recession of 2001, and to promote economic recovery. Today, nearly all economists view monetary policy as a significant stabilization tool.

9. Monetary policy has two major limitations and potential problems: (a) Recognition and operation lags complicate the timing of monetary policy. (b) In a severe recession, the reluctance of firms to borrow and spend on capital goods may limit the effectiveness of an expansionary monetary policy.

10. Some economists recommend that the United States follow the lead of several other nations, including Canada and the United Kingdom, in replacing or combining the "artful management" of monetary policy with inflation targeting. Opponents of this idea believe it may unduly reduce the Fed's flexibility in smoothing business cycles.

Terms and Concepts

monetary policy	open-market operations	prime interest rate
interest	reserve ratio	restrictive monetary policy
transactions demand	discount rate	Taylor rule
asset demand	Federal funds rate	cyclical asymmetry
total demand for money	expansionary monetary policy	inflation targeting

Study Questions

1. **KEY QUESTION** What is the basic determinant of (a) the transactions demand and (b) the asset demand for money? Explain how these two demands can be combined graphically to determine total money demand. How is the equilibrium interest rate in the money market determined? Use a graph to show the impact of an increase in the total demand for money on the equilibrium interest rate (no change in money supply). Use your general knowledge of equilibrium prices to explain why the previous interest rate is no longer sustainable.

2. **KEY QUESTION** Assume that the following data characterize a hypothetical economy: money supply = $200 billion; quantity of money demanded for transactions = $150 billion; quantity of money demanded as an asset = $10 billion at 12 percent interest, increasing by $10 billion for each 2-percentage-point fall in the interest rate.
   a. What is the equilibrium interest rate? Explain.
   b. At the equilibrium interest rate, what are the quantity of money supplied, the total quantity of money

demanded, the amount of money demanded for transactions, and the amount of money demanded as an asset?

3. **KEY QUESTION** Suppose a bond with no expiration date has a face value of $10,000 and annually pays a fixed amount of interest of $800. Compute and enter in the spaces provided in the accompanying table either the interest rate that the bond would yield to a bond buyer at each of the bond prices listed or the bond price at each of the interest yields shown. What generalization can be drawn from the completed table?

Bond Price	Interest Yield, %
$ 8,000	_____
_____	8.9
$10,000	_____
$11,000	_____
_____	6.2

4. Use commercial bank and Federal Reserve Bank balance sheets to demonstrate the impact of each of the following transactions on commercial bank reserves:
   a. Federal Reserve Banks purchase securities from banks.
   b. Commercial banks borrow from Federal Reserve Banks.
   c. The Fed reduces the reserve ratio.

5. **KEY QUESTION** In the accompanying table you will find consolidated balance sheets for the commercial banking system and the 12 Federal Reserve Banks. Use columns 1 through 3 to indicate how the balance sheets would read after each of transactions *a* to *c* is completed. Do not cumulate your answers; that is, analyze each transaction separately, starting in each case from the figures provided. All accounts are in billions of dollars.
   a. A decline in the discount rate prompts commercial banks to borrow an additional $1 billion from the Federal Reserve Banks. Show the new balance-sheet figures in column 1 of each table.
   b. The Federal Reserve Banks sell $3 billion in securities to members of the public, who pay for the bonds with checks. Show the new balance-sheet figures in column 2 of each table.
   c. The Federal Reserve Banks buy $2 billion of securities from commercial banks. Show the new balance-sheet figures in column 3 of each table.
   d. Now review each of the above three transactions, asking yourself these three questions: (1) What change, if any, took place in the money supply as a direct and immediate result of each transaction? (2) What increase or decrease in the commercial banks' reserves took place in each transaction? (3) Assuming a reserve ratio of

	Consolidated Balance Sheet: All Commercial Banks		
	(1)	(2)	(3)
Assets:			
Reserves	$ 33	_____	_____	_____
Securities	60	_____	_____	_____
Loans	60	_____	_____	_____
Liabilities and net worth:			
Checkable deposits	$150	_____	_____	_____
Loans from the Federal Reserve Banks	3	_____	_____	_____

	Consolidated Balance Sheet: The 12 Federal Reserve Banks		
	(1)	(2)	(3)
Assets:			
Securities	$60	_____	_____	_____
Loans to commercial banks	3	_____	_____	_____
Liabilities and net worth:			
Reserves of commercial banks	$33	_____	_____	_____
Treasury deposits	3	_____	_____	_____
Federal Reserve Notes	27	_____	_____	_____

20 percent, what change in the money-creating potential of the commercial banking system occurred as a result of each transaction?

6. What is the basic objective of monetary policy? What are the major strengths of monetary policy? Why is monetary policy easier to conduct than fiscal policy in a highly divided national political environment?

7. Distinguish between the Federal funds rate and the prime interest rate. Why is one higher than the other? Why do changes in the two rates closely track one another?

8. **KEY QUESTION** Suppose that you are a member of the Board of Governors of the Federal Reserve System. The economy is experiencing a sharp rise in the inflation rate. What change in the Federal funds rate would you recommend? How would your recommended change get accomplished? What impact would the actions have on the lending ability of the banking system, the real interest rate, investment spending, aggregate demand, and inflation?

9. Suppose that the Federal funds rate is 4 percent and real GDP falls 2 percent below potential GDP. Acording to the Taylor rule, in what direction and by how much should the Fed change the Federal funds rate?

10. Explain the links between changes in the nation's money supply, the interest rate, investment spending, aggregate demand, and real GDP (and the price level).

11. What do economists mean when they say that monetary policy can exhibit cyclical asymmetry? Why is this possibility significant to policymakers?

12. What is "inflation targeting," and how does it differ from "artful management"? What are the main benefits of inflation targeting, according to its supporters? Why do many economists think it is unnecessary or even undesirable?

13. **LAST WORD** How do each of the following metaphors apply to the Federal Reserve's role in the economy: Fed as a mechanic; Fed as a warrior; Fed as a fall guy?

Web-Based Questions

1. **CURRENT U.S. INTEREST RATES** Visit the Federal Reserve's Web site at **www.federalreserve.gov,** and select Economic Research and Data, then Statistics: Releases and Historical Data, Selected Interest Rates (weekly), and Historical Data to find the most recent values for the following interest rates: the Federal funds rate, the discount rate, and the prime interest rate. Are these rates higher or lower than they were 3 years ago? Have they increased, decreased, or remained constant over the past year?

2. **THE FEDERAL RESERVE ANNUAL REPORT** Visit the Federal Reserve's Web site at **www.federalreserve.gov**, and select Monetary Policy and then Monetary Policy Report to the Congress to retrieve the current annual report (Sections 1 and 2). Summarize the policy actions of the Board of Governors during the most recent period. In the Fed's opinion, how did the U.S. economy perform?

Financial Economics

Chapter 14 Web is a bonus chapter found at the book's Web site, **www.mcconnell17.com.** It extends
the analysis of Part 4, "Money, Banking, and Monetary Policy," by examining fundamental ideas
relating to financial markets. Your instructor may (or may not) assign all or parts of this chapter.

- **About the relationship between short-run aggregate supply and long-run aggregate supply.**

- **How to apply the "extended" (short-run/long-run) AD-AS model to inflation, recessions, and unemployment.**

- **About the short-run tradeoff between inflation and unemployment (the Phillips Curve).**

- **Why there is no long-run tradeoff between inflation and unemployment.**

- **The relationship between tax rates, tax revenues, and aggregate supply.**

15

Extending the Analysis of Aggregate Supply

During the early years of the Great Depression, many economists suggested that the economy would correct itself in the *long run* without government intervention. To this line of thinking, economist John Maynard Keynes remarked, "In the long run we are all dead!"

For several decades following the Great Depression, macroeconomic economists understandably focused on refining fiscal policy and monetary policy to smooth business cycles and address the problems of unemployment and inflation. The main emphasis was on short-run problems and policies associated with the business cycle.

But over people's lifetimes, and from generation to generation, the long run is tremendously important for economic well-being. For that reason, macroeconomists have refocused attention on long-run macroeconomic adjustments, processes, and outcomes. As we will see in this and the next three chapters (one is at our Internet site only), the renewed emphasis on the long run has produced significant insights on aggregate supply, economic growth, and economic development. We will also see that it has renewed historical debates over the causes of macro instability and the effectiveness of stabilization policy.

Our goals in this chapter are to extend the analysis of aggregate supply to the long run, examine the inflation-unemployment relationship, and evaluate the effect of taxes on aggregate supply. The latter is a key concern of so-called *supply-side economics*.

From Short Run to Long Run

Until now we have assumed the aggregate supply curve remains stable when the aggregate demand curve shifts. For example, an increase in aggregate demand along the upsloping short-run aggregate supply curve raises both the price level and real output. That analysis is accurate and realistic for the **short run,** which, you may recall from Chapter 10, is a period in which nominal wages (and other input prices) do not respond to price-level changes.

There are at least two reasons why nominal wages may for a time be unresponsive to changes in the price level:

- Workers may not immediately be aware of the extent to which inflation (or deflation) has changed their real wages, and thus they may not adjust their labor supply decisions and wage demands accordingly.
- Many employees are hired under fixed-wage contracts. For unionized employees, for example, nominal wages are spelled out in their collective bargaining agreements for perhaps 2 or 3 years. Also, most managers and many professionals receive set salaries established in annual contracts. For them, nominal wages remain constant for the life of the contracts, regardless of changes in the price level.

In such cases, price-level changes do not immediately give rise to changes in nominal wages. Instead, significant periods of time may pass before such adjustments occur.

Once contracts have expired and nominal wage adjustments have been made, the economy enters the **long run.** Recall that this is the period in which nominal wages are fully responsive to previous changes in the price level. As time passes, workers gain full information about price-level changes and how those changes affect their real wages. For example, suppose that Jessica received an hourly nominal wage of $10 when the price index was 100 (or, in decimals, 1.0) and that her real wage was also $10 (= $10 of nominal wage divided by 1.0). But when the price level rises to, say, 120, Jessica's $10 real wage declines to $8.33 (= $10/1.2). As a result, she and other workers will adjust their labor supply and wage demands such that their nominal wages

eventually will rise to restore the purchasing power of an hour of work. In our example, Jessica's nominal wage will increase from $10 to $12, returning her real wage to $10 (= $12/1.2). But that adjustment will take time.

Short-Run Aggregate Supply

Our immediate objective is to demonstrate the relationship between short-run aggregate supply and long-run aggregate supply. We begin by briefly reviewing short-run aggregate supply.

Consider the short-run aggregate supply curve AS_1 in Figure 15.1a. This curve is based on three assumptions: (1) The initial price level is P_1, (2) firms and workers have established nominal wages on the expectation that this price level will persist, and (3) the price level is flexible both upward and downward. Observe from point a_1 that at price level P_1 the economy is operating at its full-employment output Q_f. This output is the real production forthcoming when the economy is operating at its natural rate of unemployment (or potential output.).

Now let's review the short-run effects of changes in the price level, say, from P_1 to P_2 in Figure 15.1a. The higher prices associated with price level P_2 increase firms' revenues, and because their nominal wages remain unchanged, their profits rise. Those higher profits lead firms to increase their output from Q_f to Q_2, and the economy moves from a_1 to a_2 on aggregate supply AS_1. At output Q_2 the economy is operating beyond its full-employment output. The firms make this possible by extending the work hours of part-time and full-time workers, enticing new workers such as homemakers and retirees into the labor force, and hiring and training the structurally unemployed. Thus, the nation's unemployment rate declines below its natural rate.

How will the firms respond when the price level *falls*, say, from P_1 to P_3 in Figure 15.1a? Because the prices they receive for their products are lower while the nominal wages they pay workers are not, firms discover that their revenues and profits have diminished or disappeared. So they reduce their production and employment, and, as shown by the movement from a_1 to a_3, real output falls to

FIGURE 15.1 Short-run and long-run aggregate supply. (a) In the short run, nominal wages do not respond to price-level changes and based on the expectation that price level P_1 will continue. An increase in the price level from P_1 to P_2 increases profits and output, moving the economy from a_1 to a_2; a decrease in the price level from P_1 to P_3 reduces profits and real output, moving the economy from a_1 to a_3. The short-run aggregate supply curve therefore slopes upward. (b) In the long run, a rise in the price level results in higher nominal wages and thus shifts the short-run aggregate supply curve to the left. Conversely, a decrease in the price level reduces nominal wages and shifts the short-run aggregate supply curve to the right. After such adjustments, the economy obtains equilibrium of points such as b_1 and c_1. Thus, the long-run aggregate supply curve is vertical at the full-employment output.

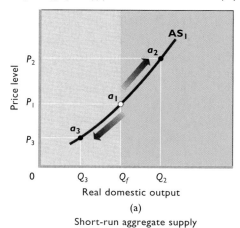
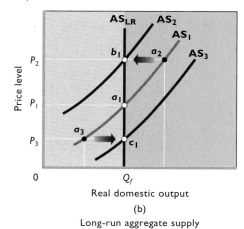

Q_3. Increased unemployment and a higher unemployment rate accompany the decline in real output. At output Q_3 the unemployment rate is greater than the natural rate of unemployment associated with output Q_f.

Long-Run Aggregate Supply

The outcomes are different in the long run. To see why, we need to extend the analysis of aggregate supply to account for changes in nominal wages that occur in response to changes in the price level. That will enable us to derive the economy's long-run aggregate supply curve.

By definition, nominal wages in the long run are fully responsive to changes in the price level. We illustrate the implications for aggregate supply in Figure 15.1b. Again, suppose that the economy is initially at point a_1 (P_1 and Q_f). As we just demonstrated, an increase in the price level from P_1 to P_2 will move the economy from point a_1 to a_2 along the short-run aggregate supply curve AS_1. In the long run, however, workers discover that their real wages (their constant nominal wages divided by the price level) have declined because of this increase in the price level. They restore their previous level of real wages by gaining nominal wage increases. Because nominal wages are one of the determinants of aggregate supply (see Figure 10.5), the short-run supply curve then shifts leftward from AS_1 to AS_2, which now reflects the higher price level P_2 and the new expectation that P_2, not P_1, will continue. The leftward shift in the short-run aggregate supply curve to AS_2 moves the economy from a_2 to b_1. Real output falls back to

its full-employment level Q_f, and the unemployment rate rises to its natural rate.

What is the long-run outcome of a *decrease* in the price level? Assuming eventual downward wage flexibility, a decline in the price level from P_1 to P_3 in Figure 15.1b works in the opposite way from a price-level increase. At first the economy moves from point a_1 to a_3 on AS_1. Profits are squeezed or eliminated because prices have fallen and nominal wages have not. But this movement along AS_1 is the short-run supply response. With enough time the lower price level P_3 (which has increased real wages) results in a drop in nominal wages such that the original real wages are restored. Lower nominal wages shift the short-run aggregate supply curve rightward from AS_1 to AS_3, and real output returns to its full-employment level of Q_f at point c_1.

By tracing a line between the long-run equilibrium points b_1, a_1, and c_1, we obtain a long-run aggregate supply curve. Observe that it is vertical at the full-employment level of real GDP. After long-run adjustments in nominal wages, real output is Q_f regardless of the specific price level. **(Key Question 3)**

Long-Run Equilibrium in the AD-AS Model

Figure 15.2 helps us understand the long-run equilibrium in the AD-AS model, now extended to include the distinction between short-run and long-run aggregate supply. (Hereafter, we will refer to this model as the extended AD-AS model,

FIGURE 15.2 Equilibrium in the extended AD-AS model. The long-run equilibrium price level P_1 and level of real output Q_f occur at the intersection of the aggregate demand curve AD$_1$, the long-run aggregate supply curve AS$_{LR}$, and the short-run aggregate supply curve AS$_1$.

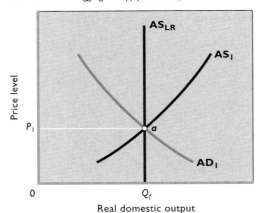

with "extended" referring to the inclusion of both the short-run and the long-run aggregate supply curves.)

In the short run, equilibrium occurs wherever the downsloping aggregate demand curve and upsloping short-run aggregate supply curve intersect. This can be at any level of output, not simply the full-employment level. Either a negative GDP or a positive GDP gap is possible in the short run.

G 15.1

Extended AD-AS model

But in the long run, the short-run aggregate supply curve adjusts as we just described. After those adjustments, long-run equilibrium occurs where the aggregate demand curve, vertical long-run aggregate supply curve, and short-run aggregate supply curve all intersect. Figure 15.2 shows the long-run outcome. Equilibrium occurs at point a, where AD$_1$ intersects both AS$_{LR}$ and AS$_1$, and the economy achieves its full-employment (or potential) output, Q_f. At long-run equilibrium price level P_1 and output level Q_f, there is neither a negative GDP gap nor a positive GDP gap.

QUICK REVIEW 15.1

- The short-run aggregate supply curve has a positive slope because nominal wages do not respond to the price-level changes.
- The long-run aggregate supply curve is vertical, because nominal wages eventually change by the same relative amount as changes in the price level.
- The long-run equilibrium GDP and price level occur at the intersection of the aggregate demand curve, the long-run aggregate supply curve, and the short-run aggregate supply curve.

Applying the Extended AD-AS Model

The extended AD-AS model helps clarify the long-run aspects of demand-pull inflation, cost-push inflation, and recession.

Demand-Pull Inflation in the Extended AD-AS Model

Recall that demand-pull inflation occurs when an increase in aggregate demand pulls up the price level. Earlier, we depicted this inflation by shifting an aggregate demand curve rightward along a stable aggregate supply curve (see Figure 10.7).

In our more complex version of aggregate supply, however, an increase in the price level eventually leads to an increase in nominal wages and thus a leftward shift of the short-run aggregate supply curve. This is shown in Figure 15.3, where we initially suppose the price level is P_1 at the intersection of aggregate demand curve AD$_1$, short-run supply curve AS$_1$, and long-run aggregate supply curve AS$_{LR}$. Observe that the economy is achieving its full-employment real output Q_f at point a.

Now consider the effects of an increase in aggregate demand as represented by the rightward shift from AD$_1$ to AD$_2$. This shift might result from any one of a number of factors, including an increase in investment spending and a rise in net exports. Whatever its cause, the increase in aggregate demand boosts the price level from P_1 to P_2 and expands real output from Q_f to Q_2 at point b. There, a positive GDP gap of $Q_2 - Q_f$ occurs.

So far, none of this is new to you. But now the distinction between short-run aggregate supply and long-run aggregate supply becomes important. Once workers have realized that their real wages have declined and their existing contracts have expired, nominal wages will rise. As they do, the short-run aggregate supply curve will ultimately shift leftward such that it intersects long-run aggregate supply at point c.[1] There; the economy has reestablished long-run equilibrium, with the price level and real output now P_3 and Q_f, respectively. Only at point c does the new aggregate demand curve AD$_2$ intersect both the short-run aggregate supply curve AS$_2$ and the long-run aggregate supply curve AS$_{LR}$.

---

[1]We say "ultimately" because the initial leftward shift in short-run aggregate supply will intersect the long-run aggregate supply curve AS$_{LR}$ at price level P_2 (review Figure 15.1b). But the intersection of AD$_2$ and this new short-run aggregate supply curve (not shown) will produce a price level above P_2. (You may want to pencil this in to make sure that you understand this point.) Again nominal wages will rise, shifting the short-run aggregate supply curve farther leftward. The process will continue until the economy moves to point c, where the short-run aggregate supply curve is AS$_2$, the price level is P_3, and real output is Q_f.

FIGURE 15.3 Demand-pull inflation in the extended AD-AS model. An increase in aggregate demand from AD$_1$ to AD$_2$ drives up the price level and increases real output in the short run. But in the long run, nominal wages rise and the short-run aggregate supply curve shifts leftward, as from AS$_1$ to AS$_2$. Real output then returns to its prior level, and the price level rises even more. In this scenario, the economy moves from a to b and then eventually to c.

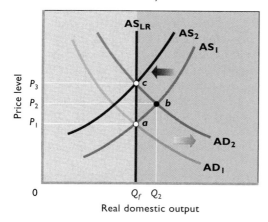

FIGURE 15.4 Cost-push inflation in the extended AD-AS model. Cost-push inflation occurs when the short-run aggregate supply curve shifts leftward, as from AS$_1$ to AS$_2$. If government counters the decline in real output by increasing aggregate demand to the broken line, the price level rises even more. That is, the economy moves in steps from a to b to c. In contrast, if government allows a recession to occur, nominal wages eventually fall and the aggregate supply curve shifts back rightward to its original location. The economy moves from a to b and eventually back to a.

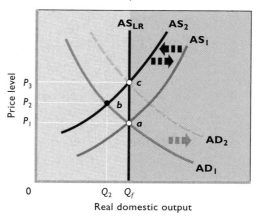

In the short run, demand-pull inflation drives up the price level and increases real output; in the long run, only the price level rises. In the long run, the initial increase in aggregate demand has moved the economy along its vertical aggregate supply curve AS$_{LR}$. For a while, an economy can operate beyond its full-employment level of output. But the demand-pull inflation eventually causes adjustments of nominal wages that return the economy to its full-employment output Q_f.

Cost-Push Inflation in the Extended AD-AS Model

Cost-push inflation arises from factors that increase the cost of production at each price level, shifting the aggregate supply curve leftward and raising the equilibrium price level. Previously (Figure 10.9), we considered cost-push inflation using only the short-run aggregate supply curve. Now we want to analyze that type of inflation in its long-run context.

Analysis Look at Figure 15.4, in which we again assume that the economy is initially operating at price level P_1 and output level Q_f (point a). Suppose that international oil producers agree to reduce the supply of oil to boost its price by, say, 100 percent. As a result, the per-unit production cost of producing and transporting goods and services rises substantially in the economy represented by Figure 15.4. This increase in per-unit production costs shifts the short-run aggregate supply curve to the left, as from AS$_1$ to AS$_2$, and the price level rises from P_1 to P_2 (as seen by comparing points a and b). In this case, the leftward shift of the aggregate supply curve is *not a response* to a price-level increase, as it was in our previous discussions of demand-pull inflation; it is the *initiating cause* of the price-level increase.

Policy Dilemma Cost-push inflation creates a dilemma for policymakers. Without some expansionary stabilization policy, aggregate demand in Figure 15.4 remains in place at AD$_1$ and real output declines from Q_f to Q_2. Government can counter this recession, negative GDP gap, and attendant high unemployment by using fiscal policy and monetary policy to increase aggregate demand to AD$_2$. But there is a potential policy trap here: An increase in aggregate demand to AD$_2$ will further raise inflation by increasing the price level from P_2 to P_3 (a move from point b to c).

Suppose the government recognizes this policy trap and decides not to increase aggregate demand from AD$_1$ to AD$_2$ (you can now disregard the dashed AD$_2$ curve) and instead decides to allow a cost-push-created recession to run its course. How will that happen? Widespread layoffs, plant shutdowns, and business failures eventually occur. At some point the demand for oil, labor, and other inputs will decline so much that oil prices and nominal wages will decline. When that happens, the initial leftward shift of the short-run aggregate supply curve will reverse itself. That is, the declining per-unit production costs caused by the recession will shift the short-run aggregate supply curve rightward from AS$_2$ to AS$_1$. The price level will return to P_1, and the full-employment level of output will be restored at Q_f (point a on the long-run aggregate supply curve AS$_{LR}$).

This analysis yields two generalizations:

- If the government attempts to maintain full employment when there is cost-push inflation, an inflationary spiral may occur.

- If the government takes a hands-off approach to cost-push inflation, a recession will occur. Although the recession eventually may undo the initial rise in per-unit production costs, the economy in the meantime will experience high unemployment and a loss of real output.

Recession and the Extended AD-AS Model

By far the most controversial application of the extended AD-AS model is its application to recession (or depression) caused by decreases in aggregate demand. We will look at this controversy in detail in Chapter 17; here we simply identify the key point of contention.

Suppose in Figure 15.5 that aggregate demand initially is AD_1 and that the short-run and long-run aggregate supply curves are AS_1 and AS_{LR}, respectively. Therefore, as shown by point a, the price level is P_1 and output is Q_f. Now suppose that investment spending declines dramatically, reducing aggregate demand to AD_2. Observe that real output declines from Q_f to Q_1, indicating that a recession has occurred. But if we make the controversial assumption that prices and wages are flexible downward, the price level falls from P_1 to P_2. The lower price level increases real wages for people who are still working, since each dollar of nominal wage has greater purchasing power. Eventually, nominal wages themselves fall to restore the previous real wage; when that happens, the short-run aggregate supply curve

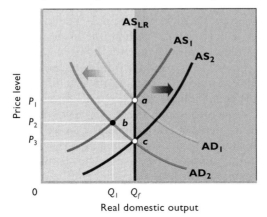

FIGURE 15.5 Recession in the extended AD-AS model. A recession occurs when aggregate demand shifts leftward, as from AD_1 to AD_2. If prices and wages are downwardly flexible, the price level falls from P_1 to P_2. That decline in the price level eventually reduces nominal wages, and this shifts the aggregate supply curve from AS_1 to AS_2. The price level declines to P_3, and real output increases back to Q_f. The economy moves from point a to b and then eventually to c.

shifts rightward from AS_1 to AS_2. The negative GDP gap evaporates without the need for expansionary fiscal or monetary policy, since real output expands from Q_1 (point b) back to Q_f (point c). The economy is again located on its long-run aggregate supply curve AS_{LR}, but now at lower price level P_3.

There is much disagreement about this hypothetical scenario. The key point of dispute is how long it would take in the real world for the necessary downward price and wage adjustments to occur to regain the full-employment level of output. For now, suffice it to say that most economists believe that if such adjustments are forthcoming, they will occur only after the economy has experienced a relatively long-lasting recession with its accompanying high unemployment and large loss of output. Therefore, economists recommend active monetary policy, and perhaps fiscal policy, to counteract recessions. **(Key Question 4)**

QUICK REVIEW 15.2

- In the short run, demand-pull inflation raises both the price level and real output; in the long run, nominal wages rise, the short-run aggregate supply curve shifts to the left, and only the price level increases.

- Cost-push inflation creates a policy dilemma for the government: If it engages in an expansionary policy to increase output, an inflationary spiral may occur; if it does nothing, a recession will occur.

- In the short run, a decline in aggregate demand reduces real output (creates a recession); in the long run, prices and nominal wages presumably fall, the short-run aggregate supply curve shifts to the right, and real output returns to its full-employment level.

The Inflation-Unemployment Relationship

Because both low inflation rates and low unemployment rates are major economic goals, economists are vitally interested in their relationship. Are low unemployment and low inflation compatible goals or conflicting goals? What explains situations in which high unemployment and high inflation coexist?

The extended AD-AS model supports three significant generalizations relating to these questions:

- Under normal circumstances, there is a short-run tradeoff between the rate of inflation and the rate of unemployment.

- Aggregate supply shocks can cause both higher rates of inflation and higher rates of unemployment.

- There is no significant tradeoff between inflation and unemployment over long periods of time.

Let's examine each of these generalizations.

The Phillips Curve

O 15.1
Phillips Curve

We can demonstrate the short-run tradeoff between the rate of inflation and the rate of unemployment through the **Phillips Curve,** named after A. W. Phillips, who developed the idea in Great Britain. This curve, generalized in Figure 15.6a, suggests an inverse relationship between the rate of inflation and the rate of unemployment. Lower unemployment rates (measured as leftward movements on the horizontal axis) are associated with higher rates of inflation (measured as upward movements on the vertical axis).

The underlying rationale of the Phillips Curve becomes apparent when we view the short-run aggregate supply curve in Figure 15.7 and perform a simple mental experiment. Suppose that in some short-run period aggregate demand expands from AD_0 to AD_2, either because firms decided to buy more capital goods or the government decided to increase its expenditures. Whatever the cause, in the short run the price level rises from P_0 to P_2 and real output rises from Q_0 to Q_2. A decline in the unemployment rate accompanies the increase in real output.

Now let's compare what would have happened if the increase in aggregate demand had been larger, say, from AD_0 to AD_3. The new equilibrium tells us that the amount of inflation and the growth of real output would both have been greater (and that the unemployment rate would have been lower). Similarly, suppose aggregate demand during the year had increased only modestly, from AD_0 to AD_1. Compared with our shift from AD_0 to AD_2, the amount of

FIGURE 15.7 The short-run effect of changes in aggregate demand on real output and the price level. Comparing the effects of various possible increases in aggregate demand leads to the conclusion that the larger the increase in aggregate demand, the higher the rate of inflation and the greater the increase in real output. Because real output and the unemployment rate move in opposite directions, we can generalize that, given short-run aggregate supply, high rates of inflation should be accompanied by low rates of unemployment.

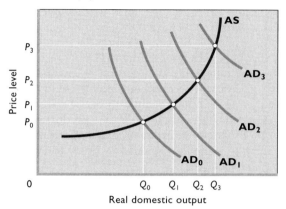

inflation and the growth of real output would have been smaller (and the unemployment rate higher).

The generalization we draw from this mental experiment is this: Assuming a constant short-run aggregate supply curve, high rates of inflation are accompanied by low rates of unemployment, and low rates of inflation are accompanied by high rates of unemployment. Other things equal, the expected relationship should look something like Figure 15.6a.

FIGURE 15.6 The Phillips Curve: concept and empirical data. (a) The Phillips Curve relates annual rates of inflation and annual rates of unemployment for a series of years. Because this is an inverse relationship, there presumably is a tradeoff between unemployment and inflation. (b) Data points for the 1960s seemed to confirm the Phillips Curve concept. (Note: Inflation rates are on a December-to-December basis.)

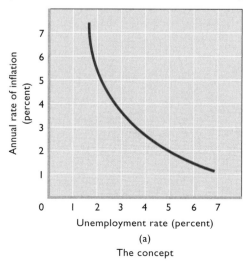

(a)
The concept

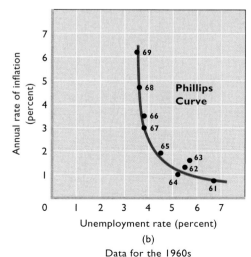

(b)
Data for the 1960s

Figure 15.6b reveals that the facts for the 1960s nicely fit the theory. On the basis of that evidence and evidence from other countries, most economists concluded there was a stable, predictable tradeoff between unemployment and inflation. Moreover, U.S. economic policy was built on that supposed tradeoff. According to this thinking, it was impossible to achieve "full employment without inflation": Manipulation of aggregate demand through fiscal and monetary measures would simply move the economy along the Phillips Curve. An expansionary fiscal and monetary policy that boosted aggregate demand and lowered the unemployment rate would simultaneously increase inflation. A restrictive fiscal and monetary policy could be used to reduce the rate of inflation but only at the cost of a higher unemployment rate and more forgone production. Society had to choose between the incompatible goals of price stability and full employment; it had to decide where to locate on its Phillips Curve.

For reasons we will soon see, today's economists reject the idea of a stable, predictable Phillips Curve. Nevertheless, they agree there is a short-run tradeoff between unemployment and inflation. Given aggregate supply, increases in aggregate demand increase real output and reduce the unemployment rate. As the unemployment rate falls and dips below the natural rate, the excessive spending produces demand-pull inflation. Conversely, when recession sets in and the unemployment rate increases, the weak aggregate demand that caused the recession also leads to lower inflation rates.

Periods of exceptionally low unemployment rates and inflation rates do occur, but only under special sets of economic circumstances. One such period was the late 1990s, when faster productivity growth increased aggregate supply and fully blunted the inflationary impact of rapidly rising aggregate demand (review Figure 10.10).

Aggregate Supply Shocks and the Phillips Curve

The unemployment-inflation experience of the 1970s and early 1980s demolished the idea of an always-stable Phillips Curve. In Figure 15.8 we show the Phillips Curve for the 1960s in blue and then add the data points for 1970 through 2005. Observe that in most of the years of the 1970s and early 1980s the economy experienced both higher inflation rates and higher unemployment rates than it did in the

FIGURE 15.8 Inflation rates and unemployment rates, 1960–2005. A series of aggregate supply shocks in the 1970s resulted in higher rates of inflation and higher rates of unemployment. So data points for the 1970s and 1980s tended to be above and to the right of the Phillips Curve for the 1960s. In the 1990s the inflation-unemployment data points slowly moved back toward the original Phillips Curve. Points for the late 1990s and 2000s are similar to those from the earlier era. (Note: Inflation rates are on a December-to-December basis.)

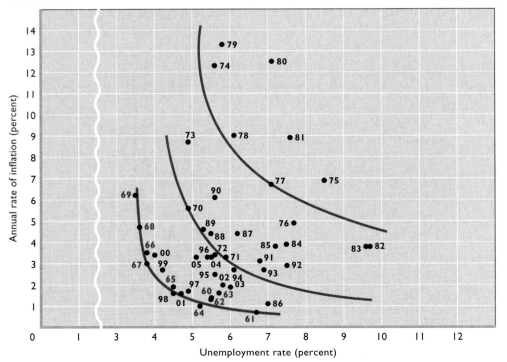

1960s. In fact, inflation and unemployment rose simultaneously in some of those years. This condition is called **stagflation**—a media term that combines the words "stagnation" and "inflation." If there still was any such thing as a Phillips Curve, it had clearly shifted outward, perhaps as shown.

Adverse Aggregate Supply Shocks The Phillips data points for the 1970s and early 1980s support our second generalization: Aggregate supply shocks can cause both higher rates of inflation and higher rates of unemployment. A series of adverse **aggregate supply shocks**—sudden, large increases in resource costs that jolt an economy's short-run aggregate supply curve leftward—hit the economy in the 1970s and early 1980s. The most significant of these shocks was a quadrupling of oil prices by the Organization of Petroleum Exporting Countries (OPEC). Consequently, the cost of producing and distributing virtually every product and service rose rapidly. (Other factors working to increase U.S. costs during this period included major agricultural shortfalls, a greatly depreciated dollar, wage hikes previously held down by wage-price controls, and declining productivity.)

These shocks shifted the aggregate supply curve to the left and distorted the usual inflation-unemployment relationship. Remember that we derived the inverse relationship between the rate of inflation and the unemployment rate shown in Figure 15.6a by shifting the aggregate demand curve along a stable short-run aggregate supply curve (Figure 15.7). But the cost-push inflation model shown in Figure 15.4 tells us that a *leftward shift* of the short-run aggregate supply curve increases the price level and reduces real output (and increases the unemployment rate). This, say most economists, is what happened in two periods in the 1970s. The U.S. unemployment rate shot up from 4.9 percent in 1973 to 8.3 percent in 1975, contributing to a significant decline in real GDP. In the same period, the U.S. price level rose by 21 percent. The stagflation scenario recurred in 1978, when OPEC increased oil prices by more than 100 percent. The U.S. price level rose by 26 percent over the 1978–1980 period, while unemployment increased from 6.1 to 7.1 percent.

Stagflation's Demise Another look at Figure 15.8 reveals a generally inward movement of the inflation-unemployment points between 1982 and 1989. By 1989 the lingering effects of the early period had subsided. One precursor to this favorable trend was the deep recession of 1981–1982, largely caused by a restrictive monetary policy aimed at reducing double-digit inflation. The recession upped the unemployment rate to 9.5 percent in 1982.

With so many workers unemployed, those who were working accepted smaller increases in their nominal wages—or, in some cases, wage reductions—in order to preserve their jobs. Firms, in turn, restrained their price increases to try to retain their relative shares of a greatly diminished market.

Other factors were at work. Foreign competition throughout this period held down wage and price hikes in several basic industries such as automobiles and steel. Deregulation of the airline and trucking industries also resulted in wage reductions or so-called wage givebacks. A significant decline in OPEC's monopoly power and a greatly reduced reliance on oil in the production process produced a stunning fall in the price of oil and its derivative products, such as gasoline.

All these factors combined to reduce per-unit production costs and to shift the short-run aggregate supply curve rightward (as from AS_2 to AS_1 in Figure 15.4). Employment and output expanded, and the unemployment rate fell from 9.6 percent in 1983 to 5.3 percent in 1989. Figure 15.8 reveals that the inflation-unemployment points for recent years are closer to the points associated with the Phillips Curve of the 1960s than to the points in

GLOBAL PERSPECTIVE 15.1

The Misery Index, Selected Nations, 1995–2005

The misery index adds together a nation's unemployment rate and its inflation rate to get a measure of national economic discomfort. For example, a nation with a 5 percent rate of unemployment and a 5 percent inflation rate would have a misery index number of 10, as would a nation with an 8 percent unemployment rate and a 2 percent inflation rate.

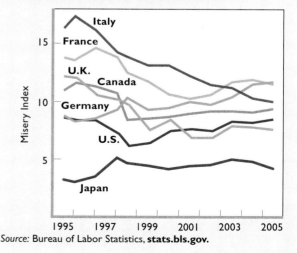

Source: Bureau of Labor Statistics, **stats.bls.gov.**

the late 1970s and early 1980s. The points for 1997–2005, in fact, are very close to points on the 1960s curve. (The very low inflation and unemployment rates in this latter period produced an exceptionally low value of the so-called *misery index*, as shown in Global Perspective 15.1.)

The Long-Run Phillips Curve

The overall set of data points in Figure 15.8 supports our third generalization relating to the inflation-unemployment relationship: There is no apparent *long-run* tradeoff between inflation and unemployment. Economists point out that when decades as opposed to a few years are considered, any rate of inflation is consistent with the natural rate of unemployment prevailing at that time. We know from Chapter 7 that the natural rate of unemployment is the unemployment rate that occurs when cyclical unemployment is zero; it is the full-employment rate of unemployment, or the rate of unemployment when the economy achieves its potential output.

How can there be a short-run inflation-unemployment tradeoff but not a long-run tradeoff? Figure 15.9 provides the answer.

Short-Run Phillips Curve

Consider Phillips Curve PC_1 in Figure 15.9. Suppose the economy initially is experiencing a 3 percent rate of inflation and a 5 percent natural rate of unemployment. Such short-term curves as PC_1, PC_2, and PC_3 (drawn as straight lines for simplicity) exist because the actual rate of inflation is not always the same as the expected rate.

Establishing an additional point on Phillips Curve PC_1 will clarify this. We begin at a_1, where we assume nominal wages are set on the assumption that the 3 percent rate of inflation will continue. But suppose that aggregate demand increases such that the rate of inflation rises to 6 percent. With a nominal wage rate set on the expectation that the 3 percent rate of inflation will continue, the higher product prices raise business profits. Firms respond to the higher profits by hiring more workers and increasing output. In the short run, the economy moves to b_1, which, in contrast to a_1, involves a lower rate of unemployment (4 percent) and a higher rate of inflation (6 percent). The move from a_1 to b_1 is consistent both with an upward-sloping aggregate supply curve and with the inflation-unemployment tradeoff implied by the Phillips Curve analysis. But this short-run Phillips Curve simply is a manifestation of the following principle: When the actual rate of inflation is higher than expected, profits temporarily rise and the unemployment rate temporarily falls.

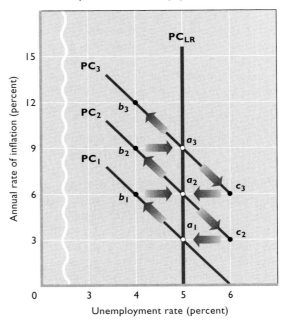

FIGURE 15.9 **The long-run vertical Phillips Curve.** Increases in aggregate demand beyond those consistent with full-employment output may temporarily boost profits, output, and employment (as from a_1 to b_1). But nominal wages eventually will catch up so as to sustain real wages. When they do, profits will fall, negating the previous short-run stimulus to production and employment (the economy now moves from b_1 to a_2). Consequently, there is no tradeoff between the rates of inflation and unemployment in the long run; that is, the long-run Phillips Curve is roughly a vertical line at the economy's natural rate of unemployment.

Long-Run Vertical Phillips Curve

But point b_1 is not a stable equilibrium. Workers will recognize that their nominal wages have not increased as fast as inflation and will therefore obtain nominal wage increases to restore their lost purchasing power. But as nominal wages rise to restore the level of real wages that previously existed at a_1, business profits will fall to their prior level. The reduction in profits means that the original motivation to employ more workers and increase output has disappeared.

Unemployment then returns to its natural level at point a_2. Note, however, that the economy now faces a higher actual and expected rate of inflation—6 percent rather than 3 percent. The higher level of aggregate demand that originally moved the economy from a_1 to b_1 still exists, so the inflation it created persists.

In view of the higher 6 percent expected rate of inflation, the short-run Phillips Curve shifts upward from PC_1 to PC_2 in Figure 15.9. An "along-the-Phillips-Curve" kind of move from a_1 to b_1 on PC_1 is merely a short-run or transient occurrence. In the long run, after nominal wages catch up with price-level increases, unemployment returns to its natural rate at a_2, and there is a new short-run Phillips Curve PC_2 at the higher expected rate of inflation.

The scenario repeats if aggregate demand continues to increase. Prices rise momentarily ahead of nominal wages, profits expand, and employment and output increase (as implied by the move from a_2 to b_2). But, in time, nominal wages increase so as to restore real wages. Profits then fall to their original level, pushing employment back to the normal rate at a_3. The economy's "reward" for lowering the unemployment rate below the natural rate is a still higher (9 percent) rate of inflation.

Movements along the short-run Phillips curve (a_1 to b_1 on PC_1) cause the curve to shift to a less favorable position (PC_2, then PC_3, and so on). A stable Phillips Curve with the dependable series of unemployment-rate–inflation-rate tradeoffs simply does not exist in the long run. The economy is characterized by a **long-run vertical Phillips Curve.**

O 15.2

Long-run vertical Phillips Curve

The vertical line through a_1, a_2, and a_3 shows the long-run relationship between unemployment and inflation. Any rate of inflation is consistent with the 5% natural rate of unemployment. So, in this view, society ought to choose a low rate of inflation rather than a high one.

Disinflation

The distinction between the short-run Phillips Curve and the long-run Phillips Curve also helps explain **disinflation**—reductions in the inflation rate from year to year. Suppose that in Figure 15.9 the economy is at a_3, where the inflation rate is 9 percent. And suppose that a decline in aggregate demand (such as that occurring in the 1981–1982 recession) reduces inflation below the 9 percent expected rate, say, to 6 percent. Business profits fall, because prices are rising less rapidly than wages. The nominal wage increases, remember, were set on the assumption that the 9 percent rate of inflation would continue. In response to the decline in profits, firms reduce their employment and consequently the unemployment rate rises. The economy temporarily slides downward from point a_3 to c_3 along the short-run Phillips Curve PC_3. When the actual rate of inflation is lower than the expected rate, profits temporarily fall and the unemployment rate temporarily rises.

Firms and workers eventually adjust their expectations to the new 6 percent rate of inflation, and thus newly negotiated wage increases decline. Profits are restored, employment rises, and the unemployment rate falls back to its natural rate of 5 percent at a_2. Because the expected rate of inflation is now 6 percent, the short-run Phillips Curve PC_3 shifts leftward to PC_2.

If aggregate demand declines more, the scenario will continue. Inflation declines from 6 percent to, say, 3 percent, moving the economy from a_2 to c_2 along PC_2. The lower-than-expected rate of inflation (lower prices) squeezes profits and reduces employment. But, in the long run, firms respond to the lower profits by reducing their nominal wage increases. Profits are restored and unemployment returns to its natural rate at a_1 as the short-run Phillips Curve moves from PC_2 to PC_1. Once again, the long-run Phillips Curve is vertical at the 5 percent natural rate of unemployment. **(Key Question 6)**

QUICK REVIEW 15.3

- As implied by the upward-sloping short-run aggregate supply curve, there may be a short-run tradeoff between the rate of inflation and the rate of unemployment. This tradeoff is reflected in the Phillips Curve, which shows that lower rates of inflation are associated with higher rates of unemployment.
- Aggregate supply shocks that produce severe cost-push inflation can cause stagflation—simultaneous increases in the inflation rate and the unemployment rate. Such stagflation occurred from 1973 to 1975 and recurred from 1978 to 1980, producing Phillips Curve data points above and to the right of the Phillips Curve for the 1960s.
- After all nominal wage adjustments to increases and decreases in the rate of inflation have occurred, the economy ends up back at its full-employment level of output and its natural rate of unemployment. The long-run Phillips Curve therefore is vertical at the natural rate of unemployment.

Taxation and Aggregate Supply

A final topic in our discussion of aggregate supply is taxation, a key aspect of **supply-side economics.** "Supply-side economists" or "supply-siders" stress that changes in aggregate supply are an active force in determining the levels of inflation, unemployment, and economic growth. Government policies can either impede or promote rightward shifts of the short-run and long-run aggregate supply curves shown in Figure 15.2. One such policy is taxation.

These economists say that the enlargement of the U.S. tax system has impaired incentives to work, save, and invest. In this view, high tax rates impede productivity growth and hence slow the expansion of long-run aggregate supply. By reducing the after-tax rewards of workers and producers, high tax rates reduce the financial attractiveness of work, saving, and investing.

Supply-siders focus their attention on *marginal tax rates*—the rates on extra dollars of income—because those rates affect the benefits from working, saving, or investing more. In 2005 the marginal tax rates varied from 10 to 35 percent in the United States. (See Table 4.1 for details.)

Taxes and Incentives to Work

Supply-siders believe that how long and how hard people work depends on the amounts of additional after-tax earnings they derive from their efforts. They say that lower marginal tax rates on earned incomes induce more work, and therefore increase aggregate inputs of labor. Lower marginal tax rates increase the after-tax wage rate and make leisure more expensive and work more attractive. The higher opportunity cost of leisure encourages people to substitute work for leisure. This increase in productive effort is achieved in many ways: by increasing the number of hours worked per day or week, by encouraging workers to postpone retirement, by inducing more people to enter the labor force, by motivating people to work harder, and by avoiding long periods of unemployment.

Incentives to Save and Invest

High marginal tax rates also reduce the rewards for saving and investing. For example, suppose that Tony saves $10,000 at 8 percent interest, bringing him $800 of interest per year. If his marginal tax rate is 40 percent, his after-tax interest earnings will be $480, not $800, and his after-tax interest rate will fall to 4.8 percent. While Tony might be willing to save (forgo current consumption) for an 8 percent return on his saving, he might rather consume when the return is only 4.8 percent.

Saving, remember, is the prerequisite of investment. Thus supply-side economists recommend lower marginal tax rates on interest earned from saving. They also call for lower taxes on income from capital to ensure that there are ready investment outlets for the economy's enhanced pool of saving. A critical determinant of investment spending is the expected *after-tax* return on that spending.

To summarize: Lower marginal tax rates encourage saving and investing. Workers therefore find themselves equipped with more and technologically superior machinery and equipment. Labor productivity rises, and that expands long-run aggregate supply and economic growth, which in turn keeps unemployment rates and inflation low.

The Laffer Curve

In the supply-side view, reductions in marginal tax rates increase the nation's aggregate supply and can leave the nation's tax revenues unchanged or even enlarge them. Thus, supply-side tax cuts need not produce Federal budget deficits.

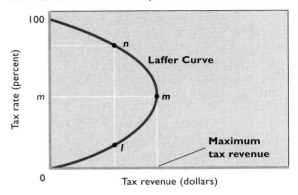

FIGURE 15.10 The Laffer Curve. The Laffer Curve suggests that up to point *m* higher tax rates will result in larger tax revenues. But tax rates higher than *m* will adversely affect incentives to work and produce, reducing the size of the tax base (output and income) to the extent that tax revenues will decline. It follows that if tax rates are above *m*, reductions in tax rates will produce increases in tax revenues.

This idea is based on the **Laffer Curve,** named after Arthur Laffer, who developed it. As Figure 15.10 shows, the Laffer Curve depicts the relationship between tax rates and tax revenues. As tax rates increase from 0 to 100 percent, tax revenues increase from zero to some maximum level (at *m*) and then fall to zero. Tax revenues decline beyond some point because higher tax rates discourage economic activity, thereby shrinking the tax base (domestic output and income). This is easiest to see at the extreme, where the tax rate is 100 percent. Tax revenues here are, in theory, reduced to zero because the 100 percent confiscatory tax rate has halted production. A 100 percent tax rate applied to a tax base of zero yields no revenue.

In the early 1980s Laffer suggested that the United States was at a point such as *n* on the curve in Figure 15.10. There, tax rates are so high that production is discouraged to the extent that tax revenues are below the maximum at *m*. If the economy is at *n*, then lower tax rates can either increase tax revenues or leave them unchanged. For example, lowering the tax rate from point *n* to point *l* would bolster the economy such that the government would bring in the same total amount of tax revenue as before.

Laffer's reasoning was that lower tax rates stimulate incentives to work, save and invest, innovate, and accept business risks, thus triggering an expansion of real output and income. That enlarged tax base sustains tax revenues even though tax rates are lowered. Indeed, between *n* and *m* lower tax rates result in increased tax revenue.

Also, when taxes are lowered, tax avoidance (which is legal) and tax evasion (which is not) decline. High marginal tax rates prompt taxpayers to avoid taxes through various tax shelters, such as buying municipal bonds, on which the interest earned is tax-free. High rates also encourage some

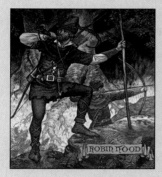

Sherwood Forest

The popularization of the idea that tax-rate reductions will increase tax revenues owed much to Arthur Laffer's ability to present his ideas simply. In explaining his thoughts to a *Wall Street Journal* editor over lunch, Laffer reportedly took out his pen and drew the curve on a napkin. The editor retained the napkin and later reproduced the curve in an editorial in *The Wall Street Journal*. The Laffer Curve was born. The idea it portrayed became the centerpiece of economic policy under the Reagan administration (1981–1989), which cut tax rates on personal income by 25 percent over a 3-year period.

Laffer illustrated his supply-side views with a story relating to Robin Hood, who, you may recall, stole from the rich to give to the poor. Laffer likened people traveling through Sherwood Forest to taxpayers, whereas Robin Hood and his band of merry men were government. As taxpayers passed through the forest, Robin Hood and his men intercepted them and forced them to hand over their money. Laffer asked audiences, "Do you think that travelers continued to go through Sherwood Forest?"

The answer he sought and got, of course, was "no." Taxpayers will avoid Sherwood Forest to the greatest extent possible. They will lower their taxable income by reducing work hours, retiring earlier, saving less, and engaging in tax avoidance and tax evasion activities. Robin Hood and his men may end up with less revenue than if they collected a relatively small "tax" from each traveler for passage through the forest.

taxpayers to conceal income from the Internal Revenue Service. Lower tax rates reduce the inclination to engage in either tax avoidance or tax evasion. **(Key Question 8)**

Criticisms of the Laffer Curve
The Laffer Curve and its supply-side implications have been subject to severe criticism.

Taxes, Incentives, and Time A fundamental criticism relates to the degree to which economic incentives are sensitive to changes in tax rates. Skeptics say ample empirical evidence shows that the impact of a tax cut on incentives is small, of uncertain direction, and relatively slow to emerge. For example, with respect to work incentives, studies indicate that decreases in tax rates lead some

people to work more but lead others to work less. Those who work more are enticed by the higher after-tax pay; they substitute work for leisure because the opportunity cost of leisure has increased. But other people work less because the higher after-tax pay enables them to "buy more leisure." With the tax cut, they can earn the same level of after-tax income as before with fewer work hours.

Inflation or Higher Real Interest Rates Most economists think that the demand-side effects of a tax cut are more immediate and certain than longer-term supply-side effects. Thus, tax cuts undertaken when the economy is at or near full employment may produce increases in aggregate demand that overwhelm any increase in aggregate supply. The likely result is inflation or restrictive monetary policy to prevent it. If the latter, real interest rates will rise and investment will decline. This will defeat the purpose of the supply-side tax cuts.

Position on the Curve Skeptics say that the Laffer Curve is merely a logical proposition and assert that there must be some level of tax rates between 0 and 100 percent at which tax revenues will be at their maximum. Economists of all persuasions can agree with this. But the issue of where a particular economy is located on its Laffer Curve is an empirical question. If we assume that we are at point *n* in Figure 15.10, then tax cuts will increase tax revenues. But if the economy is at any point below *m* on the curve, tax-rate reductions will reduce tax revenues.

Rebuttal and Evaluation
Supply-side advocates respond to the skeptics by contending that the Reagan tax cuts in the 1980s worked as Laffer predicted. Although the top marginal income tax rates on earned income were cut from 50 to 28 percent in that decade, real GDP and tax revenues were substantially higher at the end of the 1990s than at the beginning.

But the general view among economists is that the Reagan tax cuts, coming at a time of severe recession, helped boost aggregate demand and return real GDP to its full-employment output and normal growth path. As the economy expanded, so did tax revenues despite the lower tax rates. The rise in tax revenues caused by economic growth swamped the declines in revenues from lower tax rates. In essence, the Laffer Curve shown in Figure 15.10 shifted rightward, increasing net tax revenues. But the tax-rate cuts did not produce extraordinary rightward shifts of the long-run aggregate supply curve. Indeed, saving fell as a percentage of personal income during the period, productivity growth was sluggish, and real GDP growth was not extraordinarily strong.

Tax Cuts for Whom? A Supply-Side Anecdote*

Critics point out that the tax cuts advocated by supply-side economists usually provide the greatest tax relief to high-income individuals and households. An anonymous supply-side economist responds with an anecdote, circulated on the Internet.

Suppose that every day 10 people go out for breakfast together. The bill for all 10 comes to $100. If they paid their bill the way we pay our income taxes in America, it would go something like this: The first four people (the poorest) would pay nothing; the fifth would pay $1; the sixth would pay $3; the seventh would pay $7; the eighth would pay $12; the ninth would pay $18; and the tenth (the richest) would pay $59.

That is what they decided to do. The 10 people ate breakfast in the restaurant every day and seemed quite happy with the arrangement until the owner threw them a curve (in tax language, a tax cut). "Since you are all such good customers," the owner said, "I'm going to reduce the cost of your daily meal by $20." So now breakfast for the 10 people cost only $80. This group still wanted to pay their bill the way Americans pay their income taxes. So the first four people were unaffected. They would still eat breakfast for free. But what about the other six—the paying customers? How would they divvy up the $20 windfall so that everyone would get their fair share?

The six people realized that $20 divided by six is $3.33. But if they subtracted that from the share of the six who were paying the bill, then the fifth and sixth individuals would end up being paid to eat their breakfasts! The restaurant owner suggested that it would be fairer to reduce each person's meal by roughly the same share as their previous portion of the total

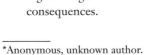

bill. Thus the fifth person would now pay nothing; the sixth would pay $2; the seventh would pay $5; the eighth would pay $9; the ninth would pay $12; and the tenth person would pay $52 instead of the original $59. Each of the six people was better off than before and the first four continued to eat free.

But once outside the restaurant, the people began to compare their savings. "I only received $1 out of the $20," declared the sixth person. "But the tenth man saved $7!" "Yeah, that's right!" exclaimed the fifth person, "I saved only $1, too. It is unfair that he received seven times as much as me." "That's true!" shouted the seventh person. "Why should he get $7 back when I got only $2. The wealthy get all the breaks!" "Wait a minute!" yelled the first four people in unison. "We didn't get anything at all. The system exploits the poor!"

The nine people angrily confronted the tenth and said, "This is not fair to us, and we are not going to put up with it." The next morning, the tenth man did not show up for breakfast, so the other nine sat down and ate without him. But when it came time to pay the bill, they discovered what was very important. They were $52 short.

Morals of this supply-side story:

- The people who pay the highest taxes get the most benefit from a general tax-rate reduction.
- Redistributing tax reductions at the expense of those paying the largest amount of taxes may produce unintended consequences.

---

*Anonymous, unknown author.

Because government expenditures rose more rapidly than tax revenues in the 1980s, large budget deficits occurred. In 1993 the Clinton administration increased the top marginal tax rates from 31 to 39.6 percent to address these deficits. The economy boomed in the last half of the 1990s, and by the end of the decade tax revenues were so high relative to government expenditures that budget surpluses emerged. In 2001, the Bush administration reduced marginal

tax rates over a series of years partially "to return excess revenues to taxpayers." In 2003 the top marginal tax rate fell to 35 percent. Also, the income tax rate on capital gains and dividends was reduced to 15 percent. Economists generally agree that the Bush tax cuts, along with a highly expansionary monetary policy, helped revive and expand the economy following the recession of 2001. Strong growth of output and income in 2004 and 2005 produced large increases in tax revenues, although large budget deficits remained. Those deficits greatly expanded the size of the public debt.

Today, there is general agreement that the U.S. economy is operating at a point below *m*—rather than above *m*—on the Laffer Curve in Figure 15.10. Personal tax-rate increases raise tax revenue and personal tax-rate decreases reduce tax revenues. But economists recognize that, other things equal, cuts in tax rates reduce tax revenues in percentage terms by less than the tax-rate reductions. And tax-rate increases do not raise tax revenues by as much in percentage terms as the tax-rate increases. Changes in marginal tax rates *do* alter taxpayer behavior and thus affect taxable income. Although these effects seem to be relatively modest, they need to be considered in designing tax policy. In that regard, supply-side economics has contributed to economists' understanding of optimal fiscal policy.

Summary

1. In macroeconomics, the short run is a period in which nominal wages do not respond to changes in the price level. In contrast, the long run is a period in which nominal wages fully respond to changes in the price level.

2. The short-run aggregate supply curve is upsloping. Because nominal wages are unresponsive to price-level changes, increases in the price level (prices received by firms) increase profits and real output. Conversely, decreases in the price level reduce profits and real output. However, the long-run aggregate supply curve is vertical. With sufficient time for adjustment, nominal wages rise and fall with the price level, moving the economy along a vertical aggregate supply curve at the economy's full-employment output.

3. In the short run, demand-pull inflation raises the price level and real output. Once nominal wages rise to match the increase in the price level, the temporary increase in real output is reversed.

4. In the short run, cost-push inflation raises the price level and lowers real output. Unless the government expands aggregate demand, nominal wages eventually will decline under conditions of recession and the short-run aggregate supply curve will shift back to its initial location. Prices and real output will eventually return to their original levels.

5. If prices and wages are flexible downward, a decline in aggregate demand will lower output and the price level. The decline in the price level will eventually lower nominal wages and shift the short-run aggregate supply curve rightward. Full-employment output will thus be restored.

6. Assuming a stable, upsloping short-run aggregate supply curve, rightward shifts of the aggregate demand curve of various sizes yield the generalization that high rates of inflation are associated with low rates of unemployment, and vice versa. This inverse relationship is known as the Phillips Curve, and empirical data for the 1960s seemed to be consistent with it.

7. In the 1970s and early 1980s the Phillips Curve apparently shifted rightward, reflecting stagflation—simultaneously rising inflation rates and unemployment rates. The higher unemployment rates and inflation rates resulted mainly from huge oil price increases that caused large leftward shifts in the short-run aggregate supply curve (so-called aggregate supply shocks). The Phillips Curve shifted inward toward its original position in the 1980s. By 1989 stagflation had subsided, and the data points for the late 1990s and first half of the first decade of the 2000s were similar to those of the 1960s.

8. Although there is a short-run tradeoff between inflation and unemployment, there is no long-run tradeoff. Workers will adapt their expectations to new inflation realities, and when they do, the unemployment rate will return to the natural rate. So the long-run Phillips Curve is vertical at the natural rate, meaning that higher rates of inflation do not permanently "buy" the economy less unemployment.

9. Supply-side economists focus attention on government policies such as high taxation that impede the expansion of aggregate supply. The Laffer Curve relates tax rates to levels of tax revenue and suggests that, under some circumstances, cuts in tax rates will expand the tax base (output and income) and increase tax revenues. Most economists, however, believe that the United States is currently operating in the range of the Laffer Curve where tax rates and tax revenues move in the same, not opposite, directions.

10. Today's economists recognize the importance of considering supply-side effects in designing optimal fiscal policy.

Terms and Concepts

short run	stagflation	disinflation
long run	aggregate supply shocks	supply-side economics
Phillips Curve	long-run vertical Phillips Curve	Laffer Curve

Study Questions

1. Distinguish between the short run and the long run as they relate to macroeconomics. Why is the distinction important?

2. Which of the following statements are true? Which are false? Explain why the false statements are untrue.
   a. Short-run aggregate supply curves reflect an inverse relationship between the price level and the level of real output.
   b. The long-run aggregate supply curve assumes that nominal wages are fixed.
   c. In the long run, an increase in the price level will result in an increase in nominal wages.

3. **KEY QUESTION** Suppose the full-employment level of real output (Q) for a hypothetical economy is $250 and the price level (P) initially is 100. Use the short-run aggregate supply schedules below to answer the questions that follow:

AS (P_{100})		AS (P_{125})		AS (P_{75})	
P	Q	P	Q	P	Q
125	$280	125	$250	125	$310
100	250	100	220	100	280
75	220	75	190	75	250

   a. What will be the level of real output in the short run if the price level unexpectedly rises from 100 to 125 because of an increase in aggregate demand? What if the price level unexpectedly falls from 100 to 75 because of a decrease in aggregate demand? Explain each situation, using figures from the table.
   b. What will be the level of real output in the long run when the price level rises from 100 to 125? When it falls from 100 to 75? Explain each situation.
   c. Show the circumstances described in parts *a* and *b* on graph paper, and derive the long-run aggregate supply curve.

4. **KEY QUESTION** Use graphical analysis to show how each of the following would affect the economy first in the short run and then in the long run. Assume that the United States is initially operating at its full-employment level of output, that prices and wages are eventually flexible both upward and downward, and that there is no counteracting fiscal or monetary policy.

   a. Because of a war abroad, the oil supply to the United States is disrupted, sending oil prices rocketing upward.
   b. Construction spending on new homes rises dramatically, greatly increasing total U.S. investment spending.
   c. Economic recession occurs abroad, significantly reducing foreign purchases of U.S. exports.

5. Assume there is a particular short-run aggregate supply curve for an economy and the curve is relevant for several years. Use the AD-AS analysis to show graphically why higher rates of inflation over this period would be associated with lower rates of unemployment, and vice versa. What is this inverse relationship called?

6. **KEY QUESTION** Suppose the government misjudges the natural rate of unemployment to be much lower than it actually is, and thus undertakes expansionary fiscal and monetary policies to try to achieve the lower rate. Use the concept of the short-run Phillips Curve to explain why these policies might at first succeed. Use the concept of the long-run Phillips Curve to explain the long-run outcome of these policies.

7. What do the distinctions between short-run aggregate supply and long-run aggregate supply have in common with the distinction between the short-run Phillips Curve and the long-run Phillips Curve? Explain.

8. **KEY QUESTION** What is the Laffer Curve, and how does it relate to supply-side economics? Why is determining the economy's location on the curve so important in assessing tax policy?

9. Why might one person work more, earn more, and pay more income tax when his or her tax rate is cut, while another person will work less, earn less, and pay less income tax under the same circumstance?

10. **LAST WORD** Suppose that a tax cut involves two alternative schemes: (*a*) a $2 tax cut or tax rebate for each of the 10 people in the breakfast club, or (*b*) a tax savings for each of the 10 in proportion to their previous bill. If the two schemes were put to a majority vote, which do you think would win? According to supply-side economists, why might that voting outcome be shortsighted? Why might this tax anecdote be more relevant to an individual state than to the Federal government?

Web-Based Questions

1. **THE LAFFER CURVE—DOES IT SHIFT?** Congress did not substantially change Federal income tax rates between 1993 and 2000. Visit the Bureau of Economic Analysis Web site, **www.bea.gov/,** and use the interactive feature for National Income and Product Accounts tables to find Table 3.2 on Federal government current receipts and expeditures. Find the annual revenues from the Federal income tax from 1993 to 2000. What happened to those revenues over those years? Given constant tax rates, what do the changes in tax revenues suggest about changes in the *location* of the Laffer Curve? If lower (or higher) tax rates do not explain the changes in tax revenues, what do you think does?

2. **DYNAMIC TAX SCORING—WHAT IS IT, AND WHO WANTS IT?** Go to **www.google.com** and search for information on "dynamic tax scoring." What is it? How does it relate to supply-side economics? Which political groups support this approach, and why? What groups oppose it, and why?

16

IN THIS CHAPTER YOU WILL LEARN:

- About the general ingredients of economic growth and how they relate to production possibilities analysis and long-run aggregate supply.

- About "growth accounting" and the specific sources of U.S. economic growth.

- Why U.S. productivity growth has accelerated since the mid-1990s.

- About differing perspectives on whether growth is desirable and sustainable.

Economic Growth

The world's capitalist countries have experienced impressive growth of real GDP and real GDP per capita during the last half of the twentieth century and the first few years of the twenty-first century. In the United States, for example, real GDP (GDP adjusted for inflation) increased from $1777 billion in 1950 to $11,135 billion in 2005. Over those same years, real GDP per capita (average output per person) rose from $11,672 to $37,537. This **economic growth** greatly increased material abundance, reduced the burden of scarcity, and raised the economic well-being of Americans.

In Chapter 7 we explained why economic growth is so important, examined economic growth in the United States, and compared growth rates among the major nations. In this chapter we will look at how growth occurs in the context of our macro model. We will also explain the various factors that have contributed to U.S. economic growth since 1950. Then in Bonus Web Chapter 16W we extend the discussion of economic growth to the special problems facing low-income developing nations.

Ingredients of Growth

There are six main ingredients in economic growth. We can group them as supply, demand, and efficiency factors.

Supply Factors

Four of the ingredients of economic growth relate to the physical ability of the economy to expand. They are:

- Increases in the quantity and quality of natural resources.
- Increases in the quantity and quality of human resources.
- Increases in the supply (or stock) of capital goods.
- Improvements in technology.

These **supply factors**—changes in the physical and technical agents of production—enable an economy to expand its potential GDP.

Demand Factor

The fifth ingredient of economic growth is the **demand factor:**

- To achieve the higher production potential created by the supply factors, households, businesses, and government must *purchase* the economy's expanding output of goods and services.

When that occurs, there will be no unplanned increases in inventories and resources will remain fully employed. Economic growth requires increases in total spending to realize the output gains made available by increased production capacity.

Efficiency Factor

The sixth ingredient of economic growth is the **efficiency factor:**

- To reach its production potential, an economy must achieve economic efficiency as well as full employment.

The economy must use its resources in the least costly way (productive efficiency) to produce the specific mix of goods and services that maximizes people's well-being (allocative efficiency). The ability to expand production, together with the full use of available resources, is not sufficient for achieving maximum possible growth. Also required is the efficient use of those resources.

The supply, demand, and efficiency factors in economic growth are related. Unemployment caused by insufficient total spending (the demand factor) may lower the rate of new capital accumulation (a supply factor) and delay expenditures on research (also a supply factor). Conversely, low spending on investment (a supply factor)

may cause insufficient spending (the demand factor) and unemployment. Widespread inefficiency in the use of resources (the efficiency factor) may translate into higher costs of goods and services and thus lower profits, which in turn may slow innovation and reduce the accumulation of capital (supply factors). Economic growth is a dynamic process in which the supply, demand, and efficiency factors all interact.

Production Possibilities Analysis

To put the six factors underlying economic growth in proper perspective, let's first use the production possibilities analysis introduced in Chapter 1.

Growth and Production Possibilities

Recall that a curve like *AB* in Figure 16.1 is a production possibilities curve. It indicates the various *maximum* combinations of products an economy can produce with its fixed quantity and quality of natural, human, and capital resources and its stock of technological knowledge. An improvement in any of the supply factors will push the production possibilities curve outward, as from *AB* to *CD*.

But the demand factor reminds us that an increase in total spending is needed to move the economy from point *a* to a point on *CD*. And the efficiency factor reminds us that we need least-cost production and an optimal location on *CD* for the resources to make their maximum possible

FIGURE 16.1 Economic growth and the production possibilities curve. Economic growth is made possible by the four supply factors that shift the production possibilities curve outward, as from *AB* to *CD*. Economic growth is realized when the demand factor and the efficiency factor move the economy from point *a* to *b*.

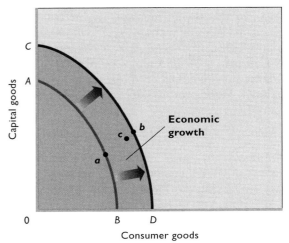

dollar contribution to total output. You will recall from Chapter 1 that this "best allocation" is determined by expanding production of each good until its marginal benefit equals its marginal cost. Here, we assume that this optimal combination of capital and consumer goods occurs at point *b*.

Example: The net increase in the size of the labor force in the United States in recent years has been 1.5 to 2 million workers per year. That increment raises the economy's production capacity. But obtaining the extra output that these added workers could produce depends on their success in finding jobs. It also depends on whether or not the jobs are in firms and industries where the workers' talents are fully and optimally used. Society does not want new labor-force entrants to be unemployed. Nor does it want pediatricians working as plumbers or pediatricians producing services for which marginal costs exceed marginal benefits.

Normally, increases in total spending match increases in production capacity, and the economy moves from a point on the previous production possibilities curve to a point on the expanded curve. Moreover, the competitive market system tends to drive the economy toward productive and allocative efficiency. Occasionally, however, the curve may shift outward but leave the economy behind at some level of operation such as *c* in Figure 16.1. Because *c* is inside the new production possibilities curve *CD*, the economy has not realized its potential for economic growth. **(Key Question 1)**

Labor and Productivity

Although demand and efficiency factors are important, discussions of economic growth focus primarily on supply factors. Society can increase its real output and income in two fundamental ways: (1) by increasing its inputs of resources, and (2) by raising the productivity of those inputs. Figure 16.2 concentrates on the input of *labor* and provides a useful framework for discussing the role of supply factors in growth. A nation's real GDP in any year depends on the input of labor (measured in hours of work) multiplied by **labor productivity** (measured as real output per hour of work):

Real GDP = hours of work × labor productivity

So, thought of this way, a nation's economic growth from one year to the next depends on its *increase* in labor inputs (if any) and its *increase* in labor productivity (if any).

Illustration: Assume that the hypothetical economy of Ziam has 10 workers in year 1, each working 2000 hours per year (50 weeks at 40 hours per week). The total input of

FIGURE 16.2 The supply determinants of real output.
Real GDP is usefully viewed as the product of the quantity of labor inputs (hours of work) multiplied by labor productivity.

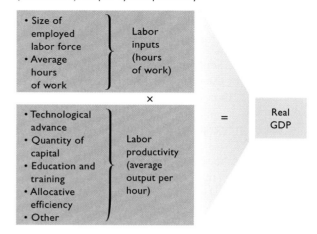

W 16.1

Productivity and economic growth

labor therefore is 20,000 hours. If productivity (average real output per hour of work) is $10, then real GDP in Ziam will be $200,000 (= 20,000 × $10). If work hours rise to 20,200 and labor productivity rises to $10.40, Ziam's real GDP will increase to $210,080 in year 2. Ziam's rate of economic growth will be about 5% [= ($210,080 − $200,000)/ $200,000] for the year.

Hours of Work What determines the number of hours worked each year? As shown in Figure 16.2, the hours of labor input depend on the size of the employed labor force and the length of the average workweek. Labor-force size depends on the size of the working-age population and the **labor-force participation rate**— the percentage of the working-age population actually in the labor force. The length of the average workweek is governed by legal and institutional considerations and by collective bargaining.

Labor Productivity Figure 16.2 tells us that labor productivity is determined by technological progress, the quantity of capital goods available to workers, the quality of the labor itself, and the efficiency with which inputs are allocated, combined, and managed. Productivity rises when the health, training, education, and motivation of workers improve, when workers have more and better machinery and natural resources with which to work, when production is better organized and managed, and when labor is reallocated from less efficient industries to more efficient industries.

Growth in the AD-AS Model

Let's now link the production possibilities analysis to long-run aggregate supply so that we can show the process of economic growth through the extended aggregate demand–aggregate supply model developed in Chapter 15.

Production Possibilities and Aggregate Supply

The supply factors that shift the economy's production possibilities curve outward also shift its long-run aggregate supply curve rightward. As shown in Figure 16.3, the outward shift of the production possibilities curve from *AB* to *CD* in graph (a) is equivalent to the rightward shift of the economy's long-run aggregate supply curve from AS_{LR1} to AS_{LR2} in graph (b). The long-run AS curves are vertical because an economy's potential output—its full-employment output—is determined by the supply and efficiency factors, not by its price level. Whatever the price level, the economy's potential output remains the same. Moreover, just as price-level changes do not shift an economy's production possibilities curve, they do not shift an economy's long-run aggregate supply curve.

Extended AD-AS Model

In Figure 16.4 we use the extended aggregate demand–aggregate supply model to depict economic growth in the United States. (The model is extended to include the distinction between short- and long-run aggregate supply. See Chapter 15.)

Suppose the economy's aggregate demand curve, long-run aggregate supply curve, and short-run aggregate supply curve initially are AD_1, AS_{LR1}, and AS_1, as shown. The equilibrium price level and level of real output are P_1 and Q_1. At price level P_1, the short-run aggregate supply is AS_1; it slopes upward because, in the short run, changes in the price level cause firms to adjust their output. In the long run, however, price-level changes do not affect the economy's real output, leaving the long-run aggregate supply curve vertical at the economy's potential level of output, here Q_1. This potential level of output depends on the supply and efficiency factors previously discussed.

Now let's assume that changes in the supply factors (quantity and quality of resources and technology) shift the long-run aggregate supply curve rightward from AS_{LR1} to AS_{LR2}. The economy's potential output has increased, as reflected by the expansion of available real output from Q_1 to Q_2.

With no change in aggregate demand, the increase in long-run aggregate supply from AS_{LR1} to AS_{LR2} in Figure 16.4 would expand real GDP and lower the price level. But declines in the price level are not a part of the U.S. growth experience. The reason? The Federal Reserve has expanded the nation's money supply over the years such that increases in aggregate demand have more than matched the increases in aggregate supply. We show this increase in aggregate demand as the shift from AD_1 to AD_2.

FIGURE 16.3 Production possibilities and long-run aggregate supply. (a) Supply factors shift an economy's production possibilities curve outward, as from *AB* to *CD*. (b) The same factors (along with the efficiency factor) shift the economy's long-run aggregate supply curve to the right, as from AS_{LR1} to AS_{LR2}.

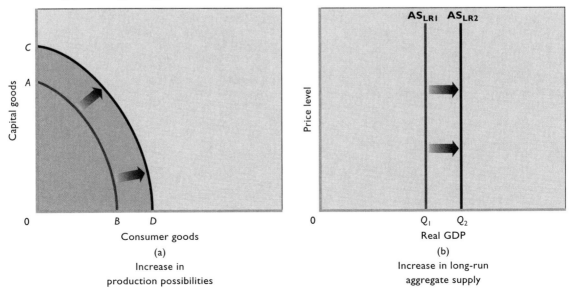

(a)
Increase in
production possibilities

(b)
Increase in long-run
aggregate supply

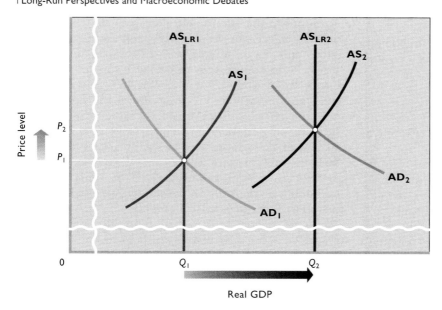

FIGURE 16.4 Depicting U.S. growth via the extended AD-AS model. Long-run aggregate supply and short-run aggregate supply have increased over time, as from AS_{LR1} to AS_{LR2} and AS_1 to AS_2. Simultaneously, aggregate demand has shifted rightward, as from AD_1 to AD_2. The actual outcome of these combined shifts has been economic growth, shown as the increase in real output from Q_1 to Q_2, accompanied by mild inflation, shown as the rise in the price level from P_1 to P_2.

The increases of aggregate supply and aggregate demand in Figure 16.4 have increased real output from Q_1 to Q_2 and have boosted the price level from P_1 to P_2. At the higher price level P_2, the economy confronts a new short-run aggregate supply curve AS_2. The changes described in Figure 16.4 describe the actual U.S. experience: economic growth, accompanied by mild inflation.

In brief, economic growth results from increases in long-run aggregate supply. Whether deflation, zero inflation, mild inflation, or rapid inflation accompanies growth depends on the extent to which aggregate demand increases relative to aggregate supply. Any inflation that occurs is the result of the growth of aggregate demand. It is not the result of the growth of real GDP. **(Key Question 5)**

O 16.1
Growth theory

U.S. Economic Growth Rates

More resources and greater productivity have fueled the growth of real GDP in the United States. Moreover, this output growth has far outstripped the population growth, resulting in a rise in real GDP per capita (= real GDP/ population). Figure 16.5 shows the average annual growth rates of real GDP and real per capita GDP in the United States from 1950 through 2005. Over all these years, real

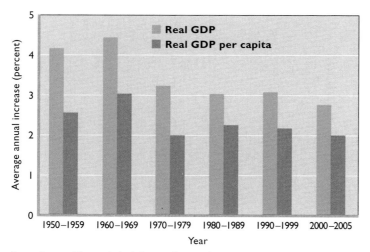

FIGURE 16.5 U.S. economic growth, annual averages for five and one-half decades. Growth of real GDP has averaged about 3.5 percent annually since 1950, and annual growth of real GDP per capita has averaged about 2.3 percent. Growth rates in the 1970s and 1980s were less than those in the 1960s, but the rates rebounded over the 1995–2005 period (not shown).

Source: Bureau of Economic Analysis, **www.bea.gov/.**

GDP grew by 3.5 percent annually, whereas real GDP per capita grew by 2.3 percent a year. Economic growth was particularly strong in the 1960s but declined during the 1970s and 1980s. Although the average annual growth rate for the 1990s only slightly exceeded that of the 1980s, real GDP surged between 1996 and 1999. Specifically, it grew by 3.7 percent in 1996, 4.5 percent in 1997, 4.2 percent in 1998, and 4.5 percent in 1999. These growth rates were higher than previous rates in the 1990s and also higher than those in most other advanced industrial nations during that period.

Economic growth continued strong in 2000 in the United States, but it collapsed during the recessionary year 2001. Specifically, the rate was 3.7 percent in 2000 and 0.8 percent in 2001. Growth rates rebounded to 1.6 percent in 2002, 2.7 percent in 2003, 4.2 percent in 2004, and 3.5 percent in 2005.

QUICK REVIEW 16.1

- The ingredients of economic growth include (a) four supply factors (increases in the quantity and quality of natural resources, increases in the quantity and quality of human resources, increases in the stock of capital goods, and improvements in technology), (b) a demand factor (increased total spending), and (c) an efficiency factor (achieving economic efficiency).
- Economic growth is shown as an outward shift of a nation's production possibilities curve (accompanied by movement from some point on the old curve to a point on the new curve) and combined rightward shifts of the long-run aggregate supply curve, the short-run aggregate supply curve, and the aggregate demand curve.
- Real GDP grew by an average of 3.5 percent annually between 1950 and 2005; over that same period, real GDP per capita grew at an average annual rate of about 2.3 percent.

Accounting for Growth

The Council of Economic Advisers uses **growth accounting** —the bookkeeping of the supply-side elements that contribute to changes in real GDP—to assess the factors underlying economic growth. Ultimately, that accounting

CONSIDER THIS ...

Economic Growth Rates Matter!

When compounded over many decades, small absolute differences in rates of economic growth add up to substantial differences in real GDP and standards of living. Consider three hypothetical countries—Alpha, Bravo, and Charlie. Suppose that in 2006 these countries have identical levels of real GDP ($6 trillion), population (200 million), and real GDP per capita ($30,000). Also, assume that annual real GDP growth is 2 percent in Alpha, 3 percent in Bravo, and 4 percent in Charlie.

How will these alternative growth rates affect real GDP and real GDP per capita over a long period, say, the 70-year average life span of an American? By 2076 the 2, 3, and 4 percent growth rates would boost real GDP from $6 trillion to:

- $24 trillion in Alpha.
- $47 trillion in Bravo.
- $93 trillion in Charlie.
- For illustration, let's assume that each country experienced an average annual population growth of 1 percent over the 70 years. Then, in 2076 real GDP per capita would be about:
- $60,000 in Alpha.
- $118,000 in Bravo.
- $233,000 in Charlie.

Economic growth rates matter!

leads to two main categories:
- Increases in hours of work.
- Increases in labor productivity.

Labor Inputs versus Labor Productivity

Table 16.1 provides the relevant data for the United States for four periods. The symbol "Q" in the table stands for

TABLE 16.1 Accounting for Growth of U.S. Real GDP, 1953–2011 (Average Annual Percentage Changes)

Item	1953 Q2 to 1973 Q4	1973 Q4 to 1995 Q2	1995 Q2 to 2001 Q1	2001 Q1 to 2005 Q3	2005 Q3 to 2011 Q4*
Increase in real GDP	3.6	2.8	3.8	2.8	3.2
Increase in quantity of labor	1.2	1.5	1.7	−0.6	0.8
Increase in labor productivity	2.4	1.3	2.1	3.4	2.4

*Rates beyond 2005 are projected rates.

Source: Derived from *Economic Report of the President, 2006,* p. 44.

"quarter" of the year. The beginning points for the first three periods are business-cycle peaks, and the last period includes future projections by the President's Council of Economic Advisers. It is clear from the table that both increases in the quantity of labor and rises in labor productivity are important sources of economic growth. Between 1953 and 2005, the labor force increased from 63 million to 142 million workers. Over that period the average length of the workweek remained relatively stable. Falling birthrates slowed the growth of the native population, but increased immigration partly offset that slowdown. As indicated in the Consider This box to the right, of particular significance was a surge of women's participation in the labor force. Partly as a result, U.S. labor-force growth averaged 1.7 million workers per year over the past 52 years.

The growth of labor productivity has also been important to economic growth. In fact, productivity growth has usually been the more significant factor, with the exception of 1973–1995 when productivity growth greatly slowed. For example, between 2001 and 2005, productivity growth was responsible for all of the 2.8 percent average annual economic growth. Between 2005 and 2011, productivity growth is projected to account for 75 percent of the growth of real GDP.

Technological Advance

The importance of productivity growth to economic growth calls for a fuller explanation of the factors that contribute to productivity growth. The largest contributor is technological advance, which is thought to account for about 40 percent of productivity growth. As economist Paul Romer stated, "Human history teaches us that economic growth springs from better recipes, not just from more cooking."

Technological advance includes not only innovative production techniques but new managerial methods and new forms of business organization that improve the process of production. Generally, technological advance is generated by the discovery of new knowledge, which allows resources to be combined in improved ways that increase output. Once discovered and implemented, new knowledge soon becomes available to entrepreneurs and firms at relatively low cost. Technological advance therefore eventually spreads through the entire economy, boosting productivity and economic growth.

Technological advance and capital formation (investment) are closely related, since technological advance usually promotes investment in new machinery and equipment. In fact, technological advance is often *embodied* within new capital. For example, the purchase of new computers brings into industry speedier, more powerful computers that incorporate new technology.

CONSIDER THIS ...

Women, the Labor Force, and Economic Growth

The substantial rise in the number of women working in the paid workforce in the United States has been one of the major labor market trends of the past half-century. In 1965, some 40 percent of women worked full-time or part-time in paid jobs. Today, that number is 59 percent.

Women have greatly increased their productivity in the workplace, mostly by becoming better educated and professionally trained. Rising productivity has increased women's wage rates. Those higher wages have raised the opportunity costs—the forgone wage earnings—of staying at home. Women have therefore substituted employment in the labor market for more expensive traditional home activities. This substitution has been particularly pronounced among married women. (Single women have always had high labor-force participation rates.)

Furthermore, changing lifestyles and the widespread availability of birth control have freed up time for greater labor-force participation by women. Women not only have fewer children, but those children are spaced closer together in age. Thus women who leave their jobs during their children's early years return to the labor force sooner.

Greater access to jobs by women has also been a significant factor in the rising labor-force participation of women. Service industries—teaching, nursing, and office work, for instance—that traditionally have employed many women have expanded rapidly in the past several decades. Also, the population in general has shifted from farms and rural regions to urban areas, where jobs for women are more abundant and more geographically accessible. An increased availability of part-time jobs has also made it easier for women to combine labor market employment with child-rearing and household activities. Also, antidiscrimination laws and enforcement efforts have reduced barriers that previously discouraged or prevented women from taking traditional male jobs such as business managers, lawyers, professors, and physicians. More jobs are open to women today than a half-century ago.

In summary, women in the United States are better educated, more productive, and more efficiently employed than ever before. Their increased presence in the labor force has contributed greatly to U.S. economic growth.

Technological advance has been both rapid and profound. Gas and diesel engines, conveyor belts, and assembly lines are significant developments of the past. So, too, are fuel-efficient commercial aircraft, integrated microcircuits, personal computers, xerography, and containerized shipping. More recently, technological advance has exploded, particularly in the areas of computers, photography, wireless communications, and the Internet. Other fertile areas of recent innovation are medicine and biotechnology.

Quantity of Capital

A second major contributor to productivity growth is increased capital, which explains roughly 30 percent of productivity growth. More and better plant and equipment make workers more productive. And a nation acquires more capital by saving some of its income and using that saving to invest in plant and equipment.

Although some capital substitutes for labor, most capital is complementary to labor—it makes labor more productive. A key determinant of labor productivity is the amount of capital goods available *per worker*. If both the aggregate stock of capital goods and the size of the labor force increase over a given period, the individual worker is not necessarily better equipped and productivity will not necessarily rise. But the quantity of capital equipment available per U. S. worker has increased greatly over time. (In 2003 it was about $83,466 per worker.)

Public investment in the U.S. **infrastructure** (highways and bridges, public transit systems, wastewater treatment facilities, water systems, airports, educational facilities, and so on) has also grown over the years. This public capital (infrastructure) complements private capital. Investments in new highways promote private investment in new factories and retail stores along their routes. Industrial parks developed by local governments attract manufacturing and distribution firms.

Private investment in infrastructure also plays a large role in economic growth. One example is the tremendous growth of private capital relating to communications systems over the years.

Education and Training

Ben Franklin once said, "He that hath a trade hath an estate," meaning that education and training contribute to a worker's stock of **human capital**—the knowledge and skills that make a worker productive. Investment in human capital includes not only formal education but also on-the-job training. Like investment in physical capital, investment in human capital is an important means of increasing labor productivity and earnings. An estimated 15% of productivity growth owes to such investment in people's education and skills.

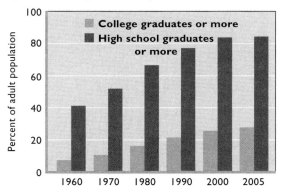

FIGURE 16.6 Changes in the educational attainment of the U.S. adult population. The percentage of the U.S. adult population, age 25 or more, completing high school and college has been rising over recent decades.

Source: U.S. Census Bureau, **www.census.gov.**

One measure of a nation's quality of labor is its level of educational attainment. Figure 16.6 shows large gains in education attainment over the past several decades. In 1960 only 41 percent of the U.S. population age 25 or older had at least a high school education; and only 8 percent had a college or postcollege education. By 2004, those numbers had increased to 85 and 28 percent, respectively. Clearly, education has become accessible to more people in the United States during the recent past.

But all is not upbeat with education in the United States. Many observers think that the quality of education in the United States has declined. For example, U.S. students in science and mathematics perform poorly on tests on those subjects relative to students in many other nations (see Global Perspective 16.1). The United States has been producing fewer engineers and scientists, a problem that may trace back to inadequate training in math and science in elementary and high schools. And it is argued that on-the-job training programs (apprenticeship programs) in several European nations are superior to those in the United States. For these reasons, much recent public policy discussion and legislation has been directed toward improving the quality of the U.S. education and training system.

Economies of Scale and Resource Allocation

Economies of scale and improved resource allocation are a third and fourth source of productivity growth, and together they explain about 15 percent of productivity growth.

Economies of Scale
Reductions in per-unit cost that result from increases in the size of markets and firms

GLOBAL PERSPECTIVE 16.1

Average Test Scores of Eighth-Grade Students in Math and Science, Top 10 Countries and the United States

The test performance of U.S. eighth-grade students did not rank favorably with that of eighth-graders in several other nations in the Third International Math and Science Study (2003).

Mathematics

Rank		Score
1	Singapore	605
2	South Korea	589
3	Hong Kong	586
4	Taiwan	585
5	Japan	570
6	Belgium	537
7	Netherlands	536
8	Estonia	531
9	Hungary	529
10	Malaysia	508
15	United States	504

Science

Rank		Score
1	Singapore	578
2	Taiwan	571
3	South Korea	558
4	Hong Kong	556
5	Estonia	552
6	Japan	552
7	Hungary	543
8	Netherlands	536
9	United States	527
10	Australia	527

are called **economies of scale.** Markets have increased in size over time, allowing firms to achieve production advantages associated with greater size. As firms expand their size and output, they are able to use larger, more productive equipment and employ methods of manufacturing and delivery that increase productivity. They also are better able to recoup substantial investments in developing new products and production methods. Examples: A large manufacturer of autos can use elaborate assembly lines with computerization and robotics, while smaller producers must settle for less advanced technologies using more labor inputs. Large pharmaceutical firms greatly reduce the average amount of labor (researchers, production workers) needed to produce each pill as they increase the number of pills produced. Accordingly, economies of scale result in greater real GDP and thus contribute to economic growth.

Improved Resource Allocation

Improved resource allocation means that workers over time have moved from low-productivity employment to high-productivity employment. Historically, much labor has shifted from agriculture, where labor productivity is low, to manufacturing, where it is quite high. More recently, labor has shifted away from some manufacturing industries to even higher productivity industries such as computer software, business consulting, and pharmaceuticals. As a result of such shifts, the average productivity of U.S. workers has increased.

Also, discrimination in education and the labor market has historically deterred some women and minorities from entering high-productivity jobs. With the decline of such discrimination over time many members of those groups have shifted from low-productivity jobs to higher-productivity jobs. The result has been higher overall labor productivity and real GDP.

Finally, we know from discussions in Chapter 5 that tariffs, import quotas, and other barriers to international trade tend to relegate resources to relatively unproductive pursuits. The long-run movement toward liberalized international trade through international agreements has improved the allocation of resources, increased labor productivity, and expanded real output, both here and abroad.

Other Factors

Several difficult-to-measure factors influence a nation's rate of economic growth. The overall social-cultural-political environment of the United States, for example, has encouraged economic growth. The market system that has prevailed in the United States has fostered many income and profit incentives that promote growth. The United States has also had a stable political system characterized by democratic principles, internal order, the right of property ownership, the legal status of enterprise, and the enforcement of contracts. Economic freedom and political freedom have been "growth-friendly."

Unlike some nations, there are virtually no social or moral taboos on production and material progress in the United States. The nation's social philosophy has embraced material advance as an attainable and desirable economic goal. The inventor, the innovator, and the businessperson are accorded high degrees of prestige and respect in American society.

Moreover, Americans have had positive attitudes toward work and risk taking, resulting in an ample supply of willing workers and innovative entrepreneurs. A flow of energetic immigrants has greatly augmented that supply. **(Key Question 6)**

QUICK REVIEW 16.2

- Improvements in labor productivity accounted for about two-thirds of increases in U.S. real GDP between 1990 and 2005; the use of more labor inputs accounted for the remainder.
- Improved technology, more capital, greater education and training, economies of scale, and better resource allocation have been the main contributors to U.S. productivity growth and thus to U.S. economic growth.
- Other factors that have been favorable to U.S. growth include reliance on the market system, a stable political system, a social philosophy that embraces material progress, an abundant supply of willing workers and entrepreneurs, and free-trade policies.

The Productivity Acceleration: A New Economy?

Figure 16.7 shows the growth of labor productivity (as measured by changes in the index of labor productivity) in the United States from 1973 to 2005, along with separate trend lines for 1973–1995 and 1995–2005. Labor productivity grew by an average of only 1.4 percent yearly over the 1973–1995 period. But productivity growth averaged 2.9 percent between 1995 and 2005. Many economists believe that this higher productivity growth resulted from a significant new wave of technological advance, coupled with global competition. Some economists say that the United States has achieved a **New Economy**—one with a higher projected trend rate of productivity growth and therefore greater potential economic growth than in the 1973–1995 period.

This increase in productivity growth is important because real output, real income, and real wages are linked to labor productivity. To see why, suppose you are alone on an uninhabited island. The number of fish you can catch or coconuts you can pick per hour—your productivity—is your real wage (or real income) per hour. By *increasing* your productivity, you can improve your standard of living because greater output per hour means there are more fish and coconuts (goods) available to consume.

So it is for the economy as a whole: Over long periods, the economy's labor productivity determines its average real hourly wage. The economy's income per hour is

FIGURE 16.7 Growth of labor productivity in the United States, 1973–2005. U.S. labor productivity (here, for the business sector) increased at an average annual rate of only 1.4 percent from 1973 to 1995. But between 1995 and 2005 it accelerated to an annual rate of 2.9 percent.

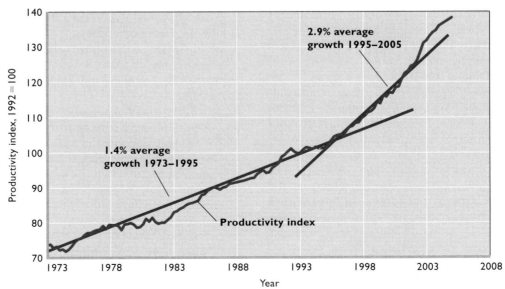

Source: U.S. Bureau of Labor Statistics, **www.bls.gov/.**

equal to its output per hour. Productivity growth therefore is its main route for increasing its standard of living. It allows firms to pay higher wages without lowering their business profits. As we demonstrated in this chapter's first Consider This box, even a seemingly small percentage change in productivity growth, if sustained over several years, can make a substantial difference as to how fast a nation's standard of living rises. We know from the *rule of 70* (Chapter 7) that if a nation's productivity grows by 2.9 percent annually rather than 1.4, its material standard of living will double in 24 years rather than 50 years.

Reasons for the Productivity Acceleration

Why has productivity growth increased relative to earlier periods? What is "new" about the New Economy?

The Microchip and Information Technology

The core element of the productivity speedup is an explosion of entrepreneurship and innovation based on the microprocessor, or *microchip*, which bundles transistors on a piece of silicon. Advocates of the New Economy liken the invention of the microchip to that of electricity, the automobile, air travel, the telephone, and television in importance and scope.

The microchip has found its way into thousands of applications. It has helped create a wide array of new products and services and new ways of doing business. Its immediate results were the pocket calculator, the bar-code scanner, the personal computer, the laptop computer, and more powerful business computers. But the miniaturization of electronic circuits also advanced the development of many other products such as cell phones and pagers, computer-guided lasers, deciphered genetic codes, global positioning equipment, energy conservation systems, Doppler radar, and digital cameras.

Perhaps of greatest significance, the widespread availability of personal and laptop computers stimulated the desire to tie them together. That desire promoted rapid development of the Internet and all its many manifestations, such as business-to-household and business-to-business electronic commerce (e-commerce). The combination of the computer, fiber optic cable, wireless technology, and the Internet constitutes a spectacular advance in **information technology,** which has been used to connect all parts of the world.

New Firms and Increasing Returns

Hundreds of new **start-up firms** advanced various aspects of the new information technology. Many of these firms created more

"hype" than goods and services and quickly fell by the wayside. But a number of firms flourished, eventually to take their places among the nation's largest firms. Examples of those firms include Intel (microchips); Apple and Dell (personal computers); Microsoft and Oracle (computer software); Cisco Systems (Internet switching systems); America Online (Internet service provision); Yahoo and Google (Internet search engines); and eBay and Amazon.com (electronic commerce). There are scores more! Most of these firms were either "not on the radar" or "a small blip on the radar" 30 years ago. Today each of them has large annual revenue and employs thousands of workers.

Successful new firms often experience **increasing returns,** which occur when a firm's output increases by a larger percentage than the increase in its inputs (resources). For example, suppose that Techco decides to double the size of its operations to meet the growing demand for its services. After doubling its plant and equipment and doubling its workforce, say, from 100 workers to 200 workers, it finds that its total output has tripled from 8000 units to 24,000 units. Techco has experienced increasing returns; its output has increased by 200 percent, while its inputs have increased by only 100 percent. That is, its labor productivity has gone up from $80 (= 8000 units/100 workers) to $120 (= 24,000 units/200 workers). Increasing returns boost labor productivity, which, other things equal, lowers per-unit costs of production. These cost reductions, as we know, are called *economies of scale.*

There are a number of sources of increasing returns and economies of scale for emerging firms:

- *More specialized inputs* Firms can use more specialized and thus more productive capital and workers as they expand their operations. A growing new e-commerce business, for example, can purchase highly specialized inventory management systems and hire specialized personnel such as accountants, marketing managers, and system maintenance experts.

- *Spreading of development costs* Firms can spread high product development costs over greater output. For example, suppose that a new software product costs $100,000 to develop and only $2 per unit to manufacture and sell. If the firm sells 1000 units of the software, its per-unit cost will be $102 [= ($100,000 + $2000)/1000], but if it sells 500,000 units, that cost will drop to only $2.20 [= ($100,000 + $1 million)/500,000].

- *Simultaneous consumption* Many of the products and services of the New Economy can satisfy many customers at the same time. Unlike a gallon of gas that needs to be produced for each buyer, a software program needs to be produced only once. It then becomes available at very low expense to thousands or even millions of buyers. The same is true of entertainment delivered on CDs, movies distributed on DVDs, and information disseminated through the Internet.

- *Network effects* Software and Internet service become more beneficial to a buyer the greater the number of households and businesses that also buy them. When others have Internet service, you can send e-mail messages to them. And when they also have software that allows display of documents and photos, you can attach those items to your e-mail messages. These system advantages are called **network effects,** which are increases in the value of the product to each user, including existing users, as the total number of users rises. The domestic and global expansion of the Internet in particular has produced network effects, as have cell phones, pagers, palm computers, and other aspects of wireless communication. Network effects magnify the value of output well beyond the costs of inputs.

- *Learning by doing* Finally, firms that produce new products or pioneer new ways of doing business experience increasing returns through **learning by doing.** Tasks that initially may have taken firms hours may take them only minutes once the methods are perfected.

Whatever the particular source of increasing returns, the result is higher productivity, which tends to reduce the per-unit cost of producing and delivering products. Table 16.2 lists a number of specific examples of cost reduction from technology in recent years.

Global Competition The recent economy is characterized not only by information technology and increasing returns but also by heightened global competition. The collapse of the socialist economies in the late 1980s and early 1990s, together with the success of market systems, has led to a reawakening of capitalism throughout the world. The new information technologies have "shrunk the globe" and made it imperative for all firms to lower their costs and prices and to innovate in order to remain competitive. Free-trade zones such as NAFTA and the European Union (EU), along with trade liberalization through the World Trade Organization (WTO), have also heightened competition internationally by removing trade protection from domestic firms. The larger geographic markets, in turn, have enabled the firms of the New Economy to expand beyond their national borders.

TABLE 16.2 Examples of Cost Reductions from Technology in the New Economy

- The cost of storing one megabit of information—enough for a 320-page book—fell from $5257 in 1975 to 17 cents in 1999.
- Prototyping each part of a car once took Ford weeks and cost $20,000 on average. Using an advanced 3-D object printer, it cut the time to just hours and the cost to less than $20.
- Studies show that telecommuting saves businesses about $20,000 annually for a worker earning $44,000—a saving in lost work time and employee retention costs, plus gains in worker productivity.
- Using scanners and computers, Weyerhaeuser increased the lumber yield and value from each log by 30 percent.
- Amoco used 3-D seismic exploration technology to cut the cost of finding oil from nearly $10 per barrel in 1991 to under $1 per barrel in 2000.
- Wal-Mart reduced the operating cost of its delivery trucks by 20 percent through installing computers, global positioning gear, and cell phones in 4300 vehicles.
- Banking transactions on the Internet cost 1 cent each, compared with $1.14 for face-to-face, pen-and-paper communication.

Source: Compiled and directly quoted from W. Michael Cox and Richard Alm, "The New Paradigm," Federal Reserve Bank of Dallas Annual Report, May 2000, various pages.

Implication: More-Rapid Economic Growth

Other things equal, stronger productivity growth and heightened global competition allow the economy to achieve a higher rate of economic growth. A glance back at Figure 16.3 will help make this point. If the shifts of the curves reflect annual changes in the old economy, then the New Economy would be depicted by an outward shift of the production possibilities curve beyond *CD* in Figure 16.3a and a shift of the long-run aggregate supply curve farther to the right than AS_{LR2} in Figure 16.3b. When coupled with economic efficiency and increased total spending, the economy's real GDP would rise by more than that shown. That is, the economy would achieve a higher rate of economic growth.

If the productivity acceleration is permanent, the economy has a higher "safe speed limit" than previously because production capacity rises more rapidly. The New Economy can grow by, say, 3.5 or 4 percent, rather than 2 or 3 percent, each year without igniting demand-pull inflation. Increases in aggregate demand that in the past would have caused inflation do not cause inflation because they are buffered by faster productivity growth. Even when wage increases rise to match the productivity increases, as is desirable and as they usually do, per-unit production costs and therefore prices can remain stable.

Global competition in the New Economy also contributes to price stability by reducing the pricing power (or market power) of U.S. firms.

A caution: Those who champion the idea of a New Economy emphasize that it does not mean that the business cycle is dead. Indeed, the economy slowed in the first two months of 2001 and receded over the following eight months of that year. The New Economy is simply one for which the *trend lines* of productivity growth and economic growth are steeper than they were in the preceding two decades. Real output may periodically deviate below and above the steeper trend lines.

Skepticism about Permanence

Although most macroeconomists have revised their forecasts for long-term productivity growth upward, at least slightly, others are still skeptical and urge a "wait-and-see" approach. Skeptics acknowledge that the economy has experienced a rapid advance of new technology, some new firms have experienced increasing returns, and global competition has increased. But they wonder if these factors are sufficiently profound to produce a 15- to 20-year period of substantially higher rates of productivity growth and real GDP growth.

Skeptics point out that productivity surged between 1975 and 1978 and between 1983 and 1986 but in each case soon reverted to its lower long-run trend. The higher trend line of productivity inferred from the short-run spurt of productivity could prove to be transient. Only by looking backward over long periods can economists distinguish the start of a new long-run secular trend from a shorter-term boost in productivity related to the business cycle and temporary factors.

What Can We Conclude?

Given the different views on the New Economy, what should we conclude? Perhaps the safest conclusions are these:

- The prospects for a continued long-run rapid trend of productivity growth are good (see Global Perspective 16.2). Studies indicate that productivity advance related to information technology has spread to a wide range of industries, including services. Even in the recession year 2001 and in 2002, when the economy was sluggish, productivity growth remained strong. Specifically, it averaged about 3.3 percent in the business sector over those two years. It rose by 4.1 percent in 2003, 3.5 percent in 2004, and 2.7 percent in 2005, as the economy vigorously expanded.
- Time will tell. Several more years must elapse before economists can declare the recent productivity acceleration a long-run, sustainable trend. (**Key Question 9**)

GLOBAL PERSPECTIVE 16.2

Growth Competitiveness Index

The World Economic Forum annually compiles a growth competitiveness index, which uses various factors (such as innovativeness, effective transfer of technology among sectors, efficiency of the financial system, rates of investment, and degree of integration with the rest of the world) to measure the ability of a country to achieve economic growth over time. Here is its top 10 list for 2005.

Country	Growth Competitiveness Ranking, 2005
Finland	1
United States	2
Sweden	3
Denmark	4
Taiwan	5
Singapore	6
Iceland	7
Switzerland	8
Norway	9
Australia	10

Source: World Economic Forum, **www.weforum.org/**.

QUICK REVIEW 16.3

- Over long time periods, labor productivity growth determines an economy's growth of real wages and its standard of living.
- Many economists believe that the United States has entered a period of faster productivity growth and higher rates of economic growth.
- The productivity acceleration is based on rapid technological change in the form of the microchip and information technology, increasing returns and lower per-unit costs, and heightened global competition that helps hold down prices.
- Faster productivity growth means the economy has a higher "economic speed limit": It can grow more rapidly than previously without producing inflation. Nonetheless, many economists caution that it is still too early to determine whether the higher rates of productivity are a lasting long-run trend or a fortunate short-lived occurrence.

Is Growth Desirable and Sustainable?

Economists usually take for granted that economic growth is desirable and sustainable. But not everyone agrees.

The Antigrowth View

Critics of growth say industrialization and growth result in pollution, global warming, ozone depletion, and other environmental problems. These adverse negative externalities occur because inputs in the production process reenter the environment as some form of waste. The more rapid our growth and the higher our standard of living, the more waste the environment must absorb—or attempt to absorb. In an already wealthy society, further growth usually means satisfying increasingly trivial wants at the cost of mounting threats to the ecological system.

Critics of growth also argue that there is little compelling evidence that economic growth has solved sociological problems such as poverty, homelessness, and discrimination. Consider poverty: In the antigrowth view, American poverty is a problem of distribution, not production. The requisite for solving the problem is commitment and political courage to redistribute wealth and income, not further increases in output.

Antigrowth sentiment also says that while growth may permit us to "make a better living," it does not give us "the good life." We may be producing more and enjoying it less. Growth means frantic paces on jobs, worker burnout, and alienated employees who have little or no control over decisions affecting their lives. The changing technology at the core of growth poses new anxieties and new sources of insecurity for workers. Both high-level and low-level workers face the prospect of having their hard-earned skills and experience rendered obsolete by an onrushing technology. High-growth economies are high-stress economies, which may impair our physical and mental health.

Finally, critics of high rates of growth doubt that they are sustainable. The planet Earth has finite amounts of natural resources available, and they are being consumed at alarming rates. Higher rates of economic growth simply speed up the degradation and exhaustion of the earth's resources. In this view, slower economic growth that is environmentally sustainable is preferable to faster growth.

In Defense of Economic Growth

The primary defense of growth is that it is the path to the greater material abundance and higher living standards desired by the vast majority of people. Rising output and incomes allow people to buy

> more education, recreation, and travel, more medical care, closer communications, more skilled personal and professional services, and better-designed as well as more numerous products. It also means more art, music, and poetry, theater,

and drama. It can even mean more time and resources devoted to spiritual growth and human development.[1]

Growth also enables society to improve the nation's infrastructure, enhance the care of the sick and elderly, provide greater access for the disabled, and provide more police and fire protection. Economic growth may be the only realistic way to reduce poverty, since there is little political support for greater redistribution of income. The way to improve the economic position of the poor is to increase household incomes through higher productivity and economic growth. Also, a no-growth policy among industrial nations might severely limit growth in poor nations. Foreign investment and development assistance in those nations would fall, keeping the world's poor in poverty longer.

Economic growth has not made labor more unpleasant or hazardous, as critics suggest. New machinery is usually less taxing and less dangerous than the machinery it replaces. Air-conditioned workplaces are more pleasant than steamy workshops. Furthermore, why would an end to economic growth reduce materialism or alienation? The loudest protests against materialism are heard in those nations and groups that now enjoy the highest levels of material abundance! The high standard of living that growth provides has increased our leisure and given us more time for reflection and self-fulfillment.

Does growth threaten the environment? The connection between growth and environment is tenuous, say growth proponents. Increases in economic growth need not mean increases in pollution. Pollution is not so much a by-product of growth as it is a "problem of the commons." Much of the environment—streams, lakes, oceans, and the air—is treated as common property, with no or insufficient restrictions on its use. The commons have become our dumping grounds; we have overused and debased them. Environmental pollution is a case of negative externalities, and correcting this problem involves regulatory legislation, specific taxes ("effluent charges"), or market-based incentives to remedy misuse of the environment.

Those who support growth admit there are serious environmental problems. But they say that limiting growth is the wrong solution. Growth has allowed economies to reduce pollution, be more sensitive to environmental considerations, set aside wilderness, create national parks and monuments, and clean up hazardous waste, while still enabling rising household incomes.

Is growth sustainable? Yes, say the proponents of growth. If we were depleting natural resources faster

[1]Alice M. Rivlin, *Reviving the American Dream* (Washington, D.C.: Brookings Institution, 1992), p. 36.

China's economic growth rate in the past 25 years is among the highest recorded for any country during any period of world history.

Propelled by capitalistic reforms, China has experienced nearly 9 percent annual growth rates over the past 25 years. Real output has more than quadrupled over that period. In 2004, China's growth rate was 10.1 percent and in 2005 it was 9.8 percent. Expanded output and income have boosted domestic saving and investment, and the growth of capital goods has further increased productivity, output, and income. The rising income, together with inexpensive labor, has attracted more direct foreign investment (a total of $150 billion between 2003 and 2005).

China's real GDP and real income have grown much more rapidly than China's population. Per capita income has increased at a high annual rate of 8 percent since 1980. This is particularly noteworthy because China's population has expanded by 14 million a year (despite a policy which encourages one child per family). Based on exchange rates, China's per capita income is now about $1390 annually. But because the prices of many basic items in China are still low and are not totally reflected in exchange rates, Chinese per capita purchasing power is estimated to be equivalent to $6300 of income in the United States.

The growth of per capita income in China has resulted from increased use of capital, improved technology, and shifts of labor away from lower-productivity toward higher-productivity uses. One such shift of employment has been from agriculture toward rural and urban manufacturing. Another shift has been from state-owned enterprises toward private firms. Both shifts have raised the productivity of Chinese workers.

Chinese economic growth had been accompanied by a huge expansion of China's international trade. Chinese exports rose from $5 billion in 1978 to $752 billion in 2005. These exports have provided the foreign currency needed to import consumer goods and capital goods. Imports of capital goods from industrially advanced countries have brought with them highly advanced technology that is embodied in, for example, factory design, industrial machinery, office equipment, and telecommunications systems.

China still faces some significant problems in its transition to the market system, however. At times, investment booms in China have resulted in too much spending relative to production capacity. The result has been some periods of 15 to 25 percent annual rates of inflation. China has successfully confronted the inflation problem by giving its central bank more power so that, when appropriate, the bank can raise interest rates to damp down investment spending. This greater monetary control has reduced inflation significantly. China's inflation rate was a mild 1.2 percent in 2003, 4.1 percent in 2004, and 1.9 percent in 2005.

Nevertheless, the overall financial system in China remains weak and inadequate. Many unprofitable state-owned enterprises owe colossal sums of money on loans made by the Chinese state-owned banks (an estimate is nearly $100 billion). Because most of these loans are not collectible, the government may need to bail out the banks to keep them in operation.

Unemployment is also a problem. Even though the transition from an agriculture-dominated economy to a more urban, industrial economy has been gradual, considerable displacement of labor has occurred. There is substantial unemployment and underemployment in the interior regions of China.

China still has much work to do to integrate its economy fully into the world's system of international finance and trade. As a condition of joining the World Trade Organization in 2001, China agreed to reduce its high tariffs on imports and remove restrictions on foreign ownership. In addition, it agreed to change its poor record of protecting intellectual property rights such as copyrights, trademarks, and patents. Unauthorized copying of products is a major source of trade friction between China and the United States. So, too, is the artificially low international value of China's currency, which has contributed to a $200 billion annual trade surplus with the United States.

China's economic development has been very uneven geographically. Hong Kong is a wealthy capitalist city with per capita income of about $24,000. The standard of living is also relatively high in China's southern provinces and coastal cities, although not nearly as high as it is in Hong Kong. In fact, people living in these special economic zones have been the major beneficiaries of China's rapid growth. In contrast, the majority of people living elsewhere in China have very low incomes. Despite its remarkable recent economic successes, China remains a relatively low-income nation. But that status is quickly changing.

than their discovery, we would see the prices of those resources rise. That has not been the case for most natural resources; in fact, the prices of most of them have declined. And if one natural resource becomes too expensive, another resource will be substituted for it.

Moreover, say economists, economic growth has to do with the expansion and application of human knowledge and information, not of extractable natural resources. In this view, economic growth is limited only by human imagination.

Summary

1. Economic growth—measured as either an increase in real output or an increase in real output per capita—increases material abundance and raises a nation's standard of living.

2. The supply factors in economic growth are (a) the quantity and quality of a nation's natural resources, (b) the quantity and quality of its human resources, (c) its stock of capital facilities, and (d) its technology. Two other factors—a sufficient level of aggregate demand and economic efficiency—are necessary for the economy to realize its growth potential.

3. The growth of production capacity is shown graphically as an outward shift of a nation's production possibilities curve or as a rightward shift of its long-run aggregate supply curve. Growth is realized when total spending rises sufficiently to match the growth of production capacity.

4. Between 1950 and 2005 the annual growth rate of real GDP for the United States averaged about 3.5 percent; the annual growth rate of real GDP per capita was about 2.3 percent.

5. U.S. real GDP has grown partly because of increased inputs of labor and primarily because of increases in the productivity of labor. The increases in productivity have resulted mainly from technological progress, increases in the quantity of capital per worker, improvements in the quality of labor, economies of scale, and an improved allocation of labor.

6. Over long time periods, the growth of labor productivity underlies an economy's growth of real wages and its standard of living.

7. Productivity rose by 2.9 percent annually between 1995 and 2005, compared to 1.4 percent annually between 1973 and

1995. Some economists think this productivity acceleration will be long-lasting and is reflective of a New Economy—one of faster productivity growth and greater noninflationary economic growth.

8. The New Economy is based on (a) rapid technological change in the form of the microchip and information technology, (b) increasing returns and lower per-unit costs, and (c) heightened global competition that holds down prices.

9. The main sources of increasing returns in recent years are (a) use of more specialized inputs as firms grow, (b) the spreading of development costs, (c) simultaneous consumption by consumers, (d) network effects, and (e) learning by doing. Increasing returns mean higher productivity and lower per-unit production costs.

10. Skeptics wonder if the recent productivity acceleration is permanent, and suggest a wait-and-see approach. They point out that surges in productivity and real GDP growth have previously occurred during vigorous economic expansions but do not necessarily represent long-lived trends.

11. Critics of rapid growth say that it adds to environmental degradation, increases human stress, and exhausts the earth's finite supply of natural resources. Defenders of rapid growth say that it is the primary path to the rising living standards nearly universally desired by people, that it need not debase the environment, and that there are no indications that we are running out of resources. Growth is based on the expansion and application of human knowledge, which is limited only by human imagination.

Terms and Concepts

economic growth

supply factors

demand factor

efficiency factor

labor productivity

labor-force participation rate

growth accounting

infrastructure

human capital

economies of scale

New Economy

information technology

start-up firms

increasing returns

network effects

learning by doing

Study Questions

1. **KEY QUESTION** What are the four supply factors of economic growth? What is the demand factor? What is the efficiency factor? Illustrate these factors in terms of the production possibilities curve.

2. Suppose that Alpha and Omega have identically sized working-age populations but that annual hours of work are much greater in Alpha than in Omega. Provide two possible explanations.

3. Suppose that work hours in New Zombie are 200 in year 1 and productivity is $8. What is New Zombie's real GDP? If work hours increase to 210 in year 2 and productivity rises to $10, what is New Zombie's rate of economic growth?

4. What is the relationship between a nation's production possibilities curve and its long-run aggregate supply curve? How does each relate to the idea of a New Economy?

5. **KEY QUESTION** Between 1990 and 2005 the U.S. price level rose by about 50 percent while real output increased by about 56 percent. Use the aggregate demand–aggregate supply model to illustrate these outcomes graphically.

6. **KEY QUESTION** To what extent have increases in U.S. real GDP resulted from more labor inputs? From higher labor productivity? Rearrange the following contributors to the growth of productivity in order of their quantitative importance: economies of scale, quantity of capital, improved resource allocation, education and training, technological advance.

7. True or false? If false, explain why.
   a. Technological advance, which to date has played a relatively small role in U.S. economic growth, is destined to play a more important role in the future.
   b. Many public capital goods are complementary to private capital goods.

   c. Immigration has slowed economic growth in the United States.

8. Explain why there is such a close relationship between changes in a nation's rate of productivity growth and changes in its average real hourly wage.

9. **KEY QUESTION** Relate each of the following to the New Economy:
   a. The rate of productivity growth
   b. Information technology
   c. Increasing returns
   d. Network effects
   e. Global competition

10. Provide three examples of products or services that can be simultaneously consumed by many people. Explain why labor productivity greatly rises as the firm sells more units of the product or service. Explain why the higher level of sales greatly reduces the per-unit cost of the product.

11. What is meant when economists say that the U.S. economy has "a higher safe speed limit" than it had previously? If the New Economy has a higher safe speed limit, what explains the series of interest-rate hikes engineered by the Federal Reserve in 2004 and 2005.

12. Productivity often rises during economic expansions and falls during economic recessions. Can you think of reasons why? Briefly explain. (Hint: Remember that the level of productivity involves both levels of output and levels of labor input.)

13. **LAST WORD** Based on the information in this chapter, contrast the economic growth rates of the United States and China over the last 25 years. How does the real GDP per capita of China compare with that of the United States? Why is there such a huge disparity of per capita income between China's coastal cities and its interior regions?

Web-Based Questions

1. **U.S. ECONOMIC GROWTH—WHAT ARE THE LATEST RATES?** Go to the Bureau of Economic Analysis Web site, **www.bea.gov,** and use the data interactivity feature to find National Income and Product Account Table 1.1. What are the quarterly growth rates (annualized) for the U.S. economy for the last six quarters? Is the average of those rates above or below the long-run U.S. annual growth rate of 3.5 percent? Expand the range of years, if necessary, to find the last time real GDP declined in two or more successive quarters. What were those quarters?

2. **WHAT'S UP WITH PRODUCTIVITY?** Visit the Bureau of Labor Statistics Web site, **www.bls.gov.** In sequence, select Productivity and Costs, Get Detailed Statistics, and Most Requested Statistics to find quarterly growth rates (annualized) for business output per hour for the last six

quarters. Is the average of those rates higher or lower than the 1.4 percent average annual growth rate of productivity during the 1973–1995 period?

3. **PRODUCTIVITY AND TECHNOLOGY—EXAMPLES OF INNOVATIONS IN COMPUTERS AND COMMUNICATIONS** Recent innovations in computers and communications technologies are increasing productivity. Lucent Technologies (formerly Bell Labs), at **www.lucent.com/minds/discoveries,** provides a timeline of company innovations over the past 80 years. Cite five technological "home runs" (for example, the transistor in 1947) and five technological "singles" (for example, free space optical switching in 1990). Which single innovation do you think has increased productivity the most? List two innovations since 1990. How might they boost productivity?

The Economics of
Developing Countries

Chapter 16 Web is a bonus chapter found at the book's Web site, **www.mcconnell17.com.** It extends the analysis of Part 5, "Long-Run Perspectives and Macroeconomic Dabates," and may or may not be assigned by your instructor.

17

IN THIS CHAPTER YOU WILL LEARN:

- **The differences between the historical Keynesian and classical macro perspectives.**

- **About alternative perspectives on the causes of macroeconomic instability, including the views of mainstream economists, monetarist, real-business cycle advocates, and proponents of coordination failures.**

- **What the equation of exchange is and how it relates to "monetarism."**

- **Why new classical economists believe the economy will "self-correct" from aggregate demand and aggregate supply shocks.**

- **The variations of the debate over "rules" versus "discretion" in conducting stabilization policy.**

Disputes over Macro Theory and Policy

As any academic discipline evolves, it naturally evokes a number of internal disagreements. Economics is no exception. In this chapter we examine a few alternative perspectives on macro theory and policy. After contrasting classical and Keynesian theories, we turn to recent disagreements on three interrelated questions: (1) What causes instability in the economy? (2) Is the economy self-correcting? (3) Should government adhere to *rules* or use *discretion* in setting economic policy?

Some History: Classical Economics and Keynes

Classical economics began with Adam Smith in 1776 and dominated economic thinking until the 1930s. It holds that full employment is the norm in a market economy and therefore a laissez-faire ("let it be") policy by government is best. Then, in the 1930s, John Maynard Keynes asserted that laissez-faire capitalism is subject to recurring recessions that bring widespread unemployment. In the Keynesian view, active government policy is required to stabilize the economy and to prevent valuable resources from standing idle.

Let's compare these two views through modern aggregate demand and aggregate supply analysis.

The Classical View

In the **classical view,** the aggregate supply curve is vertical and is the sole determinant of the level of real output. The downsloping aggregate demand curve is stable and is the sole determinant of the price level.

Vertical Aggregate Supply Curve

According to the classical perspective, the aggregate supply curve is a vertical line, as shown in Figure 17.1a. This line is located at the full-employment level of real GDP, Q_f. According to the classical economists, the economy will operate at its potential level of output because of (1) Say's law (Last

Word, Chapter 9) and (2) responsive, flexible prices and wages.

We stress that classical economists believed that Q_f does not change in response to changes in the price level. Observe that as the price level falls from P_1 to P_2 in Figure 17.1a, real output remains anchored at Q_f.

But this stability of output is at odds with the upsloping supply curves for individual products that we discussed in Chapter 3. There we found that lower prices would make production less profitable and would cause producers to offer less output and employ fewer workers. The classical response to this view is that input costs in the economy would fall along with product prices and leave real profits and output unchanged. For example, if product prices on average fall from $10 to $5 and per-unit costs decline from $8 to $4, the real profit per unit of output will remain at $2. The new $1 of nominal profit (= $5 − $4) will equal $2 of real profit because prices have been halved. With flexible wages and other input prices, costs will move up and down with prices and leave real rewards and real output constant. A change in the price level will not cause the economy to stray from full employment.

Stable Aggregate Demand

Classical economists theorize that money underlies aggregate demand. The amount of real output that can be purchased depends on (1) the quantity of money households and businesses possess and (2) the purchasing power of that money as

FIGURE 17.1 Classical and Keynesian views of the macroeconomy. (a) In classical theory, aggregate supply determines the full-employment level of real output, while aggregate demand establishes the price level. Aggregate demand normally is stable, but if it should decline, say, from AD_1 to AD_2, the price level will quickly fall from P_1 to P_2 to eliminate the temporary excess supply of ab and to restore full employment at c. (b) The Keynesian view is that aggregate demand is unstable and that prices and wages are downwardly inflexible. An AD_1 to AD_2 decline in aggregate demand has no effect on the price level. Instead, the economy moves from point x to y and real output falls to Q_u, where it can remain for long periods.

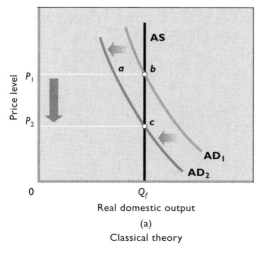

(a)
Classical theory

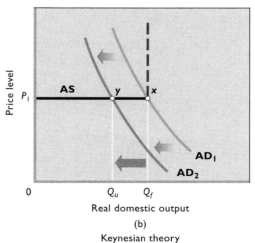

(b)
Keynesian theory

determined by the price level. The purchasing power of the dollar refers to the real quantity of goods and services a dollar will buy. Thus, as we move down the vertical axis of Figure 17.1a, the price level is falling. This means that the purchasing power of each dollar is rising. If the price level were to fall by one-half, a certain quantity of money would then purchase a real output twice as large. With a fixed money supply, the price level and real output are inversely related.

What about the location of the aggregate demand curve? According to the classical economists, aggregate demand will be stable as long as the nation's monetary authorities maintain a constant supply of money. With a fixed aggregate supply of output, increases in the supply of money will shift the aggregate demand curve rightward and spark demand-pull inflation. Reductions in the supply of money will shift the curve leftward and trigger deflation. The key to price-level stability, then, is to control the nation's money supply to prevent unwarranted shifts in aggregate demand.

Even if the money supply and therefore aggregate demand decline, the economy depicted in Figure 17.1a will not experience unemployment. Admittedly, the immediate effect of a decline in aggregate demand from AD_1 to AD_2 is an excess supply of output, since the aggregate output of goods and services exceeds aggregate spending by the amount ab. But, with the presumed downward flexibility of product and resource prices, that excess supply will reduce product prices along with workers' wages and the prices of other inputs. As a result, the price level will quickly decline from P_1 to P_2 until the amounts of output demanded and supplied are brought once again into equilibrium, this time at c. While the price level has fallen from P_1 to P_2, real output remains at the full-employment level.

The Keynesian View

The heart of the **Keynesian view** is that product prices and wages are downwardly inflexible over very long time periods. The result is graphically represented as a horizontal aggregate supply curve. Also, aggregate demand is subject to periodic changes caused by changes in the determinants of aggregate demand.

Horizontal Aggregate Supply Curve (to Full-Employment Output)
The downward inflexibility of prices and wages presumed by the Keynesians translates to the horizontal aggregate supply curve, shown in Figure 17.1b. Here, a decline in real output from Q_f to Q_u will have no impact on the price level. Nor will an increase in real output from Q_u to Q_f. The aggregate supply

curve therefore extends from zero real output rightward to point x, where real output is at its full-employment level, Q_f. Once full employment is reached, the aggregate supply curve becomes vertical. The dashed line extending upward from the horizontal aggregate supply curve at x shows this.

Unstable Aggregate Demand Keynesian economists view aggregate demand as unstable from one period to the next, even without changes in the money supply. In particular, the investment component of aggregate demand fluctuates, altering the location of the aggregate demand curve. Suppose aggregate demand in Figure 17.1b declines from AD_1 to AD_2. The sole impact is on output and employment. Real output falls from Q_f to Q_u, but the price level remains unchanged at P_1. Moreover, Keynesians believe that unless there is an offsetting increase in aggregate demand, real output may remain at Q_u, which is below the full-employment level Q_f. Active government policies to increase aggregate demand are essential to move the economy from point y to point x. Otherwise, the economy will suffer the wastes of recession and depression. **(Key Question 1)**

QUICK REVIEW 17.1

- In classical macroeconomics, the aggregate supply curve is vertical at the full-employment level of real output, and the aggregate demand curve is stable as long as the money supply is constant.
- In Keynesian macroeconomics, the aggregate supply curve is horizontal up to the full-employment level of output; then it becomes vertical. The aggregate demand curve is unstable largely because of the volatility of investment spending; such shifts cause either recession or demand-pull inflation.

What Causes Macro Instability?

As earlier chapters have indicated, capitalist economies experienced considerable instability during the twentieth century. The United States, for example, experienced the Great Depression, numerous recessions, and periods of inflation. Contemporary economists have different perspectives on why this instability occurs.

Mainstream View

For simplicity, we will use the term "mainstream view" to characterize the prevailing macroeconomic perspective of the majority of economists. According to that view, which retains a Keynesian flavor, instability in the economy arises from two sources: (1) significant changes in investment spending, which change aggregate demand, and, occasionally, (2) adverse aggregate supply shocks, which change aggregate supply. Although these factors are not new to you, let's quickly review them.

Changes in Investment Spending
Mainstream macroeconomics focuses on aggregate spending and its components. Recall that the basic equation underlying aggregate expenditures is

$$C_a + I_g + X_n + G = \text{GDP}$$

That is, the aggregate amount of after-tax consumption, gross investment, net exports, and government spending determines the total amount of goods and services produced and sold. In equilibrium, $C_a + I_g + X_n + G$ (aggregate expenditures) is equal to GDP (real output). A decrease in the price level increases equilibrium GDP and thus allows us to trace out a downsloping aggregate demand curve for the economy (see the appendix to Chapter 10). Any change in one of the spending components in the aggregate expenditures equation shifts the aggregate demand curve. This, in turn, changes equilibrium real output, the price level, or both.

Investment spending, in particular, is subject to wide "booms" and "busts." Significant increases in investment spending are multiplied into even greater increases in aggregate demand and thus can produce demand-pull inflation. In contrast, significant declines in investment spending are multiplied into even greater decreases in aggregate demand and thus can cause recessions.

Adverse Aggregate Supply Shocks
In the mainstream view, the second source of macroeconomic instability arises on the supply side. Occasionally, such external events as wars or an artificial supply restriction of a key resource can boost resource prices and significantly raise per-unit production costs. The result is a sizable decline in a nation's aggregate supply, which destabilizes the economy by simultaneously causing cost-push inflation and recession.

Monetarist View
Classical economics has reappeared in several modern

O 17.1
Monetarism

forms. One is **monetarism,** which (1) focuses on the money supply, (2) holds that markets are highly competitive, and (3) says that a competitive market system gives the economy a high degree of macroeconomic stability. Like classical economists, monetarists argue that the price and wage

flexibility provided by competitive markets would cause fluctuations in aggregate demand to alter product and resource prices rather than output and employment. Thus the market system would provide substantial macroeconomic stability *were it not for government interference in the economy.*

The problem, as monetarists see it, is that government has promoted downward wage inflexibility through the minimum-wage law, pro-union legislation, guaranteed prices for certain farm products, pro-business monopoly legislation, and so forth. The free-market system is capable of providing macroeconomic stability, but, despite good intentions, government interference has undermined that capability. Moreover, monetarists say that government has contributed to the economy's business cycles through its clumsy and mistaken attempts to achieve greater stability through its monetary policies.

Equation of Exchange
The fundamental equation of monetarism is the **equation of exchange:**

$$MV = PQ$$

where M is the supply of money; V is the **velocity** of money, that is, the average number of times per year a dollar is spent on final goods and services; P is the price level or, more specifically, the average price at which each unit of physical output is sold; and Q is the physical volume of all goods and services produced.

The left side of the equation of exchange, MV, repre-

O 17.2
Equation of exchange

sents the total amount spent by purchasers of output, while the right side, PQ, represents the total amount received by sellers of that output. The nation's money supply (M) multiplied by the number of times it is spent each year (V) must equal the nation's nominal GDP ($= P \times Q$). The dollar value of total spending has to equal the dollar value of total output.

Stable Velocity
Monetarists say that velocity, V, in the equation of exchange is relatively stable. To them, "stable" is not synonymous with "constant," however. Monetarists are aware that velocity is higher today than it was several decades ago. Shorter pay periods, widespread use of credit cards, and faster means of making payments enable people to hold less money and to turn it over more rapidly than was possible in earlier times. These factors have enabled people to reduce their holdings of cash and checkbook money relative to the size of the nation's nominal GDP.

When monetarists say that velocity is stable, they mean that the factors altering velocity change gradually and predictably and that changes in velocity from one year to the next can be readily anticipated. Moreover, they hold that velocity does not change in response to changes in the money supply itself. Instead, people have a stable desire to hold money relative to holding other financial assets, holding real assets, and buying current output. The factors that determine the amount of money the public wants to hold depend mainly on the level of nominal GDP.

Example: Assume that when the level of nominal GDP is $400 billion, the public desires $100 billion of money to purchase that output. That means that V is 4 (= $400 billion of nominal GDP/$100 billion of money). If we further assume that the actual supply of money is $100 billion, the economy is in equilibrium with respect to money; the actual amount of money supplied equals the amount the public wants to hold.

If velocity is stable, the equation of exchange suggests that there is a predictable relationship between the money supply and nominal GDP (= PQ). An increase in the money supply of, say, $10 billion would upset equilibrium in our example, since the public would find itself holding more money or liquidity than it wants. That is, the actual amount of money held ($110 billion) would exceed the amount of holdings desired ($100 billion). In that case, the reaction of the public (households and businesses) is to restore its desired balance of money relative to other items, such as stocks and bonds, factories and equipment, houses and automobiles, and clothing and toys. But the spending of money by individual households and businesses would leave more cash in the checkable deposits or billfolds of other households and firms. And they too would try to "spend down" their excess cash balances. But, overall, the $110 billion supply of money cannot be spent down because a dollar spent is a dollar received.

Instead, the collective attempt to reduce cash balances increases aggregate demand, thereby boosting nominal GDP. Because velocity in our example is 4—that is, the dollar is spent, on average, four times per year—nominal GDP rises from $400 billion to $440 billion. At that higher nominal GDP, the money supply of $110 billion equals the amount of money desired ($440 billion/4 = $110 billion), and equilibrium is reestablished.

The $10 billion increase in the money supply thus eventually increases nominal GDP by $40 billion. Spending on goods, services, and assets expands until nominal GDP has gone up enough to restore the original 4-to-1 equilibrium relationship between nominal GDP and the money supply.

W 17.1

Equation of exchange

Note that the relationship GDP/M defines V. A stable relationship between nominal GDP and M means a stable V. And a change in M causes a proportionate change in nominal GDP. Thus, changes in the money supply allegedly have a predictable effect on nominal GDP (= $P \times Q$).

An increase in M increases P or Q, or some combination of both; a decrease in M reduces P or Q, or some combination of both. **(Key Question 4)**

Monetary Causes of Instability Monetarists say that inappropriate monetary policy is the single most important cause of macroeconomic instability. An increase in the money supply directly increases aggregate demand. Under conditions of full employment, that rise in aggregate demand raises the price level. For a time, higher prices cause firms to increase their real output, and the rate of unemployment falls below its natural rate. But once nominal wages rise to reflect the higher prices and thus to restore real wages, real output moves back to its full-employment level and the unemployment rate returns to its natural rate. The inappropriate increase in the money supply leads to inflation, together with instability of real output and employment.

Conversely, a decrease in the money supply reduces aggregate demand. Real output temporarily falls, and the unemployment rate rises above its natural rate. Eventually, nominal wages fall and real output returns to its full-employment level. The inappropriate decline in the money supply leads to deflation, together with instability of real GDP and employment.

The contrast between mainstream macroeconomics and monetarism on the causes of instability thus comes into sharp focus. Mainstream economists view the instability of investment as the main cause of the economy's instability. They see monetary policy as a stabilizing factor. Changes in the money supply raise or lower interest rates as needed, smooth out swings in investment, and thus reduce macroeconomic instability. In contrast, monetarists view changes in the money supply as the main cause of instability in the economy. For example, they say that the Great Depression occurred largely because the Fed allowed the money supply to fall by 35 percent during that period. According to Milton Friedman, a prominent monetarist,

> And [the money supply] fell not because there were no willing borrowers—not because the horse would not drink. It fell because the Federal Reserve System forced or permitted a sharp reduction in the [money supply], because it failed to exercise the responsibilities assigned to it in the Federal Reserve Act to provide liquidity to the banking

system. The Great Contraction is tragic testimony to the power of monetary policy—not, as Keynes and so many of his contemporaries believed, evidence of its impotence.[1]

Real-Business-Cycle View

A third modern view of the cause of macroeconomic instability is that business cycles are caused by real factors that affect aggregate supply rather than by monetary, or spending, factors that cause fluctuations in aggregate demand. In the **real-business-cycle theory,** business fluctuations result from significant changes in technology and resource availability. Those changes affect productivity and thus the long-run growth trend of aggregate supply.

An example focusing on recession will clarify this thinking. Suppose productivity (output per worker) declines sharply because of a large increase in oil prices, which makes it prohibitively expensive to operate certain types of machinery. That decline in productivity implies a reduction in the economy's ability to produce real output. The result would be a decrease in the economy's long-run aggregate supply curve, as represented by the leftward shift from AS_{LR1} to AS_{LR2} in Figure 17.2.

As real output falls from Q_1 to Q_2, the public needs less money to buy the reduced volume of goods and services. So the demand for money falls. Moreover, the slowdown in business activity means that businesses need to borrow less from banks, reducing the part of the money supply created by banks through their lending. Thus, the supply of money also falls. In this controversial scenario, changes in the supply of money respond to changes in the demand for money. The decline in the money supply then reduces aggregate demand, as from AD_1 to AD_2 in Figure 17.2. The outcome is a decline in real output from Q_1 to Q_2, with no change in the price level.

Conversely, a large increase in aggregate supply (not shown) caused by, say, major innovations in the production process would shift the long-run aggregate supply curve rightward. Real output would increase, and money demand and money supply would both increase. Aggregate demand would shift rightward by an amount equal to the rightward shift of long-run aggregate supply. Real output would increase, without driving up the price level.

Conclusion: In the real-business-cycle theory, macro instability arises on the aggregate supply side of the economy, not on the aggregate demand side, as mainstream economists and monetarists usually claim.

[1]Milton Friedman, *The Optimum Quantity of Money and Other Essays* (Chicago: Aldine, 1969), p. 97.

FIGURE 17.2 The real-business-cycle theory. In the real-business-cycle theory, a decline in resource availability shifts the nation's long-run aggregate supply curve to the left from AS_{LR1} to AS_{LR2}. The decline in real output from Q_1 to Q_2, in turn, reduces money demand (less is needed) and money supply (fewer loans are taken out) such that aggregate demand shifts leftward from AD_1 to AD_2. The result is a recession in which the price level remains constant.

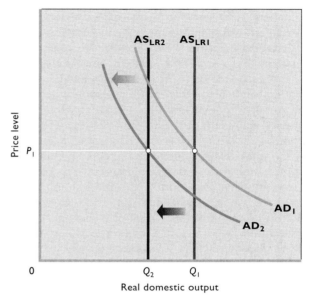

Coordination Failures

A fourth and final modern view of macroeconomic instability relates to so-called **coordination failures.** Such failures occur when people fail to reach a mutually beneficial equilibrium because they lack a way to coordinate their actions.

Noneconomic Example
Consider first a noneconomic example. Suppose you learn of an impending informal party at a nearby beach, although it looks as though it might rain. If you expect others to be there, you will decide to go. If you expect that others will not go, you will decide to stay home. There are several possible equilibrium outcomes, depending on the mix of people's expectations. Let's consider just two. If each person assumes that all the others will be at the party, all will go. The party will occur and presumably everyone will have a good time. But if each person assumes that everyone else will stay home, all will stay home and there will be no party. When the party does not take place, even though all would be better off if it did take place, a coordination failure has occurred.

Macroeconomic Example
Now let's apply this example to macroeconomic instability, specifically

recession. Suppose that individual firms and households expect other firms and consumers to cut back their investment and consumption spending. As a result, each firm and household will anticipate a reduction of aggregate demand. Firms therefore will cut back their own investment spending, since they will anticipate that their future production capacity will be excessive. Households will also reduce their own spending (increase their saving), because they anticipate that they will experience reduced work hours, possible layoffs, and falling incomes in the future.

Aggregate demand will indeed decline and the economy will indeed experience a recession in response to what amounts to a self-fulfilling prophecy. Moreover, the economy will stay at a below-full-employment level of output because, once there, producers and households have no individual incentive to increase spending. If all producers and households would agree to increase their investment and consumption spending simultaneously, then aggregate demand would rise, and real output and real income would increase. Each producer and each consumer would be better off. However, this outcome does not occur because there is no mechanism for firms and households to agree on such a joint spending increase.

In this case, the economy is stuck in an *unemployment equilibrium* because of a coordination failure. With a different set of expectations, a coordination failure might leave the economy in an *inflation equilibrium*. In this view, the economy has a number of such potential equilibrium positions, some good and some bad, depending on people's mix of expectations. Macroeconomic instability, then, reflects the movement of the economy from one such equilibrium position to another as expectations change.

QUICK REVIEW 17.2

- Mainstream economists say that macroeconomic instability usually stems from swings in investment spending and, occasionally, from adverse aggregate supply shocks.
- Monetarists view the economy through the equation of exchange ($MV = PQ$). If velocity V is stable, changes in the money supply M lead directly to changes in nominal GDP ($P \times Q$). For monetarists, changes in M caused by inappropriate monetary policy are the single most important cause of macroeconomic instability.
- In the real-business-cycle theory, significant changes in "real" factors such as technology, resource availability, and productivity change the economy's long-run aggregate supply, causing macroeconomic instability.
- Macroeconomic instability can result from coordination failures—less-than-optimal equilibrium positions that occur because businesses and households lack a way to coordinate their actions.

Does the Economy "Self-Correct"?

Just as there are disputes over the causes of macroeconomic instability, there are disputes over whether or not the economy will correct itself when instability does occur. And economists also disagree on how long it will take for any such self-correction to take place.

New Classical View of Self-Correction

New classical economists tend to be either monetarists or adherents of **rational expectations theory:** the idea that businesses, consumers, and workers expect changes in policies or circumstances to have certain effects on the economy and, in pursuing their own self-interest, take actions to

O 17.3

Rational expectations theory

make sure those changes affect them as little as possible. The **new classical economics** holds that when the economy occasionally diverges from its full-employment output, internal mechanisms within the economy will automatically move it back to that output. Policymakers should stand back and let the automatic correction occur, rather than engaging in active fiscal and monetary policy. This perspective is that associated with the vertical long-run Phillips Curve, which we discussed in Chapter 15.

Graphical Analysis Figure 17.3a relates the new classical analysis to the question of self-correction. Specifically, an increase in aggregate demand, say, from AD_1 to AD_2, moves the economy upward along its short-run aggregate supply curve AS_1 from a to b. The price level rises and real output increases. In the long run, however, nominal wages rise to restore real wages. Per-unit production costs then increase, and the short-run aggregate supply curve shifts leftward, eventually from AS_1 to AS_2. The economy moves from b to c, and real output returns to its full-employment level, Q_1. This level of output is dictated by the economy's vertical long-run aggregate supply curve, AS_{LR}.

Conversely, a decrease in aggregate demand from AD_1 to AD_3 in Figure 17.3b first moves the economy downward along its short-run aggregate supply curve AS_1 from point a to d. The price level declines, as does the level of real output. But in the long run, nominal wages decline such that real wages fall to their previous levels. When that happens, per-unit production costs decline and the short-run aggregate supply curve shifts to the right, eventually from

FIGURE 17.3 New classical view of self-correction. (a) An unanticipated increase in aggregate demand from AD₁ to AD₂ first moves the economy from *a* to *b*. The economy then self-corrects to *c*. An anticipated increase in aggregate demand moves the economy directly from *a* to *c*. (b) An unanticipated decrease in aggregate demand from AD₁ to AD₃ moves the economy from *a* to *d*. The economy then self-corrects to *e*. An anticipated decrease in aggregate demand moves the economy directly from *a* to *e*. (Mainstream economists, however, say that if the price level remains at P_1, the economy will move from *a* to *f*, and even if the price level falls to P_4, the economy may remain at *d* because of downward wage inflexibility.)

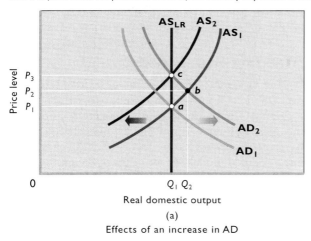

(a)
Effects of an increase in AD

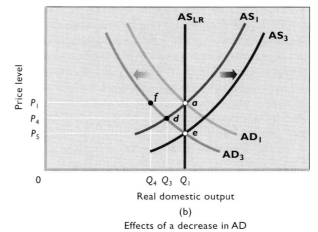

(b)
Effects of a decrease in AD

AS_1 to AS_3. The economy moves to *e*, where it again achieves its full-employment level, Q_1. As in Figure 17.3a, the economy in Figure 17.3b has automatically self-corrected to its full-employment output and its natural rate of unemployment.

Speed of Adjustment There is some disagreement among new classical economists on how long it will take for self-correction to occur. Monetarists usually hold the *adaptive* expectations view that people form their expectations on the basis of present realities and only gradually change their expectations as experience unfolds. This means that the shifts in the short-run aggregate supply curves shown in Figure 17.3 may not occur for 2 or 3 years or even longer. Other new classical economists, however, accept the rational expectations assumption that workers anticipate some future outcomes before they occur. When price-level changes are fully anticipated, adjustments of nominal wages are very quick or even instantaneous. Let's see why.

Although several new theories, including Keynesian ones, incorporate rational expectations, our interest here is the new classical version of the rational expectations theory (hereafter, RET). RET is based on two assumptions:
• People behave rationally, gathering and intelligently processing information to form expectations about things that are economically important to them. They adjust those expectations quickly as new developments affecting future economic outcomes occur. Where there is adequate information, people's

beliefs about future economic outcomes accurately reflect the likelihood that those outcomes will occur. For example, if it is clear that a certain policy will cause inflation, people will recognize that fact and adjust their economic behavior in anticipation of inflation.
• Like classical economists, RET economists assume that all product and resource markets are highly competitive and that prices and wages are flexible both upward and downward. But the RET economists go further, assuming that new information is quickly (in some cases, instantaneously) taken into account in the demand and supply curves of such markets. The upshot is that equilibrium prices and quantities adjust rapidly to unforeseen events—say, technological change or aggregate supply shocks. They adjust instantaneously to events that have known outcomes—for example, changes in fiscal or monetary policy.

Unanticipated Price-Level Changes The implication of RET is not only that the economy is self-correcting but that self-correction occurs quickly. In this thinking, unanticipated changes in the price level—so-called **price-level surprises**—do cause temporary changes in real output. Suppose, for example, that an unanticipated increase in foreign demand for U.S. goods increases U.S. aggregate demand from AD₁ to AD₂ in Figure 17.3a. The immediate result is an unexpected increase in the price level from P_1 to P_2.

But now an interesting question arises. If wages and prices are flexible, as assumed in RET, why doesn't the higher price level immediately cause nominal wages to rise, such that there is no increase in real output at all? Why does the economy temporarily move from point a to b along AS$_1$? In RET, firms increase output from Q_1 to Q_2 because of misperceptions about rising prices of their own products relative to the prices of other products (and to the prices of labor). They mistakenly think the higher prices of their own products have resulted from increased demand for those products relative to the demands for other products. Expecting higher profits, they increase their own production. But in fact *all* prices, including the price of labor (nominal wages), are rising because of the general increase in aggregate demand. Once firms see that *all* prices and wages are rising, they decrease their production to previous levels.

In terms of Figure 17.3a, the increase in nominal wages shifts the short-run aggregate supply curve leftward, ultimately from AS$_1$ to AS$_2$, and the economy moves from b to c. Thus, the increase in real output caused by the price-level surprise corrects itself.

The same analysis in reverse applies to an unanticipated price-level decrease. In the economy represented by Figure 17.3b, firms misperceive that the prices of their own products are falling due to decreases in the demand for those products relative to other products. They anticipate declines in profit and cut production. As a result of their collective actions, real output in the economy falls. But seeing that all prices and wages are dropping, firms increase their output to prior levels. The short-run aggregate supply curve in Figure 17.3b shifts rightward from AS$_1$ to AS$_3$, and the economy "self-corrects" by moving from d to e.

Fully Anticipated Price-Level Changes
In RET, fully *anticipated* price-level changes do not change real output, even for short periods. In Figure 17.3a, again consider the increase in aggregate demand from AD$_1$ to AD$_2$. Businesses immediately recognize that the higher prices being paid for their products are part of the inflation they had anticipated. They understand that the same forces that are causing the inflation result in higher nominal wages, leaving their profits unchanged. The economy therefore moves directly from a to c. The price level rises as expected, and output remains at its full-employment level Q_1.

Similarly, a fully *anticipated* price-level decrease will leave real output unchanged. Firms conclude that nominal wages are declining by the same percentage amount as the declining price level, leaving profits unchanged. The economy represented by Figure 17.3b therefore moves directly from a to e. Deflation occurs, but the economy continues to produce its full-employment output Q_1. The anticipated decline in aggregate demand causes no change in real output.

Mainstream View of Self-Correction

Almost all economists acknowledge that the new classical economists have made significant contributions to the theory of aggregate supply. In fact, mainstream economists have incorporated some aspects of RET into their own more detailed models. However, most economists strongly disagree with RET on the question of downward price and wage flexibility. While the stock market, foreign exchange market, and certain commodity markets experience day-to-day or minute-to-minute price changes, including price declines, that is not true of many product markets and most labor markets. There is ample evidence, say mainstream economists, that many prices and wages are inflexible downward for long periods. As a result, it may take years for the economy to move from recession back to full-employment output, unless it gets help from fiscal and monetary policy.

Graphical Analysis
To understand this mainstream view, again examine Figure 17.3b. Suppose aggregate demand declines from AD$_1$ to AD$_3$ because of a significant decline in investment spending. If the price level remains at P_1, the economy will not move from a to d to e, as suggested by RET. Instead, the economy will move from a to f, as if it were moving along a horizontal aggregate supply curve between those two points. Real output will decline from its full-employment level, Q_1, to the recessionary level, Q_4.

But let's assume that surpluses in product markets eventually cause the price level to fall to P_4. Will this lead to the decline in nominal wages needed to shift aggregate supply from AS$_1$ to AS$_3$, as suggested by the new classical economists? "Highly unlikely" say mainstream economists. Even more so than prices, nominal wages tend to be inflexible downward. If nominal wages do not decline in response to the decline in the price level, then the short-run aggregate supply curve will not shift rightward. The self-correction mechanism assumed by RET and new classical economists will break down. Instead, the economy will remain at d,

G 17.1
Self-correction

experiencing less-than-full-employment output and a high rate of unemployment.

Downward Wage Inflexibility
In Chapter 10 we discussed several reasons why firms may not be able to, or may not want to, lower nominal wages. Firms may not be able to cut wages because of wage contracts and the legal minimum wage. And firms may not want to lower wages if they fear potential problems with morale, effort, and efficiency.

While contracts are thought to be the main cause of wage rigidity, so-called efficiency wages and insider-outsider relationships may also play a role. Let's explore both.

Efficiency Wage Theory
Recall from Chapter 10 that an **efficiency wage** is a wage that minimizes the firm's labor cost per unit of output. Normally, we would think that the market wage is the efficiency wage since it is the lowest wage at which a firm can obtain a particular type of labor. But where the cost of supervising workers is high or where worker turnover is great, firms may discover that paying a wage that is higher than the market wage will lower their wage cost per unit of output.

Example: Suppose a firm's workers, on average, produce 8 units of output at a $9 market wage but 10 units of output at a $10 above-market wage. The efficiency wage is $10, not the $9 market wage. At the $10 wage, the labor cost per unit of output is only $1 (= $10 wage/10 units of output), compared with $1.12 (= $9 wage/8 units of output) at the $9 wage.

How can a higher wage result in greater efficiency?

- *Greater work effort* The above-market wage, in effect, raises the cost to workers of losing their jobs as a result of poor performance. Because workers have a strong incentive to retain their relatively high-paying jobs, they are more likely to provide greater work effort. Looked at differently, workers are more reluctant to shirk (neglect or avoid work) because the higher wage makes job loss more costly to them. Consequently, the above-market wage can be the efficient wage; it can enhance worker productivity so much that the higher wage more than pays for itself.
- *Lower supervision costs* With less incentive among workers to shirk, the firm needs fewer supervisory personnel to monitor work performance. This, too, can lower the firm's overall wage cost per unit of output.
- *Reduced job turnover* The above-market pay discourages workers from voluntarily leaving their jobs. The lower turnover rate reduces the firm's cost of hiring and training workers. It also gives the firm a more experienced, more productive workforce.

The key implication for macroeconomic instability is that efficiency wages add to the downward inflexibility of wages. Firms that pay efficiency wages will be reluctant to cut wages when aggregate demand declines, since such cuts may encourage shirking, require more supervisory personnel, and increase turnover. In other words, wage cuts that reduce productivity and raise per-unit labor costs are self-defeating.

O 17.4
Efficiency wages

Insider-Outsider Relationships
Other economists theorize that downward wage inflexibility may relate to relationships between "insiders" and "outsiders." Insiders are workers who retain employment even during recession. Outsiders are workers who have been laid off from a firm and unemployed workers who would like to work at that firm.

When recession produces layoffs and widespread unemployment, we might expect outsiders to offer to work for less than the current wage rate, in effect, bidding down wage rates. We might also expect firms to hire such workers in order to reduce their costs. But, according to the **insider-outsider theory,** outsiders may not be able to underbid existing wages because employers may view the nonwage cost of hiring them to be prohibitive. Employers might fear that insiders would view acceptance of such underbidding as undermining years of effort to increase wages or, worse, as "stealing" jobs. So insiders may refuse to cooperate with new workers who have undercut their pay. Where teamwork is critical for production, such lack of cooperation will reduce overall productivity and thereby lower the firms' profits.

Even if firms are willing to employ outsiders at less than the current wage, those workers might refuse to work for less than the existing wage. To do so might invite harassment from the insiders whose pay they have undercut. Thus, outsiders may remain unemployed, relying on past saving, unemployment compensation, and other social programs to make ends meet.

As in the efficiency wage theory, the insider-outsider theory implies that wages will be inflexible downward when aggregate demand declines. Self-correction may eventually occur but not nearly as rapidly as the new classical economists contend. **(Key Question 7)**

QUICK REVIEW 17.3

- New classical economists believe that the economy "self-corrects" when unanticipated events divert it from its full-employment level of real output.
- In RET, unanticipated price-level changes cause changes in real output in the short run but not in the long run.
- According to RET, market participants immediately change their actions in response to anticipated price-level changes such that no change in real output occurs.
- Mainstream economists say that the economy can get mired in recession for long periods because of downward price and wage inflexibility.
- Sources of downward wage inflexibility include contracts, efficiency wages, and insider-outsider relationships.

Rules or Discretion?

These different views on the causes of instability and on the speed of self-correction have led to vigorous debate on macro policy. Should the government adhere to policy rules that prohibit it from causing instability in an economy that is otherwise stable? Or should it use discretionary fiscal and monetary policy, when needed, to stabilize a sometimes-unstable economy?

In Support of Policy Rules

Monetarists and other new classical economists believe policy rules would reduce instability in the economy. They believe that such rules would prevent government from trying to "manage" aggregate demand. That would be a desirable trend, because in their view such management is misguided and thus is likely to *cause* more instability than it cures.

Monetary Rule Since inappropriate monetary policy is the major source of macroeconomic instability, say monetarists, the enactment of a **monetary rule** would make sense. One such rule would be a requirement that the Fed expand the money supply each year at the same annual rate as the typical growth of the economy's production capacity. That fixed-rate expansion of the money supply would occur year after year regardless of the state of the economy. The Fed's sole monetary role would then be to use its tools (open-market operations, discount-rate changes, and changes in reserve requirements) to ensure that the nation's money supply grew steadily by, say, 3 to 5 percent a year. According to Milton Friedman,

> Such a rule . . . would eliminate . . . the major cause of instability in the economy—the capricious and unpredictable impact of countercyclical monetary policy. As long as the money supply grows at a constant rate each year, be it 3,

CONSIDER THIS . . .

On the Road Again

Keynesian economist Abba Lerner (1903–1982) likened the economy to an automobile traveling down a road that had traffic barriers on each side. The problem was that the car had no steering wheel. It would hit one barrier, causing the car to veer to the opposite side of the road. There it would hit the other barrier, which in turn would send it careening to the opposite side. To avoid such careening in the form of business cycles, said Lerner, society must equip the economy with a steering wheel. Discretionary fiscal and monetary policy would enable government to steer the economy safely between the problems of recession and demand-pull inflation.

Economist Milton Friedman (b. 1912) modified Lerner's analogy, giving it a different meaning. He said that the economy does not need a skillful driver of the economic vehicle who is continuously turning the wheel to adjust to the unexpected irregularities of the route. Instead, the economy needs a way to prohibit the monetary passenger in the back seat from occasionally leaning over and giving the steering wheel a jerk that sends the car off the road. According to Friedman, the car will travel down the road just fine unless the Federal Reserve destabilizes it.

Lerner's analogy implies an internally unstable economy that needs steering through discretionary government stabilization policy. Friedman's modification of the analogy implies a generally stable economy that is destabilized by inappropriate monetary policy by the Federal Reserve. For Lerner, stability requires active use of fiscal and monetary policy. For Friedman, macroeconomic stability requires a monetary rule forcing the Federal Reserve to increase the money supply at a set, steady annual rate.*

---

*Friedman has softened his call for a monetary rule in recent years, acknowledging that the Fed has become much more skillful at keeping the rate of inflation in check through prudent monetary policy.

4, or 5 percent, any decline into recession will be temporary. The liquidity provided by a constantly growing money supply will cause aggregate demand to expand. Similarly, if the supply of money does not rise at a more than average rate, any inflationary increase in spending will burn itself out for lack of fuel.[2]

---

[2] As quoted in Lawrence S. Ritter and William L. Silber, *Money*, 5th ed. (New York: Basic Books, 1984), pp. 141–142.

FIGURE 17.4 **Rationale for a monetary rule.** A monetary rule that required the Fed to increase the money supply at an annual rate linked to the long-run increase in potential GDP would shift aggregate demand rightward, as from AD_1 to AD_2, at the same pace as the shift in long-run aggregate supply, here AS_{LR1} to AS_{LR2}. Thus the economy would experience growth without inflation or deflation.

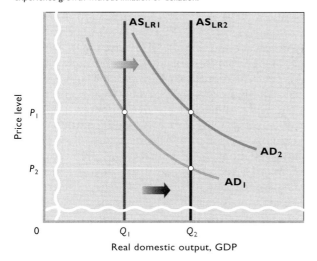

Figure 17.4 illustrates the rationale for a monetary rule. Suppose the economy represented there is operating at its full-employment real output, Q_1. Also suppose the nation's long-run aggregate supply curve shifts rightward, as from AS_{LR1} to AS_{LR2}, each year, signifying the average annual potential increase in real output. As you saw in earlier chapters, such annual increases in "potential GDP" result from added resources, improved resources, and improved technology.

Monetarists argue that a monetary rule would tie increases in the money supply to the typical rightward shift of long-run aggregate supply. In view of the direct link between changes in the money supply and aggregate demand, this would ensure that the AD curve would shift rightward, as from AD_1 to AD_2, each year. As a result, real GDP would rise from Q_1 to Q_2 and the price level would remain constant at P_1. A monetary rule, then, would promote steady growth of real output along with price stability.

Generally, rational expectations economists also support a monetary rule. They conclude that an expansionary or restrictive monetary policy would alter the rate of inflation but not real output. Suppose, for example, the Fed implements an easy money policy to reduce interest rates, expand investment spending, and boost real GDP. On the basis of past experience and economic knowledge, the public would anticipate that this policy is inflationary and would take protective actions. Workers would press for higher nominal wages; firms would raise their product

prices; and lenders would lift their nominal interest rates on loans.

All these responses are designed to prevent inflation from having adverse effects on the real income of workers, businesses, and lenders. But collectively they would immediately raise wage and price levels. So the increase in aggregate demand brought about by the expansionary monetary policy would be completely dissipated in higher prices and wages. Real output and employment would not expand.

In this view, the combination of rational expectations and instantaneous market adjustments dooms discretionary monetary policy to ineffectiveness. If discretionary monetary policy produces only inflation (or deflation), say the RET economists, then it makes sense to limit the Fed's discretion and to require that Congress enact a monetary rule consistent with price stability at all times.

In recent decades, the call for a Friedman-type monetary rule has faded. Some economists who tend to favor monetary rules have advocated *inflation targeting*, which we discussed in Chapter 14. The Fed would be required to announce a targeted band of inflation rates, say, 1 to 2 percent, for some future period such as the following 2 years. It would then be expected to use its monetary policy tools to keep inflation rates within that range. If it did not hit the inflation target, it would have to explain why it failed.

Strictly interpreted, inflation targeting would focus the Fed's attention nearly exclusively on controlling inflation and deflation, rather than on counteracting business fluctuations. Proponents of inflation targeting generally believe the economy will have fewer, shorter, and less severe business cycles if the Fed adheres to the rule "Set a known inflation goal and achieve it."

We discussed another modern monetary rule—the Taylor rule—in Chapter 14 on monetary policy. This rule specifies how the Fed should alter the Federal funds rate under differing economic circumstances. We discuss this rule in more depth in this chapter's Last Word.

Balanced Budget Monetarists and new classical economists question the effectiveness of fiscal policy. At the extreme, a few of them favor a constitutional amendment requiring that the Federal government balance its budget annually. Others simply suggest that government be "passive" in its fiscal policy, not intentionally creating budget deficits or surpluses. They believe that deficits and surpluses caused by recession or inflationary expansion will eventually correct themselves as the economy self-corrects to its full-employment output.

Monetarists are particularly strong in their opposition to expansionary fiscal policy. They believe that the deficit spending accompanying such a policy has a strong tendency to "crowd out" private investment. Suppose government runs a budget deficit by printing and selling U.S. securities—that is, by borrowing from the public. By engaging in such borrowing, the government is competing with private businesses for funds. The borrowing increases the demand for money, which then raises the interest rate and crowds out a substantial amount of private investment that would otherwise have been profitable. The net effect of a budget deficit on aggregate demand therefore is unpredictable and, at best, modest.

RET economists reject discretionary fiscal policy for the same reason they reject active monetary policy: They don't think it works. Business and labor will immediately adjust their behavior in anticipation of the price-level effects of a change in fiscal policy. The economy will move directly to the anticipated new price level. Like monetary policy, say the RET theorists, fiscal policy can move the economy along its vertical long-run aggregate supply curve. But because its effects on inflation are fully anticipated, fiscal policy cannot alter real GDP even in the short run. The best course of action for government is to balance its budget.

In Defense of Discretionary Stabilization Policy

Mainstream economists oppose both a strict monetary rule and a balanced-budget requirement. They believe that monetary policy and fiscal policy are important tools for achieving and maintaining full employment, price stability, and economic growth.

Discretionary Monetary Policy
In supporting discretionary monetary policy, mainstream economists argue that the rationale for the Friedman monetary rule is flawed. While there is indeed a close relationship between the money supply and nominal GDP over long periods, in shorter periods this relationship breaks down. The reason is that the velocity of money has proved to be more variable and unpredictable than monetarists contend. Arguing that velocity is variable both cyclically and over time, mainstream economists contend that a constant annual rate of increase in the money supply might not eliminate fluctuations in aggregate demand. In terms of the equation of exchange, a steady rise of M does not guarantee a steady expansion of aggregate demand because V—the rate at which money is spent—can change.

Look again at Figure 17.4, in which we demonstrated the monetary rule: Expand the money supply annually by a fixed percentage, regardless of the state of the economy. During the period in question, optimistic business expectations might create a boom in investment spending and thus shift the aggregate demand curve to some location to the right of AD_2. (You may want to pencil in a new AD curve, labeling it AD_3.) The price level would then rise above P_1; that is, demand-pull inflation would occur. In this case, the monetary rule will not accomplish its goal of maintaining price stability. Mainstream economists say that the Fed can use a restrictive monetary policy to reduce the excessive investment spending and thereby hold the rightward shift of aggregate demand to AD_2, thus avoiding inflation.

Similarly, suppose instead that investment declines because of pessimistic business expectations. Aggregate demand will then increase by some amount less than the increase from AD_1 to AD_2 in Figure 17.4. Again, the monetary rule fails the stability test: The price level sinks below P_1 (deflation occurs). Or if the price level is inflexible downward at P_1, the economy will not achieve its full-employment output (unemployment rises). An expansionary monetary policy can help avoid each outcome.

Mainstream economists quip that the trouble with the monetary rule is that it tells the policymaker, "Don't do something, just stand there."

Discretionary Fiscal Policy
Mainstream economists support the use of fiscal policy to keep recessions from deepening or to keep mild inflation from becoming severe inflation. They recognize the possibility of crowding out but do not think it is a serious problem when business borrowing is depressed, as is usually the case in recession. Because politicians can abuse fiscal policy, most economists feel that it should be held in reserve for situations where monetary policy appears to be ineffective or working too slowly.

As indicated earlier, mainstream economists oppose requirements to balance the budget annually. Tax revenues fall sharply during recessions and rise briskly during periods of demand-pull inflation. Therefore, a law or a constitutional amendment mandating an annually balanced budget would require that the government increase tax rates and reduce government spending during recession and reduce tax rates and increase government spending during economic booms. The first set of actions would worsen recession, and the second set would fuel inflation.

Last *Word*

The Taylor Rule: Could a Robot Replace Ben Bernanke?

Macroeconomist John Taylor of Stanford University Calls for a New Monetary Rule That Would Institutionalize Appropriate Fed Policy Responses to Changes in Real Output and Inflation.

In our discussion of rules versus discretion, "rules" were associated with a *passive* monetary policy—one in which the monetary rule required that the Fed expand the money supply at a fixed annual rate regardless of the state of the economy. "Discretion," on the other hand, was associated with an *active* monetary policy in which the Fed changed interest rates in response to actual or anticipated changes in the economy.

Economist John Taylor has put a new twist on the rules-versus-discretion debate by suggesting a hybrid policy rule that dictates the precise active monetary actions the Fed should take when changes in the economy occur. We first encountered this Taylor rule in our discussion of monetary policy in Chapter 14. The Taylor rule combines traditional monetarism, with its emphasis on a monetary rule, and the more mainstream view that active monetary pol-

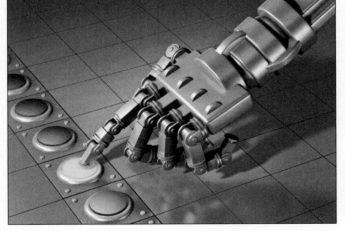

icy is a useful tool for taming inflation and limiting recession. Unlike the Friedman monetary rule, the Taylor rule holds, for example, that monetary policy should respond to changes in both real GDP and inflation, not simply inflation. The key adjustment instrument is the interest rate, not the money supply.

The Taylor rule has three parts:

- If real GDP rises 1 percent above potential GDP, the Fed should raise the Federal funds rate (the interbank interest rate of overnight loans), relative to the current inflation rate, by .5 percentage point.

- If inflation rises by 1 percentage point above its target of 2 percent, then the Fed should raise the Federal funds rate by .5 percentage point relative to the inflation rate.
- When real GDP is equal to potential GDP and inflation is equal to its target rate of 2 percent, the Federal funds rate should remain at about 4 percent, which would imply a real interest rate of 2 percent.*

Taylor has neither suggested nor implied that a robot, programmed with the Taylor rule, should replace Ben Bernanke, chairman of the Federal Reserve System. The Fed's discretion to override the rule (or "contingency plan for policy") would be retained, but the Fed would have to explain why its policies diverged from the rule. So the rule would remove the "mystery" associated with monetary policy and increase the Fed's accountability. Also, says Taylor, if used consistently, the rule would enable market participants to predict Fed behavior, and this would increase Fed credibility and reduce uncertainty.

Critics of the Taylor rule acknowledge that it is more in tune with countercyclical Fed policy than with Friedman's simple monetary rule. And they concede that the Fed's recent monetary policy closely mimics the rule. But they see no reason to limit the Fed's future discretion in adjusting interest rates as it sees fit to achieve stabilization and growth. Monetary policy must consider all risks to the economy and react accordingly. The critics also point out that the Fed has done a good job of promoting price stability, full employment, and economic growth over the past two decades. In view of this success, they conclude that a mechanical monetary rule is unnecessary and potentially detrimental.

---

*John Taylor, *Inflation, Unemployment, and Monetary Policy* (Cambridge, Mass.: MIT Press, 1998), pp. 44–47.

Increased Macro Stability

Finally, mainstream economists point out that the U.S. economy has been much more stable in the last half-century than it had been in earlier periods. It is not a coincidence, they say, that use of discretionary fiscal and monetary policies characterized the latter period but not the former. These policies have helped tame the business cycle. Moreover, mainstream economists point out several specific policy successes in the past three decades:

- A tight money policy dropped inflation from 13.5 percent in 1980 to 3.2 percent in 1983.
- An expansionary fiscal policy reduced the unemployment rate from 9.7 percent in 1982 to 5.5 percent in 1988.
- An easy money policy helped the economy recover from the 1990–1991 recession.
- Judicious tightening of monetary policy in the mid-1990s, and then again in the late 1990s, helped the economy remain on a noninflationary, full-employment growth path.
- In late 2001 and 2002, expansionary fiscal and monetary policy helped the economy recover from a series of economic blows, including the collapse of numerous Internet start-up firms, a severe decline in investment spending, the impacts of the terrorist attacks of September 11, 2001, and a precipitous decline in stock values.
- In 2004 and 2005 the Fed tempered continued expansionary fiscal policy by increasing the Federal funds rate in $\frac{1}{4}$-percentage-point increments from

1 percent to 4.25 percent. The economy expanded briskly in those years, while inflation stayed in check. The mild inflation was particularly impressive because the average price of a barrel of crude oil rose from $24 in 2002 to $55 in 2005. **(Key Question 13)**

Summary of Alternative Views

In Table 17.1 we summarize the central ideas and policy implications of three macroeconomic theories: mainstream macroeconomics, monetarism, and rational expectations theory. Note that we have broadly defined new classical economics to include both monetarism and the rational expectations theory, since both adhere to the view that the economy tends automatically to achieve equilibrium at its full-employment output. Also note that "mainstream macroeconomics" remains based on Keynesian ideas.

These different perspectives have obliged mainstream economists to rethink some of their fundamental principles and to revise many of their positions. Although considerable disagreement remains, mainstream macroeconomists agree with monetarists that "money matters" and that excessive growth of the money supply is the major cause of long-lasting, rapid inflation. They also agree with RET proponents and theorists of coordination failures that expectations matter. If government can create expectations of price stability, full employment, and economic growth, households and firms will tend to act in ways to make them happen. In short, thanks to ongoing challenges to conventional wisdom, macroeconomics continues to evolve.

TABLE 17.1 Summary of Alternative Macroeconomic Views

| Issue | Mainstream Macroeconomics (Keynesian based) | New Classical Economics | |
		Monetarism	Rational Expectations
View of the private economy	Potentially unstable	Stable in long run at natural rate of unemployment	Stable in long run at natural rate of unemployment
Cause of the observed instability of the private economy	Investment plans unequal to saving plans (changes in AD); AS shocks	Inappropriate monetary policy	Unanticipated AD and AS shocks in the short run
Appropriate macro policies	Active fiscal and monetary policy	Monetary rule	Monetary rule
How changes in the money supply affect the economy	By changing the interest rate, which changes investment and real GDP	By directly changing AD, which changes GDP	No effect on output because price-level changes are anticipated
View of the velocity of money	Unstable	Stable	No consensus
How fiscal policy affects the economy	Changes AD and GDP via the multiplier process	No effect unless money supply changes	No effect because price-level changes are anticipated
View of cost-push inflation	Possible (AS shock)	Impossible in the long run in the absence of excessive money supply growth	Impossible in the long run in the absence of excessive money supply growth

Summary

1. In classical economics the aggregate supply curve is vertical and establishes the level of real output, while the aggregate demand curve tends to be stable and establishes the price level. So the economy is relatively stable.

2. In Keynesian economics the aggregate supply curve is horizontal at less-than-full-employment levels of real output, while the aggregate demand curve is inherently unstable. So the economy is relatively unstable.

3. The mainstream view is that macro instability is caused by the volatility of investment spending, which shifts the aggregate demand curve. If aggregate demand increases too rapidly, demand-pull inflation may occur; if aggregate demand decreases, recession may occur. Occasionally, adverse supply shocks also cause instability.

4. Monetarism focuses on the equation of exchange: $MV = PQ$. Because velocity is thought to be stable, changes in M create changes in nominal GDP ($= PQ$). Monetarists believe that the most significant cause of macroeconomic instability has been inappropriate monetary policy. Rapid increases in M cause inflation; insufficient growth of M causes recession. In this view, a major cause of the Great Depression was inappropriate monetary policy, which allowed the money supply to decline by about 35 percent.

5. Real-business-cycle theory views changes in resource availability and technology (real factors), which alter productivity, as the main causes of macroeconomic instability. In this theory, shifts of the economy's long-run aggregate supply curve change real output. In turn, money demand and money supply change, shifting the aggregate demand curve in the same direction as the initial change in long-run aggregate supply. Real output thus can change without a change in the price level.

6. A coordination failure is said to occur when people lack a way to coordinate their actions in order to achieve a mutually beneficial equilibrium. Depending on people's expectations, the economy can come to rest at either a good equilibrium (noninflationary full-employment output) or a bad equilibrium (less-than-full-employment output or demand-pull inflation). A bad equilibrium is a result of a coordination failure.

7. The rational expectations theory rests on two assumptions: (1) With sufficient information, people's beliefs about future economic outcomes accurately reflect the likelihood that those outcomes will occur; and (2) markets are highly competitive, and prices and wages are flexible both upward and downward.

8. New classical economists (monetarists and rational expectations theorists) see the economy as automatically correcting itself when disturbed from its full-employment level of real output. In RET, unanticipated changes in aggregate demand change the price level, and in the short run this leads firms to change output. But once the firms realize that all prices are changing (including nominal wages) as part of general inflation or deflation, they restore their output to the previous level. Anticipated changes in aggregate demand produce only changes in the price level, not changes in real output.

9. Mainstream economists reject the new classical view that all prices and wages are flexible downward. They contend that nominal wages, in particular, are inflexible downward because of several factors, including labor contracts, efficiency wages, and insider-outsider relationships. This means that declines in aggregate demand lower real output, not only wages and prices.

10. Monetarist and rational expectations economists say the Fed should adhere to some form of policy rule, rather than rely exclusively on discretion. The Friedman rule would direct the Fed to increase the money supply at a fixed annual rate equal to the long-run growth of potential GDP. An alternative approach—inflation targeting—would direct the Fed to establish a targeted range of inflation rates, say, 1 to 2%, and focus monetary policy on meeting that goal. They also support maintaining a "neutral" fiscal policy, as opposed to using discretionary fiscal policy to create budget deficits or budget surpluses. A few monetarists and rational expectations economists favor a constitutional amendment requiring that the Federal government balance its budget annually.

11. Mainstream economists oppose strict monetary rules and a balanced-budget requirement, and defend discretionary monetary and fiscal policies. They say that both theory and evidence suggest that such policies are helpful in achieving full employment, price stability, and economic growth.

Terms and Concepts

classical view

Keynesian view

monetarism

equation of exchange

velocity

real-business-cycle theory

coordination failures

rational expectations theory

new classical economics

price-level surprises

efficiency wage

insider-outsider theory

monetary rule

Study Questions

1. **KEY QUESTION** Use the aggregate demand–aggregate supply model to compare the "old" classical and the Keynesian interpretations of (*a*) the aggregate supply curve and (*b*) the stability of the aggregate demand curve. Which of these interpretations seems more consistent with the realities of the Great Depression?

2. According to mainstream economists, what is the usual cause of macroeconomic instability? What role does the spending-income multiplier play in creating instability? How might adverse aggregate supply factors cause instability, according to mainstream economists?

3. State and explain the basic equation of monetarism. What is the major cause of macroeconomic instability, as viewed by monetarists?

4. **KEY QUESTION** Suppose that the money supply and the nominal GDP for a hypothetical economy are $96 billion and $336 billion, respectively. What is the velocity of money? How will households and businesses react if the central bank reduces the money supply by $20 billion? By how much will nominal GDP have to fall to restore equilibrium, according to the monetarist perspective?

5. Briefly describe the difference between a so-called real business cycle and a more traditional "spending" business cycle.

6. Craig and Kris were walking directly toward each other in a congested store aisle. Craig moved to his left to avoid Kris, and at the same time Kris moved to his right to avoid Craig. They bumped into each other. What concept does this example illustrate? How does this idea relate to macroeconomic instability?

7. **KEY QUESTION** Use an AD-AS graph to demonstrate and explain the price-level and real-output outcome of an anticipated decline in aggregate demand, as viewed by RET economists. (Assume that the economy initially is operating at its full-employment level of output.) Then demonstrate and explain on the same graph the outcome as viewed by mainstream economists.

8. What is an efficiency wage? How might payment of an above-market wage reduce shirking by employees and reduce worker turnover? How might efficiency wages contribute to downward wage inflexibility, at least for a time, when aggregate demand declines?

9. How might relationships between so-called insiders and outsiders contribute to downward wage inflexibility?

10. Use the equation of exchange to explain the rationale for a monetary rule. Why will such a rule run into trouble if V unexpectedly falls because of, say, a drop in investment spending by businesses?

11. Answer parts *a* and *b*, below, on the basis of the following information for a hypothetical economy in year 1: money supply = $400 billion; long-term annual growth of potential GDP = 3 percent; velocity = 4. Assume that the banking system initially has no excess reserves and that the reserve requirement is 10 percent. Also assume that velocity is constant and that the economy initially is operating at its full-employment real output.
   a. What is the level of nominal GDP in year 1?
   b. Suppose the Fed adheres to a monetary rule through open-market operations. What amount of U.S. securities will it have to sell to, or buy from, banks or the public between years 1 and 2 to meet its monetary rule?

12. Explain the difference between "active" discretionary fiscal policy advocated by mainstream economists and "passive" fiscal policy advocated by new classical economists. Explain: "The problem with a balanced-budget amendment is that it would, in a sense, require active fiscal policy—but in the wrong direction—as the economy slides into recession."

13. **KEY QUESTION** Place "MON," "RET," or "MAIN" beside the statements that most closely reflect monetarist, rational expectations, or mainstream views, respectively:
   a. Anticipated changes in aggregate demand affect only the price level; they have no effect on real output.
   b. Downward wage inflexibility means that declines in aggregate demand can cause long-lasting recession.
   c. Changes in the money supply M increase PQ; at first only Q rises because nominal wages are fixed, but once workers adapt their expectations to new realities, P rises and Q returns to its former level.
   d. Fiscal and monetary policies smooth out the business cycle.
   e. The Fed should increase the money supply at a fixed annual rate.

14. You have just been elected president of the United States, and the present chairperson of the Federal Reserve Board has resigned. You need to appoint a new person to this position, as well as a person to chair your Council of Economic Advisers. Using Table 17.1 and your knowledge of macroeconomics, identify the views on macro theory and policy you would want your appointees to hold. Remember, the economic health of the entire nation—and your chances for reelection—may depend on your selections.

15. **LAST WORD** Compare and contrast the Taylor rule for monetary policy with the older, simpler monetary rule advocated by Milton Friedman.

Web-Based Question

1. **THE EQUATION OF EXCHANGE—WHAT IS THE CUR-RENT VELOCITY OF MONEY?** In the equation of exchange, $MV = PQ$, the velocity of money, V, is found by dividing nominal GDP ($= PQ$) by M, the money supply. Calculate the velocity of money for the past 4 years. How stable was V during that period? Is V increasing or decreasing? Get current-dollar GDP data from the "Gross Domestic Product" section at the Bureau of Economic Analysis Web site, **www.bea.gov/.** Find $M1$ money supply data (seasonally adjusted) at the Fed's Web site, **www.federalreserve.gov/,** by selecting, in sequence, Economic Research and Data, Statistics: Releases and Historical Data, and Money Stock Measures—Historical Data.

PART SIX

International Economics

18

IN THIS CHAPTER YOU WILL LEARN:

- **The graphical model of comparative advantage, specialization, and the gains from trade.**

- **How differences between world prices and domestic prices prompt exports and imports.**

- **How economists analyze the economic effects of tariffs and quotas.**

- **The rebuttals to the most frequently presented arguments for protectionism.**

- **About the assistance provided workers under the Trade Adjustment Act of 2002.**

- **How the offshoring of U.S. jobs relates to the growing international trade in services.**

International Trade

The WTO, trade deficits, dumping. Exchange rates, the current account, the G8 nations. The IMF, official reserves, currency interventions. This is some of the language of international economics, the subject of Part 6. To understand the increasingly integrated world economy, we need to learn more about this language and the ideas that it conveys.

In this chapter we build on Chapter 5 by providing both a deeper analysis of the benefits of international trade and a fuller appraisal of the arguments for protectionism. Then in Chapter 19 we examine exchange rates and the U.S. balance of payments.

Some Key Facts

In Chapter 5, we provided an abundance of statistical information about U.S. international trade. The following "executive summary" reviews the most important of those facts:

- A *trade deficit* occurs when imports exceed exports. The United States has a trade deficit in goods. In 2005, U.S. imports of goods exceeded U.S. exports of goods by $782 billion.
- A *trade surplus* occurs when exports exceed imports. The United States has a trade surplus in services (such as air transportation services and financial services). In 2005, U.S. exports of services exceeded U.S. imports of services by $58 billion.
- Principal U.S. exports include chemicals, consumer durables, agricultural products, semiconductors, and computers; principal imports include petroleum, automobiles, household appliances, computers, and metals.
- Like other advanced industrial nations, the United States imports some of the same categories of goods that it exports. Examples: automobiles, computers, chemicals, semiconductors, and telecommunications equipment.
- Canada is the United States' most important trading partner quantitatively. In 2005, some 24 percent of U.S. exported goods were sold to Canadians, who in turn provided 17 percent of the U.S. imports of goods.
- The United States has a sizable trade deficit with China. In 2005, it was $202 billion.
- The U.S. dependence on foreign oil is reflected in its trade with members of OPEC. In 2005, the United States imported $125 billion of goods (mainly oil) from OPEC members, while exporting $31 billion of goods to those countries.
- The United States leads the world in the combined volume of exports and imports, as measured in dollars. Germany, the United States, China, Japan, and France are the top five exporters by dollar volume (see Global Perspective 5.1, p. 88). Currently, the United States provides about 9 percent of the world's exports (see Global Perspective 18.1).
- Exports of goods and services (on a national income account basis) make up about 11 percent of total U.S. output. That percentage is much lower than the percentage in many other nations, including Canada, Italy, France, and the United Kingdom (see Table 5.1, p. 86).
- China has become a major international trader, with an estimated $762 billion of exports in 2005. Other Asian economies—including South Korea, Taiwan, and Singapore—are also active in international trade.

GLOBAL PERSPECTIVE 18.1

Shares of World Exports, Selected Nations

Germany has the largest share of world exports, followed by the United States and China. The eight largest export nations account for nearly 50 percent of world exports.

Percentage Share of World Exports, 2004

Germany
United States
China
Japan
France
Netherlands
Italy
United Kingdom

Source: World Trade Organization, **www.wto.org.**

Their combined exports exceed those of France, Britain, or Italy.

- International trade (and finance) links world economies (review Figure 5.1, page 85). Through trade, changes in economic conditions in one place on the globe can quickly affect other places.
- International trade is often at the center of debates over economic policy, both within the United States and internationally.

With this information in mind, let's look more closely at the economics of international trade.

The Economic Basis for Trade

Chapter 5 revealed that international trade enables nations to specialize their production, enhance their resource productivity, and acquire more goods and services. Sovereign nations, like individuals and the regions of a nation, can gain by specializing in the products they can produce with greatest relative efficiency and by trading for the goods they cannot produce as efficiently. A more complete answer to the question "Why do nations trade?" hinges on three facts:

- The distribution of natural, human, and capital resources among nations is uneven; nations differ in their endowments of economic resources.

- Efficient production of various goods requires different technologies or combinations of resources.
- Products are differentiated as to quality and other nonprice attributes. A few or many people may prefer certain imported goods to similar goods made domestically.

To recognize the character and interaction of these three facts, think of Japan, for example, which has a large, well-educated labor force and abundant, and therefore inexpensive, skilled labor. As a result, Japan can produce efficiently (at low cost) a variety of **labor-intensive goods** such as digital cameras, video game players, and DVD players whose design and production require much skilled labor.

In contrast, Australia has vast amounts of land and can inexpensively produce such **land-intensive goods** as wheat, wool, and meat. Brazil has the soil, tropical climate, rainfall, and ready supply of unskilled labor that are needed for the efficient, low-cost production of coffee.

Industrially advanced economies with relatively large amounts of capital can inexpensively produce goods whose production requires much capital, including such **capital-intensive goods** as automobiles, agricultural equipment, machinery, and chemicals.

All nations, regardless of their labor, land, or capital intensity, can find special niches for individual products that are in demand worldwide because of their special qualities. Examples: fashions from Italy, luxury automobiles from Germany, software from the United States, and watches from Switzerland.

The distribution of resources, technology, and product distinctiveness among nations, however, is not forever fixed. When that distribution changes, the relative efficiency and success with which nations produce and sell goods also changes. For example, in the past few decades South Korea has upgraded the quality of its labor force and has greatly expanded its stock of capital. Although South Korea was primarily an exporter of agricultural products and raw materials a half-century ago, it now exports large quantities of manufactured goods. Similarly, the new technologies that gave us synthetic fibers and synthetic rubber drastically altered the resource mix needed to produce these goods and changed the relative efficiency of nations in manufacturing them.

As national economies evolve, the size and quality of their labor forces may change, the volume and composition of their capital stocks may shift, new technologies may develop, and even the quality of land and the quantity of natural resources may be altered. As such changes occur, the relative efficiency with which a nation can produce specific goods will also change.

Comparative Advantage: Graphical Analysis

Implicit in what we have been saying is the principle of comparative advantage, described through production possibilities tables in Chapter 5. Let's look again at that idea, now using graphical analysis.

Two Isolated Nations

Suppose the world economy is composed of just two nations: the United States and Brazil. Also for simplicity, suppose that the labor forces in the United States and Brazil are of equal size. Each nation can produce both wheat and coffee, but at different levels of economic efficiency. Suppose the U.S. and Brazilian domestic production possibilities curves for coffee and wheat are as shown in Figure 18.1a and 18.1b. Note especially three realities relating to these production possibilities curves:

- *Constant costs* The "curves" are drawn as straight lines, in contrast to the bowed-outward production possibilities frontiers we examined in Chapter 1. This means that we have replaced the law of increasing opportunity costs with the assumption of constant costs. This substitution simplifies our discussion but does not impair the validity of our analysis and conclusions. Later we will consider the effects of increasing opportunity costs.
- *Different costs* The production possibilities curves of the United States and Brazil reflect different resource mixes and differing levels of technological progress. Specifically, the differing slopes of the two curves tell us that the opportunity costs of producing wheat and coffee differ between the two nations.
- *U.S. absolute advantage in both* In view of our assumption that the U.S. and Brazilian labor forces are of equal size, the two production possibilities curves show that the United States has an *absolute advantage* in producing both products. If the United States and Brazil use their entire (equal-size) labor forces to produce either coffee or wheat, the United States can produce more of either than Brazil. The United States, using the same number of workers as Brazil, has greater production possibilities. So output per worker—labor productivity—in the United States exceeds that in Brazil in producing both products.

United States In Figure 18.1a, with full employment, the United States will operate on its production possibilities curve. On that curve, it can increase its output of wheat from 0 tons to 30 tons by forgoing 30 tons of coffee output. This

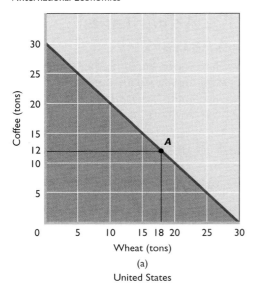
(a)
United States

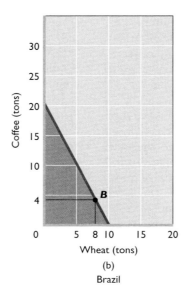
(b)
Brazil

FIGURE 18.1 Production possibilities for the United States and Brazil. The two production possibilities curves show the combinations of coffee and wheat that (a) the United States and (b) Brazil can produce domestically. The curves for both countries are straight lines because we are assuming constant opportunity costs. The different cost ratios, 1 coffee ≡ 1 wheat for the United States, and 2 coffee ≡ 1 wheat for Brazil, are reflected in the different slopes of the two lines.

means that the slope of the production possibilities curve is −1 (= −30 coffee/+30 wheat), implying that 1 ton of coffee must be sacrificed for each extra ton of wheat. In the United States the domestic exchange ratio or **opportunity-cost ratio** for the two products is 1 ton of coffee for 1 ton of wheat, or $1C ≡ 1W$. (As in Chapter 5, the "≡" sign simply means "equivalent to.") Said differently, the United States can "exchange" a ton of coffee for a ton of wheat. Our constant-cost assumption means that this exchange or opportunity-cost equation prevails for all possible moves from one point to another along the U.S. production possibilities curve.

Brazil Brazil's production possibilities curve in Figure 18.1b represents a different full-employment opportunity-cost ratio. In Brazil, 20 tons of coffee must be given up to get 10 tons of wheat. The slope of the production possibilities curve is −2 (= −20 coffee/+10 wheat). This means that in Brazil the opportunity-cost ratio for the two goods is 2 tons of coffee for 1 ton of wheat, or $2C ≡ 1W$.

Self-Sufficiency Output Mix If the United States and Brazil are isolated and are to be self-sufficient, then each country must choose some output mix on its production possibilities curve. It will choose the mix that provides the greatest total utility, or satisfaction. Assume that point A in Figure 18.1a is the optimal mix in the United States; that is, society deems the combination of 18 tons of wheat and 12 tons of coffee preferable to any other combination of the goods available along the production possibilities curve. Suppose Brazil's optimal product mix is 8 tons of wheat and 4 tons of coffee, indicated by point B in Figure 18.1b. These choices are reflected in column 1 of Table 18.1.

Specializing Based on Comparative Advantage

Although the United States has an absolute advantage in producing both goods, gains from specialization and trade are possible. Specialization and trade are mutually

TABLE 18.1 International Specialization According to Comparative Advantage and the Gains from Trade

Country	(1) Outputs before Specialization	(2) Outputs after Specialization	(3) Amounts Exported (−) and Imported (+)	(4) Outputs Available after Trade	(5) Gains from Specialization and Trade (4) − (1)
United States	18 wheat	30 wheat	−10 wheat	20 wheat	2 wheat
	12 coffee	0 coffee	+15 coffee	15 coffee	3 coffee
Brazil	8 wheat	0 wheat	+10 wheat	10 wheat	2 wheat
	4 coffee	20 coffee	−15 coffee	5 coffee	1 coffee

beneficial, or profitable, to the two nations if the *comparative* opportunity costs of producing the two products within the two nations differ, as they do in this example. The **principle of comparative advantage** says that total output will be greatest when each good is produced by the nation that has the lowest domestic opportunity cost for that good. In our two-nation illustration, the United States has the lower domestic opportunity cost for wheat; the United States need forgo only 1 ton of coffee to produce 1 ton of wheat, whereas Brazil must forgo 2 tons of coffee for 1 ton of wheat. The United States has a comparative (cost) advantage in wheat and should specialize in wheat production. The "world" (that is, the United States and Brazil) in our example would clearly not be economizing in the use of its resources if a high-cost producer (Brazil) produced a specific product (wheat) when a low-cost producer (the United States) could have produced it. Having Brazil produce wheat would mean that the world economy would have to give up more coffee than is necessary to obtain a ton of wheat.

O 18.1

Comparative advantage

Brazil has the lower domestic opportunity cost for coffee; it must sacrifice only $\frac{1}{2}$ ton of wheat in producing 1 ton of coffee, while the United States must forgo 1 ton of wheat in producing a ton of coffee. Brazil has a comparative advantage in coffee and should specialize in coffee production. Again, the world would not be employing its resources economically if coffee were produced by a high-cost producer (the United States) rather than by a low-cost producer (Brazil). If the United States produced coffee, the world would be giving up more wheat than necessary to obtain each ton of coffee. Economizing requires that any particular good be produced by the nation having the lowest domestic opportunity cost, or the comparative advantage for that good. The United States should produce wheat, and Brazil should produce coffee.

In column 2 of Table 18.1 we verify that specialized production enables the world to get more output from its fixed amount of resources. By specializing completely in wheat, the United States can produce 30 tons of wheat and no coffee. Brazil, by specializing completely in coffee, can produce 20 tons of coffee and no wheat. The world ends up with 4 more tons of wheat (30 tons compared with 26) *and* 4 more tons of coffee (20 tons compared with 16) than it would if there were self-sufficiency or unspecialized production.

Terms of Trade

But consumers of each nation want both wheat *and* coffee. They can have both if the two nations trade the two products. But what will be the **terms of trade?** At what

exchange ratio will the United States and Brazil trade wheat and coffee?

Because $1W \equiv 1C$ in the United States, the United States must get *more than* 1 ton of coffee for each ton of wheat exported; otherwise, it will not benefit from exporting wheat in exchange for Brazilian coffee. The United States must get a better "price" (more coffee) for its wheat in the world market than it can get domestically; otherwise, there is no gain from trade and it will not occur.

Similarly, because $1W \equiv 2C$ in Brazil, Brazil must get 1 ton of wheat by exporting some amount *less than* 2 tons of coffee. Brazil must be able to pay a lower "price" for wheat in the world market than it must pay domestically, or else it will not want to trade. The international exchange ratio or terms of trade must lie somewhere between

$$1W \equiv 1C \text{ (United States' cost conditions)}$$

and

$$1W \equiv 2C \text{ (Brazil's cost conditions)}$$

But where between these limits will the world exchange ratio fall? The United States will prefer a rate close to $1W \equiv 2C$, say, $1W \equiv 1\frac{3}{4}C$. The United States wants to get as much coffee as possible for each ton of wheat it exports. Similarly, Brazil wants a rate near $1W \equiv 1C$, say, $1W \equiv 1\frac{1}{4}C$. Brazil wants to export as little coffee as possible for each ton of wheat it receives in exchange. The exchange ratio or terms of trade determine how the gains from international specialization and trade are divided between the two nations.

The actual exchange ratio depends on world supply and demand for the two products. If overall world demand for coffee is weak relative to its supply and if the demand for wheat is strong relative to its supply, the price of coffee will be lower and the price of wheat higher. The exchange ratio will settle nearer the $1W \equiv 2C$ figure the United States prefers. If overall world demand for coffee is great relative to its supply and if the demand for wheat is weak relative to its supply, the ratio will settle nearer the $1W \equiv 1C$ level favorable to Brazil. (We discuss equilibrium world prices later in this chapter.)

Gains from Trade

Suppose the international terms of trade are $1W \equiv 1\frac{1}{2}C$. The possibility of trading on these terms permits each nation to supplement its domestic production possibilities curve with a **trading possibilities line** (or curve), as shown in **Figure 18.2 (Key Graph).** Just as a production possibilities curve shows the amounts of these products a full-employment economy can obtain by shifting resources from one to the other, a trading possibilities line shows the amounts of two products a nation can obtain by specializing

keygraph

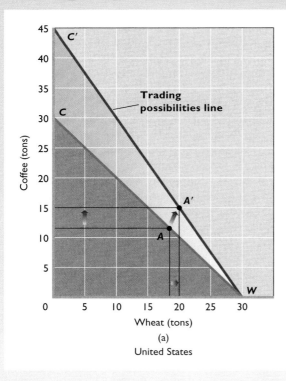

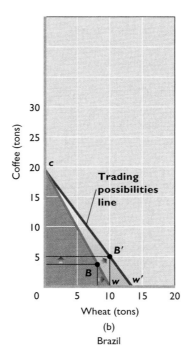

FIGURE 18.2 Trading possibility lines and the gains from trade. As a result of specialization and trade, both the United States and Brazil can have higher levels of output than the levels attainable on their domestic production possibilities curves. (a) The United States can move from point A on its domestic production possibilities curve to, say, A' on its trading possibilities line. (b) Brazil can move from B to B'.

QUICK QUIZ 18.2

1. The production possibilities curves in graphs (a) and (b) imply:
   a. increasing domestic opportunity costs.
   b. decreasing domestic opportunity costs.
   c. constant domestic opportunity costs.
   d. first decreasing, then increasing, domestic opportunity costs.
2. Before specialization, the domestic opportunity cost of producing 1 unit of wheat is:
   a. 1 unit of coffee in both the United States and Brazil.
   b. 1 unit of coffee in the United States and 2 units of coffee in Brazil.
   c. 2 units of coffee in the United States and 1 unit of coffee in Brazil.
   d. 1 unit of coffee in the United States and $\frac{1}{2}$ unit of coffee in Brazil.

3. After specialization and international trade, the world output of wheat and coffee is:
   a. 20 tons of wheat and 20 tons of coffee.
   b. 45 tons of wheat and 15 tons of coffee.
   c. 30 tons of wheat and 20 tons of coffee.
   d. 10 tons of wheat and 30 tons of coffee.
4. After specialization and international trade:
   a. the United States can obtain units of coffee at less cost than it could before trade.
   b. Brazil can obtain more than 20 tons of coffee, if it so chooses.
   c. the United States no longer has a comparative advantage in producing wheat.
   d. Brazil can benefit by prohibiting coffee imports from the United States.

Answers: 1. c; 2. b; 3. c; 4. a

---

in one product and trading for the other. The trading possibilities lines in Figure 18.2 reflect the assumption that both nations specialize on the basis of comparative advantage: The United States specializes completely in wheat (at point *W* in Figure 18.2a), and Brazil specializes completely in coffee (at point *c* in Figure 18.2b).

Improved Options Now the United States is not constrained by its domestic production possibilities line,

which requires it to give up 1 ton of wheat for every ton of coffee it wants as it moves up its domestic production possibilities line from, say, point *W*. Instead, the United States, through trade with Brazil, can get $1\frac{1}{2}$ tons of coffee for every ton of wheat it exports to Brazil, as long as Brazil has coffee to export. Trading possibilities line *WC'* thus represents the $1W \equiv 1\frac{1}{2}C$ trading ratio.

Similarly, Brazil, starting at, say, point *c*, no longer has to move down its domestic production possibilities curve, giving up 2 tons of coffee for each ton of wheat it wants. It can now export just $1\frac{1}{2}$ tons of coffee for each ton of wheat it wants by moving down its trading possibilities line cw'.

Specialization and trade create a new exchange ratio between wheat and coffee, reflected in each nation's trading possibilities line. This exchange ratio is superior for both nations to the unspecialized exchange ratio embodied in their production possibilities curves. By specializing in wheat and trading for Brazil's coffee, the United States can obtain more than 1 ton of coffee for 1 ton of wheat. By specializing in coffee and trading for U.S. wheat, Brazil can get 1 ton of wheat for less than 2 tons of coffee. In both cases, self-sufficiency is undesirable.

Added Output By specializing on the basis of comparative advantage and by trading for goods that are produced in the nation with greater domestic efficiency, the United States and Brazil can realize combinations of wheat and coffee beyond their production possibilities curves. Specialization according to comparative advantage results in a more efficient allocation of world resources, and larger outputs of both products are therefore available to both nations.

Suppose that at the $1W \equiv 1\frac{1}{2}C$ terms of trade, the United States exports 10 tons of wheat to Brazil and in return Brazil exports 15 tons of coffee to the United States. How do the new quantities of wheat and coffee available to the two nations compare with the optimal product mixes that existed before specialization and trade? Point A in Figure 18.2a reminds us that the United States chose 18 tons of wheat and 12 tons of coffee originally. But by producing 30 tons of wheat and no coffee and by trading 10 tons of wheat for 15 tons of coffee, the United States can obtain 20 tons of wheat and 15 tons of coffee. This new, superior combination of wheat and coffee is indicated by point A' in Figure 18.2a. Compared with the no-trade amounts of 18 tons of wheat and 12 tons of coffee, the United States' **gains from trade** are 2 tons of wheat and 3 tons of coffee.

Similarly, recall that Brazil's optimal product mix was 4 tons of coffee and 8 tons of wheat (point B) before specialization and trade. Now, after specializing in coffee and trading, Brazil can have 5 tons of coffee and 10 tons of wheat. It accomplishes that by producing 20 tons of coffee and no wheat and exporting 15 tons of its coffee in exchange for 10 tons of American wheat. This new position is indicated by point B' in Figure 18.2b. Brazil's gains from trade are 1 ton of coffee and 2 tons of wheat.

As a result of specialization and trade, both countries have more of both products. Table 18.1, which summarizes the transactions and outcomes, merits careful study.

The fact that points A' and B' are economic positions superior to A and B is enormously important. We know that a nation can expand its production possibilities boundary by

W 18.1

Gains from trade

(1) expanding the quantity and improving the quality of its resources or (2) realizing technological progress. We have now established that international trade can enable a nation to circumvent the output constraint illustrated by its production possibilities curve. The outcome of international specialization and trade is equivalent to having more and better resources or discovering improved production techniques.

Trade with Increasing Costs

To explain the basic principles underlying international trade, we simplified our analysis in several ways. For example, we limited discussion to two products and two nations. But multiproduct and multinational analysis yields the same conclusions. We also assumed constant opportunity costs (linear production possibilities curves), which is a more substantive simplification. Let's consider the effect of allowing increasing opportunity costs (concave-to-the-origin production possibilities curves) to enter the picture.

Suppose that the United States and Brazil initially are at positions on their concave production possibilities curves where their domestic cost ratios are $1W \equiv 1C$ and $1W \equiv 2C$, as they were in our constant-cost analysis. As before, comparative advantage indicates that the United States should specialize in wheat and Brazil in coffee. But now, as the United States begins to expand wheat production, its cost of wheat will rise; it will have to sacrifice more than 1 ton of coffee to get 1 additional ton of wheat. Resources are no longer perfectly substitutable between alternative uses, as the constant-cost assumption implied. Resources less and less suitable to wheat production must be allocated to the U.S. wheat industry in expanding wheat output, and that means increasing costs—the sacrifice of larger and larger amounts of coffee for each additional ton of wheat.

Similarly, Brazil, starting from its $1W \equiv 2C$ cost ratio position, expands coffee production. But as it does, it will find that its $1W \equiv 2C$ cost ratio begins to rise. Sacrificing a ton of wheat will free resources that are capable of producing only something less than 2 tons of coffee, because those transferred resources are less suitable to coffee production.

As the U.S. cost ratio falls from $1W \equiv 1C$ and the Brazilian ratio rises from $1W \equiv 2C$, a point will be reached where the cost ratios are equal in the two nations, perhaps at $1W \equiv 1\frac{3}{4}C$. At this point the underlying basis for further specialization and trade—differing cost ratios—has disappeared, and further specialization is therefore uneconomical. And, most important, this point of equal cost ratios may be reached while the United States is still producing some coffee along with its wheat and Brazil is producing some wheat along with its coffee. The primary effect of increasing opportunity costs is less-than-complete specialization. For this reason we often find domestically produced products competing directly against identical or similar imported products within a particular economy. **(Key Question 4)**

The Case for Free Trade

The case for free trade reduces to one compelling argument: Through free trade based on the principle of comparative advantage, the world economy can achieve a more efficient allocation of resources and a higher level of material well-being than it can without free trade.

Since the resource mixes and technological knowledge of the world's nations are all somewhat different, each nation can produce particular commodities at different real costs. Each nation should produce goods for which its domestic opportunity costs are lower than the domestic opportunity costs of other nations and exchange those goods for products for which its domestic opportunity costs are high relative to those of other nations. If each nation does this, the world will realize the advantages of geographic and human specialization. The world and each free-trading nation can obtain a larger real income from the fixed supplies of resources available to it. Government trade barriers lessen or eliminate gains from specialization. If nations cannot trade freely, they must shift resources from efficient (low-cost) to inefficient (high-cost) uses in order to satisfy their diverse wants.

One side benefit of free trade is that it promotes competition and deters monopoly. The increased competition from foreign firms forces domestic firms to find and use the lowest-cost production techniques. It also compels them to be innovative with respect to both product quality and production methods, thereby contributing to economic growth. And free trade gives consumers a wider range of product choices. The reasons to favor free trade are the same as the reasons to endorse competition.

A second side benefit of free trade is that it links national interests and breaks down national animosities. Confronted with political disagreements, trading partners tend to negotiate rather than make war.

QUICK REVIEW 18.1

- International trade enables nations to specialize, increase productivity, and increase output available for consumption.
- Comparative advantage means total world output will be greatest when each good is produced by the nation that has the lowest domestic opportunity cost.
- Specialization is less than complete among nations because opportunity costs normally rise as any given nation produces more of a particular good.

Supply and Demand Analysis of Exports and Imports

Supply and demand analysis reveals how equilibrium prices and quantities of exports and imports are determined. The amount of a good or a service a nation will export or import depends on differences between the equilibrium world price and the equilibrium domestic price. The interaction of *world* supply and demand determines the equilibrium **world price**—the price that equates the quantities supplied and demanded globally. *Domestic* supply and demand determine the equilibrium **domestic price**—the price that would prevail in a closed economy that does not engage in international trade. The domestic price equates quantity supplied and quantity demanded domestically.

In the absence of trade, the domestic prices in a closed economy may or may not equal the world equilibrium prices. When economies are opened for international trade, differences between world and domestic prices encourage exports or imports. To see how, consider the international effects of such price differences in a simple two-nation world, consisting of the United States and Canada, that are both producing aluminum. We assume there are no trade barriers, such as tariffs and quotas, and no international transportation costs.

Supply and Demand in the United States

Figure 18.3a shows the domestic supply curve S_d and the domestic demand curve D_d for aluminum in the United States, which for now is a closed economy. The intersection of S_d and D_d determines the equilibrium domestic price of $1 per pound and the equilibrium domestic quantity of 100 million pounds. Domestic suppliers produce 100 million pounds and sell them all at $1 a pound. So there are no domestic surpluses or shortages of aluminum.

FIGURE 18.3 U.S. export supply and import demand. (a) Domestic supply S_d and demand D_d set the domestic equilibrium price of aluminum at $1 per pound. At world prices above $1 there are domestic surpluses of aluminum. At prices below $1 there are domestic shortages. (b) Surpluses are exported (top curve), and shortages are met by importing aluminum (lower curve). The export supply curve shows the direct relationship between world prices and U.S. exports; the import demand curve portrays the inverse relationship between world prices and U.S. imports.

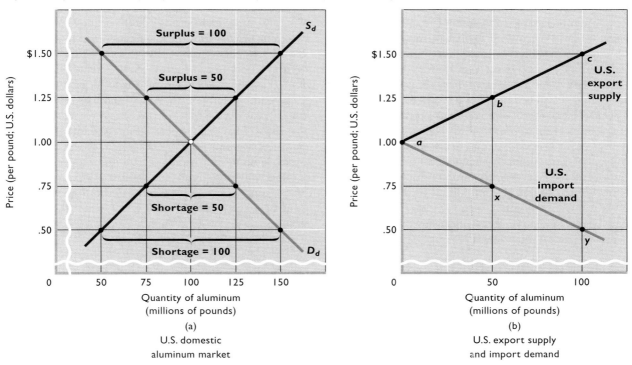

(a)
U.S. domestic
aluminum market

(b)
U.S. export supply
and import demand

But what if the U.S. economy were opened to trade and the world price of aluminum were above or below this $1 domestic price?

U.S. Export Supply
If the aluminum price in the rest of the world (that is, Canada) exceeds $1, U.S. firms will produce more than 100 million pounds and will export the excess domestic output. First, consider a world price of $1.25. We see from the supply curve S_d that U.S. aluminum firms will produce 125 million pounds of aluminum at that price. The demand curve D_d tells us that the United States will purchase only 75 million pounds at $1.25. The outcome is a domestic surplus of 50 million pounds of aluminum. U.S. producers will export those 50 million pounds at the $1.25 world price.

What if the world price were $1.50? The supply curve shows that U.S. firms will produce 150 million pounds of aluminum, while the demand curve tells us that U.S. consumers will buy only 50 million pounds. So U.S. producers will export the domestic surplus of 100 million pounds.

Toward the top of Figure 18.3b we plot the domestic surpluses—the U.S. exports—that occur at world prices above the $1 domestic equilibrium price. When the world

and domestic prices are equal (= $1), the quantity of exports supplied is zero (point *a*). There is no surplus of domestic output to export. But when the world price is $1.25, U.S. firms export 50 million pounds of surplus aluminum (point *b*). At a $1.50 world price, the domestic surplus of 100 million pounds is exported (point *c*).

The U.S. **export supply curve,** found by connecting points *a*, *b*, and *c*, shows the amount of aluminum U.S. producers will export at each world price above $1. This curve *slopes upward*, indicating a direct or positive relationship between the world price and the amount of U.S. exports. As world prices increase relative to domestic prices, U.S. exports rise.

U.S. Import Demand
If the world price is below the domestic $1 price, the United States will import aluminum. Consider a $.75 world price. The supply curve in Figure 18.3a reveals that at that price U.S. firms produce only 75 million pounds of aluminum. But the demand curve shows that the United States wants to buy 125 million pounds at that price. The result is a domestic shortage of 50 million pounds. To satisfy that shortage, the United States will import 50 million pounds of aluminum.

At an even lower world price, $.50, U.S. producers will supply only 50 million pounds. Because U.S. consumers want to buy 150 million pounds at that price, there is a domestic shortage of 100 million pounds. Imports will flow to the United States to make up the difference. That is, at a $.50 world price U.S. firms will supply 50 million pounds and 100 million pounds will be imported.

In Figure 18.3b we plot the U.S. **import demand curve** from these data. This *downsloping curve* shows the amounts of aluminum that will be imported at world prices below the $1 U.S. domestic price. The relationship between world prices and imported amounts is inverse or negative. At a world price of $1, domestic output will satisfy U.S. demand; imports will be zero (point *a*). But at $.75 the United States will import 50 million pounds of aluminum (point *x*); at $.50, the United States will import 100 million pounds (point *y*). Connecting points *a*, *x*, and *y* yields the *downsloping* U.S. import demand curve. It reveals that as world prices fall relative to U.S. domestic prices, U.S. imports increase.

Supply and Demand in Canada

We repeat our analysis in Figure 18.4, this time from the viewpoint of Canada. (We have converted Canadian dollar prices to U.S. dollar prices via the exchange rate.) Note that the domestic supply curve S_d and the domestic demand curve D_d for aluminum in Canada yield a domestic price of $.75, which is $.25 lower than the $1 U.S. domestic price.

The analysis proceeds exactly as above except that the domestic price is now the Canadian price. If the world price is $.75, Canadians will neither export nor import aluminum (giving us point *q* in Figure 18.4b). At world prices above $.75, Canadian firms will produce more aluminum than Canadian consumers will buy. Canadian firms will export the surplus. At a $1 world price, Figure 18.4b tells us that Canada will have and export a domestic surplus of 50 million pounds (yielding point *r*). At $1.25, it will have and will export a domestic surplus of 100 million pounds (point *s*). Connecting these points yields the upsloping Canadian export supply curve, which reflects the domestic surpluses (and hence the exports) that occur when the world price exceeds the $.75 Canadian domestic price.

At world prices below $.75, domestic shortages occur in Canada. At a $.50 world price, Figure 18.4a shows that Canadian consumers want to buy 125 million pounds of aluminum but Canadian firms will produce only 75 million pounds. The shortage will bring 50 million pounds of

FIGURE 18.4 Canadian export supply and import demand. (a) At world prices above the $.75 domestic price, production in Canada exceeds domestic consumption. At world prices below $.75, domestic shortages occur. (b) Surpluses result in exports, and shortages result in imports. The Canadian export supply curve and import demand curve depict the relationships between world prices and exports or imports.

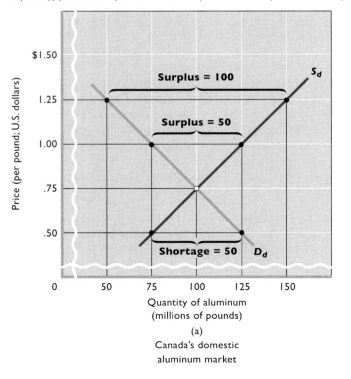

(a)
Canada's domestic
aluminum market

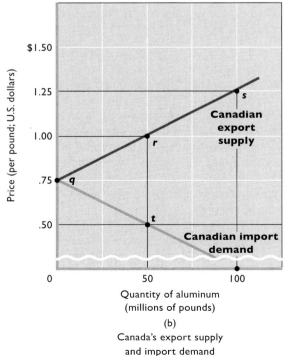

(b)
Canada's export supply
and import demand

imports to Canada (point *t* in Figure 18.4b). The Canadian import demand curve in that figure shows the Canadian imports that will occur at all world aluminum prices below the $.75 Canadian domestic price.

Equilibrium World Price, Exports, and Imports

We now have the tools for determining the **equilibrium world price** of aluminum and the equilibrium world levels of exports and imports when the world is opened to trade. Figure 18.5 combines the U.S. export supply curve and import demand curve in Figure 18.3b and the Canadian export supply curve and import demand curve in Figure 18.4b. The two U.S. curves proceed rightward from the $1 U.S. domestic price; the two Canadian curves proceed rightward from the $.75 Canadian domestic price.

W 18.2

Equilibrium world price, exports, and imports

International equilibrium occurs in this two-nation model where one nation's import demand curve intersects another nation's export supply curve. In this case the U.S. import demand curve intersects Canada's export supply curve at *e*. There, the world price of aluminum is $.88. The Canadian export supply curve indicates that Canada will export 25 million pounds

FIGURE 18.5 Equilibrium world price and quantity of exports and imports. In a two-nation world, the equilibrium world price (= $.88) is determined by the intersection of one nation's export supply curve and the other nation's import demand curve. This intersection also decides the equilibrium volume of exports and imports. Here, Canada exports 25 million pounds of aluminum to the United States.

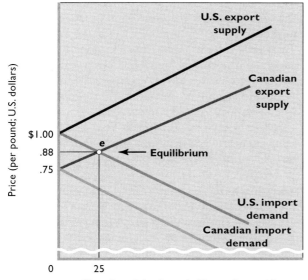

of aluminum at this price. Also at this price the United States will import 25 million pounds from Canada, indicated by the U.S. import demand curve. The $.88 world price equates the quantity of imports demanded and the quantity of exports supplied (25 million pounds). Thus there will be world trade of 25 million pounds of aluminum at $.88 per pound.

Note that after trade, the single $.88 world price will prevail in both Canada and the United States. Only one price for a standardized commodity can persist in a highly competitive world market. With trade, all consumers can buy a pound of aluminum for $.88, and all producers can sell it for that price. This world price means that Canadians will pay more for aluminum with trade ($.88) than without it ($.75). The increased Canadian output caused by trade raises Canadian per-unit production costs and therefore raises the price of aluminum in Canada. The United States, however, pays less for aluminum with trade ($.88) than without it ($1). The U.S. gain comes from Canada's comparative cost advantage in producing aluminum.

Why would Canada willingly send 25 million pounds of its aluminum output to the United States for U.S. consumption? After all, producing this output uses up scarce Canadian resources and drives up the price of aluminum for Canadians. Canadians are willing to export aluminum to the United States because Canadians gain the means—the U.S. dollars—to import other goods, say, computer software, from the United States. Canadian exports enable Canadians to acquire imports that have greater value to Canadians than the exported aluminum. Canadian exports to the United States finance Canadian imports from the United States. **(Key Question 6)**

QUICK REVIEW 18.2

* A nation will export a particular product if the world price exceeds the domestic price; it will import the product if the world price is less than the domestic price.
* In a two-country world model, equilibrium world prices and equilibrium quantities of exports and imports occur where one nation's export supply curve intersects the other nation's import demand curve.

Trade Barriers

No matter how compelling the case for free trade, barriers to free trade *do* exist. Let's expand Chapter 5's discussion of trade barriers.

Excise taxes on imported goods are called **tariffs;** they may be imposed to obtain revenue or to protect domestic firms. A **revenue tariff** is usually applied to a product that is not being produced domestically, for example, tin, coffee, or bananas in the case of the United States. Rates on revenue tariffs are modest; their purpose is to provide the Federal government with revenue. A **protective tariff** is designed to shield domestic producers from foreign competition. Although protective tariffs are usually not high enough to stop the importation of foreign goods, they put foreign producers at a competitive disadvantage in selling in domestic markets.

An **import quota** specifies the maximum amount of a commodity that may be imported in any period. Import quotas can more effectively retard international commerce than tariffs. A product might be imported in large quantities despite high tariffs; low import quotas completely prohibit imports once quotas have been filled.

A **nontariff barrier (NTB)** is a licensing requirement that specifies unreasonable standards pertaining to product quality and safety, or unnecessary bureaucratic red tape that is used to restrict imports. Japan and the European countries frequently require that their domestic importers of foreign goods obtain licenses. By restricting the issuance of licenses, imports can be restricted. The United Kingdom uses this barrier to bar the importation of coal.

A **voluntary export restriction (VER)** is a trade barrier by which foreign firms "voluntarily" limit the amount of their exports to a particular country. VERs, which have

O 18.2
Mercantilism

the effect of import quotas, are agreed to by exporters in the hope of avoiding more stringent trade barriers. In the late 1990s, for example, Canadian producers of softwood lumber (fir, spruce, cedar, pine) agreed to a VER on exports to the United States under the threat of a permanently higher U.S. tariff. Later in this chapter we will consider the arguments and appeals that are made to justify protection.

Economic Impact of Tariffs

Once again we turn to supply and demand analysis—now to examine the economic effects of protective tariffs. Curves D_d and S_d in Figure 18.6 show domestic demand and supply for a product in which a nation, say, the United States, has a comparative disadvantage—for example, digital versatile disk (DVD) players. (Disregard curve $S_d + Q$ for now.) Without world trade, the domestic price and output would be P_d and q, respectively.

Assume now that the domestic economy is opened to world trade and that the Japanese, who have a comparative advantage in DVD players, begin to sell their players in the United States. We assume that with free trade the

FIGURE 18.6 The economic effects of a protective tariff or an import quota. A tariff that increases the price of a good from P_w to P_t will reduce domestic consumption from d to c. Domestic producers will be able to sell more output (b rather than a) at a higher price (P_t rather than P_w). Foreign exporters are injured because they sell less output (bc rather than ad). The brown area indicates the amount of tariff paid by domestic consumers. An import quota of bc units has the same effect as the tariff, with one exception: The amount represented by the brown area will go to foreign producers rather than to the domestic government.

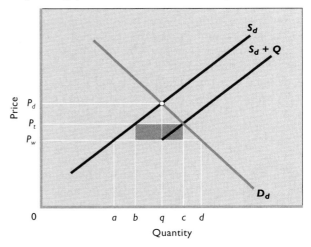

domestic price cannot differ from the world price, which here is P_w. At P_w domestic consumption is d and domestic production is a. The horizontal distance between the domestic supply and demand curves at P_w represents imports of ad. Thus far, our analysis is similar to the analysis of world prices in Figure 18.3.

Direct Effects Suppose now that the United States imposes a tariff on each imported DVD player. The tariff, which raises the price of imported players from P_w to P_t, has four effects:

- **Decline in consumption** Consumption of DVD players in the United States declines from d to c as the higher price moves buyers up and to the left along their demand curve. The tariff prompts consumers to buy fewer players, and reallocate a portion of their expenditures to less desired substitute products. U.S. consumers are clearly injured by the tariff, since they pay P_wP_t more for each of the c units they buy at price P_t.

- **Increased domestic production** U.S. producers—who are not subject to the tariff—receive the higher price P_t per unit. Because this new price is higher than the pretariff world price P_w, the domestic DVD-player industry moves up and to the right along its supply curve S_d, increasing domestic output from a to b. Domestic producers thus enjoy both a higher price and expanded sales; this explains why domestic producers lobby for protective tariffs. But from a social point of view, the greater domestic production from *a* to *b* means that the tariff permits domestic producers of players to bid resources away from other, more efficient, U.S. industries.

- **Decline in imports** Japanese producers are hurt. Although the sales price of each player is higher by P_wP_t, that amount accrues to the U.S. government, not to Japanese producers. The after-tariff world price, or the per-unit revenue to Japanese producers, remains at P_w, but the volume of U.S. imports (Japanese exports) falls from *ad* to *bc*.

- **Tariff revenue** The brown rectangle represents the amount of revenue the tariff yields. Total revenue from the tariff is determined by multiplying the tariff, P_wP_t per unit, by the number of players imported, *bc*. This tariff revenue is a transfer of income from consumers to government and does not represent any net change in the nation's economic well-being. The result is that government gains this portion of what consumers lose by paying more for DVD players.

Indirect Effect Tariffs have a subtle effect beyond what our supply and demand diagram can show. Because Japan sells fewer DVD players in the United States, it earns fewer dollars and so must buy fewer U.S. exports. U.S. export industries must then cut production and release resources. These are highly efficient industries, as we know from their comparative advantage and their ability to sell goods in world markets.

Tariffs directly promote the expansion of inefficient industries that do not have a comparative advantage; they also indirectly cause the contraction of relatively efficient industries that do have a comparative advantage. Put bluntly, tariffs cause resources to be shifted in the wrong direction—and that is not surprising. We know that specialization and world trade lead to more efficient use of world resources and greater world output. But protective tariffs reduce world trade. Therefore, tariffs also reduce efficiency and the world's real output.

Economic Impact of Quotas

We noted earlier that an import quota is a legal limit placed on the amount of some product that can be imported in a given year. Quotas have the same economic impact as a tariff, with one big difference: While tariffs generate revenue for the domestic government, a quota transfers that revenue to foreign producers.

Suppose in Figure 18.6 that, instead of imposing a tariff, the United States prohibits any imports of Japanese

DVD players in excess of *bc* units. In other words, an import quota of *bc* players is imposed on Japan. We deliberately chose the size of this quota to be the same amount as imports would be under a P_wP_t tariff so that we can compare "equivalent" situations. As a consequence of the quota, the supply of players is $S_d + Q$ in the United States. This supply consists of the domestic supply plus the fixed amount *bc* (= *Q*) that importers will provide at each domestic price. The supply curve $S_d + Q$ does not extend below price P_w, because Japanese producers would not export players to the United States at any price below P_w; instead, they would sell them to other countries at the world market price of P_w.

Most of the economic results are the same as those with a tariff. Prices of DVD players are higher (P_t instead of P_w) because imports have been reduced from *ad* to *bc*. Domestic consumption of DVD players is down from *d* to *c*. U.S. producers enjoy both a higher price (P_t rather than P_w) and increased sales (*b* rather than *a*).

The difference is that the price increase of P_wP_t paid by U.S. consumers on imports of *bc*—the brown area—no longer goes to the U.S. Treasury as tariff (tax) revenue but flows to the Japanese firms that have acquired the rights to sell DVD players in the United States. For consumers in the United States, a tariff produces a better economic outcome than a quota, other things being the same. A tariff generates government revenue that can be used to cut other taxes or to finance public goods and services that benefit the United States. In contrast, the higher price created by quotas results in additional revenue for foreign producers. **(Key Question 7)**

Net Costs of Tariffs and Quotas

Figure 18.6 shows that tariffs and quotas impose costs on domestic consumers but provide gains to domestic producers and, in the case of tariffs, revenue to the Federal government. The consumer costs of trade restrictions are calculated by determining the effect the restrictions have on consumer prices. Protection raises the price of a product in three ways: (1) The price of the imported product goes up; (2) the higher price of imports causes some consumers to shift their purchases to higher-priced domestically produced goods; and (3) the prices of domestically produced goods rise because import competition has declined.

Study after study finds that the costs to consumers substantially exceed the gains to producers and government. A sizable net cost or efficiency loss to society arises from trade protection. Furthermore, industries employ large amounts of economic resources to influence Congress to pass and retain protectionist laws. Because these rent-seeking efforts divert resources away from more socially desirable purposes, trade restrictions impose that cost on society.

Conclusion: The gains that U.S. trade barriers create for protected industries and their workers come at the expense of much greater losses for the entire economy. The result is economic inefficiency.

The Case for Protection: A Critical Review

Despite the logic of specialization and trade, there are still protectionists in some union halls, corporate boardrooms, and the halls of Congress. What arguments do protectionists make to justify trade barriers? How valid are those arguments?

Military Self-Sufficiency Argument

The argument here is not economic but political-military: Protective tariffs are needed to preserve or strengthen industries that produce the materials essential for national defense. In an uncertain world, the political-military objectives (self-sufficiency) sometimes must take precedence over economic goals (efficiency in the use of world resources).

Unfortunately, it is difficult to measure and compare the benefit of increased national security against the cost of economic inefficiency when protective tariffs are imposed. The economist can only point out that when a nation levies tariffs to increase military self-sufficiency it incurs economic costs.

All people in the United States would agree that relying on hostile nations for necessary military equipment is not a good idea, yet the self-sufficiency argument is open to serious abuse. Nearly every industry can claim that it makes direct or indirect contributions to national security and hence deserves protection from imports.

Are there not better ways than tariffs to provide needed strength in strategic industries? When it is achieved through tariffs, this self-sufficiency increases the domestic prices of the products of the protected industry. Thus only those consumers who buy the industry's products shoulder the cost of greater military security. A direct subsidy to strategic industries, financed out of general tax revenues, would distribute those costs more equitably.

Diversification-for-Stability Argument

Highly specialized economies such as Saudi Arabia (based on oil) and Cuba (based on sugar) are dependent on international markets for their income. In these economies,

CONSIDER THIS ...

Shooting Yourself in the Foot

In the lore of the Wild West, a gunslinger on occasion would accidentally pull the trigger on his pistol while retrieving it from its holster, shooting himself in the foot. Since then, the phrase "shooting yourself in the foot" implies doing damage to yourself rather than the intended party.

That is precisely how economist Paul Krugman sees a trade war:

> A trade war in which countries restrict each other's exports in pursuit of some illusory advantage is not much like a real war. On the one hand, nobody gets killed. On the other, unlike real wars, it is almost impossible for anyone to win, since the main losers when a country imposes barriers to trade are not foreign exporters but domestic residents. In effect, a trade war is a conflict in which each country uses most of its ammunition to shoot itself in the foot.*

The same analysis is applicable to trade boycotts between major trading partners. Such a boycott was encouraged by some American commentators against French imports because of the opposition of France to the U.S.- and British-led war in Iraq. But the decline of exports to the United States would leave the French with fewer U.S. dollars to buy American exports. So the unintended effect would be a decline in U.S. exports to France and reduced employment in U.S. export industries. Moreover, such a trade boycott, if effective, might lead French consumers to retaliate against American imports. As with a "tariff war," a "boycott war" typically harms oneself as much as the other party.

_____
*Paul Krugman, *Peddling Prosperity* (New York: Norton, 1994), p. 287.

wars, international political developments, recessions abroad, and random fluctuations in world supply and demand for one or two particular goods can cause deep declines in export revenues and therefore in domestic income. Tariff and quota protection are allegedly needed in such nations to enable greater industrial diversification. That way, these economies will not be so dependent on exporting one or two products to obtain the other goods they need. Such goods will be available domestically, thereby providing greater domestic stability.

There is some truth in this diversification-for-stability argument. But the argument has little or no relevance to the United States and other advanced economies. Also, the economic costs of diversification may be great; for example, one-crop economies may be highly inefficient at manufacturing.

Infant Industry Argument

The infant industry argument contends that protective tariffs are needed to allow new domestic industries to establish themselves. Temporarily shielding young domestic firms from the severe competition of more mature and more efficient foreign firms will give infant industries a chance to develop and become efficient producers.

This argument for protection rests on an alleged exception to the case for free trade. The exception is that young industries have not had, and if they face mature foreign competition will never have, the chance to make the long-run adjustments needed for larger scale and greater efficiency in production. In this view, tariff protection for such infant industries will correct a misallocation of world resources perpetuated by historically different levels of economic development between domestic and foreign industries.

Counterarguments There are some logical problems with the infant industry argument. In the developing nations it is difficult to determine which industries are the infants that are capable of achieving economic maturity and therefore deserving protection. Also, protective tariffs may persist even after industrial maturity has been realized.

Most economists feel that if infant industries are to be subsidized, there are better means than tariffs for doing so. Direct subsidies, for example, have the advantage of making explicit which industries are being aided and to what degree.

Strategic Trade Policy In recent years the infant industry argument has taken a modified form in advanced economies. Now proponents contend that government should use trade barriers to reduce the risk of investing in product development by domestic firms, particularly where advanced technology is involved. Firms protected from foreign competition can grow more rapidly and achieve greater economies of scale than unprotected foreign competitors. The protected firms can eventually dominate world markets because of their lower costs. Supposedly, dominance of world markets will enable the domestic firms to return high profits to the home nation. These profits will exceed the domestic sacrifices caused by trade barriers. Also, advances in high-technology indus-

tries are deemed beneficial, because the advances achieved in one domestic industry often can be transferred to other domestic industries.

Japan and South Korea, in particular, have been accused of using this form of **strategic trade policy.** The problem with this strategy and therefore with this argument for tariffs is that the nations put at a disadvantage by strategic trade policies tend to retaliate with tariffs of their own. The outcome may be higher tariffs worldwide, reduction of world trade, and the loss of potential gains from technological advances.

Protection-against-Dumping Argument

The protection-against dumping argument contends that tariffs are needed to protect domestic firms from "dumping" by foreign producers. **Dumping** is the selling of excess goods in a foreign market at a price below cost. Economists cite two plausible reasons for this behavior. First, firms may use dumping abroad to drive out domestic competitors there, thus obtaining monopoly power and monopoly prices and profits for the importing firm. The long-term economic profits resulting from this strategy may more than offset the earlier losses that accompany the below-cost sales.

Second, dumping may be a form of price discrimination, which is charging different prices to different customers even though costs are the same. The foreign seller may find it can maximize its profit by charging a high price in its monopolized domestic market while unloading its surplus output at a lower price in the United States. The surplus output may be needed so that the firm can obtain the overall per-unit cost saving associated with large-scale production. The higher profit in the home market more than makes up for the losses incurred on sales abroad.

Because dumping is an "unfair trade practice," most nations prohibit it. For example, where dumping is shown to injure U.S. firms, the Federal government imposes tariffs called *antidumping duties* on the specific goods. But relatively few documented cases of dumping occur each year, and specific instances of unfair trade do not justify widespread, permanent tariffs. Moreover, antidumping duties can be abused. Often, what appears to be dumping is simply comparative advantage at work.

Increased Domestic Employment Argument

Arguing for a tariff to "save U.S. jobs" becomes fashionable when the economy encounters a recession or experiences slow job growth during a recovery (as in the early

2000s in the United States). In an economy that engages in international trade, exports involve spending on domestic output and imports reflect spending to obtain part of another nation's output. So, in this argument, reducing imports will divert spending on another nation's output to spending on domestic output. Thus domestic output and employment will rise. But this argument has several shortcomings.

While imports may eliminate some U.S. jobs, they create others. Imports may have eliminated the jobs of some U.S. steel and textile workers in recent years, but other workers have gained jobs unloading ships, flying imported aircraft, and selling imported electronic equipment. Import restrictions alter the composition of employment, but they may have little or no effect on the volume of employment.

The *fallacy of composition*—the false idea that what is true for the part is necessarily true for the whole—is also present in this rationale for tariffs. All nations cannot simultaneously succeed in restricting imports while maintaining their exports; what is true for one nation is not true for all nations. The exports of one nation must be the imports of another nation. To the extent that one country is able to expand its economy through an excess of exports over imports, the resulting excess of imports over exports worsens another economy's unemployment problem. It is no wonder that tariffs and import quotas meant to achieve domestic full employment are called "beggar my neighbor" policies: They achieve short-run domestic goals by making trading partners poorer.

Moreover, nations adversely affected by tariffs and quotas are likely to retaliate, causing a "trade-barrier war" that will choke off trade and make all nations worse off. The **Smoot-Hawley Tariff Act** of 1930 is a classic example. Although that act was meant to reduce imports and stimulate U.S. production, the high tariffs it authorized prompted adversely affected nations to retaliate with tariffs equally high. International trade fell, lowering the output and income of all nations. Economic historians generally agree that the Smoot-Hawley Tariff Act was a contributing cause of the Great Depression.

Finally, forcing an excess of exports over imports cannot succeed in raising domestic employment over the long run. It is through U.S. imports that foreign nations earn dollars for buying U.S. exports. In the long run a nation must import in order to export. The long-run impact of tariffs is not an increase in domestic employment but, at best, a reallocation of workers away from export industries and to protected domestic industries. This shift implies a less efficient allocation of resources.

Cheap Foreign Labor Argument

The cheap foreign labor argument says that domestic firms and workers must be shielded from the ruinous competition of countries where wages are low. If protection is not provided, cheap imports will flood U.S. markets and the prices of U.S. goods—along with the wages of U.S. workers—will be pulled down. That is, the domestic living standards in the United States will be reduced.

This argument can be rebutted at several levels. The logic of the argument suggests that it is not mutually beneficial for rich and poor persons to trade with one another. However, that is not the case. A low-income farmworker may pick lettuce or tomatoes for a rich landowner, and both may benefit from the transaction. And both U.S. consumers and Chinese workers gain when they "trade" a pair of athletic shoes priced at $30 as opposed to a similar shoe made in the United States for $60.

Also, recall that gains from trade are based on comparative advantage, not on absolute advantage. Look back at Figure 18.1, where we supposed that the United States and Brazil had labor forces of exactly the same size. Noting the positions of the production possibilities curves, observe that U.S. labor can produce more of either good. Thus, it is more productive. Because of this greater productivity, we can expect wages and living standards to be higher for U.S. labor. Brazil's less productive labor will receive lower wages.

The cheap foreign labor argument suggests that, to maintain its standard of living, the United States should not trade with low-wage Brazil. What if it does not trade with Brazil. Will wages and living standards rise in the United States as a result? No. To obtain coffee, the United States will have to reallocate a portion of its labor from its efficient wheat industry to its inefficient coffee industry. As a result, the average productivity of U.S. labor will fall, as will real wages and living standards. The labor forces of both countries will have diminished standards of living because without specialization and trade they will have less output available to them. Compare column 4 with column 1 in Table 18.1 or points A' and B' with A and B in Figure 18.2 to confirm this point.

Trade Adjustment Assistance

A nation's comparative advantage in the production of a certain product is not forever fixed. As national economies evolve, the size and quality of their labor forces may change, the volume and composition of their capital stocks may shift, new technologies may develop, and even the quality of land and the quantity of natural resources may be altered. As these changes take place, the relative efficiency with which a nation can produce specific goods will also change. Also, new trade agreements can suddenly leave formerly protected industries highly vulnerable to major disruption or even collapse.

Shifts in patterns of comparative advantage and removal of trade protection can hurt specific groups of workers. For example, the erosion of the United States' once strong comparative advantage in steel has caused production plant shutdowns and layoffs in the U.S. steel industry. The textile and apparel industries in the United States face similar difficulties. Clearly, not everyone wins from free trade (or freer trade). Some workers lose.

The **Trade Adjustment Assistance Act** of 2002 introduced some new, novel elements to help those hurt by shifts in international trade patterns. The law provides cash assistance (beyond unemployment insurance) for up to 78 weeks for workers displaced by imports or plant relocations abroad. To obtain the assistance, workers must participate in job searches, training programs, or remedial education. Also provided are relocation allowances to help displaced workers move geographically to new jobs within the United States. Refundable tax credits for health insurance serve as payments to help workers maintain their insurance coverage during the retraining and job search period. Workers who are 50 years of age or older are eligible for "wage insurance," which replaces some of the difference in pay (if any) between their old and new jobs. Trade adjustment assistance not only helps workers hurt by international trade but also helps create the political support necessary to reduce trade barriers and export subsidies. For both reasons, many economists support it.

But not all observers are fans of trade adjustment assistance. Loss of jobs from imports or plant relocations abroad is only a small fraction (about 3 percent in recent years) of total job loss in the economy each year. Many workers also lose their jobs because of changing patterns of demand, changing technology, bad management, and other dynamic aspects of a market economy. Some critics ask, "What makes losing one's job to international trade worthy of such special treatment, compared to losing one's job to, say, technological change?" Economists can find no totally satisfying answer.

Offshoring

Not only are some U.S. jobs lost because of international trade, but some are lost because of globalization of resource markets. In recent years U.S. firms have found the outsourcing of work abroad increasingly profitable. Economists call this business activity **offshoring**: shifting work previously done by American workers to workers located in other nations. Offshoring is not a new practice but traditionally has involved components for U.S. manufacturing goods. For example, Boeing has long offshored the production of major airplane parts for its "American" aircraft.

Recent advances in computer and communications technology have enabled U.S. firms to offshore service jobs such as data entry, book composition, software coding, call-center operations, medical transcription, and claims processing to countries such as India. Where offshoring occurs, some of the value added in the production process accrues to foreign countries rather than the United States. So part of the income generated from the production of U.S. goods is paid to foreigners, not to American workers.

Offshoring is a major burden on Americans who lose their jobs, but it is not necessarily bad for the overall economy. Offshoring simply reflects a growing specialization and international trade in services. That trade has been made possible by recent trade agreements and new information and communication technologies. Like trade in goods, trade in services reflects comparative advantage and is beneficial to both trading parties. Moreover, the United States has a sizable trade surplus with other nations in services. The U.S. gains by specializing in high-valued services such as transportation services, accounting services, legal services, and advertising services, where it still has a comparative advantage. It then "trades" to obtain lower-valued services such as call-center and data entry work, for which comparative advantage has gone abroad.

Offshoring also increases the demand for complementary jobs in the United States. Jobs that are close substitutes for existing U.S. jobs are lost, but complementary jobs in the United States are expanded. For example, the lower price of writing software code in India may mean a lower cost of software sold in the United States and abroad. That, in turn, may create more jobs for U.S.-based workers such as software designers, marketers, and distributors. Moreover, the offshoring may encourage domestic investment and expansion of firms in the United States by reducing their production costs and keeping them competitive worldwide. In some instances, "offshoring jobs" may equate to "importing competitiveness." Entire firms that might otherwise disappear abroad may remain profitable in the United States only because they can offshore some of their work.

Various Protest Groups Have Angrily Targeted the World Trade Organization (WTO). What Is the Source of All the Noise and Commotion?

The WTO became known to the general public in November 1999, when tens of thousands of people took part in sometimes violent demonstrations in Seattle. Since then, international WTO meetings have drawn large numbers of angry demonstrators. The groups involved include some labor unions (which fear loss of jobs and labor protections), environmental groups (which oppose environmental degradation), socialists (who dislike capitalism and multinational corporations), and a few anarchists (who detest government authority of any kind). Dispersed within the crowds are other, smaller groups such as European farmers who fear the WTO will threaten their livelihoods by reducing agricultural tariffs and farm subsidies.

The most substantive WTO issues involve labor protections and environmental standards. Labor unions in industrially advanced countries (hereafter, "advanced countries") would like the international trade rules to include such labor standards as collective bargaining rights, minimum wages, workplace safety standards, and prohibitions of child labor. Such rules are fully consistent with the long-standing values and objectives of unions. But there is a hitch.

Imposing labor standards on low-income developing countries (hereafter, "developing countries") would raise labor and production costs in those nations. The higher costs in the developing countries would raise the relative price of their goods and make them less competitive with goods produced in the advanced countries (which already meet the labor standards). So the trade rules would increase the demands for products and workers in the advanced countries and reduce them in the developing countries. Union workers in the advanced countries would benefit; consumers in the advanced countries and workers in the developing countries would be harmed. The trade standards would contribute to poverty in the world's poorest nations.

Not surprisingly, the developing countries say "thanks, but no thanks" to the protesters' pleas for labor standards. Instead, they want the advanced countries to reduce or eliminate tariffs on goods imported from the developing countries. That would expand the demand for developing countries' products and workers, boosting developing countries' wages. As living standards in the developing countries rise, those countries then can afford to devote more of their annual productivity advances to improved working conditions.

The 149-nation WTO points out that its mandate is to liberalize trade through multilateral negotiation, not to set labor standards for each nation. That should be left to the countries themselves.

QUICK REVIEW 18.3

- A tariff on a product increases its price, reduces its consumption, increases its domestic production, reduces its imports, and generates tariff revenue for government; an import quota does the same, except a quota generates revenue for foreign producers rather than for the government imposing the quota.
- Most rationales for trade protections are special-interest requests that, if followed, would create gains for protected industries and their workers at the expense of greater losses for the economy.
- The Trade Adjustment Assistance Act of 2002 is designed to help some of the workers hurt by shifts in international trade patterns.
- Offshoring is a major burden on American workers who lose their jobs, but not necessarily negative for the overall American economy.

The World Trade Organization

As indicated in Chapter 5, the Uruguay Round of 1993 established the **World Trade Organization (WTO)**. In 2006, the WTO, which oversees trade agreements and rules on disputes relating to them, had 149 member nations. It also provides forums for further rounds of trade negotiations. The ninth and latest round of negotiations—the **Doha Round**—was launched in Doha, Qatar, in late 2001. (The trade rounds occur over several years in several geographic venues and are named after the city or country of origination.) The negotiations are aimed at further reducing tariffs and quotas, as well as agricultural subsidies that distort trade. One of this chapter's questions asks you to update the progress of the Doha Round (or, alternatively, the Doha Development Agenda) via an Internet search.

As a symbol of trade liberalization and global capitalism, the WTO has become a target of a variety of protest groups. This chapter's Last Word examines some of the reason for the protests, and we strongly suggest that you read it.

Economists suggest that protesters channel their efforts to supporting activities of the International Labour Organization (ILO), which strives to improve wages and working conditions worldwide. Demonstrators might also help local groups bring political pressure on individual nations to improve their labor protections as their standards of living rise.

Environmental standards are the second substantive WTO issue. Critics are concerned that trade liberalization will encourage more activities that degrade sensitive forests, fisheries, and mining lands and contribute to air, water, and solid-waste pollution. Critics would like the WTO to establish trade rules that set minimum environmental standards for the member nations. The WTO nations respond that environmental standards are outside the mandate of the WTO and must be established by the individual nations via their own political processes.

Moreover, imposing such standards on developing countries may simply provide competitive cost advantages to companies in the advanced countries. As with labor standards, that will simply slow economic growth and prolong poverty in the developing countries. Studies show that economic growth and rising living standards are strongly associated with greater environmental protections. In the early phases of their development, low-income developing nations typically choose to trade off some environmental damage to achieve higher real wages. But studies show that the tradeoff is usually reversed once standards of living rise beyond threshold levels.

Labor standards and environmental protections are worthy objectives. But impeding efforts to liberalize trade may be an ineffective—even detrimental—way to achieve them. Reductions in tariffs and impediments to investment increase productivity, output, and incomes worldwide. The higher living standards enable developing and developed nations alike to "buy" more protections for labor and the environment. Strong, sustained economic growth typically results not only in more goods and services but also in more socially desirable and environmentally sensitive production methods.

Summary

1. The United States leads the world in the combined volume of exports and imports. Other major trading nations are Germany, Japan, the western European nations, and the Asian economies of China, South Korea, Taiwan, and Singapore.

2. World trade is based on three considerations: the uneven distribution of economic resources among nations, the fact that efficient production of various goods requires particular techniques or combinations of resources, and the differentiated products produced among nations.

3. Mutually advantageous specialization and trade are possible between any two nations if they have different domestic opportunity-cost ratios for any two products. By specializing on the basis of comparative advantage, nations can obtain larger real incomes with fixed amounts of resources. The terms of trade determine how this increase in world output is shared by the trading nations. Increasing (rather than constant) opportunity costs limit specialization and trade.

4. A nation's export supply curve shows the quantities of a product the nation will export at world prices that exceed the domestic price (the price in a closed, no-international-trade economy). A nation's import demand curve reveals the quantities of a product it will import at world prices below the domestic price.

5. In a two-nation model, the equilibrium world price and the equilibrium quantities of exports and imports occur where one nation's export supply curve intersects the other nation's import demand curve.

6. Trade barriers take the form of protective tariffs, quotas, nontariff barriers, and "voluntary" export restrictions. Supply and demand analysis reveals that protective tariffs and quotas increase the prices and reduce the quantities demanded of the affected goods. Sales by foreign exporters diminish; domestic producers, however, gain higher prices and enlarged sales. Consumer losses from trade restrictions greatly exceed producer and government gains, creating an efficiency loss to society.

7. The strongest arguments for protection are the infant industry and military self-sufficiency arguments. Most other arguments for protection are interest-group appeals or reasoning fallacies that emphasize producer interests over consumer interests or stress the immediate effects of trade barriers while ignoring long-run consequences.

8. The Trade Adjustment Assistance Act of 2002 provides cash assistance, education and training benefits, health care subsidies, and wage subsidies (for persons age 50 or older) to qualified workers displaced by imports or plant relocations abroad.

9. Offshoring is the practice of shifting work previously done by Americans to workers located in other nations. While offshoring reduces some U.S. jobs, it lowers production costs, expands sales, and therefore may create other U.S. jobs. Less than 3 percent of all job losses in the United States each year result from imports, offshoring, and plant relocations to abroad.

10. In 2006 the World Trade Organization (WTO) consisted of 149 member nations. The WTO oversees trade agreements among the members, resolves disputes over the rules, and periodically meets to discuss and negotiate further trade liberalization. In 2001 the WTO initiated a new round of trade negotiations in Doha, Qatar. By 2006 the Doha Round (or Doha Development Agenda) was still in progress.

11. As a symbol of global capitalism, the WTO has become a target of considerable protest. The controversy surrounding the WTO is the subject of this chapter's Last Word. Most economists are concerned that tying trade liberalization to a host of other issues such as environmental and labor standards will greatly delay or block further trade liberalization. Such liberalization is one of the main sources of higher living standards worldwide.

Terms and Concepts

labor-intensive goods

land-intensive goods

capital-intensive goods

opportunity-cost ratio

principle of comparative advantage

terms of trade

trading possibilities line

gains from trade

world price

domestic price

export supply curve

import demand curve

equilibrium world price

tariffs

revenue tariff

protective tariff

import quota

nontariff barrier (NTB)

voluntary export restriction (VER)

strategic trade policy

dumping

Smoot-Hawley Tariff Act

Trade Adjustment Assistance Act

offshoring

World Trade Organization (WTO)

Doha Round

Study Questions

1. Quantitatively, how important is international trade to the United States relative to other nations?

2. Distinguish among land-, labor-, and capital-intensive commodities, citing one nontextbook example of each. What role do these distinctions play in explaining international trade? What role do distinctive products, unrelated to cost advantages, play in international trade?

3. Suppose nation A can produce 80 units of X by using all its resources to produce X or 60 units of Y by devoting all its resources to Y. Comparable figures for nation B are 60 units of X and 60 units of Y. Assuming constant costs, in which product should each nation specialize? Why? What are the limits of the terms of trade?

4. **KEY QUESTION** To the right are hypothetical production possibilities tables for New Zealand and Spain. Each country can produce apples and plums.

   Plot the production possibilities data for each of the two countries separately. Referring to your graphs, answer the following:

   a. What is each country's cost ratio of producing plums and apples.

   b. Which nation should specialize in which product?

New Zealand's Production Possibilities Table
(Millions of Bushels)

Product	Production Alternatives			
	A	B	C	D
Apples	0	20	40	60
Plums	15	10	5	0

Spain's Production Possibilities Table
(Millions of Bushels)

Product	Production Alternatives			
	R	S	T	U
Apples	0	20	40	60
Plums	60	40	20	0

c. Show the trading possibilities lines for each nation if the actual terms of trade are 1 plum for 2 apples. (Plot these lines on your graph.)

d. Suppose the optimum product mixes before specialization and trade were alternative B in New Zealand and alternative S in Spain. What would be the gains from specialization and trade?

5. "The United States can produce X more efficiently than can Great Britain. Yet we import X from Great Britain." Explain.

6. **KEY QUESTION** Refer to Figure 3.6, page 54. Assume that the graph depicts the U.S. domestic market for corn. How many bushels of corn, if any, will the United States export or import at a world price of $1, $2, $3, $4, and $5? Use this information to construct the U.S. export supply curve and import demand curve for corn. Suppose the only other corn-producing nation is France, where the domestic price is $4. Which country will export corn; which will import it?

7. **KEY QUESTION** Draw a domestic supply and demand diagram for a product in which the United States does not have a comparative advantage. What impact do foreign imports have on domestic price and quantity? On your diagram show a protective tariff that eliminates approximately one-half of the assumed imports. What are the price-quantity effects of this tariff on (*a*) domestic consumers, (*b*) domestic producers, and (*c*) foreign exporters? How would the effects of a quota that creates the same amount of imports differ?

8. "The potentially valid arguments for tariff protection are also the most easily abused." What are those arguments? Why are they susceptible to abuse? Evaluate the use of artificial trade barriers, such as tariffs and import quotas, as a means of achieving and maintaining full employment.

9. Evaluate the following statements:
   a. Protective tariffs reduce both the imports and the exports of the nation that levies tariffs.
   b. The extensive application of protective tariffs destroys the ability of the international market system to allocate resources efficiently.
   c. Unemployment in some industries can often be reduced through tariff protection, but by the same token inefficiency typically increases.
   d. Foreign firms that "dump" their products onto the U.S. market are in effect providing bargains to the country's citizens.
   e. In view of the rapidity with which technological advance is dispersed around the world, free trade will

inevitably yield structural maladjustments, unemployment, and balance-of-payments problems for industrially advanced nations.
   f. Free trade can improve the composition and efficiency of domestic output. Competition from Volkswagen, Toyota, and Honda forced Detroit to make a compact car, and foreign imports of bottled water forced American firms to offer that product.
   g. In the long run, foreign trade is neutral with respect to total employment.

10. Suppose Japan agreed to a voluntary export restriction (VER) that reduced U.S. imports of Japanese steel by 10 percent. What would be the likely short-run effects of that VER on the U.S. and Japanese steel industries? If this restriction were permanent, what would be its long-run effects in the two nations on (*a*) the allocation of resources, (*b*) the volume of employment, (*c*) the price level, and (*d*) the standard of living?

11. What forms do trade adjustment assistance take in the United States? How does such assistance promote support for free trade agreements? Do you think workers who lose their jobs because of changes in trade laws deserve special treatment relative to workers who lose their jobs because of other changes in the economy, say, changes in patterns of government spending?

12. What is offshoring of white-collar service jobs, and how does it relate to international trade? Why has it recently increased? Why do you think more than half of all the offshored jobs have gone to India? Give an example (other than that in the textbook) of how offshoring can eliminate some U.S. jobs while creating other U.S. jobs.

13. What is the WTO and how does it relate to international trade? How many nations belong to the WTO? (Update the number given in this book at **www.wto.org**.) What did the Uruguay Round (1994) of WTO trade negotiations accomplish? What is the name of the current WTO round of trade negotiations?

14. **LAST WORD** What are the main concerns of the WTO protesters? What problems, if any, arise when too many extraneous issues are tied to efforts to liberalize trade?

Web-Based Questions

1. **TRADE LIBERALIZATION—THE WTO** Go to the Web site of the World Trade Organization (**www.wto.org**) to retrieve the latest news from the WTO. List and summarize three recent news items relating to the WTO.

2. **THE U.S. INTERNATIONAL TRADE COMMISSION— WHAT IS IT AND WHAT DOES IT DO?** Go to **www.usitc. gov** to determine the duties of the U.S. International Trade

Commission (USITC). How does this organization differ from the World Trade Organization (question 13)? Go to the "Information Center" and find News Releases. Identify and briefly describe three USITC "determinations" relating to charges of unfair international trade practices that harm U.S. producers.

19

IN THIS CHAPTER YOU WILL LEARN:

- How currencies of different nations are exchanged when international transactions take place.

- About the balance sheet the United States uses to account for the international payments it makes and receives.

- How exchange rates are determined in currency markets.

- The difference between flexible exchange rates and fixed exchange rates.

- The causes and consequences of recent record-high U.S. trade deficits.

Exchange Rates, the Balance of Payments, and Trade Deficits

If you take a U.S. dollar to the bank and ask to exchange it for U.S. currency, you will get a puzzled look. If you persist, you may get a dollar's worth of change: One U.S. dollar can buy exactly one U.S. dollar. But on April 25, 2006, for example, 1 U.S. dollar could buy 2353 Colombian pesos, 1.34 Australian dollars, .56 British pounds, 1.13 Canadian dollars, .80 European euros, 114.82 Japanese yen, or 11.15 Mexican pesos. What explains this seemingly haphazard array of exchange rates?

In Chapter 18 we examined comparative advantage as the underlying economic basis of world trade and discussed the effects of barriers to free trade. Now we introduce the highly important monetary or financial aspects of international trade.

Financing International Trade

One factor that makes international trade different from domestic trade is the involvement of different national currencies. When a U.S. firm exports goods to a Mexican firm, the U.S. exporter wants to be paid in dollars. But the Mexican importer possesses pesos. The importer must exchange pesos for dollars before the U.S. export transaction can occur.

This problem is resolved in foreign exchange markets (or currency markets), in which dollars can purchase Mexican pesos, European euros, South Korean won, British pounds, Japanese yen, or any other currency, and vice versa. Sponsored by major banks in New York, London, Zurich, Tokyo, and elsewhere, foreign exchange markets facilitate exports and imports.

U.S. Export Transaction

Suppose a U.S. exporter agrees to sell $300,000 of computers to a British firm. Assume, for simplicity, that the rate of exchange—the rate at which pounds can be exchanged for, or converted into, dollars, and vice versa—is $2 for £1 (the actual exchange rate is about $1.80 = 1 pound). This means the British importer must pay the equivalent of £150,000 to the U.S. exporter to obtain the $300,000 worth of computers. Also assume that all buyers of pounds and dollars are in the United States and Great Britain. Let's follow the steps in the transaction:

- To pay for the computers, the British buyer draws a check for £150,000 on its checking account in a London bank and sends it to the U.S. exporter.
- But the U.S. exporting firm must pay its bills in dollars, not pounds. So the exporter sells the £150,000 check on the London bank to its bank in, say, New York City, which is a dealer in foreign exchange. The bank adds $300,000 to the U.S. exporter's checking account for the £150,000 check.
- The New York bank deposits the £150,000 in a correspondent London bank for future sale to some U.S. buyer who needs pounds.

Note this important point: U.S. exports create a foreign demand for dollars, and the fulfillment of that demand increases the supply of foreign currencies (pounds, in this case) owned by U.S. banks and available to U.S. buyers.

Why would the New York bank be willing to buy pounds for dollars? As just indicated, the New York bank is a dealer in foreign exchange; it is in the business of buying (for a fee) and selling (also for a fee) one currency for another.

U.S. Import Transaction

Let's now examine how the New York bank would sell pounds for dollars to finance a U.S. import (British export) transaction. Suppose a U.S. retail firm wants to import £150,000 of compact discs produced in Britain by a hot new musical group. Again, let's track the steps in the transaction:

- The U.S. importer purchases £150,000 at the $2 = £1 exchange rate by writing a check for $300,000 on its New York bank. Because the British exporting firm wants to be paid in pounds rather than dollars, the U.S. importer must exchange dollars for pounds, which it does by going to the New York bank and purchasing £150,000 for $300,000. (Perhaps the U.S. importer purchases the same £150,000 that the New York bank acquired from the U.S. exporter.)
- The U.S. importer sends its newly purchased check for £150,000 to the British firm, which deposits it in the London bank.

Here we see that U.S. imports create a domestic demand for foreign currencies (pounds, in this case), and the fulfillment of that demand reduces the supplies of foreign currencies (again, pounds) held by U.S. banks and available to U.S. consumers.

The combined export and import transactions bring one more point into focus. U.S. exports (the computers) make available, or "earn," a supply of foreign currencies for U.S. banks, and U.S. imports (the compact discs) create a demand for those currencies. In a broad sense, any nation's exports finance or "pay for" its imports. Exports provide the foreign currencies needed to pay for imports.

Postscript: Although our examples are confined to exporting and importing goods, demand for and supplies of pounds also arise from transactions involving services and the payment of interest and dividends on foreign investments. The United States demands pounds not only to buy imports but also to buy insurance and transportation services from the British, to vacation in London, to pay dividends and interest on British investments in the United States, and to make new financial and real investments in Britain. **(Key Question 2)**

The Balance of Payments

A nation's **balance of payments** is the sum of all the transactions that take place between its residents and the residents of all foreign nations. Those transactions include exports and imports of goods, exports and imports of services, tourist expenditures, interest and dividends received or paid abroad, and purchases and sales of financial or real assets abroad. The U.S. Commerce Department's

Bureau of Economic Analysis compiles the balance-of-payments statement each year. The statement shows all the payments a nation receives from foreign countries and all the payments it makes to them. It shows "flows" of in-payments to and outpayments from the United States.

Table 19.1 is a simplified balance-of-payments statement for the United States in 2005. Let's take a close look at this accounting statement to see what it reveals about U.S. international trade and finance. To help our explanation, we divide the single balance-of-payments account into two components: the *current account* and the *capital and financial account*.

Current Account

The top portion of Table 19.1 summarizes U.S. trade in currently produced goods and services and is called the **current account**. Items 1 and 2 show U.S. exports and imports of goods (merchandise) in 2005. U.S. exports have a *plus* (+) sign because they are a *credit*; they earn and make available foreign exchange in the United States. As you saw in the preceding section, any export-type transaction that obligates foreigners to make "inpayments" to the United States generates supplies of foreign currencies in the U.S. banks.

U.S. imports have a *minus* (−) sign because they are a *debit*; they reduce the stock of foreign currencies in the United States. Our earlier discussion of trade financing indicated that U.S. imports obligate the United States to make "outpayments" to the rest of the world that reduce available supplies of foreign currencies held by U.S. banks.

Balance on Goods Items 1 and 2 in Table 19.1 reveal that in 2005 U.S. goods exports of $893 billion did not earn enough foreign currencies to finance U.S. goods imports of $1675 billion. A country's *balance of trade on goods* is the difference between its exports and its imports of goods. If exports exceed imports, the result is a surplus on the balance of goods. If imports exceed exports, there is a trade deficit on the balance of goods. We note in item 3 that in 2005 the United States incurred a trade deficit on goods of $782 billion.

Balance on Services The United States exports not only goods, such as airplanes and computer software, but also services, such as insurance, consulting, travel, and brokerage services, to residents of foreign nations. Item 4 in Table 19.1 shows that these service "exports" totaled

TABLE 19.1 The U.S. Balance of Payments, 2005 (in Billions)

Current account		
(1) U.S. goods exports	$+893	
(2) U.S. goods imports	−1675	
(3) *Balance on goods*		$−782
(4) U.S. exports of services	+380	
(5) U.S. imports of services	−322	
(6) *Balance on services*		+58
(7) *Balance on goods and services*		−724
(8) Net investment income	+2	
(9) Net transfers	−83	
(10) **Balance on current account**		−805
Capital and financial account		
Capital account		
(11) *Balance on capital account*		−6
Financial account		
(12) Foreign purchases of assets in the United States	+1298*	
(13) U.S. purchases of assets abroad	−487*	
(14) *Balance on financial account*		+811
(15) **Balance on capital and financial account**		**+ 805**
		$ 0

*Includes one-half of a $10 billion statistical discrepancy that is listed in the capital account.

Source: U.S. Department of Commerce, Bureau of Economic Analysis, **www.bea.gov/**. Preliminary 2005 data. The export and import data are on a "balance-of-payment basis," and usually vary from the data on export and imports reported in the National Income and Product Accounts.

$380 billion in 2005 and are a credit (thus the + sign). Item 5 indicates that the United States "imports" similar services from foreigners; those service imports were $322 billion in 2005 and are a debit (thus the − sign). So the balance on services (item 6) in 2005 was $58 billion.

The **balance on goods and services** shown as item 7 is the difference between U.S. exports of goods and services (items 1 and 4) and U.S. imports of goods and services (items 2 and 5). In 2005, U.S. imports of goods and services exceeded U.S. exports of goods and services by $724 billion. So a **trade deficit** (or "unfavorable balance of trade") occurred. In contrast, a **trade surplus** (or "favorable balance of trade") occurs when exports of goods and services exceed imports of goods and services. (Global Perspective 19.1 shows U.S. trade deficits and surpluses with selected nations.)

Balance on Current Account Item 8, *net investment income*, represents the difference between (1) the interest and dividend payments foreigners paid the United States for the use of exported U.S. capital and (2) the interest and dividends the United States paid for the use of foreign capital invested in the United States. Observe that in 2005 U.S.

GLOBAL PERSPECTIVE 19.1

U.S. Trade Balances in Goods and Services, Selected Nations, 2004

The United States has large trade deficits in goods and services with several nations, in particular, China, Japan, and Canada.

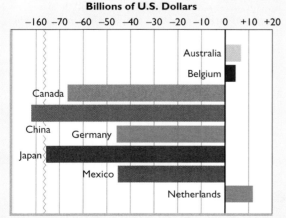

Source: Department of Commerce, Bureau of Economic Analysis, **www.bea.gov/.**

net investment income was a positive $2 billion worth of foreign currencies.

Item 9 shows net transfers, both public and private, between the United States and the rest of the world. Included here is foreign aid, pensions paid to U.S. citizens living abroad, and remittances by immigrants to relatives abroad. These $83 billion of transfers are net U.S. outpayments that decrease available supplies of foreign exchange. They are, in a sense, the exporting of goodwill and the importing of "thank-you notes."

By adding all transactions in the current account, we obtain the **balance on current account** shown in item 10. In 2005 the United States had a current account deficit of $805 billion. This means that the U.S. current account transactions (items 2, 5, 8, and 9) created outpayments of foreign currencies from the United States greater than the inpayments of foreign currencies to the United States.

Capital and Financial Account
The second account within the overall balance-of-payments account is the **capital and financial account,** which consists of two separate accounts: the *capital account* and the *financial account.*

Capital Account The capital account is a "net" account (one that can be either + or −) that mainly measures debt forgiveness. Line 11 tells us that in 2005 Americans forgave $6 billion more of debt owed to them by foreigners than foreigners forgave debt owed to them by Americans. The − sign indicates a debit; it is an "on-paper" outpayment by the net amount of debt forgiven.

Financial Account The financial account summarizes the purchase or sale of real or financial assets and the corresponding flows of monetary payments that accompany them. For example, a foreign firm may buy a real asset, say, an office building in the United States, or a financial asset, for instance, a U.S. government security. Both kinds of transaction involve the "export" of the ownership of U.S. assets from the United States in return for inpayments of foreign currency. As indicated in line 12, these "exports" of ownership of assets are designated foreign purchases of assets in the United States. They have a + sign because, like exports of U.S. goods and services, they represent inpayments of foreign currencies.

Conversely, a U.S. firm may buy, say, a hotel chain (real asset) in a foreign country or some of the common stock (financial asset) of a foreign firm. Both transactions involve the "import" of the ownership of the real or financial assets to the United States and are paid for by outpayments of foreign currencies. These "imports" are designated U.S. purchases of assets abroad and, as shown in line 13, have a − sign; like U.S. imports of goods and services, they represent outpayments of foreign currencies from the United States.

Items 11 and 12 combined yielded an $811 billion balance on the financial account for 2005 (line 14). In 2005 the United States "exported" $1298 billion of ownership of its real and financial assets and "imported" $487 billion. Thought of differently, this capital account surplus brought in inpayments of $811 billion of foreign currencies to the United States.

The **balance on the capital and financial account** (line 15) is $805 billion. It is the sum of the $6 billion deficit on the capital account and the $811 billion surplus on the financial account. Observe that this $805 billion surplus in the capital and financial account equals the $805 billion deficit in the current account. The various components of the balance of payments (the current account, the capital account, and the financial account) must together equal zero. Every unit of foreign exchange used (as reflected in a minus outpayment or debit transaction) must have a source (a plus inpayment or credit transaction).

Payments, Deficits, and Surpluses

Although the balance of payments must always sum to zero, as in Table 19.1, economists and policymakers sometimes speak of **balance-of-payments deficits and surpluses.** The central banks of nations hold quantities of **official reserves,** consisting of foreign currencies, reserves held in the International Monetary Fund, and stocks of gold. These reserves are drawn on—or replenished— to make up any net deficit or surplus that otherwise would occur in the balance-of-payment account. (This is much as you would draw on your savings or add to your savings as a way to balance your annual income and spending.) In some years, a nation must make an inpayment of official reserves to its capital and financial account in order to balance it with the current account. In these years, a *balance-of- payments deficit* is said to occur.

In other years, an outpayment of official reserves from the capital and financial account must occur to balance that account with the current account. The outpayment adds to the stock of official reserves. A *balance-of payments-surplus* is said to exist in these years.

A balance-of-payments deficit is not necessarily bad, just as a balance-of-payments surplus is not necessarily good. Both simply happen. However, any nation's official reserves are limited. Persistent payments deficits, which must be financed by drawing down those reserves, would ultimately deplete the reserves. That nation would have to adopt policies to correct its balance of payments. Such

policies might require painful macroeconomic adjustments, trade barriers and similar restrictions, or a major depreciation of its currency. For this reason, nations strive for payments balance, at least over several-year periods.

The United States held $75 billion of official reserves in 2005. The typical annual depletion or addition of official reserves is not of major concern, particularly because withdrawals and deposits roughly balance over time. For example, the stock of official U.S. reserves rose from $79 billion in 2003 to $86 billion in 2004. It fell to $75 billion in 2005.

W 19.1

Balance of payments

The historically large current account deficits that the United States has been running over the past several years are of more concern than annual balance-of-payment deficits or surpluses. The current account deficits need to be financed by equally large surpluses in the capital and financial account. Thus far, that has not been a problem. Later in this chapter, we will examine the causes and potential consequences of large current account deficits. **(Key Question 3)**

QUICK REVIEW 19.1

- U.S. exports create a foreign demand for dollars, and fulfillment of that demand increases the domestic supply of foreign currencies; U.S. imports create a domestic demand for foreign currencies, and fulfillment of that demand reduces the supplies of foreign currency held by U.S. banks.
- The current account balance is a nation's exports of goods and services less its imports of goods and services plus its net investment income and net transfers.
- The capital and financial account balance includes the net amount of the nation's debt forgiveness and the nation's sale of real and financial assets to people living abroad less its purchases of real and financial assets from foreigners.
- The current account balance and the capital and financial account balance always sum to zero.
- A balance-of-payments deficit occurs when a nation must draw down its official reserves to balance the capital and financial account with the current account; a balance-of-payments surplus occurs when a nation adds to its official reserves in order to balance the two accounts.

Flexible Exchange Rates

Both the size and the persistence of a nation's balance-of-payments deficits and surpluses and the adjustments it must make to correct those imbalances depend on the system of exchange rates being used. There are two "pure" types of exchange-rate systems:

- A **flexible- or floating-exchange-rate system** through which demand and supply determine exchange rates and in which no government intervention occurs.
- A **fixed-exchange-rate system** through which governments determine exchange rates and make necessary adjustments in their economies to maintain those rates.

We begin by looking at flexible exchange rates. Let's examine the rate, or price, at which U.S. dollars might be exchanged for British pounds. In **Figure 19.1 (Key Graph)** we show demand D_1 and supply S_1 of pounds in the currency market.

G 19.1

Flexible exchange rates

The *demand-for-pounds curve* is downward-sloping because all British goods and services will be cheaper to the United States if pounds become less expensive to the United States. That is, at lower dollar prices for pounds, the United States can obtain more pounds and therefore more British goods and services per dollar. To buy those cheaper British goods, U.S. consumers will increase the quantity of pounds they demand.

The *supply-of-pounds curve* is upward-sloping because the British will purchase more U.S. goods when the dollar price of pounds rises (that is, as the pound price of dollars falls). When the British buy more U.S. goods, they supply a greater quantity of pounds to the foreign exchange market. In other words, they must exchange pounds for dollars to purchase U.S. goods. So, when the dollar price of pounds rises, the quantity of pounds supplied goes up.

The intersection of the supply curve and the demand curve will determine the dollar price of pounds. Here, that price (exchange rate) is $2 for £1.

Depreciation and Appreciation

An exchange rate determined by market forces can, and often does, change daily like stock and bond prices. When the dollar price of pounds *rises*, for example, from $2 = £1 to $3 = £1, the dollar has *depreciated* relative to the pound (and the pound has appreciated relative to the dollar). When a currency depreciates, more units of it (dollars) are needed to buy a single unit of some other currency (a pound).

When the dollar price of pounds *falls*, for example, from $2 = £1 to $1 = £1, the dollar has *appreciated* relative to the pound. When a currency appreciates, fewer units of it (dollars) are needed to buy a single unit of some other currency (pounds).

In our U.S.-Britain illustrations, depreciation of the dollar means an appreciation of the pound, and vice versa. When the dollar price of a pound jumps from $2 = £1 to $3 = £1, the pound has appreciated relative to the dollar because it takes fewer pounds to buy $1. At $2 = £1, it took £$\frac{1}{2}$ to buy $1; at $3 = £1, it takes only £$\frac{1}{3}$ to buy $1. Conversely, when the dollar appreciated relative to the pound, the pound depreciated relative to the dollar. More pounds were needed to buy a dollar.

Determinants of Exchange Rates

What factors would cause a nation's currency to appreciate or depreciate in the market for foreign exchange? Here are three generalizations:

- If the demand for a nation's currency increases (all else equal), that currency will appreciate; if the demand declines, that currency will depreciate.
- If the supply of a nation's currency increases, that currency will depreciate; if the supply decreases, that currency will appreciate.
- If a nation's currency appreciates, some foreign currency depreciates relative to it.

With these generalizations in mind, let's examine the determinants of exchange rates—the factors that shift the demand or supply curve for a certain currency.

Changes in Tastes   Any change in consumer tastes or preferences for the products of a foreign country may alter the demand for that nation's currency and change its exchange rate. If technological advances in U.S. wireless phones make them more attractive to British consumers and businesses, then the British will supply more pounds in the exchange market in order to purchase more U.S. wireless phones. The supply-of-pounds curve will shift to the right, causing the pound to depreciate and the dollar to appreciate.

In contrast, the U.S. demand-for-pounds curve will shift to the right if British woolen apparel becomes more fashionable in the United States. So the pound will appreciate and the dollar will depreciate.

Relative Income Changes   A nation's currency is likely to depreciate if its growth of national income is more rapid than that of other countries. Here's why: A country's imports vary directly with its income level. As total income rises in the United States, people there buy both more domestic goods and more foreign goods. If the U.S. economy is expanding rapidly and the British economy is stagnant, U.S. imports of British goods, and therefore U.S. demands for pounds, will increase. The dollar price of pounds will rise, so the dollar will depreciate.

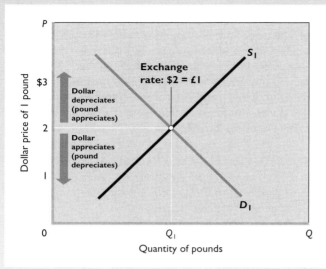

FIGURE 19.1 The market for foreign currency (pounds). The intersection of the demand-for-pounds curve D_1 and the supply-of-pounds curve S_1 determines the equilibrium dollar price of pounds, here, $2. That means that the exchange rate is $2 = £1. The upward green arrow is a reminder that a higher dollar price of pounds (say, $3 = £1, caused by a shift in either the demand or the supply curve) means that the dollar has depreciated (the pound has appreciated). The downward green arrow tells us that a lower dollar price of pounds (say, $1 = £1, again caused by a shift in either the demand or the supply curve) means that the dollar has appreciated (the pound has depreciated).

QUICK QUIZ 19.1

1. Which of the following statements is true?
   a. The quantity of pounds demanded falls when the dollar appreciates.
   b. The quantity of pounds supplied declines as the dollar price of the pound rises.
   c. At the equilibrium exchange rate, the pound price of $1 is £$\frac{1}{2}$.
   d. The dollar appreciates if the demand for pounds increases.
2. At the price of $2 for £1 in this figure:
   a. the dollar-pound exchange rate is unstable.
   b. the quantity of pounds supplied equals the quantity demanded.
   c. the dollar price of £1 equals the pound price of $1.
   d. U.S. goods exports to Britain must equal U.S. goods imports from Britain.
3. Other things equal, a leftward shift of the demand curve in this figure:
   a. would depreciate the dollar.

b. would create a shortage of pounds at the previous price of $2 for £1.
   c. might be caused by a major recession in the United States.
   d. might be caused by a significant rise of real interest rates in Britain.
4. Other things equal, a rightward shift of the supply curve in this figure would:
   a. depreciate the dollar and might be caused by a significant rise of real interest rates in Britain.
   b. depreciate the dollar and might be caused by a significant fall of real interest rates in Britain.
   c. appreciate the dollar and might be caused by a significant rise of real interest rates in the United States.
   d. appreciate the dollar and might be caused by a significant fall of interest rates in the United States.

Answers: 1. c; 2. b; 3. c; 4. c

Relative Price-Level Changes

Changes in the relative price levels of two nations may change the demand and supply of currencies and alter the exchange rate between the two nations' currencies.

The **purchasing-power-parity theory** holds that exchange rates equate the purchasing power of various currencies. That is, the exchange rates among national currencies adjust to match the ratios of the nations' price levels: If a certain market basket of goods costs $10,000 in the United States and £5,000 in Great Britain, according to this theory the exchange rate will be $2 = £1. That way,

a dollar spent on goods sold in Britain, Japan, Turkey, and other nations will have equal purchasing power.

In practice, however, exchange rates depart from purchasing power parity, even over long periods. Nevertheless, changes in relative price levels are a determinant of exchange rates. If, for example, the domestic price level rises rapidly in the United States and remains constant in Great Britain, U.S. consumers will seek out low-priced British goods, increasing the demand for pounds. The British will purchase fewer U.S. goods, reducing the supply of pounds. This combination of demand and supply

CONSIDER THIS ...

The Big Mac Index

The purchasing-power-parity (PPP) theory says that exchange rates will adjust such that a given broad market basket of goods and services will cost the same in all countries. If the market basket costs $1000 in the United States and 100,000 yen in Japan, then the exchange rate will be $1 = ¥100 (= 1000/100,000). If instead the exchange rate is $1 = ¥110, we can expect the dollar to depreciate and the yen to appreciate such that the exchange rate moves to the purchasing-power-parity rate of $1 = ¥100. Similarly, if the exchange rate is $1 = ¥90, we can expect the dollar to appreciate and the yen to depreciate.

Instead of using a market basket of goods and services, *The Economist* magazine has offered a light-hearted test of the purchasing-power-parity theory through its *Big Mac index*. It uses the exchange rates of 100 countries to convert the domestic currency price of a Big Mac into U.S. dollar prices. If the converted dollar price in, say, Britain exceeds the dollar price in the United States, the *Economist* concludes (with a wink) that the pound is overvalued relative to the dollar. On the other hand, if the adjusted dollar price of a Big Mac in Britain is less than the dollar price in the United States, then the pound is undervalued relative to the dollar.

The *Economist* finds wide divergences in actual dollar prices across the globe and thus little support for the purchasing-power-parity theory. Yet it humorously trumpets any predictive success it can muster (or is that "mustard"?):

> Some readers find our Big Mac index hard to swallow. This year (1999), however, has been one to relish. When the euro was launched at the start of the year most forecasters expected it to rise. The Big Mac index, however, suggested the euro was overvalued against the dollar—and indeed it has fallen [13 percent]. . . . Our correspondents have once again been munching their way around the globe . . . [and] experience suggests that investors ignore burgernomics at their peril.*

Maybe so—bad puns and all. Economist Robert Cumby examined the Big Mac index for 14 countries for 10 years.[†] Among his findings:

- A 10 percent undervaluation, according to the Big Mac standard, in one year is associated with a 3.5 percent appreciation of that currency over the following year.

- When the U.S. dollar price of a Big Mac is high in a country, the relative local currency price of a Big Mac in that country generally declines during the following year. Hmm. Not bad.

*"Big MacCurrencies," *The Economist*, Apr. 3, 1999; "Mcparity," *The Economist*, Dec. 11, 1999.

[†]Robert Cumby, "Forecasting Exchange Rates and Relative Prices with the Hamburger Standard: Is What You Want What You Get with Mcparity?" National Bureau of Economic Research, January 1997.

changes will cause the pound to appreciate and the dollar to depreciate.

Relative Interest Rates Changes in relative interest rates between two countries may alter their exchange rate. Suppose that real interest rates rise in the United States but stay constant in Great Britain. British citizens will then find the United States an attractive place in which to make financial investments. To undertake these investments, they will have to supply pounds in the foreign exchange market to obtain dollars. The increase in the supply of pounds results in depreciation of the pound and appreciation of the dollar.

Speculation Currency speculators are people who buy and sell currencies with an eye toward reselling or repurchasing them at a profit. Suppose speculators expect the U.S. economy to (1) grow more rapidly than the British economy and (2) experience a more rapid rise in its price level than will Britain. These expectations translate into an anticipation that the pound will appreciate and the dollar will depreciate. Speculators who are holding dollars will therefore try to convert them into pounds. This effort will increase the demand for pounds and cause the dollar price of pounds to rise (that is, cause the dollar to depreciate). A self-fulfilling prophecy occurs: The pound appreciates and the dollar depreciates because speculators act on the belief that these changes will in fact take place. In this way, speculation can cause changes in exchange rates. (We deal with currency speculation in more detail in this chapter's Last Word.)

Table 19.2 has more illustrations of the determinants of exchange rates; the table is worth careful study.

Flexible Rates and the Balance of Payments

Proponents of flexible exchange rates say they have an important feature: They automatically adjust and eventually eliminate balance-of-payments deficits or surpluses.

TABLE 19.2 Determinants of Exchange Rates: Factors That Change the Demand for or the Supply of a Particular Currency and Thus Alter the Exchange Rate

Determinant	Examples
Change in tastes	Japanese electronic equipment declines in popularity in the United States (Japanese yen depreciates; U.S. dollar appreciates).
	European tourists reduce visits to the United States (U.S. dollar depreciates; European euro appreciates).
Change in relative incomes	England encounters a recession, reducing its imports, while U.S. real output and real income surge, increasing U.S. imports (British pound appreciates; U.S. dollar depreciates).
Change in relative prices	Switzerland experiences a 3% inflation rate compared to Canada's 10% rate (Swiss franc appreciates; Canadian dollar depreciates).
Change in relative real interest rates	The Federal Reserve drives up interest rates in the United States, while the Bank of England takes no such action (U.S. dollar appreciates; British pound depreciates).
Speculation	Currency traders believe South Korea will have much greater inflation than Taiwan (South Korean won depreciates; Taiwan dollar appreciates).
	Currency traders think Norway's interest rates will plummet relative to Denmark's rates (Norway's kroner depreciates; Denmark's krone appreciates).

We can explain this idea through Figure 19.2, in which S_1 and D_1 are the supply and demand curves for pounds from Figure 19.1. The equilibrium exchange rate of $2 = £1 means that there is no balance-of-payments deficit or surplus between the United States and Britain. At that exchange rate, the quantity of pounds demanded by U.S. consumers to import British goods, buy British transportation and insurance services, and pay interest and dividends on British investments in the United States equals the amount of pounds supplied by the British in buying U.S. exports, purchasing services from the United States, and making interest and dividend payments on U. S. investments in Britain. The United States would have no need to either draw down or build up its official reserves to balance its payments.

Suppose tastes change and U.S. consumers buy more British automobiles; the U.S. price level increases relative to Britain's; or interest rates fall in the United States compared to those in Britain. Any or all of these changes will increase the U.S. demand for British pounds, for example, from D_1 to D_2 in Figure 19.2.

If the exchange rate remains at the initial $2 = £1, a U.S. balance-of-payments deficit will occur in the amount of ab. At the $2 = £1 rate, U.S. consumers will demand the quantity of pounds shown by point b but Britain will supply only the amount shown by a. There will be a shortage of pounds. But this shortage will not last because this is a competitive market. Instead, the dollar price of pounds will rise (the dollar will depreciate) until the balance-of-payments deficit is eliminated. That occurs at the new equilibrium exchange rate of $3 = £1, where the quantities of pounds demanded and supplied are again equal.

To explain why this occurred, we reemphasize that the exchange rate links all domestic (U.S.) prices with all foreign (British) prices. The dollar price of a foreign good is found by multiplying the foreign price by the exchange rate (in dollars per unit of the foreign currency). At an exchange rate of $2 = £1, a British automobile priced at £15,000 will cost a U.S. consumer $30,000 (= 15,000 × $2).

FIGURE 19.2 Adjustments under flexible exchange rates and fixed exchange rates. Under flexible exchange rates, a shift in the demand for pounds from D_1 to D_2, other things equal, would cause a U.S. balance-of-payments deficit ab. That deficit would be corrected by a change in the exchange rate from $2 = £1 to $3 = £1. Under fixed exchange rates, the United States would cover the shortage of pounds ab by using international monetary reserves, restricting trade, implementing exchange controls, or enacting a contractionary stabilization policy.

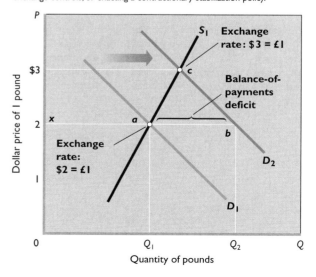

A change in the exchange rate alters the prices of all British goods to U.S. consumers and all U.S. goods to British buyers. The shift in the exchange rate (here from $2 = £1 to $3 = £1) changes the relative attractiveness of U.S. imports and exports and restores equilibrium in the U.S. (and British) balance of payments. From the U.S. view, as the dollar price of pounds changes from $2 to $3, the British auto priced at £15,000, which formerly cost a U.S. consumer $30,000, now costs $45,000 (= 15,000 × $3). Other British goods will also cost U.S. consumers more, and U.S. imports of British goods will decline. A movement from point *b* toward point *c* in Figure 19.2 graphically illustrates this concept.

From Britain's standpoint, the exchange rate (the pound price of dollars) has fallen (from £$\frac{1}{2}$ to £$\frac{1}{3}$ for $1). The international value of the pound has appreciated. The British previously got only $2 for £1; now they get $3 for £1. U.S. goods are therefore cheaper to the British, and U.S. exports to Britain will rise. In Figure 19.2, this is shown by a movement from point *a* toward point *c*.

The two adjustments—a decrease in U.S. imports from Britain and an increase in U.S. exports to Britain—are just what are needed to correct the U.S. balance-of-payments deficit. These changes end when, at point *c*, the quantities of British pounds demanded and supplied are equal. **(Key Questions 7 and 10)**

Disadvantages of Flexible Exchange Rates

Even though flexible exchange rates automatically work to eliminate payment imbalances, they may cause several significant problems.

Uncertainty and Diminished Trade

The risks and uncertainties associated with flexible exchange rates may discourage the flow of trade. Suppose a U.S. automobile dealer contracts to purchase 10 British cars for £150,000. At the current exchange rate of, say, $2 for £1, the U.S. importer expects to pay $300,000 for these automobiles. But if during the 3-month delivery period the rate of exchange shifts to $3 for £1, the £150,000 payment contracted by the U.S. importer will be $450,000.

That increase in the dollar price of pounds may thus turn the U.S. importer's anticipated profit into substantial loss. Aware of the possibility of an adverse change in the exchange rate, the U.S. importer may not be willing to assume the risks involved. The U.S. firm may confine its operations to domestic automobiles, so international trade in this product will not occur.

The same thing can happen with investments. Assume that when the exchange rate is $3 to £1, a U.S. firm invests $30,000 (or £10,000) in a British enterprise. It estimates a return of 10 percent; that is, it anticipates annual earnings of $3000 or £1000. Suppose these expectations prove correct in that the British firm earns £1000 in the first year on the £10,000 investment. But suppose that during the year, the value of the dollar appreciates to $2 = £1. The absolute return is now only $2000 (rather than $3000), and the rate of return falls from the anticipated 10 percent to only $6\frac{2}{3}$ percent (= $2000/$30,000). Investment is risky in any case. The added risk of changing exchange rates may persuade the U.S. investor not to venture overseas.[1]

Terms-of-Trade Changes

A decline in the international value of its currency will worsen a nation's terms of trade. For example, an increase in the dollar price of a pound will mean that the United States must export more goods and services to finance a specific level of imports from Britain.

Instability

Flexible exchange rates may destabilize the domestic economy because wide fluctuations stimulate and then depress industries producing exported goods. If the U.S. economy is operating at full employment and its currency depreciates, as in our illustration, the results will be inflationary, for two reasons. (1) Foreign demand for U.S. goods may rise, increasing total spending and pulling up U.S. prices. Also, the prices of all U.S. imports will increase. (2) Conversely, appreciation of the dollar will lower U.S. exports and increase imports, possibly causing unemployment.

Flexible or floating exchange rates may also complicate the use of domestic stabilization policies in seeking full employment and price stability. This is especially true for nations whose exports and imports are large relative to their total domestic output.

Fixed Exchange Rates

To circumvent the disadvantages of flexible exchange rates, at times nations have fixed or "pegged" their exchange rates. For our analysis of fixed exchange rates, we assume that the United States and Britain agree to maintain a $2 = £1 exchange rate.

The problem is that such a government agreement cannot keep from changing the demand for and the supply of pounds. With the rate fixed, a shift in demand or supply will threaten the fixed-exchange-rate system, and government must intervene to ensure that the exchange rate is maintained.

---

[1]You will see in this chapter's Last Word, however, that a trader can circumvent part of the risk of unfavorable exchange-rate fluctuations by "hedging" in the "futures market" or "forward market" for foreign exchange.

In Figure 19.2, suppose the U.S. demand for pounds increases from D_1 to D_2 and a U.S. payment deficit *ab* arises. Now, the new equilibrium exchange rate ($3 = £1) is above the fixed exchange rate ($2 = £1). How can the United States prevent the shortage of pounds from driving the exchange rate up to the new equilibrium level? How can it maintain the fixed exchange rate? The answer is by altering market demand or market supply or both so that they will intersect at the $2 = £1 rate. There are several ways to do this.

Use of Reserves

One way to maintain a fixed exchange rate is to manipulate the market through the use of official reserves. Such manipulations are called **currency interventions.** By selling part of its reserves of pounds, the U.S. government could increase the supply of pounds, shifting supply curve S_1 to the right so that it intersects D_2 at *b* in Figure 19.2 and thereby maintains the exchange rate at $2 = £1.

How do official reserves originate? Perhaps a balance-of-payments surplus occurred in the past. The U.S. government would have purchased that surplus. That is, at some earlier time the U.S. government may have spent dollars to buy the surplus pounds that were threatening to reduce the exchange rate to below the $2 = £1 fixed rate. Those purchases would have bolstered the U.S. official reserves of pounds.

Nations have also used gold as "international money" to obtain official reserves. In our example, the U.S. government could sell some of its gold to Britain to obtain pounds. It could then sell pounds for dollars. That would shift the supply-of-pounds curve to the right, and the $2 = £1 exchange rate could be maintained.

It is critical that the amount of reserves and gold be enough to accomplish the required increase in the supply of pounds. There is no problem if deficits and surpluses occur more or less randomly and are of similar size. Then, last year's balance-of-payments surplus with Britain will increase the U.S. reserve of pounds, and that reserve can be used to "finance" this year's deficit. But if the United States encounters persistent and sizable deficits for an extended period, it may exhaust its reserves, and thus be forced to abandon fixed exchange rates. Or, at the least, a nation whose reserves are inadequate must use less appealing options to maintain exchange rates. Let's consider some of those options.

Trade Policies

To maintain fixed exchange rates, a nation can try to control the flow of trade and finance directly. The United States could try to maintain the $2 = £1 exchange rate in the face of a shortage of pounds by discouraging imports (thereby reducing the demand for pounds) and encouraging exports (thus increasing the supply of pounds). Imports could be reduced by means of new tariffs or import quotas; special taxes could be levied on the interest and dividends U.S. financial investors receive from foreign investments. Also, the U.S. government could subsidize certain U.S. exports to increase the supply of pounds.

The fundamental problem is that these policies reduce the volume of world trade and change its makeup from what is economically desirable. When nations impose tariffs, quotas, and the like, they lose some of the economic benefits of a free flow of world trade. That loss should not be underestimated: Trade barriers by one nation lead to retaliatory responses from other nations, multiplying the loss.

Exchange Controls and Rationing

Another option is to adopt exchange controls and rationing. Under **exchange controls** the U.S. government could handle the problem of a pound shortage by requiring that all pounds obtained by U.S. exporters be sold to the Federal government. Then the government would allocate or ration this short supply of pounds (represented by *xa* in Figure 19.2) among various U.S. importers, who demand the quantity *xb*. This policy would restrict the value of U.S. imports to the amount of foreign exchange earned by U.S. exports. Assuming balance in the capital and financial account, there would then be no balance-of-payments deficit. U.S. demand for British imports with the value *ab* would simply not be fulfilled.

There are major objections to exchange controls:

- **Distorted trade** Like tariffs, quotas, and export subsidies (trade controls), exchange controls would distort the pattern of international trade away from the pattern suggested by comparative advantage.

- **Favoritism** The process of rationing scarce foreign exchange might lead to government favoritism toward selected importers (big contributors to reelection campaigns, for example).

- **Restricted choice** Controls would limit freedom of consumer choice. The U.S. consumers who prefer Volkswagens might have to buy Chevrolets. The business opportunities for some U.S. importers might be impaired if the government were to limit imports.

- **Black markets** Enforcement problems are likely under exchange controls. U.S. importers might want foreign exchange badly enough to pay more than the $2 = £1 official rate, setting the stage for black-market dealings between importers and illegal sellers of foreign exchange.

Domestic Macroeconomic Adjustments

A final way to maintain a fixed exchange rate would be to use domestic stabilization policies (monetary policy and fiscal policy) to eliminate the shortage of foreign currency. Tax hikes, reductions in government spending, and a high-interest-rate policy would reduce total spending in the U.S. economy and, consequently, domestic income. Because the volume of imports varies directly with domestic income, demand for British goods, and therefore for pounds, would be restrained.

If these "contractionary" policies served to reduce the domestic price level relative to Britain's, U.S. buyers of consumer and capital goods would divert their demands from British goods to U.S. goods, reducing the demand for pounds. Moreover, the high-interest-rate policy would lift U.S. interest rates relative to those in Britain.

Lower prices on U.S. goods and higher U.S. interest rates would increase British imports of U.S. goods and would increase British financial investment in the United States. Both developments would increase the supply of pounds. The combination of a decrease in the demand for and an increase in the supply of pounds would reduce or eliminate the original U.S. balance-of-payments deficit. In Figure 19.2 the new supply and demand curves would intersect at some new equilibrium point on line *ab*, where the exchange rate remains at $2 = £1.

Maintaining fixed exchange rates by such means is hardly appealing. The "price" of exchange-rate stability for the United States would be a decline in output, employment, and price levels—in other words, a recession. Eliminating a balance-of-payments deficit and achieving domestic stability are both important national economic goals, but to sacrifice stability to balance payments would be to let the tail wag the dog.

QUICK REVIEW 19.2

- In a system in which exchange rates are flexible (meaning that they are free to float), the rates are determined by the demand for and supply of individual national currencies in the foreign exchange market.
- Determinants of flexible exchange rates (factors that shift currency supply and demand curves) include changes in (a) tastes, (b) relative national incomes, (c) relative price levels, (d) real interest rates, and (e) speculation.
- Under a system of fixed exchange rates, nations set their exchange rates and then maintain them by buying or selling reserves of currencies, establishing trade barriers, employing exchange controls, or incurring inflation or recession.

International Exchange-Rate Systems

In recent times the world's nations have used three different exchange-rate systems: a fixed-rate system, a modified fixed-rate system, and a modified flexible-rate system.

The Gold Standard: Fixed Exchange Rates

Between 1879 and 1934 the major nations of the world adhered to a fixed-rate system called the **gold standard.** Under this system, each nation must:

- Define its currency in terms of a quantity of gold.
- Maintain a fixed relationship between its stock of gold and its money supply.
- Allow gold to be freely exported and imported.

If each nation defines its currency in terms of gold, the various national currencies will have fixed relationships to one another. For example, if the United States defines $1 as worth 25 grains of gold, and Britain defines £1 as worth 50 grains of gold, then a British pound is worth 2×25 grains, or $2. This exchange rate was fixed under the gold standard. The exchange rate did not change in response to changes in currency demand and supply.

Gold Flows If we ignore the costs of packing, insuring, and shipping gold between countries, under the gold standard the rate of exchange would not vary from this $2 = £1 rate. No one in the United States would pay more than $2 = £1 because 50 grains of gold could always be bought for $2 in the United States and sold for £1 in Britain. Nor would the British pay more than £1 for $2. Why should they when they could buy 50 grains of gold in Britain for £1 and sell it in the United States for $2?

Under the gold standard, the potential free flow of gold between nations resulted in fixed exchange rates.

Domestic Macroeconomic Adjustments When currency demand or supply changes, the gold standard requires domestic macroeconomic adjustments to maintain the fixed exchange rate. To see why, suppose that U.S. tastes change such that U.S. consumers want to buy more British goods. The resulting increase in the demand for pounds creates a shortage of pounds in the United States (recall Figure 19.2), implying a U.S. balance-of-payments deficit.

What will happen? Remember that the rules of the gold standard prohibit the exchange rate from moving from the fixed $2 = £1 rate. The rate cannot move to, say, a new equilibrium at $3 = £1 to correct the imbalance. Instead, gold will flow from the United States to Britain to correct the payments imbalance.

But recall that the gold standard requires that participants maintain a fixed relationship between their domestic money supplies and their quantities of gold. The flow of gold from the United States to Britain will require a reduction of the money supply in the United States. Other things equal, that will reduce total spending in the United States and lower U.S. real domestic output, employment, income, and, perhaps, prices. Also, the decline in the money supply will boost U.S. interest rates.

The opposite will occur in Britain. The inflow of gold will increase the money supply, and this will increase total spending in Britain. Domestic output, employment, income, and, perhaps, prices will rise. The British interest rate will fall.

Declining U.S. incomes and prices will reduce the U.S. demand for British goods and therefore reduce the U.S. demand for pounds. Lower interest rates in Britain will make it less attractive for U.S. investors to make financial investments there, also lessening the demand for pounds. For all these reasons, the demand for pounds in the United States will decline. In Britain, higher incomes, prices, and interest rates will make U.S. imports and U.S. financial investments more attractive. In buying these imports and making these financial investments, British citizens will supply more pounds in the exchange market.

In short, domestic macroeconomic adjustments in the United States and Britain, triggered by the international flow of gold, will produce new demand and supply conditions for pounds such that the $2 = £1 exchange rate is maintained. After all the adjustments are made, the United States will not have a payments deficit and Britain will not have a payments surplus.

So the gold standard has the advantage of maintaining stable exchange rates and correcting balance-of-payments deficits and surpluses automatically. However, its critical drawback is that nations must accept domestic adjustments in such distasteful forms as unemployment and falling incomes, on the one hand, or inflation, on the other hand. Under the gold standard, a nation's money supply is altered by changes in supply and demand in currency markets, and nations cannot establish their own monetary policy in their own national interest. If the United States, for example, were to experience declining output and income, the loss of gold under the gold standard would reduce the U.S. money supply. That would increase interest rates, retard borrowing and spending, and produce further declines in output and income.

Collapse of the Gold Standard The gold standard collapsed under the weight of the worldwide Depression of the 1930s. As domestic output and employment fell worldwide, the restoration of prosperity became the primary goal of afflicted nations. They responded by enacting protectionist measures to reduce imports. The idea was to get their economies moving again by promoting consumption of domestically produced goods. To make their exports less expensive abroad, many nations redefined their currencies at lower levels in terms of gold. For example, a country that had previously defined the value of its currency at 1 unit = 25 ounces of gold might redefine it as 1 unit = 10 ounces of gold. Such redefining is an example of **devaluation**—a deliberate action by government to reduce the international value of its currency. A series of such devaluations in the 1930s meant that exchange rates were no longer fixed. That violated a major tenet of the gold standard, and the system broke down.

The Bretton Woods System

The Great Depression and the Second World War left world trade and the world monetary system in shambles. To lay the groundwork for a new international monetary system, in 1944 major nations held an international conference at Bretton Woods, New Hampshire. The conference produced a commitment to a modified fixed-exchange-rate system called an *adjustable-peg system*, or, simply, the **Bretton Woods system.** The new system sought to capture the advantages of the old gold standard (fixed exchange rate) while avoiding its disadvantages (painful domestic macroeconomic adjustments).

Furthermore, the conference created the **International Monetary Fund (IMF)** to make the new exchange-rate system feasible and workable. The new international monetary system managed through the IMF prevailed with modifications until 1971. (The IMF still plays a basic role in international finance; in recent years it has performed a major role in providing loans to developing countries, nations experiencing financial crises, and nations making the transition from communism to capitalism.)

IMF and Pegged Exchange Rates How did the adjustable-peg system of exchange rates work? First, as with the gold standard, each IMF member had to define its currency in terms of gold (or dollars), thus establishing rates of exchange between its currency and the currencies of all other members. In addition, each nation was obligated to keep its exchange rate stable with respect to every other currency. To do so, nations would have to use their official currency reserves to intervene in foreign exchange markets.

Assume again that the U.S. dollar and the British pound were "pegged" to each other at $2 = £1. And suppose again that the demand for pounds temporarily increases so that a shortage of pounds occurs in the United States (the United States has a balance-of-payments deficit). How can the United States keep its pledge to maintain a $2 = £1 exchange rate when the new equilibrium rate is, say, $3 = £1? As we noted previously, the United States can supply additional pounds to the exchange market, increasing the supply of pounds such that the equilibrium exchange rate falls back to $2 = £1.

Under the Bretton Woods system there were three main sources of the needed pounds:

- **Official reserves** The United States might currently possess pounds in its official reserves as the result of past actions against a payments surplus.
- **Gold sales** The U.S. government might sell some of its gold to Britain for pounds. The proceeds would then be offered in the exchange market to augment the supply of pounds.
- **IMF borrowing** The needed pounds might be borrowed from the IMF. Nations participating in the Bretton Woods system were required to make contributions to the IMF based on the size of their national income, population, and volume of trade. If necessary, the United States could borrow pounds on a short-term basis from the IMF by supplying its own currency as collateral.

Fundamental Imbalances: Adjusting the Peg

The Bretton Woods system recognized that from time to time a nation may be confronted with persistent and sizable balance-of-payments problems that cannot be corrected through the means listed above. In such cases, the nation would eventually run out of official reserves and be unable to maintain its fixed-exchange-rate system. The Bretton Woods remedy was correction by devaluation, that is, by an "orderly" reduction of the nation's pegged exchange rate. Also, the IMF allowed each member nation to alter the value of its currency by 10 percent, on its own, to correct a so-called fundamental (persistent and continuing) balance-of-payments deficit. Larger exchange-rate changes required the permission of the Fund's board of directors.

By requiring approval of significant rate changes, the Fund guarded against arbitrary and competitive currency devaluations by nations seeking only to boost output in their own countries at the expense of other countries. In our example, devaluation of the dollar would increase U.S. exports and lower U.S. imports, correcting its persistent payments deficit.

Demise of the Bretton Woods System

Under this adjustable-peg system, nations came to accept gold and the dollar as international reserves. The acceptability of gold as an international medium of exchange derived from its earlier use under the gold standard. Other nations accepted the dollar as international money because the United States had accumulated large quantities of gold, and between 1934 and 1971 it maintained a policy of buying gold from, and selling gold to, foreign governments at a fixed price of $35 per ounce. The dollar was convertible into gold on demand, so the dollar came to be regarded as a substitute for gold, or "as good as gold." And since the discovery of new gold was limited, the growing volume of dollars helped provide a medium of exchange for the expanding world trade.

But a major problem arose. The United States had persistent payments deficits throughout the 1950s and 1960s. Those deficits were financed in part by U.S. gold reserves but mostly by payment of U.S. dollars. As the amount of dollars held by foreigners soared and the U.S. gold reserves dwindled, other nations began to question whether the dollar was really "as good as gold." The ability of the United States to continue to convert dollars into gold at $35 per ounce became increasingly doubtful, as did the role of dollars as international monetary reserves. Thus the dilemma was: To maintain the dollar as a reserve medium, the U.S. payments deficit had to be eliminated. But elimination of the payments deficit would remove the source of additional dollar reserves and thus limit the growth of international trade and finance.

The problem culminated in 1971 when the United States ended its 37-year-old policy of exchanging gold for dollars at $35 per ounce. It severed the link between gold and the international value of the dollar, thereby "floating" the dollar and letting market forces determine its value. The floating of the dollar withdrew U.S. support from the Bretton Woods system of fixed exchange rates and, in effect, ended the system.

The Current System: The Managed Float

The current international exchange-rate system (1971–present) is an "almost" flexible system called **managed floating exchange rates.** Exchange rates among major currencies are free to float to their equilibrium market levels, but nations occasionally use currency interventions in the foreign exchange market to stabilize or alter market exchange rates.

Normally, the major trading nations allow their exchange rates to float up or down to equilibrium levels based on supply and demand in the foreign exchange market. They recognize that changing economic conditions among nations require continuing changes in equilibrium exchange rates to avoid persistent payments deficits or surpluses. They rely on freely operating foreign exchange markets to accomplish the necessary adjustments. The result has been considerably more volatile exchange rates than those during the Bretton Woods era.

But nations also recognize that certain trends in the movement of equilibrium exchange rates may be at odds with national or international objectives. On occasion, nations therefore intervene in the foreign exchange market by buying or selling large amounts of specific currencies. This way, they can "manage" or stabilize exchange rates by influencing currency demand and supply.

The leaders of the *G8 nations* (Canada, France, Germany, Italy, Japan, Russia, United Kingdom, and United States) meet regularly to discuss economic issues and try to coordinate economic policies. At times they have collectively intervened to try to stabilize currencies. For example, in 2000 they sold dollars and bought euros in an effort to stabilize the falling value of the euro relative to the dollar. In the previous year the euro (€) had depreciated from €1 = $1.17 to €1 = $.87.

The current exchange-rate system is thus an "almost" flexible exchange-rate system. The "almost" refers mainly to the periodic currency interventions by governments; it also refers to the fact that the actual system is more complicated than described. While the major currencies such as dollars, euros, pounds, and yen fluctuate in response to changing supply and demand, some developing nations peg their currencies to the dollar and allow their currencies to fluctuate with it against other currencies. Also, some nations peg the value of their currencies to a "basket" or group of other currencies.

How well has the managed float worked? It has both proponents and critics.

In Support of the Managed Float

Proponents of the managed-float system argue that is has functioned far better than many experts anticipated. Skeptics had predicted that fluctuating exchange rates would reduce world trade and finance. But in real terms world trade under the managed float has grown tremendously over the past several decades. Moreover, as supporters are quick to point out, currency crises such as those in Mexico and southeast Asia in the last half of the 1990s were not the result of the floating-exchange-rate system itself. Rather, the abrupt currency devaluations and depreciations resulted from internal problems in those nations, in conjunction with the nations' tendency to peg their currencies to the dollar or to a basket of currencies. In some cases,

flexible exchange rates would have made these adjustments far more gradual.

Proponents also point out that the managed float has weathered severe economic turbulence that might have caused a fixed-rate system to break down. Such events as extraordinary oil price increases in 1973–1974 and again in 1981–1983, inflationary recessions in several nations in the mid-1970s, major national recessions in the early 1980s, and large U.S. budget deficits in the 1980s and the first half of the 1990s all caused substantial imbalances in international trade and finance, as did the large U.S. budget deficits and soaring world oil prices that occurred in the middle of the first decade of the 2000s. Flexible rates enabled the system to adjust to all these events, whereas the same events would have put unbearable pressures on a fixed-rate system.

Concerns with the Managed Float

There is still much sentiment in favor of greater exchange-rate stability. Those favoring more stable exchange rates see problems with the current system. They argue that the excessive volatility of exchange rates under the managed float threatens the prosperity of economies that rely heavily on exports. Several financial crises in individual nations (for example, Mexico, South Korea, Indonesia, Thailand, Russia, and Brazil) have resulted from abrupt changes in exchange rates. These crises have led to massive "bailouts" of those economies via IMF loans. The IMF bailouts, in turn, may encourage nations to undertake risky and inappropriate economic policies since they know that, if need be, the IMF will come to the rescue. Moreover, some exchange-rate volatility has occurred even when underlying economic and financial conditions were relatively stable, suggesting that speculation plays too large a role in determining exchange rates.

Perhaps more important, assert the critics, the managed float has not eliminated trade imbalances, as flexible rates are supposed to do. Thus, the United States has run persistent trade deficits for many years, while Japan has run persistent surpluses. Changes in exchange rates between dollars and yen have not yet corrected these imbalances, as is supposed to be the case under flexible exchange rates.

Skeptics say the managed float is basically a "nonsystem"; the guidelines concerning what each nation may or may not do with its exchange rates are not specific enough to keep the system working in the long run. Nations inevitably will be tempted to intervene in the foreign exchange market, not merely to smooth out short-term fluctuations in exchange rates but to prop up their currency if it is chronically weak or to manipulate the exchange rate to achieve domestic stabilization goals.

So what are we to conclude? Flexible exchange rates have not worked perfectly, but they have not failed miserably. Thus far they have survived, and no doubt have eased, several major shocks to the international trading system. Meanwhile, the "managed" part of the float has given nations some sense of control over their collective economic destinies. On balance, most economists favor continuation of the present system of "almost" flexible exchange rates.

QUICK REVIEW 19.3

- Under the gold standard (1879–1934), nations fixed exchange rates by valuing their currencies in terms of gold, by tying their stocks of money to gold, and by allowing gold to flow between nations when balance-of-payments deficits and surpluses occurred.
- The Bretton Woods exchange-rate system (1944–1971) fixed or pegged exchange rates but permitted orderly adjustments of the pegs under special circumstances.
- The managed floating system of exchange rates (1971–present) relies on foreign exchange markets to establish equilibrium exchange rates. The system permits nations to buy and sell foreign currency to stabilize short-term changes in exchange rates or to correct exchange-rate imbalances that are negatively affecting the world economy.

Recent U.S. Trade Deficits

As indicated in Figure 19.3a, the United States has experienced large and persistent trade deficits over the past several years. These deficits climbed steadily between 1997 and 2000, fell slightly in the recessionary year 2001, and rose sharply between 2002 and 2005. In 2005 the trade deficit on goods was $782 billion and the trade deficit on goods and services was $724 billion. The current account deficit (Figure 19.3b) reached a record $805 billion in 2005. It rose from 5.7 percent of GDP in 2004 to 6.4 percent of GDP in 2005. Large trade deficits are expected to continue for many years, both in absolute and relative terms.

Causes of the Trade Deficits

Several reasons account for these large trade deficits. First, between 1997 and 2000, and again between 2003 and 2005, the U.S. economy grew more rapidly than the economies of several of its major trading partners. That strong growth of U.S. income enabled Americans to buy more imported goods. In contrast, Japan and some European nations either suffered recession or experienced slower income growth. So their purchases of U.S. exports did not keep pace with the growing U.S. imports.

Also, large trade deficits with China have emerged, reaching $202 billion in 2005. This amount is even greater than the U.S. trade imbalance with Japan ($83 billion in

FIGURE 19.3 U.S. trade deficits, 1994–2005. (a) The United States experienced large deficits in *goods* and in *goods and services* between 1997 and 2005. (b) The U.S. current account, generally reflecting the goods and services deficit, was also in substantial deficit. These trade deficits are expected to continue throughout the current decade.

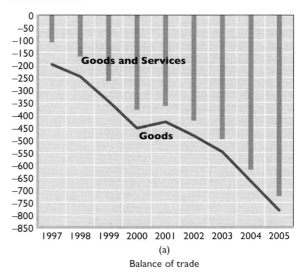

Billions of Dollars

(a)
Balance of trade

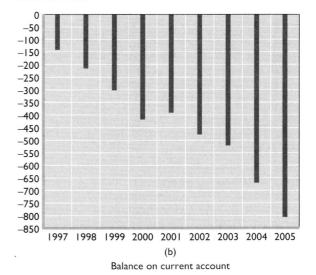

Billions of Dollars

(b)
Balance on current account

2005). The United States is China's largest export market, and although China has increased its imports from the United States, its standard of living has not yet increased enough for its citizens to afford large quantities of U.S. goods and services. Adding to the problem, China has fixed the exchange rate of it currency, the yuan, to a basket of currencies that includes the dollar. Therefore its large trade surplus with the United States has not caused the yuan to

Speculation in Currency Markets

Are Speculators a Negative or a Positive Influence in Currency Markets and International Trade?

Most people buy foreign currency to facilitate the purchase of goods or services from another country. A U.S. importer buys Japanese yen to purchase Japanese autos. A Hong Kong financial investor purchases Australian dollars to invest in the Australian stock market. But there is another group of participants in the currency market—speculators—that buys and sells foreign currencies in the hope of reselling or rebuying them later at a profit.

Contributing to Exchange-Rate Fluctuations Speculators were much in the news in late 1997 and 1998 when they were widely accused of driving down the values of the South Korean won, Thailand baht, Malaysian ringgit, and Indonesian rupiah. The value of these currencies fell by as much as 50 percent within 1 month, and speculators undoubtedly contributed to the swiftness of those declines. The expectation of currency depreciation (or appreciation) can be self-fulfilling. If speculators, for example, expect the Indonesian rupiah to be devalued or to depreciate, they quickly sell rupiah and buy currencies that they think will increase in relative value. The sharp increase in the supply of rupiah indeed reduces its value; this reduction then may trigger further selling of rupiah in expectation of further declines in its value.

But changed economic realities, not speculation, are normally the underlying causes of changes in currency values. That was largely the case with the southeast Asian countries in which actual and threatened bankruptcies in the financial and manufacturing sectors undermined confidence in the strength of the currencies. Anticipating the eventual declines in currency values, speculators simply hastened those declines. That is, the declines in value probably would have occurred with or without speculators.

Moreover, on a daily basis, speculation clearly has positive effects in foreign exchange markets.

Smoothing Out Short-Term Fluctuations in Currency Prices When temporarily weak demand or strong supply reduces a currency's value, speculators quickly buy the currency, adding to its demand and strengthening its value. When temporarily strong demand or weak supply increases a currency's value, speculators sell the currency. That selling increases the supply of the currency and reduces its value. In this way speculators smooth out supply and demand, and thus exchange rates, over short time periods. This day-to-day exchange-rate stabilization aids international trade.

Absorbing Risk Speculators also absorb risk that others do not want to bear. Because of potential adverse changes in exchange rates, international transactions are riskier than domestic trans-

appreciate in value relative to the U.S. dollar. That appreciation would make Chinese goods more expensive in the United States and reduce U.S. imports of Chinese goods. In China a stronger yuan would reduce the dollar price of U.S. goods and increase Chinese purchases of U.S. exports. Reduced U.S. imports from China and increased U.S. exports to China would reduce the large U.S. trade deficit.

Another factor causing the large U.S. trade deficits has been the rapid rise of the price of oil. Because the United States imports a large percentage of its oil, rising prices tend to aggravate trade deficits. For example, in 2005 the United States had a $94 billion trade deficit with the OPEC countries.

Finally, a declining U.S. saving rate (= saving/total income) has also contributed to U.S. trade deficits. In recent years, the saving rate has declined while the investment rate (= investment/total income) has remained stable or even increased. The gap has been met through foreign

purchases of U.S. real and financial assets, creating a large capital and financial account surplus. Because foreign savers are willingly financing a larger part of U.S. investment, Americans are able to save less than otherwise and consume more. Part of that added consumption spending is on imported goods. Also, many foreigners view U.S. real assets favorably because of the relatively high risk-adjusted rates of return they generate. The purchase of those assets provides foreign currency to Americans to finance their strong appetite for imported goods.

The point is that the capital account surplus may be a partial cause of the trade deficits, not just a result of those deficits.

Implications of U.S. Trade Deficits

The recent U.S. trade deficits are the largest ever run by a major industrial nation. Whether the large trade deficits should be of significant concern to the United States and actions. Suppose AnyTime, a hypothetical retailer, signs a contract with a Swiss manufacturer to buy 10,000 Swatch watches to be delivered in 3 months. The stipulated price is 75 Swiss francs per watch, which in dollars is $50 per watch at the present exchange rate of, say, $1 = 1.5 francs. AnyTime's total bill for the 10,000 watches will be $500,000 (= 750,000 francs).

But if the Swiss franc were to appreciate, say, to $1 = 1 franc, the dollar price per watch would rise from $50 to $75 and AnyTime would owe $750,000 for the watches (= 750,000 francs). AnyTime may reduce the risk of such an unfavorable exchange-rate fluctuation by hedging in the futures market. Hedging is an action by a buyer or a seller to protect against a change in future prices. The futures market is a market in which currencies are bought and sold at prices fixed now, for delivery at a specified date in the future.

AnyTime can purchase the needed 750,000 francs at the current $1 = 1.5 francs exchange rate, but with delivery in 3 months when the Swiss watches are delivered. And here is where speculators come in. For a price determined in the futures market, they agree to deliver the 750,000 francs to AnyTime in 3 months at the $1 = 1.5 francs exchange rate, regardless of the exchange rate then. The speculators need not own francs when the agreement is made. If the Swiss franc depreciates to, say, $1 = 2 francs in this period, the speculators profit. They can buy the 750,000 francs stipulated in the contract for $375,000, pocketing the difference between that amount and the $500,000 AnyTime has agreed to pay for the 750,000 francs. If the Swiss franc appreciates, the speculators, but not AnyTime, suffer a loss.

The amount AnyTime must pay for this "exchange-rate insurance" will depend on how the market views the likelihood of the franc depreciating, appreciating, or staying constant over the 3-month period. As in all competitive markets, supply and demand determine the price of the futures contract.

The futures market thus eliminates much of the exchange-rate risk associated with buying foreign goods for future delivery. Without it, AnyTime might have decided against importing Swiss watches. But the futures market and currency speculators greatly increase the likelihood that the transaction will occur. Operating through the futures market, speculation promotes international trade.

In short, although speculators in currency markets occasionally contribute to swings in exchange rates, on a day-to-day basis they play a positive role in currency markets.

the rest of the world is debatable. Most economists see both benefits and costs to trade deficits.

Increased Current Consumption

At the time a trade deficit or a current account deficit is occurring, American consumers benefit. A trade deficit means that the United States is receiving more goods and services as imports from abroad than it is sending out as exports. Taken alone, a trade deficit allows the United States to consume outside its production possibilities curve. It augments the domestic standard of living. But here is a catch: The gain in present consumption may come at the expense of reduced future consumption. When and if the current account deficit declines, Americans may have to consume less than before and perhaps even less than they produce.

Increased U.S. Indebtedness

A trade deficit is considered unfavorable because it must be financed by borrowing from the rest of the world, selling off assets, or dipping into official reserves. Recall that current account deficits are financed primarily by net inpayments of foreign currencies to the United States. When U.S. exports are insufficient to finance U.S. imports, the United States increases both its debt to people abroad and the value of foreign claims against assets in the United States. Financing of the U.S. trade deficit has resulted in a larger foreign accumulation of claims against U.S. financial and real assets than the U.S. claim against foreign assets. Today, the United States is the world's largest debtor nation. In 2004 foreigners owned $2.5 billion more of U.S. assets (corporations, land, stocks, bonds, loan notes) than U.S. citizens and institutions owned in foreign assets.

If the United States wants to regain ownership of these domestic assets, at some future time it will have to export more than it imports. At that time, domestic consumption will be lower because the United States will need to send more of its output abroad than it receives as imports. Therefore, the current consumption gains delivered by U.S. current account deficits may mean permanent debt, permanent foreign ownership, or large sacrifices of future consumption.

We say "may mean" above because the foreign lending to U.S. firms and foreign investment in the United States increases the U.S. capital stock. U.S. production capacity therefore might increase more rapidly than otherwise because of a large surplus on the capital and financial account. Faster increases in production capacity and real GDP enhance the economy's ability to service foreign debt and buy back real capital, if that is desired.

In short, trade deficits are a mixed blessing. The long-term impacts of the record-high U.S. trade deficits are largely unknown. That "unknown" worries some economists, who are concerned that foreigners will lose financial confidence in the United States. If that happens, they would restrict their lending to American households and businesses and also reduce their purchases of U.S. assets. Both actions would decrease the demand for U.S. dollars in the foreign exchange market and cause the U.S. dollar to depreciate. A sudden, large depreciation of the U.S. dollar might disrupt world trade and negatively affect economic growth worldwide. Other economists, however, downplay this scenario. Because any decline in the U.S. capital and financial account surplus is automatically met with a decline in the current account deficit, the overall impact on the American economy would be slight.

Summary

1. U.S. exports create a foreign demand for dollars and make a supply of foreign exchange available to the United States. Conversely, U.S. imports create a demand for foreign exchange and make a supply of dollars available to foreigners. Generally, a nation's exports earn the foreign currencies needed to pay for its imports.

2. The balance of payments records all international trade and financial transactions taking place between a given nation and the rest of the world. The balance on goods and services (the trade balance) compares exports and imports of both goods and services. The current account balance includes not only goods and services transactions but also net investment income and net transfers.

3. The capital and financial account includes (a) the net amount of the nation's debt forgiveness and (b) the nation's sale of real and financial assets to people living abroad less its purchases of real and financial assets from foreigners.

4. The current account and the capital and financial account always sum to zero. A deficit in the current account is always offset by a surplus in the capital and financial account. Conversely, a surplus in the current account is always offset by a deficit in the capital and financial account.

5. A balance-of-payments deficit is said to occur when a nation must draw down its official reserves, making inpayments to its balance of payments, in order to balance the capital and financial account with the current account. A balance-of-payments surplus occurs when a nation must increase its official reserves, making outpayments from its balance of payments, to balance the two accounts. The desirability of a balance-of-payments deficit or surplus depends on its size and its persistence.

6. Flexible or floating exchange rates between international currencies are determined by the demand for and supply of those currencies. Under flexible rates a currency will depreciate or appreciate as a result of changes in tastes, relative income changes, relative price changes, relative changes in real interest rates, and speculation.

7. The maintenance of fixed exchange rates requires adequate reserves to accommodate periodic payments deficits. If reserves are inadequate, nations must invoke protectionist trade policies, engage in exchange controls, or endure undesirable domestic macroeconomic adjustments.

8. The gold standard, a fixed-rate system, provided exchange-rate stability until its disintegration during the 1930s. Under this system, gold flows between nations precipitated sometimes painful changes in price, income, and employment levels in bringing about international equilibrium.

9. Under the Bretton Woods system, exchange rates were pegged to one another and were stable. Participating nations were obligated to maintain these rates by using stabilization funds, gold, or loans from the IMF. Persistent or "fundamental" payments deficits could be resolved by IMF-sanctioned currency devaluations.

10. Since 1971 the world's major nations have used a system of managed floating exchange rates. Market forces generally set rates, although governments intervene with varying frequency to alter their exchange rates.

11. Between 1997 and 2005, the United States had large and rising trade deficits, which are projected to last well into the future. Causes of the trade deficits include (a) more rapid income growth in the United States than in Japan and some European nations, resulting in expanding U.S. imports relative to exports, (b) the emergence of a large trade deficit

with China, (c) rising prices of imported oil, and (d) a large surplus in the capital and financial account, which enabled Americans to reduce their saving and buy more imports.

12. U.S. trade deficits have produced current increases in the living standards of U.S. consumers. The accompanying sur-

pluses on the capital and financial account have increased U.S. debt to the rest of the world and increased foreign ownership of assets in the United States. This greater foreign investment in the United States, however, has undoubtedly increased U.S. production possibilities.

Terms and Concepts

balance of payments	balance on current account	flexible- or floating-exchange-rate system	gold standard
current account	capital and financial account	fixed-exchange-rate system	devaluation
balance on goods and services	balance on capital and financial account	purchasing-power-parity theory	Bretton Woods system
trade deficit	balance-of-payments deficits and surpluses	currency interventions	International Monetary Fund (IMF)
trade surplus	official reserves	exchange controls	managed floating exchange rates

Study Questions

1. Explain how a U.S. automobile importer might finance a shipment of Toyotas from Japan. Trace the steps as to how a U.S. export of machinery to Italy might be financed. Explain: "U.S. exports earn supplies of foreign currencies that Americans can use to finance imports."

2. **KEY QUESTION** Indicate whether each of the following creates a demand for or a supply of European euros in foreign exchange markets:
   a. A U.S. airline firm purchases several Airbus planes assembled in France.
   b. A German automobile firm decides to build an assembly plant in South Carolina.
   c. A U.S. college student decides to spend a year studying at the Sorbonne in Paris.
   d. An Italian manufacturer ships machinery from one Italian port to another on a Liberian freighter.
   e. The U.S. economy grows faster than the French economy.
   f. A U.S. government bond held by a Spanish citizen matures, and the loan amount is paid back to that person.
   g. It is widely believed that the euro will depreciate in the near future.

3. **KEY QUESTION** Alpha's balance-of-payments data for 2006 are shown below. All figures are in billions of dollars. What are the (*a*) balance on goods, (*b*) balance on goods and services, (*c*) balance on current account, and (*d*) balance on capital and financial account? Suppose Alpha needed to deposit $10 billion of official reserves into the capital and financial account to balance it against the current account. Does Alpha have a balance-of-payments deficit or surplus? Explain.

Goods exports	+$40
Goods imports	−30
Service exports	+15
Service imports	−10
Net investment income	−5
Net transfers	+10
Balance on capital account	0
Foreign purchases of Alpha assets	+20
Alpha purchases of assets abroad	−40

4. China had a $150 billion overall current account surplus in 2005. Assuming that China's net debt forgiveness was zero in 2005 (its capital account balance was zero), what can you specifically conclude about the relationship of Chinese purchases of financial and real assets abroad versus foreign purchases of Chinese financial and real assets? Explain.

5. "A rise in the dollar price of yen necessarily means a fall in the yen price of dollars." Do you agree? Illustrate and elaborate: "The critical thing about exchange rates is that they provide a direct link between the prices of goods and services produced in all trading nations of the world." Explain the purchasing-power-parity theory of exchange rates.

6. Suppose that a Swiss watchmaker imports watch components from Sweden and exports watches to the United States. Also suppose the dollar depreciates, and the Swedish krona appreciates, relative to the Swiss franc. Speculate as to how each would hurt the Swiss watchmaker.

7. **KEY QUESTION** Explain why the U.S. demand for Mexican pesos is downward-sloping and the supply of pesos to

Americans is upward-sloping. Assuming a system of flexible exchange rates between Mexico and the United States, indicate whether each of the following would cause the Mexican peso to appreciate or depreciate:

a. The United States unilaterally reduces tariffs on Mexican products.

b. Mexico encounters severe inflation.

c. Deteriorating political relations reduce American tourism in Mexico.

d. The U.S. economy moves into a severe recession.

e. The United States engages in a high-interest-rate monetary policy.

f. Mexican products become more fashionable to U.S. consumers.

g. The Mexican government encourages U.S. firms to invest in Mexican oil fields.

h. The rate of productivity growth in the United States diminishes sharply.

8. Explain why you agree or disagree with the following statements:

a. A country that grows faster than its major trading partners can expect the international value of its currency to depreciate.

b. A nation whose interest rate is rising more rapidly than interest rates in other nations can expect the international value of its currency to appreciate.

c. A country's currency will appreciate if its inflation rate is less than that of the rest of the world.

9. "Exports pay for imports. Yet in 2005 the nations of the world exported about $724 billion more worth of goods and services to the United States than they imported from the United States." Resolve the apparent inconsistency of these two statements.

10. **KEY QUESTION** Diagram a market in which the equilibrium dollar price of 1 unit of fictitious currency zee (Z) is $5 (the exchange rate is $5 = Z1). Then show on your diagram a decline in the demand for zee.

a. Referring to your diagram, discuss the adjustment options the United States would have in maintaining the exchange rate at $5 = Z1 under a fixed-exchange-rate system.

b. How would the U.S. balance-of-payments surplus that is created (by the decline in demand) get resolved under a system of flexible exchange rates?

11. Compare and contrast the Bretton Woods system of exchange rates with that of the gold standard. What caused the collapse of the gold standard? What caused the demise of the Bretton Woods system?

12. Describe what is meant by the term "managed float." Did the managed-float system precede or follow the adjustable-peg system? Explain.

13. What have been the major causes of the large U.S. trade deficits since 1997? What are the major benefits and costs associated with trade deficits? Explain: "A trade deficit means that a nation is receiving more goods and services from abroad than it is sending abroad." How can that be called "unfavorable"?

14. **LAST WORD** Suppose Winter Sports—a hypothetical French retailer of snowboards—wants to order 5000 snowboards made in the United States. The price per board is $200, the present exchange rate is 1 euro = $1, and payment is due in dollars when the boards are delivered in 3 months. Use a numerical example to explain why exchange-rate risk might make the French retailer hesitant to place the order. How might speculators absorb some of Winter Sports' risk?

Web-Based Questions

1. **THE U.S. BALANCE ON GOODS AND SERVICES—WHAT ARE THE LATEST FIGURES?** The U.S. Census Bureau reports the latest data on U.S. trade in goods and services at its Web site, **www.census.gov/indicator/www/ustrade. html.** In the latest month, did the trade balance in goods and services improve (that is, yield a smaller deficit or a larger surplus) or deteriorate? Was the relative trade strength of the United States compared to the rest of the world in goods or in services? Which product groups had the largest increases in exports? Which had the largest increases in imports?

2. **THE YEN-DOLLAR EXCHANGE RATE** The Federal Reserve Board of Governors provides exchange rates for various currencies for the last decade at **www.federalreserve.gov/ releases** (Foreign Exchange Rates; Historical bilateral rates). Has the dollar appreciated, depreciated, or remained constant relative to the Canadian dollar, the European euro, the Japanese yen, the Swedish krona, and the Swiss franc since 2000?

Note: Terms set in *italic* type are defined separately in this glossary.

actual investment The amount that *firms* invest; equal to *planned investment* plus *unplanned investment*.

actual reserves The funds that a bank has on deposit at the *Federal Reserve Bank* of its district (plus its *vault cash*).

adjustable pegs The device used in the *Bretton Woods system* to alter *exchange rates* in an orderly way to eliminate persistent payments deficits and surpluses. Each nation defined its monetary unit in terms of (pegged it to) gold or the dollar, kept the *rate of exchange* for its money stable in the short run, and adjusted its rate in the long run when faced with international payments disequilibrium.

aggregate A collection of specific economic units treated as if they were one. For example, all prices of individual goods and services are combined into a *price level*, or all units of output are aggregated into *gross domestic product*.

aggregate demand A schedule or curve that shows the total quantity of goods and services demanded (purchased) at different *price levels*.

aggregate demand–aggregate supply (AD-AS) model The macroeconomic model that uses *aggregate demand* and *aggregate supply* to determine and explain the *price level* and the real *domestic output*.

aggregate expenditures The total amount spent for final goods and services in an economy.

aggregate expenditures–domestic output approach Determination of the equilibrium *gross domestic product* by finding the real GDP at which *aggregate expenditures* equal *domestic output*.

aggregate expenditures schedule A schedule or curve showing the total amount spent for final goods and services at different levels of *real GDP*.

aggregate supply A schedule or curve showing the total quantity of goods and services supplied (produced) at different *price levels*.

aggregate supply shocks Sudden, large changes in resource costs that shift an economy's aggregate supply curve.

allocative efficiency The apportionment of resources among firms and industries to obtain the production of the products most wanted by society (consumers); the output of each product at which its *marginal cost* and *price* or *marginal benefit* are equal.

anticipated inflation Increases in the price level *(inflation)* that occur at the expected rate.

appreciation (of the dollar) An increase in the value of the dollar relative to the currency of another nation, so a dollar buys a larger amount of the foreign currency and thus of foreign goods.

asset Anything of monetary value owned by a firm or individual.

asset demand for money The amount of *money* people want to hold as a *store of value*; this amount varies inversely with the *interest rate*.

average propensity to consume Fraction (or percentage) of *disposable income* that households plan to spend for consumer goods and services; consumption divided by *disposable income*.

average propensity to save (APS) Fraction (or percentage) of *disposable income* that households save; *saving* divided by *disposable income*.

average tax rate Total tax paid divided by total (taxable) income, as a percentage.

balance of payments (See *international balance of payments*.)

balance-of- payments deficit The amount by which *inpayments* from a nation's stock of *official reserves* are required to balance that nation's *capital and financial account* with its *current account* (in its *balance of payments*).

balance-of- payments surplus The amount by which *outpayments* to a nation's stock of *official reserves* are required to balance that nation's *capital and financial account* with its *current account* (in its *international balance of payments*).

balance on current account The exports of goods and services of a nation less its imports of goods and services plus its *net investment income* and *net transfers* in a year.

balance on goods and services The exports of goods and services of a nation less its imports of goods and services in a year.

balance sheet A statement of the *assets*, *liabilities*, and *net worth* of a firm or individual at some given time.

bank deposits The deposits that individuals or firms have at banks (or thrifts) or that banks have at the *Federal Reserve Banks*.

bankers' bank A bank that accepts the deposits of and makes loans to *depository institutions*; in the United States, a *Federal Reserve Bank*.

bank reserves The deposits of commercial banks and thrifts at *Federal Reserve Banks* plus bank and thrift *vault cash*.

barter The exchange of one good or service for another good or service.

base year The year with which other years are compared when an index is constructed; for example, the base year for a *price index*.

Board of Governors The seven-member group that supervises and controls the money and banking system of the United States; the Board of Governors of the Federal Reserve System; the Federal Reserve Board.

bond A financial device through which a borrower (a firm or government) is obligated to pay the principal and interest on a loan at a specific date in the future.

break-even income The level of *disposable income* at which *households* plan to consume (spend) all their income and to save none of it; also, in an income transfer program, the level of earned income at which subsidy payments become zero.

Bretton Woods system The international monetary system developed after the Second World War in which *adjustable pegs* were employed, the *International Monetary Fund* helped stabilize foreign exchange rates, and gold and the dollar were used as *international monetary reserves*.

budget deficit The amount by which the expenditures of the Federal government exceed its revenues in any year.

budget surplus The amount by which the revenues of the Federal government exceed its expenditures in any year.

built-in stabilizer A mechanism that increases government's budget deficit (or reduces its surplus) during a recession and increases government's budget surplus (or reduces its deficit) during an expansion without any action by policymakers. The tax system is one such mechanism.

Bureau of Economic Analysis (BEA) An agency of the U.S. Department of Commerce that compiles the national income and product accounts.

business cycle Recurring increases and decreases in the level of economic activity over periods of years; consists of peak, recession, trough, and expansion phases.

business firm (See *firm*.)

capital Human-made resources (buildings, machinery, and equipment) used to produce goods and services; goods that do not directly satisfy human wants; also called capital goods.

capital and financial account The section of a nation's *international balance of payments* that records (1) debt forgiveness by and to foreigners and (2) foreign purchases of assets in the United States and U.S. purchases of assets abroad.

capital and financial account deficit A negative balance on its *capital and financial account* in a country's *international balance of payments*.

capital and financial account surplus A positive balance on its *capital and financial account* in a country's *international balance of payments*.

capital gain The gain realized when securities or properties are sold for a price greater than the price paid for them.

capital goods (See *capital*.)

capital-intensive commodity A product that requires a relatively large amount of *capital* to be produced.

capitalism An economic system in which property resources are privately owned and markets and prices are used to direct and coordinate economic activities.

capital stock The total available *capital* in a nation.

cartel A formal agreement among firms (or countries) in an industry to set the price of a product and establish the outputs of the individual firms (or countries) or to divide the market for the product geographically.

causation A relationship in which the occurrence of one or more events brings about another event.

CEA (See *Council of Economic Advisers*.)

central bank A bank whose chief function is the control of the nation's *money supply*; in the United States, the Federal Reserve System.

central economic planning Government determination of the objectives of the economy and how resources will be directed to attain those goals.

***ceteris paribus* assumption** (See *other-things-equal assumption*.)

change in demand A change in the *quantity demanded* of a good or service at every price; a shift of the *demand curve* to the left or right.

change in quantity demanded A change in the amount of a product that consumers are willing and able to purchase because of a change in the product's price.

change in quantity supplied A change in the amount of a product that producers offer for sale because of a change in the product's price.

change in supply A change in the *quantity supplied* of a good or service at every price; a shift of the *supply curve* to the left or right.

checkable deposit Any deposit in a *commercial bank* or *thrift institution* against which a check may be written.

checkable-deposit multiplier (See *monetary multiplier*.)

check clearing The process by which funds are transferred from the checking accounts of the writers of checks to the checking accounts of the recipients of the checks.

checking account A *checkable deposit* in a *commercial bank* or *thrift institution*.

circular flow diagram An illustration showing the flow of resources from *households* to *firms* and of products from firms to households. These flows are accompanied by reverse flows of money from firms to households and from households to firms.

classical economics The macroeconomic generalizations accepted by most economists before the 1930s that led to the conclusion that a capitalistic economy was self-regulating and therefore would usually employ its resources fully.

closed economy An economy that neither exports nor imports goods and services.

coincidence of wants A situation in which the good or service that one trader desires to obtain is the same as that which another trader desires to give up and an item that the second trader wishes to acquire is the same as that which the first trader desires to surrender.

COLA (See *cost-of-living adjustment*.)

command system A method of organizing an economy in which property resources are publicly owned and government uses *central economic planning* to direct and coordinate economic activities; command economy; communism.

commercial bank A firm that engages in the business of banking (accepts deposits, offers checking accounts, and makes loans).

commercial banking system All *commercial banks* and *thrift institutions* as a group.

communism (See *command system*.)

comparative advantage A lower relative opportunity cost than that of another producer or country.

compensation to employees *Wages* and salaries plus wage and salary supplements paid by employers to workers.

competition The presence in a market of independent buyers and sellers competing with one another along with the freedom of buyers and sellers to enter and leave the market.

complementary goods Products and services that are used together. When the price of one falls, the demand for the other increases (and conversely).

conglomerates Firms that produce goods and services in two or more separate industries.

constant opportunity cost An *opportunity cost* that remains the same for each additional unit as a consumer (or society) shifts purchases (production) from one product to another along a straight-line *budget line* (*production possibilities curve*).

consumer goods Products and services that satisfy human wants directly.

Consumer Price Index (CPI) An index that measures the prices of a fixed "market basket" of some 300 goods and services bought by a "typical" consumer.

consumer sovereignty Determination by consumers of the types and quantities of goods and services that will be produced with the scarce resources of the economy; consumers' direction of production through their dollar votes.

consumer surplus The difference between the maximum price a consumer is (or consumers are) willing to pay for an additional unit of a product and its market price; the triangular area below the demand curve and above the market price.

consumption of fixed capital An estimate of the amount of *capital* worn out or used up (consumed) in producing the *gross domestic product*; also called depreciation.

consumption schedule A schedule showing the amounts *households* plan to spend for *consumer goods* at different levels of *disposable income*.

contractionary fiscal policy A decrease in *government purchases* for goods and services, an increase in *net taxes*, or some combination of the two, for the purpose of decreasing *aggregate demand* and thus controlling inflation.

coordination failure A situation in which people do not reach a mutually beneficial outcome because they lack some way to jointly coordinate their actions; a possible cause of macroeconomic instability.

corporate income tax A tax levied on the net income (accounting profit) of corporations.

corporation A legal entity ("person") chartered by a state or the Federal government that is distinct and separate from the individuals who own it.

correlation A systematic and dependable association between two sets of data (two kinds of events); does not necessarily indicate causation.

cost-of-living adjustment (COLA) An automatic increase in the incomes (wages) of workers when inflation occurs; guaranteed by a collective bargaining contract between firms and workers.

cost-push inflation Increases in the price level (inflation) resulting from an increase in resource costs (for example, raw-material prices) and hence in *per-unit production costs*; inflation caused by reductions in *aggregate supply*.

Council of Economic Advisers (CEA) A group of three persons that advises and assists the president of the United States on economic matters (including the preparation of the annual *Economic Report of the President*).

creative destruction The hypothesis that the creation of new products and production methods simultaneously destroys the market power of existing monopolies.

credit An accounting item that increases the value of an asset (such as the foreign money owned by the residents of a nation).

credit union An association of persons who have a common tie (such as being employees of the same firm or members of the same labor union) that sells shares to (accepts deposits from) its members and makes loans to them.

crowding-out effect A rise in interest rates and a resulting decrease in *planned investment* caused by the Federal government's increased borrowing to finance budget deficits and refinance debt.

currency Coins and paper money.

currency appreciation (See *exchange-rate appreciation*.)

currency depreciation (See *exchange-rate depreciation*.)

currency intervention A government's buying and selling of its own currency or foreign currencies to alter international exchange rates.

current account The section in a nation's *international balance of payments* that records its exports and imports of goods and services, its net *investment income*, and its *net transfers*.

cyclical asymmetry The idea that *monetary policy* may be more successful in slowing expansions and controlling *inflation* than in extracting the economy from severe recession.

cyclical deficit A Federal *budget deficit* that is caused by a recession and the consequent decline in tax revenues.

cyclical unemployment A type of *unemployment* caused by insufficient total spending (or by insufficient *aggregate demand*).

debit An accounting item that decreases the value of an asset (such as the foreign money owned by the residents of a nation).

deflating Finding the *real gross domestic product* by decreasing the dollar value of the GDP for a year in which prices were higher than in the *base year*.

deflation A decline in the economy's *price level*.

demand A schedule showing the amounts of a good or service that buyers (or a buyer) wish to purchase at various prices during some time period.

demand curve A curve illustrating *demand*.

demand factor (in growth) The increase in the level of *aggregate demand* that brings about the *economic growth* made possible by an increase in the production potential of the economy.

demand management The use of *fiscal policy* and *monetary policy* to increase or decrease *aggregate demand*.

demand-pull inflation Increases in the price level (inflation) resulting from an excess of demand over output at the existing price level, caused by an increase in *aggregate demand*.

demand schedule (See *demand*.)

dependent variable A variable that changes as a consequence of a change in some other (independent) variable; the "effect" or outcome.

depository institutions Firms that accept deposits of *money* from the public (businesses and persons); *commercial banks, savings and loan associations, mutual savings banks*, and *credit unions*.

depreciation (See *consumption of fixed capital*.)

depreciation (of the dollar) A decrease in the value of the dollar relative to another currency, so a dollar buys a smaller amount of the foreign currency and therefore of foreign goods.

derived demand The demand for a resource that depends on the demand for the products it helps to produce.

determinants of aggregate demand Factors such as consumption spending, *investment*, government spending, and *net exports* that, if they change, shift the aggregate demand curve.

determinants of aggregate supply Factors such as input prices, *productivity*, and the legal-institutional environment that, if they change, shift the aggregate supply curve.

determinants of demand Factors other than price that determine the quantities demanded of a good or service.

determinants of supply Factors other than price that determine the quantities supplied of a good or service.

devaluation A decrease in the governmentally defined value of a currency.

developing countries Many countries of Africa, Asia, and Latin America that are characterized by lack of capital goods, use of nonadvanced technologies, low literacy rates, high unemployment, rapid population growth, and labor forces heavily committed to agriculture.

direct foreign investment The building of new factories (or the purchase of existing capital) in a particular nation by corporations of other nations.

direct relationship The relationship between two variables that change in the same direction, for example, product price and quantity supplied; positive relationship.

discount rate The interest rate that the *Federal Reserve Banks* charge on the loans they make to *commercial banks* and *thrift institutions*.

discouraged workers Employees who have left the *labor force* because they have not been able to find employment.

discretionary fiscal policy Deliberate changes in taxes (tax rates) and government spending by Congress to promote full employment, price stability, and economic growth.

discrimination The practice of according individuals or groups inferior treatment in hiring, occupational access, education and training, promotion, wage rates, or working conditions even though they have the same abilities, education, skills, and work experience as other workers.

disinflation A reduction in the rate of *inflation*.

disposable income (DI) *Personal income* less personal taxes; income available for *personal consumption expenditures* and *personal saving*.

dissaving Spending for consumer goods and services in excess of *disposable income*; the amount by which *personal consumption expenditures* exceed disposable income.

dividends Payments by a corporation of all or part of its profit to its stockholders (the corporate owners).

division of labor The separation of the work required to produce a product into a number of different tasks that are performed by different workers; *specialization* of workers.

Doha Round The latest, uncompleted (as of fall 2006) sequence of trade negotiations by members of the *World Trade Organization*; named after Doha, Qatar, where the set of negotiations began.

dollar votes The "votes" that consumers and entrepreneurs cast for the production of consumer and capital goods, respectively, when they purchase those goods in product and resource markets.

domestic capital formation The process of adding to a nation's stock of *capital* by saving and investing part of its own domestic output.

domestic output *Gross* (or net) *domestic product*; the total output of final goods and services produced in the economy.

domestic price The price of a good or service within a country, determined by domestic demand and supply.

dumping The sale of a product in a foreign country at prices either below cost or below the prices commonly charged at home.

durable good A consumer good with an expected life (use) of 3 or more years.

earnings The money income received by a worker; equal to the *wage* (rate) multiplied by the amount of time worked.

economic cost A payment that must be made to obtain and retain the services of a *resource*; the income a firm must provide to a resource supplier to attract the resource away from an alternative use; equal to the quantity of other products that cannot be produced when resources are instead used to make a particular product.

economic efficiency The use of the minimum necessary resources to obtain the socially optimal amounts of goods and services; entails both *productive efficiency* and *allocative efficiency*.

economic growth (1) An outward shift in the *production possibilities curve* that results from an increase in resource supplies or quality or an improvement in *technology*; (2) an increase of real output *(gross domestic product)* or real output per capita.

economic law An *economic principle* that has been tested and re-tested and has stood the test of time.

economic model A simplified picture of economic reality; an abstract generalization.

economic perspective A viewpoint that envisions individuals and institutions making rational decisions by comparing the marginal benefits and marginal costs associated with their actions.

economic policy A course of action intended to correct or avoid a problem.

economic principle A widely accepted generalization about the economic behavior of individuals or institutions.

economic profit The *total revenue* of a firm less its *economic costs* (which include both *explicit costs* and *implicit costs*); also called "pure profit" and "above-normal profit."

economic resources The *land, labor, capital,* and *entrepreneurial ability* that are used in the production of goods and services; productive agents; factors of production.

economics The social science concerned with how individuals, institutions, and society make optimal (best) choices under conditions of scarcity.

economic system A particular set of institutional arrangements and a coordinating mechanism for solving the economizing problem; a method of organizing an economy, of which the *market system* and the *command system* are the two general types.

economic theory A statement of a cause-effect relationship; when accepted by all or nearly all economists, an *economic principle*.

economies of scale Reductions in the *average total cost* of producing a product as the firm expands the size of plant (its output) in the *long run;* the economies of mass production.

economizing problem The choices necessitated because society's economic wants for goods and services are unlimited but the resources available to satisfy these wants are limited (scarce).

efficiency factors (in growth) The capacity of an economy to combine resources effectively to achieve growth of real output that the *supply factors* (of growth) make possible.

efficiency loss Reductions in combined consumer and producer surplus caused by an underallocation or overallocation of resources to the production of a good or service. Also called deadweight loss.

efficiency wage A wage that minimizes wage costs per unit of output by encouraging greater effort or reducing turnover.

efficient allocation of resources That allocation of an economy's resources among the production of different products that leads to the maximum satisfaction of consumers' wants, thus producing the socially optimal mix of output with society's scarce resources.

electronic payments Purchases made by transferring funds electronically. Examples: Fedwire transfers, automated clearinghouse transactions (ACHs), payments via the PayPal system, and payments made through stored-value cards.

employment rate The percentage of the *labor force* employed at any time.

entrepreneurial ability The human resource that combines the other resources to produce a product, makes nonroutine decisions, innovates, and bears risks.

equation of exchange $MV = PQ$, in which M is the supply of money, V is the *velocity* of money, P is the *price level*, and Q is the physical volume of *final goods and services* produced.

equilibrium GDP (See *equilibrium real domestic output*.)

equilibrium price The *price* in a competitive market at which the *quantity demanded* and the *quantity supplied* are equal, there is neither a shortage nor a surplus, and there is no tendency for price to rise or fall.

equilibrium price level The price level at which the aggregate demand curve intersects the aggregate supply curve.

equilibrium quantity (1) The quantity demanded and supplied at the equilibrium price in a competitive market; (2) the profit-maximizing output of a firm.

equilibrium real domestic output The *gross domestic product* at which the total quantity of final goods and services purchased *(aggregate expenditures)* is equal to the total quantity of final goods and services produced (the real domestic output); the real domestic output at which the aggregate demand curve intersects the aggregate supply curve.

equilibrium real output (See *equilibrium real domestic output*)

euro The common currency unit used by 12 European nations (as of 2006) in the Euro zone, which consists of Austria, Belgium, Finland, France, Germany, Greece, Ireland, Italy, Luxembourg, the Netherlands, Portugal, and Spain.

European Union (EU) An association of 25 European nations that has eliminated tariffs and quotas among them, established common tariffs for imported goods from outside the member nations, eliminated barriers to the free movement of capital, and created other common economic policies.

excess reserves The amount by which a bank's or thrift's *actual reserves* exceed its *required reserves;* actual reserves minus required reserves.

exchange control (See *foreign exchange control*.)

exchange rate The *rate of exchange* of one nation's currency for another nation's currency.

exchange-rate appreciation An increase in the value of a nation's currency in foreign exchange markets; an increase in the *rate of exchange* for foreign currencies.

exchange-rate depreciation A decrease in the value of a nation's currency in foreign exchange markets; a decrease in the *rate of exchange* for foreign currencies.

exchange-rate determinant Any factor other than the *rate of exchange* that determines a currency's demand and supply in the *foreign exchange market*.

excise tax A tax levied on the production of a specific product or on the quantity of the product purchased.

exhaustive expenditure An expenditure by government resulting directly in the employment of *economic resources* and in the absorption by government of the goods and services those resources produce; a *government purchase*.

expansion A phase of the *business cycle* in which *real GDP*, *income*, and employment rise.

expansionary fiscal policy An increase in *government purchases* of goods and services, a decrease in *net taxes*, or some combination of the two for the purpose of increasing *aggregate demand* and expanding real output.

expansionary monetary policy Federal Reserve system actions to increase the *money supply*, lower *interest rates*, and expand *real GDP*; an easy money policy.

expectations The anticipations of consumers, firms, and others about future economic conditions.

expected rate of return The increase in profit a firm anticipates it will obtain by purchasing capital (or engaging in research and development); expressed as a percentage of the total cost of the investment (or R&D) activity.

expenditures approach The method that adds all expenditures made for *final goods and services* to measure the *gross domestic product*.

expenditures-output approach (See *aggregate expenditures–domestic output approach*.)

exports Goods and services produced in a nation and sold to buyers in other nations.

export subsidies Government payments to domestic producers to enable them to reduce the *price* of a good or service to foreign buyers.

export supply curve An upward-sloping curve that shows the amount of a product that domestic firms will export at each *world price* that is above the *domestic price*.

export transaction A sale of a good or service that increases the amount of foreign currency flowing to a nation's citizens, firms, and government.

external benefit (See *positive externality*.)

external cost (See *negative externality*.)

external debt Private or public debt owed to foreign citizens, firms, and institutions.

externality A cost or benefit from production or consumption, accruing without compensation to someone other than the buyers and sellers of the product (see *negative externality* and *positive externality*) .

external public debt The portion of the public debt owed to foreign citizens, firms, and institutions.

face value The dollar or cents value placed on a U.S. coin or piece of paper money.

factors of production *Economic resources: land, capital, labor,* and *entrepreneurial ability.*

fallacy of composition The false notion that what is true for the individual (or part) is necessarily true for the group (or whole).

FDIC (See *Federal Deposit Insurance Corporation*.)

Federal Deposit Insurance Corporation (FDIC) The federally chartered corporation that insures deposit liabilities (up to $100,000 per account) of *commercial banks* and *thrift institutions* (excluding *credit unions*, whose deposits are insured by the *National Credit Union Administration*).

Federal funds rate The interest rate banks and other depository institutions charge one another on overnight loans made out of their *excess reserves*.

Federal government The government of the United States, as distinct from the state and local governments.

Federal Open Market Committee (FOMC) The 12-member group that determines the purchase and sale policies of the *Federal Reserve Banks* in the market for U.S. government securities.

Federal Reserve Banks The 12 banks chartered by the U.S. government to control the *money supply* and perform other functions. (See *central bank, quasi-public bank,* and *bankers' bank*.)

Federal Reserve Note Paper money issued by the *Federal Reserve Banks*.

Federal Reserve System The U.S. central bank, consisting of the *Board of Governors* of the Federal Reserve and the 12 *Federal Reserve Banks*, which controls the lending activity of the nation's banks and thrifts and thus the *money supply*; commonly referred to as the "Fed."

fiat money Anything that is *money* because government has decreed it to be money.

final goods and services Goods and services that have been purchased for final use and not for resale or further processing or manufacturing.

financial capital (See *money capital*.)

financial services industry The broad category of firms that provide financial products and services to help households and businesses earn *interest*, receive *dividends*, obtain *capital gains*, insure against losses, and plan for retirement. The industry includes *commercial banks, thrift institutions*, insurance companies, mutual fund companies, pension funds, and securities firms.

firm An organization that employs resources to produce a good or service for profit and owns and operates one or more *plants*.

fiscal policy Changes in government spending and tax collections designed to achieve a full-employment and noninflationary domestic output; also called *discretionary fiscal policy*.

fixed exchange rate A *rate of exchange* that is set in some way and therefore prevented from rising or falling with changes in currency supply and demand.

flexible exchange rate A *rate of exchange* determined by the international demand for and supply of a nation's money; a rate free to rise or fall (to float).

floating exchange rate (See *flexible exchange rate*.)

foreign competition (See *import competition*.)

foreign exchange control The control a government may exercise over the quantity of foreign currency demanded by its citizens and firms and over the *rates of exchange* in order to limit its *outpayments* to its *inpayments* (to eliminate a *payments deficit*).

foreign exchange market A market in which the money (currency) of one nation can be used to purchase (can be exchanged for) the money of another nation; currency market.

foreign exchange rate (See *rate of exchange*.)

foreign purchase effect The inverse relationship between the *net exports* of an economy and its price level relative to foreign price levels.

45° line A line along which the value of *GDP* (measured horizontally) is equal to the value of *aggregate expenditures* (measured vertically).

fractional reserve banking system A *reserve requirement* that is less than 100 percent of the checkable-deposit liabilities of a *commercial bank* or *thrift institution*.

freedom of choice The freedom of owners of property resources to employ or dispose of them as they see fit, of workers to enter any line of work for which they are qualified, and of consumers to spend their incomes in a manner that they think is appropriate.

freedom of enterprise The freedom of *firms* to obtain economic resources, to use those resources to produce products of the firm's own choosing, and to sell their products in markets of their choice.

free-rider problem The inability of potential providers of an economically desirable good or service to obtain payment from those who benefit, because of *nonexcludability*.

free trade The absence of artificial (government-imposed) barriers to trade among individuals and firms in different nations.

frictional unemployment A type of unemployment caused by workers voluntarily changing jobs and by temporary layoffs; unemployed workers between jobs.

full employment (1) The use of all available resources to produce want-satisfying goods and services; (2) the situation in which the *unemployment rate* is equal to the *full-employment unemployment rate* and there is *frictional* and *structural* but no *cyclical unemployment* (and the *real GDP* of the economy equals *potential output*).

full-employment unemployment rate The *unemployment rate* at which there is no *cyclical unemployment* of the *labor force*; equal to between 4 and 5 percent in the United States because some *frictional* and *structural unemployment* is unavoidable.

functional distribution of income The manner in which *national income* is divided among the functions performed to earn it (or the kinds of resources provided to earn it); the division of national income into wages and salaries, proprietors' income, corporate profits, interest, and rent.

gains from trade The extra output that trading partners obtain through specialization of production and exchange of goods and services.

GDP (See *gross domestic product*.)

GDP gap Actual *gross domestic product* minus potential output; may be either a positive amount (a *positive GDP gap*) or a negative amount (a *negative GDP gap*).

GDP price index A *price index* for all the goods and services that make up the *gross domestic product*; the price index used to adjust *nominal gross domestic product* to *real gross domestic product*.

G8 nations A group of eight major nations (Canada, France, Germany, Italy, Japan, Russia, United Kingdom, and United States) whose leaders meet regularly to discuss common economic problems and try to coordinate economic policies.

General Agreement on Tariffs and Trade (GATT) The international agreement reached in 1947 in which 23 nations agreed to give equal and nondiscriminatory treatment to one another, to reduce tariff rates by multinational negotiations, and to eliminate *import quotas*. It now includes most nations and has become the *World Trade Organization*.

generalization Statement of the nature of the relationship between two or more sets of facts.

gold standard A historical system of fixed exchange rates in which nations defined their currencies in terms of gold, maintained a fixed relationship between their stocks of gold and their money supplies, and allowed gold to be freely exported and imported.

government purchases (G) Expenditures by government for goods and services that government consumes in providing public goods and for public (or social) capital that has a long lifetime; the expenditures of all governments in the economy for those *final goods and services*.

government transfer payment The disbursement of money (or goods and services) by government for which government receives no currently produced good or service in return.

gross domestic product (GDP) The total market value of all *final goods and services* produced annually within the boundaries of the United States, whether by U.S.- or foreign-supplied resources.

gross private domestic investment (Ig) Expenditures for newly produced *capital goods* (such as machinery, equipment, tools, and buildings) and for additions to inventories.

growth accounting The bookkeeping of the supply-side elements such as productivity and labor inputs that contribute to changes in *real GDP* over some specific time period.

guiding function of prices The ability of price changes to bring about changes in the quantities of products and resources demanded and supplied.

horizontal axis The "left-right" or "west-east" measurement line on graph or grid.

household An economic unit (of one or more persons) that provides the economy with resources and uses the income received to purchase goods and services that satisfy economic wants.

human capital The knowledge and skills that make a person productive.

human capital investment Any expenditure undertaken to improve the education, skills, health, or mobility of workers, with an expectation of greater productivity and thus a positive return on the investment.

hyperinflation A very rapid rise in the price level; an extremely high rate of inflation.

hypothesis A tentative explanation of cause and effect that requires testing.

IMF (See *International Monetary Fund*.)

import competition The competition that domestic firms encounter from the products and services of foreign producers.

import demand curve A downsloping curve showing the amount of a product that an economy will import at each *world price* below the *domestic price*.

import quota A limit imposed by a nation on the quantity (or total value) of a good that may be imported during some period of time.

imports Spending by individuals, *firms*, and governments for goods and services produced in foreign nations.

import transaction The purchase of a good or service that decreases the amount of foreign money held by citizens, firms, and governments of a nation.

income A flow of dollars (or purchasing power) per unit of time derived from the use of human or property resources.

income approach The method that adds all the income generated by the production of *final goods and services* to measure the *gross domestic product*.

income effect A change in the quantity demanded of a product that results from the change in *real income (purchasing power)* caused by a change in the product's price.

income inequality The unequal distribution of an economy's total income among households or families.

increase in demand An increase in the *quantity demanded* of a good or service at every price; a shift of the *demand curve* to the right.

increase in supply An increase in the *quantity supplied* of a good or service at every price; a shift of the *supply curve* to the right.

increasing returns An increase in a firm's output by a larger percentage than the percentage increase in its inputs.

independent goods Products or services for which there is little or no relationship between the price of one and the demand for the other. When the price of one rises or falls, the demand for the other tends to remain constant.

independent variable The variable causing a change in some other (dependent) variable.

individual demand The demand schedule or *demand curve* of a single buyer.

individual supply The supply schedule or *supply curve* of a single seller.

industrially advanced countries High-income countries such as the United States, Canada, Japan, and the nations of western Europe that have highly developed *market economies* based on large stocks of technologically advanced capital goods and skilled labor forces.

industry A group of (one or more) *firms* that produce identical or similar products.

inferior good A good or service whose consumption declines as income rises (and conversely), price remaining constant.

inflating Determining *real gross domestic product* by increasing the dollar value of the *nominal gross domestic product* produced in a year in which prices are lower than those in a *base year*.

inflation A rise in the general level of prices in an economy.

inflationary expectations The belief of workers, firms, and consumers that substantial inflation will occur in the future.

inflationary expenditure gap The amount by which the *aggregate expenditures schedule* must shift downward to decrease the *nominal GDP* to its full-employment noninflationary level.

inflation premium The component of the *nominal interest rate* that reflects anticipated inflation.

inflation targeting The annual statement by a *central bank* of a goal for a specific range of inflation in a future year, coupled with monetary policy designed to achieve the goal.

information technology New and more efficient methods of delivering and receiving information through use of computers, fax machines, wireless phones, and the Internet.

infrastructure The capital goods usually provided by the *public sector* for the use of its citizens and firms (for example, highways, bridges, transit systems, wastewater treatment facilities, municipal water systems, and airports).

injection An addition of spending to the income-expenditure stream: *investment, government purchases*, and *net exports*.

innovation The first commercially successful introduction of a new product, the use of a new method of production, or the creation of a new form of business organization.

inpayments The receipts of domestic or foreign money that individuals, firms, and governments of one nation obtain from the sale of goods and services abroad, as investment income and remittances, and from foreign purchases of its assets.

insider-outsider theory The hypothesis that nominal wages are inflexible downward because firms are aware that workers ("insiders") who retain employment during recession may refuse to work cooperatively with previously unemployed workers ("outsiders") who offer to work for less than the current wage.

interest The payment made for the use of money (of borrowed funds).

interest income Payments of income to those who supply the economy with *capital*.

interest rate The annual rate at which interest is paid; a percentage of the borrowed amount.

interest-rate effect The tendency for increases in the *price level* to increase the demand for money, raise interest rates, and, as a result, reduce total spending and real output in the economy (and the reverse for price-level decreases).

intermediate goods Products that are purchased for resale or further processing or manufacturing.

internally held public debt *Public debt* owed to citizens, firms, and institutions of the same nation that issued the debt.

international balance of payments A summary of all the transactions that took place between the individuals, firms, and government units of one nation and those of all other nations during a year.

international balance-of-payments deficit (See *balance-of-payments deficit*.)

international balance-of-payments surplus (See *balance-of-payments surplus*.)

international gold standard (See *gold standard*.)

International Monetary Fund (IMF) The international association of nations that was formed after the Second World War to make loans of foreign monies to nations with temporary *payments deficits* and, until the early 1970s, to administer the *adjustable pegs*. It now mainly makes loans to nations facing possible defaults on private and government loans.

international monetary reserves The foreign currencies and other assets such as gold that a nation can use to settle a *balance-of-payments deficit*.

international value of the dollar The price that must be paid in foreign currency (money) to obtain one U.S. dollar.

intrinsic value The market value of the metal within a coin.

inventories Goods that have been produced but remain unsold.

inverse relationship The relationship between two variables that change in opposite directions, for example, product price and quantity demanded; negative relationship.

investment Spending for the production and accumulation of *capital* and additions to inventories.

investment demand curve A curve that shows the amounts of *investment* demanded by an economy at a series of *real interest rates*.

investment goods Same as *capital* or capital goods.

investment in human capital (See *human capital investment*.)

investment schedule A curve or schedule that shows the amounts firms plan to invest at various possible values of *real gross domestic product*.

"invisible hand" The tendency of firms and resource suppliers that seek to further their own self-interests in competitive markets to also promote the interest of society.

Joint Economic Committee (JEC) Committee of senators and representatives that investigates economic problems of national interest.

Keynesian economics The macroeconomic generalizations that lead to the conclusion that a capitalistic economy is characterized by macroeconomic instability and that *fiscal policy* and *monetary policy* can be used to promote *full employment*, *price-level stability*, and *economic growth*.

Keynesianism The philosophical, ideological, and analytical views pertaining to *Keynesian economics*.

labor People's physical and mental talents and efforts that are used to help produce goods and services.

labor force Persons 16 years of age and older who are not in institutions and who are employed or are unemployed and seeking work.

labor-force participation rate The percentage of the working-age population that is actually in the *labor force*.

labor-intensive commodity A product requiring a relatively large amount of *labor* to be produced.

labor market discrimination (See *discrimination*.)

labor productivity Total output divided by the quantity of labor employed to produce it; the *average product* of labor or output per hour of work.

labor union A group of workers organized to advance the interests of the group (to increase wages, shorten the hours worked, improve working conditions, and so on).

Laffer Curve A curve relating government tax rates and tax revenues and on which a particular tax rate (between zero and 100 percent) maximizes tax revenues.

laissez-faire capitalism (See *capitalism*.)

land Natural resources ("free gifts of nature") used to produce goods and services.

land-intensive commodity A product requiring a relatively large amount of *land* to be produced.

law of demand The principle that, other things equal, an increase in a product's price will reduce the quantity of it demanded, and conversely for a decrease in price.

law of increasing opportunity costs The principle that as the production of a good increases, the *opportunity cost* of producing an additional unit rises.

law of supply The principle that, other things equal, an increase in the price of a product will increase the quantity of it supplied, and conversely for a price decrease.

leakage (1) A withdrawal of potential spending from the income-expenditures stream via *saving*, tax payments, or *imports*; (2) a withdrawal that reduces the lending potential of the banking system.

learning by doing Achieving greater *productivity* and lower *average total cost* through gains in knowledge and skill that accompany repetition of a task; a source of *economies of scale*.

legal tender A legal designation of a nation's official currency (bills and coins). Payment of debts must be accepted in this monetary unit, but creditors can specify the form of payment, for example, "cash only" or "check or credit card only."

lending potential of an individual commercial bank The amount by which a single bank can safely increase the *money supply* by making new loans to (or buying securities from) the public; equal to the bank's excess reserves.

lending potential of the banking system The amount by which the banking system can increase the *money supply* by making new loans to (or buying securities from) the public; equal to the *excess reserves* of the banking system multiplied by the *monetary multiplier*.

liability A debt with a monetary value; an amount owed by a firm or an individual.

limited liability Restriction of the maximum loss to a predetermined amount for the owners (stockholders) of a *corporation*. The maximum loss is the amount they paid for their shares of stock.

liquidity The ease with which an asset can be converted quickly into cash with little or no loss of purchasing power. Money is said to be perfectly liquid, whereas other assets have a lesser degree of liquidity.

long run (1) In *microeconomics*, a period of time long enough to enable producers of a product to change the quantities of all the resources they employ; period in which all resources and costs are variable and no resources or costs are fixed. (2) In *macroeconomics*, a period sufficiently long for *nominal wages* and other input prices to change in response to a change in the nation's *price level*.

long-run aggregate supply curve The aggregate supply curve associated with a time period in which input prices (especially *nominal wages*) are fully responsive to changes in the *price level*.

long-run vertical Phillips Curve The *Phillips Curve* after all nominal wages have adjusted to changes in the rate of inflation; a line emanating straight upward at the economy's *natural rate of unemployment*.

lump-sum tax A tax that is a constant amount (the tax revenue of government is the same) at all levels of GDP.

M1 The most narrowly defined *money supply*, equal to *currency* in the hands of the public and the *checkable deposits* of commercial banks and thrift institutions.

M2 A more broadly defined *money supply*, equal to *M1* plus *noncheckable savings accounts* (including *money market deposit accounts*), small *time deposits* (deposits of less than $100,000), and individual *money market mutual fund* balances.

macroeconomics The part of economics concerned with the economy as a whole; with such major aggregates as the household, business, and government sectors; and with measures of the total economy.

managed floating exchange rate An *exchange rate* that is allowed to change (float) as a result of changes in currency supply and demand but at times is altered (managed) by governments via their buying and selling of particular currencies.

marginal analysis The comparison of marginal ("extra" or "additional") benefits and marginal costs, usually for decision making.

marginal benefit The extra (additional) benefit of consuming 1 more unit of some good or service; the change in total benefit when 1 more unit is consumed.

marginal cost (MC) The extra (additional) cost of producing 1 more unit of output; equal to the change in *total cost* divided by the change in output (and, in the short run, to the change in total *variable cost* divided by the change in output).

marginal propensity to consume (MPC) The fraction of any change in *disposable income* spent for *consumer goods*; equal to the change in consumption divided by the change in disposable income.

marginal propensity to save (MPS) The fraction of any change in *disposable income* that households save; equal to the change in *saving* divided by the change in disposable income.

marginal tax rate The tax rate paid on each additional dollar of income.

marginal utility The extra *utility* a consumer obtains from the consumption of 1 additional unit of a good or service; equal to the change in total utility divided by the change in the quantity consumed.

market Any institution or mechanism that brings together buyers (demanders) and sellers (suppliers) of a particular good or service.

market demand (See *total demand*.)

market economy An economy in which the private decisions of consumers, resource suppliers, and firms determine how resources are allocated; the *market system*.

market failure The inability of a market to bring about the allocation of resources that best satisfies the wants of society; in particular, the overallocation or underallocation of resources to the production of a particular good or service because of *externalities* or informational problems or because markets do not provide desired *public goods*.

market system All the product and resource markets of a *market economy* and the relationships among them; a method that allows the prices determined in those markets to allocate the economy's scarce resources and to communicate and coordinate the decisions made by consumers, firms, and resource suppliers.

Medicaid A Federal program that helps finance the medical expenses of individuals covered by the *Supplemental Security Income (SSI)* and *Temporary Assistance for Needy Families (TANF)* programs.

Medicare A Federal program that is financed by *payroll taxes* and provides for (1) compulsory hospital insurance for senior citizens, (2) low-cost voluntary insurance to help older Americans pay physicians' fees, and (3) subsidized insurance to buy prescription drugs.

medium of exchange Any item sellers generally accept and buyers generally use to pay for a good or service; *money;* a convenient means of exchanging goods and services without engaging in *barter*.

menu costs The reluctance of firms to cut prices during recessions (that they think will be short lived) because of the costs of altering and communicating their price reductions; named after the cost associated with printing new menus at restaurants.

microeconomics The part of economics concerned with decision making by individual units such as a *household*, a *firm*, or an *industry* and with individual markets, specific goods and services, and product and resource prices.

minimum wage The lowest *wage* that employers may legally pay for an hour of work.

monetarism The macroeconomic view that the main cause of changes in aggregate output and price level is fluctuations in the *money supply;* espoused by advocates of a *monetary rule.*

monetary multiplier The multiple of its *excess reserves* by which the banking system can expand *checkable deposits* and thus the *money supply* by making new loans (or buying securities); equal to 1 divided by the *reserve requirement.*

monetary policy A central bank's changing of the *money supply* to influence interest rates and assist the economy in achieving price stability, full employment, and economic growth.

monetary rule The rule suggested by *monetarism.* As traditionally formulated, the rule says that the *money supply* should be expanded each year at the same annual rate as the potential rate of growth of the *real gross domestic product;* the supply of money should be increased steadily between 3 and 5 percent per year. (Also see *Taylor rule.*)

money Any item that is generally acceptable to sellers in exchange for goods and services.

money capital Money available to purchase *capital;* simply *money,* as defined by economists.

money income (See *nominal income.*)

money market The market in which the demand for and the supply of money determine the *interest rate* (or the level of interest rates) in the economy.

money market deposit accounts (MMDAs) Bank- and thrift-provided interest-bearing accounts that contain a variety of short-term securities; such accounts have minimum balance requirements and limits on the frequency of withdrawals.

money market mutual funds (MMMFs) Interest-bearing accounts offered by investment companies, which pool depositors' funds for the purchase of short-term securities. Depositors can write checks in minimum amounts or more against their accounts.

money supply Narrowly defined, *M*1; more broadly defined, *M*2 and *MZM.* (See each.)

monopoly A market structure in which the number of sellers is so small that each seller is able to influence the total supply and the price of the good or service. (Also see *pure monopoly.*)

most-favored-nation (MFN) status An agreement by the United States to allow some other nation's *exports* into the United States at the lowest tariff level levied by the United States.

multinational corporations Firms that own production facilities in two or more countries and produce and sell their products globally.

multiple counting Wrongly including the value of *intermediate goods* in the *gross domestic product;* counting the same good or service more than once.

multiplier The ratio of a change in the equilibrium GDP to the change in *investment* or in any other component of *aggregate expenditures* or *aggregate demand;* the number by which a change in

any such component must be multiplied to find the resulting change in the equilibrium GDP.

multiplier effect The effect on equilibrium GDP of a change in *aggregate expenditures* or *aggregate demand* (caused by a change in the *consumption schedule, investment,* government expenditures, or *net exports*).

MZM A definition of the *money supply* that includes monetary balances immediately available at zero cost to households and businesses for making transactions. *MZM* (money zero maturity) equals *M*2 minus small *time deposits* plus *money market mutual fund* balances owned by businesses.

national bank A *commercial bank* authorized to operate by the U.S. government.

National Credit Union Administration (NCUA) The federally chartered agency that insures deposit liabilities (up to $100,000 per account) in *credit unions.*

national income Total income earned by resource suppliers for their contributions to *gross domestic product* plus *taxes on production and imports;* the sum of wages and salaries, *rent, interest, profit, proprietors' income,* and such taxes.

national income accounting The techniques used to measure the overall production of the economy and other related variables for the nation as a whole.

natural monopoly An industry in which *economies of scale* are so great that a single firm can produce the product at a lower average total cost than would be possible if more than one firm produced the product.

natural rate of unemployment (NRU) The *full-employment unemployment rate;* the unemployment rate occurring when there is no cyclical unemployment and the economy is achieving its potential output; the unemployment rate at which actual inflation equals expected inflation.

near-money Financial assets, the most important of which are *noncheckable savings accounts, time deposits,* and U.S. short-term securities and savings bonds, which are not a medium of exchange but can be readily converted into money.

negative externality A cost imposed without compensation on third parties by the production or consumption of sellers or buyers. Example: A manufacturer dumps toxic chemicals into a river, killing the fish sought by sports fishers; an external cost or a spillover cost.

negative GDP gap A situation in which actual *gross domestic product* is less than *potential output.*

negative relationship (See *inverse relationship.*)

net domestic product *Gross domestic product* less the part of the year's output that is needed to replace the *capital goods* worn out in producing the output; the nation's total output available for consumption or additions to the *capital stock.*

net exports (X_n) *Exports* minus *imports.*

net foreign factor income Receipts of resource income from the rest of the world minus payments of resource income to the rest of the world.

net investment income The interest and dividend income received by the residents of a nation from residents of other nations less the interest and dividend payments made by the residents of that nation to the residents of other nations.

net private domestic investment *Gross private domestic investment* less *consumption of fixed capital;* the addition to the nation's stock of *capital* during a year.

net taxes The taxes collected by government less *government transfer payments.*

net transfers The personal and government transfer payments made by one nation to residents of foreign nations less the personal and government transfer payments received from residents of foreign nations.

network effects Increases in the value of a product to each user, including existing users, as the total number of users rises.

net worth The total *assets* less the total *liabilities* of a firm or an individual; for a firm, the claims of the owners against the firm's total assets; for an individual, his or her wealth.

new classical economics The theory that, although unanticipated price-level changes may create macroeconomic instability in the short run, the economy is stable at the full-employment level of domestic output in the long run because prices and wages adjust automatically to correct movements away from the full-employment, noninflationary output.

New Economy The label attached by some economists and the popular press to the U.S. economy since 1995. The main characteristics are accelerated *productivity growth* and *economic growth,* caused by rapid technological advance and the emergence of the global economy.

nominal gross domestic product (GDP) The *GDP* measured in terms of the price level at the time of measurement (unadjusted for *inflation*).

nominal income The number of dollars received by an individual or group for its resources during some period of time.

nominal interest rate The interest rate expressed in terms of annual amounts currently charged for interest and not adjusted for inflation.

nominal wage The amount of money received by a worker per unit of time (hour, day, etc.); money wage.

nondiscretionary fiscal policy (See *built-in stabilizer.*)

nondurable good A *consumer good* with an expected life (use) of less than 3 years.

nonexcludability The inability to keep nonpayers (free riders) from obtaining benefits from a certain good; a *public good* characteristic.

nonexhaustive expenditure An expenditure by government that does not result directly in the employment of economic resources or the production of goods and services; see *government transfer payment.*

nonincome determinants of consumption and saving All influences on consumption and saving other than the level of *GDP.*

noninterest determinants of investment All influences on the level of investment spending other than the *interest rate.*

noninvestment transaction An expenditure for stocks, bonds, or secondhand *capital goods.*

nonmarket transactions The production of goods and services excluded in the measurement of the *gross domestic product* because they are not bought and sold.

nonproduction transaction The purchase and sale of any item that is not a currently produced good or service.

nonrivalry The idea that one person's benefit from a certain good does not reduce the benefit available to others; a *public good* characteristic.

nontariff barriers (NTBs) All barriers other than *protective tariffs* that nations erect to impede international trade, including *import quotas,* licensing requirements, unreasonable product-quality standards, unnecessary bureaucratic detail in customs procedures, and so on.

normal good A good or service whose consumption increases when income increases and falls when income decreases, price remaining constant.

normal profit The payment made by a firm to obtain and retain *entrepreneurial ability;* the minimum income entrepreneurial ability must receive to induce it to perform entrepreneurial functions for a firm.

normative economics The part of economics involving value judgments about what the economy should be like; focused on which economic goals and policies should be implemented; policy economics.

North American Free Trade Agreement (NAFTA) A 1993 agreement establishing, over a 15-year period, a free-trade zone composed of Canada, Mexico, and the United States.

official reserves Foreign currencies owned by the central bank of a nation.

offshoring The practice of shifting work previously done by American workers to workers located abroad.

Okun's law The generalization that any 1-percentage-point rise in the *unemployment rate* above the *full-employment unemployment rate* will increase the GDP gap by 2 percent of the *potential output* (GDP) of the economy.

OPEC (See *Organization of Petroleum Exporting Countries.*)

open economy An economy that exports and imports goods and services.

open-market operations The buying and selling of U.S. government securities by the *Federal Reserve Banks* for purposes of carrying out *monetary policy.*

opportunity cost The amount of other products that must be forgone or sacrificed to produce a unit of a product.

opportunity-cost ratio An equivalency showing the number of units of two products that can be produced with the same resources; the cost 1 corn $\equiv$ 3 olives show that the resources required to produce 3 units of olives must be shifted to corn production to produce 1 unit of corn.

Organization of Petroleum Exporting Countries (OPEC) A cartel of 11 oil-producing countries (Algeria, Indonesia, Iran, Iraq, Kuwait, Libya, Nigeria, Qatar, Saudi Arabia, Venezuela, and the UAE) that controls the quantity and price of crude oil exported by its members and that accounts for a large percentage of the world's export of oil.

other-things-equal assumption The assumption that factors other than those being considered are held constant; *ceteris paribus* assumption.

outpayments The expenditures of domestic or foreign currency that the individuals, firms, and governments of one nation make to purchase goods and services, for remittances, to pay investment income, and for purchases of foreign assets.

paper money Pieces of paper used as a *medium of exchange;* in the United States, *Federal Reserve Notes.*

partnership An unincorporated firm owned and operated by two or more persons.

patent An exclusive right given to inventors to produce and sell a new product or machine for 20 years from the time of patent application.

payments deficit (See *balance-of-payments deficit*.)

payments surplus (See *balance-of-payments surplus*.)

payroll tax A tax levied on employers of labor equal to a percentage of all or part of the wages and salaries paid by them and on employees equal to a percentage of all or part of the wages and salaries received by them.

peak The point in a business cycle at which business activity has reached a temporary maximum; the economy is near or at full employment and the level of real output is at or very close to the economy's capacity.

per capita GDP *Gross domestic product* (GDP) per person; the average GDP of a population.

per capita income A nation's total income per person; the average income of a population.

personal consumption expenditures The expenditures of *households* for *durable* and *nondurable consumer goods* and *services.*

personal distribution of income The manner in which the economy's *personal* or *disposable income* is divided among different income classes or different households or families.

personal income (PI) The earned and unearned income available to resource suppliers and others before the payment of personal taxes.

personal income tax A tax levied on the taxable income of individuals, households, and unincorporated firms.

personal saving The *personal income* of households less personal taxes and *personal consumption expenditures; disposable income* not spent for *consumer goods.*

per-unit production cost The average production cost of a particular level of output; total input cost divided by units of output.

Phillips Curve A curve showing the relationship between the *unemployment rate* (on the horizontal axis) and the annual rate of increase in the *price level* (on the vertical axis).

planned investment The amount that *firms* plan or intend to invest.

plant A physical establishment that performs one or more functions in the production, fabrication, and distribution of goods and services.

policy economics The formulation of courses of action to bring about desired economic outcomes or to prevent undesired occurrences.

political business cycle The alleged tendency of Congress to destabilize the economy by reducing taxes and increasing government expenditures before elections and to raise taxes and lower expenditures after elections.

positive economics The analysis of facts or data to establish scientific generalizations about economic behavior.

positive externality A benefit obtained without compensation by third parties from the production or consumption of sellers or buyers. Example: A beekeeper benefits when a neighboring farmer plants clover. An *external benefit* or a spillover benefit.

positive GDP gap A situation in which actual *gross domestic product* exceeds *potential output.*

positive relationship (See *direct relationship*.)

***post hoc, ergo propter hoc* fallacy** The false belief that when one event precedes another, the first event must have caused the second event.

potential output The real output *(GDP)* an economy can produce when it fully employs its available resources.

poverty A situation in which the basic needs of an individual or family exceed the means to satisfy them.

poverty rate The percentage of the population with incomes below the official poverty income levels that are established by the Federal government.

price The amount of money needed to buy a particular good, service, or resource.

price index An index number that shows how the weighted-average price of a "market basket" of goods changes over time.

price level The weighted average of the prices of all the final goods and services produced in an economy.

price-level stability A steadiness of the price level from one period to the next; zero or low annual inflation; also called "price stability."

price-level surprises Unanticipated changes in the price level.

price war Successive and continued decreases in the prices charged by firms in an oligopolistic industry. Each firm lowers its price below rivals' prices, hoping to increase its sales and revenues at its rivals' expense.

prime interest rate The benchmark *interest rate* that banks use as a reference point for a wide range of loans to businesses and individuals.

principal-agent problem A conflict of interest that occurs when agents (workers or managers) pursue their own objectives to the detriment of the principals' (stockholders') goals.

private good A good or service that is individually consumed and that can be profitably provided by privately owned firms because they can exclude nonpayers from receiving the benefits.

private property The right of private persons and firms to obtain, own, control, employ, dispose of, and bequeath *land, capital,* and other property.

private sector The *households* and business *firms* of the economy.

producer surplus The difference between the actual price a producer receives (or producers receive) and the minimum acceptable price; the triangular area above the supply curve and below the market price.

production possibilities curve A curve showing the different combinations of two goods or services that can be produced in a *full-employment, full-production* economy where the available supplies of resources and technology are fixed.

productive efficiency The production of a good in the least costly way; occurs when production takes place at the output at which *average total cost* is a minimum and *marginal product* per dollar's worth of input is the same for all inputs.

productivity A measure of average output or real output per unit of input. For example, the productivity of labor is determined by dividing real output by hours of work.

productivity growth The percentage increase in *productivity* from one period to another.

product market A market in which products are sold by *firms* and bought by *households.*

profit The return to the resource *entrepreneurial ability* (see *normal profit*); *total revenue* minus *total cost* (see *economic profit*).

progressive tax A tax whose *average tax rate* increases as the taxpayer's income increases and decreases as the taxpayer's income decreases.

property tax A tax on the value of property (*capital, land, stocks* and *bonds,* and other *assets*) owned by *firms* and *households.*

proportional tax A tax whose *average tax rate* remains constant as the taxpayer's income increases or decreases.

protective tariff A *tariff* designed to shield domestic producers of a good or service from the competition of foreign producers.

public debt The total amount owed by the Federal government to the owners of government securities; equal to the sum of past government *budget deficits* less government *budget surpluses.*

public good A good or service that is characterized by *nonrivalry* and *nonexcludability;* a good or service with these characteristics provided by government.

public investments Government expenditures on public capital (such as roads, highways, bridges, mass-transit systems, and electric power facilities) and on *human capital* (such as education, training, and health).

public sector The part of the economy that contains all government entities; government.

purchasing power The amount of goods and services that a monetary unit of income can buy.

purchasing power parity The idea that exchange rates between nations equate the purchasing power of various currencies. Exchange rates between any two nations adjust to reflect the price-level differences between the countries.

pure rate of interest An essentially risk-free, long-term interest rate that is free of the influence of market imperfections.

quantity demanded The amount of a good or service that buyers (or a buyer) desire to purchase at a particular price during some period.

quantity supplied The amount of a good or service that producers (or a producer) offer to sell at a particular price during some period.

quasi-public bank A bank that is privately owned but governmentally (publicly) controlled; each of the U.S. *Federal Reserve Banks.*

quasi-public good A good or service to which excludability could apply but that has such a large *positive externality* that government sponsors its production to prevent an underallocation of resources.

R&D Research and development activities undertaken to bring about *technological advance.*

rate of exchange The price paid in one's own money to acquire 1 unit of a foreign currency; the rate at which the money of one nation is exchanged for the money of another nation.

rate of return The gain in net revenue divided by the cost of an investment or an *R&D* expenditure; expressed as a percentage.

rational behavior Human behavior based on comparison of marginal costs and marginal benefits; behavior designed to maximize total utility.

rational expectations theory The hypothesis that firms and households expect monetary and fiscal policies to have certain effects on the economy and (in pursuit of their own self-interests) take actions that make these policies ineffective.

rationing function of prices The ability of market forces in competitive markets to equalize *quantity demanded* and *quantity supplied* and to eliminate shortages and surpluses via changes in prices.

real-balances effect The tendency for increases in the *price level* to lower the real value (or purchasing power) of financial assets with fixed money value and, as a result, to reduce total spending and real output, and conversely for decreases in the price level.

real-business-cycle theory A theory that *business cycles* result from changes in technology and resource availability, which affect *productivity* and thus increase or decrease long-run aggregate supply.

real capital (See *capital.*)

real GDP (See *real gross domestic product.*)

real GDP per capita *Inflation*-adjusted output per person; *real GDP*/population.

real gross domestic product (GDP) *Gross domestic product* adjusted for inflation; gross domestic product in a year divided by the GDP *price index* for that year, the index expressed as a decimal.

real income The amount of goods and services that can be purchased with *nominal income* during some period of time; nominal income adjusted for inflation.

real interest rate The interest rate expressed in dollars of constant value (adjusted for *inflation*) and equal to the *nominal interest rate* less the expected rate of inflation.

real wage The amount of goods and services a worker can purchase with his or her *nominal wage*; the purchasing power of the nominal wage.

recession A period of declining real GDP, accompanied by lower real income and higher unemployment.

recessionary expenditure gap The amount by which the *aggregate expenditures schedule* must shift upward to increase the real *GDP* to its full-employment, noninflationary level.

Reciprocal Trade Agreements Act A 1934 Federal law that authorized the president to negotiate up to 50 percent lower tariffs with foreign nations that agreed to reduce their tariffs on U.S. goods. (Such agreements incorporated the *most-favored-nation* clause.)

refinancing the public debt Paying owners of maturing government securities with money obtained by selling new securities or with new securities.

regressive tax A tax whose *average tax rate* decreases as the taxpayer's income increases and increases as the taxpayer's income decreases.

rental income The payments (income) received by those who supply *land* to the economy.

required reserves The funds that banks and thrifts must deposit with the *Federal Reserve Bank* (or hold as *vault cash*) to meet the legal *reserve requirement*; a fixed percentage of the bank's or thrift's checkable deposits.

reserve requirement The specified minimum percentage of its checkable deposits that a bank or thrift must keep on deposit at the Federal Reserve Bank in its district or hold as *vault cash*.

resource A natural, human, or manufactured item that helps produce goods and services; a productive agent or factor of production.

resource market A market in which *households* sell and *firms* buy resources or the services of resources.

restrictive monetary policy Federal Reserve system actions to reduce the *money supply*, increase *interest rates*, and reduce *inflation*; a tight money policy.

revenue tariff A *tariff* designed to produce income for the Federal government.

rule of 70 A method for determining the number of years it will take for some measure to double, given its annual percentage increase. Example: To determine the number of years it will take for the *price level* to double, divide 70 by the annual rate of *inflation*.

sales tax A tax levied on the cost (at retail) of a broad group of products.

saving Disposable income not spent for consumer goods; equal to *disposable income* minus *personal consumption expenditures*.

savings account A deposit in a *commercial bank* or *thrift institution* on which interest payments are received; generally used for saving rather than daily transactions; a component of the *M2* money supply.

savings and loan association (S&L) A firm that accepts deposits primarily from small individual savers and lends primarily to individuals to finance purchases such as autos and homes; now nearly indistinguishable from a *commercial bank*.

saving schedule A schedule that shows the amounts *households* plan to save (plan not to spend for *consumer goods*), at different levels of *disposable income*.

savings deposit A deposit that is interest-bearing and that the depositor can normally withdraw at any time.

savings institution (See *thrift institution*.)

Say's law The largely discredited macroeconomic generalization that the production of goods and services (supply) creates an equal *demand* for those goods and services.

scarce resources The limited quantities of *land*, *capital*, *labor*, and *entrepreneurial ability* that are never sufficient to satisfy people's virtually unlimited economic wants.

scientific method The procedure for the systematic pursuit of knowledge involving the observation of facts and the formulation and testing of hypotheses to obtain theories, principles, and laws.

seasonal variations Increases and decreases in the level of economic activity within a single year, caused by a change in the season.

secular trend A long-term tendency; a change in some variable over a very long period of years.

self-interest That which each firm, property owner, worker, and consumer believes is best for itself and seeks to obtain.

seniority The length of time a worker has been employed absolutely or relative to other workers; may be used to determine which workers will be laid off when there is insufficient work for them all and who will be rehired when more work becomes available.

separation of ownership and control The fact that different groups of people own a *corporation* (the stockholders) and manage it (the directors and officers).

service An (intangible) act or use for which a consumer, firm, or government is willing to pay.

shirking Workers' neglecting or evading work to increase their *utility* or well-being.

shortage The amount by which the *quantity demanded* of a product exceeds the *quantity supplied* at a particular (below-equilibrium) price.

short run (1) In microeconomics, a period of time in which producers are able to change the quantities of some but not all of the resources they employ; a period in which some resources (usually plant) are fixed and some are variable. (2) In macroeconomics, a period in which nominal wages and other input prices do not change in response to a change in the price level.

short-run aggregate supply curve An aggregate supply curve relevant to a time period in which input prices (particularly *nominal wages*) do not change in response to changes in the *price level.*

simple multiplier The *multiplier* in any economy in which government collects no *net taxes*, there are no *imports*, and *investment* is independent of the level of income; equal to 1 divided by the *marginal propensity to save.*

simultaneous consumption The same-time derivation of *utility* from some product by a large number of consumers.

slope of a line The ratio of the vertical change (the rise or fall) to the horizontal change (the run) between any two points on a line. The slope of an upward-sloping line is positive, reflecting a direct relationship between two variables; the slope of a downward-sloping line is negative, reflecting an inverse relationship between two variables.

Smoot-Hawley Tariff Act Legislation passed in 1930 that established very high tariffs. Its objective was to reduce imports and stimulate the domestic economy, but it resulted only in retaliatory tariffs by other nations.

Social Security The social insurance program in the United States financed by Federal payroll taxes on employers and employees and designed to replace a portion of the earnings lost when workers become disabled, retire, or die.

Social Security trust fund A Federal fund that saves excessive Social Security tax revenues received in one year to meet Social Security benefit obligations that exceed Social Security tax revenues in some subsequent year.

sole proprietorship An unincorporated *firm* owned and operated by one person.

specialization The use of the resources of an individual, a firm, a region, or a nation to concentrate production on one or a small number of goods and services.

speculation The activity of buying or selling with the motive of later reselling or rebuying for profit.

SSI (See *Supplemental Security Income.*)

stagflation Inflation accompanied by stagnation in the rate of growth of output and an increase in unemployment in the economy; simultaneous increases in the *inflation rate* and the *unemployment rate.*

standardized budget A comparison of the government expenditures and tax collections that would occur if the economy operated at *full employment* throughout the year; the full-employment budget.

start-up (firm) A new firm focused on creating and introducing a particular new product or employing a specific new production or distribution method.

stock (corporate) An ownership share in a corporation.

store of value An *asset* set aside for future use; one of the three functions of *money.*

strategic trade policy The use of trade barriers to reduce the risk inherent in product development by domestic firms, particularly that involving advanced technology.

structural unemployment Unemployment of workers whose skills are not demanded by employers, who lack sufficient skill to obtain employment, or who cannot easily move to locations where jobs are available.

subsidy A payment of funds (or goods and services) by a government, firm, or household for which it receives no good or service in return. When made by a government, it is a *government transfer payment.*

substitute goods Products or services that can be used in place of each other. When the price of one falls, the demand for the other product falls; conversely, when the price of one product rises, the demand for the other product rises.

substitution effect (1) A change in the quantity demanded of a *consumer good* that results from a change in its relative expensiveness caused by a change in the product's price; (2) the effect of a change in the price of a *resource* on the quantity of the resource employed by a firm, assuming no change in its output.

supply A schedule showing the amounts of a good or service that sellers (or a seller) will offer at various prices during some period.

supply curve A curve illustrating *supply.*

supply factor (in growth) An increase in the availability of a resource, an improvement in its quality, or an expansion of technological knowledge that makes it possible for an economy to produce a greater output of goods and services.

supply schedule (See *supply.*)

supply-side economics A view of macroeconomics that emphasizes the role of costs and *aggregate supply* in explaining *inflation, unemployment,* and *economic growth.*

surplus The amount by which the *quantity supplied* of a product exceeds the *quantity demanded* at a specific (above-equilibrium) price.

tariff A tax imposed by a nation on an imported good.

tax An involuntary payment of money (or goods and services) to a government by a *household* or *firm* for which the household or firm receives no good or service directly in return.

taxes on production and imports A *national income accounting* category that includes such taxes as *sales, excise,* business property taxes, and *tariffs* which firms treat as costs of producing a product and pass on (in whole or in part) to buyers by charging a higher price.

tax incidence The person or group that ends up paying a tax.

tax-transfer disincentives Decreases in the incentives to work, save, invest, innovate, and take risks that allegedly result from high *marginal tax rates* and *transfer payments.*

Taylor rule A modern monetary rule proposed by economist John Taylor that would stipulate exactly how much the Federal

Reserve should change interest rates in response to divergences of real GDP from potential GDP and divergences of actual rates of inflation from a target rate of inflation.

technological advance New and better goods and services and new and better ways of producing or distributing them.

technology The body of knowledge and techniques that can be used to combine *economic resources* to produce goods and services.

terms of trade The rate at which units of one product can be exchanged for units of another product; the price of a good or service; the amount of one good or service that must be given up to obtain 1 unit of another good or service.

theoretical economics The process of deriving and applying economic theories and principles.

thrift institution A *savings and loan association, mutual savings bank,* or *credit union.*

till money (See *vault cash.*)

time deposit An interest-earning deposit in a *commercial bank* or *thrift institution* that the depositor can withdraw without penalty after the end of a specified period.

total demand The demand schedule or the *demand curve* of all buyers of a good or service; also called market demand.

total demand for money The sum of the *transactions demand for money* and the *asset demand for money.*

total product (TP) The total output of a particular good or service produced by a firm (or a group of firms or the entire economy).

total revenue (TR) The total number of dollars received by a firm (or firms) from the sale of a product; equal to the total expenditures for the product produced by the firm (or firms); equal to the quantity sold (demanded) multiplied by the price at which it is sold.

total spending The total amount that buyers of goods and services spend or plan to spend; also called *aggregate expenditures.*

total supply The supply schedule or the *supply curve* of all sellers of a good or service; also called market supply.

Trade Adjustment Assistance Act A U.S. law passed in 2002 that provides cash assistance, education and training benefits, health care subsidies, and wage subsidies (for persons age 50 or older) to workers displaced by imports or relocations of U.S. plants to other countries.

trade balance The export of goods (or goods and services) of a nation less its imports of goods (or goods and services).

trade bloc A group of nations that lower or abolish trade barriers among members. Examples include the *European Union* and the nations of the *North American Free Trade Agreement.*

trade controls *Tariffs, export subsidies, import quotas,* and other means a nation may employ to reduce *imports* and expand *exports.*

trade deficit The amount by which a nation's *imports* of goods (or goods and services) exceed its *exports* of goods (or goods and services).

tradeoff The sacrifice of some or all of one economic goal, good, or service to achieve some other goal, good, or service.

trade surplus The amount by which a nation's *exports* of goods (or goods and services) exceed its *imports* of goods (or goods and services).

trading possibilities line A line that shows the different combinations of two products that an economy is able to obtain (consume) when it specializes in the production of one product and trades (exports) it to obtain the other product.

transactions demand for money The amount of money people want to hold for use as a *medium of exchange* (to make payments); varies directly with the *nominal GDP.*

transfer payment A payment of *money* (or goods and services) by a government to a *household* or *firm* for which the payer receives no good or service directly in return.

unanticipated inflation Increases in the price level (*inflation*) at a rate greater than expected.

underemployment A situation in which workers are employed in positions requiring less education and skill than they have.

undistributed corporate profits After-tax corporate profits not distributed as dividends to stockholders; corporate or business saving; also called retained earnings.

unemployment The failure to use all available *economic resources* to produce desired goods and services; the failure of the economy to fully employ its *labor force.*

unemployment compensation (See *unemployment insurance*).

unemployment insurance The social insurance program that in the United States is financed by state *payroll taxes* on employers and makes income available to workers who become unemployed and are unable to find jobs.

unemployment rate The percentage of the *labor force* unemployed at any time.

unit labor cost Labor cost per unit of output; total labor cost divided by total output; also equal to the *nominal wage* rate divided by the *average product* of labor.

unit of account A standard unit in which prices can be stated and the value of goods and services can be compared; one of the three functions of *money.*

unlimited liability Absence of any limits on the maximum amount that an individual (usually a business owner) may become legally required to pay.

unlimited wants The insatiable desire of consumers for goods and services that will give them satisfaction or *utility.*

unplanned changes in inventories Changes in inventories that firms did not anticipate; changes in inventories that occur because of unexpected increases or decreases of aggregate spending (of *aggregate expenditures*).

unplanned investment Actual investment less *planned investment;* increases or decreases in the *inventories* of firms resulting from production greater than sales.

Uruguay Round A 1995 trade agreement (fully implemented in 2005) that established the *World Trade Organization (WTO),* liberalized trade in goods and services, provided added protection to intellectual property (for example, *patents* and *copyrights*), and reduced farm subsidies.

U.S. securities U.S. Treasury bills, notes, and bonds used to finance *budget deficits*; the components of the *public debt*.

utility The want-satisfying power of a good or service; the satisfaction or pleasure a consumer obtains from the consumption of a good or service (or from the consumption of a collection of goods and services).

value added The value of the product sold by a *firm* less the value of the products (materials) purchased and used by the firm to produce the product.

value judgment Opinion of what is desirable or undesirable; belief regarding what ought or ought not to be (regarding what is right or just and wrong or unjust).

value of money The quantity of goods and services for which a unit of money (a dollar) can be exchanged; the purchasing power of a unit of money; the reciprocal of the *price index*.

vault cash The *currency* a bank has in its vault and cash drawers.

velocity The number of times per year that the average dollar in the *money supply* is spent for *final goods and services;* nominal GDP divided by the money supply.

vertical axis The "up-down" or "north-south" measurement line on a graph or grid.

vertical intercept The point at which a line meets the vertical axis of a graph.

very long run A period in which *technology* can change and in which *firms* can introduce new products.

voluntary export restrictions (VER) Voluntary limitations by countries or firms of their exports to a particular foreign nation to avoid enactment of formal trade barriers by that nation.

wage The price paid for the use or services of *labor* per unit of time (per hour, per day, and so on).

wage rate (See *wage.*)

wages The income of those who supply the economy with *labor*.

wealth Anything that has value because it produces income or could produce income. Wealth is a stock; income is a flow. Assets less liabilities; net worth.

wealth effect The tendency for people to increase their consumption spending when the value of their financial and real assets rises and to decrease their consumption spending when the value of those assets falls.

world price The international market price of a good or service, determined by world demand and supply.

World Trade Organization (WTO) An organization of 149 nations (as of fall 2006) that oversees the provisions of the current world trade agreement, resolves trade disputes stemming from it, and holds forums for further rounds of trade negotiations.

WTO (See *World Trade Organization.*)

Credits

Index

Page numbers followed by n indicate notes.

Selected Economics Statistics for Various Years, 1981–2005

Statistics in rows 1–5 are in billions of dollars in the year specified. Details may not add to totals because of rounding

GDP AND INCOME DATA	1981	1982	1983	1984	1985	1986	1987	1988	1989	1990	1991
1 Gross domestic product	3,128.4	3,255.0	3,536.7	3,933.2	4,220.3	4,462.8	4,739.5	5,103.8	5,484.4	5,803.1	5,995.9
1A Personal consumption expenditures	1,941.1	2,077.3	2,290.6	2,503.3	2,720.3	2,899.7	3,100.2	3,353.6	3,598.5	3,839.9	3,986.1
1B Gross private domestic investment	572.4	517.2	564.3	735.6	736.2	746.5	785.0	821.6	874.9	861.0	802.9
1C Government purchases	627.5	680.5	733.5	797.0	879.0	949.3	999.5	1039.0	1,099.1	1,180.2	1,234.4
1D Net exports	−12.5	−20.0	−51.7	−102.7	−115.2	−132.7	−145.2	−110.4	−88.2	−78.0	−27.5
2 Net domestic product	2,740.4	2,828.1	3,092.9	3,460.6	3,713.5	3,931.5	4,177.5	4,506.2	4,840.1	5,120.6	5,270.0
3 National income	2,742.4	2,864.3	3,084.2	3,482.3	3,723.4	3,902.3	4,173.7	4,549.4	4,826.6	5,089.1	5,227.9
3A Wages and salaries	1,825.8	1,925.8	2,042.6	2,255.6	2,424.7	2,570.1	2,750.2	2,967.2	3,145.2	3,338.2	3,445.2
3B Rent	38.0	38.8	37.8	40.2	41.9	33.5	33.5	40.6	43.1	50.7	60.3
3C Interest	232.3	271.1	285.3	327.1	341.3	366.8	366.4	385.3	432.1	442.2	418.2
3D Profits	223.1	209.7	264.2	318.6	330.3	319.5	368.8	432.6	426.6	437.8	451.2
3E Proprietor's income	183.0	176.3	192.5	243.3	262.3	275.7	302.2	341.6	363.3	380.6	377.1
3F Taxes on production and imports*	237.2	222.4	261.9	297.4	322.8	336.8	352.7	440.8	416.2	439.7	475.8
4 Personal income	2,591.3	2,775.3	2,960.7	3,289.5	3,526.7	3,722.4	3,947.4	4,253.7	4,587.8	4,878.6	5,051.0
5 Disposable income	2,246.1	2,421.2	2,608.4	2,912.0	3,109.3	3,285.1	3,458.3	3,748.7	4,021.7	4,285.8	4,464.3
6 Disposable income per capita	9,765.0	10,426.0	11,131.0	12,319.0	13,037.0	13,649.0	12,241.0	15,297.0	16,237.0	17,131.0	17,609.0
7 Personal saving as percent of DI	10.9	11.2	9.0	10.8	9.0	8.2	7.0	7.3	7.1	7.0	7.3

OTHER STATISTICS	1981	1982	1983	1984	1985	1986	1987	1988	1989	1990	1991
8 Real GDP (billions of 2002 dollars)	5,291.7	5,189.3	5,423.8	5,813.6	6,053.7	6,263.6	6,475.1	6,742.7	6,981.4	7,112.5	7,100.5
9 Economic growth rate (change in real GDP)	2.5	3.5	1.9	−0.2	3.3	2.7	4.0	2.5	3.5	1.9	−0.2
10 Consumer Price Index (1982–1984 = 100)	90.9	96.5	99.6	103.9	107.6	109.6	113.6	118.3	124.0	130.7	136.2
11 Rate of inflation (percent change in CPI)	10.3	6.2	3.2	4.3	3.6	1.9	3.6	4.1	4.8	5.4	4.2
12 Money supply, M1 (billions of $)	436.7	474.8	521.4	551.6	619.8	724.6	750.2	786.6	792.9	824.7	897.1
13 Federal funds interest rate (%)	16.39	12.24	9.09	10.23	8.1	6.8	6.66	7.57	9.21	8.1	5.69
14 Prime interest rate (%)	18.87	14.86	10.79	12.04	9.93	8.33	8.21	9.32	10.87	10.01	8.46
15 Population (millions)	230.0	232.2	234.3	236.3	238.5	240.7	242.8	245.0	247.3	250.1	253.5
16 Civilian labor force (millions)	108.7	110.2	111.6	113.5	115.5	117.8	119.9	121.7	123.9	125.8	126.3
16A Employment (millions)	100.4	99.5	100.8	105.0	107.1	109.6	112.4	115.0	117.3	118.8	117.7
16B Unemployment (millions)	8.3	10.7	10.7	8.5	8.3	8.2	7.4	6.7	6.5	7.0	8.6
17 Unemployment rate (%)	7.6	9.7	9.6	7.5	7.2	7.0	6.2	5.5	5.3	5.6	6.8
18 Productivity growth, business sector (%)	2.1	−0.8	3.6	2.7	2.3	3.0	0.6	1.5	1.0	2.0	1.5
19 After-tax manufacturing profit per dollar of sales (cents)	4.7	3.5	4.1	4.6	3.8	3.7	4.9	5.9	4.9	3.9	2.4
20 Price of crude oil (U.S. average, dollars per barrel)	35.75	31.83	29.08	28.75	26.92	14.44	17.75	14.87	18.33	23.19	20.2
21 Federal budget surplus (+) or deficit (−) (billions of dollars)	−79.0	−128.0	−207.8	−185.4	−212.3	−221.2	−149.7	−155.2	−152.6	−221.0	−269.2
22 Public debt (billions of dollars)	994.8	1,137.3	1,371.7	1,564.7	1,817.5	2,120.6	2,346.1	2,601.3	2,868.0	3,206.6	3,598.5
23 Trade balance on current account (billions of dollars)	5.0	−5.5	−38.7	−94.3	−118.2	−147.2	−160.7	−121.1	−99.5	−79.0	2.9

*includes a statistical discrepancy.